CHRONOLOGY
OF SCIENCE

LISA REZENDE, PH.D.

Facts On File

An imprint of Infobase Publishing

*To my teachers for introducing me to science
and my family for supporting my pursuits*

Chronology of Science

Copyright © 2006 by Lisa Rezende, Ph.D.
Illustrations © 2006 by Infobase Publishing

Facts On File, Inc.
An imprint of Infobase Publishing
132 West 31st Street
New York NY 10001

Library of Congress Cataloging-in-Publication Data
Rezende, Lisa.
    Chronology of science / Lisa Rezende.
       p.   cm.
    Includes bibliographical references and index.
    ISBN 0-8160-5342-1
    1. Science—Chronology. 2. Science—History. 3. Scientists—
Biography. I. Title.
    Q125.R455 2006
    502'.02—dc22   2005015982

Facts On File books are available at special discounts when
purchased in bulk quantities for businesses, associations,
institutions, or sales promotions. Please call our Special Sales
Department in New York at 212/967-8800 or 800/322-8755.

You can find Facts On File on the World Wide Web at
http://www.factsonfile.com

Text design by Erika K. Arroyo
Cover design by Dorothy M. Preston
Illustrations by Sholto Ainslie

Printed in the United States of America

VB FOF 10 9 8 7 6 5 4 3 2 1

This book is printed on acid-free paper.

CONTENTS

ACKNOWLEDGMENTS

This book is the product of efforts by many different people. I am grateful to my literary agent, Jodie Rhodes, who encouraged me to write the proposal and put me in contact with Facts On File, Inc. The book took shape under the patient pen of my editor, Frank K. Darmstadt, who conceived the project, suggested the format for each entry, and helped maintain consistency across the many pages of this book. The photographs were obtained with the assistance of Samantha van Gerbig at the Museum of the History of Science, Anita Duncan at Photo Researchers, and Lori Cox-Paul and Gwen Pattison at the National Archives. Finally, I owe a great deal of thanks to my many colleagues, friends, and family members who immediately told me their favorite scientists, experiments, and achievements when they heard about this project. In particular, I have to thank my partner in scientific and personal endeavors, Tsu-Shuen Tsao, who looked over the proposal, helped me generate the list of entries, and read various drafts of this book. I will always be grateful for his constant support.

INTRODUCTION

Chronology of Science serves as a reference for middle and high school students looking for accurate, up-to-date information on the major achievements in science history. The information presented is intended to supplement the science taught in the classroom. Each entry presents the student with a concise description of a scientific discovery, the problem it addressed, and the impact it had on the field and, where appropriate, beyond. The complete scope of a scientific story cannot be told in a chronology entry, so a list of print and Internet references is included to point the reader to further information. Supplementing the short entries are essays providing more in-depth discussion of major topics ranging from the scientific achievements of ancient civilizations to modern fields of study such as quantum mechanics. While each entry and essay is written with the goal of eliminating all unnecessary jargon, a glossary of common scientific terms is included to help the student become conversant in the vocabulary of science.

Middle and high school students are often introduced to science as a series of distinct subjects, choosing among courses in biology, chemistry, physics, and Earth science. While educational goals make it necessary to segregate scientific subjects in this way, in fact scientific thinking and discoveries are not limited to specific fields. The tech-

niques used and the consequences of many discoveries are often felt across scientific disciplines. *Chronology of Science* complements the standard middle and high school curriculum by presenting scientific discoveries in a chronological and integrated fashion. Students will discover that ancient Greeks, natural philosophers, and Renaissance scientists often put forth theories in a number of disciplines. Similarly, today's scientists often consider themselves a specialist in a hybrid field, such as a biochemistry or astrophysics. The integrated approach of *Chronology of Science* is intended to give students a taste of the cross-pollination between fields that they may not get in their courses. At the end of each entry, we have added a code denoting the scientific discipline(s) that the entry directly affects. The key to the code is as follows:

- B-biology
- C-chemistry
- ES-Earth science
- M-mathematics
- MS-marine science
- P-physics
- SA-space and astronomy
- W-weather and climate

A chronological presentation of events poses a particular challenge when discussing scientific advances. By nature, scientific theories and discoveries are not one-day events, but are rather a more slowly evolving convergence of an idea and experimental evidence. Before a discovery becomes public knowledge, it is scrutinized, with experiments performed repeatedly when possible and manuscripts reviewed by colleagues before their official publications. During these processes, ideas are refined, theories altered, and new findings discovered. As a result, one can rarely pinpoint the day a scientific discovery occurred. Today, this difficulty is apparent in legal battles over who has the right to claim that they invented a hot and profitable new technology. Similar battles have been waged in laboratories and places of higher learning for centuries. In the pages of this book, students will learn of the long-standing argument over who invented *calculus* over 300 years ago. These examples illustrate how pinpointing the date of a scientific discovery is not as easy as pinpointing the date of other historical events such as battles, treaties, or changes in government. In this chronology, the dates listed often reflect when the discovery was announced through a speech, letter, patent, or publication. In some cases, the primary work detailed in the entry may have been done years before, in others merely weeks. Where documentation of the actual date of the discovery could be found, through interviews with the scientist or publication of laboratory notes, those dates are used. Where no date could be accurately pinpointed, the entry is listed by year, decade, or century.

Finally, the student must be aware that any selection of 2,000 scientific discoveries is inherently subjective. In this volume, the student will read about discoveries made by leading scientists from Aristotle to the engineers who built the Mars Rover. Most of these events would appear in any similar volume. However, in other cases, the decision to include or omit a given event could be more controversial. The selection of entries included in this volume is based upon the author's research, and decisions were made after consulting other published chronology and time lines, as well as major awards given to scientists in a variety of fields. Despite these efforts, omissions are inevitable. For example, the majority of the entries describe science that took place in Europe and the United States, reflecting the Western bias of our culture. Great effort has been made to include the major scientific advances made in China, India, Arab nations, and the Americas, particularly in the early sections. Unfortunately, many events are likely to be missed. For more information on the scientific achievement of these societies, the reader is directed to references on non-Western science included in the back matter.

SETTING THE FOUNDATION
Science in Antiquity through the First Century B.C.E.

∽ INTRODUCTION ∽

The scientific and technological advances that are chronicled in this section range from seemingly simple steps taken by humans as civilizations developed, such as the use of tools, to the work of Greek philosophers, ranging from mathematics to the nature of matter, which set the foundation for modern science in the West. Perhaps the most obvious advances of this period are technological, including agricultural tools, such as the plow and seed drill, and the development of new materials from bronze to iron and steel. Using simple tools and instruments and without the benefit of regular communication with other societies, early scholars make stunning advances, particularly in astronomy and mathematics. By the end of this period, the roots of mathematics, physics, chemistry, and biology are firmly in place, and many important astronomical observations are made.

Today's scientific research drives technological advances; however, for most of the period covered in this section, scientific advances are a consequence of technology. For example, the seeds of modern chemistry are found in the development of materials from bronze to glass. The development of materials is so significant to the advance of early civilization that eras are named after them. The "Bronze Age" is heralded by the discovery that mixing molten copper and tin together generates bronze, a metal *alloy* that is both strong and malleable. Similarly, the "Iron Age" sees the invention and widespread use of steel, an alloy of iron and copper.

Ancient astronomy, which flourishes in many ancient cultures, is often associated with religious beliefs and ceremonies. Astronomers from China to South America record the movement of celestial bodies visible to the naked eye. Scholars studying the Sun and the Moon make observations that lead to the development of solar and lunar calendars. Early scientists and engineers build observatories and other structures to aid in these observations, from Stonehenge in England to Mayan temples in South America.

Others use simple scientific instruments, such as the *gnomon* and the *astrolabe,* to aid in their astronomical calculations. Chinese and Babylonian astronomers make notable advances during this era. The astronomical records of Chinese scholars have survived until today, and show that ancient astronomers also observed *comets* and *supernovae.* Meanwhile, Babylonian astronomers use mathematics to describe the movement of celestial bodies, beginning the union of astronomy and mathematics that continues today.

Scientific research begins to take a form more recognizable today in ancient Greece. Western science is born during this era, as natural philosophers develop theories in scientific disciplines from physics to biology. One of the key questions pondered by these early scholars is the nature of matter. During this period, philosophers argue that matter can be reduced to essential *elements*, although the exact identity of these elements is disputed. Some argue that matter comes from fire, others water, and still others say that there are myriad elements, including skin, bone, and earth. Greek natural philosopher Aristotle famously describes four elements: fire, air, water, and earth. His description of the elements dominates scientific thought for centuries.

Ancient Greek philosophers also excel in mathematics, particularly *geometry.* Perhaps the most famous mathematical work of this era is the *Pythagorean theorem,* which describes the mathematical relationship between the sides of a *right triangle.* Mathematicians and engineers in Egypt, Babylon, and China study this relationship for centuries before the mathematicians of the Pythagorean School in ancient Greece provide a proof for the theorem that now bears their name. Greek mathematicians establish many other theorems, which are summarized in *The Elements,* a treatise on geometry written by the mathematician Euclid. Today's high school students continue to study the geometry outlined in Euclid's *The Elements. Euclidean geometry,* as the field is now known, centers on five assumptions or *axioms.* Using these axioms, Greek mathematicians prove the relationship between points, lines, and angles. Also recognizable to today's students is the work on *conic sections,* the curves that are generated when a plane intersects a cone. The study of conic sections represents an early step in the intersection of geometry and *algebra.* In the next centuries, Arab mathematicians will preserve and advance this vital work of Greek mathematicians.

TIME LINE OF SCIENTIFIC ACHIEVEMENTS BEFORE THE FIRST CENTURY C.E.

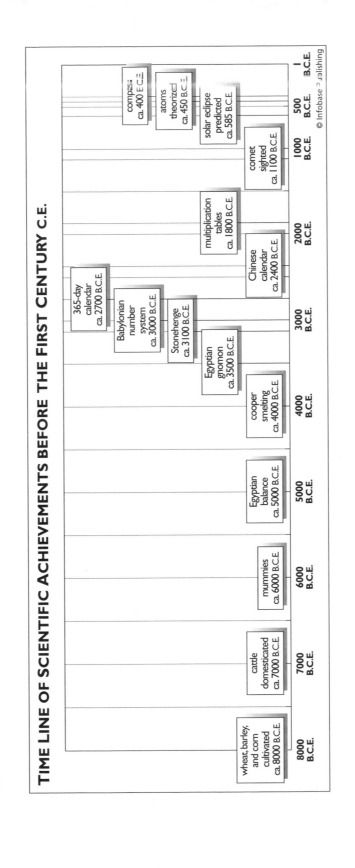

wheat, barley, and corn cultivated
ca. 8000 B.C.E.

cattle domesticated
ca. 7000 B.C.E.

mummies
ca. 6000 B.C.E.

Egyptian balance
ca. 5000 B.C.E.

cooper smelting
ca. 4000 B.C.E.

Egyptian gnomon
ca. 3500 B.C.E.

Stonehenge
ca. 3100 B.C.E.

Babylonian number system
ca. 3000 B.C.E.

365-day calendar
ca. 2700 B.C.E.

Chinese calendar
ca. 2400 B.C.E.

multiplication tables
ca. 1800 B.C.E.

comet sighted
ca. 1100 B.C.E.

solar eclipse predicted
ca. 585 B.C.E.

atoms theorized
ca. 450 B.C.E.

compass
ca. 400 B.C.E.

8000 B.C.E.　7000 B.C.E.　6000 B.C.E.　5000 B.C.E.　4000 B.C.E.　3000 B.C.E.　2000 B.C.E.　1000 B.C.E.　500 B.C.E.　I B.C.E.

∾ CHRONOLOGY ∾

ca. 1,800,000 B.C.E.

Homo habilis uses stone tools.

Members of the species *Homo habilis,* an ancestor of *Homo sapiens* or modern man, first used tools millions of years ago. Archaeological evidence suggests that around 1,800,000 B.C.E., *Homo habilis* makes and uses the first stone tools. Scholars believe that these ancestors of modern man chipped stones to give them a sharp edge. Such primitive tools are likely used to hunt animals. The use of stone tools continues for many thousands of years until advances in metallurgy and material science provides more malleable starting materials.

(ES)

Stone tools are one of the first innovations by early man. These ancient Paleolithic stone hand axes were discovered in Olduvai Gorge, Tanzania, Africa. *(John Reader/Photo Researchers, Inc)*

ca. 30,000 B.C.E.

Early Europeans devise a method of counting.

Mathematics was born when ancient man learned how to count. Some of the earliest evidence of counting comes from central Europe, dating to about 30,000 B.C.E. Archaeologists have found a bone with tick marks carved into it. The ticks are arranged into 11 groups of five, suggesting that the bone was used as a tally.

(M)

ca. 20,000 B.C.E.

French cave paintings depict daily life.

As described in the sidebar "Discovering the Scientific Achievements of the Ancient World," the current understanding of the ancient world comes from the artifacts discovered by modern archaeologists. For example, cave paintings found in France provide clues to the lives of early humans thousands of years ago. These early artworks, which date back to around 20,000 B.C.E., depict ancient people playing musical instruments. Other drawings show the animals of the ancient world, including what appear to be oxen.

(B, P)

ca. 12,000 B.C.E.

Hunters in the Middle East domesticate dogs.

Animals have been used to perform work such as pulling carts and hunting game for centuries. Dogs were one of the first animals to be domesticated, most likely by hunters who used them to help find and kill other animals. As early as 12,000 B.C.E., people in modern-day Iraq begin domesticating dogs. Scholars believe that dogs are one of the first animals to be domesticated because they naturally form packs with leaders and followers, making it easier for them to accept commands from a human.

(B)

ca. 9000 B.C.E.

Farmers in the Middle East domesticate goats.

The domestication of animals allowed ancient civilizations to have a dependable supply of food. Around 9000 B.C.E., farmers in the Middle East domesticate goats, using them as a source of milk. Goat milk is used to make cheeses and butter, giving the owner a renewable source of nutrients without having to kill the animal.

(B)

ca. 8000 B.C.E.

Early civilizations build houses in the Middle East.

As early man began to domesticate animals and cultivate fruits and vegetables, civilizations could stay in one place rather than constantly move in search of food. Archaeologists have discovered the remnants of houses built in the Middle East around 8000 B.C.E. The small houses are made from sun-dried mud bricks. As discussed in the sidebar "Discovering the Scientific Achievements of the Ancient World," such artifacts are essential to the current understanding of early history.

(P)

Middle Eastern farmers cultivate wheat and barley.

Early advances in agriculture allowed civilizations to move from a migratory culture to one that remained in a single location. Around 8000 B.C.E., early farmers in the Middle East begin to cultivate wheat and barley, grains that grew wild in the region. Planting and sowing these crops gives civilizations a dependable and renewable source of food. The crops last well beyond harvest because these grains can be ground into flour then stored for long periods of time without spoiling.

(B)

Farmers in the Americas cultivate maize.

Some of the earliest scientific discoveries came in the field of agriculture, where the domestication of animals and the cultivation of crops allowed cultures to flourish. Around 8000 B.C.E., farmers in North and South America begin to cultivate and harvest maize, a breed of corn. Similar to the wheat and barley cultivated in the Middle East (See entry for CA. 8000 B.C.E.), maize can be ground into flour and stored without spoiling. The crop remains an important agricultural product today.

(B)

ca. 7000 B.C.E.

Early farmers domesticate cattle.

The domestication of animals was an important advance for many ancient cultures, allowing people to use animals for work and raise them for food. Around 7000 B.C.E., farmers in modern-day Turkey domesticate wild oxen. Domesticated cattle can carry cargo, pull plows, provide milk, and serve as a source of meat.

(B)

ca. 6000 B.C.E.

South American cultures preserve corpses as mummies.

Ancient cultures in regions of South America, including modern-day Chile and Peru, attempted to preserve the bodies of the deceased by wrapping them with cloth before burial. These corpses, known as mummies, retained many of the body's living features for far longer than an unpreserved body. The climate and soil conditions in South America helped to preserve these bodies.

(B)

Farmers in Mesopotamia make beer from barley.

As agriculture developed, people began to stay in one place to hunt and harvest food and produce other goods. Among the first domesticated crops is the grain barley (*See* entry for CA. 8000 B.C.E.). Around 6000 B.C.E., farmers in Mesopotamia use barley to make beer. Beer making is an early example of *fermentation,* where microorganisms digest sugars in food and release alcohol as a byproduct.

(B, C)

ca. 5000 B.C.E.

Farmers in the Middle East and Egypt develop irrigation.

In ancient times, reliably growing crops such as wheat (*See* entry for CA. 8000 B.C.E.) depended upon the availability of fresh water. As more crops are grown, farmers in the Middle East and Egypt develop methods of harnessing water from nearby rivers, called irrigation. By digging ditches around the crop, farmers direct the water from the river to the crops, providing a steady supply of water. In Egypt, farmers harness the floodwaters from the Nile River. The development of irrigation marks a major step in the expansion of agriculture.

(B, ES)

Ancient Egyptians develop the balance.

Accurate measurements were essential for trade, agriculture, and the advancement of science. Around 5000 B.C.E., scholars in ancient Egypt develop the balance to determine the weight of an object. Eventually a system of weight develops based on a unit called a kite. The standard weight of a kite varies throughout Egyptian history, ranging from 0.14 ounces (4 g) to just over a single ounce (30 g).

(P)

ca. 4000 B.C.E.

Ancient Egyptians mine and smelt copper.

Homo habilis, an ancestor of modern humans, first used stone tools around 1,800,000 B.C.E. (*See* entry for CA. 1,800,000 B.C.E.). As civilizations became more advanced, craftsmen found that metals were more useful for making tools than stones. An important early advance was the mining of metal ores. Around 4000 B.C.E., ancient Egyptians begin to mine copper ores. Ores are not pure metal and must be purified. Heating metal ores to the point of melting allows metalworkers to recover pure metal from an ore, a process known as smelting. The ancient Egyptians who performed this work began the science of metallurgy.

(C, ES)

Ships sail in Mesopotamia and Egypt.

The development of transportation relied upon a basic understanding of physics, as vehicles were essentially simple machines that helped humans perform work. Engineers and scholars designed vehicles that could easily move goods and people. Rather than carry goods by land, some opted to use the water, building hollowed-out boats and rafts. Around 4000 B.C.E., scholars design ships with sails that move by wind power. The development of sailing ships improves communication between societies and leads to the exploration of distant lands.

(MS, P)

Craftsmen in Mesopotamia devise a kiln.
In the ancient world, bricks were made from mud, then "baked" in the sun. As *heat* is an important component in brick making, craftsmen soon realized that bricks that are burned are stronger than those that are sun-dried. Around 4000 B.C.E., craftsmen in Mesopotamia develop an oven or kiln to burn bricks.

(C)

Ancient Chinese develop the plow.
Early advances in agriculture helped ancient civilizations survive and thrive. By 4000 B.C.E., farmers in ancient China use mechanical plows to turn soil in the fields. While Chinese make their first plows out of wood, later plows are built from new materials such as bronze and iron. Plows are pulled either by men or by domesticated animals such as oxen. During the Middle Ages, European farmers replicate Chinese design.

(P)

ca. 3600 B.C.E.

Sumerians use bronze.
The first tools were made from stone (*See* entry for CA. 1,800,000 B.C.E.). With the dis-

ELEMENTS KNOWN TO ANCIENT SCHOLARS

Metal	Date of discovery	Main ore from which metal is obtained	Main method of extraction	Main uses
Iron	Ancient	Haematite, Fe_2O_3	Reduce Fe_2O_3 with carbon monoxide	Most important structural metal (as steel), vehicles, engines, tools
Tin	Ancient	Tinstone, SnO_2	Reduce SnO_2 with carbon	Tin plate (coating iron), alloys (e.g., solder, pewter, bronze, etc.)
Lead	Ancient	Galena, PbS	Heat sulfide in air → oxide. Reduce oxide with carbon	Roof and cable covering, battery plates, alloys (e.g., solder, printing metals)
Copper	Ancient	Copper pyrites, $CuFeS_2$ (CuS + FeS)	Controlled heating with correct amount of air → Cu + SO_2	Electrical wires, cables, etc., water pipes, alloys, (e.g., brass, bronze)
Mercury	Ancient	Cinnabar, HgS	Heat in air → Hg + SO_2	Scientific equipment (e.g., barometers, thermometers, etc.), mercury vapor lamps, chlor-alkali cells

This table shows some of the elements discovered by ancient cultures and their modern-day uses.

covery of metal ores, early craftsmen used metals in lieu of stone to make tools. Around 3600 B.C.E., Sumerian craftsmen discover bronze, an *alloy* of copper and tin. Bronze is both stronger and easier to manipulate than copper. By 3600 B.C.E., the use of bronze spreads across the Middle East, heralding what is now called the "Bronze Age."

(C)

ca. 3500 B.C.E.

Ancient Egyptians develop a timekeeping device.

As described in the sidebar "Measuring Time in the Ancient World," early timekeeping devices and calendars depended on the movement of the Sun and Moon. Around 3500 B.C.E., one of the first timekeeping devices, the *gnomon,* is developed in ancient Egypt. A gnomon is composed of a vertical stick that casts a shadow on the ground or a stone base when left in the sunlight. Scholars estimate the time by looking at the position of the shadow. The gnomon is a precursor to the sundial.

(SA)

Sumerians write using pictograms.

Writing was an essential development in ancient civilizations, allowing people to record observations, rituals, and other information for future generations. Around 3500 B.C.E., the Sumerian people begin using pictograms as a form of writing. Pictograms are a series of symbols depicting various objects and animals that are used to convey information. Eventually the system expands to include more than 1,000 different symbols.

(B, C, ES, M, MS, P, SA, W)

Sumerians use wheeled carts.

Advances in transportation allowed ancient cultures to move goods and people. Around 3500 B.C.E., Sumerian craftsmen make a great advance in land transportation when they develop wheeled carts. Wheels roll along the ground, making it easier for a person or an animal to pull a heavy cart. The use of the wheel soon spreads to the movement of water, where waterwheels become an important aid for irrigation.

(P)

ca. 3200 B.C.E.

Sumerians develop cuneiform writing.

As described in the sidebar "Discovering the Scientific Advances of the Ancient World," the development of writing in ancient civilizations allowed scholars to pass on important information to future generations. Sumerians developed a system of pictographs by 3500 B.C.E. (*See* entry for CA. 3500 B.C.E.). Around 3200 B.C.E., the system evolves into a more systematic form of writing known as cuneiform. Using a blunt-ended stylus, Sumerians imprint wedgelike strokes into a clay tablet. Today, scholars use the cuneiform records to help them understand the way of life and achievements in the Middle East thousands of years ago.

(B, C, ES, M, MS, P, SA, W)

ca. 3100 B.C.E.

Egyptians develop a hieroglyphic system of writing.

Much of our knowledge of ancient civilizations comes from the writings they left behind. By 3100 B.C.E., ancient Egyptians develop the hieroglyphic system of writing. Hieroglyphics consists of pictures that depict common objects. As a more sophisticated system develops, pictures are used to represent sounds so the writing could be read phonetically. As discussed in the sidebar

MEASURING TIME IN THE ANCIENT WORLD

Today, the opportunity to glance at a watch or calendar and find out the day and time is easily taken for granted. In ancient civilizations, devices that mark time represent a major technological and scientific advance. Timekeeping is intimately related to astronomy, with the observation of the Sun and Moon serving as important markers for the month and year. The seasons of the year are marked by the summer and winter solstices, which correlate to the longest and shortest days of the year, respectively, and by the vernal and autumnal *equinoxes,* defined as the dates when day and night are the same length. Similarly, early timekeeping devices, such as the sundial, monitor the position of the Sun in the sky. Other clocks are based on the flow of water over time.

The timekeeping devices used by different cultures are remarkably similar. The first of these devices is the *gnomon,* an early sundial. The gnomon is essentially a large stick placed in direct sunlight. The time of day is determined by following the position of the shadow cast by the gnomon. Gnomons are used in Egypt for thousands of years. The next advance in timekeeping also comes in Egypt with the invention of the sundial. Improving upon the basic design of the gnomon, sundials feature a crosspiece that casts a shadow upon an inscribed stone. Time is kept by reading the markings on the stone. A third timekeeping device found in the ancient world is the water clock. The first water clocks keep time by marking the passage of water from one vessel to another through a small hole. The second vessel is marked so that the time that has passed can be read. This basic design is improved upon in Greece around 270 B.C.E., when the flow of water is used to turn a rod and time is read by the position of the rod. This improved water clock, called a clepsydra, is used until the Renaissance.

Ancient cultures also develop calendars to keep track of longer stretches of time that coincide with the four seasons. Calendars are based upon astronomical observations, marking the passage of time using the phases of the Moon and movement of the Sun. Civilizations from Asia to the Americas develop calendars based upon the phases of the Moon. These lunar calendars divide time into a series of 30-day months. Calendars based completely upon the phases of the Moon have an inherent problem, as over time the months begin to fall out of line with the seasons. The planting and harvesting of crops depends upon accurate calendars, therefore scholars soon devise methods to reconcile the lunar calendar with the four seasons. One solution is to change the length of months, with some lasting 30 days and other 29 days. Other civilizations insert extra days into the calendar to help reconcile this discrepancy. The second type of calendar found in the ancient world is the solar calendar, which measures time based upon the position of the Sun in the sky. Calendars based solely on the position of the Sun, known as solar calendars, correlate well with the growing season and are more adaptable to agriculture than

"Discovering the Scientific Advances of the Ancient World," translating scrolls and other hieroglyphic writings has allowed modern scholars to learn about the achievements of the ancient Egyptians.

(B, C, ES, M, MS, P, SA, W)

Ancient craftsmen begin building Stonehenge.

As described in the sidebar "Discovering the Scientific Advances of the Ancient World," much of what is now known of ancient cultures came from structures built thousands

Ancient cultures around the world develop calendars based upon astronomical observations. This photograph depicts a stone showing the Aztec calendar. *(Chris R. Sharp/Photo Researchers, Inc)*

are lunar calendars. However, the length of the solar year, 365¼ days, makes it difficult to divide time into months. As a result, scholars combine the lunar and solar calendars. These lunar-solar calendars divide a 365-day year into 12 30-day months. In Egypt, five extra days are added to the year to reconcile the lunar and solar calendars. China also adopts a lunar-solar calendar, but they use a slightly differ- ent means to reconcile the length of the year. The Chinese calendar, still in use today, adds an extra month or leap month every few years to assure that the calendar stays in step with the seasons. Western calendars are currently based on the 365-day year with an extra day added every four years. This "leap year" is first adopted in Rome when the Julian calendar is developed around 46 B.C.E.

of years ago. In some cases, a few clues that hint at the purpose of these structures have been found, and their function is a mystery today. One of the most famous structures is the circular arrangement of rocks known as Stonehenge. The construction of this monument begins around 3100 B.C.E. and continues over 10,000 years. Modern astron- omers have noted that the northeast axis of the monument aligns with the Sun dur- ing the summer solstice, suggesting that the site may have been used for astronomical observations. Other scholars believe the site was used for religious worship.

(P, SA)

ca. 3000 B.C.E.

Egyptians predict the Nile floods.

Agriculture in ancient Egypt depended upon the flooding of the Nile River. Around 3000 B.C.E., Egyptian scholars invent a device called the nilometer to predict the extent of the flood. The nilometer is used to determine the depth of the Nile at a given point and time, allowing scholars to predict whether or not the flood will supply a sufficient amount of water for the crops. The nilometer also helps determine if a flood has the potential to put nearby cities in danger.

(W)

Egyptians develop a standard measure of length.

Standard systems of measure are essential for commerce, engineering, and science. Around 3000 B.C.E., ancient Egyptian scholars develop the cubit, a standard measure of length. Defined as the length of an arm from the elbow to the tip of the middle finger, the cubit measures approximately 18 inches (46 cm).

(P)

Chinese domesticate the silkworm.

The domestication of animals led to a revolution in agriculture for civilizations throughout the ancient world. Domesticated animals helped perform heavy work, such as driving a plow, aided with hunting, and served as food sources. Around 3000 B.C.E., Chinese craftsmen domesticate the silkworm and begin using them to produce silk. Today, silk makers around the world continue to use the Chinese silkworm.

(B)

Babylonian mathematicians adopt a sexagesimal number system.

As writing spread, scholars developed number systems to represent quantities. One of the first is found in Babylon around 3000 B.C.E. The Babylonian system is based on quantities of 60 or a sexagesimal system. In *base* 60, the numbers one through 59 are each represented by a unique character, while numbers larger than 59 are expressed by grouping smaller numbers using *positional notation*. The development of a positional notation system facilitates calculations that involve large numbers.

(M)

ca. 2800 B.C.E.

Mesopotamian astronomers develop a lunar calendar.

The sidebar "Measuring Time in the Ancient World," describes how the development of clocks and calendars required an understanding of astronomy. Around 2800 B.C.E., astronomers in Mesopotamia develop a calendar based upon the motion of the Moon. According to their lunar calendar, a year is 354 days long. Such purely lunar calendars are not used for long, because the length of the year exceeds that of a solar year, and the calendar falls out of phase with the four seasons.

(SA)

ca. 2700 B.C.E.

Sumerian astronomers add a solar year to the calendar.

As described in the sidebar "Measuring Time in the Ancient World," astronomers played a critical role in the development of calendars. The first calendars developed in Mesopotamia (*See* entry for CA. 2800 B.C.E.) were based on the cycles of the Moon, with each month beginning at the first appearance of

DISCOVERING THE SCIENTIFIC ADVANCES OF THE ANCIENT WORLD

Ancient civilizations left behind many clues to their achievements, including monuments such as Stonehenge and the pyramids of Egypt, and writings that have been found in the Middle East and China. Modern archaeologists continue to uncover artifacts and written records that provide clues as to the scientific knowledge of early cultures. This research traditionally focuses on tracing the roots of Western science from Mesopotamia to ancient Greece, then culminating in the Renaissance in Europe. However, many of the same scientific and technological advances were also made in India, China, and the Americas, and the achievements of early cultures in Africa and Australia are still being uncovered. The history of science in the ancient world continues to be written as today's scholars use a combination of archaeology, history, and science to uncover the scientific advances of the ancient world.

Ancient civilizations from Europe to the Americas left behind buildings and monuments that remain standing today. Such monu-

One of the methods that modern historians use to learn about ancient science is archaeological excavation. This photograph is from an excavation in Ashkelon, Israel, that uncovered pottery at the site of an ancient Canaanite city. *(Richard T. Nowitz/ Photo Researchers, Inc)*

ments are a testament to some of the scientific and engineering achievements of these early cultures. Perhaps the best-known architectural achievement of the ancient world is the pyramids of Egypt and South America. Similar structures are found in India, Ethiopia, Mexico, and southern Europe. Modern scholars have noted that many of these structures represent astronomical as well as architectural achievements. Among the most famous are Stonehenge, an arrangement of stones found in modern-day England, where the northeast axis of the monument is in alignment with the Sun during the summer solstice, as well as temples in Mexico and Central America, where the structures are aligned with the Sun during the two equinoxes. By studying these and other structures, today's scholars gain insight into the scientific knowledge of ancient cultures.

In addition to buildings, archaeologists study artifacts found at the sites of ancient cities, which provide insight into the tools a civilization had developed, the materials craftsmen used, and how these achievements affected the everyday way of life of the people. The discovery of scientific instruments, such as the gnomon, gives scholars a sense of how early scientists studied the world around them. Other artifacts, such as paintings found inside caves and tombs, show how citizens used tools for hunting, agriculture, building, or other tasks needed for survival.

While structures and artifacts tell part of the story of scientific achievement in the ancient world, most of our knowledge comes from the written record. The ability of modern scholars to decipher and translate the cuneiform writings of Sumerian scholars, the hieroglyphs found in Egyptian tombs and scrolls, and the existing records from Chinese dynasties provides a wealth of information about the

(continues)

(continued)

mathematical and astronomical achievements of these societies. Similarly, the works of the ancient Greek natural philosophers survived through careful translation by Arab scholars. While a wealth of information and insight has been gained through these records, the potential to understand even more about these cultures has likely been lost. Throughout history, the written records of cultures have been destroyed, from the destruction of the library at Alexandria and the burning of mathematics books in China centuries ago, to the destruction of libraries and museums in war-torn nations today. The loss of such important documents impairs the ability of historians and scientists to understand the achievements of the ancient world.

Modern scholars will probably never know much of the science of the ancient world. The archaeological records that have been extensively studied give today's historians a picture of the achievements of civilization in the Middle East, Egypt, and ancient Greece. Western scholars have recently taken a greater interest in the work of early Chinese and Hindu scientists, as well as the achievements of the Maya, Aztec, and Olmec cultures in the Americas. Future studies may broaden the current picture of scientific achievement and include a greater understanding of cultures in Africa and Australia. However, no amount of research will quell the controversy over the assignment of what civilization "first discovered" various tools, materials, mathematical principles, and celestial bodies.

the Moon. Around 2700 B.C.E., astronomers in Mesopotamia refine the calendar, basing the length of the year on the motion of the Sun, and the length of each month on the cycle of the Moon. This lunar-solar calendar is used throughout most of the Middle East.

(SA)

Ancient Egyptians introduce the 365-day calendar.

The sidebar "Measuring Time in the Ancient World," describes the development of the modern calendar. Thousands of years ago, lunar calendars were used throughout the Middle East. By reconciling the motions of both the Moon and the Sun, Sumerians developed a calendar dividing the year into twelve 30-day months. However, this calendar was five days short of the 365-day cycle of the Sun. Around 2700 B.C.E., the government of ancient Egypt institutes a 365-day calendar,

with twelve 30-day months and five extra days.

(SA)

ca. 2680 B.C.E.

Egyptians build a step pyramid.

As described in the sidebar "Discovering the Scientific Advances of the Ancient World," many ancient civilizations built pyramids that remain standing today. Among the most famous are those found in Egypt. Pyramids are large structures with a rectangular base and four triangular sloping sides. Around 2680 B.C.E., the ancient Egyptians build their first pyramid, a tomb for the pharaoh King Djoser (ca. 2700 B.C.E.). Known as a step pyramid, the structure features a large tomb within the interior and a series of connected underground rooms, including the burial chamber.

(P)

ca. 2500 B.C.E.

Egyptian physicians use false teeth.
Modern knowledge of medical practices in the ancient world comes from both the written and fossil record (*See* sidebar "Discovering the Scientific Advances of the Ancient World"). For example, a fossilized human jawbone found in what was ancient Egypt contained an early form of false teeth. Around 2500 B.C.E., ancient Egyptian dentists use real teeth held together with wire and attached to the jaw through a hole drilled in an adjacent tooth.

(B)

Egyptians develop hieratic script.
Egyptian hieroglyphs are one of the earliest known writing systems. Around 2500 B.C.E., the ancient Egyptians develop a second system of writing, hieratic script, based on hieroglyphs. Hieratic script, which is less detailed and faster to write than hieroglyphs, is used for everyday tasks, while hieroglyphs are saved for tombs and other monuments.

(B, C, ES, M, MS, P, SA, W)

Egyptians make wine from grapes.
The discovery of *fermentation,* the process by which alcohol is produced by microorganisms that digest sugar, allowed ancient cultures to produce alcoholic beverages such as beer (*See* entry for CA. 6000 B.C.E.). Around 2500 B.C.E., ancient Egyptians grow grapes and use them to make wine. Winemaking spreads across the Middle East, where grapes had been harvested for centuries, and plays an important role in many religious ceremonies.

(B, C)

ca. 2400 B.C.E.

Chinese adopt a calendar based upon the movement of the Sun and the Moon.
As described in the sidebar "Measuring Time in the Ancient World," accurate calendars depended upon the availability of astronomical observations. Astronomers in China made and recorded observations of the Sun and Moon. Around 2400 B.C.E., these observations are used to design a lunar-solar calendar. The Chinese calendar sets the length of a year to the position of the Sun in sky, while movement of the Moon sets the length of a month. Leap months are added periodically to reconcile the lunar and solar calendars. The system is so accurate that a version of this calendar continues to be used today.

(SA)

ca. 2250 B.C.E.

Egyptian physicians describe surgery.
Physicians and healers have used surgery since ancient times. Around 2250 B.C.E., Egyptian scholars describe a variety of surgical techniques, known as *The Book of Surgery.* The scroll describes how to diagnose and treat a variety of disorders. Scholars describe how to use bandages, splints, and compresses, as well as set broken bones and saw through skulls.

(B)

ca. 2000 B.C.E.

Egyptian farmers use plows driven by oxen.
Ancient scholars made many advances in agriculture that allowed their civilizations to thrive. Around 2000 B.C.E., farmers in ancient Egypt domesticate oxen and harness them to plows. The oxen-driven plows replace plows dragged along by humans, freeing workers to take on other tasks in the field.

(B, P)

Babylonians expand their system of weights and measures.
Reproducible standards of weights and measures are essential for activities from

commerce to construction. The Babylonians developed the first known unit of weight, the mina, which weighed around 640 grams. Around 2000 B.C.E., Babylonian scholars develop standards of length as well. The kus is the basic unit of length in Babylon, measuring approximately 20.1 inches (53 cm).

(P)

ca. 1950 B.C.E.

Babylonians discover the relationship between the sides of a right triangle.

The ancient Greeks were known for their achievements in *geometry*. Some of the basic theorems of the field, however, were known by other ancient cultures. Around 1950 B.C.E., Babylonian mathematicians realize the relationship between the sides of a *right triangle:* the sum of the squares of the sides are equal to the square of the angle opposite the *right angle,* now known as the *Pythagorean theorem* (*See* entry for CA. 550 B.C.E.), or $a^2 + b^2 = c^2$. Babylonian mathematicians note a number sets of whole numbers (for example 3, 4, and 5) that fulfill this relationship.

(M)

ca. 1800 B.C.E.

Mathematicians in Mesopotamia develop multiplication tables.

Early mathematics focused on the development of number systems as well as basic operations in *arithmetic* and early studies in *geometry*. In Mesopotamia, Babylonian scholars developed a number system based around groups of 60. Such a system with *place value notation* facilitated arithmetical calculations. For example, around 1800 B.C.E., Babylonian mathematicians develop multiplication tables listing the

multiples of the whole numbers from one through 20.

(M)

ca. 1750 B.C.E.

Egyptian mathematicians describe geometry problems.

The ancient Greeks excelled in the study of *geometry,* but many other cultures also made advances in the field. For example, papyri dating to approximately 1750 B.C.E. show that ancient Egyptian mathematicians study geometry, focusing on ways to calculate areas and volumes. The Egyptian mathematicians develop methods to calculate the area of a circle and the volume of a truncated pyramid.

(M)

ca. 1700 B.C.E.

Babylonian mathematicians solve the quadratic equation.

Ancient mathematicians contemplated problems, including the solutions of basic equations that are now considered part of the study of *algebra.* One common problem was the *quadratic equation,* which takes the form $ax^2 + bx + c = 0$. Around 1700 B.C.E., Babylonian mathematicians become the first to solve quadratic equations.

(M)

Ahmes writes a mathematics text.

In ancient Egypt, most mathematics revolved around everyday tasks, such as construction or trade. Around 1700 B.C.E., the Egyptian scribe Ahmes (ca. 1700 B.C.E.) writes a mathematics text, *How to Obtain Information About All Things Mysterious and Dark.* He describes basic mathematics, including *arithmetic,* fractions, and simple geometry such as calculating areas and volumes.

(M)

ca. 1650 B.C.E.

Egyptian mathematicians solve simple equations and use fractions.

Our knowledge of mathematics in ancient Egypt comes from a series of papyri that detail problems and their solutions. The Rhind papyrus, which dates to approximately 1650 B.C.E., describes the solutions to a number of simple equations that do not have whole number solutions. These problems demonstrate that ancient Egyptian mathematicians knew how to use fractions.

(M)

ca. 1600 B.C.E.

Babylonian astronomers identify constellations in the zodiac.

Early astronomers studied stars and groups of stars called constellations. Around 1600 B.C.E., Babylonian astronomers name specific constellations based upon the animals they resemble. The first constellations recorded are the lion (Leo), the bull (Taurus), and the scorpion (Scorpio). Eventually, these constellations, along with nine others, are used to name the 12 regions of the skies that Babylonian astrologers call the zodiac.

(SA)

ca. 1500 B.C.E.

Egyptians construct "Cleopatra's Needles."

As described in the sidebar "Measuring Time in the Ancient World," early astronomical devices calculated the movement of the Sun by providing a method to measure the shadows cast by long pillars. Ancient Egyptians built large granite pillars called obelisks that stood at the entrance of some temples. Around 1500 B.C.E., crafts-

men in Heliopolis build one of the most famous pairs of obelisks, known as "Cleopatra's Needles." The shadow cast by the obelisks allows scholars to calculate time, the length of seasons, and the timing of solstices. Today one of the pillars stands in Central Park in New York City and the other resides on the banks of the Thames River in London.

(SA)

ca. 1450 B.C.E.

Egyptian scholars develop the water clock.

Ancient cultures developed a number of methods to measure time, such as the *gnomon* and the sundial (*See* the sidebar "Measuring Time in the Ancient World" for more details). Around 1450 B.C.E., scholars in ancient Egypt devise a new type of clock, called the water clock, which measures the passing of time by tracking the flow of water between two vessels. Early Egyptian water clocks follow water flowing from a full vessel through a hole and into a second vessel. The second vessel has graduated marks that allow scholars to calculate how much time has passed.

(P)

ca. 1400 B.C.E.

Egyptian craftsmen produce glass vases.

Ancient Egyptian craftsmen knew how to make glass from silica sand. Around 1400 B.C.E., they make glass vases, the first useful vessels made from this material. The vases are made from what is now known as mosaic glass, fusing many individual pieces of glass together to form a complete object. Today, these objects are considered the first examples of modern glassmaking.

(C)

ca. 1300 B.C.E.

Chinese mathematicians use the decimal system.

Arithmetical calculations are easier using *place value notation* systems, where quantities are represented in particular places in a number. For example, the place value notation system commonly used today is a *decimal system,* where each place in a number represents a power of 10. The first use of the decimal system dates to the 13th century B.C.E. in China, when an inscription describing 547 days is written as 500 days plus 40 days plus seven days.

(M)

Chinese develop lacquer.

Synthetic materials such as plastics are often considered to be modern inventions. However, ancient cultures also developed processed materials. Around 1300 B.C.E., Chinese craftsmen invent a plastic varnish called lacquer, which is made from the sap of the lacquer tree. The rubberlike substance is used to make, among other things, utensils, furniture, coffins, and trinkets.

(C)

ca. 1100 B.C.E.

Chinese astronomers observe a comet.

Many ancient cultures studied the skies for religious rather than for scientific reasons. Regardless of their motivations, these early astronomers made many important scientific observations. For example, Chinese astronomers made key astronomical observations and recorded many of the first known sightings of celestial bodies. Around 1100 B.C.E., Chinese astronomers record the observation of a *comet.*

(SA)

ca. 1000 B.C.E.

The use of iron spreads through Europe.

The use of metals purified from ores greatly expanded the ability of ancient craftsmen to make tools. By 1000 B.C.E., civilizations in Europe learn how to smelt iron ores to obtain pure iron. Iron is one of the most abundant metals on the Earth and is found in greater quantities than copper, one of two metals used to make bronze (*See* entry for CA. 3600 B.C.E.). The widespread use of iron in Europe marks the beginning of the "Iron Age."

(C, ES)

Farmers begin breeding domesticated animals.

Domesticated animals performed a variety of tasks in the ancient world, from serving as a food source to helping with hard labor such as pulling a plow. Different animals were better suited to certain tasks, and within a group of the same species, some individuals would excel. Around 1000 B.C.E., farmers begin specifically breeding animals in hopes that their offspring will have the same or better traits than their parents. Animal breeding remains an important technique in agriculture today.

(B)

Babylonian and Chinese mathematicians use the abacus.

Calculating devices have been used to aid mathematicians performing complex calculations for centuries. The earliest of these devices is the abacus or counting board. Both Babylonian and Chinese mathematicians develop an abacus around 1000 B.C.E. Many believe the Babylonians first developed the abacus; however, this remains controversial. Chinese mathematicians, students, and bankers excel using the abacus, and it continues to be used into the 20th century.

(M)

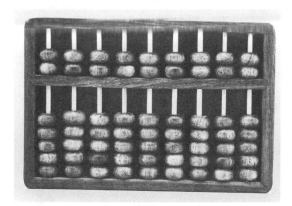

Chinese and Babylonian mathematicians develop the abacus ca. 10th century B.C.E. Many Chinese people continue to use the abacus well into the 20th century C.E. This example comes from 19th-century China. *(Museum of the History of Science, Oxford)*

ca. 900 B.C.E.

Olmec engineers build pyramids in Teotihuacán.
As described in the sidebar "Discovering the Scientific Advances of the Ancient World," civilizations throughout the world built massive pyramids. Around 900 B.C.E., in what is now Mexico, the Olmec build two stone pyramids, known as the Pyramid of the Sun and the Pyramid of the Moon in Teotihuacán. The exteriors of the pyramids are stone, which coat walls made of mud bricks.

(P)

Ancient Egyptians temper steel.
Widespread use of iron and its *alloys* for making tools began around 1000 B.C.E. (*See* entry for CA. 1000 B.C.E.). Steel, an alloy of carbon and iron, was widely used by craftsmen at this time. Early steel was very brittle, limiting its usefulness. Around 900 B.C.E., ancient Egyptians develop a method to make steel less brittle by reheating it, a process known as tempering. Tempered steel is stronger than other alloys and is used to make knives and other weapons.

(C)

June 15, 763 B.C.E.

Babylonian astronomers record a solar eclipse.
An *eclipse* is observed when Earth and two other bodies become aligned. During an eclipse, the view of one of these objects is blocked as observed from Earth. Ancient astronomers recorded solar eclipses, which occur when the Moon comes between the Sun and the Earth. The first record of a solar eclipse can be traced to ancient Babylon. Modern scholars have concluded that the eclipse referred to in these ancient documents occurred on June 15, 763 B.C.E. By 720 B.C.E., Chinese astronomers also record a solar eclipse.

(SA)

ca. 700 B.C.E.

Sushruta describes surgical techniques.
Surgery has been used to treat medical conditions for centuries. In India, the first description of surgical techniques comes around 700 B.C.E. In the text *Sushruta Samhita,* the Hindu physician Sushruta describes more than 100 different surgical instruments, and many common surgical procedures including amputating limbs, stitching cuts, extracting teeth, draining wounds, and removing cataracts.

(B)

Egyptians develop the sundial.
As described in the sidebar "Measuring Time in the Ancient World," early clocks measured time by tracking the movement of the Sun in sky. The *gnomon* is one such device.

SOLAR AND LUNAR ECLIPSES

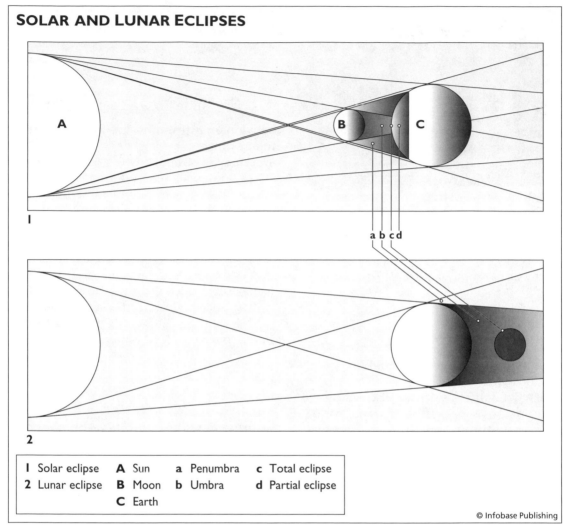

I	Solar eclipse	**A**	Sun	**a**	Penumbra	**c**	Total eclipse
2	Lunar eclipse	**B**	Moon	**b**	Umbra	**d**	Partial eclipse
		C	Earth				

© Infobase Publishing

Ancient astronomers recorded both solar and lunar eclipses. Solar eclipses (top) occur when the Moon comes between the Earth and the Sun; lunar eclipses (bottom) occur when the Earth passes between the Sun and the Moon.

Around 700 B.C.E., ancient Egyptians develop the sundial, a more precise timekeeper. The sundial consists of a base inscribed with time divisions and a raised crosspiece that casts a shadow upon the base when the device is exposed to the Sun.

(SA)

ca. 691 B.C.E.

Assyrian engineers build an aqueduct.
As ancient cities grew larger, engineers began building conduits or aqueducts to channel water from the hillsides to the fields below. Around 691 B.C.E., Assyrian engineers build an aqueduct across a valley that feeds into

the city of Nineveh. The 900 foot long channel is a precursor to the modern aqueducts used to supply water to cities and farms.

(P)

ca. 600 B.C.E.

Chinese use gnomons to measure the length of the year.

As described in the sidebar "Measuring Time in the Ancient World," the instruments that allowed scholars to make astronomical observations aided accurate timekeeping. Around 600 B.C.E., Chinese astronomers use a *gnomon* to measure the length of the summer and winter solstice. Using data collected with the gnomon, scholars calculate the length of the solar year. The gnomon consists of a large stick or pillar placed upright in the Sun, where it can cast a shadow on a marked tablet used to measure the length of the shadow.

(SA)

Chinese develop the iron plow.

Plows, one of the great agricultural advances of the ancient world, appeared in many cultures. China is believed to be the first civilization to develop the plow (*See* entry for CA. 4000 B.C.E.). Around 600 B.C.E., the Chinese develop the first iron plows, known as *kuan,* which are pulled by oxen.

(P)

Chinese use plants to identify the minerals in soil.

Plants are sensitive to the mineral composition of soil in which they grow. Soil composition is not uniform across the land; in fact different areas can have strikingly different concentrations of a host of minerals. Certain species of plants grow well near mineral deposits, while others will not grow at all. Ancient Chinese scholars make this observation around 600 B.C.E. and begin to study plant life as mark-

ers for lands that are rich in specific minerals. *The Classic of Mountains and Seas* describes the plant life that tends to grow near gold ore. Such observations help engineers determine the best sites to establish mines.

(B, ES)

May 28, 585 B.C.E.

Thales of Miletus correctly predicts a solar eclipse.

Eclipses were studied by astronomers in many different ancient cultures, from China to Babylon. Greek scholar Thales of Miletus (ca. 625–547 B.C.E.) is credited with successfully predicting that a solar eclipse would occur on May 28, 585 B.C.E. Thales becomes one of the most famous scientists of ancient Greece. Today, many scholars believe he used methods developed by Babylonian astronomers to predict when the eclipse would occur.

(SA)

ca. 580 B.C.E.

Thales of Miletus states that all matter is made primarily of water.

For centuries, philosophers and scientists pondered the nature of matter. One of the first Western scholars to tackle this question was Greek philosopher Thales of Miletus. Around 580 B.C.E., Thales proposes that all matter is made primarily of water. He uses this theory to explain natural phenomena such as earthquakes. His theory is soon supplanted by the work of Aristotle and other Greek philosophers.

(C)

Thales of Miletus introduces geometry to ancient Greece.

Ancient Greek mathematicians were renowned for their accomplishments in *geometry.* Around 580 B.C.E., Greek philosopher Thales of Miletus brings the study of geometry to Greece from Egypt. Thales describes the basic rules of angles and triangles, defines the diameter of a circle, and uses geometry to solve practical problems such as calculating heights and distances.

(M)

ca. 550 B.C.E.

Pythagoras describes the mathematics of acoustics.

Mathematicians in ancient Greece studied the relationship between mathematics and the natural world. One of the first to apply mathematics to natural phenomena was Greek mathematician Pythagoras (ca. 580–500 B.C.E.). Around 550 B.C.E., Pythagoras and his followers use simple experiments to investigate how sounds are made by a variety of instruments. The Pythagoreans describe the relationship between the length of a wind instrument and the pitch of the note it produces. Similarly, the sound of a string instrument varies with the length of the string. The Pythagoreans are among the first to recognize the numerical relationship between musical harmonies.

(M, P)

Pythagoreans describe the relationship between the sides of a right triangle.

The Greek school founded by Pythagoras made advances in mathematics and physics but was probably best known for the *Pythagorean theorem* describing the relationship between the sides of a *right triangle*. The theorem states that the square of the length of the side opposite the *right angle,* called the *hypotenuse,* is equal to the sum of the squares of the length of the other two sides, or $a^2 + b^2 = c^2$ where c is the length of the hypotenuse and a and b are the length of the other sides. This relationship was known in many cultures before the Pythagoreans embarked

Bust of the ancient Greek philosopher Pythagoras. The Pythagorean School is famous for work in mathematics, most notably lending its name to the theorem describing the relationship between the sides of the right triangle. *(SPL/Photo Researchers, Inc)*

upon their study of geometry; however the name endures.

(M)

Anaximander models the Earth based on scientific principles.

Philosophers in ancient Greece studied a wide range of natural phenomena from mathematics to Earth science. Around 550 B.C.E., Greek astronomer Anaximander (610–ca. 547 B.C.E.), a pupil of Thales of Miletus (*See* entry for CA. 580 B.C.E.), presents a model of Earth, describing it as cylindrical in shape. Anaximander hypothesizes that Earth is unsuspended in the universe. He believes in a *geocentric* model of the universe, with Earth at the center of the universe and stars and other heavenly bodies rotating around it.

(SA)

Anaximander presents a theory for the origin of the universe.

Greek philosopher Anaximander, a student of Thales of Miletus (*See* entry for CA. 580 B.C.E.), described theories of the Earth and the universe. Around 550 B.C.E., he presents his theory for the origin of the universe. According to Anaximander, the universe forms by a mechanical *force* that separates matter into opposite components such as hot and cold or earth and ether.

(SA)

Anaximander describes the origins of life.

Natural philosophers in ancient Greece pondered many of the questions that are still studied by scientists today. For example, Greek philosopher Anaximander presents his ideas on the origin and *evolution* of life around 550 B.C.E. Anaximander believes that life first develops in the mud, evolving into fish and other marine life that eventually makes the leap to land. His theory represents an early theory of evolution.

(B)

ca. 545 B.C.E.

Anaximenes of Miletus states that all matter is made of air.

For centuries, philosophers and scientists have pondered the nature of matter. Ancient Greek philosophers and scientists believed that matter is made of one or more fundamental substances. Around 545 B.C.E., Greek philosopher Anaximenes of Miletus (ca. 545 B.C.E.) proposes that air is the primary substance in all matter.

He points to the condensation of water as a mechanism by which air can be transformed from one substance to another.

(C)

ca. 530 B.C.E.

Xenophanes observes fossils of sea life on mountaintops.

Modern geologists and paleontologists study fossils to understand early life. This tradition begins in ancient Greece around 530 B.C.E., when Greek philosopher Xenophanes (ca. 560–ca. 478 B.C.E.) describes finding fossilized seashells and fish on mountaintops. He suggests that the land on the mountaintops was once underwater. Xenophanes uses fossil evidence to develop his theory that the Earth formed from a condensation of water and mud.

(ES)

ca. 520 B.C.E.

Pythagorean mathematicians note irrational numbers.

Ancient Greek mathematicians excelled in the field of *geometry*. The mathematicians who were part of the Pythagorean school studied the numerical relationships found in geometry, with the belief that all objects can be expressed using *integers* or ratios of integers. Around 520 B.C.E., Pythagorean mathematicians realize the length of a diagonal of a square cannot be expressed as a *ratio* of integers, suggesting the existence of *irrational numbers*.

(M)

ca. 510 B.C.E.

Hecataeus of Miletus describes the geography of Europe, Africa, and Asia.

As people in ancient civilizations began to travel to distant lands, scholars wrote works of geography, describing the terrain and culture of the known cultures. Around 510 B.C.E., Greek scholar Hecataeus of Miletus (sixth–fifth century B.C.E.) writes *Periegesis* (Tour around the world), one of the first works of geography. The three-volume work describes the geography of Europe, Asia, and Africa, focusing on the regions bordering the Mediterranean Sea.

(ES)

ca. 500 B.C.E.

Kashyapa describes units of matter.

Scholars and philosophers in many ancient cultures described how matter could be broken down into fundamental units. Around 500 B.C.E., Indian scholar Kashyapa states that the ancient elements, fire, water, earth, air, and ether, can be further broken down into fundamental units he calls *parmanus*. Kashyapa believes that the properties of different *parmanus* determine the properties of matter. Today, Kashyapa's concept of *parmanus* is viewed as being an ancient predecessor to modern *atomic theory*.

(C)

Alcmaeon studies the body through dissection.

Medicine relies upon the knowledge of *anatomy*. Around 500 B.C.E., Greek physiologist Alcmaeon (sixth century B.C.E.) studies human anatomy through dissection. He identifies and describes arteries and veins, as well as nerves. His studies lead him to suggest that the brain is the intellectual center of the body. Some evidence suggests he may have also practiced the dissection of live animals called vivisection.

(B)

Lao-tzu describes double-acting piston bellows.

The manufacturing of different metal *alloys* often requires a continuous stream of air that can be blown over or through molten metals. Around 500 B.C.E., Chinese scholar Lao-tzu (fl. sixth century B.C.E.) describes a device, known as a double-acting piston bellow, which produces a continuous stream of air. A similar device is later used to provide a stream of liquid, a critical component to the Chinese weapon known as the flame-thrower. Despite its widespread use in China, the double-acting piston does not reach Europe until the 16th century.

(P)

ca. 480 B.C.E.

Oenopides of Chios calculates the obliquity of the Earth.

Ancient astronomers realized that the Earth is tilted with respect to the plane of orbit, known as the *obliquity*, and try to calculate the angle that it is tipped. Around 480 B.C.E., Greek philosopher Oenopides of Chios (fifth century B.C.E.) calculates that the obliquity of the Earth is 24 degrees. Today, scholars realize his value is remarkably close to the actual value of 23.5 degrees.

(SA)

Heracleitus states that fire is the primary substance in the universe.

Many ancient Greek philosophers contemplated the primary substances that make up the universe. By 480 B.C.E., Greek philosopher Heracleitus (ca. 540–ca. 480 B.C.E.) proposes that the universe is made from fire. He describes a chain of transformation from fire to air to water and finally to earth. Heracleitus says that these substances are in continual flux; however, equilibrium is established between these substances, keeping the world in balance.

(C, SA)

Anaxagoras states that matter is made from an infinite number of elements.

A number of ancient Greek philosophers described their ideas of how matter forms, proposing that fire, water, earth, and air are fundamental substances. Around 480 B.C.E., Greek philosopher Anaxagoras (ca. 500–ca. 428 B.C.E.) says that matter is made from an infinite number of basic substances. His theory accounts for the vast diversity and dynamic changes found in the natural world.

(C, ES, SA)

ca. 450 B.C.E.

Philolaus describes heavenly bodies circling a central fire.

For centuries, scholars debated whether or not the Earth is the center of the universe. One of the first suggestions that the Earth moves through space comes around 450 B.C.E., when Greek philosopher Philolaus (fifth century B.C.E.) says that the Earth, Moon, Sun, and other planets move around a central fire. His work anticipates the later debate of whether the universe is Sun-centered, known as *heliocentric,* or Earth-centered, called *geocentric.*

(SA)

Empedocles describes the movement of blood.

Blood, pumped by the heart, flows through the body, delivering oxygen and other nutrients to organs and tissues. The first step toward understanding the nature of blood's circulation through the body occurs around 450 B.C.E., when Greek natural philosopher Empedocles (ca. 490–430 B.C.E.) describes the movement of blood through the heart. Despite this early first step, a thorough explanation of circulation does not come until the 17th century.

(B)

Empedocles describes how the elements undergo changes.

For centuries, philosophers and scientists pondered the nature of matter. Ancient Greek philosophers and scientists believed that matter is made of one or more fundamental substances. Around 450 B.C.E., Greek natural philosopher Empedocles states that all matter is made from a combination of four fundamental substances: fire, water, air, and earth. Empedocles further describes how the forces of love and hate cause these *elements* to undergo changes.

(C)

Leucippus of Miletus describes atoms.

Ancient Greek philosophers and scientists believed that matter is made of one or more fundamental substances. Around 450 B.C.E., Greek philosopher Leucippus of Miletus (fifth century B.C.E.) proposes that all matter can be reduced to indivisible units he calls *atoms.* At first, his work is embraced by other Greek philosophers, but later falls out of favor. When the 18th-century English scientist John Dalton (1766–1844) describes modern *atomic theory,* he recalls Leucippus when he names the fundamental units atoms.

(C)

ca. 440 B.C.E.

Democritus describes the universe in terms of atoms and voids.

Ancient Greek philosophers and scientists believed all matter is composed of indivisible units called *atoms.* Around 440 B.C.E., Leucippus's student, Democritus (ca. 460–ca. 370 B.C.E.), describes how atoms and the void between atoms make up the universe. Democritus asserts that movement and changes of matter come from the movement of atoms.

(C, SA)

Meton of Athens develops a 19-year calendar cycle.

As described in the sidebar "Measuring Time in the Ancient World," ancient astronomers used their observations of the heavens to develop calendars. Around 440 B.C.E., Greek astronomer Meton of Athens (fl. 432 B.C.E.) develops a 19-year calendar cycle, based upon the movement of the Sun and the Moon. Meton uses his calendar, now known as the Metonic cycle, to predict *eclipses*. The Metonic cycle becomes the basis of the Greek and Hebrew calendars.

(SA)

ca. 430 B.C.E.

Hippocrates of Chios describes Greek geometry.

Ancient Greek mathematicians made several notable advances in the study of *geometry*. Around 430 B.C.E., Greek mathematician Hippocrates of Chios (fl. 460 B.C.E.) writes *Elements of Geometry*. His work considers two leading problems of the day: the duplication of a cube and the squaring of a circle. His work is later supplanted when Greek mathematician Euclid summarizes Greek geometry in *The Elements* (*See* entry for CA. 300 B.C.E.).

(M)

ca. 420 B.C.E.

Hippocrates of Cos describes the natural causes of disease.

Physicians and scientists are always searching for the causes of disease. In ancient Greece, physician Hippocrates of Cos (ca. 460– ca. 377 B.C.E.) believed that all diseases had natural causes. In his work *Nature of Man*, Hippocrates describes how disorders in one or more of the four humors, phlegm, blood, yellow bile, and black bile, lead to a diseased state. In most cases, Hippocrates prefers to treat diseases with changes in diet and environment rather than prescribing drugs. He becomes one of the first Western physicians

to apply scientific reason to the study and treatment of disease.

(B)

Hippias of Elis discovers the quadratix.

Ancient Greek mathematicians excelled in the study of *geometry*. One problem that garnered much attention in this era was the construction of curves and other geometric figures using a compass and straightedge. Around 420 B.C.E., Greek mathematician Hippias of Elis (fifth century B.C.E.) discovers a curve that can be used to divide an angle into three equal parts, known as trisecting an angle. The curve, now known as a quadratix, is the first curve studied by ancient Greek mathematicians that cannot be constructed using a straightedge and compass.

(M)

ca. 400 B.C.E.

Hippocrates of Cos develops the Hippocratic oath.

In ancient Greece, medicine was not a formal field of study but rather a profession learned through apprenticeships. As a result, the quality and types of medical practices varied greatly. Around 400 B.C.E., Greek physician Hippocrates of Cos attempts to establish guidelines for medical practices. He develops what becomes known as the Hippocratic oath, outlining the principles which medical practitioners should practice, from treating the sick to the best of one's ability to preserving a patient's privacy. New physicians take a modern version of the Hippocratic oath today.

(B)

Chinese invent the compass.

Magnets are attracted to the poles of the Earth, an observation that has been used to build compasses for navigation. The first compass, made from a magnetic *lodestone,* appears in China around 400 B.C.E. A book from this era, *Book of the Devil Valley Master,* mentions people carrying "south-pointers" on their travels. Many scholars believe these early compasses were used for divination rather than navigation.

(ES)

Kan Te observes sunspots.

Ancient Chinese astronomers made a number of important astronomical observations. Around 400 B.C.E., Chinese astronomer Kan Te (fourth century B.C.E.) records darkened regions on the surface of the Sun. He wrongly believes that they arise from *eclipses* that begin at discrete regions of the Sun then spread to cover the entire surface. Today, scholars recognize that Kan Te had observed sunspots rather than an eclipse.

(SA)

Chinese invent cast iron.

Cast iron is a strong material used to build everything from pots and pans to field plows. The first use of cast iron appears in China around 400 B.C.E., when Chinese engineers build large furnaces capable of heating iron to over 1800°F (1000°C). The cast iron made by the Chinese is flexible, allowing craftsman to make a variety of objects, and strong enough to be used in farm equipment and buildings. The use of cast iron does not spread to Europe until the 14th century.

(C)

Mohist philosophers describe the first law of motion.

Sir Isaac Newton (1642–1727) described the tendency of objects in motions to stay in motion and objects at rest to stay at rest, which is known as the first law of motion (*See* entry for 1687). The first articulation of this principle comes around 400 B.C.E., when Chinese scholars who follow the philosopher Mo-tzu (ca. 470–ca. 321 B.C.E.), known

as the Mohist philosophers, write *Mo Ching.* Their work is soon lost and therefore does not affect subsequent studies by Chinese physicists.

(P)

Theodorus of Cyrene describes why the square roots of many numbers are irrational.

Ancient Greek mathematicians were renowned for their work in geometry, but they also made advances in other mathematical disciplines. Around 400 B.C.E., Greek mathematician Theodorus of Cyrene (ca. 465–ca. 398 B.C.E.) demonstrates that the square roots of the numbers 3, 5, 6, 8, 10, 11, 12, 14, 15, and 17 are *irrational numbers.* His work follows the tradition of the Pythagorean mathematicians who had previously shown that the square root of 2 was irrational.

(M)

Lu Pan constructs kites.

Today, most kites are flown for recreation. In ancient China, kites were used as a form of communication, sending signals between cities and to distant armies. Around 400 B.C.E., Chinese scholar Lu Pan (also know as Kungshu P'an) constructs the first kites. He renders the kites in the shape of birds and uses them to send messages between military units. Through the next centuries, kites are used by Chinese scholars for communication, fishing, and attempts at manned flight, a precursor to the modern hang glider.

(P)

Democritus describes the cosmos.

Perhaps the greatest problem facing philosophers and scientists is understanding the nature of the universe. Around 400 B.C.E., Greek scholar Democritus presents a theory of the universe based upon his previous hypothesis that all matter is composed of *atoms* (*See* entry for CA. 440 B.C.E.).

Democritus says the cosmos forms when a group of atoms are brought together into a specific structure. According to his theory, the cosmos consists of the Sun, the Moon, the planets, and the stars all revolving around the Earth. His theory is one of many early *geocentric*, or Earth-centered, models of the universe.

(SA)

Mo-tzu describes the use of poison gas in warfare.

Chemical weapons are a modern problem, but their use dates back to antiquity. Around 400 B.C.E., Chinese philosopher Mo-tzu describes the use of poison gases to attack enemies. According to Mo-tzu, armies use bellows to pump the fumes from burning mustard into tunnels that lead to enemy headquarters. Poison gases are also used to fumigate houses, either to prevent insect infestation or to clear the house of a particular disease.

(C)

399 B.C.E.

Greek engineers develop the catapult.

Engineers use the basic principles of physics to make devices that can carry and transport heavy objects. One such object, the catapult, first appears in 399 B.C.E., when Greek engineers under the direction of Dionysius the Elder (ca. 430–ca. 367 B.C.E.) construct the weapon. A catapult uses a bow or a wooden arm to project an object into the air. Greek soldiers use catapults to project both spears and stones at enemies.

(P)

387 B.C.E.

Plato establishes the Academy at Athens.

Throughout history, philosophers and later scientists have come together at great centers of learning. In 387 B.C.E., Greek philosopher

Plato (ca. 428–ca. 347 B.C.E.) establishes one of the great schools of the ancient world, the Academy at Athens. Plato's Academy thrives until the first century B.C.E. Among the scholars trained at the Academy is Greek philosopher Aristotle (384–322 B.C.E.), who goes on to found a rival school after Plato's death (*See* entry for 335 B.C.E.).

(B, C, ES, M, MS, SA, W)

ca. 370 B.C.E.

Eudoxus of Cnidus describes proportions.

Mathematicians in ancient Greece excelled in the study of *geometry*. Many of their accomplishments are recorded in Greek philosopher Euclid's great work *The Elements* (*See* entry for CA. 300 B.C.E.). Included in this work is a theory of proportions put forth by Greek mathematician Eudoxus of Cnidus (ca. 395–ca. 342 B.C.E.) around 370 B.C.E. Eudoxus describes a proof demonstrating how two quantities are proportional to each other that has a great effect on the study of *irrational numbers*.

(M)

Aristotle describes free falling bodies.

Natural philosophers in ancient Greece pondered questions of physics and developed ways to describe motion. One of the early theories of motion appears around 370 B.C.E., when Greek philosopher Aristotle describes the motion of free falling bodies. He correctly observes that objects accelerate as they fall. However, he believes that heavier objects fall faster than lighter objects, an idea that is later disproved by modern scientists.

(P)

ca. 350 B.C.E.

Shi Shen describes the coordinates of stars.

Chinese astronomers made many key observations of celestial bodies and were the first to record the existence of sunspots and comets. Around 330 B.C.E., Chinese astronomer Shi Shen publishes a star catalog describing the coordinates of 121 different stars. Shi's work is the first of many important star catalogs recorded in China.

(SA)

Heracleides of Ponticus states that the Earth rotates on its axis.

Early astronomers proposed many explanations for the movement of heavenly bodies. Around 350 B.C.E., Greek scholar Heracleides of Ponticus (ca. 390–ca. 322 B.C.E.) claims that the Earth rotates on its axis once every 24 hours. He uses this theory to explain how objects in the sky rise and set each day. While Heracleides's theory becomes widely known, Greek scholars do not generally accept his idea.

(SA)

Heracleides of Ponticus states that Venus and Mercury orbit the Sun.

Astronomers have pondered the nature and order of the universe since antiquity. Around 350 B.C.E., Greek natural philosopher Heracleides of Ponticus describes his schema for the solar system, with the planets now called Venus and Mercury orbiting the Sun and the Sun orbiting the Earth. His work is helps establish the *geocentric* theory of the universe, which states that the Earth is the center of the universe.

(SA)

Aristotle presents evidence that the Earth is a sphere.

Early natural philosophers developed a wide array of theories about the Earth and its position in the universe. Around 350 B.C.E., Greek philosopher Aristotle states that the planet Earth is spherical and tends to move toward the center of the universe. Aristotle backs his theory with observational evidence, including the circular shadow cast by the Earth

Ancient Greek naturalist Aristotle used observations made during a lunar eclipse as part of his argument that the Earth is spherical. This photograph of a lunar eclipse as viewed from Merritt Island, Florida, was taken centuries later, on December 20, 2000. *(NASA Kennedy Space Center)*

during a lunar *eclipse* as evidence supporting the Earth's spherical shape. He concludes by estimating that the *circumference* of the Earth is about 45,000 miles (72,000 km), 1.8 times larger than the value known today.

(SA)

Aristotle classifies more than 500 animal species.

Biologists develop classification systems for living organisms based upon their common features. Around 350 B.C.E., Greek philosopher Aristotle presents one of the first of these classification systems in his classic work *History of Animals*. He categorizes more than 500 animal species, placing each in one of nine groups: egg-laying quadrupeds, viviparous quadrupeds (which give birth to live animals), marine mammals, birds, fish, mollusks, crustacea, tesracea, and insects.

Aristotle's system is the first to recognize the difference between fish and marine mammals.

(B)

Eudoxus of Cnidus develops a geometric model of the universe.

Early astronomers both observed the movement of stars and planets and tried to develop models to explain them. Around 350 B.C.E., Greek astronomer Eudoxus of Cnidus develops a geometric model of the universe. Eudoxus explained the motion of a planet as a series of circular movements. Eudoxus's view of the universe persists after his death and is further developed by Greek astronomer Callippus (fourth century B.C.E.) and Greek philosopher Aristotle.

(SA)

Dinostratus squares a circle.

Ancient Greeks excelled in mathematics, particularly the field of *geometry.* Around 350 B.C.E., Greek scholar Dinostratus (ca. 390–ca. 320 B.C.E.) finds a circle with the same area as a square, known as squaring a circle. He uses a curve called a quadratix (*See* entry for CA. 420 B.C.E.). The quadratix, discovered by Hippias of Elis, is the first curve known to ancient Greek mathematicians that could not be constructed using a compass and straightedge.

(M)

Menaechmus discovers conic sections.

Scholars in ancient Greece were renowned for their work in mathematics. Around 350 B.C.E., Greek mathematician Menaechmus (fourth century B.C.E.) shows that intersecting a plane with a cone generates four different curves: the circle, the ellipse, the hyperbola, and the parabola. These curves, known as *conic sections,* are frequently used by modern scientists and continue to be studied by high school students today.

(M)

Aristotle describes the elements.

Philosophers in ancient Greece made many attempts to define the fundamental units of matter. Around 350 B.C.E., Greek natural philosopher Aristotle describes the chemical elements. Aristotle agrees with many of his predecessors, stating there are four elements, earth, water, air, and fire, which combine to form all types of matter. He claims that each element is characterized by the fundamental qualities hot, cold, wet, and dry and argues any agent that can change a fundamental

Ancient Greek natural philosopher Aristotle contributes to a wide variety of scientific disciplines, including biology and meteorology. This historical portrait was first published in 1702. *(George Bernard/Photo Researchers, Inc)*

quality can transmute an element. For example, the element earth is cold and dry; if a process makes it wet, the element becomes water. Aristotle states that such transformations are constantly occurring in nature.

(C)

347 B.C.E.

Ch'ang Ch'ü describes the use of natural gas as fuel.

Methane, or natural gas, is commonly used for fuel today. The first use of natural gas is believed to have occurred in ancient China. In his 347 B.C.E. work, *Records of the Country South of Mount Hua*, Chinese scholar Ch'ang Ch'ü (fourth century B.C.E.) describes a substance from the ground that burns brightly and leaves behind no ashes. By the first century B.C.E., Chinese drill for natural gas and use it to purify salts.

(C)

ca. 345 B.C.E.

Sun-tzu describes the crossbow.

The crossbow allowed a soldier to shoot several bolts in a short period of time, enabling a much more efficient attack than a single bow and arrow. Around 345 B.C.E., Chinese scholar Sun-tzu (fourth century B.C.E.) describes the use of a crossbow in *Ping-fa* (The art of war). The device Sun-tzu describes has a trigger that allows arrows to be fired quickly and with great *force*.

(P)

ca. 340 B.C.E.

Callippus describes the movement of heavenly bodies.

Ancient astronomers studied the motions of the Moon, stars, and the visible planets. Around 340 B.C.E., Greek astronomer Callippus studies the motion of the planets. He concludes that at least 34 spheres are necessary to account for the movement of heavenly bodies. Callippus also constructs a 76-year cycle that includes both the solar and lunar years.

(SA)

Aristotle writes *Meteorology.*

Many ancient Greek philosophers applied their reasoning abilities to a wide variety of scientific questions. Greek natural philosopher Aristotle, for example, published theories on a wide range of topics, including biology, physics, and astronomy. Around 340 B.C.E., he presents his theories about the weather in *Meterologica* (Meteorology). His work encompasses meteorological phenomena such as rainbows, rainstorms, thunder, and lightning, as well as other events in the sky, including the appearance of *comets* and shooting stars.

(W)

335 B.C.E.

Aristotle establishes a school at the Lyceum.

Ancient Greece was home to some of the greatest centers of learning in the ancient world. In 335 B.C.E., Greek philosopher Aristotle establishes a school at the Lyceum in Athens. The Lyceum soon rivals the Academy, where Aristotle once studied. Scholars at the Lyceum are known for a more cooperative approach to research than those at the Academy. Work at the Lyceum also reflects Aristotle's interest in natural philosophy, particularly biology.

(B, P, W)

ca. 330 B.C.E.

Pytheas of Massalia notes the relationship between tides and the Moon.

Throughout history, important scientific observations have been made during voyages.

Around 330 B.C.E., Greek geographer Pytheas of Massalia (ca. 300 B.C.E.) sails from Greece to the North Atlantic, and then explores the North and Baltic Seas. On his voyage, Pytheas encounters much stronger tides than are found on the Mediterranean Sea. He notes that the strength of the tides seems to be correlated with the phases of the Moon.

(ES, MS, SA, W)

Aristaeus describes the theory of conic sections.
Ancient Greek mathematicians were renowned for their work in the field of *geometry*. The discovery that four different curves can be formed from a plane intersecting a cone (*See* entry for CA. 350 B.C.E.) stimulated research into the properties of these curves, known as *conic sections*. Around 330 B.C.E., Greek mathematician Aristaeus (ca. 370–ca. 300) writes one of the first treatises on the subject, *Five Books Concerning Conic Sections*, outlining some early theories of these interesting curves.

(M)

ca. 320 B.C.E.

Theophrastus classifies plant species.
Biologists classify organisms based upon their common characteristics. Around 320 B.C.E., Greek philosopher Theophrastus (ca. 372–ca. 287 B.C.E.) classifies more than 500 species of plants into one of four categories: trees, shrubs, under shrubs, and herbs. His work includes detailed descriptions of plant species and how they grow.

(B)

ca. 312 B.C.E.

Zeno of Citium establishes the Stoa.
Centers of learning thrived in Athens during the fourth century B.C.E. Around 312 B.C.E., Greek philosopher Zeno of Citium (ca.

335–ca. 263 B.C.E.) establishes a school of philosophy that becomes known as the Stoa. Scholars at the school embrace the Stoic philosophy, which is based upon logic, ethics, and physics. The Stoic school survives until the second century C.E.

(P)

ca. 310 B.C.E.

Tsou Yen describes five elements.
Ancient scholars in many cultures attempted to define the *elements* that make up matter. Around 310 B.C.E., Chinese scholar Tsou Yen (ca. 340–ca. 260 B.C.E.) describes the five elements or *Wu hsing*. Tsou states that the elements, water, metal, wood, fire, and earth, exist within a cycle, the elements intimately associated with natural phenomena from sounds and colors to plants and animals.

(C)

ca. 307 B.C.E.

Epicurus of Samos founds a school of philosophy.
Advances in science often occur at centers of learning. During the fourth century B.C.E., many of the great schools of ancient Greece were founded, including Plato's Academy and the Lyceum. Around 307 B.C.E., Epicurus of Samos (342–270 B.C.E.) establishes a school of philosophy on the grounds of his home. At the school, which becomes known as the Garden of Epicurus, the idea that atoms are fundamental units of matter plays a prominent role in many theories of natural philosophy. The Garden of Epicurus remains open until the third century C.E.

(C, P)

Ptolemy establishes the library of Alexandria.
The explosion of philosophical and scientific work in ancient Greece coincided with the

founding of many famous centers of learning in Athens, including Plato's Academy and the Stoa. Arguably, the most famous center of learning in the Greek empire was the library of Alexandria. Around 307 B.C.E., the king of Egypt Ptolemy I (ca. 367–ca. 283 B.C.E.) establishes the library, which houses the scholarly works of the ancient Greeks and serves as a place where philosophers gather and work.

(B, C, ES, M, MS, P, SA, W)

ca. 300 B.C.E.

Chen Zuo describes stars and constellations.

Chinese astronomers made many early observations of stars, planets, and celestial bodies such as *comets.* These observations led to the development of star catalogs, detailing the coordinates of stars and clusters of stars known as constellations (*See* entry for CA. 350 B.C.E.). Around 300 B.C.E., Chinese astronomer Chen Zuo publishes a star catalog describing the coordinates of 1,464 stars, as well as 283 constellations.

(SA)

Chinese physicians describe the pulse.

Physicians use external indicators such as temperature and heart rate to determine the health of a patient. The use of the heart rate as assessed by taking a pulse is introduced in China around 300 B.C.E. Chinese physicians feel that the pulse indicates the flow of two important fluids through the body, the blood or yin, and the energy (ch'i) or yang. This ancient Chinese medical practice indicates an early understanding of circulation.

(B)

Praxagoras of Cos distinguishes between veins and arteries.

In ancient Greece, many early medical practitioners made important observations about the anatomy and physiology of living organisms. Around 300 B.C.E., Greek physician Praxagoras of Cos (fourth century B.C.E.) notes that there is a difference between two types of blood vessels, arteries and veins. Praxagoras believes that air flows through arteries, while blood flows through veins. Today, scientists realize that arteries carry blood rich in oxygen to the body while veins carry blood deprived of oxygen back to the heart and lungs.

(B)

Herophilus dissects human cadavers.

The study of *anatomy* relies upon the knowledge gained from dissecting organisms and studying various organs and tissues. Around 300 B.C.E., Greek scholar Herophilus (ca. 335–ca. 280 B.C.E.) dissects human cadavers and studies the *anatomy* of the brain and peripheral nervous system. Among his discoveries are the *membranes* in the brain and the distinction between sensory neurons, nerves that send signals to the brain, and motor neurons, nerves that direct muscles to relax or contract. Herophilus also studies the abdominal organs, providing detailed descriptions of the liver, pancreas, intestines, and reproductive organs.

(B)

Chinese scholars harness horses.

Land transportation in the ancient world relied upon the domestication of animals and the development of effective vehicles. The development of the horse-drawn carriage and the chariot depended upon the ability to harness large animals to the vehicle. Around 300 B.C.E., Chinese scholars develop a harness that effectively attaches horses to a carriage. The so-called collar harness is strapped around the horse's torso, allowing the horse to pull from the chest.

(P)

Euclid writes a work of geometry.

Ancient Greek mathematicians excelled in mathematics, particularly *geometry*. Around 300 B.C.E., Greek scholar Euclid (ca. 300 B.C.E.) writes his classic text *The Elements* describing the definitions, *postulates,* and problems that characterize geometry. Euclid's work, encompassing 13 books, covers the geometry of both planes and solids. His work is based upon five assumptions or postulates describing points, lines, circles, and angles. The geometry described in *The Elements* closely resembles the geometry taught in high schools today.

(M)

Diocles of Carystus writes the first anatomy text.

Ancient Greek medical practitioners made many advances in the understanding of *anatomy*. Around 300 B.C.E., Greek physician Diocles of Carystus (fourth century B.C.E.) writes the first anatomy text. Diocles describes the workings of the human body in terms of the four elements, fire, air, water, and earth. He says that a proper balance of these elements is essential for good health.

(B)

Ancient Chinese scholars describe the planting of crops.

Many early scientific advances centered on agricultural practices that help civilizations thrive. Around 300 B.C.E., the Chinese treatise *Master Lu's Spring and Autumn Annals* describes the practice of growing crops in rows. Planting crops in rows facilitates planting, weeding, and harvesting. The practice, which likely began in China during the sixth century B.C.E., is not embraced in Europe until the 18th century.

(B)

Shih Lu constructs the Magic Canal.

Engineers in many different ancient civilizations, including Babylon and Greece, built canals to transport goods by water. Around 300 B.C.E., Chinese engineer Shih Lu constructs the first contour canal, linking two rivers that flow in different directions by following the contours of the surrounding hills. The canal, known as the Ling Ch'ü or the Magic Canal, continues to be used today.

(ES, P)

Dicaearchus of Messina develops a map of the Earth.

Many ancient Greeks saw the Earth as a sphere. The philosopher Aristotle presented scientific evidence supporting this theory around 350 B.C.E. (*See* entry for CA. 350 B.C.E.). Around 300 B.C.E., Dicaearchus of Messina (ca. 320 B.C.E.), a student of Aristotle, develops a map of the Earth. He depicts the Earth as a sphere and estimates its *circumference* and the height of various mountains.

(ES, M)

ca. 286 B.C.E.

Strato of Lampsacus describes falling bodies.

Many ancient Greek philosophers developed theories to explain the physical world. For example, Aristotle put forth one of the first theories to explain the motion of falling bodies, stating that bodies accelerate as they fall and that the rate of this acceleration is a function of the bodies' weight (*See* entry for CA. 350 B.C.E.). Around 286 B.C.E., Greek natural philosopher Strato of Lampsacus (d. 270 B.C.E.) revisits Aristotle's work. Strato confirms Aristotle's theory of falling bodies, adding that the impact of an object's fall is affected by both the weight of the object and the distance the object falls.

(P)

ca. 280 B.C.E.

Egyptians complete the Pharos Lighthouse.

As civilizations built ships capable of sailing far from land, they needed a way to guide ships at night. Around 280 B.C.E., Egyptian engineers complete a lighthouse on the island of Pharos, and it becomes the model for the lighthouses used today. The lighthouse stands 350 feet (107 m) high and is topped by a cylinder where a fire burns at night. Sailors entering the harbor at Alexandria use the light of the fire to guide their way.

(P)

Aristarchus of Samos proposes that the Sun is the center of the universe.

Ancient astronomers studied the motions of the stars and planets and began to develop theories to explain the universe and the Earth's place within it. Many of these theories were *geocentric*, stating that the Earth was the center of the universe. Around 280 B.C.E., Greek philosopher Aristarchus of Samos (ca. 270 B.C.E.) proposes a *heliocentric* model of the universe, stating that the Earth revolves around the Sun. Despite his work, the geocentric model continues to dominate astronomical thinking for centuries.

(SA)

Erasistratus of Ceos studies the heart and circulatory system.

Advances in the field of *anatomy* depend upon the dissection of organisms. Around 280 B.C.E., Greek scholar Erasistratus of Ceos (ca. 250 B.C.E.), following the work of Herophilus of Chalcedon, studies human anatomy by dissecting cadavers. Erasistratus focuses on the human heart, describing how its valves assure that fluid flows in one direction through the organ. He states that arteries and veins are found throughout the body

and that they serve as channels assuring the spread of vital nutrients.

(B)

Ptolemy Philadelphus completes a canal connecting the Nile with the Red Sea.

Engineers in ancient civilizations from Babylon to China designed and built canals to expand the reach of water transportation. Around 280 B.C.E., Egyptian King Ptolemy Philadelphus (308–246 B.C.E.) oversees the completion of a canal that connects the Nile River to the Red Sea, a project that began 350 years earlier.

(P)

ca. 270 B.C.E.

Ctesibius of Alexandria invents an accurate water clock.

As described in the sidebar "Measuring Time in the Ancient World," scientists and engineers worked hard at developing devices that could accurately keep time. Around 270 B.C.E., Greek inventor Ctesibius of Alexandria (ca. 270 B.C.E.) invents an accurate water clock called the clepsydra. The clock uses dripping water to turn a rod that measures passing time. The clepsydra is so accurate that it remains in use until the Renaissance.

(P)

ca. 260 B.C.E.

Archimedes describes buoyancy.

Many ancient Greek scholars developed theories describing the physical world. One of the most famous scholars, Archimedes (ca. 287–212 B.C.E.), writes *On Floating Bodies* around 260 B.C.E., describing his theory of buoyancy. Archimedes notes that a body floating in a liquid is lighter than it is on Earth. In what is now known as Archimedes' principle, he states that the weight of a floating body is equal to the weight of the liquid it displaces. Archimedes' principle is not widely accepted by his peers, but his work continues to be studied today.

(P)

Archimedes proves the law of the lever.
A lever, consisting of a beam balanced upon a support, can be used to move heavy objects. Around 260 B.C.E., Greek scholar Archimedes describes how the lever works. He shows that if the point of support is in the middle of the lever, two objects on either end must be the same weight to balance each other out. However, if the point of support is away from the center, two objects of differing weights can balance each other. The law of the lever says that the lever is in balance when the weights at the ends are inversely proportional to their distance from the support. Archimedes' proof the law of the lever continues to be studied today.

(P)

Philo of Byzantium improves the catapult.
The study of physics has led to the development and improvement of devices that make many kinds of work easier. For example, the catapult is a machine that uses a sling to project a heavy object into the air. Around 260 B.C.E., Greek scholar Philo of Byzantium (ca. 250 B.C.E.) studies the application of physics to military problems. In his work *Mechanics,* he describes the catapult and presents his design for a chain drive that allows for repeat loading of the machine.

(P)

ca. 240 B.C.E.

Eratosthenes of Cyrene calculates the circumference of the Earth.
From the time of Aristotle, ancient Greek scholars believed that the Earth was a sphere. Around 240 B.C.E., Greek astronomer Era-tosthenes of Cyrene (ca. 276–ca. 194 B.C.E.) states that the *circumference* of the Earth is approximately 29,000 miles (47,000 km). He describes his calculation in the work *On the Measurement of the Earth,* which scholars study for centuries after his death. Today, scientists calculate the circumference of the Earth to be just less than 25,000 miles (40,000 km).

(M, SA)

Chinese astronomers observe Halley's comet.
Astronomers in China were renowned for their careful recording of celestial bodies, including some of the first descriptions of masses of ice and dirt called *comets*. In 240 B.C.E., Chinese astronomers record the first known sighting of Halley's comet. During the 18th century, British astronomer Edmond Halley (1656–1742) correctly predicts that this comet is visible from the Earth every 76 years (*See* entry for 1705).

(SA)

ca. 230 B.C.E.

Eratosthenes of Cyrene develops a method for finding prime numbers.
Prime numbers are numbers that are divisible only by themselves and the number one. Mathematicians interested in *number theory* have studied prime numbers for centuries. Around 230 B.C.E., Greek mathematician Era-tosthenes of Cyrene develops a method for finding prime numbers known as the "Sieve of Eratosthenes." His method continues to be used today.

(M)

ca. 214 B.C.E.

Construction begins on the Great Wall of China.
Building walls around cities provided a useful means of defense against enemy invaders.

Beginning around 700 B.C.E., Chinese states built large walls to guard against invasion from one another. By the time China was unified under a single emperor around 221 B.C.E., walls protected at least seven different states. Around 214 B.C.E., Emperor Cheng (ca. 259–ca. 210 B.C.E.) orders workers to take down the walls that separate states within the Chinese empire and connect the walls that define the borders of China. The construction of what is now known as the Great Wall of China continues for the next 10 years.

(P)

ca. 200 B.C.E.

Ancient Chinese farmers develop the seed drill.

Early advances in agriculture allowed ancient civilizations to survive and thrive. By 200 B.C.E., Chinese farmers develop the seed drill to facilitate the planting of crops. The seed drill is pulled behind a large animal, such as a horse or mule, and evenly distributes seed along the rows of crops (*See* entry for CA. 300 B.C.E.). Use of the seed drill economizes the use of seeds, as the alternative method, the spreading of seeds by hand, wastes seeds because plants often grow in clumps.

(B)

Chinese physicians describe the circulation of blood.

The notion that blood is pumped by the heart and circulates through the body first appeared in Western medicine in the 17th century. However, the idea is first found in the ancient Chinese medial text *Su wen* (The yellow emperor's manual of corporeal medicine) around 200 B.C.E. The text describes the flow of two substances through the body, blood, and an energy called *ch'i*.

(B)

Beginning in the third century B.C.E., Chinese engineers combine a series of walls surrounding Chinese cities to build what is now called the Great Wall of China (here photographed in the fall of 1979). *(George Saxton, NESDIS, NOAA)*

Chinese mathematicians use negative numbers.

Chinese mathematicians built counting boards, also known as abacuses, to facilitate arithmetical calculations. Around 200 B.C.E., Chinese counting boards begin using black rods to represent positive numbers and red rods denoting negative numbers. The use of negative numbers does not become widespread in the West until the 16th century.

(M)

ca. 190 B.C.E.

Apollonius of Perga presents a theory of conic sections.

Ancient Greek mathematicians excelled in the field of *geometry.* Around 350 B.C.E., Greek scholar Menaechmus recognized that when a plane intersects a cone, four different curves can be formed (*See* entry of CA. 350 B.C.E.). These curves, the circle, the ellipse, the parabola, and the hyperbola, are collectively known as *conic sections.* Around 190 B.C.E., Greek mathematician Apollonius of Perga (ca. 262–ca. 190 B.C.E.) writes *Conics,* an eight-book treatise on these curves. Mathematicians study his work until the Renaissance.

(M)

ca. 180 B.C.E.

Hypsicles of Alexandria introduces the 360-degree circle to Greek mathematics.

The study of astronomy requires advanced knowledge of mathematics. As a result, advances in mathematics are made by scholars trying to solve astronomical problems. Around 180 B.C.E., Greek mathematician Hypsicles of Alexandria (second century B.C.E.) divides the path the Sun takes through a celestial sphere, known as the *ecliptic,* into 360 parts or degrees. His work is the first introduction of the 360-degree circle to Greek mathematics. Hypsicles describes

his work in *Anaphorikos* (On the ascension of stars).

(M, SA)

Diocles attempts to duplicate the cube.

Ancient Greek mathematicians excelled in mathematics, particularly *geometry.* One of the classic problems they studied involved using a compass and straightedge to construct a cube that has twice the volume of a given cube. Around 180 B.C.E., Greek mathematician Diocles (ca. 190 B.C.E.) attempts to solve this problem using the *conic section* called the parabola and a new curve known as a cissoid curve. While he does not successfully solve the problem, his work leads to a better understanding of these curves. Diocles publishes his investigation as part of the work *On Burning Mirrors.*

(M)

ca. 170 B.C.E.

Librarians at Pergamum transcribe books onto parchment.

Transmission of knowledge in the ancient world required scholars to faithfully transcribe the works of others and store those works in libraries. The Greeks established a great library at Pergamum. Unfortunately, they lacked a sufficient supply of papyrus to transcribe all the works they wished to catalog. To fill their need for more writing materials, craftsmen developed parchment from animal skins. Unlike papyrus, which is rolled into scrolls, parchment could be bound together to make books.

(C)

ca. 150 B.C.E.

Hipparchus of Rhodes calculates the distance from the Earth to the Moon.

Eclipses occur when one celestial body blocks the light traveling to another. Around 150

B.C.E., Greek astronomer Hipparchus of Rhodes (ca. 146–127 B.C.E.) uses data he collects during a solar eclipse to calculate the distance from the Earth to the Sun. Hipparchus estimates that the distance is between 59 and 67 times the radius of Earth. Today, astronomers know the distance is 60 times the radius of the Earth.

(M, SA)

ca. 140 B.C.E.

Chinese make paper.
Paper has been used in many different cultures. The oldest known piece of paper, dating to around 140 B.C.E., is found in a Chinese tomb. The first Chinese paper is made from hemp fibers. The paper contains no words and appears to be unsuitable for writing. Around 200 years later, Chinese scholars begin to use paper for writing.

(C)

ca. 135 B.C.E.

Han Ying describes the hexagonal nature of snowflakes.
Each snowflake, a *crystal* of water, has six sides. The first description of this hexagonal nature appears around 135 B.C.E., when Chinese scholar Han Ying writes *Moral Discourses Illustrating the Han Text of the "Book of Songs."* Han states that snowflakes are always six-sided. He calls the fact common knowledge, suggesting that Chinese scholars knew of the shape of snowflakes many years before.

(C, ES, W)

ca. 129 B.C.E.

Hipparchus of Rhodes discovers the precession of the equinox.
Twice a year the Sun crosses the equator on a date known as the *equinox.* Greek astronomer

Works from China dating to the second century B.C.E. refer to the fact that snowflakes are hexagons. These photographs, from *Studies among Snow Crystals* by Wilson Bentley (1902), show 12 examples of the different forms a hexagonal snowflake can take. *(Historic NWS Collection, NOAA)*

Hipparchus of Rhodes recorded his observation of both the vernal and autumnal equinoxes. Around 129 B.C.E., he discovers that the equinox is slowly moving westward due to the movement of the Earth's axis, a phenomenon known as the precession of the equinox. Over 200 years later Greek astronomer Ptolemy (second century C.E.) describes Hipparchus's work in *The Almagest.*

(SA)

ca. 125 B.C.E.

Chinese isolate hormones.
Hormones are biological molecules that allow the organs of an animal to communicate

with one another. Today, physicians use synthetic hormones as drugs, such as birth control pills. The first medicinal use of hormones appeared in ancient China. By 125 B.C.E., Chinese physicians learn how to isolate sex hormones from human urine. Physicians use these hormones to treat a variety of disorders including impotence, menstrual problems, and hair growth.

(B)

ca. 100 B.C.E.

Ko Yu invents the wheelbarrow.
The wheelbarrow is used to facilitate the transportation of heavy objects everywhere from farms to battlefields. The first description of a wheelbarrow appears around 100 B.C.E. in Liu Hsiang's work *Lives of Famous Immortals.* Liu describes the invention of the wheelbarrow by the artesian Ko Yu, who builds a "wooden ox." Soon wheelbarrows are used to transport supplies on the battlefield and carry materials through city streets.

(P)

Hindu scholars write the first yoga text.
In ancient India, health practices often intersected with religious practices. Around 100 B.C.E., Hindu scholars write the first text describing the practice of yoga. The program includes strict dietary guidelines as well as an exercise routine that involves breathing and assuming specific positions. Hindu scholars believe that yoga helps people stay fit and thus avoid illness. Yoga continues to be practiced for both religious and health purposes today.

(B)

Chinese engineers drill for brine and natural gas.
The invention of cast iron allowed Chinese engineers to build a variety of new and useful tools. Around 100 B.C.E., Chinese craftsmen develop cast iron drill bits capable of boring holes up to 4,800 feet (1500 m) deep. The drills are initially used to find salt water (brine), which is used as a source of salt. Brine must be heated for a long period of time so that the water evaporates, leaving the salt behind. Building such fires is expensive until engineers drill deeper and find natural gas. By burning natural gas, Chinese efficiently and inexpensively produce salt.

(C, ES, P)

Chinese mathematicians find the cube root of large numbers.
Early mathematicians devised many methods to simplify complex arithmetical calculations. Around 100 B.C.E., Chinese mathematicians develop a method to find the cube root of a large number. In the mathematical text *Nine Chapters on the Mathematical Art,* Chinese mathematicians show that 123 is the cube root of 1,860, 867.

(M)

Chinese astronomers build an armillary sphere.
Chinese astronomers made many key observations, including the first recorded sightings of *comets* and sunspots. Chinese scholars also made instruments to aid in their studies of the skies. Around 100 B.C.E., Chinese astronomers build a device that models astronomical landmarks called an *armillary* sphere. This early armillary sphere consists of circles representing the equator and the horizon, and a polar axis.

(SA)

Babylonian astronomers use mathematics to describe the movement of the Sun and the Moon.
Mathematics and astronomy are intimately related, with modern astronomers and physicists using mathematical models to describe

celestial phenomena. This tradition begins in Babylon, where by 100 B.C.E. astronomers have applied mathematics to describe apparent changes in the speed of the Sun and the Moon at different times of the year.

(SA)

ca. 90 B.C.E.

Asclepiades of Bithynia claims disease is caused by disruption of atoms.
Early physicians developed theories on the origin of disease. Hippocrates stated that disease is caused by an imbalance of the four humors, blood, phlegm, yellow bile, and black bile (*See* entry for CA. 420 B.C.E.). Around 90 B.C.E., Greek scholar Asclepiades of Bithynia (second century–first century B.C.E.) contradicts this theory by describing disease as a disruption of the small particles called *atoms* that make up the body (*See* entry for CA. 440 B.C.E.). Asclepiades is one of the first to apply Leucippus's theory of atoms to disease.

(B, C)

Ssuma Ch'ien describes the parachute.
Parachutes allow humans to safely fall from great distances. Around 90 B.C.E., Chinese historian Ssuma Ch'ien describes the first parachute in his work *Historical Records*. According to Ssuma, parachutes are used throughout Chinese history. The first mention of a parachute in the West does not appear until the 15th century in the notebooks of Italian scholar Leonardo da Vinci.

(P)

ca. 60 B.C.E.

Lucretius describes the atomic nature of matter.
Ancient Greek philosophers developed a variety of theories describing the nature of matter. Around 450 B.C.E., Leucippus of Miletus stated that all matter is made of indivisible particles called *atoms*. Nearly 400 years later, Greek philosopher Lucretius (ca. 100–ca. 53 B.C.E.) writes *On the Nature of Things*, reviving the theory of atoms. His work touches upon all areas of science, including a theory of the origin of the cosmos, plants, and animals; a description of light and mirrors; and a history of earthquakes, volcanoes, and storms.

(C, ES, P, W)

ca. 46 B.C.E.

Romans institute the Julian calendar.
As described in the sidebar "Measuring Time in the Ancient World," ancient Egyptians scholars developed solar calendars. Around 46 B.C.E., Greek astronomer Sosigenes (first century B.C.E.) devises a new calendar based upon the solar year. He calculates that the year is actually 365¼ days long. To reconcile the lengths of the month and year, Sosigenes adds an extra day every four years. The year with the extra day is now known as the leap year. Roman statesman Julius Caesar backs the adoption of the calendar, now known as the Julian calendar.

(SA)

ca. 20 B.C.E.

Vitruvius describes building materials.
Architecture requires the development of materials that are strong enough to be used in buildings and other structures. Around 20 B.C.E., Roman architect Vitruvius (first century B.C.E.) writes *De architectura* (On architecture), a 10-book treatise describing the history of architecture, recipes for building materials, and the design of clocks and dials. In his work, Vitruvius describes how to mix concrete and how to

dissolve gold in mercury to make a gold amalgam.

(C, P)

ca. 15 B.C.E.

Yang Hsiung describes the belt drive.

Many cultures used the wheel for both manufacturing and transportation. Around the first century B.C.E., Chinese engineers develop the belt drive, which allows power to be transmitted from one wheel to another. The belt drive is first described in the work *Dictionary of Local Expressions* in 15 B.C.E. Chinese use the belt drive in the manufacture of silk and other garments.

(P)

ca. 9 B.C.E.

Liu Hui uses decimal fractions.

Arithmetic is much easier in systems that use *place value notation,* where each place in a numeral has a specific value. Chinese mathematicians developed a place value notation system based on values of 10, called a *decimal system,* in the 14th century B.C.E. Around 9 B.C.E., Chinese mathematician Liu Hui writes *Nice Chapters on the Mathematical Art,* describing how fractions can be expressed using decimals. Liu's system is not widely adopted, and Chinese mathematicians continue using traditional fractions until the 15th century.

(M)

∾ CONCLUSION ∾

As civilizations were established and advanced, a set of key scientific discoveries were made by many different cultures. These included the domestication of crops and animals, the use of tools, basic skills of mathematics and writing, the development of calendars and timekeeping devices, and astronomical observations of the Sun, the Moon, and other celestial bodies. By the end of the period chronicled in this section, civilizations began to distinguish themselves in particular fields. In Babylon, astronomers used mathematics to explain the movement of objects in the sky. The natural philosophers in ancient Greece were renowned for their achievements in *geometry* as well as their work in physics and theories on the *elements* that make up matter. Chinese astronomers recorded the first known sightings of *comets* and supernovae.

The work of these early civilizations sets the foundation for modern science. In mathematics, the development of *arithmetic, number theory, algebra,* and geometry during this time period leads to the development of *trigonometry* and the expansion of algebra that takes place in the Middle Ages. Astronomical observations lead to the development of calendars in the Middle East and China. Babylonian astronomers begin the tradition of using mathematics to explain their observations, work that will be expanded by Arab mathematicians in later centuries. In chemistry, craftsmen foreshadow the modern field of *metallurgy* when they develop bronze and steel. Similarly, natural philosophers in ancient Greece, India, and China debate the elements that make up matter, pondering questions that are not answered until the 17th century. Early physicists apply their knowledge, building simple machines such as the catapult, and begin to use mathematics to explain buoyancy and other physical phenomena. Their work is expanded by Arab physicists in the Middle Ages and serves as a starting point for the classical *mechanics* developed in Europe during the 16th century. Early biology focuses primarily on medicine and agriculture. Ancient Greek philosophers begin the tradition of classifying living organisms and propose theories to explain the origin of life. Biologists in the coming centuries will continue to catalog and classify living organisms. The greatest advances in biology are made by early physicians describing the *anatomy* of humans and performing surgery to treat diseases such as cataracts. The work of these early physicians is greatly expanded during the Renaissance, when the dissection of cadavers for the study of anatomy becomes a common practice.

2

EXPANDING KNOWLEDGE
First Century C.E.–13th Century C.E.

∾ INTRODUCTION ∾

Through the collapse of the Roman Empire to the rise of Islam in the Middle East, science continues to flourish. The early centuries of the Christian Era sees the last of the great Greek thinkers, a huge body of work by Islamic scientists, and the spread of scientific knowledge and technologies westward from India and China to the Middle East and eventually Europe. During this time period, great institutions of learning are created and destroyed.

Many of the achievements chronicled in this chapter are attributed to Arab scientists in the Middle East. After the seventh century, the Islamic religion spreads throughout the Middle East and eventually into Europe. Islamic scientists know the work of the ancient Greeks and are able to expand upon their knowledge. Arab mathematicians excel at *algebra* and solve problems using the *quadratic equation*. Alchemists look for a method to turn base metals into gold. In their quest they amass knowledge of chemistry and techniques to study the elements. Arguably the greatest achievement of the era is in the field of *optics*. Arab scientist Abu 'Ali al-Hasan ibn al-Haytham explains vision, demonstrating that eyes perceive light reflected from objects. Many of the works of Arab scholars are translated into Latin and studied in medieval Europe. Even their names are "Latinized." For example, Arab scholar Abu 'Ali al-Hasan ibn al-Haytham became known as Alhazen. European scientists learn about the science and philosophy of the great Greek and Arab scholars through these translations.

Science and technology continues to flourish in China during this era. Scholars study *magnetism,* develop the compass, and use it for navigation. Chinese mathematicians study *number theory,* calculate the value of pi, and work to improve the Chinese calendar. Astronomers in China, and around the world, record a guest star, now known to be a supernova. Knowledge of chemistry also expands during this period. Chinese alchemists search for a substance that would confer everlasting life. The most notable application of chemistry is the invention of gunpowder and its use by the military.

Scholars in India make notable contributions to mathematics during this period. Hindu mathematicians establish a numeral system that resembles the system commonly used today. Like the number system used in Western societies today, the Hindu system is a *decimal system* and includes zero. Hindu numbers spread to the Middle East and finally reach Europe in the 13th century.

The focus of this chapter is upon the scientific achievements in Europe, the Middle East, India, and Asia. There was undoubtedly a wealth of scientific knowledge collected by civilizations in Africa, the Americas, and other parts of Asia. This book, however, focuses upon discoveries, innovations, and scientific works that influence the state of science and technology as found in the Western world today. Many scientific studies of this era focused upon mathematics and astronomy. As such, a number of civilizations uncovered similar facts. Truly knowing who "discovered" these scientific truths first is a difficult task and must be kept in mind when studying this era. Regardless, the discoveries made during this critical period profoundly influenced subsequent generations, and many of the ideas developed by these scholars still influence Western science today.

TIME LINE OF SCIENTIFIC ACHIEVEMENTS BETWEEN THE FIRST CENTURY C.E. AND THE THIRTEENTH CENTURY

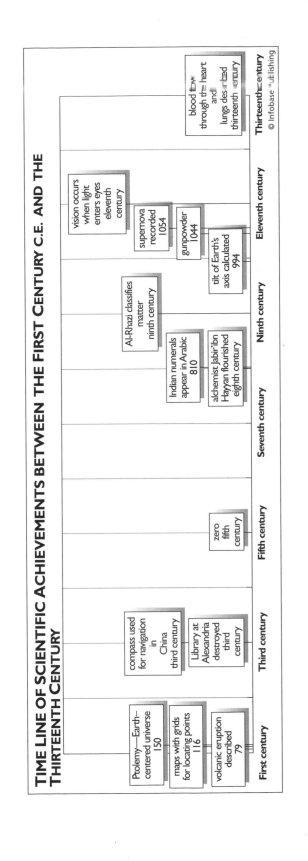

First century

Ptolemy—Earth-centered universe
150

maps with grids for locating points
116

volcanic eruption described
79

Third century

compass used for navigation in China
third century

Library at Alexandria destroyed third century

Fifth century

zero
fifth century

Seventh century

Ninth century

Al-Rhazi classifies matter ninth century

Indian numerals appear in Arabic
810

alchemist Jabir ibn Hayyan flourished eighth century

Eleventh century

vision occurs when light enters eyes eleventh century

supernova recorded
1054

gunpowder
1044

tilt of Earth's axis calculated 994

Thirteenth century

blood flow through the heart and lungs described thirteenth century

© Infobase Publishing

CHRONOLOGY

First Century

The invention of the ambix improves distillation.

Alchemists sought to separate complex mixtures and isolate pure liquids from them. One of the most common methods used for this purpose is known as *distillation.* Around 100 C.E., alchemists in Alexandria develop the ambix, an apparatus that allowed for efficient distillation. The ambix resembles modern distillation devices in that it contains a vessel in which the mixture is placed and heated, then connected to a long arm in which gases collect and condense leading to a vessel to collect the isolated substance. This basic design is improved upon over the centuries allowing performance of more complex distillation procedures.

(C)

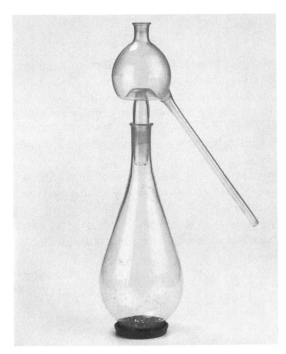

Chemists use distillation apparatus to separate mixtures of liquids. The ambix (or alembic) was first developed by Greek scholars for this purpose. Improved versions of their basic design continue to be used today. This example was built in the mid-19th century. *(Museum of the History of Science, Oxford)*

Hero of Alexandria investigates pneumatics.

Many simple machines use air pressure, steam, and vacuums to do their work. The study of the mechanical properties of air is called pneumatics. During the first century (ca. 100), Greek scholar Hero of Alexandria (ca. 62 C.E.) conducts a series of experiments on air pressure and vacuums. He describes his work, and the work of others, in *Pneumatics.* Hero includes descriptions of a number of simple machines, including the siphon and the pump, as well as theories explaining how they work.

(P)

Chinese mathematicians discover the magic square.

Mathematicians sometimes discover interesting relationships among numbers that are not immediately apparent. Chinese mathematicians discover one such relationship, the *magic square,* during the first century. The magic square is an arrangement of numbers in the shape of a square where the sum along any side, row, or diagonal is the same. Early work on the subject is compiled in the text *Ta tai li chi* (Records of the rites compiled by Tai the Elder). While such squares are now considered interesting puzzles, they make up a field of intense mathematical research for centuries.

(M)

Egyptian astrologers study the stars.

Astrologers attempt to correlate events on Earth with the movements of stars and planets in the sky. In the first century, the work of Dorothieus of Sidon (ca. 100 C.E.) forms the basis of Egyptian *astrology*. His five-book work influences astrologers throughout the Arab world. A number of other significant works of astrology dating to this period are attributed to an astrologer known as Pseudo-Petosiris. These works combine astrology, numerology, and religious studies.

(M, SA)

Menelaus of Alexandria defines the spherical triangle.

Trigonometry, the mathematics of triangles, was developed and used by astronomers. However, geometry and trigonometry deal with flat surfaces. Astronomers need to understand the properties of triangles on curved surfaces. During the first century, Menelaus of Alexandria (ca. first century) defines a spherical triangle in his work *Spherics*. Arcs on the surface of spheres, rather than three straight lines, define spherical triangles. Menelaus of Alexandria develops theorems and mathematics using spherical triangles that are still studied today.

(M)

ca. 7

Strabo describes the geography of Europe, Asia, and Africa.

Knowledge of other civilizations was once limited by the ability to travel to other lands. During the first century (ca. 7–18), Greek geographer Strabo (ca. 64 B.C.E.–ca. 23 C.E.) compiles the Greek knowledge of *geography* in his multivolume work *Geographia* (Geography). The 17-book work includes his observations as well as descriptions attributed to other scholars. His work describes what was known of the geography and history of Europe, Asia, and Africa. Strabo also chronicles the development of geography as a science.

(ES)

ca. 43

Pomponius Mela divides the Earth into five zones.

Geographers are interested in not only mapping civilizations but also the natural features of different regions. During the first century (ca. 43), Roman geographer Pomponius Mela divides the Earth into five different regions in his work *De situ orbis habitabilis* (Descriptive account of the habitable world). He describes two regions suitable for life, called temperate zones, one to the north of a torrid zone and the other to the south of it. He also describes two frigid zones bordering each of temperate zones.

(ES, W)

ca. 62

Lucius Annaeus Seneca writes an account of Greek Earth science.

The Greeks amassed theories and knowledge about the Earth and its atmosphere. During the first century (ca. 62), Roman philosopher Lucius Annaeus Seneca (ca. 4 B.C.E.–65 C.E.) chronicles much of this knowledge in his seven-book work *Naturales quaestiones*. Seneca describes the work of many Greek scholars, and their understanding of a number of natural phenomena, including weather patterns, earthquakes, and heavenly bodies.

(ES, SA, W)

ca. 70

Dioscorides describes the medicinal use of plants.

Many biologists today focus their research on subjects with implications in the field of medicine. Such a tradition dates back to ancient times. In the first century (ca. 70 C.E.), Greek biologist Pedanius Dioscorides (40–ca. 90) writes the text *De materia med-*

ica (On medical matters), describing the medicinal uses of more than 600 plants and herbs. Rather than writing from a theoretical standpoint, Dioscorides insists upon actual observation of a plant and its medical uses. Dioscorides's works are later translated and read throughout the Middle Ages.

(B)

ca. 77

Pliny the Elder writes an account of ancient science.

For science to advance, scholars must be able to look back at authoritative accounts of the work of those that came before them. This was true in ancient times as well as today. In the first century (ca. 77), Roman scholar Pliny the Elder (23–79) writes *Naturalis historia* (Natural history), a 37-book treatise covering the accumulated knowledge of science from cosmology to physiology. His work is translated and used throughout the Middle Ages. Today, *Naturalis historia* stands out as one of the classic texts of ancient times.

(B, C, ES, MS, SA, W)

ca. 79

Pliny the Younger describes a volcanic eruption and its aftermath.

The eruption of a volcano is a spectacular natural phenomenon. In 79, Roman author Pliny the Younger (61–113) witnesses and describes the eruption of Mount Vesuvius. His writings include a description of an earthquake before the eruption, the volcanic eruption, and a subsequent tsunami. Pliny's work is considered the first detailed description of a volcanic eruption. The eruption of Mount Vesuvius in 79 remains famous today for burying the city of Pompeii.

(ES)

ca. 84

The armillary sphere assists ancient astronomers.

The astronomical device known as the *armillary sphere* was found in many different ancient cultures. Armillary spheres allowed ancient astronomers to locate specific stars. The first armillary spheres consisted of a ring marking the equator. During the first century (ca. 84), Chinese astronomers add a second ring, representing the path of the Sun, to the instrument.

(SA)

Second Century

Chinese farmers control pests with an insecticide.

Farmers and gardeners share the need to protect the food they grow from insects. By the second century, Chinese farmers develop an effective means to kill insects that would damage their crops. They release other insects into their fields that prey upon the pests that consume their crops. The most famous example is the carnivorous citrus ant that kills black ants, which would otherwise destroy mandarin orange trees. Thus Chinese farmers develop the first effective insecticide.

(B)

Nichomachus of Gerasa describes perfect numbers.

Studies of *number theory* have been found in many civilizations. During the second century, Roman mathematician Nichomachus of Gerasa (ca. 100) writes *Introduction to Arithmetic*. In his work, he describes a perfect number, defined as a number that is equal to the sum of all numbers that it can be evenly divided by. The four perfect numbers known to Nichomachus of Gerasa

INNOVATIONS IN NUMBERS FIRST CENTURY–THIRTEENTH CENTURY

$6 = 1 + 2 + 3$
$28 = 1 + 2 + 4 + 7 + 14$

Perfect numbers

220 and 284
$220 = 1 + 2 + 4 + 71 + 142$
$284 = 1 + 2 + 4 + 5 + 10 + 11 + 20 + 22 + 44 + 55 + 110$

Amicable numbers

```
        1
      1   1
    1   2   1
  1   3   3   1
1   4   6   4   1
1  5  10 10  5   1
```

Pascal's triangle

4	9	2
3	5	7
8	1	6

Magic square: sum of each column, row, and the two diagonals is 15

© Infobase Publishing

Some examples of discoveries in arithmetic and number theory made during the Middle Ages. Among the achievements in number theory during this era are the discoveries of perfect numbers (top left) amicable numbers (top right), Yanghui Triangle (better known in the West as Pascal's triangle) (bottom left), and magic squares (bottom right).

were 6, 28, 496, and 8,128. Today, 39 perfect numbers are known, and computers continue to search for more.

(M)

Galen describes human anatomy.

One of the greatest Western physicians was Greek scholar Galen of Pergamum (129–ca. 216), who wrote more than 300 books during the second century. Galen's most famous texts are in the field of *anatomy*. His studies of anatomy lead to a greater understanding of how the body works. Among his discoveries, Galen shows that arteries carry blood through the body. He also uncovers the function of nerves by severing them in animals and observing the results. Arab scholars translate Galen's works, making his influence felt through the Renaissance.

(B)

ca. 105

Tsai Lun presents paper to Chinese emperor.

The recording of scholarly works requires writing and a medium to write upon. The invention of paper is widely believed to have occurred in China by 105. This is when Tsai Lun presents paper made from bamboo fibers to the emperor. The oldest known paper in China is made of hemp pulp and dates to approximately 100 B.C.E. Centuries pass before the Chinese invention moves westward to Arab and European cultures.

(C)

116

Chang Heng uses grids to locate points on a map.

Geographers use maps to record the location of cities and natural features of the land. Different methods of locating specific points developed as civilizations became more advanced. During the second century, Chinese scientist Chang Heng uses grids as a method for locating specific points on his maps. His work *Discourse on New Calculations* explains how grids could be used to scientifically calculate the distance between two points. In 116, he presents one of his maps to the emperor.

(ES, M)

ca. 132

Chang Heng improves the armillary sphere.

The *armillary sphere* was found in many different cultures. Astronomers used it to locate stars. In China, scholars developed an armillary sphere consisting of a ring that aligned with the equator and another that aligned with the *ecliptic*. During the second century, Chinese astronomer Chang Heng improves the device by adding more rings—one correlating with the meridian and the other with the horizon. He also devises a water-powered armillary sphere (ca. 132), allowing Chinese astronomers to compute the movement of the stars.

(SA)

Chang Heng invents the seismograph.

Scholars and scientists have long looked for ways to predict and locate earthquakes in the hope that they could limit the destruction they cause. In 132, Chinese scholar Chang Heng devises the first *seismograph,* an instrument that detects earthquakes. The device consists of a cylinder with eight dragons' heads, each facing in a different direction along the top, and eight frogs with open mouths on the bottom. The dragons each have a ball in their mouth. When an earthquake occurs, one or more of the balls would drop into the frog's mouth. The direction of the earthquake is deduced from the direction

that the ball dropped. Chang's seismograph allows the local government to send help to the region affected by the earthquake.

(ES)

150

Ptolemy writes *The Almagest.*

The science of astronomy developed independently in different ancient civilizations. In 150, Greek scholar Ptolemy (100–170) summarizes the work of Greek astronomers in his classic work *The Almagest. The Almagest* contains both astronomical observations and mathematical descriptions of them. Notably, Ptolemy argues for a *geocentric,* or Earth-centered, universe. Scholars in both Europe and the Arab world study *The Almagest* through the Middle Ages. Ptolemy's Earth-centered model of the universe dominates astronomical thinking for centuries.

(SA)

Ptolemy creates an atlas of the known world.

Maps are important tools in politics and commerce. As civilizations developed, so did their knowledge of the world around them. Thus, more accurate maps began to be produced. In 150, Greek scholar Ptolemy devises his atlas of the known world and presents it in his work *Geography*. Ptolemy's atlas is notable for using gridlines to locate specific points on his maps, and accounting for the curvature of the Earth.

(ES)

Third Century

The library at Alexandria is destroyed.

From the third century B.C.E., the library at Alexandria houses the academic work of the ancient Greeks, as well as that of other cultures. The library is part of a complex of buildings that includes a number of libraries and a museum and is believed to have housed approximately 1 million works from the Greeks and Romans, as well as translations of works from other cultures. The exact date and cause of the library's destruction is a subject of some controversy, dating to the period between the late third century and the early seventh century.

(B, C, ES, M, MS, P, SA, W)

Liu Hui calculates pi to 3.14.

Many of the basic principles of mathematics developed independently in several cultures. During the third century, Chinese mathematician Liu Hui writes *Chiu-chang suan-shu* (Nine chapters on the mathematical art), now considered a classic of Chinese mathematics. His work includes a calculation of pi (π) to 3.14, calculations using fractions, methods of obtaining square roots and cube roots, and applications of what is now known as the *Pythagorean theorem* (See entry for CA. 550 B.C.E.).

(M)

Diophantus studies algebra.

Mathematics flourished in ancient Greece; however, most works were studies of *geometry*. In later centuries, mathematicians in the Roman empire and the Middle East turned their focus to numbers and equations, making advances in the fields of *arithmetic* and *algebra*. During the third century, Greek mathematician Diophantus (ca. 250) writes *Arithmetica*, one of the first known treatises on algebra. His work inspires Arab mathematicians in the Middle Ages, and is read in Europe during the Renaissance.

(M)

Mayan civilization migrates after Mount Ilopango erupts.

The Mayan civilization was one of the great cultures of the Western Hemisphere. During the third century, the civilization faces relocation when the volcano Mount Ilopango erupts. A mass migration of survivors from the area of the volcano, the modern-day country of El Salvador, northward to what is now Belize follows. The result is a blending of two previously separate populations of Mayan people. Today, this event is believed to have helped bring about the classic period of Mayan culture.

(ES)

Chinese travelers use a compass to aid navigation.

Around 400 B.C.E., Chinese scholars discovered that certain rocks, called *lodestones,* are drawn to a particular direction (See entry for CA. 400 B.C.E.). The naturally magnetic lodestones are attracted to the magnetic poles of the Earth. Chinese scholars used lodestones to devise early compasses. Interestingly, the early compasses are not used for navigation until sometime during the third century C.E. The device is referred to as the "south-pointer."

(ES)

Chang Chi studies vitamin deficiency diseases.

Physicians today know that a number of diseases occur when one's diet is missing certain nutrients called vitamins. Chinese physician Chang Chi first records such deficiency diseases during the third century. In *Systematic Treatise of Medicine*, Chang describes a number of diseases that could be treated by adding specific foods to the patient's diet. Today, physicians recognize that the foods he recommended are rich in specific vitamins. Chang's work begins the study of vitamin deficiency disease in China.

(B)

Fourth Century

Wai Tan alchemists search for eternal life.

As described in the sidebar "The Alchemists," Chinese *alchemy* focused on finding a path to immortality. In the fourth century, Wai Tan alchemy develops in China. Practitioners of Wai Tan alchemy look for a substance that would give a person everlasting life. This form of alchemy eventually spreads to Western civilizations. In Europe, alchemists begin a similar quest, the search for what is known as the Elixir of Life.

(B, C)

Pappus of Alexandria summarizes Greek mathematics.

The accomplishments of the ancient Greeks in *geometry* are well known. During the fourth century, Roman mathematician Pappus of Alexandria (ca. 320) writes a treatise on Greek mathematics called *Synagoge* (Collection), which is considered one of the most complete summaries of ancient Greek geometry. *Synagoge* is translated into Latin during the sixth century, influencing generations of mathematicians.

(M)

Chen Zhou develops star maps.

Ancient Chinese astronomers excelled at developing star maps for centuries. During the fourth century, Chen Zhou develops the

THE ALCHEMISTS

The roots of modern chemistry can be traced to the ancient science of *alchemy*. Alchemists were found in many civilizations: Greek, Arab, and Chinese. They investigate chemical reaction in the pursuit of two lofty goals: turning base metals into gold ("Philosopher Stone") and finding a formula for eternal life ("Elixir of Life.") Although they fail to attain these goals, they leave behind a rich heritage of chemical knowledge including fundamental chemical reactions and important laboratory techniques.

Scholars believe that Greek alchemy grew from a combination of practical chemistry discovered in Egypt, such as metal work and the creations of dyes, and Greek philosophy. Many Egyptian alchemists study Aristotle, who believed there were four primary elements (air, fire, water, and earth) and that transformations between them were possible. They reason that if an element can be transformed into another, then it should be possible to transform one metal into another. Using a variety of laboratory techniques, the early alchemists change the visible properties of metal. For example, the color of a metal will change as the metal oxidizes or rusts. They believe that if they find the right catalyst, the elusive Philosopher Stone, they can transform a metal into the purest form, gold.

As centuries pass and the Islamic religion spreads across the Middle East, the science of alchemy continues to flourish. One of the most prominent Arab alchemists of this era is Jabir ibn Hayyan, known in Latin as Geber. The exact identity of Jabir ibn Hayyan is unclear. Historians now believe that the ninth-century works attributed to him are actually the works of many alchemists. Regardless of their origin, the importance of the works remains clear. The Jabir texts describe the combination of metals in search for the proper proportions to find gold. In the course of these studies, they describe basic chemistry procedures that could be found in a high school chemistry class today, such as *distillation,* crystallization, calcinations, creating solutions, sublimation, and reduction. Other Arab alchemists of this era develop important techniques to study matter. For example, Arab alchemist Ibn Sina, also known by the name Avicenna, does not believe in transmutation of elements, but rather believes that an element can be extracted from another substance. The work

(continues)

(continued)

of Avicenna and like-minded alchemists leads to the development of techniques to refine metals and separate mixtures.

Alchemy also thrives in China. The goals of Chinese alchemists differs from the goals of their Greek, Egyptian, and Arab counterparts. Rather than seeking a way to turn base metals to gold, Chinese alchemists search for a chemical that would make people immortal. Such a substance is known in the West as the Elixir of Life. With this goal in mind, two distinct forms of alchemy develop in China, Wai Tan or external alchemy, and Nei Tan or internal alchemy. Wai Tan alchemists look for physical substances that can confer eternal life upon those who took them. Nei Tan alchemy, on the other hand, focuses on the spirit. Its practitioners look for ways to harness the body's own energy to bring about eternal life.

The goals of Chinese alchemy spread to Europe in the 13th century. In this era, Europeans turn their attention to the search for both the Elixir of Life and the Philosopher Stone. The work of European alchemists leads to great advances in a number of chemical laboratory techniques. In particular, the European alchemists make great improvements upon distillation, a technique that allows them to separate mixtures of liquids into their individual components. Distillation and other techniques pioneered by the alchemists remain important tools in chemistry laboratories today.

The story of the alchemists ends with the development of modern chemistry in the 17th century. Despite chasing what seem today to be impossible goals, the alchemists laid the foundation for modern chemical analysis. They developed apparatus and techniques to perform chemical reactions, separate complex mixtures, and analyze the products of their work. Modern chemists owe a debt to the work of these early scientists.

---

most complete Chinese star map to date by combining the work of other astronomers. His map includes 283 constellations and 1,464 individual stars.

(SA)

Serenus studies the sections of a cylinder.

The study of *conic sections,* the curves generated from a plane intersecting a cone, dates back to the ancient Greeks (*See* entry for CA. 350 B.C.E.). During the fourth century, Egyptian mathematician Serenus writes two major works on conic sections. His work *On the Sections of a Cylinder* successfully argues that an important conic section, the ellipse, could also be generated as a section of a cylinder. Before Serenus's work, mathematicians believed that these curves were different. Serenus also writes *On the Sections of a Cone,* describing the sections of cones with *right angles.*

(M)

Zosimos writes an encyclopedia of alchemy.

As described in the sidebar "The Alchemists," *alchemy* flourished in Arab countries during the Middle Ages, but its origins date back to ancient Greece. During the fourth century, Greek alchemist Zosimos of Panopolis (ca. 300) writes an encyclopedia of alchemy. His work covers not only what is now considered the "scientific" aspects of alchemy, namely laboratory apparatus and procedures, but also the more mystical aspects of the discipline. Zosimos's writing on alchemy are translated and studied throughout the Middle Ages.

(C)

Fifth Century

Proclus proposes a new postulate in geometry.

Euclidean *geometry* is based upon five assumptions, or *postulates,* concerning the nature of lines, circles, and angles (*See* entry for CA. 300 B.C.E.). Later mathematicians proposed related postulates, particularly concerning nonintersecting or parallel lines. During the fifth century, Greek philosopher Proclus (410–485) begins this tradition when he proposes that given a line and a point not on the line, only one parallel line can be drawn through the point. Today, the postulate is now known as Playfair's Postulate, named after the 18th-century mathematician who revived Proclus's work.

(M)

T'ao Hung-ching writes a compendium of Chinese pharmacology.

Chinese *alchemy* focused upon finding substances that could be taken to ensure eternal life. During the fifth century, Chinese alchemist T'ao Hung-ching (451–536) writes a compendium of the drugs known to Chinese physicians, *Bencao jing jizhu* (Collected commentaries to the canonical pharmacopoeia). His study of pharmacology includes dividing drugs into six categories, discussing drugs no longer in use, and describing alchemical practices.

(C)

415

The mathematician Hypatia is murdered.

Alexandria was one of the great centers of learning in the Roman Empire. Early in the fifth century, the Neoplatonist school of philosophy in Alexandria is led by a Greek mathematician named Hypatia (ca. 370–415). Although none of her works survive today, scholars know that she wrote widely on *arithmetic* and had a particular interest in *conic sections.* Her belief in science and rationalism leads to her murder in 415 by a mob of Christians, effectively ending the teaching of Plato in Alexandria.

(M)

450

Tsu Ch'ung-Chih calculates pi to 10 decimal places.

Mathematicians constantly look for more accurate approximations of a number of constants. In particular, great effort has gone into calculating the *ratio* of the circle's *circumference* to its diameter, a value known as *pi* (π). Many ancient mathematicians worked to derive values of pi accurate to many decimal places. In 450, Chinese mathematician Tsu Ch'ung-Chih creates a circle nearly 10 feet (3 m) in diameter and uses it to calculate a value of pi to 10 decimal places. His work is documented in *Sui Shu* (History of the Sui dynasty, 630).

(M)

499

Aryabhata summarizes Indian mathematics.

Indian civilization made a great number of advances in mathematics. Indian mathematician Aryabhata I (476–550) in his treatise *Aryabhatiya* summarizes these works in 499. His work describes methods for calculating *pi,* solving a *quadratic equation,* as well as some basic concepts in *trigonometry.* He also details an alphabet-numeral system of mathematical notations, where numbers are assigned to letters of the alphabet, allowing mathematicians to write in poetic form for centuries. Today, Aryabhata I is considered one of the pioneers of Indian mathematics.

(M)

500

Indian mathematicians introduce zero.

The development of the modern numeral system is predicated on the creation of a *place value notation* system and the use of zero. By 500, Indian mathematicians develop the concept of zero and incorporate it into their numeral system. Zero acts as a placeholder in a numeral where no numeric value is assigned to that place in the number. Today, the development of zero is considered one of the most fundamentally important advances in mathematics.

(M)

Sixth Century

Chinese scholars develop Nei Tan alchemy.

As described in the sidebar "The Alchemists," Chinese alchemists endeavored to find the means to eternal life. Wai Tan *alchemy* focused on finding substances that would bring about immortality. Around the sixth century, a more spiritual form of alchemy called Nei Tan alchemy develops. Rather than looking for substances to extend life, Nei Tan practitioners look for ways to harness the body's energy. While Wai Tan alchemy serves as a basis for modern chemistry, Nei Tan alchemy acts as the foundation for spiritual healing.

(B)

Chinese develop woodblock printing.

The development of woodblock printing in China during the sixth century facilitated the recording of history. This early form of printing is performed by creating woodblocks with the reverse images of characters attached to them. The blocks are then painted and the images pressed upon paper. Derivations of this method are used in the Far East for centuries.

(B, C, ES, M, MS, P, SA, W)

Varahamihira describes Indian astrology.

Throughout many civilizations, mathematics developed alongside astronomy and astrology. Indian scholar Varahamihira (505–587) writes one of the great treatises in Indian astrology, *Panca-siddhantika* (Five treatises), during the sixth century. Varahamihira describes Indian *astrology,* calendar development, and mathematics. His work also summarizes much of what was known of Greek astronomy.

(SA)

Seventh Century

Indian mathematicians develop the predecessor to the modern numeral system.

As described in the sidebar "The Origin of Modern Numerals," the numeral system used in Western cultures today was developed in India by the seventh century. The system has zero, uses *place value notations,* and is based upon the quantity of 10. In addition, the written Indian numerals resemble today's Arabic numbers. Use of this system spreads from India to the Arab world and finally to Europe.

(M)

Chinese invent porcelain.

Pottery is an invention that is critical to daily life. In addition to its practical uses, pottery is also kept as art. The crafting of translucent pottery known as porcelain dates back to ancient China. While the exact time of the invention is unclear, scholars believe porcelain was available by the seventh century. To make porcelain, crafters used pure clay and heated it to a high temperature. As trade opened up to the West, European artisans began looking for ways to replicate Chinese porcelain.

(C)

Sun Simo writes Chinese medical texts.

The practice of medicine draws knowledge from a variety of disciplines, including biology, chemistry, and religion. During the seventh century, Chinese physician Sun Simo writes a series of medical texts that are studied in China for hundreds of years. In addition to describing diseases, his major works, *Qianjin fang* (Prescriptions worth a thousand) and *Qianjing yifang* (Revised prescriptions worth a thousand) discuss Chinese *alchemy* and medical ethics. His works on medical ethics spread, influencing medical practices throughout the Far East.

(B, C)

Brahmagupta approximates the sine of an angle.

Trigonometry, the study of the relationship between the sides of a triangle, arose independently in a number of different civilizations. The field was developed primarily by astronomers to aid in calculating celestial distances. During the seventh century, Indian mathematician and astronomer Brahmagupta (598–ca. 665) devises a method to approximate the *sine*.

(M)

628

Brahmagupta describes planetary motion.

The study of astronomy is found across cultures. In 628, one of the great works of early Indian science appears when Indian astronomer Brahmagupta writes *Brahma sphuta siddhanta* (Brahma's correct system). In his work, Brahmagupta describes planetary motion along with mathematics relevant to astronomers. His work is translated in Baghdad during the eighth century and spreads across the Arab world.

(SA)

635

Chinese astronomers observe that a comet's tail points away from the Sun.

Chinese astronomers not only tracked the positions of stars and constellations, they were also known as keen observers of *comets*. Chinese astronomers mapped the position and paths of approximately 40 different comets. One of the obvious characteristics of a comet is its tail. In 635, Chinese scholars record the observation that a comet's tail always points away from the Sun. This observation is critical to the discovery of solar wind.

(SA)

673

Callinicus of Heliopolis introduces Greek fire to warfare.

The application of scientific knowledge to the tools of warfare is not a modern occurrence but a tradition that began in ancient civilizations. During the seventh century, Syrian architect Callinicus of Heliopolis is a refugee in Constantinople who introduces a flaming material known as Greek fire. The first known use of Greek fire occurs during an attack on Constantinople by Arab ships in 673. Reports claim the fire could not be extinguished by water. There is no record of how Greek fire was made, and its composition remains a mystery today.

(C)

Eighth Century

Muhammad ibn Ibrahim al-Fazari introduces the astrolabe to Arab astronomers.

Mapping the stars requires the development of precise instruments. The *astrolabe* is one such instrument that appears in many cultures. The astrolabe allows astronomers to calculate the position and movement of heavenly bodies by reflecting the way the sky looks at a particular time. Muhammad ibn Ibrahim al-Fazari is believed to have introduced the astrolabe to Arab astronomy during the eighth century. Astronomers throughout the Middle Ages use various forms of the astrolabe.

(SA)

Masha Allah writes a classic study of astronomy and astrology.

Many works of Arab science were later translated and widely read in Europe, thus influencing the course of European science. The work of the eighth-century Arab astronomer known by his Latinized name Masha Allah (762–ca. 815) is one such case. His most famous work on *astronomy* and *astrology, De scientia motus orbis,* introduces Persian astrology to the Arab world. His work is translated into Latin and becomes widely quoted in the writings of 16th-century European scientists.

(SA)

Ancient astronomers from many different cultures, including China and the Middle East, used astrolabes to help map the positions of heavenly bodies. This example of an astrolabe comes from the Middle East ca. 1227. *(Museum of the History of Science, Oxford)*

I Hsing develops the mechanical clock.

One of the most important instruments developed by scientists was the mechanical clock. Precise measurements of time are important for scientific experiments, religious observances, and daily activities. Chinese scholar I Hsing devises the first known mechanical clock in China during the eighth century. Chinese scholars continually improve upon this design. Accounts of Chinese clocks reach Europe, where mechanical clocks are finally developed during the 14th century.

(P)

Jabir ibn Hayyan writes about alchemy.

As described in the sidebar "The Alchemist," Arab alchemists devised a number of important techniques for chemical analysis while trying to change base metals into gold. The most famous writings of Arab *alchemy* are attributed to Jabir ibn Hayyan (ca. 721–ca. 815) during the eighth century. Many scholars now believe they were produced by a number of different like-minded alchemists. Regardless, texts written under the name of Jabir, particularly *The Book of the Kingdom, The Little Book of Balances, The Book of Mercy, The Book of Concentration,* and *The Book of Eastern Mercury,* record important advances in Arab alchemy that are later translated and studied in medieval Europe.

(C)

750

Jabir ibn Hayyan describes the distillation of vinegar.

Like the chemists of today, alchemists sought out methods to obtain pure substances from naturally occurring mixtures. *Distillation*, the heating of a liquid in order to separate it into its components, is one technique that is used by both alchemists and modern chemists. Often, alchemists tried to prepare *acids* to use in further experiments. In 750, work attributed to Arab alchemist Jabir ibn Hayyan (ca. 721–ca. 815) describes the distillation of vinegar to obtain acetic acid.

(C)

772–777

Indian astronomy texts are introduced to Arab astronomers.

Spreading of scientific knowledge in the ancient world required the interaction of scientists capable of translating one another's work. In 772, Arab astronomer Muhammad ibn Ibrahim al-Fazari translates the work of Indian astronomer Brahmagupta (*See* entry for 628). The work becomes known as *Great sindhind*. In 777, astronomer Ya'qub ibn Tariq meets with a Hindu astronomer in Baghdad and arranges for the translation of other Hindu texts. These events lead to the introduction of Indian astronomy texts into the Arab world.

(SA)

Ninth Century

Ya-qub ibn Ishaq as-Sabah al-Kindi expands Arab knowledge of Greek philosophy.

In the course of translating the works of ancient Greeks, many Arab scholars both commented upon them and extended their work. During the ninth century, Arab philosopher Ya-qub ibn Ishaq as-Sabah al-Kindi (d. ca. 870) writes extensively about Greek philosophy and science. His work resembles an encyclopedia of Greek philosophy. Notably, he presents an improved explanation of mirrors in his commentary on Greek *optics*.

(P)

Muhammad ibn Musa al-Khwarizmi summarizes the work of Indian astronomers.

While astronomy developed independently across cultures and flourishes, the knowledge also spread from one civilization to the next. During the early ninth century, Arab astronomer Muhammad ibn Musa al-Khwarizmi writes a treatise of astronomy that summarizes and expands the work of Indian astronomers. His works are translated into Latin and studied by European astronomers for centuries.

(SA)

Hunayn ibn Ishaq al-Ibadi writes medical texts.

Arab scholars and translators sustained Greek medical knowledge, like many other sciences, through many generations. During the ninth century, Hunayn ibn Ishaq al-Ibadi (808–873) translates the works of a number of ancient medical texts, including the works of Hippocrates (*See* entry for CA. 420 B.C.E.) and Galen (*See* entry for SECOND CENTURY C.E.). He also writes an original text, *Questions on Medicine for Beginners*. His works are translated into Latin and influences the course of Western medicine.

(B)

Al-Battani uses trigonometry in astronomical calculations.

Mathematics is an important component of astronomy and astrology. In the first century, Greek astronomer Ptolemy (*See* entry for 150) used geometry in his astronomical calculations. During the ninth century, Arab astronomer al-Battani (known in Latin as Albategni, ca. 858–929) improves upon Ptolemy's methods by applying *trigonometry* to similar problems. His treatise *On the Motion of Stars* is studied until the 16th century. Among the notable achievements of al-Battani's work are improved calculations of *eclipses* and an estimation of the diameter of the Sun.

(SA)

Abu Ma'shar argues the validity of astrology.

For centuries and across cultures, astrologists have tried to correlate events on Earth with the movement of stars and planets. During the ninth century, a leading Arab astrologer, Abu Ma'shar (also known by the Latinized name Albumasar, 787–886), attempts to prove the validity of *astrology* as a science. His arguments appear in his work *Kitab ithbat 'ilm al-nujum* (Book of the establishment of astrology). Abu Ma'shar bases his argument on philosophy and not on experimental observations.

(SA)

Thabit ibn Qurrah develops a method to determine amicable numbers.

Mathematicians have studied *number theory* for centuries. During the ninth century, Arab mathematicians study pairs of amicable numbers. A pair of numbers is amicable if each is equal to the sum of the numbers evenly divisible by the other. Arab mathematician Thabit ibn Qurrah (ca. 836–901) develops a formula to determine amicable numbers, described in *Book on the Determination of Amicable Numbers.* Thabit uses his formula to calculate one set of amicable numbers. His work is rediscovered centuries later by European mathematicians who use it to uncover other pairs of these interesting numbers.

(M)

Abu Bakr Muhammad ibn Zakariya ar-Razi develops methods to analyze and classify chemicals.

Alchemists made countless advances in the analysis and purification of chemicals (*See* sidebar "The Alchemists"). During the ninth century, prominent Arab alchemist Abu Bakr Muhammad ibn Zakariya ar-Razi (ca. 865–ca. 935) writes a treatise on the instrumentation used to analyze chemicals as well a systematic method to classify matter and its reactions. Ar-Razi's works are translated into Latin and influence alchemists, and later chemists in Europe.

(C)

Abu'L-Abbas Ahmad ibn Muhammad ibn Kathir al-Farghani writes a treatise on astronomy.

Advances in astronomy continued in the Arab world during the Middle Ages, with many scholars translating and building upon the works of the ancient Greeks. During the ninth century, Arab astronomer Abu'L-Abbas Ahmad ibn Muhammad ibn Kathir al-Farghani (d. ca. 861) writes *Jawami* (Elements), a treatise on astronomy. Al-Farghani takes a nonmathematical approach to the work of Ptolemy (*See* entry for 150). His work includes an estimate of the *obliquity* of the *ecliptic,* as well as the *circumference* and diameter of the Earth. His work is translated into Latin and read widely in Europe until the 15th century.

(SA)

Arab brothers known as Banu Musa develop a method to trisect an angle.

Arab mathematicians reexamined many of the classic problems in *geometry* posed by the Greeks. During the ninth century, three brothers known collectively as Banu Musa work on many of the same problems studied by the Greeks. They write *Book on the Mea-*

surement of Plane and Spherical Figures. Among the important developments described in this book is a method to divide an angle into three equal parts.

(M)

810

Muhammad ibn Musa al-Khwarizmi introduces Hindu numerals to Arab mathematics.
Our modern numeral system, known as Arabic numerals, had its origins in ancient India (*See* entry for SEVENTH CENTURY). During the ninth century, Arab scholars become aware of Indian numerals and their system of decimal place notation. In 810, mathematician and astronomer Muhammad ibn Musa al-Khwarizmi (ca. 780–ca. 850) writes *Algorithmi de numero indorum* (Calculations with Indian numerals), which introduces the *decimal system* and the concept of zero first to the Arab world, and later, through translations, to Europe.

(M)

813–833

The House of Wisdom is created in Baghdad.
Science has always flourished when governments support centers of learning where scholars can gather for research and teaching. In the period from 813 to 833, Caliph Abu al-Abbas Abd Allah al-Ma'mun (786–833) organizes an academy known as the House of Wisdom in Baghdad. Significant work is carried out in astronomy, including calculations of the diameter of the Earth and tables of planetary movement. The academy is also the home to many great mathematicians of the era.

(M, SA)

825–835

Ahmad ibn Abdallah al-Marwazi Habash al-Hasib keeps time by measuring the altitude of the Sun.
Astronomy has been studied for many purposes. As described in the sidebar "Measuring Time in the Ancient World," a common use of astronomy is timekeeping. Arab astronomer and mathematician Ahmad ibn Abdallah al-Marwazi Habash al-Hasib (ninth century) works in Baghdad from 825 to 835. Among his many accomplishments in mathematics and astronomy is the development of a method of timekeeping based upon the altitude of the Sun. His method is widely accepted by Arab astronomers of his era.

(SA)

ca. 870

Abu 'Abd Allah Muhammad ibn Isa al-Mahani develops the cubic equation.
The classic problems of Greek mathematics have been investigated through the ages. Around 870, Arab mathematician Abu 'Abd Allah Muhammad ibn Isa al-Mahani sets out to find an algebraic solution to a classic problem posed by Archimedes, dividing a sphere with a plane. He develops an equation containing a term to the third power, known as a *cubic equation,* to help him solve the problem. However, he was unable to develop a method to solve the cubic equation, so the problem remained.

(M)

10th Century

Abu al-Wafa' al-Buzajani writes about mathematical applications in everyday life.
Mathematics has been a part of daily life for centuries. During the 10th century, Arab mathematician Abu al-Wafa' al-Buzajani

(940–998) writes books describing the applications of mathematics in various trades. His works, *Book on What Is Necessary from the Science of Arithmetic for Scribes and Businessmen* and *Book on What Is Necessary from Geometric Construction for the Artisan,* describe the mathematics used in everyday life at that time and give insight into the development of mathematics in Arab world.

(M)

Abu Kamil develops a method to solve quadratic equations.

Arab mathematicians excelled in the field of *algebra.* During the 10th century, Arab mathematician Abu Kamil (ca. 850–ca. 930) develops methods to deal with high-power numbers. In *Book on Algebra,* he presents a method to solve *quadratic equations.* Quadratic equations have a term expressed to the second power and generally take the form of $ax^2 + bx + c = 0$. Abu Kamil becomes known for his ability to deal with unknown quantities of higher powers.

(M)

Abu al-Wafa' al-Buzajani describes the six trigonometric functions.

The study of triangles, known as *trigonometry,* has its roots in Indian and Arab cultures. Mathematicians calculated the relationships between the sides of a triangle, known as trigonometric functions. Early mathematicians focused on the *sine* and *cosine* of a given angle. In the 10th century, Arab mathematician Abu al-Wafa' al-Buzajani explores all six trigonometric functions including the *secant* and *cosecant.* His work marks the beginning of work with these lesser used but important functions in Arab trigonometry.

(M)

Abu Nasr al-Farabi spreads the ideas of Greek philosophers.

The works of Greek philosophers have remained in the public eye for centuries. In the early 10th century, Arab philosopher Abu Nasr al-Farabi is primarily responsible for translating, defending, and expanding ideas of Greek philosophers. Al-Farabi bases his teaching on Aristotle, Plato, Ptolemy, and other Greek philosophers and scientists.

(B, C, M, SA, W)

Ahmad ibn Yusuf writes a treatise on ratios and proportions.

The study of ratios and proportions has many uses beyond pure mathematics. During the 10th century, Arab mathematician Ahmad ibn Yusuf (d. ca. 912) writes a treatise on this subject. His work is greatly influenced by the ideas of Euclid (*See* entry for CA. 300 B.C.E.), and is subsequently translated into Latin, influencing mathematicians in Europe until the 16th century.

(M)

Abu'L-Hasan 'Ali ibn Abbas al-Majusi writes an encyclopedia of medicine.

Arab physicians drew from the texts of Greek physicians such as Galen (*See* entry for SECOND CENTURY C.E.) and Hippocrates (*See* entry for CA. 420 B.C.E.), as well as their own observations. During the 10th century, Arab physician Abu'L-Hasan 'Ali ibn Abbas al-Majusi (10th century) compiles a multivolume encyclopedia of medicine, known as *The Royal Book.* His work covers a wide range of medical topics, including the history of medicine, anatomy, disease symptoms, treatments, nutrition, and hygiene. *The Royal Book* is later translated into Latin and studied by European scholars.

(B)

Abu Sahl Wayjan ibn Rustam al-Quhi uses algebra to solve problems posed by Greek mathematicians.

Many problems posed by Greek mathematicians required knowledge of *algebra,* which was not known in ancient Greece. Arab mathematicians reexamined many of these problems in later centuries. For example,

10th-century Arab mathematician Abu Sahl Wayjan ibn Rustam al-Quhi studies a number of problems posed by Archimedes and Apollonius. He applies algebra to these problems and offers solutions using *quadratic* and *cubic equations.*

(M)

ca. 900

Abu'L-Abbas al-Fadl ibn Hatim al-Nayrizi calculates astronomical distances using the tangent.

Trigonometry, the study of triangles, developed alongside astronomy. In the early 10th century (ca. 900–902), Arab astronomer al-Nayrizi (ca. 897–ca. 922) becomes one of the first to use the *tangent,* a trigonometric function, in his astronomical calculations. The tangent is equal to the *ratio* of the sides opposite and adjacent to an angle in a *right triangle.*

(M, SA)

ca. 964

Abu'L-Husayn 'Abd al-Rahman al-Sufi describes the Andromeda galaxy.

Astronomy developed independently in many cultures. Tenth-century Arab astronomer Abu'L-Husayn 'Abd al-Rahman al-Sufi (903–986) attempts to match the stars identified by the Greeks to those known to Arabs in his astronomical treatise *Book of Fixed Stars* (ca. 964). He also describes the Andromeda galaxy, which Arab astronomers identify during the 10th century. The Andromeda galaxy is not known in Europe until the 17th century.

(SA)

ca. 968–977

Abu Mansur Muwaffak describes drugs from many cultures.

Medical practitioners are always searching for substances that will cure disease. As hap-

pens today, many physicians and healers look to the medical practices of other cultures to complement the practices of their own culture. During the 10th century, Arab scholar Abu Mansur Muwaffak gathers the current knowledge of pharmacology from Persia and parts of India and compiles it in *Book of Remedies* (ca. 968–977). He classifies drugs based upon their source and their mode of action.

(B, C)

985

Muhammad ibn Ahmad al-Maqdisi creates an accurate map of the Arab world.

Mapmaking requires in-depth knowledge of the geography of a region. In the ancient world, this task was far more difficult than it is today as transportation was more cumbersome. In 985, Arab geographer Muhammad ibn Ahmad al-Maqdisi (also known as Muqaddasi, ca. 946–ca. 1000) generates accurate maps of the Arab world. His work *Kitab ahsan al-taqasim fi ma'rifat al-aqalim* (The best division for knowledge of the regions) divides the Arab world into 14 regions.

(ES)

994

Abu Mahmud Hamid ibn al-Khidr al-Khujandi builds the largest-known sextant.

Astronomy relies upon the development of instruments to aid scientists in the study of the stars. The sextant, which is used to measure the angular distance between two objects, is one such instrument. During the 10th century, Arab astronomer Abu Mahmud Hamid ibn al-Khidr al-Khujandi (d. 1000) builds the largest-known sextant in his observatory, located in modern-day Iran. In 994, he uses the instrument to calculate the angle formed by the Earth's axis and the equator, known as the *obliquity* of the *ecliptic*.

(SA)

997

Abu Rayhan Muhammad ibn Ahmad al-Biruni calculates the difference in latitude between two cities.

Mapmakers use the distance of a geographical point from the equator to mark its *latitude*. Scholars have developed a number of methods to calculate latitude. In 997, Arab astronomer Abu Rayhan Muhammad ibn Ahmad al-Biruni (973–1048) uses the timing of a lunar *eclipse* to calculate the difference in latitude between observation points in the cities of Kath and Baghdad. al-Biruni's later works, which include discussions of Indian numerals (*See* entry for SEVENTH CENTURY), are influential in the spread of Indian numerals in the Arab world.

(SA)

11th Century

Shen Kua describes the use of a compass to make maps.

Compasses that point toward the magnetic poles are important navigational tools. Chinese scientists noticed that magnetic stones, called *lodestones,* point southward (*See* entry for CA. 400 B.C.E.). During the early 11th century, Chinese scholar Shen Kua describes the use of the magnetic compass to make maps. The magnetic compass remains an important tool for mapmaking for centuries to follow.

(ES)

Al-Baghdadi writes about Greek and Hindu mathematics.

Mathematicians in the Arab world had access to the mathematical advances of both Indian and Greek civilizations. Thus, they were able to draw upon and expand their works. During the 11th century, Arab mathematician

al-Baghdadi (d. 1037) writes a treatise on *arithmetic, al-Takmila fi'l-hisab,* which describes the arithmetic of both civilizations. Notably, his work includes a description of fractions, *irrational numbers,* and *number theory.*

(M)

Abu'L-Hasan 'Ali ibn Ali ibn Ja'Afar al-Misri ibn Ridwan writes Arab medical texts based on Hippocrates and Galen.

During the Middle Ages, many Arab physicians studied and built upon the medical work of the ancient Greeks. During the 11th century, Egyptian physician Abu'L-Hasan 'Ali ibn Ali ibn Ja'Afar al-Misri ibn Ridwan (998–ca. 1068) writes medical texts recounting and expanding the works of Hippocrates (*See* entry for CA. 420 B.C.E.) and Galen (*See* entry for SECOND CENTURY C.E.). His work *On the Prevention of Bodily Ills in Egypt* survives today. Ibn Ridwan's writings expand medical knowledge while keeping alive the work of Greek physicians.

(B)

Abu Bakr ibn Muhammad ibn al-Husayn al-Karaji solves the quadratic equation.

Arab mathematicians excelled in *algebra*. During the early 11th century, Arab mathematician Abu Bakr ibn Muhammad ibn al-Husayn al-Karaji (10th century–11th century) develops a form of algebra that allows him to solve an important problem in algebra, the *quadratic equation*. Quadratic equations take the form of $ax^2 + bx + c = 0$. Al-Karaji is one of the first mathematicians to apply the rules of arithmetic to the unknown quantities in algebraic equations.

(M)

Abu Ishaq Ibrahim ibn Yahya al-Naqqash al-Zarqali creates the Toledo Tables.

Ancient astronomers were constantly striving to gain a greater understanding of the universe. In the Middle Ages, this led to the continual refinement of astronomical tables. In the 11th century, Arab astronomer Abu Ishaq Ibrahim ibn Yahya al-Naqqash al-Zarqali (d. 1100) collaborates with other astronomers of the era to create the astronomical tables that became known as the Toledo Tables. He includes an introduction to relevant topics in *trigonometry*. The tables are translated into Latin and read widely throughout Europe.

(SA)

Yaqut al-Hamawi al-Rumi writes a study of the Islamic and Western lands.

Our knowledge of Arab culture during the Middle Ages depends upon the work of many scholars. In the late 11th century, Arab geographer Yaqut al-Hamawi al-Rumi (1179–1229), known for his biographies of Islamic scientists, studies *geography*. His travels lead him to write *Mujam al-buldan* (Dictionary of lands), a study of geography used in both the Islamic and Western world.

(ES, MS)

Abu 'Ali al-Hasan ibn al-Haytham explains vision.

How humans can see is a question that scientists have pondered for centuries. One prominent theory was that the eyes send out rays that allowed them to see objects. During the 11th century, Arab scientist Abu 'Ali al-Hasan ibn al-Haytham (also known by the Latinized name Alhazen, 965–1039) establishes that this was not the case. Using an experimental rather than theoretical approach, Abu 'Ali al-Hasan ibn al-Haytham demonstrates that light falling upon the eye allows vision. His discovery is included in his multivolume work, known in Latin as *Opticae thesaurus Alhazen,* which influences scientists for many centuries.

(B, P)

Ibn Sina proposes that erosion of land creates sediments.

Studies of the Earth show that different layers or *sediments* appear in bodies of water.

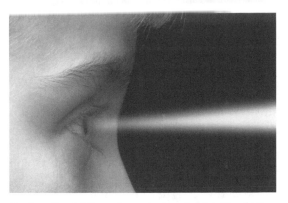

During the 11th century, Arab scientist Abu 'Ali al-Hasan ibn al-Haytham establishes that vision occurs by the eyes perceiving light, as depicted in this photograph. *(Victor de Schwanberg/Photo Researchers, Inc)*

During the 11th century, Arab scientist Ibn Sina (also known by the Latinized name Avicenna, 980–1037) proposes that sediments formed from the *erosion* of nearby land. He further speculates that the sediments became rocks. This explanation of land changes brought about by sedimentation, and erosion is also found in Chinese literature of this era (*See* entry for 1085).

(ES)

Constantine the African translates Greek and Arab medical texts into Latin.

The transmission of ideas between cultures depended upon translations of important works. Toward the end of the 11th century, a Latin scholar known as Constantine the African (ca. 1020–1087) translates many of the great works of Greek and Arab medicine into Latin. His translations are used in Western Europe until the Renaissance.

(B)

1000–1007

Abu'L-Hasan 'Ali ibn Abd al-Rahman ibn Ahmad ibn Yunus al-Sadafi ibn Yunus

creates astronomical charts that are used in timekeeping.

During the Middle Ages, astronomers made observations that are critical for timekeeping. From 1000 to 1007, Arab astronomer Abu'L-Hasan 'Ali ibn Abd al-Rahman ibn Ahmad ibn Yunus al-Sadafi ibn Yunus (d. 1009) studies the relationship of the planets to lunar and solar *eclipses*. Through careful study he is able to calculate astronomical constants with greater accuracy than had been previously achieved. His work culminates in the creation of astronomical charts that are used in timekeeping for the next 800 years.

(SA)

1025

Abu'L-Hassan al-Nasawi calculates cube roots.

Through the study of *arithmetic,* mathematicians develop methods to perform complex arithmetical operations such as calculating the square and cube roots of numbers. In 1025, Arab mathematician Abu'L-Hassan al-Nasawi develops a method to solve the cube root of a given number. Al-Nasawi's method resembles a method developed in ancient China as well as the one used by mathematicians today.

(M)

1044

Tseng Kung-Liang devises a compass for navigation.

Chinese scholars were instrumental in the development of the magnetic compass. First, they discovered that certain stones, called *lodestones,* point toward the south (*See* entry for CA. 400 B.C.E.). Later scholars described the use of these stones to determine direction. In 1044, Chinese scholar Tseng Kung-Liang records the use of a compass by the military for navigation. Tseng describes a "south-pointing fish," whose tail points to the north. The term refers to the fish shape that the lodestone takes in these early compasses.

(ES)

Chinese scholars describe gunpowder.

Gunpowder was developed in China during the Middle Ages. The first description on how to produce gunpowder appears in 1044 as part of Chinese scholar Tseng Kung-Liang's book *Most Important Military Techniques*. Tseng explains how to use gunpowder to produce three different types of bombs. At the time of his work, gunpowder had been used in China for at least 100 years. Over the next three centuries, the formula and use of gunpowder spread from China to the Arab world and finally to Europe.

(C)

Chinese astronomers observe a supernova.

In 1054, Chinese astronomers recorded the appearance of a guest star that was visible in daylight for the next 23 days. Chinese records show that the guest star remains in night sky for at least a year. Today, the guest star is known to be the explosion of a star, called a *supernova,* that created the Crab Nebula. References to the same astronomical event have been found in a number of Native American cultures as well.

(SA)

1086

Omar Khayyám devises the Muslim calendar.

Devising an accurate calendar requires precise astronomical observations in addition to mathematical calculations (*See* sidebar "Measuring Time in the Ancient World"). As science advances, civilizations are able to reform their calendars. In 1086, Persian scholar Omar Khayyám (ca.

1048–1131) devises a new Muslim calendar. He calculates the length of the solar year to be 365.24219858156 days, a value remarkably close to the one used today. In fact, his calculation of the solar year is more accurate than the Gregorian calendar that was instituted in Europe nearly 500 years later.

(SA)

Shen Kua explains land formation in terms of erosion and sedimentation.

Since ancient times, scientists have proposed theories on how structures on the Earth are formed and changed. One of the early theories resembling modern understanding appears in 11th-century China. In 1086, Chinese scholar Shen Kua explains land formation in terms of *erosion* of land and sedimentation of soils. He describes these processes in *Dream Pool Essays*. His explanations of these processes resemble modern ideas put forth by James Hutton in the 18th century. Similar theories appear in Arab science during the same era.

(ES)

12th Century

Abu'L-Fath 'Abd al-Rahman al-Khazini invents hydrostatic balance.

Experimental science requires precision instruments. Measuring the weight of an object is important both for science and trade. To this end, scientists and engineers try to improve balances used to weigh objects. In the early 12th century, Arab scientist Abu'L-Fath 'Abd al-Rahman al-Khazini invents the hydrostatic balance to obtain precise measurements of weight.

(P)

Bhaskara II proposes a design for a perpetual motion machine.

For centuries, scientists and engineers searched for the most efficient means of generating *energy*, and dreamed of a machine that could produce energy without consuming it. One of the first proposals for a perpetual motion machine comes in the 12th century, when Indian mathematician Bhaskara II (1114–ca. 1185) devises a model for a wheel that could turn forever. While such a wheel could not be built, over the next centuries several other scientists tried, and failed, to develop their own perpetual motion machine.

(P)

Abu'L-Fath 'Abd al-Rahman al-Khazini proposes that gravity acts toward the center of the Earth.

How do the Earth and other planets move through space? Since ancient Greece, scholars and scientists have studied the *forces* that cause the motion of planets. Today, scientists recognize these forces as *gravity*. One of the first to propose the role of gravity in planetary motion is Arab scientist Abu'L-Fath 'Abd al-Rahman al-Khazini. During the 12th century, he proposes that gravity acts toward the center of the Earth.

(P, SA)

Roman architects design the flying buttress.

Architecture applies the lessons of science with the sensibility of art. During the 12th century in Europe, the beginnings of Gothic architecture are seen as Roman architects design a distinct type of arch known as the flying buttress. Examples of this architecture can be seen today in cathedrals throughout France, England, and Germany.

(P)

Oxford University is founded.

Centers of learning aid the advancement of science by bringing together scholars for the purpose of teaching and research. During the 12th century, Oxford University is founded in

England. Today, Oxford University still stands as the world's oldest English-speaking university and a center where students learn from some of the great scholars of their time.

(B, C, ES, M, MS, P, SA, W)

ca. 1150

Chinese scholars invent the rocket.
The development of gunpowder added planned explosions to the arsenal of techniques that Chinese soldiers had at their disposal (*See* entry for 1044). Just as today, gunpowder was also used in fireworks during the Middle Ages. By the middle of the 12th century, Chinese scholars devise rockets to propel fireworks into the air. In 1206, rockets are used to propel arrows in war. They become known as "Chinese arrows." The use of these early rockets spreads westward to Europe in the 13th century.

(C)

1190

Compass reaches Europe.
Chinese scholars and inventors discovered magnets and developed the compass for navigation (*See* entry for CA. 400 B.C.E.). At the end of the 12th century, the first description of the magnetic compass appears in Europe. In 1190, English scholar Alexander Neckam (1157–1217) describes the compass in *De naturis rerum* (On the nature of things). Neckam describes sailors using a compass to find their direction when clouds obscure the Sun.

(ES)

13th Century

Jordanus de Nemore uses letters to denote variables.
Arab mathematicians excelled in the study of *algebra* and greatly advanced the field during the Middle Ages. In this era, algebra problems were posed in writing with numerical examples given for each equation. During the 13th century, German mathematician Jordanus de Nemore (1225–60) uses numerical examples and variables denoted by letters in place of numbers interchangeably in *De numeris datis* (On given numbers). Today's students would feel familiar with problems in his work as he describes quantities in terms of variables such as x and y.

(M)

Jordanus de Nemore explains levers.
Ancient Greek scholars proposed many explanations of *mechanics* that continued to be studied in the Middle Ages. During the 13th century, German mathematician Jordanus de Nemore writes *Mechanica* (Mechanics), a study of physics based upon the ideas of Aristotle and subsequent works by Arab scientists. *Mechanica* contains physical and mathematical explanations of tools such as levers, and also discusses the physics of movement.

(P)

Albertus Magnus declares scholars should rely upon personal observations.
As European science began to develop in the Middle Ages, scholars looked to the texts of the ancient Greeks and Islamic scholars as a starting place for their studies. During the 13th century, German scholar Albertus Magnus (1208–80) studies a variety of subjects in the natural world, including *botany*, zoology, and geology. He begins his work with ideas and principles espoused by Aristotle and other scholars of the past. However, he emphasizes that personal observation should take precedence over past works.

(B, C, ES, M, MS, P, SA, W)

Ibn an-Nafis describes blood flow through the heart and lungs.
For centuries, the works of physician Galen influenced medical thinking (*See* entry for SECOND CENTURY C.E.). During the 13th

century, Arab physician Ibn an-Nafis (d. 1288) describes the flow of blood through the heart and lungs in a manner that contradicts Galen. Galen believed that blood flows directly from the right *ventricle* of the heart to the left ventricle. Ibn an-Nafis shows that blood actually enters the right ventricle, then goes to the lungs before returning to the heart. While his explanation of blood flow is correct, Ibn an-Nafis's ideas on circulation are not widely accepted for centuries.

(B)

The *Alfonsine Tables* aid astronomers.

Greek astronomer Ptolemy made planetary tables to aid in the study of the heavens (*See* entry for 150). A number of Arab astronomers improved upon these tables. In the 13th century, Spanish king Alfonso X of Castile (1221–84) orders the creation of new planetary tables. The resulting *Alfonsine Tables* are influential in European astronomy for many years.

(SA)

Roger Bacon emphasizes observation over reason.

Throughout history, scientific scholars have developed theories based upon observations, experiments, and reasoning. At different times in history, one aspect of scientific inquiry has been favored over others. For example, Greek natural philosophers valued reasoning when developing scientific theories. In the 13th century, Roger Bacon (ca. 1220–92) argues empiricism should be favored over reasoning in the absence of observation. Bacon's ideas influence experimentalists during the Renaissance.

(B, C, ES, M, MS, P, SA, W)

Nasir ad-Din al-Tusi describes the theorem of sines.

Mathematicians and astronomers developed *trigonometry,* the mathematical field that studies triangles. During the 13th century,

Arab mathematician Nasir ad-Din al-Tusi (1201–74) writes the landmark work of trigonometry, *Book of the Principle of Transversal.* The book includes a description of the theorem of *sines.*

(M)

Chiu-Shao Ch'in determines the start of the Chinese calendar.

The Chinese calendar begins on a date known as the "Grand Cycle." The calculation of this date, one on which the winter solstice occurs at midnight on a specific date, requires both astronomical observation and specialized mathematics. In the 13th century, Chinese mathematician Chiu-Shao Ch'in describes a method for determining the Grand Cycle in his work *Shu-shu chiu-chang* (Mathematical treatise in nine sections). The work also contains methods for financial calculations and land measurements.

(M)

1202

Leonardo Fibonacci introduces Hindu-Arabic numerals to European scholars.

European scholars in the Middle Ages used the Roman numeral system for their calculations. Meanwhile, the Arab world adopted the number system developed in India, now known as Hindu-Arabic numerals (*See* sidebar "The Origin of Modern Numerals"). This system is introduced to European scholars in 1202, when Italian mathematician Leonardo Fibonacci (also known as Leonardo of Pisa) writes *Liber abbaci* (The book of calculation). His work demonstrates the usefulness of Indian numerals (*See* entry for SEVENTH CENTURY), particularly for commercial calculations. Although calculations are less cumbersome using Hindu-Arabic numerals, Roman numerals continued to be widely used for the next 200 years.

(M)

Italian mathematician Leonardo Fibonacci introduces Hindu-Arabic numerals to Europe, using them in his book, *Liber abbaci* (The book of calculation). *(SPL/Photo Researchers, Inc)*

1261

Yang Hui describes Pascal's triangle.
The method of *algebra* now known as *Pascal's triangle* is an arithmetical array of numbers that allows one to calculate the coefficient of the exponents for the equation $(a+b)^n$. The numbers are arrayed in rows such that each number is equal to the sum of the two numbers diagonally above it. Scholars believe that the first description of Pascal's triangle came from Chinese mathematician Yang Hui in 1261. Yang introduces his triangle, known as Yanghui Triangle in China, in the classic work *Hsiang-chieh chiu-chang suan-fa* (Detailed analysis of the mathemati-

cal rules in the nine chapters). Yang Hui later publishes theories and methods of multiplication and division, and work with decimals.

(M)

1276

Roger Bacon proposes using lenses for eyeglasses.
Lenses can be made that magnify views of images. Scholars interested in *optics* have studied the properties of lenses for centuries. One practical application of such studies was the invention of eyeglasses to correct sight deficiencies. While scholars are uncertain where and when eyeglasses were first made, the first written proposal to use lenses to correct vision is attributed to English scholar Roger Bacon in 1276.

(P)

ca. 1269

Pierre le Pèlerin de Maricourt studies magnets.
Chinese scholars studied magnetism for centuries. They used the Earth's magnetism to develop the magnetic compass (*See* entry for CA. 400 B.C.E.). During the 13th century (ca. 1269), the first scientific study of magnets appears in Europe when French scholar Pierre le Pèlerin de Maricourt writes *Epistola de magnete* (Letter on the magnet.) Notably, Pèlerin de Maricourt describes the poles of a magnet.

(ES)

ca. 1276

Guo constructs the tower gnomon.
The development of calendars required proper calculation of the motion of the Sun with respect to the Earth (*See* sidebar "Measuring Time in the Ancient World").

THE ORIGIN OF MODERN NUMERALS

Numerals make up an important system of notation for basic operations in *arithmetic,* which is used every day. The number system used by Western society, Hindu-Arabic numerals, has its roots in ancient India. The number system developed in India spread southward into the Islamic world, then westward to Europe. Eventually, Hindu-Arabic numerals replaced both the more cumbersome Roman numeral system used in Europe and the Babylonian system used in many Arab countries. While the form of the numbers change as time passes, the basic components of the system remain intact today.

Modern numerals are written using a *place value notation,* meaning the same numeral to denote different quantities depending upon its place in the number. Specifically, Hindu-Arabic numbers use a decimal system. Elementary school students learn that the decimal system has places for each power of 10. For instance, the numeral *2* appears in the number *20* where it is understood to denote $(2 \times 10^1) + (0 \times 10^0)$. Effective use of place value notation depends upon the numeral zero, which fills the place where no quantity is indicated. Without a zero, a single numeral such as *2* could represent the number *2, 20,* or even *2,000,000*. From this example, one can easily see that the use of zero is one of the most important innovations in mathematics. Scholars widely believe that zero appears in ancient India by the sixth century.

Indian numerals are introduced to Arab scholars through the works of Arab mathematician al-Khwarizmi during the ninth century. Before this time, the Babylonian number system was used for astronomical calculations. Over the next few centuries, Arab mathematicians write a number of works on arithmetic using Indian numerals. Some evidence shows that nonscholars use Indian numerals to perform arithmetic during the late 10th century.

While Islamic scholars adopt the Hindu number system, Europeans continue to use Roman numerals. Roman numerals are an example of an aggregate system of numerals. That is, each number is represented as a sum of a series of numbers. For instance the number *16* in Roman numerals is represented by XVI, or *10 + 5 + 1*. Calculations are difficult to perform using an aggregate system of numbers. Although there are recorded instances of Indian numbers before the 13th century, scholars widely believed that Italian mathematician Leonardo Fibonacci introduced them in the 13th century. Fibonacci was taught by Arab teachers and traveled widely. In 1202, he wrote *Liber abaci* (The book of calculation), introducing Indian numbers to European scholars. Over the next few centuries, Indian and Roman numerals are both used in Europe. Eventually, the Hindu-Arabic numbers become the dominant number system, and remain so today.

During the 13th century (ca. 1276), Chinese astronomer Guo Shou-Jing constructs the tower *gnomon* to aid in these calculations. The tower gnomon is a sundial that measures 43.6 feet (13.3 m) in height. Using this instrument, Guo calculates the length of the solar year. His calculation differs from the value accepted today by only 26 seconds.

(SA)

ca. 1284

Witelo describes the reflection and refraction of light.

The ancient Greeks initiated studies on *optics* that were extended by Arab scientists. During the 13th century (ca. 1284), Polish scientist Witelo (ca. 1230–1275) writes *Perspectiva,* a treatise on optics. His work includes experiments using devices designed by Arab

The gnomon, a device used to measure time, is developed by many ancient civilizations, including China and Egypt. This example of a horizontal string-gnomon dial is believed to come from China ca. the 19th century. *(Museum of the History of Science, Oxford)*

scholar Abu 'Ali al-Hasan ibn al-Haytham, who showed that vision occurs by the eyes perceiving light (*See* entry for 11TH CENTURY). Notably, Witelo provides physical and mathematical descriptions of the *refraction* and *reflection* of light.

(P)

∾ CONCLUSION ∾

During the 1,300 years chronicled in this chapter, the focus of scientific learning shifts from Greek philosophers and the Roman Empire to the growing Arab world, India, and China. Knowledge spreads at a pace many times slower than it does today, and many of the innovations made by Chinese and Indian scholars do not reach Europe until the 13th century.

Advances in mathematics are prominent in this era, with the expansion of study in *arithmetic* and *algebra* and the development of *trigonometry*. Arab and Indian astronomers both discover the properties of the triangle and its usefulness in astronomical calculations. Soon trigonometry is established as a branch of mathematics. Arab mathematicians reexamine the *geometry* of the ancient Greeks and apply their skills in algebra to find solutions to problems that were previously unsolved. By the 13th century, the numerals used first by Indian and then by Arabic mathematicians find their way to Europe, where they slowly begin to replace the Roman numerals that had been used for centuries.

Chinese excelled not only in the sciences but also in technological innovations. During the period chronicled in this chapter, the Chinese develop the compass for navigation, paper and the wood-block method to print upon it, and gunpowder. These discoveries and their uses in both war and peacetime slowly spread across Asia and into Europe during the Middle Ages.

The era also saw the beginning of a shift in how scientific discoveries are made. Ancient Greek philosophers applied logic in their study of the natural world. While logic certainly continues to take a large role in scientific pursuits, many scholars begin to value observation as well. A notable example of using observation to advance knowledge is Arab scientist Abu 'Ali al-Hasan ibn al-Haytham's discovery that vision is a result of light entering the eyes rather than the eyes sending out rays to visually detect objects. By the 13th century, a number of scholars begin arguing for the importance of observation in understanding the natural world. This trend would continue to help advance science in the coming decades.

3

SCIENCE IN THE RENAISSANCE
1300–1633

∾ INTRODUCTION ∾

During the fifth through 14th centuries, most scientific advances occur in Asia and Middle East, while European scholars focus primarily on studying the classic texts of the ancient Greeks. This changes in the 14th century. The period of European history traditionally known as the Renaissance sees a huge expansion in scientific research, discovery, and knowledge. A number of critical discoveries are made in the fields of *astronomy*, physics, and biology. Meanwhile, scholars begin to take an experimental approach to science. The new emphasis on scientific experiments leads many to design instruments that make such experiments easier. At the same time, Asian scholars and scientists continue to make advances in science and technology.

Some of the most famous scientific advances of this period come in the field of astronomy. The era opens with European scholars espousing the Earth-centered or *geocentric* view of the universe proposed by Greek astronomer Ptolemy. During the 16th

century, this view begins to shift when Polish astronomer Nicholas Copernicus (1473–1543) presents his Sun-centered, or *heliocentric*, view of the cosmos. The astronomers who follow Copernicus, notably Tycho Brahe (1546–1601), Johannes Kepler (1571–1630), and Galileo Galilei (1564–1642), embrace and expand Copernicus's view of the universe. Tycho builds a great observatory and makes some of the most accurate observations known at the time. Upon his death, he passes his observations to his student Kepler. Kepler uses the data to describe planetary motion. At the same time, Galileo provides additional evidence for the heliocentric universe with the observations he makes using a telescope.

Astronomy is one of the scientific disciplines that benefits from the many inventions of the era. The Renaissance sees the invention of the telescope and an early microscope, instruments that allow scholars to see things that were once too distant or too small to observe. Renaissance scientists also develop instruments to measure the physical properties of matter. The era sees the invention of the thermometer, or thermoscope, and the hygrometer, which measures humidity. One of the most important inventions of the era is Johannes Gutenberg's (ca. 1390–1468) printing press, which allows scientific knowledge to be rapidly disseminated. As a result, scholars have the opportunity to study the work of others, and either advance or refute their work in a timely manner.

Renaissance scholars begin taking a new approach to scientific endeavors. European scholars of earlier eras studied the works of ancient Greek philosophers, such as Aristotle, Galen, and Ptolemy. During the Renaissance, many scholars advocate experimental science rather than relying upon the work of ancient scholars. The writings of two natural philosophers, Paracelsus (1493–1541) and Francis Bacon (1561–1626), demonstrate this trend. Followers of these philosophers begin conducting experiments that challenge the work of the ancient Greeks and lead to many great scientific advances, from the application of chemistry to the search for new drugs to the early works of physics that lead to an understanding of *gravity*.

Biology and chemistry are two fields that benefit from the experimental approach to science. Italian medical schools become centers of research into human *anatomy* and physiology. Their studies lead to one of the most significant discoveries of the era, the description of the circulation of blood. Other physicians make observations that lead them to suspect that some diseases are transmitted from person to person by microscopic organisms. Medical studies also lead to advances in chemistry. During the Renaissance, some physicians begin trying to find substances that will treat diseases. These searches lead to new methods to quantify and analyze chemicals. The experimental approach taken to study matter leads to a new understanding of the air around us. Experiments show that water vapor is present in the air and that the air is actually a mixture of distinct gases that have different properties.

Finally, the emphasis on experimentation leads to new discoveries in physics. Galileo studies motion, describing the effect of gravity on falling bodies and introducing the concept of *inertia*. Others study the properties of light, proposing theories to explain rainbows, and describing how light refracts. The era also sees the first explanation of magnetism, and the proposal that the Earth itself is a giant magnet. These and other advances in physics set the stage for the great work in physics that will come in the next century.

TIME LINE OF SCIENTIFIC ACHIEVEMENTS BETWEEN 1300 AND 1635

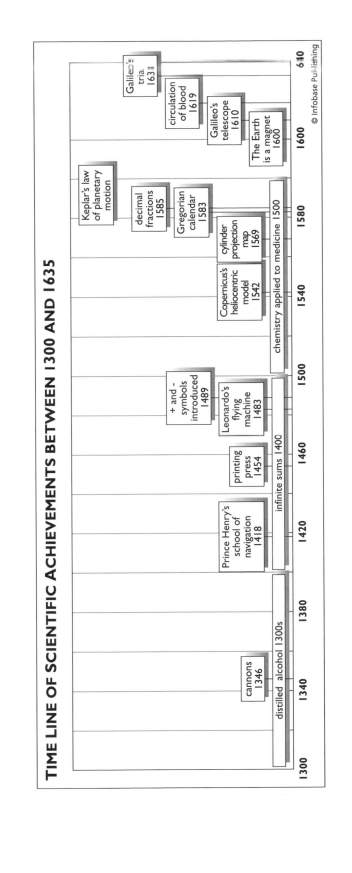

cannons 1346

distilled alcohol 1300s

Prince Henry's school of navigation 1418

infinite sums 1400

printing press 1454

Leonardo's flying machine 1483

+ and − symbols introduced 1489

chemistry applied to medicine 1500

Copernicus's heliocentric model 1542

cylinder projection map 1569

Gregorian calendar 1583

decimal fractions 1585

Keplar's law of planetary motion

The Earth is a magnet 1600

Galileo's telescope 1610

circulation of blood 1619

Galileo's trial 1633

1300   1340   1380   1420   1460   1500   1540   1580   1600   1610

~ CHRONOLOGY ~

1300s

False Geber discovers sulfuric acid.

Alchemists in the Middle East and Europe searched for a means to transform base metals into gold. In pursuit of their goal, many developed important techniques in classifying and analyzing chemicals. Many studied the properties of corrosive solutions known as *acids* and *bases*. In the early 14th century, an unknown alchemist discovers a particularly strong acid, sulfuric acid. The alchemist used the name Geber, which is also the Latin name of the eighth-century alchemist Jabir Ibn Hayyan (*See* entry for 11TH CENTURY). He is now known as False Geber. Sulfuric acid remains a widely used chemical today.

(C)

The spinning wheel is brought to Europe.

Many innovations introduced in Europe trace their roots to other cultures. Many believe that the mechanical spinning wheel was first developed in India, then introduced into Europe in the early 14th century, where it revolutionized garment making. Rather than spinning natural fibers, such as cotton, into thread by hand, the mechanical spinning wheel allows this task to be performed by a simple machine operated by a foot pedal.

(P)

Arnau de Villanova distills wine.

Alchemists developed a number of techniques to separate complex mixtures (*See* sidebar "The Alchemists"). One popular method, *distillation,* was used to divide a mixture of liquids into its separate components. During the early 14th century, Catalan alchemist Arnau de Villanova (ca. 1235–1312) applies this technique to wine. When wine is heated, the alcohol boils off first. Arnau de Villanova captures the alcohol vapors, then cools them. The resulting liquid, now called brandy, has a much higher alcohol content than the original wine. Distillation becomes widely used to make beverages with high alcohol content.

(C)

Italian craftsmen build a mechanical clock.

Timekeeping posed a problem for many early inventors and engineers (*See* sidebar "Measuring Time in the Ancient World"). Sundials were replaced by water clocks that were controlled by changes in water level over time. In 14th-century Europe, the first mechanical clocks appear. Mechanical clocks use weights driven by *gravity* to keep the time. An early mechanical clock, featuring bells that chime at the beginning of each hour, is mounted in a tower in Milan, Italy.

(P)

1304

Giotto di Bondone depicts a comet.

Astronomers have observed *comets* since ancient times. During the seventh century (*See* entry for 635), Chinese astronomers noted that a comet's tail always points away from the Sun. The first realistic depiction of a comet in Europe occurs in 1304, when Italian painter Giotto di Bondone (ca. 1266–1337) draws the star of Bethlehem as a comet in his painting *The Adoration of the Magi.* Modern scholars believe that di Bondone based his depiction of a comet on one that was visible in the European sky in 1301.

(SA)

ca. 1305

Dietrich von Freiberg describes rainbows.

Where do rainbows come from? Early in the 14th century (ca. 1305), Dietrich von

Freiberg (1250–1310) performs experiments designed to explain this natural phenomena. To study rainbows, he passes light through flasks filled with water. He proposes that each color of the rainbow is generated from a different drop of water. Dietrich von Freiberg's experiments allow him to conclude that rainbows stem from two different *refractions* of light at the surface of raindrops and a *reflection* of light within the drop. He describes his studies in *De iride et radialibus impressionibus* (On the rainbow and radiant impressions).

(P)

1316

Mondino Dei Liucci writes anatomy text.
The study of *anatomy* requires scholars to dissect a wide variety of organisms. During the early 14th century, medical schools in Italy reintroduce the practice of dissecting human cadavers. Such dissections lead to a new understanding of human anatomy. In 1316, Italian anatomist Mondino Dei Liucci (ca. 1270–ca. 1326) writes an anatomy text. He bases his writing on both the studies of Greek and Arab scholars as well as the observations made at Italian medical schools. His text is widely studied in Europe until the 17th century.

(B)

1346

English army uses a cannon.
Chinese scholars invented gunpowder and gave it to the Chinese army, which used it in battle (*See* entry for 1044). Knowledge of gunpowder spreads to Europe by the 13th century. In 1346, English forces use gunpowder to hurl a ball toward French forces during a battle in the Hundred Years' War. This is the first known instance of a cannon being used in battle. Soon the cannon replaces the catapult in European battles.

(C)

1400s

Madhava of Sangamagramma describes infinite sums.
Indian mathematicians described many mathematical processes that were not known in Europe until centuries later. In particular, they excelled in the study of the triangle, *trigonometry*. In the early 15th century, Hindu mathematician Madhava of Sangamagramma (1350–1425) describes infinite series as they relate to trigonometric functions. Sir Isaac Newton describes the equations he works out in the 17th century.

(M)

Leonardo da Vinci points to fossils as evidence that the mountains were once part of the sea.
How do mountains form? Scholars studying geology have put forth a number of theories. During the 15th century, Italian scholar Leonardo da Vinci (1452–1519) embraces the theory that the mountains were once a part of the ocean. He carefully studies fossils found on mountaintops. Leonardo notes that fossilized sea creatures such as oysters, fish, and coral are found on mountains near the sea. Furthermore, he sees that the arrangement of the fossils is similar to patterns of shells scattered on the shore. He points to these fossils as evidence that the land on the mountains had once been a part of the sea.

(ES)

1403

Venetian officials quarantine visitors.
Bubonic plague struck Europe in the late 14th and early 15th centuries, killing nearly

one-third of the population. Death often occurred only days after the infection was first detected. In 1403, officials in the Italian city of Venice decide that the best method to halt the spread of the plague is to keep visitors out of the city until they are sure they do not have the disease. They institute a 40-day quarantine for visitors. If the visitor did not develop the plague during the quarantine period, they were allowed into the city.

(B)

1418

Prince Henry of Portugal establishes a school of navigation.

In the early 15th century, trade between China and Europe depended upon travel across the land of Europe and Asia. Some Europeans began to look for ways to bypass the Middle East and trade directly with China. In 1418, Prince Henry of Portugal (1394–1460) begins this process when he opens his school of navigation. His ships begin exploring the world by sea, ushering in an age of European exploration.

(MS)

1436

Leone Battista Alberti describes how to draw three-dimensional objects.

The depiction of three-dimensional objects on a two-dimensional page is a problem that plagues artists, architects, and mathematicians. Artists refer to this process as achieving proper perspective, making the object appear more lifelike. In 1436, Italian artist Leone Battista Alberti (1404–72) describes a method for achieving perspective. His method is not only artistically pleasing but also mathematically correct.

(M)

ca. 1450

Nicholas of Cusa designs the hygrometer.

As described in the sidebar "Developing the Tools and Methods of Modern Science," during the Renaissance many natural philosophers realized that in order to truly understand the world around them, they had to make precise measurements of a variety of conditions. For instance, one of the important factors in studying the weather is measuring the amount of moisture in the air. During the 15th century (ca. 1450), German scholar Nicholas of Cusa (1401–64) designs the first hygrometer. He uses his device experimentally to demonstrate that there is water vapor in the air.

(P, W)

Nicholas of Cusa posits that the Earth is in motion and the universe is infinite.

As described in the sidebar "Astronomy in the Renaissance," *astronomy* flourished in Europe during the Renaissance. In the 15th century, most scholars believed that the Earth was the center of the universe. In 1450, German scholar Nicholas of Cusa rejects this view. He states that the Earth is in constant motion. He goes on to describe an infinite universe where all heavenly bodies are constantly moving. Today, scholars are unsure how Nicholas of Cusa developed this modern view of the universe.

(SA)

1454

Johannes Gutenberg introduces the movable type printing press.

While writing allowed scholars to record their ideas, producing multiple copies of a written document presented a formidable challenge. Chinese inventors developed wood-block printing during the sixth century to facilitate this process (*See*

DEVELOPING THE TOOLS AND METHODS OF MODERN SCIENCE

The Renaissance is a time when European scholars discover, question, and expand the work of their Greek and Arab predecessors. Many great discoveries are made during this era, and the work of the natural philosophers lay the basis for modern science. Some of the most important achievements during this period are not specific discoveries, but the development of the experimental approach to science. Scholars begin developing theories based upon their observations, rather than relying solely on deductive reasoning. Unlike pursuits in logic, experimental science often requires specialized instruments. Astronomers need telescopes to look beyond the planets and stars visible to the eye. Physicists need accurate measurement of physical properties such as temperature and pressure. Thus to conduct and repeat their scientific experiments, Renaissance scholars develop a number of scientific instruments that are still used by scientists today.

While there are notable examples of theories developed from observation before the Renaissance, many early scholars valued logic over observation. Greek philosophers were renowned for their achievements in logic. Consequently, many of the scientific theories developed in ancient Greece did not

come from direct observations. However, a number of philosophers applied both logic and observation to their explanations of natu-

The 16th-century natural philosopher Paracelsus is one of the first European scholars to emphasize performing experiments over studying the texts of the ancient Greeks. *(Museum of the History of Science, Oxford)*

entry for SIXTH CENTURY). These early devices are improved upon in 1454, when German inventor Johannes Gutenberg introduces the movable type printing press. He demonstrates the usefulness of his invention by printing 300 copies of the Bible. Gutenberg's printing press revolutionizes publishing in Europe.

(B, C, ES, M, MS, P, SA, W)

1472

Johann Müller writes a treatise on trigonometry.

Like their Arab predecessors, European Renaissance astronomers relied upon *trigonometry* to measure celestial distances. During the 15th century, German astronomer and mathematician Johann Müller (also known as Regiomontanus, 1436–76) studied

ral phenomenon. Studies of *astronomy* have always relied upon observations of the heavens. Similarly, biologists classify plants and animal based upon their physical attributes. Alchemists in the Middle East developed a number of techniques that will later be applied to chemistry. Observations of the physical world led to explanations of vision and buoyancy that still apply today. However, the tradition of experimental science truly gains wide acceptance in Europe during the Renaissance.

At the end of the Middle Ages and the beginning of the Renaissance, a number of prominent European scholars began to embrace experimental science. During the 13th century, English scholar Roger Bacon argued that observation should be used over logic when investigating the natural world. Other scholars apply these principles. Notably, 13th-century scholar Witelo takes an experimental approach to explaining the *reflection* and *refraction* of light. By the 16th century, the place of experimental science is reinforced as scholars begin rejecting the works of the ancient Greek and developing their own view of the natural world. German scholar Paracelsus implores his students to learn from nature rather than relying upon texts. Meanwhile, prominent English philosopher Francis Bacon declares that the ancient texts must be reviewed and theories not supported by experimental evidence should be rejected. He advocates a new catalog of facts based upon observation and experiments. He describes his analysis of the scientific method in his classic work *Novum organum* (The new logic). French philosopher and mathematician René Descartes, who proposes that scholars completely reject the work of the ancient Greeks and start developing natural philosophy from scratch, espouses similar views. Through the influence of Bacon, Descartes, and other advocates of observation, experimental science begins to flourish.

Scholars soon find that they need precision instruments to conduct experiments and make observations of the natural world. During the Renaissance, a number of scientific instruments are developed. A central figure in the development and use of scientific instruments is Italian scientist Galileo Galilei. He is renowned for his early use of the telescope to observe the Moon, planets, and Sun. Galileo also conducts experiments in the field of physics. He develops the thermoscope, an early thermometer, to measure temperature. Other important instruments developed during this time period are the hygrometer, used to measure humidity, and the first microscope. Using these and other tools, Renaissance scholars begin a tradition of experimental science that continues today.

the daily movements of celestial bodies. In 1472, he writes his treatise *De triangulis omnimodis* (On all classes of triangles) to provide a mathematical basis to help astronomers.

(M, SA)

Johann Müller traces the path of a comet. Astronomers have observed *comets*, bodies of ice and dust, for centuries. In 1472, German astronomer Johann Müller (also known as Regiomontanus) makes nightly observation of a comet that is visible in the European sky and plots its position with respect to the known stars. Müller's observations are the first known description of the path of a comet, and marks the beginning of the study of comets by European astronomers.

(SA)

ca. 1483

Leonardo da Vinci describes a flying machine.

Many of the great scholars of the Renaissance excelled in a variety of fields. The artist and scientist Leonardo da Vinci is a classic example of what is commonly referred to as a Renaissance man. In addition to being one of the greatest artists in history, Leonardo designed many different machines. During the late 15th century (ca. 1483), he begins a series of designs describing a flying machine. The most famous of his proposed flying machines is the aerial screw, which became a resemblance to a helicopter. Although there is no evidence that he ever attempted to build the flying machine, the aerial screw remains famous for being centuries ahead of its time.

(P)

Leonardo da Vinci designs a parachute.

Leonardo da Vinci's notebooks are filled with designs for machines and devices. Although many of his designs are hypothetical, they are notable for their resemblance to modern-day devices. In the late 15th century (ca. 1483), Leonardo describes and sketches a parachute that looks remarkably similar to the device used by modern skydivers. He notes that the parachute should be made of linen, and has a base of approximately 36 feet (11 m). Leonardo believes his parachute will allow anyone to jump from any height without being injured.

(P)

1492

Christopher Columbus notes that magnetic north is not the true north.

The 15th century marked the beginning of the age of exploration in Europe. Many explorers made important contributions to science as well. In 1492, Italian explorer Christopher Columbus (1451–1506) uses a magnetic compass in his voyage across the Atlantic Ocean. During his voyages, he notices that the compass did not point to true north. In fact, at the beginning the compass points slightly westward, but as the journey continues the needle points eastward. Thus, he notes that magnetic north is not necessarily true north.

(ES, MS)

1500s

Geronimo Cardano describes probabilities.

The *probability* that a random event will occur can be calculated mathematically. Many mathematicians apply these principles to games of chance. During the 16th century, Italian mathematician Geronimo Cardano (1501–76) describes some of the basic mathematics of probability in his work *Liber de ludo aleae* (The book on games of chance), which is not published until 1663, almost 90 years after his death. Today, Cardano's work is considered one of the first works describing the mathematics behind gambling.

(M)

Peter Henlein invents the pocket watch.

Inventors and engineers exploit observations in physics to improve timekeeping. Early clocks were powered by water. In the 14th century, mechanical clocks driven by weights replaced them. During the early 16th century, German inventor Peter Henlein (1480–1542) notes that a tightly wound spring loosens over time and could be used to drive a clock. Since a spring is much smaller than the weights required to power a mechanical clock, Henlein's timekeeping device is small enough to carry, and he is widely credited with inventing the pocket watch.

(P)

Tobacco use spreads throughout Europe.

The age of exploration led to many native plants and animals being transported to non-native lands. The spread of tobacco is a clear example of this practice. The tobacco plant is native to Central America, but spreads to North America centuries before the arrival of European explorers. By the 16th century, sailors who visit the Americas bring tobacco to Europe. Soon physicians touting its medicinal properties present tobacco seeds to monarchs. By the late 16th century, smoking becomes popular in Europe, sealing tobaccos place in Western society.

(B)

Robert Recorde introduces the "=" sign.

Mathematics was once described in words rather than symbols. The mathematical

European explorers introduce tobacco to Western culture in the 16th century. Initially, physicians tout the supposed medical benefits of smoking tobacco, and the drug becomes widely used. This photograph, taken in 1941, depicts tobacco drying in Charles County, Maryland. *(Department of Agriculture/National Archives)*

symbols used today developed as mathematics became widely published. One of the great mathematical writers of the 16th century was English mathematician Robert Recorde (ca. 1510–58). He writes a series of textbooks that are used widely by scholars and students, including *The Whetstone of Witte* (1557). Among his accomplishments is the introduction of the modern sign = representing the words *equal to.*

(M)

Paracelsus advocates applying chemistry to medicine.

For centuries, herbs and other plant products were used to treat diseases. During the 16th century, German physician and scholar Bombast von Hohenheim (1493–1541), commonly known as Paracelsus, revolutionizes medicine when he applies chemistry to the search for drugs. He believes that disease stems from external rather than internal causes, and applies his knowledge of chemistry to search for treatments. As his views gain popularity, medical students begin training in chemistry rather than the study of herbs. Today, chemistry remains a critical component of drug discovery.

(B, C)

1501

Georgius Agricola publishes a mineralogy text.

Mining has led to many discoveries in chemistry and geology. During the 16th century, Georgius Agricola (1494–1555) becomes interested in studying minerals while serving as a physician in a mining town. He studies the geology and chemistry of mines. His work culminates in the book *De re metallica* (Concerning ametallic things), which is widely

considered to be the first book devoted to mineralogy.

(C, ES)

1514

Vander Hoecke uses the + and – symbols.

During the Renaissance, mathematicians began moving away from describing mathematical calculations using words, and instead applied symbols. Many of the symbols used today first appeared in works from this era. The origin of symbols for addition (+) and (–) is unclear. The actual symbols first appear in a work by German mathematician Johannes Widman (ca. 1462–ca. 1498) in 1489, but they do not indicate addition and subtraction as they do today. Generally, the use of these symbols for addition and subtraction is credited to Dutch mathematician Vander Hoecke in 1514.

(M)

1522

Ferdinand Magellan's expedition travels around the Earth.

European explorers traveled to the continents of the world during the 14th and 15th centuries. In 1519, an expedition led by Portuguese navigator Ferdinand Magellan (ca. 1480–1521) set out westward, looking for a route to China. In 1522, a single ship from his expedition returns to Spain, having sailed around the Earth. Magellan, however, does not survive the voyage. The expedition is a success, both in reaching China, and in bringing back important information about the Earth. Observers aboard Magellan's ships determine that the Earth contains a continuous ocean and estimate the Earth's *circumference* to be 25,000 miles (40,000 km).

(MS)

1535

Niccolò Tartaglia solves cubic equations.
Problems in *algebra* often lead to equations involving an exponent on a variable. One of the most common is an equation with an unknown raised to the third power, known as a *cubic equation*. Such equations are difficult to solve. Mathematicians often devised methods to solve a specific cubic equation. In 1535, Italian mathematician Niccolò Tartaglia (1499–1557) devises a general method to solve cubic equations. His work is published 10 years later and leads to a famous debate with mathematician Lodovico Ferrari (1522–65), who published his own method of solving cubic equations in 1545.

(M)

1538

William Turner takes a scientific approach to botany.
The study of plants has many practical applications, ranging from the breeding of specific species as agricultural crops, to the use of herbs and plant products as drugs. During the Renaissance, the scientific discipline of *botany* developed. One of the first scholars to publish a scientific analysis of plants was English botanist William Turner (1510–68). In 1538, he writes *Libellus de re herbaria novus* (New letter on the properties of herbs). Today, he is considered the father of English botany.

(B)

1540

Vannoccio Biringuccio describes inorganic chemistry.
Alchemists in the Middle Ages laid much of the basis of modern chemistry, developing techniques to separate, analyze, and transform matter. However, scholars studying the properties of metals, known as metallurgy, also influenced chemists in later generations. In 1540, Italian scientist Vannoccio Biringuccio (1480–ca. 1539) writes *Pirotechnia*, a treatise on working with metals. He describes methods to create mixtures of metals known as *alloys*, as well as other experimental techniques. Biringuccio was not an alchemist; in fact, he criticizes much of their philosophy, including their goal of finding a way to transform metals into gold.

(C)

1542

Nicholas Copernicus describes a heliocentric view of the universe.
As described in the sidebar "Astronomy in the Renaissance," many astronomers at the dawn of the Renaissance believed

Polish astronomer Nicholas Copernicus is considered the father of modern astronomy. *(Museum of the History of Science, Oxford)*

the work of Greek scholar Ptolemy, who described an Earth-centered, or *geocentric,* universe (*See* entry for 150 C.E.). Polish astronomer Nicholas Copernicus challenges this view in 1542, when he publishes his classic work *De revolutionibus orbium coelestium* (On the revolutions of the heavenly spheres). Copernicus advocates a *heliocentric* view of the universe, stating that the Earth and other known planets orbit the Sun. He correctly describes the orbits of Mercury and Venus as being closer to the Sun than the Earth, while Mars, Jupiter, and Saturn travel in orbits farther from the Sun. Today, Copernicus is known as the father of modern astronomy.

(SA)

1543

The first botanical garden opens in Pisa.

Just as astronomers need observatories and chemists need laboratories, scholars interested in plants need a place to study and conduct experiments. In 1543, the first botanical garden opens at the university in Pisa. The garden serves as a place to grow herbal medicines and train students who are interested in studying the properties of herbs. Botanical gardens soon spread across Europe where early botanists studied plants. By the 19th century, however, botanical gardens become better known as places to observe ornamental

ASTRONOMY IN THE RENAISSANCE

Until the 16th century, European astronomers embraced the Earth-centered, or *geocentric,* view of the universe described by Greek astronomer Ptolemy. During the Renaissance, a number of astronomers begin to question this view. The next two centuries see a collection of theories and observations that refutes Ptolemy and leads many to believe that the Earth revolves around the Sun.

The work of Polish astronomer Nicholas Copernicus is largely responsible for this new view of the world. Copernicus questions the work of Ptolemy because he thinks his theory lacks consistency and does not adhere to the established laws of physics. He tries to improve upon Ptolemy's model by developing a view of the universe that is consistent with his understanding of physics. He makes a number of assumptions while developing his model, the most famous of which is that the Sun is the center around which the Earth and planets revolve. By making the Sun the center of the universe, Copernicus avoids many of the difficulties that introduced inconsistencies in Ptolemy's model. He presents his *heliocentric* model in his work *On the Revolutions of the Heavenly Spheres* in 1542.

Danish astronomer Tycho Brahe calls another firmly held belief of the ancient Greek astronomer, the immutability of the stars, into question. Tycho is renowned as one of the greatest astronomical observers of all time. He makes a series of careful observations of a new star that is visible in Europe during the late 16th century. According to Greek astronomical theory, the stars are fixed and constant. For this reason, many believe the new star is actually a *comet.* Tycho's observation proves otherwise. Tycho continues to make some of the most accurate observations of the stars ever recorded. Today, astronomers know that the new star Tycho observed was a *supernova* that occurred within the Milky Way.

Astronomer Johannes Kepler combines Copernicus's heliocentric model of the universe with Tycho's astronomical observations

plants than as sites to conduct scientific experiments.

(B)

Andreas Vesalius describes human anatomy.

For centuries, scholars studied the work of Galen to understand human *anatomy* (*See* entry for SECOND CENTURY C.E.). During the 16th century, Belgian physician Andreas Vesalius (1514–64) dissects many human cadavers. He concludes that the work of Galen contains many errors, such as a drawing of the human liver with five lobes rather than two, suggesting that his work was based on dissecting animals. Vesalius states that human anatomy can be learned only by dis-

section, not from textbooks. In 1543, Vesalius describes his work in *De humani corporis fabrica* (On the fabric of the human body). Today, medical students learn anatomy the way Vesalius advocated, by dissecting human cadavers.

(B)

1545

Ambroise Paré stops bleeding by tying off arteries.

Early surgeons stopped infections by amputating the infected limbs. To stop the bleeding, surgeons would burn the arteries shut. In 1545, French surgeon Ambroise

---

as he attempts to develop a physical explanation of planetary motion. Kepler firmly believes that mathematical relationships can accurately describe physical phenomena. His work culminates in his three laws of planetary motion: first, that planets orbit the Sun in an elliptical pattern; second, a mathematical relationship describes how the speed of a planet decreases as it moves away from the Sun; and third, a mathematical relationship exists between the length of the planetary year and the distance a planet is from the Sun. Together, Kepler's laws give a physical and mathematical basis for the Copernican view of the universe.

One of the most famous astronomers of the Renaissance period is Italian scholar Galileo Galilei. He builds one of the first telescopes and makes a number of astronomical observations that are not possible with the naked eye. By viewing the Moon and the Sun with a telescope, Galileo sees that they are not the perfect spheres that they appear to be from the Earth. Instead, he sees the craters of the Moon and sunspots on the Sun, further

evidence that the heavenly bodies are not perfect. He makes a second critical discovery while observing the planet Jupiter, discovering its four moons. The observation of these moons introduces the idea that there can be more than one center in the universe, that is the planets can revolve around the Sun, while moons revolve around the planets. Galileo's work supports Copernicus's view of the universe. This support gets him in trouble. He writes a dialogue contrasting the Ptolemaic system to the Copernican system that angers the Catholic Church. Eventually, Galileo is forced to face the Inquisition and renounce the heliocentric view of the universe.

During the Renaissance, the current model of the solar system is developed. Through the work of Copernicus, Tycho, Kepler, Galileo, and others, the ancient Greek view of an Earth-centered unchanging universe is overturned. By the 17th century, adherents to the geocentric view of the universe have a difficult time defending themselves against the mounting evidence that the planets revolve around the Sun.

Paré (1510–90) advocates tying off arteries rather than burning them shut. Paré works as a military surgeon where he develops his surgical techniques. He publishes his work in French, rather than the scholarly language of Latin. His work is translated and influences physicians throughout Europe.

(B)

1546

Girolamo Fracastoro states that infectious diseases spread through microscopic agents.

Before the development of modern drugs, infectious diseases were a major cause of death. Physicians and scientists worked to understand how infections start and spread. In 1546, Italian physician Girolamo Fracastoro (ca. 1478–1553) writes *De contagione et contagiosis morbis et curatione* (On con-tagion and the cure of contagious disease). Fracastoro describes a number of infectious diseases, including syphilis, and proposes that organisms too small to be seen cause these diseases. Today, biologists have clearly established that microscopic protozoa, *bacteria,* and *viruses* cause infectious diseases.

(B)

Niccolò Tartaglia describes the trajectory of a bullet.

Science and technology have been applied to warfare throughout the ages. In some cases, the study of military weapons led to advances in physics. One case occurs in 1546, when Italian mathematician Niccolò Tartaglia describes the trajectory of a bullet. Tartaglia falsely assumes that the trajectory is a curved line throughout the path of a bullet. He calculates that the maximum firing range can be obtained by firing the weapon at a 45-degree angle. His pioneering work on

projectile motion is described in *Quesiti et invenzioni diverse.*

(M, P)

1551

Georg Rhäticus publishes trigonometric tables with all six functions.

Astronomers rely upon *trigonometry,* the mathematical study of triangles, to aid their astronomical calculations. Mathematicians describe the relationship between the sides of a triangle as trigonometric functions. There are six such functions, *sine, cosine, tangent, secant, cosecant,* and *cotangent,* each representing the *ratio* of one side to another. Mathematicians and astronomers have developed a number of trigonometric tables that list values for one or more of the six functions of a triangle. In 1551, German mathematician Georg Rhäticus publishes *Cannon of the Doctrine of Triangles,* the first known table that describes all six trigonometric functions.

(M)

Pierre Belon notes similarities between different species.

During the 16th century, the study of the natural world became more systematic. In 1551, French naturalist Pierre Belon (1517–64) pioneers the field of comparative *anatomy.* In *Histoire naturelle des estranges poissons marins* (Natural history of strange marine animals), he classifies fish based upon similarities among species. Belon dissects a number of different species, identifies different organs, and notes similar organs among species.

(B)

1553

Giovanni Benedetti proposes that bodies fall at the same rate.

As modern physics began to develop, scholars increasingly applied mathematics to their study of the physical world. In 1553, Italian mathematician Giovanni Benedetti (1530–90) uses mathematics to describe how bodies fall to the Earth. In his works *Resolutio* (Resolution) and *Demonstratio* (Description), he applies the works of Archimedes and Aristotle to his study of falling bodies. He states that the surface area contributes more to the resistance of a falling body than its volume. Furthermore, he maintains that bodies of the same material will fall at the same rate.

(P)

1555

Renaldo Colombo describes blood circulation between the lungs and the heart.

During the Renaissance, physicians and scholars began applying dissection to the study of *anatomy*. Like many of his contemporaries, Italian anatomist, Renaldo Colombo (ca. 1516–59) relied upon his own dissections rather than the study of ancient texts to support his theories. In 1555, he describes the circulation of blood between the heart and lungs. Now known as the pulmonary circuit, the blood in the right *ventricle* of the heart passes through the lungs before entering the left atrium. He publishes some of the leading work in the anatomy of the circulatory system of his time, including *De re anatomica* (On anatomy, 1559).

(B)

1564

Bartolomeo Eustachi describes the anatomy of the kidney.

Physicians and scholars in the 16th century relied upon dissection to understand *anatomy*. The great anatomy teachers described the organs in the body in great detail. In 1564, Italian physician Bartolomeo Eustachi (1520–74) writes a treatise on the kidney. He describes the anatomy of the organ and its relationship to the adrenal glands. Today, two parts of the kidney, the Eustachian tube and the Eustachian valve, are named for Eustachi.

(B)

1565

Giambattista della Porta establishes the first scientific society.

During the Renaissance, many scholars interested in the natural world began taking an experimental approach to their studies. Italian natural philosopher Giambattista della Porta (ca. 1535–1615) carried out experiments trying to replicate what he calls "natural magic." In 1565, he establishes the first scientific society called Accademia dei Segreti. While many other societies exist during this era, Porta's is believed to be the first dedicated exclusively to science. The Inquisition shuts down Accademia dei Segreti in 1578.

(B, C, ES, M, MS, P, SA, W)

Conrad Gesner studies fossils.

Natural historians study fossils to understand the plants and animals that populated the prehistoric world. During the Renaissance, a few scholars began to study the fossil record. One of the first was Swiss natural philosopher Conrad Gesner (1516–65). In 1565, he publishes *On Fossil Objects,* a work that includes illustrations that compare the fossils of ancient sea creatures with those found during his time. Unlike today's definition, Gesner includes stones and gems in his definition of fossils. However, he does divide fossils into several categories, separating crystals and gems from fossils that resemble living animals.

(B, ES)

1569

August

Gerardus Mercator designs the cylinder projection map.

As the European explorers and sailors began making regular voyages to distant lands, a need grew for more maps that were both accurate and easy to use. In August 1569, Flemish cartographer Gerardus Mercator (1512–94) designs the cylinder projection map. The projection maps depicts the spherical globe in a manner that allows sailors to chart a course without changing compass settings. The Mercator map is notable for the straight lines that represent the parallels and meridians. One of the drawbacks of the projection map is that the sizes of landmasses become distorted, with the greater distortions occurring as the distance from the equator increases.

(ES)

Danish astronomer Tycho Brahe builds a great observatory during the 16th century.
(Museum of the History of Science, Oxford)

1572

November 11

Tycho Brahe observes a supernova.

As described in the sidebar "Astronomy in the Renaissance," astronomy flourished in Europe during the Renaissance. On November 11, 1572, Danish astronomer Tycho Brahe observes a new star in the sky. He makes careful observation of the star and maps it to a known constellation. In 1573, he publishes his observations in *De nova stella* (A new star). Today, scholars realize that Tycho observed an exploding star or *supernova* that was visible in Europe for nearly two years.

(SA)

16th-century Europe. Advances in the field depended upon accurate observations and descriptions of the movement of heavenly bodies. In 1576, Danish astronomer Tycho Brahe secures funding from the Danish government to build an astronomical observatory off the coast of Sweden. The observatory, which Tycho calls Uraniborg, is built between 1576 and 1580. At the observatory, Tycho makes some of the most accurate observations known at the time. Astronomer Johannes Kepler works out his laws of planetary motion based upon Tycho's observations.

(SA)

1576

Tycho Brahe builds an astronomical observatory.

As described in the sidebar "Astronomy in the Renaissance," astronomy flourished in

1581

Robert Norman notes the dip of a compass.

The discovery of the compass revolutionized navigation, allowing sailors to chart a course when clouds obscured the stars. Later, the compass became an important tool for the study of *magnetism*. In 1581, British sailor Robert Norman describes the dip of the compass needle. In *The Newe Attractive,* Norman calculates the dip of the compass needle in London, which leads to the demonstration that the Earth is a magnet.

(ES, MS)

1582

Galileo Galilei describes the motion of a pendulum.

As described in the sidebar "Developing the Tools and Methods of Modern Science," Renaissance scholars began to rely upon observation and experiments rather than upon pure logic when they investigated the natural world. In 1582, Galileo Galilei is a young budding scholar. One of his first notable works describes the motion of a pendulum. A pendulum is a weight suspended from a fixed point that allows it to swing back and forth. Galileo notices that the time the pendulum takes to complete one swing, known as the period, is constant. His observation leads to the invention of pendulum clocks, and stands as some of his earliest work on *gravity*.

(P)

1583

Christoph Clavius creates the Gregorian calendar.

The development of accurate calendars requires knowledge of both mathematics and astronomy. In 1583, Bavarian mathematician Christoph Clavius (1537–1612) reforms the calendar used in Europe, known as the Julian calendar. He presents his work to Pope Gregory XIII (1502–85), who adopts the calendar. Clavius's calendar, now called

the Gregorian calendar, is used widely in the Western world.

(SA)

Simon Stevin describes hydrostatics.

During the Renaissance, many scholars began performing experiments to help them understand natural phenomena. Such work led to the creation of new scientific disciplines. In 1583, Flemish mathematician Simon Stevin (1548–1620) creates the field known as hydrostatics with the publication of *De beghinselen der weeghconst* (Statics and hydrostatics). His work is notable for describing triangle *forces* and the downward pressure on a liquid.

(P)

1585

Simon Stevin uses decimals to describe fractions.

During the Renaissance, much of the representation used in mathematical calculations today began to be widely used. During this period, mathematicians began representing fractions with *decimals*. In 1585, Flemish mathematician Simon Stevin writes two works, *La thiende* (The tenth) and *La disme* (The decimal), which lead to widespread use of decimals. Stevin's work shows how the decimal system simplifies calculations with fractions. He correctly predicts that they will soon be used to represent weights and measures.

(M)

1586

Simon Stevin observes gravity.

During the Renaissance, many scholars began performing careful experiments to help them understand natural phenomena. In 1586, Flemish mathematician Simon Stevin conducts a series of experiments on falling bodies. He drops lead balls of different weights and observes that they strike the ground at the same time. His observation of *gravity* is published a few years before Galileo's extensive study on the subject.

(P)

1590

Galileo Galilei describes falling bodies.
During the Renaissance, many scholars began performing experiments to test their theories about the natural world. In 1590, Italian scholar Galileo Galilei begins his study of falling bodies. He shows that objects of different weights actually fall to Earth at the same speed, a conclusion that contradicts the work of Aristotle. Galileo's early observations of *gravity* include mathematical descriptions of the motion of falling bodies. He describes these experiments in *De motu* (On motion).

(P)

Galileo Galilei invents the thermoscope.
As described in the sidebar "Developing the Tools and Methods of Modern Science," experimental science that flourished in Europe depended upon the development of instruments to accurately measure the physical characteristics of matter. In 1590, Italian scholar Galileo Galilei invents the thermoscope to measure the temperature of the air. While his thermoscope is not very accurate, the invention is notable both as one of the first instruments devised for scientific measurements and as the forerunner to the modern thermometer.

(C, P, W)

Lens makers invent the first microscope.
As described in the sidebar "Developing the Tools and Methods of Modern Science,"

the growing emphasis on experimental science during the Renaissance led many scientists to devise instruments that helped them observe the natural world. In 1590, the Janssen family makes lenses for eyeglasses. Scholars believe that they constructed the first compound microscope at this time, although the only evidence are drawings and the reports of others. According to the drawings, the microscope consists of a long tube with a lens on each end, and is capable of magnifying objects to nine times their actual size. The actual identity of the inventor of the microscope is controversial. Many reports state that Zacharias Janssen (1580–ca. 1638) invented this compound microscope, but others credit the invention to Dutch lens maker Hans Lippershey (ca. 1570–ca. 1619), the inventor of the telescope (*See* entry for 1609).

(B, P)

1592

François Viète introduces the use of symbols to algebra.
Mathematicians who study *algebra* use equations to determine the value of unknown quantities. For centuries, algebra was written in words. In 1592, French mathematician François Viète (1540–1603) introduces the use of symbols to write algebraic equations. In his work *In artem analyticem isagoge* (Introduction to the analytical arts), he uses consonants to represent known quantities and vowels to represent unknown quantities. While the system differs from the one used today, the work is considered to be the first book of algebra that would seem recognizable to a modern high school student. His work lays the groundwork for symbolic algebra.

(M)

1596

Ludolf van Ceulen calculates pi to 20 decimal places.

The *ratio* of the *circumference* of a circle to its diameter is represented by the constant called *pi* (p). Pi is an *irrational number* that cannot be represented as a fraction. Throughout history, mathematicians have devised methods to calculate the value of pi with greater accuracy. In 1596, German mathematician Ludolf van Ceulen (1540–1610) uses a *polygon* with 2^{62} sides to calculate the value of pi to 35 decimal places. The value he obtains is engraved on his tombstone.

(M)

David Fabricius discovers the first variable star.

Astronomy thrived in Europe during the Renaissance. In 1596, German astronomer David Fabricius (1564–1617) observes a star that displays changes in the intensity of light. He calls the star Mira, the first *variable*

Variable stars, stars that change intensity, are first observed by the 16th-century German astronomer David Fabricius. This photograph, taken aboard the Hubble Space telescope, shows a variable star in a distant spiral galaxy. *(NASA, HST Key Project Team)*

star to be observed. His observation is controversial because it is counter to the classical view that the stars are unchanging.

(SA)

1597

Andreas Libau summarizes medieval alchemy.

Alchemy, characterized by the search for a chemical that will turn metals to gold, thrived during the Middle Ages (*see* sidebar "The Alchemists"). Alchemists from the Middle East to Europe developed a large body of knowledge about a variety of substances. Much of their work laid the basis for modern chemistry. In 1597, German chemist Andreas Libau (ca. 1540–1616) summarizes the work of medieval alchemists in his famous treatise *Alchemia*.

(C)

1600s

Galileo Galilei states the principle of inertia.

During the 17th century, many scholars began to understand the laws of motion. In the course of his experiments on motion, Italian scholar Galileo Galilei develops the principle of *inertia*. He notes that a body that is in motion tends to remain in motion unless something physically stops it; while a body at rest stays at rest unless something moves it. Sir Isaac Newton later expands Galileo's concept of inertia (*See* entry for 1687).

(P)

1600

Giordano Bruno burns at the stake for his heliocentric views.

As described in the sidebar "Astronomy in the Renaissance," Renaissance astronomers began to reject the classical view that the Earth is the center of the universe. After Nicholas Copernicus's work stated that the Sun is the center of the universe, many began to embrace this *heliocentric* view (*See* entry for 1542). Italian scholar Giordano Bruno (1548–1600) not only espouses the heliocentric view of the solar system, but his writings also suggest the modern idea that the universe is infinite. His views contradict the teachings of the Catholic Church, leading to his arrest and trial. Upon refusing to refute his ideas, Bruno is burned at the stake in 1600.

(SA)

William Gilbert describes the Earth as a magnet.

Magnetism has been known since the invention of the compass. During the Renaissance, many European scholars began performing experiments to study magnetism. In 1600, English scholar William Gilbert (1544–1603) publishes his classic work *De magnete, magneticisque corporibus, et de magno magnete tellure* (On the magnet, magnetic bodies, and the great magnet of the Earth). Gilbert's work is notable for describing the Earth as a giant magnet, and studying the relationship between magnetism and *electricity*.

(ES, P)

1608

Girolamo Fabrici describes blood flow in the legs.

During the Renaissance, physicians began studying *anatomy* by making their own observations using cadavers, rather than relying on medical texts alone. Italian surgeon Girolamo Fabrici (1573–1619) is widely considered one of the great Italian anatomists. In 1608, he publishes *De*

venarum ostiolis (On the valves of the veins), describing blood flow in the legs. He notes that leg veins have small valves that assure that blood flows upward. His work provides the basis for later descriptions of circulation.

(B)

1609

Galileo Galilei uses a telescope to study astronomy.

Astronomy benefited greatly from the invention of the telescope, which helped scholars identify more objects in the sky. In 1609, Italian scholar Galileo Galilei builds the first telescope used for astronomical observations. His telescope magnifies objects up to 20 times. Among his early findings using the telescope are a more complete understanding of the phases of the Moon, the realization that there are more stars than those visible with the naked eye, and the discovery of moons surrounding Jupiter and Saturn. In January 1610, he publishes these observations in *Sidereus nuncius* (The sidereal messenger).

(SA)

Hans Lippershey invents the telescope.

As described in the sidebar "Developing the Tools and Methods of Modern Science," the Renaissance saw the invention of many new devices that helped scientists. For example, the telescope provided astronomers with a means to observe more bodies in the sky. The identity of the actual inventor of the telescope is controversial. Many believe that Dutch lens maker Hans Lippershey (also known as Hans Lippersheim) invented the telescope in 1609. He envisioned using the

KEPLER'S LAWS OF PLANETARY MOTION

path of planets

planet   Sun

equal area of paths traveled in same amount of time

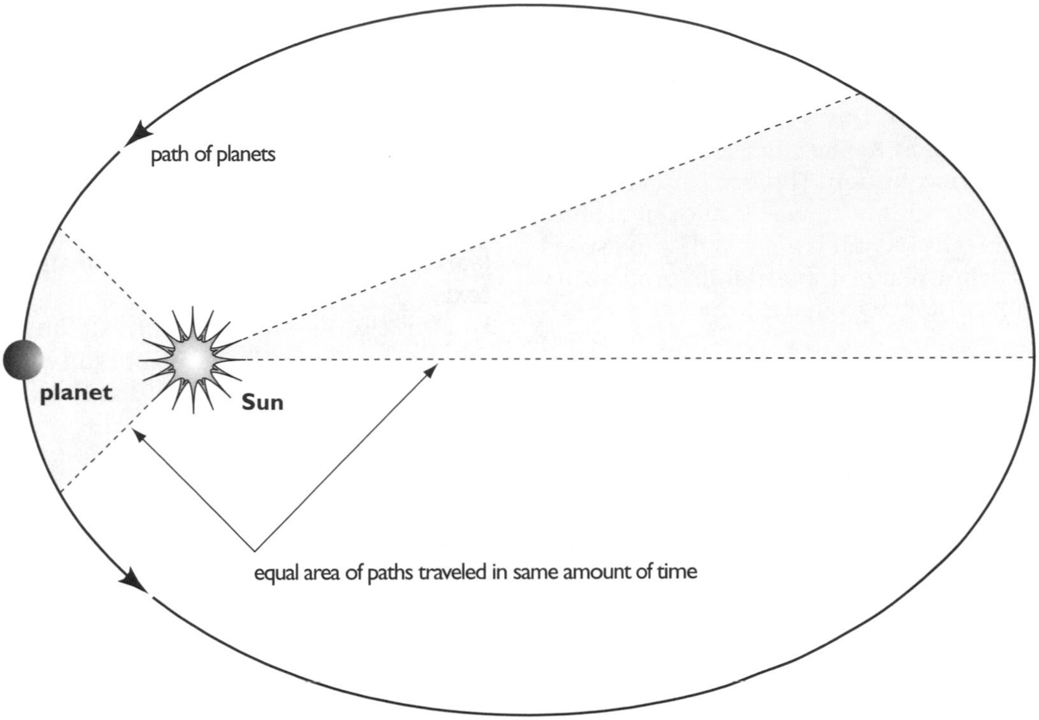

Law 1: The planets follow an elliptical path around the Sun.
Law 2: A line joining the planet and the Sun covers an equal area in an equal amount of time, regardless of its position in the ellipse.
Law 3: The square of the time it takes a planet to orbit the Sun (p) is proportional to the cube of its average distance from the Sun (a) or $p^2 = a^3$.

© Infobase Publishing

During the 17th century, German astronomer Johannes Kepler describes three laws of planetary motion. The first law says that planets follow an elliptical path. The second and third laws mathematically describe the relationship between the time a planet takes to orbit the Sun and its distance from the Sun.

instrument not as a scientific tool but as an aid for the military, and he gave his design to the Dutch government. Word of his telescope spread through Europe, and soon Galileo builds one for astronomical observations.

(P, SA)

Johannes Kepler describes his first and second laws of planetary motion.

As described in the sidebar "Astronomy in the Renaissance," during the Renaissance the idea that the Earth travels around the Sun, known as the *heliocentric* theory, gained wider acceptance with astronomers. In 1609, German astronomer Johannes Kepler publishes *Astronomica nova* (New astronomy) describing how the planets move around the Sun. His laws are based upon the observations of Danish astronomer Tycho Brahe. In this work, he states what are now known as Kepler's first and second laws of planetary motion. The first law states that all planets follow an elliptical orbit around the Sun. His second law states that the speed at which a planet travels in its orbit varies with its distance from the Sun.

(P, SA)

1610

Galileo Galilei describes the phases of Venus.

The invention of the telescope greatly increased knowledge of astronomy (*See* entry for 1609). In 1610, Italian scholar Galileo Galilei uses a telescope he built to study the planet Venus. Looking at Venus over time, he shows that the planet has a full range of phases, similar to those of the Moon. Galileo realizes that this finding implies that Venus revolves around the Sun. He uses these observations in support of Polish astronomer Nicholas Copernicus's *heliocentric* view of the universe (*See* entry for 1542).

(SA)

Simon Mayr discovers and names the moons of Jupiter.

Astronomical observations were greatly improved with the invention of the telescope at the beginning of the 17th century (*See* entry for 1609). In 1610, German astronomer Simon Mayr (also known as Simon Marius, 1573–1624) builds a telescope and uses it to view the planet Jupiter. He sees that Jupiter has four moons and names them Io, Europa, Ganymede, and Callisto. In 1614, he describes his observations of Jupiter in *Mundus iovialis* (Jovian world). Although his names for the moons are used today, scholars disagree as to whether Marius or Galileo was the first to observe the moons of Jupiter.

(SA)

1611

Jean Beguin writes the first chemistry text.

During the Renaissance, physicians and scholars emulating Paracelsus began looking to chemistry rather than herbs as they try to find new treatments for diseases. In 1611, French scholar Jean Beguin (1550–1620) writes *Tyrocinium chymicum* (Beginning chemistry), the first chemistry text. Beguin's work focuses on methods to prepare drugs, and is primarily concerned with the consistency of preparations and methods to determine the quantity of substances.

(C)

1613

Galileo Galilei observes sunspots.

During the Renaissance, scholars supported their theories of the natural world with data collected through observation and experimentation. The invention of the telescope allowed Italian scholar Galileo Galilei to make a number of key observations that advance the field of astronomy. In 1613, he publishes *Istoria e dimostrazioni intorno alle macchie solari e loro accidenti* (History and demonstrations concerning sunspots and their properties) describing his observations of sunspots. Galileo argues that sunspots are part of the Sun itself rather than satellites of the Sun. His work is controversial because it challenges the popular notion that the Sun is perfect.

(SA)

1614

John Napier publishes tables of logarithms.

During the Renaissance, many of the methods used in mathematical calculations today were developed. In 1614, Scottish mathematician John Napier (1550–1617) describes the use of *logarithms* to simplify complex calculations. Logarithms are a way of simplifying large numbers by expressing them as the number a given *base* (usually 10) must be raised in order to obtain the larger number. For example, three is the logarithm of 1,000 because $10^3 = 1,000$. His work *Mirifici logarithmorum canonis descriptio* (Description of the marvelous canon of logarithms) describes how to obtain logarithms and their many uses.

(M)

1616

Santorio Santorio publishes results of metabolic experiments.

During the Renaissance, many physicians and scholars began performing experiments to help them understand how the human body works. In the early 17th century, Italian physician Santorio Santorio (also known as Sanctorius 1561–1636) shows interest in how the body's metabolism works. Santorio chooses to experiment on himself. He constructs a large scale and over a long period of time measures the fluctuations of his own weight. He also measures the food and liquid he consumes, and the amount of waste products he excretes. From these experiments, he concludes that the body takes in more material than it secretes. In 1616, Santorio describes his experiment in *De statica medicina* (On medical measurement).

(B)

1617

John Napier simplifies calculations with Napier's bones.

Work in astronomy and physics often requires complex calculation that can be quite cumbersome if they are performed by hand. Scottish mathematician John Napier searched for methods to make complex calculations simpler. He devised a method to perform multiplication and division using small rods known as "Napier's bones." In 1617, he describes the use of Napier's bones in *Rabdologiae* (Study of divining rods). Today, Napier's bones is considered an important predecessor to the slide rule.

(M)

1619

Johannes Kepler publishes his third law of planetary motion.

During the Renaissance, the field of astronomy benefited from the invention of the telescope and advances in mathematics that simplify complex calculations. During this period, German astronomer Johannes Kepler works with Danish astronomer Tycho Brahe to describe the motion of the planets. Initially, his work leads to two laws of planetary motion. In 1619, Kepler articulates a third law of planetary motion, which states that there is an exact relationship between the time it takes a planet to orbit the Sun and the radius of its orbit.

(SA)

1620

Francis Bacon argues for the use of experimental evidence in science.

During the Renaissance, many scholars began to reject the work of ancient philosophers and instead commenced their own studies of the natural world based upon experimental evidence. In 1620, British philosopher Francis Bacon (1561–1626) publishes *Novum organum* (The new logic). Bacon argues against the sole use of logic and deductive reasoning. Instead, he states that science should be based upon inductive reasoning, i.e., learning how something works in a number of specific instances and using that information to make generalizations. He advocates the use of experiments to obtain evidence of how the natural world works.

(B, C, ES, M, MS, P, SA)

1622

Willebrord Snel describes the refraction of light.

The field of *optics* is concerned with the properties of light. In 1622, Dutch scholar Willebrord Snel (1580–1626) describes one of the fundamental relationships in optics. Snel studies the way light bends as it passes from one medium to another. He describes the relationship between the degree of *refraction*, known as the refractive index, and the path the light takes into the medium. This relationship, known as Snel's Law, is not widely known until 1690, when Dutch mathematician Christiaan Huygens includes Snel's work in his book *Traité de la lumière.*

(P)

Jan Baptista van Helmont recognizes the existence of different gases.

For centuries, air was believed to be a form of matter unto itself, rather than a mixture of different gases. In 1627, Belgian chemist Jan Baptista van Helmont (1579–1644) realizes that many vapors are made of different substances. He recognizes the existence of distinct gases and coins the term *gas.*

Continuing his work on vapors, Helmont becomes the first to discover carbon dioxide. He compares the vapors released by burning wood to those released during *fermentation,* and finds that they have the same properties. Today, scientists know that this gas is carbon dioxide.

(C)

1628

Johannes Kepler publishes planetary tables.

During the early 17th century, German astronomer Johannes Kepler described three laws of planetary motion based upon the observations of Danish astronomer Tycho Brahe. In 1628, Kepler publishes a set of planetary tables, the *Rudolphine Tables,* also based upon Tycho's observation. Kepler uses *logarithms* developed by John Napier to make the calculations necessary for the work. The tables are notable for their *heliocentric* view of the universe.

(SA)

William Harvey describes the circulation of the blood.

Until the Renaissance, most European physicians learned *anatomy* from the ancient Greek texts. By the 16th century, however, physicians and scholars began to dissect cadavers to better understand how the human body works. In 1628, English physician William Harvey (1578–1657) describes the circulation of the blood in *Exercitatio anatomica de motu cordis et sanguinis in animablius* (An anatomical exercise on the motion of the heart and blood in animals). Harvey describes the heart as the pump that helps the blood circulate. He also describes the function of valves and the circulation of blood between the heart and lungs.

(B)

1631

Thomas Harriot introduces signs for "greater than" and "less than."

During the 17th century, many of the symbols used in mathematical calculations today were introduced. In 1631, the symbol "<" for "less than" and ">" for "greater than" first appear in English mathematician Thomas Harriot's (1560–1621) work *Artis analyticae praxis ad aequationes algebraicas resolvenda* (Application of analytical art to solving algebraic equations). Although the symbols are widely credited as being Harriot's, there is evidence to suggest his editor added them to the text.

(M)

William Oughtred introduces the symbol for multiplication.

A number of the mathematical symbols used today were introduced during the Renaissance. In 1631, English mathematician William Oughtred (1574–1660) introduces the symbol for multiplication (x) in *Clavis mathematicae* (Key to mathematics). His book describes basic *arithmetic* and *algebra* and is used widely throughout the 17th century.

(M)

1632

William Oughtred develops the slide rule.

Throughout the Renaissance, developments in physics and astronomy led to an increasing need to perform complex mathematics. John Napier developed *logarithms* to make such calculations easier. In 1632, English mathematician William Oughtred uses logarithms in his calculating device known as the slide rule. His slide rule is in the shape of a circle. He describes his device and its use in *Circles of Proportion and the Horizontal Instrument*.

(M)

1633

April

Galileo Galilei renounces the heliocentric view of the universe.

Throughout the 16th and 17th centuries, astronomers gathered evidence that the Sun is the center of the universe rather than the Earth. The invention of the telescope strengthened these arguments. In 1632, Italian scholar Galileo Galilei publishes *Dialogue Concerning the Two Chief World Systems, Ptolemaic and Copernican,* outlining the evidence for the *heliocentric* view of the universe. The Catholic Church asserts that the Ptolemaic or *geocentric* view is not portrayed favorably in his book. In April 1633, Galileo is forced to appear before the Inquisition, where he retracts his heliocentric view.

(SA)

⚬ CONCLUSION ⚬

The European Renaissance was notable for great scientific achievements, groundbreaking inventions, and the beginnings of a more experimental approach to scientific discovery. During this era, mathematics books begin to resemble modern high school texts, while common scientific knowledge also starts to resemble the facts taught in elementary school. Some Renaissance scientists also suffer because their theories go against the teachings of the Catholic Church, beginning centuries of conflict between science and religion.

Some of the most notable scientific achievements of the Renaissance were in astronomy, notably the *heliocentric* view of the universe and the laws of planetary motion. However, other fields saw hints of great advances soon to come. Galileo Galilei makes notable achievements in astronomy, including some of the first views of the solar system using a telescope. In addition, he uncovers some basic physical principles, including descriptions of the period of pendulum and *inertia* that foreshadow great advances in physics. Likewise, the invention of the microscope is the first step that opens the world of cells and microorganisms to biologists.

Even without the great discoveries, the Renaissance would be notable for changing the way scholars approach science. Rather than studying the texts of Greek philosophers, Renaissance scholars began the tradition of exploring the natural world through experimentation. The experimental approach was essential for the great achievements in chemistry that occurred in the 17th and 18th centuries.

Throughout the Renaissance, scholars embracing the heliocentric view of the solar system face conflict with the Catholic Church. Unfortunately, such conflicts are not unique to this era. While scientists of later eras do not face trials and imprisonment, as Galileo and others did, many find themselves at odds with church teachings. In the next centuries, geologists who estimate the age of the Earth and biologists who advocate *evolution,* and now stem cell research, also face opposition from religious institutions.

4

BUILDING THE BASE OF MODERN SCIENCE

1635–1759

∽ INTRODUCTION ∾

The 17th and 18th centuries were a time of great expansion in all fields of science. The era saw the development of chemistry as a rigorous science, the fundamental laws of physics explained, a new field of mathematics developed, a deeper understanding of biological organism through the use of microscopes, an expanded view of the universe through more powerful telescopes, and the beginning of scientific arguments of how the Earth was formed and changes over time.

Chemistry as a formal field of study begins in the 17th century with the publication of Robert Boyle's (1627–91) *The Skeptical Chymist* in 1661. Boyle differentiates modern chemistry from the science of the past by rejecting the classic definition of elements and countering the secrecy of the alchemists by advocating precise measurements and careful documentation for understanding how chemical reactions work. After the publication of Boyle's work, chemistry develops rapidly. French chemist Antoine-Laurent Lavoisier (1743–94) provides a modern definition of an element, calling it a substance that cannot be further broken down in a chemical reaction. Soon, chemists begin identifying these fundamental substances. Others study how matter changes and develop the *phlogiston* theory, which says that a substance called phlogiston helps matter change from one form to another. While the theory is incorrect, the search for the elusive phlogiston guides the research of many chemists and eventually leads to the discovery of the element oxygen in the 18th century.

As the science of chemistry is being born, chemists work with physicists and mathematicians to understand the physical and chemical behavior of gases. The era sees a description of atmospheric pressure and the development of methods to study the pressure of gases. These advances lead to the elucidation of the physical laws that govern the behavior of gases. The physics of light, known as *optics,* also advances during this era with scholars providing explanations of rainbows to presenting arguments that support both the particle and wave theory of light. The greatest achievement in physics comes in the 17th century with the publication of English physicist Sir Isaac Newton's (1642–1727) classic work *Philosophiae naturalis principia mathematica* (Mathematical principles of natural philosophy; known as *Principia mathematica*). Today, high school students still study Newton's work, particularly his laws of motion and description of universal gravitation.

Sir Isaac Newton also leaves his mark on mathematics, as one of the two scholars of the era who were instrumental in developing *calculus.* Newton develops a form of calculus, called the method of fluxions, to help him describe motion. Ironically, he relies almost exclusively on *geometry* to describe his laws of motion and *gravity* in *Principia mathematica.* The other mathematician credited with the development of calculus, German mathematician Gottfried Leibniz (1646–1716), presents his work in a format that becomes widely adopted and is recognizable to mathematics students today. Other mathematical achievements of the era include the development of *probability* and *statistics* and the explanation of *Pascal's triangle.*

During the 17th century, biologists look at organisms under the microscope, uncovering cells, the fundamental units of life, and discovering a wide range of microorganisms, from *bacteria* to algae. Microscopic observations lead to the discovery of capillaries, the small blood vessels that connect arteries and veins, and red blood cells, the cells responsible for carrying oxygen throughout the body.

Just as microscopes uncover the world of cells and microorganisms, telescopes provide astronomers with an expanded view of the universe. Some astronomers turn their telescopes to the planets, discovering moons surrounding Jupiter and Saturn. Others, including English astronomer Edmond Halley, follow *comets.* During this era, Halley notices that a particular comet seems to appear in the sky at regular intervals and predicts that it will once again be visible. Fifty-three years later, an amateur astronomer spots "Halley's comet," near the time and place Halley had predicted. The reappearance of Halley's comet gives widespread credence to the notion that scientific observations and research can predict the behavior of nature in the future.

Scientists of this era also begin to develop theories of how the Earth and its many characteristic features were formed. By looking at geological landmarks, such as mountains and valleys, Earth scientists develop theories that the Earth changes because of natural occurrences, such as water eroding soil or volcanoes heating rock and changing its appearance. Such arguments continue into the next century. In addition, naturalists study the various *sediments* found in the Earth, noting that each layer of sediment seems to contain specific types of fossils and developing theories as to how the sediments form. Other scholars who study the Earth focus on changes in the weather, such as American scientist Benjamin Franklin, who tracks storm movements and invents the lightning rod.

TIME LINE OF SCIENTIFIC ACHIEVEMENTS BETWEEN 1636 AND 1759

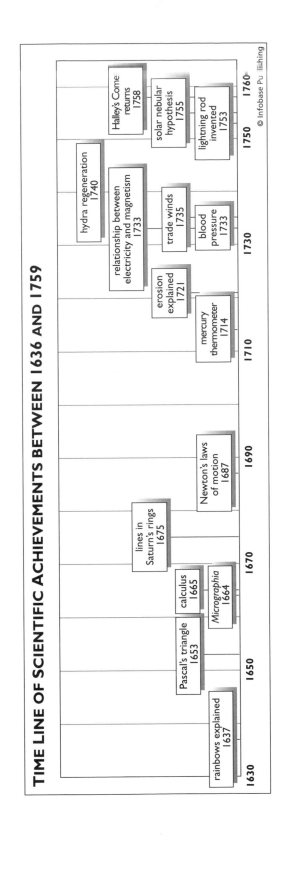

rainbows explained 1637

Pascal's triangle 1653

calculus 1665

Micrographia 1664

lines in Saturn's rings 1675

Newton's laws of motion 1687

mercury thermometer 1714

erosion explained 1721

relationship between electricity and magnetism 1733

trade winds 1735

blood pressure 1733

hydra regeneration 1740

Halley's Comet returns 1758

solar nebular hypothesis 1755

lightning rod invented 1753

1630   1650   1670   1690   1710   1730   1750   1760

© Infobase Publishing

∽ CHRONOLOGY ∾

1635

Henry Gellibrand shows the Earth's magnetic field changes over time.

The widespread use of compasses for navigation set off a flurry of studies on *magnetism.* Scientists studying the Earth's *magnetic field* noticed a difference between true north and magnetic north, known as magnetic declination (*See* entry for 1580). British scientists independently measured the magnetic declination in London; however, each obtained a slightly different value. In 1635, English astronomer Henry Gellibrand (1597–1636) studies these differences and realizes that the Earth's magnetic field actually changes over time, explaining the discrepancy in past results.

(ES)

Francesco Bonaventura Cavalieri finds a relationship between the volumes of solids.

Mathematicians have devised ways to calculate the volume of three-dimensional objects, or solids. In 1635, Italian mathematician Francesco Bonaventura Cavalieri (1598–1647) describes "Cavalieri's principle," which states that two solids of equal height have the same volume if a plane that intersects them both at the same altitude has the same area. He articulates his principle in *Geometria indivisibilibus continuorum nova quadam ratione promota* (A certain method for the development of a new geometry of continuous indivisibles). This work represents an early step on the path to developing *calculus.*

(M)

1636

Marin Mersenne calculates the frequency of audible sounds.

Hearing occurs when the ear perceives sound waves that travel at specific frequencies. Seventeenth-century French scholar Marin Mersenne (1588–1648) pioneered the scientific study of sound, known as *acoustics.* In 1636, he publishes *Harmonie universelle* (Universal harmony), a treatise on music, harmonics, and acoustics. In this work, Mersenne publishes his calculation of the frequency of the lowest audible tones. Today, Mersenne is considered the father of acoustics.

(P)

1637

René Descartes describes analytic geometry.

Mathematicians have studied the *geometry* of the ancient Greeks for centuries. During the 17th century, many began to apply the principles of *algebra* to geometry, leading to the development of analytic geometry. In 1637, French philosopher and mathematician René Descartes (1596–1650) writes one of the first

The 17th-century French scholar René Descartes makes key contributions to the field of geometry as well as to the philosophy of modern science. *(Museum of the History of Science)*

descriptions of analytic geometry *Géométrie* (Geometry).

(M)

René Descartes describes how rainbows appear as arcs.

The array of colors seen in a rainbow can be explained using physics and mathematics. By the 17th century, scholars know that the colors appear when light passing through water drops undergoes a specific sequence of *refractions* and *reflections*. However, physicists cannot explain why rainbows always appear as circular arcs. In his 1637 work *Les météores* (Meteorology), French mathematician René Descartes calculates the angle at which light leaves a water drop. He explains the rainbows are caused by light passing through many different raindrops, causing the rainbow to take on the appearance of an arc.

(P)

Pierre de Fermat describes a method to determine the maximum and minimum value of a function.

During the 17th century, scholars applied mathematics to their understanding of the physical world. In 1637, French mathematician Pierre de Fermat (1601–65) studies the *refraction* of light. In the course of this work, he develops a new method to calculate the maximum and minimum value of a *function*. His method is an important predecessor to the *derivative,* a basic operation in differential *calculus*.

(M)

Pierre de Fermat writes his last theorem but leaves out the proof.

Some mathematical puzzles persist for centuries. One of the most famous is known as Fermat's last theorem. Around 1637, French mathematician Pierre de Fermat writes his theorem in the margins of a book, stating that the equation $x^n + y^n = z^n$ has no non-

zero integer solutions for x, y, and z when $n > 2$. Fermat states he has a proof for the theorem, but no room to write it. For more than 300 years, mathematicians search for the elusive proof to this theorem. In 1993, English mathematician Andrew Wiles (b. 1953) presents a proof to the theorem (*See* entry for DECEMBER 1993).

(M)

1638

The countess of Chinchon introduces a malaria treatment to Europe.

Malaria is an infectious disease transmitted by mosquitoes. While malaria is most prominent in tropical countries, malaria was also found in Europe prior to the introduction of insect management techniques. In the 17th century, Europeans traveling to Peru learn that some South American Indians treat malaria with the bark of cinchona tree. In 1638, the countess of Chinchon brings some of this bark, which contains the drug quinine (*See* entry for 1820), back to Spain, where it soon becomes the first drug used to treat an infectious disease in Europe. Quinine is still widely used to treat malaria and other disorders today.

(B)

1639

Gérard Desargues develops projection geometry.

The ancient Greeks excelled in *geometry,* and for generations mathematicians adhered to the views of Euclid (*See* entry for CA. 300 B.C.E.). The 17th-century French mathematician Gérard Desargues (1591–1661) developed a *derivative* of Euclidean geometry, known as projection *geometry*. Projection geometry considers the possibility that two parallel lines meet at an infinitely distant point. Desargues describes his work on projection geometry in *Brouillon project d'une atteinte aux evenemens des rencontres du cone avec un plan* (Rough draft for an essay on the results of taking plane sections of a cone).

(M)

1641

William Gascoigne invents the crosshairs.
Astronomy relies upon the ability to make accurate and reproducible observations of the heavens. The invention of the telescope (*See* entry for 1609) gave astronomers a powerful tool for looking at the skies. In 1641, English astronomer William Gascoigne (ca. 1612–44) is observing the stars when a spiderweb falls on his telescope. He notices that the thin line of the web is magnified, giving him a reference to align the images he views through the telescope. Gascoigne then constructs a telescope with crosshairs, thin wires that help the user align images and measure distances.

(SA)

1643

Evangelista Torricelli invents the barometer and describes atmospheric pressure.
The discovery of gases during the 17th century (*See* entry for 1627) led to new investigations of the air around us. In 1643, Italian physicist Evangelista Torricelli (1608–47) studies atmospheric gases. He wonders if the gases in the atmosphere exert pressure on the Earth. To answer this question, he creates the first barometer, a glass tube with liquid mercury, and places it in a pool of mercury that is open to the air. Torricelli finds that the mercury level in the tube is always 30 inches (76 cm) higher than that in the tube. He reasons that the pressure of the atmo-

Italian scholar Evangelista Torricelli invents the barometer in 1643. Here, an early barometer is depicted in the 1688 work *Traittez de barometres, thermometers, et notiometres, ou hydgrometres* by Joachim d'Alence. *(Steve Nicklas/NOS, NGS)*

sphere must be causing mercury in the tube in rise and maintain that height.

(P, W)

1645

Blaise Pascal invents the adding machine.
Mathematicians often need to perform simple yet cumbersome arithmetical calculations. Traditionally, complex calculations

were performed with the help of an abacus. In 1645, French mathematician Blaise Pascal (1623–62) invents an adding machine to simplify such calculations. Pascal's machine performs addition and subtraction of up to eight figures, using moving gears.

(CS, M)

1648

September 19

Blaise and Périer Pascal show that atmospheric pressure drops at high altitudes.

The news of Evangelista Torricelli's invention of the barometer and his demonstration of atmospheric pressure traveled quickly. French scholar Blaise Pascal wonders if the pressure of the atmosphere is the same at all altitudes. His brother, Périer, carries a barometer to the top of Puy-de-Dôme mountain in central France, approximately 5,000 feet (1,500 m) above sea level. Together, they demonstrate that the atmospheric pressure is lower at high altitudes.

(P, W)

1650

Giambattista Riccioli observes the first double star.

The invention of the telescope at the beginning of the 17th century greatly expanded astronomers' abilities to study the stars (See entry for 1609). In 1650, Italian astronomer Giambattista Riccioli (1598–1671) uses a telescope to study the famous constellation known as the Big Dipper. He discovers that what appears to be a single star when viewed with the naked eye, is actually two stars. Such formations become known as double stars.

(SA)

1651

Giambattista Riccioli names the craters on the Moon.

With the invention of the telescope, astronomers began to study formations on the Moon and the planets. In 1651, Italian astronomer Giambattista Riccioli publishes *Almagestum novum* (New almagest). His book includes a map of the Moon, based upon his telescopic observations. Riccioli names the various craters he observes after famous astronomers of the past, including Ptolemy, Tycho Brahe, and Nicholas Copernicus, as well as naming one after himself.

(SA)

1652

Thomas Bartholin discovers the lymphatic system.

The immune system protects humans and other animals from *bacteria, viruses,* and other foreign agents. One of the first clues as to how the immune system works comes in 1652, when Danish physiologist Thomas Bartholin (1616–80) discovers the lymphatic system. The lymphatic system protects the body from foreign agents by producing and distributing immune cells that fight infection.

(B)

1653

Blaise Pascal describes "Pascal's triangle."

Pascal's triangle, an arithmetical array of numbers that allows one to calculate the coefficient of the exponents for the equation $(x + 1)^n$, was first described in the 13th century (See entry for 1261). The numbers are arrayed in rows such that each number is equal to the sum of the two numbers diagonally above it. In 1653, French mathematician Blaise Pascal describes "Pascal's triangle" and how it can be used in mathematics in *Treatise on the Arithmetical Triangle*. Uses for the "Pascal's triangle" include combinatorics and finding binomial coefficients.

(M)

May

Blaise Pascal states Pascal's Law describing hydraulics.

During the 17th century, scientists began to investigate the effects of pressure on liquids and gases. In May 1653, French scholar Blaise Pascal summarizes his experiments on pressure in what is now known as Pascal's Law. Pascal's Law states that pressure placed upon one point of fluid confined to a container is spread to every point in the fluid. The principle is used to develop the hydraulic press. Pascal describes his principle in *Traités de l'équilibre des liqueurs et de la pesanteur de la masse de l'air* (Treatise on the equilibrium of liquids).

(P)

1654

Blaise Pascal and Pierre de Fermat describe probability.

The branch of mathematics known as *statistics* traces its roots to early studies on the mathematics of chance, or *probability*. The basic concepts in probability are developed in 1654 through a series of correspondences between the mathematicians Blaine Pascal and Pierre de Fermat. They describe the mathematics of games of chance and show that they are governed by natural laws. Their work is published in 1657 as part of a treatise written by the mathematician Christiaan Huygens (1629–95).

(M)

Grand Duke Ferdinand II establishes the first weather observatory network.

During the 17th century, scientific advances flourished in Italy. In 1654, the Grand Duke Ferdinand II of Tuscany (1610–70) establishes a weather observation network with stations across Italy and extending into France and Poland. The stations record observations on current weather conditions along with scientific measurements such as air pressure, wind direction, temperature, and humidity.

(W)

May 8

Otto von Guericke demonstrates a vacuum.

The discovery of gases (*See* entry for 1627) prompted scientists to try and understand their behavior. During this era, German physicist Otto von Guericke (1602–86) invents an air pump, which removes air from a vessel, creating a vacuum. Guericke uses his air pump to perform public demonstrations. On May 8, 1654, he carries out a series of experiments for the German emperor, showing that two hemisphere brought together and sealed by a vacuum cannot be pulled apart. He then allows air to reenter the sphere, and the pieces can be separated. News of Guericke's public demonstration of a vacuum spreads throughout Europe, increasing awareness of gases and their properties.

(P)

1655

John Wallis describes infinity.

The concept of *infinity* is demonstrated by the fact that each number can be doubled and there is an infinite amount of space between two points. In 1655, English mathematician John Wallis (1616–1703) considers the concept of infinity in *Arithmetica infinitorum* (Arithmetic of infinitesimals). The work is notable for using the symbol ∞ to represent infinity. Wallis's work is an important step toward the development of *calculus*.

(M)

Christiaan Huygens discovers a moon orbiting Saturn.

The invention of the telescope at the beginning of the 17th century allowed astronomers to study objects in the sky that they previously could not see (*See* entry for 1609). In 1655, Dutch astronomer Christiaan Huygens builds a powerful telescope and uses it to observe Saturn. He discovers a moon orbiting the planet, now known as Titan. Today, astronomers know that 18 moons orbit Saturn.

(SA)

1656

Christiaan Huygens describes the rings of Saturn.

When Renaissance astronomers such as Galileo Galilei viewed Saturn through a telescope, they noticed that other matter seemed to be attached to the planet. In 1655, Dutch astronomer Christiaan Huygens builds a powerful telescope and uses it to observe Saturn. In 1656, he realizes that a set of rings surround the planet. His observations also help him explain why the visibility of Saturn's rings varies by season.

(SA)

Christiaan Huygens builds the first pendulum clock.

Scientists and engineers apply their knowledge of physics to improve the accuracy of clocks. In 1656, Dutch scholar Christiaan Huygens studies Galileo Galilei's work on the

European astronomers first note Saturn's ring during the 17th century. The *Hubble Space Telescope* took this view of Saturn in October 1999. *(NASA and the Hubble Heritage Team)*

pendulum (*See* entry for 1582). He realizes that the motion of a pendulum can be used as a timekeeping device and builds the first pendulum clock. His work is described in the 1673 book *Horologium oscillatorium* (The pendulum clock).

(P)

1657

Pierre de Fermat describes the movement of light.

As described in the sidebar "Physics and Mathematics," mathematics and physics are intimately related. During the 17th century, French mathematician Pierre de Fermat investigates the nature of light. Fermat believes that natural events occur in the shortest possible time. Applying this logic to *optics*, he states that light travels along a path in the shortest possible time, known as Fermat's "principle of least time." His ideas arc later applied to Sir Isaac Newton's view of *mechanics* (*See* entry for 1687).

(P)

1659

Johann Rahn introduces the division sign.

Many of the symbols used in mathematics today trace their origins to the 17th century. In 1659, Swiss mathematician Johann Rahn (1622–76) writes *Teutsche algebra,* an *algebra* text in which he introduces the obelus (÷) to signify the arithmetical operation division, and an asterisk (*) to signify multiplication. Today, some scholars believe the symbols were actually developed by British mathematician John Pell (1611–85), who worked with Rahn on the book. Regardless of who actually developed the symbols, the publication of Rahn's works marks their first appearance in print.

(M)

1660

Otto von Guericke demonstrates static electricity.

As science became more experimental, scholars began to investigate the *forces* that underlie physical phenomena. In 1660, German physicist Otto von Guericke (1602–86) studies magnetic forces in hopes of explaining the motion of the stars. To perform his experiments, he manufactures a sphere from sulfur-containing minerals. Sparks flow from the sphere when it rotates. Although he does not realize it at the time, von Guericke is the first to demonstrate static *electricity,* and his device is later used to perform electrical experiments.

(P)

Franz Dele Boë describes the chemical basis of disease.

Many different theories have been proposed to explain diseases. In 1660, German physician Franz Dele Boë (1614–72) tries to relate disease to chemical reactions in the body. He claims that disease occurs when there is an imbalance of *acids* and *bases* in the blood. Dele Boë advocates giving patients drugs that will correct the chemistry of their blood.

(B, C)

Charles II of England establishes the Royal Society.

Scientific advances depend upon the ability of scientists to communicate their results and theories with one another. One mechanism for such communication is the establishment of scientific societies. In 1660, Charles II of England (1630–85) establishes the Royal Society, assembling the great scientific minds of the era. The Royal Society still exists today, serving as the United Kingdom's national academy of sciences with approximately 1,400 members.

(B, C, ES, M, MS, P, SA)

1661

Marcello Malpighi describes the flow of blood through capillaries.

As described in the sidebar "The Microscope and Biology," 17th-century biologists used the microscope to study body parts and fluids. For example, the blood carries cells, nutrients, and gases throughout the body. During this era, physiologists know about two types of blood vessels: arteries that carry blood from the heart to the tissues, and veins that circulate blood back to the heart. How are arteries and veins connected? In 1661, Italian physician Marcello Malpighi (1628–94) uses a microscope to observe blood flowing through a third type of vessel, now called capillaries. Capillaries are extremely small vessels that bring blood directly to the tissues.

(B)

Robert Boyle lays the foundation for modern chemistry.

Before the 17th century, scholars ranging from philosophers to alchemists studied matter and its reactions, pursuits considered part of the field of chemistry today. However, the field itself is born in 1661, when English chemist Robert Boyle writes *The Skeptical Chymist*. He argues against Aristotle's theory of four elements, which leads to the development of the modern definition of an element, a substance that cannot be broken down to a simpler substance. He states that *elements* combine with one another to form more complex chemicals known as compounds. In his work, Boyle also advocates careful recording and reporting of scientific experiments, a critical practice in modern science.

(C)

1662

Robert Boyle states his gas law.

Seventeenth-century scholars began to uncover the nature of gases and how they are mixed together to form the air around us.

The 17th-century English chemist Robert Boyle is considered the father of modern chemistry. *(Museum of the History of Science)*

English chemist Robert Boyle tried to understand the Earth's atmosphere by studying the pressure of air when it is compressed. Gases can be compressed into a smaller volume when outside pressure is applied. In 1662, Boyle describes the relationship between pressure and volume in what is now known as Boyle's Law, which states that if a gas is kept at a constant temperature, the pressure multiplied by its volume remains constant.

(C, P)

1664

Robert Hooke observes the Great Red Spot on Jupiter.

The invention of the telescope at the beginning of the 17th century led to more detailed descriptions of the planets (*See* entry for 1609). In 1664, English physicist Robert Hooke (1635–1703) observes the planet Jupiter through a telescope. He notes that on the surface of the planet there appears to be a large red spot. In the same year, Jean-Dominique Cassini (*See* entry for JULY 1664) also observes the spot, leading to some controversy as to who should be credited with the observation. Today, astronomers know that the Great Red Spot on Jupiter is caused by a perpetual storm system in the planet's atmosphere.

(SA)

July

Jean-Dominique Cassini studies Jupiter.

As the 17th century progressed, astronomers benefited from the ever-increasing power of telescopes. In July 1664, French astronomer Jean-Dominique Cassini (1625–1712) studies the planet Jupiter. He observes the bands and spot on the surface of Jupiter (also observed by Robert Hooke), notes that the poles of the planet are flat, and calculates the period of rotation on its axis.

(SA)

November 23

Robert Hooke describes cells.

As described in the sidebar "The Microscope and Biology," during the 17th century advances in *optics* led to the invention of the telescope (*See* entry for 1609) and the microscope. One of the pioneers of microscopy was English physicist Robert Hooke. On November 23, 1664, he publishes *Micrographia*, describing the observations he makes using the microscope. Among the most important aspects of the work are the observations of cork under the microscope. Hooke notes that cork appears to be divided into discrete units, which he calls cells.

(B)

1665

Sir Isaac Newton works on fluxions.

As described in the sidebar "Physics and Mathematics," physics and mathematics

were intimately connected in the 17th century. In 1665, Sir Isaac Newton begins to develop his work on finite quantities, or fluxions. He uses fluxions to study the velocity and acceleration of bodies. In the course of his studies, he develops a number of methods used in modern differential *calculus*. Credit for the invention of differential calculus is shared between Newton and Gottfried Leibniz (*See* entry for 1673). The controversy over who developed differential calculus is complicated because Newton did not publish his work on fluxions. Instead, his work appears nine years after his death in *Method of Fluxions* (1736).

(M)

Francesco Maria Grimaldi describes the diffraction of light.

One of the great quests in physics throughout the ages has been to understand the nature and properties of light. In 1665, Italian physicist Francesco Maria Grimaldi (1618–63) shows that light can be bent, a process known as *diffraction*. Grimaldi passes light through two small holes and shows that the resulting band of light is wider than the one that entered the holes, demonstrating the light had been diffracted. Grimaldi's result suggests that light travels in *waves*, contradicting the corpuscle theory of light (*See* entry for 1666). His results are published in *Physicomathesis de lumine, coloribus, et iride* (Physicomathematical thesis of light, colors, and the rainbow).

(P)

1666

Sir Isaac Newton explains why rainbows are multicolored.

As described in the sidebar "Physics and Mathematics," the array of colors seen in a rainbow can be explained using physics

PHYSICS AND MATHEMATICS

Mathematics is the language of science and has been so since the days of ancient Greece. As science grows more experimental during the Renaissance, the need for mathematics becomes greater. With the development of precision instruments, scientists can make reproducible measurements of physical parameters such as temperature and pressure, and use them to check the mathematical relationships that had been theoretically derived. For instance, as chemistry develops into a science of its own, mathematics becomes an important tool for explaining the rates of chemical reactions and the energy needed for a reaction to occur. By the 19th century, even biologists begin using mathematics, as demonstrated by the careful statistics kept by Austrian botanist Gregor Mendel when he develops his laws of genetics. The reliance upon mathematics is most obvious in the field of physics, as it is often easier to describe the *forces* that control the physical world using mathematical equations than it is to describe physics in words.

For centuries, *geometry* is widely used by scholars trying to understand the physical world.

During the 17th and 18th centuries, geometry is widely used by scientists interested in *optics,* or the behavior of light. In fact, until the 18th century, many scholars consider optics a branch of mathematics. For example, French mathematician René Descartes develops a mathematical description of rainbows in 1637. His explanation relies upon calculating the angle at which light is bent, or refracted, as it passes through a water droplet, and the angle at which the observer is viewing the rainbow. At the same time, another great French mathematician, Pierre de Fermat, uses geometry to explain how light travels. He shows that light will follow the fastest path between two points—known as Fermat's principle. Interestingly, both Descartes' work on the *refraction* of light and Fermat's principle can be used to derive the law of refraction, a mathematical relationship that describes how light is refracted as it travels through different media, which was first proposed by Dutch scholar Willebrord Snel in 1622.

Perhaps no one advanced physics and mathematics more than Sir Isaac Newton. During the mid-17th century, Newton describes

and mathematics. By the 17th century, scholars know that the colors appear when light passing through prisms or water drops undergoes a specific sequence of *refractions* and *reflections*. In 1666, English physicist Sir Isaac Newton notes that not all light in a prism is refracted to the same extent. He reasons that light actually contains all the colors of the rainbow, and that prisms separate light into its component colors. Newton's corpuscular theory of light is published in *Opticks* (1704).

(P)

1667

Sir Isaac Newton builds the first reflecting telescope.

New scientific principles are often applied to the design of new technologies. In 1667, English physicist Sir Isaac Newton applies his principles of *optics* (*See* entry for 1666) when he builds the reflecting telescope. The reflecting telescope uses mirrors rather than curved lenses to collect light and magnify images. The mirrors prevent light from separating into its component colors. At first the reflecting telescope is not widely used by

the physical world, including light, gravity, and motion. In addition, he develops a form of *calculus,* called the method of fluxions. Newton invents a method to determine the *ratio* between two velocities, or fluxions, and applies it to his study of motion. When considering a curve describing a particular motion, Newton uses the ratio between fluxions to determine the tangent to the curve as well as the area under the curve. Thus, the method of fluxions is one of the first works of calculus—a branch of mathematics that becomes essential for the study of physics. Ironically, Newton rarely uses the method of fluxions in his great work *Principia Mathematica,* preferring to rely upon the more commonly known rules of geometry to explain his work on motion and gravitational forces. In fact, Newton did not publish his work on fluxions during his lifetime, which leads to some controversy as to who invented calculus.

At the same time that Newton worked on fluxions, German mathematician Gottfried Leibniz also developed mathematical methods to consider infinitely small changes in values, find tangents to curves, and calculate areas under a curve. Leibniz's first publication introducing his calculus appears in 1673. Mathematicians Jacob and Johann Bernoulli notice his work and help develop the field by applying calculus to physics. As described above, a controversy as to whether Leibniz or Newton invented calculus develops in the late 17th century. Soon Newton's method of fluxions is used throughout England, while scientists on the European continent adopt Leibniz's calculus. In the 18th century, Swiss mathematician Leonhard Euler uses calculus to describe motion, while the Scottish mathematician Colin Maclaurin shows how the method of fluxions can be used to study problems in physics. By the 19th century, the method of fluxions is abandoned in favor of Leibniz's calculus. Today, historians credit both Newton and Leibniz with the development of calculus.

The work of Newton and others shows that motion and gravity can be described using geometry, *algebra,* or calculus. In the 20th century, a new physics, called *quantum mechanics,* develops. Quantum mechanics relies upon calculus to describe the forces that govern the behavior of extremely small particles. Today, while a beginning physics course can be taught using only algebra and geometry, a true understanding of modern physics requires that a student be well versed in calculus as well.

---

astronomers; however, by the 18th century they become more popular.

(P, SA)

November

Niels Stensen describes sedimentation.
During the 16th and 17th centuries, scholars began to study fossils found within the Earth (*See* entry for 1565). In 1667, Danish scientist Niels Stensen (1638–86) collects fossils in Italy. He begins to wonder how the different layers of earth called *strata* are formed. In November of that year, he writes *De solido intra solidum naturaliter contento disserationis prodromus* (Forerunner of a dissertation of a solid naturally contained within a solid), describing the process of sedimentation. Steno says that one layer of *stratum* must be complete before the next layer forms.

(ES)

1668

John Wallis describes conservation of momentum.
It is more difficult to stop a heavy body moving at a fast rate than a lighter body that

travels at the same speed because the heavier body has more *momentum*. During the 1660s, physicists and mathematicians consider how momentum is affected when two bodies collide. In 1668, English mathematician John Wallis suggests that the momentum is always conserved. Today, conservation of momentum is one of the fundamental laws of physics.

(P)

Francesco Redi shows that insects are not produced by spontaneous generation.

For centuries, scholars believed that some small living things, such as insects, could arise spontaneously from nonliving things. Advocates of the theory of spontaneous generation pointed to the common observation that maggots will arise from rotting meat. In 1668, Italian biologist Francesco Redi (1626–97) performs a series of experiments demonstrating that the maggots actually arise from flies that land on the meat and lay eggs, thus disproving spontaneous generation. His experiments are published in *Esperienze intorno alla generazione degli insetti* (Experiments concerning the generation of insects).

(B)

Jean Picard calculates the circumference and diameter of the Earth.

Astronomers must develop methods to measure the large distances between planets, as well as their dimensions. In 1668, French astronomer Jean Picard (1620–82) gathers recent observations made with telescopes to arrive at a new estimate for the circumference and diameter of the Earth. Picard's results are published in *Mesure de la terre* (The measurement of Earth) in 1671. Sir Isaac Newton later uses this work when he develops his principle of gravitation (*See* entry for 1687).

(SA)

September 15

Robert Hooke states that earthquakes caused fossils to be found on mountaintops.

Fossils are remnants of past life on Earth. During the 17th century, the origin of fossils causes some controversy, as some scientific interruptions do not agree with biblical teachings, which explain the distribution of fossils by maintaining that they were brought to the mountaintops during the Great Flood. On September 15, 1668, English scientist Robert Hooke presents a lecture arguing that earthquakes, not the Great Flood, caused fossils to be distributed to the mountains. Hooke's work on earthquakes is controversial, and he avoids publishing it. The paper finally appears after his death in the collection *Posthumous Works,* published in 1705.

(ES)

1669

Isaac Barrow proves the fundamental theorem of calculus.

Calculus, as it is developed during the 17th century, involves two basic functions, *differentiation* and *integration*. The fundamental theorem of calculus states that these two functions are inverse opposites of each other; just as the arithmetical operations addition and subtraction are inverse operations. The theorem is represented by the equation:

$$\int_a^b f(x)\,dx = F(b) - F(a).$$

In 1669, English mathematician Isaac Barrow (1614–77) uses geometry to prove the fundamental theorem of calculus in his work *Lectiones opticae et geometricae.*

(M)

Hennig Brand isolates phosphorus.
Ancient scholars and alchemists knew many of the *elements* that make up matter. The first known element to be isolated was phosphorus. In 1669, German chemist Hennig Brand (d. ca. 1692) evaporates urine then heats the residue until a gas is released. He collects the phosphorous gas in water, making phosphoric acid.

(C)

Niels Stensen claims fossils are the remains of living organisms.

The study of fossils in the 17th century pitted scholars against church teachings. Danish scientist Niels Stensen (also known as Nicolaus Steno) studied fossils found on his travels through Italy. He compared fossils with the living creatures and noticed many similarities. In 1669, he publishes *De solido intra solidum naturaliter contento dissertationis prodromus* (The prodromus of Nicolaus Steno's dissertation concerning a solid body enclosed by a process of nature within a solid), in which he states that fossils are the remains of living organisms.

(B, ES)

Eramus Bartholin studies the Icelandic spar.

During the 17th century, physicists continued to address long-standing questions about the nature of light. In 1669, Danish scholar Eramus Bartholin (1625–98) discovers that objects viewed through a *crystal* of calcium carbonate, known as an Icelandic spar, appear to be doubled. He theorizes that the light passing through the Icelandic spar is split into two independent rays, resulting in a double *refraction.*

(P)

Richard Lower shows that contact with air turns blood bright red.

The blood vessels that can be seen through the skin appear blue, yet when a wound bleeds the blood appears red. What causes the change in color? In 1669, English physiologist Richard Lower (1631–91) shows that blood turns bright red when it comes into contact with the air. He explains that the blood that flows through arteries is red because it has recently contacted air in the lungs, while the blood flowing through veins appears blue because it has not been in contact with air for some time. He describes his work in *Tractatus de corde* (A treatment of the heart).

(B)

1671

Jean-Dominique Cassini discovers Saturn's moons.

The invention of the telescope in the early 17th century allowed astronomers to identify new heavenly bodies. In 1655, Dutch astronomer Christiaan Huygens discovers a moon orbiting Saturn (*See* entry for 1655). Beginning in 1671, French astronomer Jean-Dominique Cassini finds more moons surrounding Saturn. Cassini discovers the moon Iapetus in 1671, followed by the discovery of three more satellites of Saturn over the next 13 years.

(SA)

1673

Reinier de Graaf describes the ovaries.

Understanding how the human body works requires accurate descriptions of anatomy. In 1673, Dutch physician Reinier de Graaf (1641–73) describes the anatomy and physiology of the ovaries. He discovers the ovarian follicles, which are known today as Graafian follicles in his honor. For many years, physiologists believe the ovarian follicles are the female reproductive cells in mammals, until the mammalian egg is discovered in 1826 (*See* entry for 1826).

(B)

Gottfried Leibniz develops differential calculus.

Calculus was developed during the 17th century. Sir Isaac Newton's work on fluxions (*See* entry for 1665) is considered to be the first approach to the subject, although his terminology and symbolism differ greatly from what is used today. In 1673, German mathematician Gottfried Leibniz describes calculus in terms that would be familiar to high school students today. He first publishes his method in 1684. The publication focuses on *differentiation,* and is notable for its use of common symbols in calculus, including *dx,* and *dy,* for *derivative.* Two years later, he published an account of *integration,* using the symbol ∫ to represent that operation.

(M)

January

Gottfried Leibniz demonstrates his calculating machine.

Many arithmetical calculations are more cumbersome than difficult, so scholars have always tried to find a way to simplify them. In January 1673, German mathematician Gottfried Leibniz presents his attempt, a calculating machine, to the Royal Society of London. Although some reacted unfavorably to Leibniz's invention, he is nevertheless elected to the society later that year. Leibniz continued to improve his machine throughout his career, and eventually it was able to perform addition, subtraction, multiplication, division, and calculate square roots.

(M)

1674

Jean-Dominique Cassini calculates the distance from the Earth to the Sun.

Throughout the 16th and 17th centuries, astronomers tried to estimate the distance between the Earth, the Sun, and the other planets. In 1674, French astronomer Jean-Dominique Cassini calculates the distance between the Earth and other heavenly bodies by calculating the apparent shift in Mars, known as the *parallax,* when it is viewed at the same time from France and French Guinea. Cassini calculates the distance from the Earth to the Sun to be 87 million miles (140 million km), close to the 93 million miles (150 million km) used today.

(SA)

September 7

Antoni van Leeuwenhoek describes microorganisms.

As described in the sidebar "The Microscope and Biology," during the 17th century advances in *optics* led to the invention of the telescope and the microscope. One of the first great microscopists was Dutch scholar Antoni van Leeuwenhoek (1632–1723). In 1674, he uses a microscope to examine pond water and observes "little animals," or microorganisms as they are now known. He describes the movement of algae in a letter dated September 7, 1674. In subsequent studies, he describes other microorganisms including *bacteria* and protozoa.

(B)

1675

Jean-Dominique Cassini discovers the line that divides Saturn's rings.

Christiaan Huygens used a powerful new telescope to show that the planet Saturn is surrounded by rings (*see* entry for 1656). In 1675, Italian astronomer Jean-Dominique Cassini examines Saturn's rings from the Paris Observatory. He discovers that a dark line, which is now called Cassini's Division in his honor, separates the rings.

(SA)

1676

Ole Rømer describes the speed of light.

While 17th-century scholars realized that light travels at a rapid velocity, they were uncertain whether or not the speed of light is a finite value. In 1676, Danish astronomer

THE MICROSCOPE AND BIOLOGY

The invention of the microscope at the end of the 16th century allowed biologists to study the components of living organisms that are too small to see, and established a new field, microbiology. Before the invention of the microscope, organisms were classified by noting visible similarities and differences. Physiologists and anatomists dissected plants and animals, and developed methods to study biological processes in living organisms. The microscope provides a tool to examine individual cells, microorganisms, and fine details of tissues and organs. However, microscopes were not widely available at universities as they are today. Instead, a microscope had to be built specifically by individuals interested in examining small objects. For this reason, trained physicists who specialized in optics performed many of the early works of microscopy.

English physicist Robert Hooke publishes the most famous early work in microscopy, *Micrographia,* in 1664. Hooke devises a compound microscope and uses it to examine many different household items, including needles and razor blades. His work is famous, however, for his description and illustrations of a thin section of cork as viewed under the microscope. Hooke describes small units within the structure of cork, which he calls cells. In the next two centuries, cells will become known as the fundamental units of life.

One of the first uses of a microscope in biology solves an open question left by Wil-

liam Harvey's famous theory of the circulation of blood. Harvey had shown that blood travels from the heart in arteries and back to the heart in veins, and proposed that small vessels serve as links between them, yet he could not prove that these vessels exist. In 1661, Italian physician Marcello Malpighi uses a microscope to examine the heart and blood vessels and finds the vessels, now called capillaries, that Harvey had proposed. Malpighi continues his microscopic observations throughout his career, describing the structure of tissues, including the liver and skin, studying embryos under the microscope, and examining the cells found in the blood.

The 17th century also witnesses the discovery of single-celled organisms known as microorganisms. In 1674, Dutch scholar Antoni van Leeuwenhoek describes microscopic organisms that he calls animalcules (which were likely algae and protozoa) when he uses a microscope to examine pond water. Leeuwenhoek continues to enthusiastically examine a variety of biological specimens and fluids. During his study of dental plaque, he discovers another type of microorganism, *bacteria.* By the end of his career, Leeuwenhoek describes not only a wide range of microorganisms, but also cells found in the blood, and spermatozoa found in semen.

The early investigations described here set the stage for a deeper understanding of cells

(continues)

(continued)

and microorganisms that develops during the 18th and 19th centuries. As physicists learn to make more powerful microscopes, biologists are able to probe deeper into the structure of organisms. With the aid of the microscope, they can classify microorganisms based upon their cell structure, and identify the different parts of the cell. Such studies are critical for the development of the germ theory of disease at the end of the 19th century and for the advances in cell and *molecular biology* made during the end of the 20th century.

Ole Rømer (1644–1710) studies the timing of *eclipses* of one of Jupiter's moons. In the course of these studies, he shows that the speed of light is constant, and he uses his data to approximate its value. Rømer's value for the speed of light is approximately 75 percent of the value known today.

(P, SA)

1677

Antoni van Leeuwenhoek describes spermatozoa.
As described in the sidebar "The Microscope and Biology," during the 17th century advances in *optics* led to the invention of the telescope and the microscope. One of the first great microscopists was Dutch scholar Antoni van Leeuwenhoek. In 1677, he examines semen under a microscope and describes the male reproductive cell, the spermatozoa, for the first time. Based upon his observations, he proposes that during fertilization, the spermatozoa move toward an egg and penetrate it.

(B)

1678

Edmond Halley studies the stars in the southern sky.
During the 17th century, European astronomers focused exclusively on the sky as viewed from the Northern Hemisphere. In 1676, English astronomy student Edmond Halley (1656–1742) leaves school and travels to an island in the Southern Atlantic Ocean. He brings along his telescope and uses his journey to study the stars from the Southern Hemisphere. Upon his return to England in 1678, he publishes *Catalogue of the Southern Stars,* which maps 341 stars in the southern sky.

(SA)

Jan Swammerdam discovers the red blood cell.
The blood is a complex organ that circulates cells and nutrients throughout the body. One important function of the blood is carrying oxygen from the lungs to the various cells and tissues throughout the body. In 1678, Dutch physiologist Jan Swammerdam (1637–80) uses a microscope and discovers the red blood cell. Today, scientists know that the red blood cell is responsible for carrying oxygen and carbon dioxide throughout the body.

(B)

1679

Robert Hooke explains elasticity.
As described in the sidebar "Physics and Mathematics," the 17th century saw great advances in the understanding of the *forces*

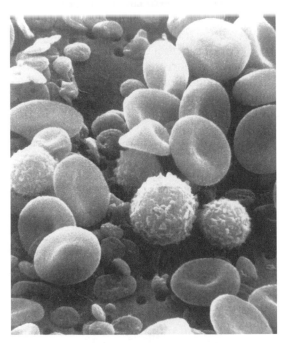

Dutch physiologist Jan Swammerdam first describes red blood cells in the 17th century. This scanning electron micrograph, from 1982, shows the doughnut shaped red blood cells among a variety of white blood cells. *(Bruce Wetzel and Harry Schaefer/National Cancer Institute)*

that underlie physical phenomena and the mathematical relationships that can be used to describe them. During this era, English physicist Robert Hooke studies the ability of an object to regain its original form after an outside force has caused it to change shape, a property known as elasticity. He uncovers what is now known as "Hooke's Law," which explains elasticity. Hooke's Law states that the extent that an object becomes deformed is proportional to the amount of force applied to the object. In 1679, Hooke publishes his work on elasticity in *Lectiones cutlerianae* (Collection of lectures).

(P)

1680

Giovanni Alfonso Borelli describes the mechanics of muscle action.

During the 17th century, physicists studied *mechanics,* or the *forces* that act upon bodies in motion or at rest. Italian physicist Giovanni Alfonso Borelli (1608–79) applies mechanics to physiology, using physics and mathematics to describe how muscles work. He develops a mathematical description of movements such as running and jumping. His work is published in 1680 as *De motu animalium* (On the movement of animals), one year after his death.

(B)

November 14

Gottfried Kirsch uses a telescope to discover a new comet.

Astronomers have observed *comets,* celestial bodies made from dirt and ice, for centuries. The invention of the telescope (*See* entry for 1609) allowed scholars to learn more about their behavior. On November 14, 1680, Gottfried Kirsch is the first astronomer using a telescope to discover a comet. Soon many different astronomers follow the comet and study its orbit around the Sun.

(SA)

1682

Nehemiah Grew describes plant anatomy.

As described in the sidebar "The Microscope and Biology," in the 17th century the invention of the microscope helped scholars gain a deeper understanding of how biological organisms work. English scientist Nehemiah Grew (1641–1712) used a microscope to study plant tissues. In 1682, he publishes his observations in *The Anatomy of Plants.* Grew describes sexual reproduction in plants, describing the reproductive function of flowers, and likening pollen to human sperm.

(B)

1683

September 17

Antoni van Leeuwenhoek describes bacteria.

During the 17th century, advances in *optics* led to the invention of the telescope and the microscope. One of the first great microscopists is Dutch scholar Antoni van Leeuwenhoek. On September 17, 1683, he reports the results of his observations of tooth plaque under the microscope. He describes the motion of two different microorganisms, now known to be *bacteria,* that are found in the mouth.

(B)

1686

John Ray classifies the plant species of Europe.

During the 17th century, scholars developed classification systems for everything from minerals to clouds. In 1686, English naturalist John Ray (1627–1705) publishes the first volume of his great work *Historia plantarum* (History of plants). Ray's goal is to classify all the plants in Europe. Eventually, the work is expanded to three volumes and classifies more than 18,600 different plant species. Ray is the first to divide plants into several subclassifications beyond flowering and nonflowering.

(B)

Edmond Halley describes the trade winds.

As more people began to travel beyond their native lands, European scholars began to investigate how nature differs from place to place. In 1676, English student Edmond Halley travels to the Southern Hemisphere

(*See* entry for 1678). On this voyage, he observes the trade winds at the equator. In 1686, he publishes a description of the trade winds and suggests that the *air current* moves because of *radiation* from the Sun.

(W)

1687

Sir Isaac Newton publishes *Principia mathematica.*

During the 17th century, English physicist Sir Isaac Newton made a number of fundamental observations that explain how the physical world works. Unlike many other scholars, Newton rarely published his work. In 1687, with much encouragement from his colleagues, he publishes *Philosophiae naturalis principia mathematica* (Mathematical principles of natural philosophy), a work widely referred to as *Principia mathematica.* In *Principia mathematica,* Newton outlines his work on physics, which is based upon a small set of simple assumption, and uses mathematics to describe the physical world. *Principia mathematica* is considered today one of the most influential scientific works in the area of physics.

(P)

Sir Isaac Newton describes inertia.

The first book of Sir Isaac Newton's classic work *Principia mathematica* describes the three fundamental laws of motion. Newton's first law of motion is an articulation of Galileo Galilei's concept of *inertia.* He states that in the absence of an external force, a body in motion will remain in motion, while a body at rest will stay at rest.

(P)

Sir Isaac Newton explains the relationship between force and acceleration.

Sir Isaac Newton's second law describes the relationship between a force acting upon

TRADE WINDS

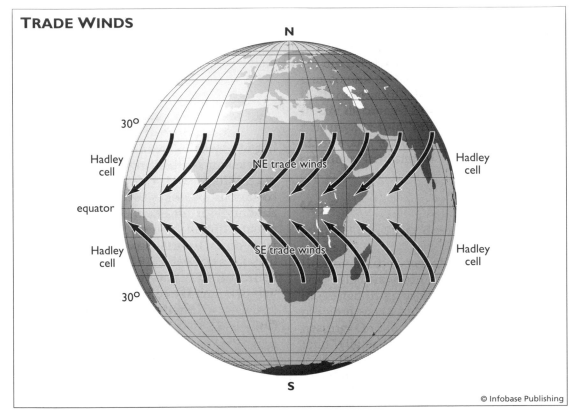

While a student, English astronomer Edmond Halley describes the trade winds, tropical winds that move toward the equator. In the Northern Hemisphere, the trade winds blow from the northeast, while in the Southern Hemisphere, the winds blow from the southeast.

an object and its acceleration. Clearly, more force is needed to move a heavy object than to move a lighter one. Newton expresses this relationship mathematically with the equation $F = ma$, where F is the force acting upon an object, m is its mass, and a is the acceleration.

(P)

Sir Isaac Newton states that for every action there is an equal and opposite reaction.

Sir Isaac Newton's third law of motion, simply put, states that for every action there is an equal and opposite reaction. Therefore, if

one object exerts a force on a second object, that object will exert that same force back. A modern example of the third law of motion is a rocket launch, where burning fuel exerts a strong downward force on the air, and the air exerts an equally strong force back onto the rocket, allowing it to escape *gravity* and launch into the sky.

(P)

Sir Isaac Newton describes universal gravitation.

During the 17th century, scholars began to study falling bodies and the forces of *gravity*. English physicist Sir Isaac Newton famously described gravity as the force that causes an apple to fall to the Earth. In 1687, he outlines his theory of universal gravitation in *Principia mathematica.* Newton states that the rate at which an object falls is proportional to the gravitational force. He also suggests that gravity causes the Moon to orbit the Earth, and develops a mathematical relationship to describe the gravitational forces between two objects.

(P)

Sir Isaac Newton states that the Earth is flat at the poles and bulges at the equator.

In 1687, English scholar Sir Isaac Newton published his great work, *Principia mathematica.* Among the important ideas present in *Principia* is a calculation showing that the effects of gravity causes the Earth to be flat at the North and South Poles, and bulge at the equator. Newton's calculations take into account the rotation of the Earth, and he states that the length of a planet's day can be calculated from the flatness of the poles. Newton's theory is proven during the 18th century by a group of French mathematicians (*See* entry for 1738).

(ES, P)

1696

Guillaume-François-Antoine de Marquis de L'Hôspital publishes a method for finding limits.

Calculus was developed during the 17th century (*See* entry for 1673). In 1696, French mathematician Guillaume-François-Antoine de Marquis L'Hôspital (1661–1704) writes the first textbook on the subject, *Analyse des infiniment petits* (Analysis of the infinitely small). L'Hôspital describes a method for finding the *limit* of certain fractions.

The idea becomes known as "L'Hôspital's Rule," although scholars believe that it was actually developed by Johann Bernoulli (1667–1748).

(M)

1697

Edward Llwyd creates the first catalog comparing fossils to living organisms.

During the 17th century, scholars studied fossils, questioning their origin and how they become distributed across the land. Nicolas Steno proposed that fossils are the remains of living organisms that are no longer on the Earth. In 1696, a Welsh museum curator named Edward Llwyd (1660–1709) writes a catalog of fossils, comparing them with living organisms. His work, *Lithophylacii britannici ichnographia,* is not widely distributed, but today stands as a landmark in the study of fossils.

(B, G)

1698

Edmond Halley leads the first scientific expedition.

Throughout the 17th century, scholars depended upon observations to generate and test theories about the natural world. Many of these observations were made in observatories, gardens, or laboratories, while others were made during voyages. In 1698, English astronomer Edmond Halley leads the first purely scientific expedition on his ship *Paramore Pink.* During the voyage across the Atlantic Ocean, Halley studies the Earth's *magnetic field,* observing and charting the variation between magnetic north and true north.

(ES)

Thomas Savery invents the steam engine.
Mining has led to scientific advances, such as the discovery of new minerals and elements, as well as technological advances. In 1698, English engineer Thomas Savery (ca. 1650–1715) invents the steam engine to power a pump that removes water from mines. Savery's engine uses steam to create a vacuum that then pumps water from the mines. Unfortunately, Savery's engine could not remove water at depths over 50 feet (15 m), nor could it be run continuously.

(P)

1702

Guillaume Amontons shows water boils at the same temperature.
The invention of the thermometer gave scientists the opportunity to study how increases in temperature affect natural processes. In 1702, French scholar Guillaume Amontons (1663–1705) builds his own thermometer and uses it to study boiling water. He finds that once water begins to boil, its temperature stops increasing. Amontons proposes that the boiling point of water be used to fix a temperature scale.

(P)

1703

George Stahl explains how matter changes.
The founding of modern chemistry in the 17th century led many scholars to examine matter and the reactions that it undergoes. In 1703, German physician George Stahl (1660–1734) studies the chemistry of mining. He describes the mining of ores to obtain metals as a process analogous to the burning of wood. He proposes the *phlogiston* theory to explain both processes. Stahl's theory says that an unknown material, called phlogiston, causes matter to be transformed. Although it is incorrect, Stahl's theory guides chemical research for decades and leads to the discovery of the *element* oxygen.

(C)

Gottfried Leibniz denotes numbers in the binary system.
The number system used by modern mathematicians is a *decimal system,* meaning the *place value notation* is based on sets of 10. Other number systems can be used; for example, the Babylonians used a base of 60. In 1703, German mathematicians demonstrate that a base of two, called a *binary system,* can also be used to denote numbers. Today, the binary system serves as a basis for modern computers.

(M)

1705

Edmond Halley predicts the return of a comet.
Astronomers have observed *comets,* celestial bodies made of ice and dirt, for centuries. The invention of the telescope allowed more comets to be studied. During the late 17th century, astronomers studied a series of comets and charted their paths. English astronomer Edmond Halley began to study the paths of comets recorded from 1337 to 1698. He noted that a comet appears in the same region of the sky every 76 years. In 1705, he publishes his work in *Synopsis of the Astronomy of Comets.* During that year, he also makes his famous prediction that the comet, now known as Halley's comet, will reappear in 1758. While he does not live to see its return, the observation of Halley's comet in that year serves as a demonstration of science's ability to predict natural phenomena.

(SA)

The 18th-century English astronomer Edmond Halley accurately predicts the appearance of the comet now known as Halley's comet, demonstrating the ability of scientists to predict natural phenomena. *(Museum of the History of Science)*

1712

Thomas Newcomen improves the steam engine.
The steam engine, which uses steam to drive mechanical work, was invented at the end of the 17th century (*See* entry for 1698). In 1712, English inventor Thomas Newcomen (1663–1729) makes significant improvements to the steam engine, known as the atmospheric engine because the steam is kept near atmospheric pressure. Like the Savory engine, Newcomen's engine uses steam to pump water from mines. Newcomen's engine is quite effective and remains in use throughout the 18th century.

(P)

1714

Daniel Fahrenheit invents the mercury thermometer.
Accurate instruments are essential for scientific experiments. Temperature is a critical parameter for chemists, physicists, and meteorologists. In 1714, German physicist Daniel Fahrenheit (1686–1736) improves the measurement of temperature when he invents the mercury thermometer. His thermometer is much more accurate than earlier devices, such as the thermoscope. Fahrenheit uses his thermometer to develop a temperature scale, known as the Fahrenheit scale, which is still used in the United States today.

(P)

1715

Brook Taylor describes the Taylor expansion.
In *arithmetic,* numbers can be considered as part of a *sequence.* The arithmetic operations that lead to a particular sequence are known as a *series.* Certain infinite series, known as power series, take the form: $a_0 + a_1x +\text{-.-.-.} + a_nx^n$. In 1715, English mathematician Brook Taylor (1685–1731) considers the expansion of a *function, f(x)*, into a power series in *Methodus incrementorum directa et inversa* (Direct and indirect methods of incrimination). His work becomes an important component of both differential equations and later, the theory of functions.

(M)

1716

August 20

Stephen Hales describes the circulation of water in plants.
Biologists in the 17th and 18th centuries compared the circulation of water in plants

to the circulation of blood in the animals. In 1716, the biologist Stephen Hales (1677–1761) experimentally demonstrates that water is brought into the plant through the roots, and then circulates throughout the plant. He finds that the rate at which water circulates is much faster than blood circulation in the body.

1718

Lady Mary Wortley Montagu describes a method to prevent smallpox.

In the 18th century, the infectious disease smallpox caused extreme illness and death throughout Europe. In 1718, Lady Mary Wortley Montagu (1689–1762), wife of the British ambassador to the Ottoman Empire, returns to England and describes an Arab method for preventing smallpox. The process, known as variolation, involves exposing noninfected individuals to the pus from lesions of infected individuals, thus inducing a mild case of the disease and protecting the patient from a potentially lethal illness. The technique is used in England, but it is replaced by Edward Jenner's smallpox vaccine by the end of the century.

(B)

Edmond Halley shows that the position of stars is not fixed.

Records of astronomical observations have been kept throughout history. In 1710, English astronomer Edmond Halley studied the position of stars noted by Greek astronomer Ptolemy (*See* entry for CA. 150). He noticed that the positions did not correlate with his own observations, inspiring him to look for evidence of stellar motion. In 1718, Halley provides evidence that at least three stars can move, demonstrating that the positions of stars are not fixed.

(SA)

1721

Henri Gautier describes erosion.

How old is the Earth? Scholars have devised many methods to answer this question. In 1721, French civil engineer Henri Gautier (1660–1737) proposes that the age of the Earth can be estimated by studying the *erosion* of mountains. In *Nouvelles conjectures sur le globe de la Terre,* Gautier describes the continual erosion of mountains and the deposit of *sediments* in the oceans. He bases his theories on the sedimentation patterns that he observes while building bridges for the French government. The book also includes

The 18th-century French engineer Henri Gautier attempts to measure the age of the Earth by studying erosions. This photograph shows how erosion has caused tree roots on the north end of Sapelo's beach to become exposed. *(Brooke Vallaster/Sapelo Island National Estuarine Research Reserve, NOAA)*

Gautier's theory that the Earth is hollow, which leads to the book's being widely discredited at the time.

(ES)

1727

Stephen Hales states that air is essential for plant growth.

During the 17th and 18th centuries, scientists began to recognize the importance of gases. The study of gases began with the air, which was shown to be a mixture of several different gases. In 1727, English physiologist Stephen Hales studies plants, and concludes that air is essential for their growth. He includes these experiments in his 1727 work *Vegetable Staticks*.

(B)

1728

Pierre Fauchard describes dentistry.

Modern dentistry began in the 18th century. French dentist Pierre Fauchard (1678–1761) is widely considered the founder of the field. In 1728, he publishes *Le chirurgien dentiste* (The surgeon dentist), which serves as the major dentistry text throughout the century. Among the advances described in the book is an improved dental drill.

(B)

1729

Stephan Gray studies materials that conduct electricity.

During the 17th century, scientists began to investigate the properties of *electricity*. One of the pioneers of the field was an Englishman named Stephan Gray (1666–1736) who worked as a cloth dyer. After his retirement in 1719, Gray begins conducting amateur scientific experiments. In 1729, he classi-

fies materials on the basis of their ability to conduct electricity. His work leads to the distinction between conductors, which conduct electricity, and insulators, which do not.

(P)

James Bradley estimates the speed of light.

The positions of heavenly bodies appear to be different when observed from different points in the Earth's orbit around the Sun. The shift in apparent position is known as the *parallax*. In 1726, English astronomer James Bradley (1693–1762) attempted to calculate the parallax of a set of stars and noticed that the observed shift was far greater than the shift he predicted using his calculations. In 1729, he argues that the shift is caused by a combination of the speed of light traveling from the stars and the speed of the Earth in its orbit. Using his data, he arrives at an estimate for the speed of light that is within 5 percent of today's value.

(P, SA)

1733

Stephen Hales describes blood pressure.

The circulation of blood is critical for an animal's survival. English physiologist Stephen Hales studied the circulation of blood in animals and discovered blood pressure. Hales measured blood pressure in animals, demonstrating that the blood pressure of an artery differs from that of a vein. He presents his work in the 1733 book *Hemostaticks*.

(B)

Charles-François de Cisternay du Fay suggests that electricity and magnetism are related.

During the 18th century, physicists performed many experiments aimed at understanding the properties of *electricity*. In 1733, French physicist Charles-François de Cisternay du Fay (1698–1739) shows that electrically charged bodies can attract or repel one another in a manner similar to a magnet. Du Fay's experiment suggests a relationship between electricity and *magnetism* that becomes more clearly defined as the century progresses.

(P)

Johann Gmelin conducts a scientific study of Siberia.

Different climates host vastly different types of organisms. In 1733, German naturalist Johann Gmelin (1709–55) commences a scientific expedition to eastern Siberia, an area characterized by extreme cold. During his trip, he catalogs more than 1,000 species of plants and notices a new type of terrain, permafrost. His voyage provides the first scientific description of permafrost, soil that is kept at a temperature below freezing for more than two years.

(ES)

1735

Carolus Linnaeus introduces a new system of taxonomy.

During the 17th and 18th centuries, scholars developed systems to classify the things they found in nature. In 1735, Swedish biologist Carolus Linnaeus (also known as Carl von Linné, 1707–78) describes a system taxonomy that classifies organisms not only by species, but also by genus, order, class, and kingdom. His system is introduced in the first edition of *Systema naturae* (Natural classification), a work that he revised to include the classification of new organisms throughout his career.

(B)

George Hadley describes the motion of the trade winds.

The movement of winds puzzled scholars for centuries. In 1735, English meteorologist George Hadley (1685–1768) describes the effect of the Earth's rotation on the trade winds at the equator in his paper "Concerning the Cause of General Trade Winds." Hadley reasons that the rotation of the Earth causes the winds to blow in a westerly direction rather than due north as one might expect.

(W)

1736

Giovanni Arduino classifies rocks.

Classification systems facilitate the study of the natural world. In 1736, Italian engineer Giovanni Arduino (1714–95) devises a system to classify rocks, based upon observations made while studying mines. Arduino divides rocks into three classes: primary, secondary, and tertiary. His system is based upon both the appearance of the rock and the presence or absence of fossils. Primary rocks contain metallic ores and do not contain fossils. Secondary rocks are dense and contain some fossils of marine life. Tertiary rocks are volcanic rocks that contain many fossils.

(ES)

Leonhard Euler uses calculus to describe mechanics.

Today, physics depends upon higher mathematics such as *calculus*. In the 18th century, however, most scholars still tried to solve physical problems using *geometry*. In 1736, Swiss mathematician Leonhard Euler (1707–83) writes *Mechanics*. His work revolutionizes the field by using calculus to describe the *forces* that act on bodies, and continues to be studied today.

(M, P)

Robert Marsham begins keeping records of seasonal changes.

The blooming of flowers and return of birds heralds the beginning of spring. Changes in the behavior and life cycle of different species can be observed throughout the four seasons. The study of these changes is known as phenology. In 1736, naturalist Robert Marsham begins recording the seasonal changes in a variety of plants, birds, and insects near his home in England. The records become a family tradition, and the next six generations continue keeping annual records until 1947. The Marsham family records are the longest known phenological records in the world.

(B)

1737

John Harrison uses a clock to fix longitude.

Accurate navigation at sea requires devices that help sailors determine where they are and the direction in which they are traveling. Knowing the *longitude* or distance from the Greenwich meridian greatly improves navigation. At the beginning of the 18th century, the governments of England, Italy, Spain, and France offered a prize to anyone who developed a device that can accurately fix longitude. In 1737, English inventor John Harrison (1693–1776) succeeds in fixing longitude on a voyage from England to Portugal. After a long period of controversy, he is finally awarded the prize in 1762.

(ES)

August 20

Pierre-Louis Moreau de Maupertuis shows that the Earth's poles are flat.

The publication of Sir Isaac Newton's *Principia mathematica* in 1687 (*See* entry for 1687) affected many different fields of science. Newton presented calculations that

suggested that the Earth is flat at the poles, an idea widely criticized by the leading scholars of the day. In 1733, French mathematician Pierre-Louis Moreau de Maupertuis (1698–1759) devises an experiment to verify Newton's theory. He sends his colleagues on a series of expeditions to make the measurements that were needed to experimentally demonstrate that the Earth's poles are flat. On August 20, 1737, Maupertuis reports his confirmation of Newton's theory at a meeting of the Paris Academy.

(ES, P)

1738

Daniel Bernoulli describes the kinetic theory of gases.

During the 18th century, scientists began to study the properties of gases. Robert Boyle described the relationship between the volume of a gas and the pressure exerted upon it (*See* entry for 1662). In 1738, Swiss mathematician Daniel Bernoulli (1700–82) puts forth his kinetic theory of gases, which gives a quantitative explanation to Boyle's Law. He states that gas molecules move faster at higher temperatures. Physicists throughout the 19th century, forming the basis for today's view of gas behavior, extend Bernoulli's work.

(C, P)

1739

Georg Brandt identifies cobalt as an element.

Many of the *elements* have been known for centuries. The deep blue metal cobalt has been found among ancient artifacts. In 1739, chemists first identify cobalt as a metal. At that time, Swedish chemist Georg Brandt (1694–1768) analyzes cobalt ores that are found in copper mines. Brandt demonstrates that it is an element, although it is years before his work gains wide acceptance.

(C)

1740

Abraham Trembley shows that the freshwater hydra will reproduce if cut in half.

Today, physicians and scientists are interested in finding methods that will allow damaged organs to regenerate themselves. The history of regeneration dates back to 1740, when Swiss zoologist Abraham Trembley (1700–84) shows that the small water creature known as the freshwater hydra will reproduce if cut in half. He publishes his study of freshwater hydra as part of his work *Mémoires* in 1742.

(B)

Anton-Lazzaro Moro describes the formation of rocks.

During the 17th and 18th centuries, scientific theories on the creation of the Earth were often at odds with the teaching of the Catholic Church. In 1740, Italian priest Anton-Lazzaro Moro (1687–1764) publishes *De crostacei e degli altri marini corpi marini che si trovano sui monti libri due* (Crustaceans and other marine bodies found on mountains), in which he describes the formation of rocks and fossils in scientific terms. Despite his religious connections, Moro believes that fossils are the remnants of animal and plant life that lived in the past. He also proposes that all rocks are derived from volcanic activity.

(ES)

1742

Anders Celsius introduces a new temperature scale.

During the 18th century, the mercury thermometer was invented (*See* entry for 1714), allowing for the accurate measurement of temperature. In 1742, Swiss scholar Anders Celsius (1701–44) uses the mercury thermometer to define points on a new temperature scale. Celsius originally sets the boiling point of water at 0°C and the freezing point of water at 100°C. A few years later, the scale is reversed, with water boiling at 100°C and freezing at 0°C. Today, the Celsius scale is used throughout the world.

(P)

Colin Maclaurin describes Newton's calculus.

As described in the sidebar "Physics and Mathematics," Sir Isaac Newton invented *calculus* to help him describe the physical world (*See* entry for 1665). In 1742, Scottish mathematician Colin Maclaurin (1698–1746) explains and expands Newton's calculus in his work *Treatise of Fluxions*. Maclaurin uses calculus to solve problems in *geometry* and physics and demonstrates a method to find the maximum and minimum value of a *function*.

(M)

June 7

Christian Goldbach states that every number greater than two is the sum of three prime numbers.

Mathematicians have studied *number theory* since ancient times. In a letter to Leonhard Euler dated June 7, 1742, Prussian mathematician Christian Goldbach (1690–1764) proposes that every number greater than two is the sum of three *prime numbers*, an idea that is now known as Goldbach's conjecture. While many mathematicians have approached the problem in the last three centuries, it remains unproven.

(M)

1743

Alexis-Claude Clairaut describes the relationship between the Earth's gravity and latitude.

Sir Isaac Newton described how the force of *gravity* causes the Earth to be flat at the poles (*See* entry for 1687). The mathematician Pierre Louis Moreau de Maupertuis verified this experimentally (*See* entry for 1738). French mathematician Alexis-Claude Clairaut (1713–65) helped Maupertuis by collecting data on the *latitude* at various points on the Earth. In 1743, he describes the relationship between the gravitational force of the Earth and latitude. He publishes his theory in *Théorie de la figure de la Terre* (Theory of the shape of the Earth).

(ES, P)

October

Benjamin Franklin demonstrates storm movements.

Watch any weather report today, and you will see storm systems being tracked across the country. The ability of a storm to move was first recorded in the 18th century. American scholar Benjamin Franklin (1706–90) studies newspaper accounts of a storm during October 1743. Based upon these accounts, he traces the movement of a storm from Georgia to Massachusetts, the first recorded analysis of storm movements.

(W)

1744

Mikhail Lomonosov describes heat as a form of motion.

During the 18th century, physicists addressed questions about *energy*. In 1744, Russian scientist Mikhail Lomonosov (1711–65) describes changes in temperature. He states that *heat* can be explained as a condition in which

particles have an increase in motion, while cold is a condition in which the motion of particles decreases.

(P)

1745

Pieter van Musschenbroek and Ewald Georg von Kleist develop a capacitor.

During the 18th century, physicists began to investigate the nature and properties of *electricity*. In 1745, German physicist Ewald Georg von Kleist (1700–48) invents a device to store electrical charges, known as a *capacitor*. Dutch physicist Pieter van Musschenbroek (1692–1761) at the University of Leyden also creates a similar device, and it becomes known as a Leyden jar.

(P)

1746

Leonhard Euler espouses a wave theory of light.

During the 18th century, physicists believed light traveled in particles or corpuscles as described by Sir Isaac Newton (*See* entry for 1666). In 1746, Swiss mathematician Leonhard Euler describes light as being generated from oscillation in space, espousing a wave theory of light. He argues that the *refraction* of light can only be explained using waves. Euler's work on *optics* is described in *Nova theoria lucis et colorum* (A new theory of light and colors).

(P)

César-François Cassini de Thury commences a geographic survey of France.

Accurate maps are needed for trade, military uses, and scientific investigations of *geography*. In 1746, French scholar César-François Cassini de Thury (1714–84) commences a scientitic geographic survey of France. Work on the new map of France continues for nearly 40 years, and is completed after his death in 1784.

(ES)

Andreas Marggraf shows that zinc is an element.

During the 18th century, scientists identified many of the *elements* that make up matter. Some elements are isolated from substances that have been known since ancient times. Descriptions of metal zinc and compounds containing it are found in the writings of Roman scholars such as Pliny the Elder. In 1746, German chemist Andreas Marggraf (1709–82) proves that zinc is an element.

(C)

1747

May 20

James Lind treats scurvy with citrus fruit.

Scurvy, a disease characterized by swollen and bleeding gums, plagued sailors until the 18th century. On May 20, 1747, Scottish physician James Lind (1716–94) treats sailors with scurvy by adding new foods into their diets. He finds that only the sailors who receive citrus fruit recover from the disease, a treatment that resembles the lime juice that had been consumed by sailors for centuries. Today, physicians know that scurvy is caused by a deficiency in vitamin C, an abundant nutrient in citrus fruit.

(B)

1748

Jean-Antoine Nollet describes osmosis.

If a semipermeable membrane—one that will allow the passage of some molecules while retaining others—separates two solutions, water moves from the side of the membrane where there are fewer molecules in solution to the side of the membrane where there are more molecules in solution. French scholar Jean-Antoine Nollet (1700–70) discovers this process, known as *osmosis*, in 1748. He conducts his experiments using a pig's bladder showing that the bladder is a semipermeable membrane, allowing the flow of water but restricting the passage of dissolved molecules.

(B, C)

Leonhard Euler describes trigonometric functions.

Trigonometry, the study of triangles, has been used since the Middle Ages. The first representation of trigonometry in the form used today comes in 1748, when Swiss mathematician Leonhard Euler publishes *Introductio in analysin infinitorum* (Introduction to the analysis of the infinite). He describes the six trigonometric functions, *sine, cosine, tangent, secant, cosecant,* and *cotangent,* as *ratios.* The work is also notable for its description of the infinite series sin x and cos x.

(M)

1749

Georges-Louis Leclerc, Comte de Buffon, states the Earth formed when a comet collided with the Sun.

In the 18th century, scholars studying natural systems rarely contradicted the church's teachings about the creation of the Earth. French geologist Georges-Louis Leclerc, Comte de Buffon (1707–88), attempted to take supernatural forces out of creation theories. In his work *Histoire naturelle* (Natural history) he describes the formation of the Earth and the solar system. He claims the planets formed when a *comet* collided with the Sun.

(ES)

The 18th-century French geologist Georges-Louis Leclerc, Comte de Buffon, proposes an early scientific explanation for the formation of the Earth. *(Museum of the History of Science, Oxford)*

1751

Axel Fredrik Cronstedt identifies nickel as an element.

During the 18th century, many *elements* were identified. During this time, chemists and mineralogists studied the different ores discovered in mines. In 1751, Swedish mineralogist Axel Fredrik Cronstedt (1722–65) analyzes an ore found in cobalt mines. He extracts a new metal from the ore and names it nickel. The discovery of nickel does not gain wide acceptance until 1754, when Cronstedt demonstrates that it is not an *alloy* of cobalt.

(C)

Jean-Étienne Guettard identifies extinct volcanoes in France.

As described in the sidebar "Theories of Geological Change," during the 18th century scholars debated how the Earth changes. One idea, known as the *Vulcanist theory,* states that geological features form from the cooling of a molten liquid. In 1751, French naturalist Jean-Étienne Guettard (1715–86) observes volcanic stones during a trip to central France, and realizes that the region housed many extinct volcanoes. The discovery leads him to suggest that changes in the Earth are brought about by heating and cooling, supporting the Vulcanist point of view.

(ES)

Nicolas Desmarest claims a land bridge once connected France and England.

During the 18th century, geologists studied land formations and developed theories on how they formed. In 1751, French geologist Nicolas Desmarest (1725–1815) studies the coastlines of France and England. He proposes that the two countries were once connected by a land bridge that had been recently destroyed.

(ES)

1752

René-Antoine Ferchault de Réaumur describes the chemistry of digestion.

Animals derive *energy* from the food they consume. Thus, the process of digestion is critical to life. French scholar René-Antoine Ferchault de Réaumur (1683–1757) studied the process of digestion in birds. He isolated the fluids found in the stomach, called gastric juices, and showed how they chemically break down food.

(B, C)

1753

Claude-François Geoffroy demonstrates that bismuth and lead are distinct elements.

As chemistry and mineralogy developed, scientists began finding that many metals that had been used for centuries are actually *elements*. For instance, the element bismuth, which often occurs naturally with lead, was not believed to be a separate element. Many speculated that bismuth and lead were two individual elements. In 1753, French chemist Claude-François Geoffroy (1729–53) proves that bismuth is not lead.

(C)

Benjamin Franklin invents the lightning rod.

Lightning storms can be beautiful and dangerous. American scientist Benjamin Franklin showed that lightning is an electrical discharge. In 1753, he invents the lightning rod, a device that protects houses from the damaging effects of lightning. By attaching a metal rod to the top of the roof and connecting a wire from the rod to the ground, Franklin assures that the lightning bypassed the house and passed to the ground.

(W)

1754

Joseph Black describes the release of carbon dioxide from solids.

During the 18th century, scientists studied the properties of gases. One of the first gases to be identified was carbon dioxide. In 1754, Scottish chemist Joseph Black (1728–99) studies carbon dioxide and finds that it is released during some chemical reactions that involve solids. He concludes that the carbon dioxide is a constituent of some solids. He describes his work in his 1756 paper "Experi-

ments Upon Magnesia Alba, Quicklime, and Some Other Alcaline Substances."

(C)

1755

Immanuel Kant proposes the solar nebular hypothesis.

Theories on the creation of the Earth and the stars have been proposed throughout history. Advances in astronomy that occurred in the 17th and 18th centuries allowed scholars to base their theories on experimental observations. In 1755, German philosopher Immanuel Kant (1724–1804) writes *Theory of the Heavens,* in which he proposes that the solar system was created from a condensing and flattening of *nebula*. The theory, known as the solar nebular hypothesis, is also put forth by Pierre Laplace (*See* entry for 1796), and it still exists in a modified form today.

(SA)

Joseph Black shows that magnesium is an element.

During the 18th century, chemists began discovering many of the *elements* that make up matter on Earth. In 1755, the chemist Joseph Black analyzes two common chemicals, magnesia and lime. At the time, they were thought to contain the same elements. Black shows that magnesia is chemically distinct from lime, and that it contains a new element, now known as magnesium. Later in the century, chemists begin developing methods to isolate magnesium from magnesia.

(C)

Leonhard Euler describes differential equations.

As described in the sidebar "Physics and Mathematics," physicists and engineers as well as mathematicians use *calculus*. In 1755, the mathematician Leonhard Euler describes a particularly useful application of calculus, the differential equation, in his work *Institutiones calculi differentialis* (Foundations of differential calculus). Euler describes three types of differential equations: linear, exact, and homogeneous.

(M)

1755

November 1

John Michell claims earthquakes are caused by volcanic activity.

During the 18th century, many geologists believed that earthquakes were related to changes in the weather. On November 1, 1755, a massive earthquake destroyed much of Lisbon, the capital of Portugal. The earthquake inspired English geologist John Michell (1724–93) to study earthquakes. In 1760, he publishes a paper suggesting that earthquakes are caused by volcanic activity. His paper also includes the idea that earthquakes travel in waves, and that the waves can be used to determine the origin of the quake.

(ES)

1756

Johann Lehmann describes mountain formation.

During the 18th century, geologists debated theories on how geographical features of the Earth formed. In 1756, German geologist Johann Lehmann (1719–67) presents his theory of mountain formation in the book *Versuch einer geschichte von flötz-gebürgen*. Lehman classifies mountains into three different classes based upon his theory of how they were formed. The first class consists of

mountains that were formed when the Earth was created; the second class is made up of mountains that form from the deposition of *sediments*; and the third class consists of volcanic mountains.

(ES)

1758

December 25

Johann Palitzsch observes the return of Halley's comet.

Astronomers have observed *comets,* celestial bodies made of ice and dirt, and charted their course for centuries. In 1705 (*See* entry for 1705), English astronomer Edmond Halley noticed that a comet appeared in the same region of the sky every 76 years. He predicted that it would return in 1758; however, he did not live to see it. Many astronomers search for the comet until finally amateur Johann Palitzsch (1723–88) sees it on December 25, 1758. The return of Halley's comet demonstrates the ability of scientists to predict natural phenomena.

(SA)

1759

Caspar Wolff describes embryo development.

The field of embryology, or the study of how organisms develop, was founded in the 18th century. In 1759, German biologist Caspar Wolff (1733–94) describes the development of chick embryos in his work *Theoria generationis* (Theory of generation). Wolff's observations that specialized organs develop from more general tissues refute the theory that organs are preformed in the embryo, a theory that dominated biology at the time.

(B)

∾ CONCLUSION ∾

The period from the early 17th century to the middle of the 18th century saw a variety of changes in science—from the development of chemistry as a formal field of study to the confirmation that science can be used to predict natural phenomena, illustrated by the predicted return of Halley's *comet*. These and other achievements set the stage for new lines of investigations. As scientific study grows and gains credibility, it continues to conflict with religious teachings. Just as Galileo Galilei and other astronomers found themselves at odds with the church about the nature of the solar system, geologists of the 18th and 19th centuries begin to contradict the church's teachings about the history of the Earth, and how it was created. For the next several centuries, scientists and church leaders will debate the age of the Earth, and how it was created. Advances in mathematics, such as the development of *calculus* and statistics during the 17th century affects all fields of science until this day. In the 20th century, calculus becomes indispensable for physicists trying to understand the *forces* that hold together the *atom*. The study of biology is revolutionized during this era as the physicist Robert Hooke and the microscopist Antoni von Leeuwenhoek describe cells and organisms too small to see. In the next century, scientists will use the microscope to identify the structures that are common to plant and animal cells, and characterize microorganisms based upon their appearance. Such studies lead directly to the germ theory of disease, and to the advances in molecular and cellular biology that are made at the end of the 20th century.

5

Science in the Age of Revolutions

1760–1850

∽ INTRODUCTION ∽

From the middle of the 18th century to the middle of the 19th century, there was a great expansion of the young field of chemistry, an increasing interest in the study of *electricity* and *magnetism,* the discovery of two new planets in the solar system, the debate of various theories of geological change, and the beginnings of theories of biological change through *evolution.*

Chemists of this era continue to identify the *elements* that make up all matter, while also establishing some of the basic laws that govern chemical reactions. The hunt for elements leads to the discovery of gases, such as hydrogen, chlorine, and oxygen. In addition, a number of elements, such as strontium and uranium are found while analyzing minerals. Through studying chemical reactions, scientists also uncover some of the basic laws of chemistry, including the observation that matter is neither created nor destroyed in a chemical reaction. The most fundamental achievement in chemistry, arguably of any era, comes in 1801, when English scholar John Dalton describes his theory that all matter is made up of indestructible units he calls *atoms.*

The field of physics is dominated by the study of *forces,* particularly electricity and magnetism. The discovery that a *magnetic field* can affect *electric currents* leads to a flurry of studies in the first part of the 19th century. Soon, the phenomenon of electrical induction, the generation of an electric current by a magnetic field, is demonstrated. Electrical induction serves as the basis for the electric motor, which uses magnets to generate the electric current that powers movement. English scholar William Herschel studies the spectrum of light and finds there is *radiation* outside of the *visible spectrum.* In 1801, physicist Thomas Young shows that light travels in waves, and the wave theory of light is studied through the end of the century.

141

Astronomers of the 18th century continue to view the stars through increasingly powerful telescopes. In 1781, English astronomer Sir William Herschel discovers Uranus, the first planet that can be viewed only with the aid of a telescope. Soon, astronomers calculate the orbit of Uranus and find that evidence of its existence could be found in many older records. In fact, through examining old observations and conducting new studies of Uranus, many realize that yet another planet likely lies beyond Uranus, leading to the discovery of the planet Neptune in 1846.

Earth scientists of this era study the local changes that occur with weather systems as well as the more global changes that lead to the formation of geological features. Studies of wind currents lead to the description of both the Gulf Stream and of hurricane whirlwinds. Other geologists debate the way the Earth changes over time. During the 18th and 19th centuries, naturalists collect evidence that the Earth changes due to effects of *heat* and water, and argue over whether such changes occur slowly, or all at once. Proponents of various theories of geological change continue to study rock formations, *sediments,* and strata. Their work leads to the classification of various stages in geological time, based upon the mineral and fossil components of various layers of the Earth.

While geologists debate changes in the Earth, biologists also begin to consider how organisms change over time. This era sees the discovery of new fossils, including the first dinosaur bones. French naturalist Jean-Baptiste de Lamarck puts forth an early theory of evolution at the beginning of the 19th century. His work will be surpassed by the theories of Charles Darwin, who embarks upon his famous journey around the world in 1831. Other biologists continue to study organisms that are alive today. During the 1830s, the cell theory of biology becomes fully formed, and one of the main cellular structures, the *nucleus* is identified. Chemists also begin to study biological systems, identifying such important biological molecules as *proteins* and *enzymes.*

TIME LINE OF SCIENTIFIC ACHIEVEMENTS FROM 1760 TO 1850

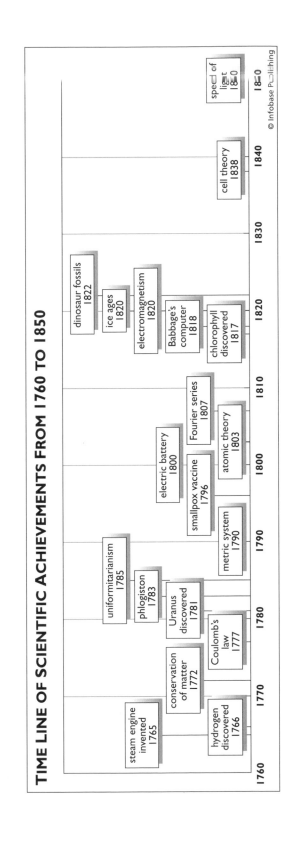

∽ CHRONOLOGY ∾

1760

Joseph Black discovers latent heat.
During the 18th century, scientists studied the way matter changes from one form to another. Such phase transitions accompany changes in temperature. In 1760, Scottish chemist Joseph Black (1728–99) studies the transition between liquid and solids. He notes that for a solid to become a liquid, *heat* must be transferred in excess of the amount required to raise the temperature to the melting point. The additional heat needed to allow the phase transition to occur is known as latent heat. Black's work is instrumental in defining the difference between heat and temperature.

(C)

1761

June 5

Mikhail Lomonosov describes the atmosphere of Venus.
The transit of Venus across the Sun has occurred 52 times during recorded history. On June 5, 1761, Russian scholar Mikhail Lomonosov (1711–65) views one such transit of Venus. He notices that Venus does not look like a black disk crossing the Sun, but instead looks fuzzy and appears to have a halo. He deduces that the planet must have an atmosphere, and describes it as being filled with a layer of clouds.

(SA)

1762

Peter Simon Pallas describes the formation of mountains.
During the 18th century, scholars began to study how geographical formation came to be. In 1762, German naturalist Peter Simon Pallas (1741–1811) describes the formation of mountains. He proposes that mountains are formed by volcanic activity that causes the granite to emerge from the Earth.

(ES)

1765

James Watt improves the steam engine.
During the early 18th century, English inventors worked to harness the power of steam to drive an engine and perform work. In 1765, Scottish inventor James Watt (1736–1819) greatly improves the efficacy of the steam engine by adding a separate condenser that helps the steam to cool. Over the next 50 years, he continues to make improvements to the engine, including the addition of insulation and lubrication. His influence on the utility of the steam engine is so great that he is often inaccurately credited as the inventor of the steam engine.

(P)

Nicolas Desmarest provides evidence that heat causes geological changes.
As described in the sidebar "Theories of Geological Change," two main theories explaining how the Earth changes were debated during the 18th century. *Neptunism* states that the movement of water causes geological changes, while the *Vulcanist theory* states that *heat* is the key to such changes. In 1765, French geologist Nicolas Desmarest (1755–1815) studies basalt near extinct volcanoes (*See* entry for 1751). He realizes that the only way the basalt could have formed is by the cooling of a stream of lava, providing a key piece of evidence supporting the Vulcanist theory.

(ES)

1766

Henry Cavendish discovers hydrogen.

As described in the sidebar "Discovering the Elements," chemists identified many of the *elements* that make up matter during the 18th century. In 1766, English chemist Henry Cavendish (1731–1810) discovers the lightest element hydrogen. He identifies the element during an experiment when he treats iron filings with an *acid*. He analyzes the gas that is released and finds it to be lighter than any known gases. Later, he shows that when hydrogen burns it gives off water as a byproduct. Today, scientists realize that water is formed from the chemical reaction between the burning hydrogen gas and oxygen in the air.

(C)

DISCOVERING THE ELEMENTS

While the term *element* has been used to describe the fundamental units of matter since the time of ancient Greece, scholars in the 17th century argued about the number of elements and their identities. Such debates are quieted in 1661, when English chemist Robert Boyle writes *The Scepitcal Cymist,* rejecting the ancient notion of elements. Soon, chemists begin to define elements as the fundamental components of the different substances they study in the laboratory. During the 18th century, French chemist Antoine-Laurent Lavoisier defines elements as substances that cannot be further decomposed in chemical reactions. Several substances that have been used and studied since ancient times—including gold, lead, silver, zinc, mercury, iron, copper, tin, arsenic, and antimony—fit Lavoisier's definition of an element. Others, such as lime, borax, and most notably water, are subsequently shown to be the products of chemical reactions. Soon, scientists look everywhere from seawater to lead mines to find and define more elements.

Advances in methods of chemical analysis, particularly the development of *electrolysis* and the discovery of *spectral lines,* aid in the search for elements. Electrolysis breaks compounds apart and separates the *ions* of salt molecules by passing an electric current through a solution. In 1800, English chemist William Nicholson uses electrolysis to break water molecules into hydrogen and oxygen, proving that water is not an element. English chemist Humphry Davy uses the same technique to show that the compound lime can be broken down to the element calcium, and to isolate the elements sodium, potassium, and barium. During the 18th century, chemists detect the presence of new elements in a mixture, such as a mineral, by using what is known as a flame test, heating the element and looking at the color that is produced. Using this method, Johan August Arfvedson discovers the element lithium in 1817. In the 19th century, chemists Robert Bunsen and Gustav Kirchhoff show that each element emits a characteristic wavelength of *light* when it is heated, known as a spectral line, which can be observed as a particular color. They use the analysis of spectral lines to identify the elements cesium and rubidium. Spectral lines also play a critical role in the discovery of elements, such as helium, that occur naturally as gases.

The set of elements known as the inert or *noble gases* get their name because they do not readily undergo chemical reactions and are found in the gas phase in nature. Helium, the

Albrecht von Haller shows that nerves control muscle.

Physiologists have investigated the action and control of muscles for centuries. In 1766, Swiss biologist Albrecht von Haller (1708–77) demonstrates that nerves control muscle action. He also traces the nerves of the body back to the spinal cord. Haller's work on neurophysiology is published as part of *Elementa physiologiae corporis humani*

(The physiological elements of the human body) in 1766.

(B)

1767

Joseph-Louis Lagrange studies algebraic equations.

Arab mathematicians developed *algebra* during the Middle Ages, but questions about

first noble gas discovered, is found in 1868 by Pierre-Jules-César Janssen, who was examining the spectral lines given off by the Sun. Almost 30 years later, English scientist William Ramsay finds helium on Earth. Working with John Strutt (also known as Lord Raleigh), Ramsay discovers the noble gas argon, which makes up approximately 1 percent of the Earth's atmosphere, in 1898. Ramsay and colleagues discover the remaining noble gases, neon, xenon, and krypton as contaminants in a sample of argon gas, identifying each by its unique spectral lines.

English chemist Humphrey Davy identifies many elements including chlorine and potassium. This photograph depicts Davy's Apparatus for Soil Analysis. *(Museum of the History of Science, Oxford)*

Another set of elements, the *lanthanides* or rare earth elements, are discovered as parts of minerals found in different mines. Chemists Jöns Jakob Berzelius and Wilhelm Hisinger identify the element cerium in 1803; however, they are unable to obtain a pure sample. Through the remainder of the 19th century, the reason for their difficulty becomes readily apparent, as chemists identify and isolate the new elements lanthanum, samarium, and didymium from samples of cerium. A sample of didymium also yields two other elements, neodymium and praseodymium. A similar analysis of samples of the element yttrium leads to the discovery of several other previously unknown elements, including erbium and terbium. At first, cerium and its related elements are called the rare earth elements; although subsequent analysis show that many are far from rare. In fact, cerium itself is the 25th-most abundant element in the Earth's crust, more common that the element tin, which has been known since ancient times. Today, the elements are known as the lanthanides, named after lanthanum, the lightest of the group.

As will be described in later sections, today's new elements are not discovered on Earth, but rather are generated by physicists in the laboratory. Elements such as curium, americium, and berkelium, are truly rare, often existing only for seconds.

how algebraic equations are solved persisted for centuries. In 1767, French mathematician Joseph-Louis Lagrange (1736–1813) considers what kinds of equations can be solved in *On the Solution of Numerical Equations*. His work provides the first method that can be reliably used to solve equations of a high degree.

(M)

1768

Joseph Priestley creates seltzer water.
As research in chemistry blossomed during the 17th century, chemists devised new methods to isolate and study gases. English chemist Joseph Priestley (1733–1804) performed a number of experiments using gases. In 1768, he isolates the gas carbon dioxide from vats of fermenting beer at a local brewery. When he dissolves carbon dioxide into water, he finds that it creates bubbles, and gives the water a distinctive taste.

(C)

1769

Antoine-Laurent Lavoisier demonstrates that water cannot be converted into a mineral.
During the 17th century, the modern science of chemistry was born, maturing during the 18th century. At this time, many scholars still believed that one substance could change, or transmute, into another. In 1769, French chemist Antoine-Laurent Lavoisier (1743–94) uses quantitative techniques to demonstrate that water cannot transmute into a mineral (or earth as it is called at the time), by proving that the *sediment* left behind after water is boiled actually originated in the vessel where the boiling took place.

(C)

1771

Joseph-Louis Lagrange describes permutations.
While *algebra* had been studied since the Middle Ages, it continued to be an active area of mathematical scholarship in the 18th century. In 1771, French mathematician Joseph-Louis Lagrange (1736–1813) tries to determine why *cubic* and *quadratic equations* can be solved algebraically. In the discussion presented in the paper "Réflexions sur la résolution algébrique des equations" (Reflection on the algebraic resolution of equations), he considers permutations, or rearrangements of values within an ordered set. Today, this work is considered the first step in applying the study of sets, known as group theory, to algebra.

(M)

Ignatius Kaim isolates manganese metal.
Many of the *elements* that make up common chemicals were isolated during the 18th century. For centuries, glassmakers used compounds containing the element manganese to help them clarify glass. In 1771, Ignatius Kaim, a graduate student in Vienna, becomes the first person to isolate manganese metal from the compound called chemical pyrolusite.

(C)

1772

Joseph Priestley collects water-soluble gases.
During the 18th century, scientists developed methods to study matter in the gaseous form. One of the difficulties in performing experiments with gases is devising methods to collect pure samples of a gas. In 1772, English chemist Joseph Priestley (1733–1804) invents the pneumatic trough, a device that collects water-soluble gases. He uses his device to iso-

into a number of new gases including oxygen (*See* entry for 1774).

(C)

Antoine-Laurent Lavoisier demonstrates conservation of matter.

One of the great problems addressed by chemists in the 18th century was the question of how matter changes through chemical reactions. In 1772, French chemist Antoine-Laurent Lavoisier (1743–94) performs a series of experiments in which he burns chemicals, such as phosphorus, then weighs the samples to show that no new matter is made and no matter is lost during the reaction. His experiments demonstrate that the principle conservation of matter, a law that states that matter is neither created nor destroyed during a chemical reaction.

(C)

Daniel Rutherford discovers nitrogen.

During the 18th century, scientists investigated the gases that make up the air. In 1772, Scottish chemist Daniel Rutherford (1749–1814) studies the component of air by depleting a sample of its known components, oxygen and carbon dioxide. He begins by burning a candle to consume all the oxygen, and then passes the remaining gas through a solution that absorbs carbon dioxide. He finds another gas remaining in the vessel. Today, that gas is known as nitrogen. Rutherford describes his experiments in the paper "Dissertatio inauguralis de aere fixo dicto, aut mephitico" (Inaugural dissertation on the air called fixed or mephite).

(C)

November 22

James Cook sails across the Antarctic Circle.

Modern scientists interested in topics ranging from global warming to how organisms adapt to extreme conditions travel to Antarctica to perform their studies. British explorer James Cook (1728–79) becomes

British explorer James Cook is acknowledged to be the first to sail across the Antarctic Circle. Today, scientists continue to study the biology, climate, and geology of Antarctica, including the active volcano Mount Erebus, shown here in November 1978. *(Commander John Bortniak/NOAA)*

the first to approach the continent when he sails across the Antarctic Circle aboard the ship *Resolution*. Cook's ability to sail past Antarctica puts to rest lingering doubts that the South Pole is home to a great land mass.

(MS)

1774

Charles Messier catalogs celestial bodies.

Astronomers have recorded the position of *comets,* planets, and stars. With the invention of the telescope, the pace of discovery increased. One of the most prolific astronomers of this era is Charles Messier (1730–1817). Throughout his career, he discovers dozens of new celestial bodies. In 1774, Messier publishes a catalog of celestial bodies, known today as Messier's catalog, which includes galaxies and *nebulae,* as well as planets, comets, and stars. The first version of his catalog maps 45 celestial bodies, while the final version, published in 1784, describes 110 different objects.

(SA)

Antoine-Laurent Lavoisier shows air is made up of five parts nitrogen to one part oxygen.

As 18th-century scientists learned how to isolate and study gases, they turned their attention toward studying the air. Joseph Priestley and Daniel Rutherford identified two components of air: oxygen and nitrogen. In 1774, French chemist Antoine-Laurent Lavoisier (1743–94) performs quantitative experiments demonstrating that air is made up of five parts nitrogen to one part oxygen.

(C)

Franz Mesmer uses a form of hypnosis to treat illness.

Throughout history, physicians have investigated both physical and spiritual cures to diseases. In 1774, German physician Franz Mesmer (1734–1815) attempts to cure a disease using magnets. In the course of this investigation, he develops techniques to cause waves of "fluids" to flow through the patient's body. His treatment, known as animal *magnetism* or mesmerism, is an early form of hypnosis. While Mesmer's work has a great following at first, it quickly loses credibility.

(B)

August 1

Joseph Priestley discovers oxygen.

For centuries, scholars believed that air was one of the *elements* that make up all matter. The rise of experimental science began to unveil the presence of other substances in air, such as water. On August 1, 1774, English chemist Joseph Priestley (1733–1804) studies the effects of sunlight on different chemicals. He collects a gas that is emitted after a chemical reaction and finds that it has different properties than "normal" air. Other chemists of his era including Carl Wilhelm Scheele, and Antoine-Laurent Lavoisier also report isolating this new air, which Lavoisier calls oxygen in 1777.

(C)

1775

Torbern Olof Bergman describes chemical affinities.

As 18th-century chemists studied chemical reactions, they began to uncover the rules governing them. In 1775, Swedish scientist Torbern Olof Bergman (1735–84) publishes a study of chemical behavior entitled *Disquistio de attractionibus electives* (Dissertation on elective attractions). His work provides the first table of chemical affinities, showing the likelihood that specific chemicals will react with one another.

(C)

1777

Charles-Augustin de Coulomb measures electric forces.
During the 18th century, many physicists investigated the properties of *electricity* and its relationship to *magnetism*. Experiments performed in the 1730s showed that bodies carry an electric charge that can attract or repel one another in a fashion similar to a magnet. In 1777, French physicist Charles-Augustin de Coulomb (1736–1806) invents the torsion balance, which can determine the size and charge of sphere. He uses this device to measure the repulsion between two charged objects. Coulomb demonstrates that the *forces* between the objects vary with the distance, in a manner similar to gravitational forces. Today, this relationship is known as Coulomb's Law.

(P)

1779

Lazzaro Spallanzani describes fertilization.
Physiologists studying reproduction make observations on the behavior of sperm and the nature of ovarian follicles that lead to a greater understanding of process. In 1779, Italian biologist Lazzaro Spallanzani (1729–99) builds upon this knowledge through a series of studies on the fertilization of amphibian eggs. He concludes that contact between the sperm and the ovarian follicles are required for fertilization to take place. Spallanzani successfully performs artificial inseminations, first using amphibians, and then using dogs.

(B)

Jan Ingen-Housz discovers photosynthesis.
Photosynthesis is the process whereby plants take *energy* from the Sun and convert it to chemical energy within their own cells. During photosynthesis, plants consume carbon dioxide and produce oxygen. In 1779, Dutch scholar Jan Ingen-Housz (1730–99) discovers photosynthesis through a series of experiments showing that plants consume carbon dioxide and excrete oxygen only when exposed to light. He describes the results in his book *Experiments upon Vegetables,* published in 1779.

(B, C)

1781

Sir William Herschel describes binary stars.
The invention of the telescope in the 17th century gave astronomers a powerful new tool to use while studying celestial bodies. One discovery that relied upon the telescope was double stars—a pair of stars that appears as a single star when viewed with the unaided eye, but is clearly two stars when observed using a telescope. In 1781, English astronomer Sir William Herschel (1738–1822) studies such pairs of stars, now called *binary stars,* and realizes that most rotate around a common center of gravity.

(SA)

Peter Jacob Hjelm shows that molybdenum is an element.
During the 18th century, many *elements* were discovered. Chemist Carl Wilhelm Scheele studied the chemical molybdenite. Scheele

showed that the compound is neither carbon in the form of graphite nor an ore of lead, as many believed. Unfortunately, he was unable to identify and isolate the substance. In 1781, Peter Jacob Hjelm (1746–1813) isolates a pure metal from a sample of molybdenite. Today, the element is known as molybdenum.

(C)

March 13

Sir William Herschel discovers the planet Uranus.

During the 18th century, astronomers used telescopes to search for balls of dirt and ice known as *comets*. On March 13, 1781, English astronomer Sir William Herschel (1738–1822) discovers what he believes to be a new comet. Later that summer, Anders Lexell notices that the body Herschel discovered has none of the characteristics of a comet (*See* entry for AUGUST 31, 1781). Herschel had in fact discovered the first planet that cannot be observed without the aid of a telescope, now called Uranus.

(SA)

August 31

Anders Lexell calculates the orbit of Uranus.

In March 1781 (*See* entry for MARCH 13, 1781), English astronomer Sir William Herschel (1738–1822) observed what he believed to be a new *comet*. The body he discovered, however, traveled more slowly than most comets and had a different shape. Mathematician Anders Lexell (1740–84) calculates the orbit of the body and shows that it is a circle. On August 31, 1781, he announces that Herschel did not discover a comet; instead he discovered the planet Uranus.

(SA)

1782

May 20

Lazzaro Spallanzani studies the regeneration of body parts in animals.

Eighteenth-century biologists learned that some animals can regenerate lost body parts such as claws or antennae. Italian physiologist Lazzaro Spallanzani (1729–99) systematically investigated regeneration in a number of organisms including earthworms and snails. In 1782, he describes the regeneration of snails' heads in his work *Promdromo di un opera da imprimersi sopra le riproduzioni animali* (An essay on animal reproduction). On May 20 of that year, a newspaper reports Spallanzani's finding, spawning naturalists and amateur scientists to decapitate snails in hopes of seeing a new head grow. However, the experiment is not so simple, as regenera-

The 18th-century Italian biologist Lazzaro Spallanzani shows that some lower animals, such as starfish, can regenerate lost body parts. This photograph, taken off the coast of Massachusetts in 1988, shows starfish and anemones. *(L. Steward/OAR/Undersea Research Program/NOAA)*

tion is possible only in certain species and when the cut is made in a specific manner.

(B)

1783

Antoine-Laurent Lavoisier describes combustion.

During the 18th century, many chemists used the *phlogistin* theory to explain chemical reactions. They believed that phlogiston was carried in the air and isolated gases thought to be enriched or devoid of the substance. When Joseph Priestley discovered oxygen, he believed it to be a gas lacking phlogiston. In 1783, French chemist Antoine-Laurent Lavoisier (1743–94) performs a series of experiments showing that dephlogisticated air (oxygen) is a component of the air around us. He shows that the gas makes up one-fifth of the air, and that it is essential for combustion.

(C)

Juan José Elhuyar and Fausto Elhuyar discover tungsten.

During the 18th century, chemists began identifying the *elements* that make up matter. Scientists who studied rocks and minerals also discovered some of the elements. In 1783, Spanish mineralogists Juan José Elhuyar (1754–1804) and Fausto Elhuyar (1755–1833) study a mineral thought to contain an unknown metal. They isolate the new metal and name it wolfram, which is later changed to tungsten.

(C)

Antoine-Laurent Lavoisier and Pierre-Simon de Laplace show that respiration is a form of combustion.

As scientists began to understand the nature of gases that make up the air around us, they were able to study the physiologi-cal process of *respiration*. French chemist Antoine-Laurent Lavoisier (1743–94) studied the process and believed that animals took in oxygen when they inhaled and expelled carbon dioxide as they exhaled. In 1783, he devises an ice-calorimeter with French mathematician Pierre-Simon de Laplace (1749–1827), and they measure the *heat* produced during respiration. Their experiments, described in the article "Memoir on Heat," shows that respiration is a form of combustion.

(B, C, P)

June 5

Jacques-Étienne de Montgolfier and Joseph-Michael Montgolfier demonstrate the hot-air balloon.

The dream of flight was realized in the 18th century when two French brothers, Jacques-Étienne de Montgolfier (1745–99) and Joseph-Michael Montgolfier (1740–1810) invented the hot-air balloon. They used a small fire to heat the air that fills a silk bag, allowing it to rise from the ground. On June 5, 1783, they hold the first public demonstration, sending an unmanned balloon on a journey of just over a mile. The first human flight takes place later that year.

1784

Henry Cavendish shows that water is formed when hydrogen burns.

During the 18th century, chemists began identifying the *elements* that make up matter. Classically, water had been considered an element. In 1784, English scholar Henry Cavendish (1731–1810) shows that water is actually a compound that can be produced when hydrogen is burned. He burns hydrogen gas mixed with air in a vessel, and finds residues of water left behind.

Today, scientists know that the compound water is produced when two *atoms* of the element hydrogen combine with one atom of the element oxygen.

(C)

1785

Benjamin Franklin describes the Gulf Stream.

Sailors have known about the Gulf Stream, a warm ocean current off of the east coast of the United States, since Europeans began exploring North America. From 1753 until 1785, American scientist Benjamin Franklin (1706–90) studied the Gulf Stream, at first through reports he received from sailors, then by taking his own temperature measurements while at sea. In 1785, he provides a scientific description of the Gulf Stream in his work *Maritime Observations*.

(W)

Henry Cavendish accurately describes the composition of air.

During the 18th century, scientists investigated the composition and properties of air. In 1785, Henry Cavendish (1731–1810) publishes an accurate accounting of the composition of air in his paper "Experiments on Air." Through a series of careful analyses, Cavendish shows that air is made up of 79.167 percent phlogisticated air (now known to be a mixture of nitrogen and argon) and 20.833 percent dephlogisticated air (now known to be oxygen).

(C)

William Withering uses digitalis to treat congestive heart failure.

Traditional herbal remedies are often effective because the plant makes natural products that can act as drugs. In 1785, English physician William Withering (1741–99) describes an herbal remedy, the juice of the foxglove plant, to treat congestive heart failure in *An Account of the Foxglove and Some of its Medicinal Uses*. Foxglove plant makes a chemical called digitalis, which is still used to treat heart disease today.

(B)

James Hutton proposes the principle of uniformitarianism.

As described in the sidebar "Theories of Geological Change," 18th-century scientists proposed many theories to explain how the Earth changes over time. Some geologists argued that water mediates geological changes; others believed that *heat* brings about changes in the Earth. In 1785, Scottish geologist James Hutton (1726–97) proposes that geologic changes occur slowly over time, and that a range of natural processes, including both heat and water, affect these changes. Ten years later, he publishes his ideas in the classic work *Theory of the Earth* (1795). His ideas, known collectively as the principle of *Uniformitarianism*, continue to guide geological thinking today.

(ES)

1786

Franz Joseph Müller von Reichenstein discovers tellurium.

During the 18th century, many *elements* were identified. During this time, scientists studied different minerals found in mines. In 1786, Franz Joseph Müller von Reichenstein (1742–1845) analyzes a metallic mineral, believing it contains the element antimony. He soon realizes the mineral is a mixture of gold and a previously unknown element, now called tellurium.

(C)

1787

Jacques-Alexandre-César Charles describes the relationship between the temperature and volume of a gas.

During the 18th century, scientists began to understand the properties of gases. Robert Boyle described the relationship between the pressure of a gas and its volume (*See* entry for 1662). In 1787, French chemist Jacques-Alexandre-César Charles (1746–1823) shows that the volume of a gas is also related to its temperature, finding that the same quantity of a gas takes up a greater volume as the temperature increases. Almost 20 years later, in 1808, Joseph-Louis Gay-Lussac (1778–1850) publishes a similar finding. Today, the principle is known as Charles's Law.

(C, P)

Antoine-Laurent Lavoisier and others devise a system of chemical nomenclature.

Rapid advances in chemistry and the discovery of *elements* throughout the 18th century created the need for a widely accepted system of nomenclature. In 1787, a group of scientists led by French chemist Antoine-Laurent Lavoisier (1743–94) writes *Method of Chemical Nomenclature,* proposing a system for naming new chemicals. The proposed names for a compound includes both the name and proportion of the elements found in the compound.

(C)

Adair Crawford discovers strontium.

Scientists analyzing minerals found in mines discovered many of the *elements* that make up matter. Some of these minerals are used to treat diseases. In 1787, physician Adair Crawford studies a new mineral, hoping to extract a barium-containing compound from it. He finds that it does not contain barium but a previously unidentified element. He names the element strontium after the lead mine where it was found.

(C)

August 22

John Fitch invents the steamboat.

Advances in the development of the steam engine throughout the 18th century triggered the Industrial Revolution and opened the possibility that steam could be used for travel. On August 22, 1787, American inventor John Fitch (1743–89) makes this possibility a reality when he tests his steamboat on the Delaware River. While Fitch continues to build steamboats, they do not gain wide use until the early 19th century, when Robert Fulton popularizes the mode of travel.

(P)

1788

Joseph-Louis Proust states the law of definite proportions.

During the 18th century, scientists began to understand the laws that govern the interactions of matter. In 1788, French chemist Joseph-Louis Proust (1754–1826) studies the chemical reactions that occur between gases. He notes that the compounds created in such reactions always contain whole number ratios of each element. Proust develops the law of definite proportions stating that elements combine in simple *ratios* to form compounds. His law holds true today.

(C)

Joseph-Louis Lagrange applies algebra to mechanics.

As described in the sidebar "Physics and Mathematics," mathematics and physics are intimately related. While physicists tend to use calculus, in 1788, French mathematician Joseph-Louis Lagrange (1736–1813) uses *algebra* to solve problems in *mechanics*. His work,

American inventor John Fitch invents the steamboat in 1787, but the mode of transportation does not become popular until the 19th century. This photograph shows the Steamboat *Cochan* on the Colorado River near Yuma, Arizona, in 1900. *(L.C. Easton/Department of Defense, National Archives)*

described in the treatise *Méchanique analytique* (Analytical mechanics), focuses on *energy* rather than on *motion,* which characterizes the mechanics of Sir Isaac Newton (*See* entry for 1687).

(M, P)

1789

Antoine-Laurent Lavoisier describes the conservation of mass.

During the 18th and 19th centuries, many of the rules governing chemical reactions were elucidated. In 1789, French chemist Antoine-Laurent Lavoisier (1743–94) writes *Traité élementaire de chimie* (Elementary treatise of chemistry) describing his research

in chemistry. One of the principles explained in the work is the law of conservation of mass. Lavoisier, a great analytical chemist, shows that mass of the *reactants* in a chemical reaction is equal to the mass of the *products.*

(C)

Martin Heinrich Klaproth discovers uranium and zirconium.

As described in the sidebar "Discovering the Elements," 18th-century chemists and mineralogists identified many of the *elements* that make up matter. In 1789, German pharmacist Martin Heinrich Klaproth (1743–1817) analyzes a mineral found in silver mines called pitchblende. Through a series of chemical reactions, he isolates a previously unknown metal, which he calls uranium, after the recently discovered planet Uranus. Pitchblende remains an important source of uranium today. In the same year, Klaproth analyzes the mineral zircon and finds another previously unknown element he calls zirconium.

(C)

1790

French Academy of Sciences establishes the metric system of measurement.
Scientific experiments rely upon accurate and reproducible methods and systems of measurement. Many of the units of measure used in the 18th century had evolved over time and were not set up in a logical or consistent fashion. In 1790, the French Academy of Sciences establishes a new system of measurement, called the metric system. The base of the metric system is the unit of length known as a meter, which is set to be one ten-millionth of the distance from the North Pole to the equator. The units of weight and volume are also derived from the meter, with a gram defined as the mass of one cubic centimeter of water, and a liter defined as the volume of a cubic decimeter. Today, the metric system is the standard method of measurement in scientific laboratories and has been adopted by countries throughout the world.

(B, C, ES, P, SA, W)

1791

William Gregor discovers titanium.
As described in the sidebar "Discovering the Elements," during the 18th century chemists and mineralogists began identifying many of the *elements* that make up matter. Soon even amateur scientists joined the hunt for new elements. In 1791, Reverend William Gregor (1761–1817) studies black sand. He shows

that it is made up of two metal-containing compounds, iron oxide and the oxide of a previously unknown element, now called titanium.

(C)

Luigi Galvani shows that nerves can be stimulated with electricity.
The function of nerve cells puzzled biologists for centuries. In 1791, Italian physiologist Luigi Galvani (1737–98) notices that the legs of a dissected frog twitch if it is near an electric generator. He then performs a number of experiments showing that the leg of a frog will contract if it contacts two different metals. Galvani believes he discovered a force in animal tissues that he called "animal electricity." Today, scientists know he demonstrated that nerves could be stimulated by *electricity*.

(B, P)

1794

Adrien-Marie Legendre describes Euclidean geometry.
The ancient Greek mathematician Euclid laid the foundation for the study of *geometry* in his book *The Elements* (*See* entry for CA. 300 B.C.E.). In 1794, French mathematician Adrien-Marie Legendre (1752–1833) writes the text *Eléments de géométrie* (Element of geometry), providing modern treatment of *Euclidean geometry*. Legendre does not expand Euclid's work, but rather puts it into modern mathematical terms. As such, his text serves as the basis for the geometry textbooks studied in high schools today.

(M)

Ernst Chladni says meteorites come from space.
In the 18th century, geologists believed the meteorites found on Earth came from

volcanic activity or the breaking of rocks by lightning. German physicist Ernst Chladni (1756–1827) looked at the minerals found in meteorites while trying to determine their origin. In 1794, he publishes his work *On the Origin of Pallas Iron and Other Similar to It and Some Associated Natural Phenomenon,* proposing that meteorites are actually rocks that crashed to Earth from outer space. His theory is widely mocked by the scientific community, until witnesses report seeing meteorites falling from the sky.

(ES, SA)

Johan Gadolin discovers yttrium.

During the 18th century, many of the *elements* that make up matter were discovered. Scientists analyzing minerals discovered a number of new metals during this time. In 1794, Finnish chemist Johan Gadolin (1760–1852) studies a tungsten-containing mineral. He finds that more than one-third of the mineral is made up of a previously unknown metal, now known as yttrium.

(C)

1795

Alexander von Humboldt describes fossils from the Jurassic period.

During the 19th century, geologists identified fossils in different layers of *strata* and grouped them according to age. In 1795, German scholar Alexander von Humboldt (1769–1859) finds a layer of fossil in limestone from the Jura Mountains in Switzerland. He calls the time period corresponding to this layer of fossils the Jurassic period. Today, paleontologists have determined that the Jurassic period began 206 million years ago and ended 144 million years ago.

(ES)

1796

Smithson Tennant demonstrates that diamonds are made from pure carbon.

Chemists and mineralogists in the 17th and 18th centuries studied diamonds, gemstones characterized by their hardness. They discovered that diamonds can be destroyed by *heat*. In fact, a burnt diamond leaves behind no ashes. In 1796, English chemist Smithson Tennant (1761–1815) shows that diamonds are a pure form of the *element* carbon. When diamonds burn, the carbon is converted to carbon dioxide gas, so there are no solid residues.

(C, ES)

Pierre-Simon de Laplace presents a theory describing the origin of the solar system.

The origin of the universe remains a question pondered by scholars. During the 18th century, French mathematician and astronomer Pierre-Simon de Laplace (1749–1827) describes the solar nebular hypothesis, explaining the formation of the solar system, in his 1796 work *Exposition du système du monde* (Exposition of the systems of the world). The hypothesis states that the solar system formed from a giant gaseous cloud. The philosopher Immanuel Kant proposed a similar theory in 1755 (*See* entry for 1755). A version of the solar nebular hypothesis is still relevant today.

(SA)

Carl Friedrich Gauss develops a method to construct a 17-sided polygon.

The ancient Greeks excelled in *geometry* and described methods to construct many *polygons* using a compass and straightedge. However, they were unable to construct some polygons such as the 17-sided polygon called a heptadecagon. In 1796, 19-year-old budding German mathematician Carl Friedrich Gauss (1777–1855) develops a method to construct a heptadecagon. He later provides a proof that if the number of sides of a polygon is a *prime number,* it can be constructed using a compass and straightedge.

(M)

May

Edward Jenner develops a vaccine to prevent smallpox.

The infectious disease smallpox once afflicted millions of people each year. During the 18th century, English physician Edward Jenner (1749–1823) treated many patients afflicted with the disease. He had grown up in the country, where it was believed that milkmaids did not get smallpox because they were previously infected with cowpox, a similar disease that afflicted cattle. Jenner reasons that he can prevent smallpox before patients contract the disease by exposing them to cowpox. In May 1796, he inoculates a boy with cowpox, and the boy becomes resistant to smallpox. Jenner calls his treatment to prevent smallpox vaccination, and the name has carried on until today.

(B)

1797

Sir James Hall shows that molten glass will crystallize if cooled slowly.

As described in the sidebar "Theories of Geological Change," 18th-century geologists

---

THEORIES OF GEOLOGICAL CHANGE

For centuries, religious leaders rather than scientists offered explanations for how the Earth was formed. As scholars examined old theories during the Renaissance, they began to develop theories on how the various layers of the Earth were formed and the origin of fossils that are found everywhere from the seaside to mountaintops. By the 18th century, Earth scientists begin debating different theories that seek to explain how the Earth's features, such as mountains and valleys, were formed. Some theories align with biblical teachings, while others rely solely on the empirical evidence uncovered by naturalists. These theories of geological changes are argued throughout the early 19th century.

One of the first theories of geological change, known as Vulcanism, explains the origin of the various types of rocks, stating that rock formations are the product of a universal fluid, similar to lava. Prominent 18th-century Vulcanists, such as French geologist Nicolas Desmarest, look for evidence of extinct volcanoes to explain the origin of various rock formations. Others, such as Scottish geologist Sir James Hall, turn to the laboratory to find evidence to support their theory. In 1797, Hall shows that molten glass will form crystals when cooled. While the *Vulcanist theory* falls out of favor by the middle of the 18th century, it is notable for bringing forth the idea that rocks and other geological features visible today were formed from natural process, rather than divine intervention.

During the 18th century, the Vulcanists debated scholars who believed that changes in the Earth are caused by water, known as the Neptunist theory. Early Neptunists believed that changes in the Earth's surface, such as the formation of mountain and valleys, were formed by water, and many believed they were the result of the Great Flood described in the Bible. By the 18th century, the theory evolves to include the idea that the Earth and its features originate in an ocean created by a divine being. Rather than relying solely on biblical interruptions, other Neptunists, such as German geologist Abraham Gottlob Werner, described the formation

(continues)

(continued)

of rock, such as granite and limestone, from an ocean that eventually receded. Neptunists also pointed to the shrinking of an original ocean to explain the existence and distribution of fossils. Despite evidence to the contrary, such as the existence of volcanic rocks that clearly formed from the cooling of molten lava, Neptunist theories persist into the early 19th century.

A third theory, Plutonism, was argued in the late 18th century, as Vulcanism fell out of favor. Rather than cite the existence of a hypothetical fluid that serves as the origin of rocks, like Vulcanists, *Plutonists* claim that *heat* alone brings about changes in the Earth. One prominent Plutonist, Scottish geologist James Hutton, claims that the immense heat at the *core* of the Earth causes different rocks and minerals to thrust up to the surface, forming landmasses and geological formations.

In addition to debating the source of changes in the Earth, scholars also debated the timing of such changes. Many early geologists were catastrophists, believing that the features of the Earth were the result of a single event,

again citing the flood described in the Bible. Over time, catastrophists, such as the 19th-century French naturalist Georges Cuvier, favor the notion that one or more sudden events, or catastrophes, led to physical changes in the Earth. Such a series of changes are used to explain the various sediments of rocks that naturalists find in the Earth. During the late 18th century, Scottish geologist James Hutton writes *Theory of the Earth,* in which he proposes that the Earth changed slowly over time, a theory known as *Uniformitarianism.* Over the next half century, scholars begin to adopt Hutton's view. In 1820, a follower of Hutton, Sir Charles Lyell, writes *Principles of Geology,* which influences a generation of naturalists, including Charles Darwin, who includes the idea that changes occur gradually over time in his theory of *evolution.* Today, the majority of geologists adhere to a Uniformitarian view of the geological changes, although many remain open to the possibility that one or more sudden changes have also influenced the formation of geological features.

argued over the *forces* that shape changes in the Earth. Some believed that water is the cause of geologic changes, while others argued that *heat* brings about changes in the Earth. In 1797, Scottish geologist Sir James Hall (1761–1823) lends support to the *Vulcanist,* and later the *Plutonist,* views of geologic change when he demonstrates that molten glass will form crystals if it is allowed to cool slowly.

(C, ES)

1798

Louis-Nicolas Vauquelin discovers chromium.

Chemists and mineralogists identified and isolated many *elements* during the 18th and

19th centuries. In 1798, French chemist Louis-Nicolas Vauquelin (1763–1829) studies a mineral known as Siberian red lead. He separates the lead from the sample and finds that the remaining material retained the red color. Vauquelin isolates the red substance and shows that it is an element. Vauquelin calls the element chromium to reflect its bright color. Today, scholars know that chromium gives some gemstones, including emeralds and rubies, their color.

(C, ES)

Henry Cavendish calculates the mass of the Earth.

Sir Isaac Newton described the way to calculate the gravitational *forces* between two objects (*See* entry for 1687). In 1798, English scholar

Henry Cavendish (1731–1810) uses measurements of gravitational forces to calculate the mass of the Earth. He arrives at a value close to the value accepted today. Cavendish also estimates the density of the Earth, stating it is more than five times denser than water.

(ES, P)

Louis-Bernard Guyton de Morveau liquefies ammonia.

While liquids and solids are relatively easy to study in the laboratory, investigations of the nature of the gaseous phase of matter require specialized techniques that were not available until the 18th century. For example, one can easily observe water freeze to form ice, then melt back to water, and finally boil to form steam. Yet, until the late 18th century, no one had been able to demonstrate that a gas could become a liquid. In 1798, French chemist Louis Bernard Guyton de Morveau (1737–1816) shows that, with sufficient chilling, the gas ammonia can be liquefied.

(C, P)

February 15

Louis-Nicolas Vauquelin identifies the element beryllium.

Beryllium is found in emeralds as well as a mineral called beryl. While the minerals that contain beryllium have been known for centuries, it was not until the 18th century that scientists identified it as an element. French mineralogist Louis-Nicolas Vauquelin worked with René-Just Haüy to analyze emeralds. On February 15, 1798, he announces that he has identified the element beryllium in these gemstones. The element eludes isolation until 1828.

(C)

1799

William Smith maps strata.

The Earth is made up of layers of rock known as *strata*. Geologists find different types of fossils when they look in different strata. In 1799, English engineer and geologist William Smith (1769–1839) draws a map describing the different strata found in a region of England. He shows that each stratum has different types of fossils. Using Smith's map, the approximate age of a fossil could be calculated based upon the stratum in which it was found.

(ES)

Humphry Davy demonstrates the uses of nitrous oxide.

During the 18th century, chemists developed methods to isolate and study gases. English chemist Humphry Davy tried to find medical uses for gases. In 1799, he studies nitrous oxide, known as laughing gas for its intoxicating effects. Experimenting on himself, Davy finds that long-term exposure to laughing gas causes a person to lose consciousness. Davy suggests that nitrous oxide can be used as an anesthetic. Despite his work, 40 years pass before surgeons start regularly administering the gas to patients.

(B, C)

Gaspard Monge outlines descriptive geometry.

Problems in geometry often have practical applications. During the late 18th century, French mathematician Gaspard Monge (1746–1818) studied methods to fortify a building so that it would not be directly exposed to a military attack. To solve this problem, he develops a method to represent three-dimensional objects on paper. His work, which marks the beginning of descriptive geometry, is outlined in the work *Géométrie descriptive* (Descriptive geometry, 1799).

(M)

July

French soldiers discover the Rosetta stone.

Our knowledge of ancient cultures comes from the discovery and study of artifacts found by archaeologists. The remnants of ancient Egypt contain inscriptions in hieroglyphics. In July 1799, the key to reading hieroglyphics is found when French soldiers discover the Rosetta stone. The stone contains the same passage written in two languages, Egyptian and Greek, using three different scripts: hieroglyphics, the common Egyptian script, and Greek letters. Scholars use the Rosetta stone to translate Egyptian hieroglyphics, a key step in understanding ancient Egypt.

(ES)

1800

Sir William Herschel discovers infrared radiation.

At the beginning of the 19th century, scientists studying light knew that it can be separated into a spectrum that appears to the eye as different colors. In 1800, English astronomer Sir William Herschel (1738–1822) studies the ability of light to change temperature. He notes that the greatest increase in temperature occurs outside of the *visible spectrum* of light. Herschel concludes that there are rays of light that the eye cannot see. Since the point in the spectrum is just beyond what appears red to the eye, the light he observes becomes known as *infrared radiation.*

(P, SA)

Marie-François-Xavier Bichat describes the organization of tissues.

Until the 19th century, biologists looked at the function of organs to understand how physiological processes take place. In 1800, French physiologist Marie-François-Xavier Bichat (1771–1802) argues that the tissues that make up the organs are essential for the organ to function properly. In his work *Traité des membranes* (Treatise on membranes), he shows that tissues differ in their structure and organization, and classifies them into 21

different categories. Bichat's work forms the basis for the modern study of histology.

(B)

Abraham Gottlob Werner classifies rocks by age.

The formation of layers of rock fascinated geologists in the 18th and 19th centuries. In 1800, German mineralogist Abraham Gottlob Werner (1750–1817) devises a system to classify rocks by their age and properties. His classification system relates rocks to their origins, the oldest stemming from the primordial sea, and the youngest formed from volcanic activity. Unlike some of his contemporaries who adhere, at least in part, to Christian teachings on the formation of the Earth, Werner takes a completely scientific view of rock formation and never mentions a supreme being in his work.

(ES)

Alessandro Volta develops the electric battery.

During the 18th century, physicists began to understand the movement of *electric current.* Italian physicist Alessandro Volta (1779–1804) was particularly interested in studies by Luigi Galvani showing that a frog's leg will move when it contacts two different metals (*See* entry for 1791). Volta believed that each metal has a different *electric potential,* creating a weak *electric current.* In 1800, he applies this principle to create the first electric battery, using the metals silver and zinc.

(P)

July

William Nicholson breaks apart water molecules by electrolysis.

For centuries, scholars and philosophers believed that all of matter was made from a pool of simple substance called *elements.* As late as the 17th century, many adhered to the ancient belief that water is one of these elements. However, experiments by Henry Cavendish and others (*See* entry for 1784) showed that water is actually a compound of hydrogen and oxygen. In July 1800, English chemist William Nicholson (1753–1815) uses *electricity* to break apart water molecules into *atoms* of hydrogen and water, by a process known as *electrolysis*.

(C)

1801

Jean-Baptiste de Lamarck suggests organisms change over time.

By the beginning of the 19th century, scholars were actively debating how the Earth changes over time, and biologists studying fossils noticed that the organisms of the past are not identical to their modern-day counterparts. In 1801, French biologist Jean-Baptiste de Lamarck (1744–1829) publishes *Système des animaux sans vertebras* (System for animals without vertebras), a work primarily concerned with classifying invertebrates. He discusses the origins of these simple creatures and suggests that changes in the environment over time lead to gradual changes in the organism's appearance.

(B)

Philippe Pinel studies mental illness.

For centuries, mental illnesses were not looked upon as physical diseases. During the 18th century, French physician Philippe Pinel (1745–1826) began to change that outlook. While treating patients in an insane asylum, he took into account a number of factors that could precipitate their illness, including heredity and emotional sensitivity. In 1801, Pinel describes his techniques and his method of classifying mental illness in *Traité medico-philosophique de l'aliénation mentale* (Medical-philosophical treatise on mental alienation). Today, Pinel is considered one of the founders of psychiatry.

(B)

René-Just Haüy describes the geometry of crystals.

Minerals take the form of beautiful crystals, with regular shapes and geometries. In 1801, French mineralogist René-Just Haüy (1743–1822) establishes the *geometry* and mathematics of *crystal* structure in his work *Traité de mineralogy* (Treatise on mineralogy). Haüy groups crystals into six categories based upon their symmetry and establishes that the form of the crystal is a reflection of its chemical composition.

(C, ES)

Johann Wilhelm Ritter discovers ultraviolet radiation.

At the beginning of the 19th century, physicists began to discover that the spectrum of light is larger than what can be viewed by the eye. In 1801, German scientist Johann Wilhelm Ritter (1776–1810) studies how light can break down a certain chemical compound. He separates light into its different components and notices that the most powerful part of the spectrum cannot be seen. Since the light Ritter discovers lies beyond the violet part of the spectrum, scientists call it *ultraviolet radiation*.

(P)

Thomas Young describes light traveling in waves.

Throughout the 18th century, Sir Isaac Newton's theory of the corpuscular nature of light (*See* entry for 1666) dominated the field of *optics*. In 1801, English physicist Thomas Young (1772–1829) presents experimental evidence that suggests light travels in waves. The wave theory of light, which explains many of its physical properties—including polarization, interference, and diffraction—is generally accepted until the birth of quantum mechanics calls the nature of light into question once again.

(P)

John Dalton states the law of partial pressures.

As the atmosphere is made up of a variety of gases, meteorologists are interested in the properties of this form of matter. In 1801, English meteorologist John Dalton (1766–1844) describes the pressure of mixtures of gases. In his law of partial pressures, he states that the pressure of a mixture of gases is equal to the sum of the pressures of each individual gas. His law assumes the gases each occupy the same volume. Today, this is known as Dalton's law of partial pressures.

(C, P, W)

January 1

Giuseppi Piazzi discovers the first asteroid.

The invention of the telescope at the beginning of the 17th century greatly expanded the understanding of the stars and planets. Italian astronomer Giuseppi Piazzi (1746–1826) used a telescope to determine the coordinates of stars. On January 1, 1801, he observes what appears to be a small planet, and names it Ceres. Soon more of these "small planets" are discovered in the same area, between Mars and Jupiter, and they are eventually reclassified as *asteroids*.

(SA)

November

Charles Hatchett discovers niobium.

As described in the sidebar "Discovering the Elements," scientists during the 18th and 19th centuries discovered many of the *elements* that make up matter. In 1801, English chemist Charles Hatchett (1756–1847) studies minerals that are part of the British Museum's collection. He analyzes one of the minerals, using a variety of chemistry techniques, and finds that it is made up of iron, manganese, and an unidentified metal. In November of the same year he announces

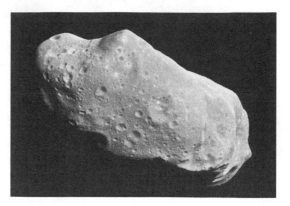

At the dawn of the 19th century, European astronomers begin to discover asteroids. This photograph, taken by cameras aboard the spacecraft *Galileo* on August 28, 1993, shows the asteroid Ida and its moon, Gaspra. *(NASA-JPL)*

his discovery. Today, the metal Hatchet isolated is known to be a mixture of two elements: niobium and tantalum.

(C)

1803

Luke Howard classifies clouds.

Throughout the 17th and 18th centuries, naturalists developed systems to classify a variety of rocks, plants, and animals. English meteorologist Luke Howard (1772–1864) was the first person to systematically classify clouds. In 1803, Howard proposes a classification system based upon the shape of clouds and altitude of clouds. He outlines the main types of clouds known today, including cumulus, stratus, cirrus, and nimbus.

(W)

Claude-Louis Berthollet describes the reversibility of chemical reactions.

The rules that govern chemical reactions were uncovered during the 18th and 19th centuries. In 1803, French chemist Claude-Louis

Berthollet (1740–1822) writes *Essai de statique chimique* (Essay on chemical statics). His work describes a number of basic concepts in chemistry, including the reversibility of chemical reactions. He outlines the factors that drive chemical reactions, including chemical affinity and the quantity of the *reactants*.

(C)

Jöns Jakob Berzelius and Wilhelm Hisinger discover the element cerium.

During the 18th and 19th centuries, chemists and mineralogist tried to identify *elements*. In 1803, Swedish chemists Jöns Jakob Berzelius (1779–1848) and Wilhelm Hisinger (1766–1852) work together to identify the element cerium. However, they were unable to obtain a pure preparation of cerium. In fact, cerium cludes isolation for nearly 75 years. Cerium belongs to the *lanthanide* series of elements, which were once known as the rare earth elements. Today, chemists recognize that cerium is far from rare; it is actually the 25th-most abundant element in the Earth's crust.

(C)

Smithson Tennant discovers iridium and osmium.

As described in the sidebar "Discovering the Elements," many of the *elements* that make up matter were identified during the 18th and 19th centuries. In 1803, English chemist Smithson Tennant (1761–1815) studies the element platinum. After making a solution of platinum, he finds a black residue. He treats the residue with *acids* and *bases* and finds

The 19th-century English meteorologist Luke Howard classifies clouds based on size and shape. This photograph, taken in 1949, depicts an anvil-shaped cumulonimbus cloud. *(Indianapolis Times/NOAA)*

that it can be separated into two elements. He calls the elements iridium and osmium.

(C)

William Hyde Wollaston discovers palladium and rhodium.

Chemists and mineralogists analyzing minerals that are found in mines discovered many of the *elements* that make up matter (See sidebar "Discovering the Elements"). In the early 19th century, English chemist William Hyde Wollaston (1766–1828) studied ways to extract the valuable metal platinum from different *alloys*. In 1803, he isolates two new metals from a platinum sample, using a series of chemical reactions. He calls one palladium, after the *asteroid* Pallas that was discovered the previous year. The second metal is named rhodium, for the color of its *crystals*.

(C)

October 21

John Dalton proposes modern atomic theory.

Throughout the 18th century, chemistry advanced rapidly as scientists found new *elements* and discovered how they combine to form more complex chemicals called compounds. In the late 18th century, French chemist Joseph-Louis Proust showed that compounds are made up of simple *ratios* of elements. English scientist John Dalton studied this and other work and realized that all matter must be made up of indestructible units. On October 21, 1803, Dalton presents his theory, calling his indestructible units of matter *atoms* after the atoms proposed by Greek philosopher Democritus (*See* entry for CA. 440 B.C.E.). Although 20th-century physicists showed that atoms are made of even smaller fundamental particles, Dalton's theory remains one of the most important in the history of science.

(C)

1804

Joseph-Louis Gay-Lussac and Jean-Baptiste Biot study the Earth's magnetic field from a balloon.

The development of the hydrogen balloon provided scientists with a valuable tool for studying the Earth and its atmosphere. In 1804, French scholars Joseph-Louis Gay-Lussac (1778–1850) and Jean-Baptiste Biot (1774–1862) travel in a hydrogen balloon and conduct scientific studies on their journey. During the voyage, they discover that the intensity of the Earth's *magnetic field* is constant up to elevations of 13,000 feet (4,000 m).

(ES, P)

1805

Sir William Herschel claims that the Sun is moving toward a specific point in space.

The invention of the telescope in the 17th century provided astronomers with the opportunity to observe the motion of distant stars. In 1805, English astronomer Sir William Herschel (1738–1822) studies the motion of the Sun in relation to a number of stars. He observes that the Sun appears to be moving toward the same point in space as the stars, suggesting that the solar system is actually traveling through space.

(SA)

Friedrich Sertürner isolates morphine from opium.

Physicians have used herbs and other plant products to treat disease for centuries. During the 19th century, scientists began to pinpoint the chemical components that make these herbs effective treatments. In 1805, German pharmacist Friedrich Sertürner (1783–1841) isolates what he calls "sleep-inducing factor" from an opium plant. The drug he isolates, now called morphine, is the first of many plant products to be purified by pharmacists.

(B, C)

1806

Louis-Nicolas Vauquelin isolates the first amino acid.

Just as compounds are made from simpler elements, biological molecules are synthesized from smaller components. *Proteins*, the molecules that perform most of the work in cells, are composed of many subunits called *amino acids*. In 1806, French chemist Louis-Nicolas Vauquelin (1763–1829) isolates an abundant compound from asparagus, and calls it asparagine. However, he does not know what role the compound plays in plant physiology. Today, scientists know that asparagine is one of 20 amino acids found in proteins.

(B, C)

1807

Jean-Baptiste-Joseph Fourier describes a Fourier series.

As described in the sidebar "Physics and Mathematics," scholars often needed to create new methods of mathematical analysis to describe physical phenomena. In the early 19th century, French scholar Jean-Baptiste-Joseph Fourier (1768–1830) was interested in describing how *heat* spreads through solids (*See* entry for 1822). He develops what is now known as the Fourier series to help solve the problems he encounters. A Fourier series describes *functions* that can be represented by the equation:

$$Y = a_0 + a_1 cos x + a_2 cos 2x + a_3 cos 3x.\text{-}.\text{-}.\text{-}.. + b_1 sin x + b_2 sin 2x + b_3 sin 3x$$

Fourier analysis continues to be used today.

(M)

Humphry Davy identifies chlorine as an element.

As described in the sidebar "Discovering the Elements," many *elements* were identified and isolated throughout the 18th and 19th centuries. While many were isolated after they were discovered, in some cases known substances were shown to be elements. Chlorine gas was first produced in 1774. However, chlorine was not shown to be an element until English chemist Humphry Davy identifies it as one in 1807. It takes nearly 10 years for his conclusion to gain wide acceptance.

(C)

Jöns Jakob Berzelius classifies compounds as organic and inorganic.

As chemists began to elucidate the structures of different compounds, they noticed that common chemicals, such as salts, are much simpler than compounds isolated from living organisms. In 1807, French chemist Jöns Jakob Berzelius (1779–1848) classifies all compounds as either *organic*—i.e., derived from living organism—or *inorganic*. Studies soon show that the organic compounds have carbon, and soon the definition evolved from compounds that are derived from living organisms to compounds that contain carbon, regardless of their origin.

(C)

October

Humphry Davy isolates sodium.

As described in the sidebar "Discovering the Elements," scientists from a variety of fields searched for new *elements* during the 19th century. Chemists devised methods to separate compounds into elements and analyzed their chemical composition. In October 1807, English chemist Humphry Davy passes an *electric current* through a solution containing the *base* sodium hydroxide. Using this technique, known as *electrolysis,* he isolates sodium.

(C)

October 6

Humphry Davy isolates potassium.

As described in the sidebar "Discovering the Elements," during the early 19th century chemists searched for the *elements* that make up all matter. English chemist Humphry Davy searched for elements by studying simple chemicals. On October 6, 1807, he passes *electricity* through a damp sample of a chemical called potash and isolates a previously unknown metal, now called potassium.

(C)

1808

Humphry Davy isolates elemental barium.

As described in the sidebar "Discovering the Elements," during the 19th century chemists began isolating pure forms of the *elements.* Barium is a metal that had been found in lead mines. In 1808, English chemist Humphry Davy isolates pure barium. He uses a techniques called *electrolysis,* which involves passing an *electric current* through a solution, in this case barium hydroxide. Today, scientists know that barium in the 14th-most abundant element on the Earth.

(C)

Humphry Davy shows that lime is made from the element calcium.

As described in the sidebar "Discovering the Elements," many *elements* were discovered and isolated during the 17th and 18th centuries. For many years, the compound known as lime was thought to be an element. In 1808, English chemist Humphry Davy shows that lime is, in fact, an oxide of the element calcium. He isolates pure calcium by passing an *electric current* through a solution contain-

ing lime, a technique known as *electrolysis.* Today, scientists know that calcium is the fifth-most abundant element in the Earth's crust.

(C)

Étienne-Louis Malus discovers polarized light.

Physicists studied the nature of light throughout the 18th and 19th centuries. In 1808, French scholar Étienne-Louis Malus (1775–1812) discovers *polarized light* while studying the *refraction* of light. He shows that when light passes through a *crystal* that is double refracting (*See* entry for 1669) and is then reflected by a mirror, only a single image is observed. He explains this phenomenon by saying that the light is separated into poles, thus calling it polarized light.

(P)

June

Scientists isolate boron.

Boron-containing compounds, such as borax, have been known since ancient times. However, elemental boron was not obtained until the 19th century. On June 21, 1808, French scientists Louis-Joseph Gay-Lussac and Louis-Jacques Thénard (1777–1857) report that they have isolated boron in the laboratory. Nine days later, on June 30, English chemist Humphry Davy independently reports similar findings.

(C)

1809

Jean-Baptiste de Lamarck proposes the acquired characteristic theory of evolution.

During the 19th century, biologists began to suggest that organisms change slowly over time, just as geologists had shown the Earth changes over time. One of the pioneers in such theories of *evolution* is French scholar Jean-Baptiste de Lamarck (1744–1829). In 1809, he proposes what is known as the acquired characteristic theory of evolution in his work *Philosophie zoologique* (Zoological philosophy). Lamarck suggests that organisms change characteristics in response to their environment, and that subsequent generations inherit these new characteristics.

(B)

Sir George Cayley describes aerodynamics.

As scholars understood more about *gravity* and other physical forces, the possibility of flight drew closer to reality. In 1809, English scientist Sir George Cayley (1773–1857) publishes the paper "On Aerial Navigation," outlining the physics of flight. Among the achievements of Cayley's work is the definition of the physical *forces* required for flight and the design of a functional glider. Today, Cayley is considered the father of aerodynamics.

(P)

1810

Franz Joseph Gall describes the brain.

By the 19th century, scientists recognized the central role that the brain plays in controlling physiological activities. In 1810, German physician Franz Joseph Gall (1758–1828) publishes *Anatomie et physiologie du système nerveux en general* (The anatomy and physiology of the nervous system in general), a treatise on the brain. Gall correctly identifies the function of gray matter, which is a network of nerves, and white matter. He also begins assigning functions to specific regions of the brain.

(B)

1811

Amedeo Avogadro describes the nature of gases.

During the 18th century, chemists began to understand the properties of gases. Gas laws developed by Robert Boyle and Jacques-Alexandre-César Charles described the behavior of gases, their temperature and pressure changes (*See* entry for 1662). In 1811, Italian scholar Amedeo Avogadro (1776–1856) states that two samples of gases that occupy the same volume and are kept at the same pressure and temperature have an equal number of particles. Today, this idea is known as Avogadro's hypothesis.

(C, P)

Bernard Courtois discovers iodine.

As described in the sidebar "Discovering the Elements," scientists discovered many of the *elements* that make up matter during the 19th century. In 1811, French chemist Bernard Courtois (1777–1838) manufactures gunpowder for the Napoleonic War. A critical step of the manufacturing process is extracting potassium salt from seaweed. After extracting the potassium, he adds *acid* to the sample and finds that a purple gas is released. He isolates the gas and proposes that it is a new element. Later experiments confirm his hypothesis, and the element is named iodine.

(C)

1812

Georges Cuvier claims species become extinct rather than evolve.

During the 19th century, scholars began questioning the biblical teachings describing the origins of life. However, some looked for scientific evidence that the Bible is correct. During this era, French naturalist Georges Cuvier (1769–1832) collects and catalogs fossils. He notes that the fossils found around the city of Paris did not resemble modern-day animals. He uses this observation to argue that the fossils represent species that become extinct rather than evolving into new species. In 1812, he publishes his work in *Recherches sur les ossemens fossils des quadrupeds* (Inquiry into fossil remains).

(B, ES)

Friedrich Mohs classifies minerals based on hardness.

Scientists develop systems to classify everything from clouds to fossils. In 1812, German mineralogist Friedrich Mohs (1773–1839) develops a system to classify minerals, based upon hardness. Mohs categorizes minerals by the hardest material that one can scratch, rather than by chemical composition. Although it takes a decade for his system to be widely accepted, the Mohs scale of mineral hardness is still in use today.

(C, ES)

1814

Joseph von Fraunhofer discovers spectral lines.

At the beginning of the 19th century, scientists interested in *optics* studied the spectrum of light. In 1814, German physicist Joseph von Fraunhofer (1787–1826) notices several dark lines while studying the spectrum of light as it passes through a fine prism. He maps the lines and notices that different patterns of lines are observed depending on the source of light. Today, the lines are known as *spectral lines*.

(P)

Augustin-Jean Fresnel explains polarized light.

Physicists interested in *optics* study the *refraction* of light through prisms as well as the *reflection* of light by mirrors. In 1808, Étienne Louis Malus showed that light can be polarized when it undergoes a double refraction followed by a reflection. In 1814, French physicist Augustin-Jean Fresnel (1788–1827) explains how the refraction of light results in polarization. Using the wave theory of light, Fresnel suggests that the prism separates light into two components: the vertical component and the horizontal component. These two components travel through the prism at different speeds, and thus emerge from the prism separately.

(P)

1815

Jean-Baptiste Biot shows that some molecules can rotate polarized light.

The three-dimensional structure of molecules refers to the spatial arrangement of atoms. Some *organic* molecules display chirality, meaning molecules with the same composition of atoms and arrangement of chemical bonds can have a different atomic arrangement in three-dimensional space. The first clue that chiral molecules exist comes in 1815, when French chemist Jean-Baptiste Biot (1774–1862) shows that some organic solutions can rotate *polarized light*. Biot classifies molecules as being either right-handed or left-handed depending upon the direction that they polarize light.

(C)

William Prout suggests that hydrogen is the fundamental atom.

As described in the sidebar "Discovering the Elements," scientists in the 18th and 19th centuries searched for the *elements* that make up matter. In 1815, English chemist William Prout (1785–1850) calculates the *atomic weight* of various elements and reports that they are all whole numbers. Since hydrogen is the smallest number, with an atomic weight of one, Prout suggests that it is the fundamental *atom* from which all other atoms are derived. While his hypothesis is incorrect, it inspires decades of research into the nature of atoms.

(C, P)

1816

René-Théophile-Hyacinthe Laënnec invents the stethoscope.

For centuries, physicians have evaluated a patient's overall health by listening to the heart and lungs. In 1816, French physician René-Théophile-Hyacinthe Laënnec (1781–1826) invents the stethoscope when he uses wooden tubes to magnify the sound of a patient's heartbeat. Laënnec becomes an expert in chest diseases, writing *De l'auscultation mediate* (On mediate auscultation), a treatise on the subject, in 1819.

(B)

Heinrich Brandes records pressure systems over Europe.

Modern weather forecasting relies upon the study of pressure systems. Polish scholar Heinrich Brandes (1777–1834) prepared the first maps of high and low pressure systems. In 1816, he begins generating maps based upon meteorological observations throughout Europe.

(W)

1817

Pierre-Joseph Pelletier and Joseph-Bienaimé Caventou isolate chlorophyll.

Plants capture *energy* from sunlight through a process known as *photosynthesis*. In 1817, French chemists Pierre-Joseph Pelletier (1788–1842) and Joseph-Bienaimé Caventou (1795–1877) isolate chlorophyll, which is the green pigment in plant leaves. At the time of their work, scientists know that green plants consume carbon dioxide and release oxygen. Later work shows that chlorophyll is an essential chemical for photosynthesis to occur.

(B, C)

Friedrich Strohmeyer discovers cadmium.

Analyzing compounds that contaminated preparations of other substances led chemists to discover many elements. In 1817, German chemist Friedrich Strohmeyer (1776–1835) studies a contaminant of the medically important chemical zinc oxide that causes it to turn yellow. He demonstrates that the yellow color is caused by a new element that he calls cadmium. Today, cadmium is considered an environmental pollutant. Not surprisingly, one of the main sources of cadmium release into the environment is zinc mines.

(C)

Johan August Arfvedson discovers lithium.

As described in the sidebar "Discovering the Elements," scientists during the 19th century discovered many of the *elements* that make up matter. In 1817, Johan August Arfvedson (1792–1841) analyzes minerals found on an island off of Sweden. He finds that they give off a bright red flame when treated with fire. He realizes that the color of the flame indicates the presence of a previously unknown element. Later work shows that the element, which Arfvedson calls lithium, is chemically similar to the element sodium, but it appears to be much lighter.

(C)

Jöns Jakob Berzelius discovers selenium.

As described in the sidebar "Discovering the Elements," 19th-century scientists raced to identify many of the *elements* that make up matter. In 1817, Swedish chemist Jöns Jakob Berzelius (1779–1848) studies the residue that is left behind in some glass vessels during the production of sulfuric acid. He shows that the residue contains a previously unidentified element. Berzelius calls it selenium because it behaves chemically like another element, tellurium.

(C)

1818

Jöns Jakob Berzelius determines atomic weights.

Advances in chemistry during the 18th century led to John Dalton's theory that all matter is made up of *atoms* (*See* entry for 1803). Dalton included a definition of the weight of a single atom of each element, known as the *atomic weight*. He set the atomic weight of hydrogen, the lightest element, as one, then determined the atomic weight of other elements experimentally. Swedish chemist Jöns Jakob Berzelius (1779–1848) also determined the atomic weights of elements. In 1818, he publishes accurate atomic weights for nearly all of the elements known at the time.

(C)

Charles Babbage conceives of a modern computer.

Since arithmetical calculations can often be cumbersome, mathematicians have designed a variety of devices, from the abacus to adding machines, to simplify the process. In 1818, English mathematician Charles Babbage (1792–1871) conceives of an adding machine that resembles modern computers. The analytical engine, as he calls it, would perform calculations of up to 20 decimal places, using a punch card system to code quantities. While Babbage never completed his machine, today it is considered a forerunner to the modern computer.

(M)

Jöns Jakob Berzelius develops a system of chemical symbols.

As scientists continued to discover the *elements* that make up matter, they also began to understand the chemical reactions that lead to the creation of new compounds. Soon, chemists realized that there needs to be a standard system of symbols to represent chemical reactions. In 1818, Swedish chemist Jöns Jakob Berzelius (1779–1848) devises a simple system to represent chemicals. He uses either one- or two-letter abbreviations for each element, and then denotes the number of atoms of a particular element present in the compound by a subscript numeral. For instance, carbon dioxide, which has one carbon atom and two oxygen atoms, is denoted as CO_2. Berzelius's system continues to be used today.

(C)

Henri Braconnot discovers glycine.

During the 19th century, chemists began to discover the molecules that are important for biological reactions. In 1818, French chemist Henri Braconnot (1780–1855) isolates a sweet-tasting substance from gelatin that he believes is a sugar. Further analysis shows that the chemical contains *atoms* of nitrogen, which are not found in sugars. The chemical he isolated, now called glycine, is one of 20 *amino acids,* which serve as building blocks for *proteins.*

(B, C)

English mathematician Charles Babbage conceives of a device resembling the modern computer at the beginning of the 19th century. His son builds Babbage's analytical engine, depicted here, in 1910. *(SPL/Photo Researchers, Inc)*

1819

Pierre-Louis Dulong and Alexis Thérèse Petit show that specific heat and atomic weight are related.

As chemists discovered more of the *elements* that make up matter, they tried to determine the *atomic weight* of each one. In 1819, French chemists Pierre-Louis Dulong (1785–1838) and Alexis Thérèse Petit (1791–1820) show that specific heat, or quantity of *heat* required to raise one gram of a substance by a single degree Celsius, is inversely proportional to its atomic weight. In other words, the heavier the *atom,* the less heat required to raise its temperature. The law of Dulong and Petit simplified the determination of atomic weights.

(C, P)

1820

Pierre-Joseph Pelletier and Joseph-Bienaimé Caventou isolate the drug quinine.

The infectious disease malaria is endemic in tropical regions of the world. Mosquitoes spread the disease, and many countries have reduced the number of cases by instituting insect control measures. During the 17th century, Europeans learned that Native Americans use the bark of the cinchona tree to treat the disease (*See* entry for 1638). In 1820, French chemists Pierre-Joseph Pelletier (1788–1842) and Joseph-Bienaimé Caventou (1795–1877) isolate the drug quinine from cinchona bark. Quinine is still used to treat malaria today.

(B, C)

Hans Christian Ørsted demonstrates electromagnetism.

Physicists in the 19th century began to understand the laws governing *electricity.* In 1820, Danish physicist Hans Christian Ørsted (1777–1851) makes a critical discovery when he links electricity to *magnetism.* Ørsted notices that an *electric current* will alter the direction of the needle of a compass. He finds that the needle will move away from the wire, forming a 90° angle. Ørsted's discovery is the first demonstration of *electromagnetism.*

(P)

André-Marie Ampère shows electromagnetism in wires carrying current.

During the 19th century, the relationship between *electricity* and *magnetism* was elucidated. After Hans Christian Ørsted demonstrated *electromagnetism* (*See* entry for 1820), physicists worked to confirm his observation. In 1820, French physicist André-Marie Ampère (1775–1836) shows that two wires carrying a current in the same direction attract each other, while those carrying a current in the opposite direction repel each other. Amprère's experiment serves as the basis of the electric motor.

(P)

Ignatz Venetz proposes that glaciers once extended into Europe.

As described in the sidebar "Theories of Geological Change," many 19th-century geologists were concerned with how structures in the Earth, such as mountains and valleys were formed. The movement of glaciers is known to cause dramatic changes in the Earth, including the formation of valleys and the mixing of *sediments.* In 1820, Swiss engineer Ignatz Venetz (1788–1859) proposes that glaciers had once reached into Europe, suggesting a time when the climate was far colder than it is now.

(ES)

1821

Michael Faraday describes magnetic fields.

Hans Christian Ørsted's demonstration of *electromagnetism* (*See* entry for 1820) set off a wave of experiments by physicists wishing to better understand the relationship between *electricity* and *magnetism*. In 1821, English physicist Michael Faraday (1791–1867) studies the effect of magnetism on *electric currents*. He introduces the concept of a *magnetic field* to explain his data. In Faraday's view, the magnetic field consists of the lines of *force* that lead to the interaction between the electric current and the magnet.

(P)

Augustin-Louis Cauchy describes complex analysis.

Mathematicians define an *imaginary number* as the square root of a negative number. The *real numbers* and imaginary numbers are both part of a system known as *complex numbers*. French mathematician Augustin-Louis Cauchy (1789–1857) studied the mathematics of complex numbers. In 1821, he publishes *Cours d'analyse*, (Course on analysis) describing how to perform algebraic operations, find limits, and define *functions* using complex numbers.

(M)

September 3

William Redfield describes storm winds.

Hurricanes are destructive storms characterized by strong winds. On September 3, 1821, American meteorologist William Redfield (1789–1857) observes a hurricane and notices that the winds travel in a counterclockwise direction. Thus he is the first to observe that these tropical storms are cyclones. Over the next eight years, he tests his theory by observing the pattern that objects are scattered by the storm. In 1831, he publishes his description of the whirlwind nature of hurricanes in the paper "Remarks on the Prevailing Storms of the Atlantic Coast of the North American States."

(W)

1822

Thomas Seebeck demonstrates thermoelectricity.

The 1820s saw a wave of experiments designed to understand *magnetism*. In 1822, German physicist Thomas Seebeck (1770–1831) studies the relationship between temperature and magnetism. He shows that when a circuit made up of two different metals is heated, a steel needle will be deflected away from the metals. Seebeck calls the phenomena thermomagnetism. However, as the relationship between *electricity* and magnetism became clearer, others realize that the magnetism was merely a by-product of the *electric current,* and that Seebeck actually observed the conversion of *heat* into electricity, which is now known as thermoelectricity.

(P)

Jean-Baptiste-Joseph Fourier uses mathematics to describe heat.

As described in the sidebar "Physics and Mathematics," physics and mathematics are intimately related. The 19th-century French scholar Jean-Baptiste-Joseph Fourier (1768–1830) devoted decades of his career to the study of *heat*. In 1822, he publishes his treatise on heat, *Théorie analytique de la chaleur* (Analytical theory of heat). In this work, Fourier uses *calculus* to describe how heat is transferred in solids.

(M, P)

Jean-Victor Poncelet describes projective geometry.

The ancient Greeks laid the foundations for *geometry*. During the 18th and 19th centuries, mathematicians reexamined the work of Euclid (*See* entry for CA. 300 B.C.E.) and other Greek scholars, and developed new ways to view geometry. In 1822, French mathematician Jean-Victor Poncelet (1788–1867) publishes *Traité des propriétés projectives des figure* (Treatise on the projective properties of figures). His work describes the attributes of figures that do not change when they are projected, and leads to an increase in the study of projective geometry.

(M)

Gideon Algernon Mantell and Mary Ann Mantell discover a dinosaur fossil.

Scientists collect and study fossils to help them develop theories on the origins of the Earth and of life. In 1822, English physician Gideon Algernon Mantell (1790–1852) and his wife, Mary Ann, find a group of fossilized teeth that resemble those of an iguana. Gideon Mantell describes the fossil, and calls it *Iguanodon*, in a paper published in 1825, "On the Teeth of the Iguanodon." Soon, his discovery is recognized as one of the first of the extinct reptiles known as dinosaurs.

(B, ES)

The study of dinosaurs begins in the mid-19th century when Gideon Algernon Mantell and his wife, Mary Ann, discover fossilized teeth that resemble an iguana. This photograph, taken in 1955, depicts a dinosaur fossil discovered in the United States. *(Department of the Interior. National Park Service Midwest Region)*

William Daniel Conybeare and William Phillips identify the Carboniferous period.
During the 19th century, geologists studied layers of fossils found in the Earth's *strata,* searching for clues about the origin of life. At first, the fossils associated with coal deposit garnered the most attention, with layers being mapped across Great Britain. Geologists William Daniel Conybeare (1787–1857) and William Phillips (1775–1828) call the time period corresponding to this layer of fossils the Carboniferous period. They describe their work in *Outlines of the Geology of England and Wales* (1822). Today, scientists recognize that the era spanned the period 354 million to 290 million years ago.

(ES)

Jean-Baptiste-Julian d'Omalius d'Halloy identifies fossils from the Cretaceous period.
Geologists classify fossils based upon the *stratum* where they are isolated. In 1822, Belgian geologist Jean-Baptiste-Julian d'Omalius d'Halloy (1783–1875) finds fossils in a chalky stratum near Paris. The fossils are believed to be the first identified from the geological period called the Cretaceous period. Today, scholars recognize the Cretaceous period as spanning the time between 144 million and 65 million years ago.

(ES)

1823

William Sturgeon invents the electromagnet.
The discovery of *electromagnetism* in 1820 (*See* entry for 1820) set off a wave of experiments designed to better understand the relationship between *electricity* and *magnetism.* In 1823, English scientist William Sturgeon (1783–1850) passes an *electric current* through copper wire wrapped around a metal bar and

shows that the current magnetizes the metal. In fact, his electromagnet, as it came to be called, can lift 20 times its own weight.

(P)

Adam Sedgwick identifies the Cambrian period.
Naturalists in the 18th and 19th centuries studied fossils found in *sediments* and grouped them by approximate age. In 1823, English naturalist Adam Sedgwick (1785–1873) studies the fossils found in some of the oldest known rocks in Wales. He names the era correlating to these fossils the Cambrian period, after the Latin name for Wales. Today, paleontologists have established that the Cambrian period began over 540 million years ago and lasted until 490 million years ago.

(ES)

1824

Augustin-Pyrame de Candolle classifies plants.
During the 18th and 19th centuries, scientists classified all forms of matter, from rocks to organisms. In 1824, Swiss botanist Augustin-Pyrame de Candolle (1778–1841) publishes the first volume of his treatise *Prodromus systematis naturalis regni vegetabilis* (Treatise on the classification of the plant kingdom). By 1839, the work expands to 21 volumes. Candolle describes the systemic classifications of plants, along with a discussion of plant evolution.

(B)

Nicolas-Léonard-Sadi Carnot analyzes heat engines.
The invention of the steam engine in the 18th century inspired physicists and engineers to investigate the scientific principles that govern their function. In 1824, French physicist Nicolas-Léonard-Sadi Carnot analyzes

the function of heat engines in his work *Réflexions sur la puissance motrice du feu et sur les machines propres à developer cette puissance* (On the motive power of fire). Carnot describes what is now known as a "Carnot engine," an idealized machine that can be used to calculate the maximum amount of work a heat engine can perform.

(P)

Niels Henrik Abel proves that is impossible to solve a quintic equation.

Some problems in mathematics persist for centuries. One such problem that eluded an answer is the solution to an equation that takes the form $ax^5 + bx^4 + cx^3 + dx^2 + ex + f = 0$, known as a quintic equation. In 1824, Norwegian mathematician Niels Henrik Abel (1802–29) proves in an article entitled "On the algebraic resolution of equations" that a quintic equation cannot be solved. Italian mathematician Paolo Ruffini publishes a similar work, which is now known as the Abel-Ruffini theorem.

(M)

Jöns Jakob Berzelius discovers silicon.

As described in the sidebar "Discovering the Elements," scientists identified many of the *elements* that make up matter during the 18th and 19th centuries. Some elements are isolated from substances that have been known since ancient times. For example, silica is an important compound that is used to manufacture glass. Before the 19th century, many scholars believed that it was an element. Humphry Davy later showed that this was not true, but he could not separate the compound into its components. In 1824, Swedish chemist Jöns Jakob Berzelius (1779–1848) shows that silica is in fact a compound, which includes new element, silicon.

(C)

February 20

William Buckland describes the first dinosaur fossil.

The 19th century was an active period for the study of fossils. During the early 1820s, English scholar William Buckland (1784–1856) finds part of the jaw and teeth of what appears to be an ancient reptile. On February 20, 1824, he presents his findings to the Geological Society of London and calls the animal *Megalosaurus*. Today, *Megalosaurus* is known to be the first dinosaur described by scientists.

(B, ES)

1825

September 17

George Stephenson demonstrates the steam locomotive.

By the early 19th century, steam engines were used to power everything from pumps to steamboats. Many inventors tried to devise ways to use them for land transportation as well. On September 17, 1825, English inventor George Stephenson (1781–1848) demonstrates a steam locomotive that can pull multiple cars and travel up to 16 miles (26 km) per hour, ushering in the era of the railroad. Today, Stephenson is considered the founder of the railways.

(P)

1826

Joseph-Diez Gergonne articulates the principle of duality.

During the 19th century, mathematicians devised new types of *geometry* that differed from the work of Euclid (*See* entry for CA. 300 B.C.E.). One of these, called *projective geometry*, is particularly useful for describing perspective. Like all geometries, projective geometry is based upon a set of *axioms,* or statements that are assumed to be true. In 1826, French mathematician Joseph-Diez Gergonne (1771–1859) notices that in projective geometry, the words *point* and *line* can be interchanged in any axiom. His observation is now known as the principle of duality.

(M)

Antoine-Jérôme Balard discovers bromine.

As described in the sidebar "Discovering the Elements," many of the *elements* that make up matter were discovered during the 18th and 19th centuries. In 1826, French chemist Antoine-Jérôme Balard (1802–76) analyzes seawater. During his investigations, he discovers bromine, an element that is closely related to two known elements, chlorine and iodine, also found in the salty waters of the sea. Scientists soon discover that bromine is abundant is seawater, which later becomes an important source for isolating bromine for commercial applications.

(C)

Karl Ernst von Baer discovers the mammalian egg.

Biologists studying development rely upon animal studies. By the early 19th century, physiologists found that reproduction occurs when sperm cells from the male fertilizes eggs from the female. However, eggs were not thought to be from mammals until 1826, when German biologist Karl Ernst von Baer (1792–1876) breaks open an ovarian follicle from a dog and discovers the egg cell inside. Baer's work shows that mammalian reproduction is not fundamentally different from the reproduction of lower animals.

(B)

1827

Georg Simon Ohm describes the flow of electric current.

Physicists in the 19th century performed a series of experiments to explain *electricity.* In 1827, German scientist Georg Simon Ohm (1789–1854) focuses his work on the flow of *electric current.* He shows that electric current is proportional to the *electric potential* between its origins and where it ends. Ohm further shows that the current is inversely proportional to the resistance, or *heat* produced while the current flows. Today, this work is known as Ohm's Law.

(P)

William Prout divides foods into four categories.

During the 19th century, chemists began to isolate specific chemicals from natural products and try to understand how they work. In 1827, English chemist William Prout (1785–1850) divides food into four categories, now called *carbohydrates,* fats, *proteins,* and water, based upon chemical compositions. Prout's categories remain in place today, and his work is the first step in understanding how the body derives energy from food.

(B, C)

Robert Brown observes intrinsic motion of particles.

Living things can power their own motion, but for many years it was assumed that particles remain stationary until an observation in the 19th century suggested otherwise. In 1827, English botanist Robert Brown (1773–1858) studies pollen grains suspended in a liquid and notices that they appear to be moving. He then performs a series of experiments that show that the motion is intrinsic to the pollen grain, and later that particles of dye display the same motion. The motion of particles, now known as "brownian motion" extends all the way to *atoms*.

(B, C, P)

of organic molecules to include carbon-containing molecules that are produced outside the body.

(C)

1828

Friedrich Wöhler synthesizes urea in the laboratory.

Swedish chemist Jöns Jakob Berzelius (1779–1848) classified molecules as either *organic,* produced by living systems, or *inorganic.* At the time, the chemical reactions studied in the laboratory involved inorganic molecules. In 1828, German chemist Friedrich Wöhler (1800–82) mixes two inorganic molecules together and unexpectedly synthesizes the organic molecule urea. His discovery demonstrates that organic molecules can be produced outside the body. Soon, other chemists expand the definition

1829

Nikolay Ivanovich Lobachevsky develops non-Euclidean geometry.

Euclid and other ancient Greek mathematicians excelled in the study of *geometry.* During the 17th and 18th centuries, European mathematicians began questioning the *postulates* that *Euclidean geometry* is based upon and developed new geometries based on new sets of assumptions. In 1829, Russian mathematician Nikolay Ivanovich Lobachevsky (1792–1856) develops *non-Euclidean geometry,* which he calls "imaginary geometry." He describes this new geometry in his 1835

GEOMETRIES OF THE NINETEENTH CENTURY

Euclidean geometry
Parallel lines never intersect.

Projective geometry
Any two lines intersect at a unique point.

Euclidean geometry
Given a line and point not on the line, there is one line going through the point that is parallel to the line.

Imaginary geometry
Given a line and point not on the line, there is more than one line going through the point that is parallel to the line.

© Infobase Publishing

Until the 19th century, most mathematicians studied Euclidean geometry based upon the axioms of the Greek mathematician Euclid (left). The 19th-century French mathematician Jean-Victor Poncelet replaces Euclid's assumption that parallel lines never intersect (top left) with the axiom that any two lines intersect at a unique point (top right), and develops projective geometry based upon this axiom. Russian mathematician Nikolay Ivanovich Lobachevsky challenges Euclid's axiom that there is only a single line going through a point that is parallel to a given line (bottom left). In his imaginary geometry, more than one line going through that point can be parallel to a given line.

work *Voobrazhaemaya geometriya* (Imaginary geometry).

(M)

Jöns Jakob Berzelius discovers thorium.

As described in the sidebar "Discovering the Elements," scientists analyzing minerals discovered many of the *elements* that make up matter. In 1829, Swedish chemist Jöns Jakob Berzelius (1779–1848) analyzes a mineral given to him by a collector and shows that it contains a new element, which he calls thorium. Berzelius then prepares a sample of pure thorium metal through a series of chemical reactions. At the end of the century, scientists show that thorium is radioactive.

(C)

Thomas Graham describes the diffusion of gases.

Gases and liquids mix by a slow process called *diffusion,* a process that depends upon the intrinsic motion of the molecules. In 1829, English scientist Thomas Graham (1805–69) studies the diffusion of gases. He shows that the rate of diffusion is inversely related to the density. Later work generalizes Graham's law to state that the velocity of a gas is inversely related to its *molecular weight.*

(C, P)

1830

Joseph Jackson Lister invents the achromatic microscope.

The invention of the microscope gave biologists a means to visualize organisms too small to see with the unaided eye. The resolution of such images, however, suffered because of fuzziness at higher magnifications. In 1830, English optician Joseph Jackson Lister (1786–1869) devises the achromatic lens, which allows scientists to view microscopic images with greater clarity. His

invention leads to an increased interest in microbiology research.

(B, P)

Sir Charles Lyell popularizes Uniformitarianism.

As described in the sidebar "Theories of Geological Change," 18th- and 19th-century scholars debated the way the Earth changes. Scottish geologist James Hutton proposed that changes in the Earth are the result of both water and fire, and occur gradually over time, a theory known as *Uniformitarianism* (*See* entry for 1785). At first, Hutton's theory is added to the ongoing debate on geological changes. Then, in 1830, British scholar Sir Charles Lyell (1797–1875) publishes *Principles of Geology,* effectively arguing in favor of Uniformitarianism. Lyell's work is so convincing that the argument is effectively settled, and his work influences the next generation of naturalists.

(ES)

February

Evariste Galois describes group theory.

While *algebra* has been studied since the Middle Ages, the solutions to certain types of equations remained elusive until the 19th century. In February 1830, a young French mathematician named Evariste Galois (1811–32) submits a paper describing how an equation can be solved by basic arithmetical operations (addition, subtraction, multiplication, division, or square roots). His paper lays the basis for the modern study of group theory.

(M)

1831

Michael Faraday discovers electric induction.

Nineteenth-century physicists studied the relationship between *electricity* and *magne-*

tism. Many focused on the magnetic properties of charged objects or wires carrying *electric current.* English physicist Michael Faraday focused his work on the effects of magnetism on electricity. In 1831, he demonstrates that a magnet can be used to generate electricity, a process known as electromagnetic induction. He studies the phenomenon and develops law of electromagnetic induction that describes the relationship between the electric current and the *magnetic field.*

(P)

Jöns Jakob Berzelius describes isomers.

Chemists use formulas to describe the proportion of chemicals that make up a compound. Swiss chemist Jöns Jakob Berzelius (1779–1848) cataloged these chemical formulas and by 1828 published the composition of nearly 2,000 different compounds. In 1831, he describes his discovery that two compounds with different chemical properties can have the same chemical formulas, and calls these pairs of chemicals *isomers.*

(C)

Joseph Henry invents the electric motor.

At the beginning of the 19th century, many physicists investigated the relationship between *electricity* and *magnetism.* In 1831, American physicist Joseph Henry (1797–1878) exploits the ability of electricity to induce a *magnetic field* when he invents the electric motor. Henry's motor uses an electric current to create a rotary motion that can be harnessed to perform work.

(P)

Nils Gabriel Sefström discovers vanadium.

During the 19th century, scientists discovered many of the *elements* that make up matter. Some were found while investigating the properties of other material. In 1831, Swedish chemist Nils Gabriel Sefström (1787–1854) tries to find out why some preparations of cast iron are brittle while other preparations are strong. Sefström finds that the brittle cast iron contains a small amount of a previously unknown element. He calls the new element vanadium.

(C)

June 1

Sir James Clark Ross reaches the north magnetic pole.

Compasses point toward the magnetic north pole, but the exact location of the pole was unclear for centuries. In 1831, English explorer Sir James Clark Ross (1800–62) travels beyond the Arctic Circle in search of the north magnetic pole. On June 1, he knows he has reached the north magnetic pole because his compass points straight down. The site is more than 2,000 miles (3,200 km) from the geographical North Pole, much farther than had been previously assumed.

(ES)

December 7

Charles Darwin sets sail on the HMS *Beagle.*

As described in the sidebar "Theories of Evolution," one of the most important scientific developments of the 19th century was English naturalist Charles Darwin's (1809–82) theory of *evolution.* Darwin's scientific career begins with a nearly five-year journey around the world aboard the HMS *Beagle.* He sets sail on December 7, 1831, on a voyage that takes him to South America, Australia, New Zealand, and Africa. During his trip, Darwin collects fossils, observes geological formations, plant and animal life, and witnesses a volcanic eruption.

(B, ES)

Darwin's voyage aboard the HMS *Beagle* takes him to the Galápagos Islands, where he gathers data for his theory of natural selection. *(NOAA)*

1832

Michael Faraday describes the process of electrolysis.

Salts are made up of charged particles called *ions*. During the process of *electrolysis,* ions are separated when an *electric current* is passed through a salt solution. In 1832, English physicist Michael Faraday studies *electrolysis*. He finds that during electrolysis, salt solutions break apart into ions. These ions then separate from one another, with the negatively charged particles migrating to the positive electrode and the positively charged ions moving toward the negative electrode. His works suggests that the electrical charges in a molecule are balanced.

(C, P)

1833

Anselme Payen and Jean-François Persoz isolate the first enzyme.

Enzymes are biological molecules that catalyze a wide range of reactions in cells. In 1833, French chemists Anselme Payen (1795–1871) and Jean-François Persoz (1805–68) isolate a substance from malt that can convert starch to sugar, and they call the substance distase. Today, scientists recognize that distase was the first enzyme isolated.

(B, C)

William Beaumont describes the process of digestion in humans.

Biologists often use animal models to understand physiological processes that occur in humans. In 1833, American physician William Beaumont (1785–1853) has the opportunity to observe digestion directly in the human stomach. He treats a patient who had been shot in the stomach. While the patient survives, the hole in his stomach remains, and Beaumont uses this opportunity to understand digestion. Over a period of 10 years, Beaumont studies the time it takes for different foods to be digested, the types of foods that irritate the stomach lining, and the chemistry of gastric juices.

(B)

Robert Brown describes the cell nucleus.

The invention of the microscope led to the discovery of cells. As microscopes became more powerful, scientists began to identify specific structures within cells. In 1833, English botanist Robert Brown publishes a study of orchid cells. He describes a structure found in all the cells he observes, and calls it the *nucleus*. In the next century, the nucleus will grow in prominence as the cellular structure that houses the cells' genetic material.

(B)

1834

Anselme Payen describes plant starches.

During the 19th century, chemists began isolating different substances from plants. The complex *carbohydrate* commonly called starch was found in all plants. In 1834, French chemist Anselme Payen analyzes starches from a variety of different plants and shows that they have the same chemical composition. In 1838, he isolates cellulose, the major carbohydrate in the woody tissues in plants.

(B, C)

Friedrich August von Alberti recognizes the Triassic period.

Geologists classify fossils found in various *strata* as belonging to distinct periods in the Earth's history. In 1834, German geologist Friedrich August von Alberti (1795–1878) describes three independent clusters of fossils that appear to belong to the same geological era, which he calls the Triassic period. Today, paleontologists recognize the Triassic period as spanning the period from 248 million years to 206 million years ago.

(ES)

Thomas Hussey proposes that another planet lies beyond Uranus.

Ancient astronomers knew five planets: Mercury, Venus, Mars, Jupiter, and Saturn. In 1781, English astronomer Sir William Herschel (1738–1822) (*See* entry for MARCH 1781) discovered a sixth planet, Uranus. Throughout the early 19th century, astronomers began finding previous records of the celestial body now known to be Uranus, and used these records to map the planet's orbit. They noted that its actual orbit differs from the orbit they predicted it should take. In 1834, Thomas Hussey proposes that yet another planet lies beyond Uranus, affecting its orbit. His proposal leads to the discovery of the planet Neptune (*See* entry for 1846).

(SA)

Charles Saint-Ange Thilorier prepares dry ice.

Matter can exist in three forms: gas, liquid, or solid. During the 19th century, scientists studied the transition between these phases. In 1834, French chemist Charles Saint-Ange Thilorier (1797–1852) cools the gas carbon dioxide, first to a liquid, and then to a solid. When the solid carbon dioxide is brought to room temperature, it does not melt to form the liquid. Instead, solid carbon dioxide

MAJOR GEOLOGICAL ERAS

Era	Period	Epoch	Age (Millions of years)	First Life Forms	Geology
Cenozoic	Quaternary	Holocene	0.01		
		Pleistocene	3	Humans	Ice age
		Pliocene	11	Mastodons	Cascades
		Neogene			
	Tertiary	Miocene	26	Saber-toothed tigers	Alps
		Oligocene	37		
		Paleogene			
		Eocene	54	Whales	
		Paleocene	65	Horses, Alligators	Rockies
Mesozoic	Cretaceous		135	Birds	Sierra Nevada
	Jurassic		210	Mammals	Atlantic
	Triassic		250	Dinosaurs	
Paleozoic	Permian		280	Reptiles	Appalachians
	Pennsylvanian		310		Ice age
				Trees	
	Carboniferous				
	Mississippian		345	Amphibians	Pangaea
				Insects	
	Devonian		400	Sharks	
	Silurian		435	Land plants	Laursia
	Ordovician		500	Fish	
	Cambrian		570	Sea plants	Gondwana
				Shelled animals	
Proterozoic			700	Invertebrates	
			2500	Metazoans	
			3500	Earliest life	
Archaean			4000		Oldest rocks
			4600		Meteorites

Investigations into the Earth's strata during the 19th century lead to the classification of the major geological eras. Later work has traced the emergence of different life-forms to each era.

transitions directly to the gas form, a process known as sublimation. Soon, solid carbon dioxide becomes known as dry ice.

(C)

1835

Gaspard-Gustave de Coriolis describes the flow of weather systems.

One of the differences between the Northern and Southern Hemispheres is that air and water currents move in opposite directions. In 1835, French scholar Gaspard-Gustave de Coriolis (1792–1843) explains that the flow of weather systems is affected by the rotation of the Earth. He notes that air and water currents cannot travel in a straight line because the rotation of the Earth will cause them to turn. In the Northern Hemisphere, currents turn to the right; in the Southern Hemisphere, they turn to the left. Today, this effect is known as the Coriolis effect.

(W)

1836

Theodor Schwann discovers enzymes in animals.

Enzymes catalyze a wide array of reaction in biological systems. In 1833, Anselme Payen and Jean-François Persoz discovered the first enzyme, distase, which catalyzes the conversion of starch to sugar. Three years later, German physiologist Theodor Schwann (1810–82) isolates an enzyme pepsin from the stomach lining of an animal. Pepsin is an important enzyme in the digestion of dietary *proteins* in the stomach.

(B, C)

John Frederic Daniell invents the zinc-copper battery.

During the 19th century, many physicists investigated the properties of *electricity*.

The invention of the battery by Alexander Volta (*See* entry for 1800) gave scientists a source of electricity, but Volta's battery could not maintain a constant current. In 1836, English scientist John Frederic Daniell (1790–1845) introduces a new tool for electrical research when he invents the zinc-copper battery, or Daniell cell as it came to be called. Daniell's battery maintains a constant and continuous current, making electricity available both for scientific experiments and as a power source for new technologies.

(P)

Charles Cagniard de la Tour shows that yeast is a living organism.

Cultures throughout history have fermented sugars to produce alcohol. During the 19th century, chemists began studying the chemistry of this process. In 1836, French physicist Charles Cagniard de la Tour (1777–1859) studies *fermentation* by brewer's yeast, a process used to make beer. He correctly deduces that the yeast is a living organism that releases carbon dioxide and alcohol as byproducts of fermentation.

(B)

1837

Jan Evangelista Purkinje describes nerve cells.

The invention of the microscope in the 17th century and subsequent improvements in the technology gave 19th-century biologists a powerful tool to explore the physiology of various organisms. In 1837, Czech biologist Jan Evangelista Purkinje (1787–1869) studies the cells of the nervous system. He discovers large nerve cells with branching extensions that originate in the cerebral cortex. Today, these cells are known as Purkinje cells.

(B)

René-Joachim-Henri Dutrochet describes photosynthesis.
Plants convert sunlight into usable *energy* through a process known as *photosynthesis*. Chemists isolated the green pigment from plant leaves, called chlorophyll, in 1817 (*See* entry for 1817). In 1837, French scholar René-Joachim-Henri Dutrochet (1776–1847) shows that only cells that contain chlorophyll are capable of performing photosynthesis. His work leads to the discovery that nonplant cells, such as algae, that contain chlorophyll also get their energy from photosynthesis.

(B)

1838

Mathias Jakob Schleiden states that plants are made of cells.
Robert Hooke first identified cells while viewing cork under a microscope and noting that it divides into discrete units. In the 19th century, Robert Brown described a structure in plant cells he called the *nucleus*. In 1838, German botanist Mathias Jakob Schleiden (1804–81) provides a description of plant cells, stating that a cell forms around a nucleus. His work *Beiträge zur phytogenesis* (Contributions of phytogenesis) describes his theory of the genesis of plant cells, and today is considered one of the seminal works in the development of cell theory.

(B)

Robert Remak describes how nerve cells and nerve fibers are connected.
The nervous system is responsible for transmitting information from the brain to the various organs and muscles of the body. By dissecting animals, anatomists observed nerve fibers attached to muscles and nerve cells in the brain and spinal cord. In 1838, German physiologist Robert Remak (1815–65) realizes that the nerve fibers and nerve cells are actually connected.

(B)

Gerardus Johannes Mulder describes proteins.
During the 19th century, scientists began to identify the molecules that are essential for life. One particularly important class of molecules, *proteins*, plays a vital role in all cells. In 1838, Dutch chemist Gerardus Johannes Mulder (1802–80) describes an abundant substance in cells that is composed of carbon, oxygen, and nitrogen. Mulder correctly believes that these substances, which he calls proteins, are essential building blocks of cells.

(B, C)

Fall

Friedrich Wilhelm Bessel accurately measures the distance from Earth to a star.
Astronomers have studied stars for centuries; however, the first accurate calculation of the distance between the Earth and a star was not made until the 19th century. In the 1830s, German astronomer Friedrich Wilhelm Bessel (1784–1846) begins observing the movement of a relatively small star. After 18 months of observations, he calculates the distance between the star and the Earth. Bessel publishes his results in fall 1838.

(SA)

1839

Theodor Schwann proposes cell theory.
Biological organisms are made up of one or more cells that perform the various functions that are essential to life. While Robert Hooke first identified cells when he examined cork under the microscope, modern cell theory was not born until the 19th cen-

tury. In 1839, German physiologist Theodor Schwann proposes that every living thing is made up of cells in his work *Mikroskopische untersuchungen über die übereinstimmung in der struktur und dem wachstum der thiere und pflanze* (Microscopic researches on the conformity in structure and growth between animals and plants).

(B)

Christian Friedrich Schönbein discovers ozone.

Ozone, a chemical made up of three oxygen *atoms,* is a major component of the upper atmosphere known as the *ozone layer.* Ozone gas is first identified in 1839 by German chemist Christian Friedrich Schönbein (1799–1868). Schönbein identifies the new gas based upon its distinctive smell, but he does not uncover its chemical composition.

(C)

Sir Roderick Murchison describes the Silurian period.

During the early 19th century, naturalists studied fossils found in *sediments* of rock and classified them based upon their approximate age. During the 1820s, Adam Sedgwick and Sir Roderick Murchison (1792–1871) look for fossils below previously studied sediments. They discover a group of fossils that contain no fossilized land plants. They call the period Silurian after an ancient Roman tribe. Murchison publishes *The Silurian System,* describing the fossils of this age, in 1839. Today, paleontologists have determined that the Silurian period began about 443 million years ago and lasted until 417 million years ago.

(ES)

John William Draper takes a photograph of the Moon.

During the 19th century, scientists developed methods of capturing light images on paper and set off a wave of research into photography. One of the earliest applications of photography to scientific research occurs in 1839, when American chemist John William Draper (1811–82) takes a photograph of the Moon. Today, astronomers can study a wide range of celestial bodies using photographs taken with the aid of powerful telescopes.

(P, SA)

Charles Goodyear vulcanizes rubber.

The rubber products of today can withstand large shifts in temperature because they undergo a process known as vulcanization. In 1839, American inventor Charles Goodyear (1800–60) discovers how to vulcanize rubber when he leaves a mixture of sulfur and rubber near a hot stove. He finds that the rubber remains flexible in cold weather. Goodyear's process expands the uses of rubber, and soon it becomes an important industrial product.

(C)

Sir William Grove devises the gas battery.

During the 19th century, scientists studied the properties of *electricity.* In 1839, English scholar Sir William Grove (1811–96) devises a fuel cell that generates electricity by burning hydrogen and oxygen gasses. Because Grove's fuel cell couples the generation of *energy* to the burning of gases, it is often called the gas battery.

(P)

Sir Charles Lyell identifies the Pleistocene period.

During the 19th century, scholars began studying the layers of fossils that can be found in *sediments* and classifying them by date. In 1839, English naturalist Sir Charles Lyell (1797–1875) proposes that the fossils found just below the volcanic rocks at the surface of some sediments be grouped together as belonging to the Pleistocene period. Lyell finds fossils of marine animals in this layer of *stratum* while looking for fossils in Italy. Today, scholars have determined that the Pleistocene period began 1.8 million years ago and lasted until 10,000 years ago.

(ES)

January

Carl Gustav Mosander discovers lanthanum.

During the 19th century, chemists discovered a number of *elements* known as the rare earth elements or *lanthanides*. Many are isolated from preparations of other lanthanides that were previously thought to be pure. In January of 1839, Swedish chemist Carl Gustav Mosander (1797–1858) analyzes a sample of the lanthanide cerium. He finds that it is contaminated with another element, which he called lanthanum. Later scientists isolate a number of other lanthanides from lanthanum. Today, scholars know that lanthanum is the lightest of the lanthanides, and thus gives the group of elements its name.

(C)

August 19

Louis-Jacques-Mandé Daguerre demonstrates photography.

During the early 19th century, French inventor Louis-Jacques-Mandé Daguerre (1789–1851) used his knowledge of chemistry to invent a process that will permanently record images. When he exposed plates coated with light-sensitive chemicals to light, he found they can capture images. Daguerre worked for many years to find the correct combination of chemicals that would create clear images, known as photographs. News of his work spreads to the French Academy of Science, and they announce the invention of photography on August 19, 1839.

(P)

1840

James Prescott Joule describes the conservation of energy.

One of the fundamental laws of nature is that *energy* cannot be created or destroyed; it is instead converted from one form to another. English scientist James Prescott Joule (1818–89) develops the law of conservation of energy in 1840. Through a series of precise measurements of energy in the form of *heat* and work, Joule comes to understand that it is neither created nor destroyed. Today, units of energy are called joules in his honor.

(C, P)

Germain Henri Hess studies the heat released in chemical reactions.

Chemical reactions either generate or consume *heat*. In 1840, Russian chemist Germain Henri Hess (1802–50) studies the heat released when an *acid* is neutralized. He shows that the same amount of heat is generated, regardless of how the chemical reaction occurs. His conclusions, now known as Hess's law of constant heat summation, lay the groundwork for the study of *thermodynamics*.

(C, P)

Sir Roderick Murchison and Adam Sedgwick identify fossils from the Devonian period.

During the 19th century, geologists began to study fossils from different layers of *sediments*, grouping them by age. In 1840, English geologists Sir Roderick Murchison (1792–1871) and Adam Sedgwick (1785–1873) study fossils in Devonshire, England. They discover a new layer in a *stratum* of slate. They name the period Devonian after the town where the fossils are discovered. Today, paleontologists refer to the Devonian period as the time spanning 417 million years to 454 million years ago.

(ES)

Carl Ernst Claus isolates ruthenium.

During the 19th century, scientists analyzing the components of different ores discovered many *elements*. Many chemists analyzed platinum ores, which led to the discoveries of rhodium, palladium, osmium, and iridium. In 1840, Russian chemist Carl Ernst Claus purifies a fifth element from platinum ores. Today, the metal is known as ruthenium.

(C)

1841

Jean Louis Rodolphe Agassiz describes ice ages.

Geologists try to understand how landmasses are formed and change over time. Glaciers, slow-moving masses of ice, extend and recede, moving land along with them. Such movement often leads to the formation of valleys and large rocks. In 1820, American naturalist Jean Louis Rodolphe Agassiz (1807–73) heard of Ignatiz Venetz's theory that glaciers once extended into Europe. Agassiz began a study of the effects of glaciers, looking for evidence that during a past ice age Europe was covered with them. In 1841, he publishes his results in *Untersuchungen über die gletscher* (Studies on glaciers).

(ES)

Sir Roderick Murchison identifies the Permian period.

During the mid-19th century, geologists classified fossils found in layers of rock based upon their relative age. English scholar Sir Roderick Murchison (1792–1871) played a central role in the identification of fossils from many different ages in England and Wales. In 1841, he travels to the Ural Mountains in Russia and discovers a new layer of fossils that had not been found in the British Isles. He calls the fossils from this period Permian, after the town of Perm near the site

where they are found. Today, paleontologists know that the Permian period began approximately 290 million years ago and ended about 248 million years ago.

(ES)

August 2

Sir Richard Owen classifies fossils as dinosaurs.

Scholars began to identify fossils of ancient reptiles during the 19th century (*See* entries for 1822 and 1824). English anatomist Sir Richard Owen (1804–92) studied these fossils and concluded that they came from giant reptiles. In an address given on August 2, 1841, he proposes that the fossils be grouped into a new subclass of reptiles. He calls the group *Dinosauriai*, meaning terrible lizard. Soon after Owen's address, dinosaur fossils are discovered throughout the world.

(B, ES)

1842

Sir John Bennet Lawes and Sir Joseph Henry Gilbert identify a chemical fertilizer.

Advances in chemistry and biology often find important application in the field of agriculture. In the 1840s, chemists looked for the components in manure that make it an effective fertilizer. In 1842, English agricultural chemists Sir John Bennet Laws (1814–1900) and Sir Joseph Henry Gilbert (1817–1901) identify nitrogen as a critical chemical in fertilizer. Using nitrogen, they develop and patent the first chemical fertilizer, which changes the way crops are grown.

(B, C)

Christian Doppler explains the Doppler effect.

When you hear a whistle of a train moving toward you, it appears to change in pitch, sounding higher as it approaches and lower as it moves away, a classic example of the *Doppler effect*. In 1842, Austrian scientist Christian Doppler (1803–53) describes the Doppler effect. He notes that the observed frequency of waves, specifically sound waves and light waves, changes if either the source or the observer is moving.

(P)

Charles Darwin classifies coral reefs and describes the formation of atolls.

During his famous voyage aboard the HMS *Beagle,* English naturalist Charles Darwin (1809–82) had an opportunity to examine the growth of coral. At the time, the prevailing theory stated that corral grows around the rims of underwater volcanoes.

Through his observations, Darwin showed this is not true. He classifies corral into three classes: atolls, barrier reefs, and fringing reefs. He presents his study of coral in the 1842 work *The Structure and Distribution of Corral Reefs.*

(B, ES)

1843

Samuel Heinrich Schwabe describes the cycling of sunspots.

Sunspots appear on the Sun at regular intervals. The first scientific confirmation that sunspots go through cycles comes in 1843, when German pharmacist and amateur astronomer Samuel Heinrich Schwabe (1789–1875) publishes the results of a 17-year study

English naturalist Charles Darwin completes a study of coral reefs during his famed voyage on the HMS *Beagle. (Mike White/Florida Keys National Marine Sanctuary/NOAA)*

of the surface of the Sun. He estimates the cycle of sunspot appearance and disappearance to be 10 years. Later studies show the interval to be closer to 11 years.

(SA)

Carl Gustav Mosander discovers erbium and terbium.

During the 19th century, a number of new *elements* were discovered in mines. The rare earth elements, now called *lanthanides,* proved to be challenging to identify. In 1843, chemist Carl Gustav Mosander analyzes samples of the metal yttrium. He finds that it can be separated into two different elements, which he calls erbium and terbium. However, chemists later find these preparations are also contaminated with other rare earth metals, extracting ytterbium and scandium from samples of erbium.

(C)

Arthur Cayley develops geometry in three or more dimensions.

The ancient Greeks laid the foundations for *geometry.* During the 18th and 19th centuries, mathematicians reexamined the work of Euclid (*See* entry for CA. 300 B.C.E.) and other Greek scholars and developed new ways to view geometry. In 1843, English mathematician Arthur Cayley develops methods to study geometry in more than three dimensions.

(M)

October 16

Sir William Hamilton develops algebra for complex numbers.

During the 17th century, mathematicians began to consider *imaginary numbers,* which are the square root of negative numbers. The *real numbers* and imaginary numbers are both part of the number system known as *complex numbers.* In 1843, Irish mathematician Sir William Hamilton (1805–65) develops an *algebra* for complex numbers. He introduces the concept of quaternions, a set of symbols that allow operations in what is now known as noncommunative algebra.

(M)

1844

Friedrich Wilhelm Bessel proposes that in some pairs of binary stars only one is visible.

The invention of the telescope led to the discovery of pairs of stars that have gravitational influence over one another, called *binary stars.* In 1844, German astronomer Friedrich Wilhelm Bessel (1784–1846) notes that some stars appear to be under the influence of a second star, but no other star is visible. He proposes that such stars are part of a binary pair, where one star is nearing extinction and thus not visible from the Earth.

(SA)

May 24

Samuel Morse transmits a telegraph message from Washington, D.C., to Baltimore, Md.

During the 19th century, the ability to communicate over long distances was revolutionized by the invention of the telegraph. American inventor Samuel Morse (1791–1872) developed the device, which uses electromagnetic impulses to transmit messages across a wire. Morse also developed a language for telegraphic communications, known as Morse code. On May 24, 1844, Morse demonstrates the usefulness of the telegraph by transmitting a message from Washington, D.C., to Baltimore, Md., a distance of 40 miles (64 km).

(P)

1845

William Parsons observes spiral nebula.
During the 19th century, astronomers built powerful telescopes and discovered new celestial bodies. In 1845, Irish astronomer William Parsons (1800–67) builds a large telescope and uses it to study celestial bodies known *nebulae*. With the unaided eye, nebulae resemble clouds, but using a telescope Parsons could describe their structure. He becomes the first person to observe a nebula with a spiral shape, eventually identifying 15 spiral nebulae.

(SA)

September

John Couch Adams and Urbain-Jean-Joseph Leverrier predict the existence of Neptune.
Ancient astronomers knew five planets: Mercury, Venus, Mars, Jupiter, and Saturn. After the official discovery of a sixth planet, Uranus, astronomers uncovered previous sightings of the planet. They used these records to plot its orbit, and noted that it differed from the one they predicted. Some proposed that the orbit of Uranus is influenced by another planet (*See* entry for 1834). In September 1845, English astronomer John Couch Adams (1819–92) and French astronomer Urbain-Jean-Joseph Leverrier (1811–77) independently study the orbit of Uranus and calculate the location of a new planet. The planet they predict is now known as Neptune.

(SA)

1846

Sir William Thomson calculates the age of the Earth.
Scientists have used many different methods to estimate the age of the Earth. In 1846, English scholar Sir William Thomson (1824–1907), also known as Lord Kelvin, estimates that the Earth is 100 million years old. He calculates the age of the Earth based upon the current temperature, assuming that the Earth was once part of the Sun, and has been cooling since it was separated.

(ES)

Heinrich Rose isolates tantalum.
Scientists analyzing minerals found in mines discovered many of the *elements* that make up matter. Minerals are made up of a number of different elements, making their separation challenging. For example, minerals containing the element tantalum often also have significant quantities of the chemically similar element niobium. For years, many scientists believed that they were the same chemical. In 1846, German chemist Heinrich Rose (1795–1864) isolates tantalum from niobium, proving that they are two distinct elements.

(C, ES)

September 23

Johann Galle discovers Neptune.
Ancient astronomers observed five planets: Mercury, Venus, Mars, Jupiter, and Saturn. A sixth planet, Uranus, was discovered during the 18th century, using a telescope. Two astronomers, John Couch Adams and Urbain Jean Joseph Leverrier, independently studied the orbit of Uranus. They each predicted the existence of a seventh planet and calculated its position in the sky (*See* entry for SEPTEMBER 1845). On September 23, 1846, German astronomer Johann Galle (1812–1910) uses Leverrier's calculations to discover the planet Neptune.

(SA)

October 14

William Morton demonstrates the use of ether as an anesthesia.
Until the 19th century, patients were given alcohol or painkillers before surgery, but

they were not always effective in dulling the extreme pain. In the 1840s, inhaling gases such as nitrous oxide, or laughing gas, became popular, and people noticed that they did not feel pain if they were injured while high on gas. In 1846, American dentist William Morton (1819–68) intends to use laughing gas to ease the pain of dental surgery, but the pharmacist has none, so he uses ether instead. When the patient feels no pain, Morton realizes the ether could be useful in all types of surgeries. On October 14 of that year, he demonstrates the use of ether in a surgical theater at Massachusetts General Hospital. Soon after, ether becomes a critical part of surgical procedures.

(B)

1847

George Boole introduces symbolic logic.
In 1847, English mathematician George Boole (1815–64) developed a method to represent logic using algebraic expressions. He introduces the symbols and rules of his system in *Mathematical Analysis of Logic*. His system, now known as Boolean *algebra*, is critical to computer programs.

(M)

July 23

Hermann von Helmholtz describes the mathematics of the conservation of energy.
During the 19th century, many of the laws that govern chemical reactions were elucidated. Using careful measurements, English scientist James Joule demonstrated that *energy* is neither created nor destroyed when work is performed. On July 23, 1847, German scholar Hermann von Helmholtz reads his paper "Über die erhaltung der kraft" (On the conservation of force) describing the conservation of energy in mathematical terms.

Today, his work is considered a statement of the first law of *thermodynamics*.

(C, P)

1848

Louis Pasteur discovers chiral molecules.
Atoms come together to form molecules. The function of a molecules depends upon the three-dimensional arrangement of atoms. During the 1840s, French chemist Louis Pasteur (1822–95) studies the effects of *polarized light* on different molecules. He finds that two molecules that have the same chemical structure and form identical *crystals* rotate polarized light into different directions. Pasteur's study shows that the two molecules are mirror images of each other. The molecules, which differ only in the three-dimensional arrangement of atoms, are said to be *chiral* molecules. The chirality of a molecule is an important component of the biological activity.

(C)

Sir William Thomson describes absolute zero.
Scientists studying the behavior of gases discovered that there is a relationship between the volume of gas and its temperature. In 1843, English scholar Sir William Thomson, also known as Lord Kelvin, proposes that the volume of a gas is related to its *energy*. He believes that if the temperature is low enough, the gas will lose its energy. He calls this temperature *absolute zero* and calculates it to be −523°F (−273°C). Kelvin devises a new temperature scale with that point serving as zero. This "Kelvin scale" continues to be used by scientists today.

(P)

Armand-Hippolyte-Louis Fizeau applies Doppler effect to all waves.
Christian Doppler first articulated the *Doppler effect*, describing how the frequency of a

wave shifts if either the source of the waves or the observer moves, in 1842 (*See* entry for 1842). Doppler primarily described the shift in sound waves. In 1848, French physicist Armand-Hippolyte-Louis Fizeau (1819–96) describes Doppler shifts in the spectrum of light emanating from stars. His work confirms that the Doppler effect applies to all types of waves, and the study of shifts in *spectral lines* becomes an important tool in astronomy.

(P, SA)

1849

Édouard-Albert Roche explains the origin of Saturn's rings.

The discovery of Saturn's rings in the 17th century led many astronomers to develop theories on how they formed. In 1849, French scholar Édouard-Albert Roche (1820–83) states that the rings were once a satellite orbiting Saturn. Roche argues that a satellite held in place by *gravity* can break apart, and the particles will continue to orbit the planet. In the 1850s, James Maxwell mathematically confirms Roche's theory.

(P, SA)

1850

Eilhardt Mitscherlich describes bacteria infecting plants.

As described in the sidebar "Finding the Microorganisms that Cause Disease," biologists in the 19th century began to pinpoint the cause of many infectious diseases. In 1850, German chemist Eilhardt Mitscherlich studies diseased potatoes. He notes that the cell walls of diseased potatoes are degraded. After finding no evidence of a fungal infection, Mitscherlich proposes that *bacteria* cause the disease.

(B)

Rudolf Clausius introduces the concept of entropy.

During the 19th century, many physicists studied the nature of *energy* and its ability to perform work. In 1850, German physicist Rudolf Clausius (1822–88) lays the basis for the field of *thermodynamics* when he describes the concept of *entropy*. Clausius defines entropy as the extent that energy that can be converted to work. In his view, higher entropy means that less work can be performed. He states that entropy of a system continually grows, and thus the amount of work that can be done continually decreases. His work forms the basis for what is now known as the second law of thermodynamics.

(C, P)

Jean-Bernard-Léon Foucault calculates the speed of light.

Since the Renaissance, scientists have tried to determine the speed at which light travels. In 1850, French physicist Jean-Bernard-

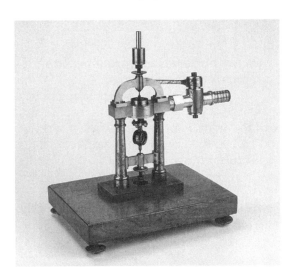

Model of the apparatus used by French scientist Jean-Bernard-Léon Foucault to calculate the speed of light in 1850. Paul Gustave Froment made this apparatus, in Paris ca. 1855. *(Museum of the History of Science, Oxford)*

Léon Foucault (1819–68) measures the speed of light to within 1 percent of the value used today. Foucault improves upon a method developed by Armand-Hippolyte-Louis Fizeau. Their methods involve calculating the velocity of light as it travels between two mirrors placed on different hilltops. Foucault later sets up a similar system under water, and shows that the speed of light in water is lower than the speed of light in air.

(P)

Macedonio Melloni shows that infrared radiation has the properties of light.

During the 19th century, physicists studying the spectrum of light noted that there appears to be light outside of the *visible spectrum.* One type, known as *infrared radiation* or *heat* rays, can transfer heat better than visible light. In 1850, Italian physicist Macedonio Melloni (1798–1854) studies infrared radiation and shows that it has all the properties of visible light.

(P)

November

James Joseph Sylvester introduces the term *matrix* to mathematics.

In mathematics, a *matrix* is a rectangular array of numbers. While the use of matrices dates back to the study of *magic squares,* it was not until the 17th century that mathematicians began to seriously consider the study of its use. Mathematician James Joseph Sylvester (1814–97) introduces the mathematical term *matrix* in the paper "On a New Class of Theorems" in November 1850.

(M)

✑ CONCLUSION ✑

By the middle of the 19th century, scientists developed theories to explain phenomena as small as the generation of an *electric current,* and as large as the formation of landmasses. In the next 50 years, these theories will be reexamined, refined, and expanded. For example, English scholar James Maxwell puts the concept of *electricity* and *magnetic fields,* proposed by English physicist Michael Faraday, into a mathematical context. Subsequent studies of electricity lead to the discovery of the *electron* at the end of the 19th century, an important milestone on the road toward understanding the structure of the *atom.* Advances made in the field of geology also lay the groundwork for subsequent studies, such as the determination of the geologic time scale. During the 19th century, Earth scientists and naturalists map the fossils they find to particular strata, and assign these fossils to one of a number of geologic eras. The geologic time scale continues to be used by paleontologists today. Similar studies of fossils play an important role in the development and acceptance of the theory of *evolution* in the second half of the 19th century. Finally, the work of 19th-century mathematicians, described in this section, has a great impact on 20th-century computer design. Two prominent achievements are Charles Babbage's counting machine, which is considered a forerunner to today's computers, and George Boole's symbolic logic, which continues to be used in software design today.

6

Science Expands as the World Grows Smaller

1851–1899

∼ INTRODUCTION ∼

The last half of the 19th century was a time of great expansion of scientific knowledge. Some of the most famous work in science—from Charles Darwin's theory of *evolution* to the discovery of *radioactivity* and *X-rays*—takes place during this period. Scientists develop new methods to study and analyze everything from tiny microorganisms to distant *nebula.*

Chemists continue to identify the *elements* that make up matter, and a system to organize the elements, the periodic table of the elements, is developed. Others characterize chemical reactions and interactions, such as Swedish chemist Svante Arrhenius, who explains how salts dissolve in water. A new method of identifying chemicals by analyzing the characteristic *spectral lines* emitted when an element is heated gives scientists a new tool to describe the make up of various compounds on Earth and in the universe.

During the late 19th century, astronomers take advantage of the discovery of atomic spectra and begin to analyze the elemental components of the universe. In an early study, English astronomer Sir William Huggins shows that the universe contains some of the same elements, such as hydrogen and carbon that are found on Earth. Soon, scientists study the spectra of the Sun, and show that it contains the elements hydrogen and helium, as well as nebula. Astronomers also study the skies with the aid of photography, with the first pictures of a solar *eclipse* being taken in 1861. Both of these tools will also play a prominent role in 20th-century astronomy.

The microscope continues to help advance understanding of living organisms as the 19th century draws to a close. Biologists discover that some cells are divided into several compartments, called *organelles*. They also observe cells dividing under the microscope, and begin to uncover how the cells that make up the nervous system of animals connect with one another to allow communication throughout the body. Microorganisms play a key role in 19th-century biology, with French scientist Louis Pasteur describing the germ theory of disease. During this era, scientists identify the microorganisms that cause a number of human and animal diseases, including anthrax, leprosy, tuberculosis, and malaria. In addition to identifying diseases caused by *bacteria* and protozoa, scientists studying mosaic disease in tobacco plants discover a new infectious agent, the *virus*.

While the advances in cellular and microbiology are impressive, Charles Darwin and Gregor Mendel make the largest impact on biology with their theories of evolution and heredity. In 1858, Darwin presents his theory of *natural selection* with Alfred Wallace, who had independently developed a similar theory. By the end of the century, biologists embrace Darwin's theory. Gregor Mendel's work on heredity, on the other hand, is not widely known during his lifetime. Through careful study of the pea plants, Mendel shows that traits are inherited independently of one another. Twentieth-century biologists will accept his work as the field of genetics grows in prominence.

TIME LINE OF SCIENTIFIC ACHIEVEMENTS BETWEEN 1851 AND 1899

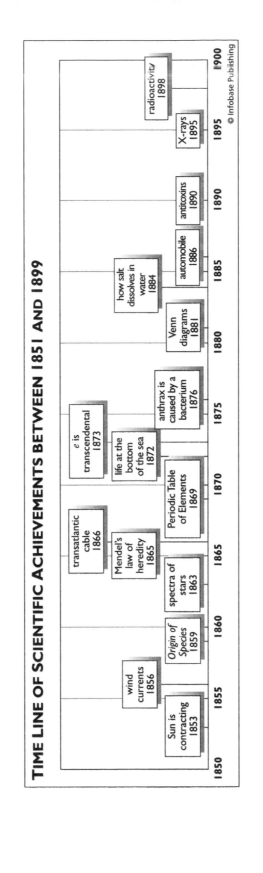

© Infobase Publishing

❧ CHRONOLOGY ❧

1851

Jean-Bernard-Léon Foucault uses Foucault's pendulum to demonstrate the rotation of the Earth.

The rotation of the Earth can be observed by viewing the movement of objects in the sky. In 1851, French physicist Jean-Bernard-Léon Foucault (1819–68) makes an experiment that demonstrates the rotation of the Earth. He designs what is now called Foucault's pendulum, a huge pendulum hanging over a bed of sand. Foucault adds a spike to the pendulum, so a mark in the sand is made as it swings. By following the pattern left in the sand, Foucault and anyone else watching the pendulum could easily observe the rotation of the Earth.

(ES, P)

1852

Sir William Thomson demonstrates the Joule-Thomson effect.

Scientists have developed a number of theories describing the behavior of gases and its relationship to pressure and temperature. As scientists realized that *heat* can be distinguished from temperature, gas behavior was reevaluated. In 1852, Sir William Thomson (also known as Lord Kelvin, 1824–1907) demonstrates what becomes known as the Joule-Thomson effect. He shows that the temperature of a gas decreases when it expands in a vacuum.

(C, P)

Sir Edward Frankland describes the valence theory of chemical reactions.

During the 19th century, chemists analyzed the chemical composition of various compounds and developed theories on how they combine. In 1852, English chemist Sir Edward Frankland (1825–99) studies the chemical reactions and notices that some *reactants* always combine with the same number of oxygen *atoms*. He describes his theory of valency, stating that a particular atom always interacts with the same number of atoms. Later studies of chemistry will show that Frankland's *valence* theory actually describes the sharing of *electrons* in chemical bonds.

(C)

April 6

Sir Edward Sabine describes the relationship between variations in the Earth's magnetic field and sunspots.

The Earth's *magnetic field* is not constant; it varies over time. On April 6, 1852, British scientist Sir Edward Sabine (1788–1883) describes his observations of the variations in the magnetic field. He notes that over an 11-year period, the variation in the Earth's magnetic field follows the cycling of sunspots that had been noted by Samuel Heinrich Schwabe nine years earlier (*See* entry for 1843).

(ES, SA)

1853

Hermann von Helmholtz states that the Sun is contracting.

As physicists studied the laws governing *energy*, they also began to question from where the Sun's energy comes. In 1853, German scholar Hermann von Helmholtz (1821–94) proposes that *gravity* causes the Sun to contract. He estimates that this process would supply enough energy to power the Sun for 20 million years. In the 20th century, research into nuclear physics replaces Helmholtz's view of the Sun's energy source, but scientists still believe that gravity causes the Sun to contract.

(P, SA)

1854

Heinrich Ernst von Beyrich describes the Oligocene period.

During the 19th century, geologists studied fossils from different layers of *strata* and assigned them to different periods in the Earth's history. In 1854, German scientist Heinrich Ernst von Beyrich (1815–96) describes fossils he finds in northern Germany from an era that he calls the Oligocene period. Today, paleontologists recognize the Oligocene period as beginning 34 million years ago and ending 23.8 million years ago.

(ES)

June 10

Georg Riemann describes geometry in *n*-dimensional space.

During the 19th century, mathematicians reconsidered the *geometry* of the ancient Greeks and developed new ways of thinking about the subject, known as non-Euclidean geometries. On June 10, 1854, German mathematician Georg Riemann (1826–66) presents his lecture *Über die hypothesen welche der geometrie zu grunde liegen* (On the hypotheses that lie at the foundations of geometry), introducing a geometry he developed. During the lecture, he describes *n*-dimensional space, now known as Riemann space. While not appreciated during his lifetime, modern physicists apply Riemann geometry to a number of important problems, including *relativity.*

(M, P)

September 7

John Snow identifies the source of a cholera outbreak.

Cholera is an infectious disease that can lead to severe gastrointestinal problems and the potentially fatal loss of body fluids. In summer 1854, a neighborhood of London suffered a widespread outbreak of the disease. English physician John Snow (1813–58), who had been considering the transmission of cholera since the 1840s, traces the source of the epidemic to a sewage-contaminated water pump. When he examines the water from the pump under a microscope, he observes small particles. Today, scientists believe the particles were the cholera-causing *bacteria.*

(B)

1855

Johann Geissler creates Geissler tubes.

Scientific experiments rely upon instruments that can set up proper conditions as well as take accurate measurements. Physicists often want to observe physical phenomena in a vacuum. In 1855, German glassblower Johann Geissler (1815–79) helps create these conditions when he invents the Geissler tube. A strong vacuum that Geissler generates using a mercury air pump evacuates the air from tubes. His work allows experiments using *cathode rays* to be performed later in the century.

(P)

Luigi Palmieri builds a seismograph.

Devices to detect earthquakes have been around since the time of ancient China, but the first device to record seismic activity was not built until 1855. Italian meteorologist Luigi Palmieri (1807–96) creates a *seismograph* by partially filling tubes with mercury and arranging them around the points of a compass. If there is sufficient seismic activity to move the mercury to the end of the tube, electrical contact is made, and the movement is recorded. Palmieri's seismographs are the first capable of detecting earthquakes too small to be perceived by humans.

(ES)

Sir William Logan finds Precambrian rocks.

Geologists in the 19th century classified fossils by age based upon the various *strata* where they were found. In 1855, Canadian geologist Sir William Edmond Logan (1798–1875) finds rocks that appear to be older than those from the Cambrian period, the first geologic age known at the time. Logan finds fossils in some of these rocks, suggesting that there was life on Earth more than 543 million years ago. Fossils from this era are now called *Precambrian*.

(ES)

Matthew Fontaine Maury describes scientific observations of the ocean.

Most 19th-century geologists focused their attention on the land as they debated the origins of mountains and valleys. This era also saw some of the first scientific studies of the sea. An early scholarly work describing the sea appears in 1855, when American oceanographer Matthew Fontaine Maury (1806–73) publishes *Physical Geography of the Sea*. Maury was the head of the United States Naval Observatory, where he kept track of the temperature and wind currents of the Atlantic Ocean. His work also included a relief map of the ocean floor.

(ES, MS)

December

James Maxwell mathematically describes lines of force.

Physicist Michael Faraday explained *electromagnetism* by using what he called lines of force to represent the direction of the force (*See* entry for 1821). In December 1855, Scottish physicist James Maxwell (1831–79) presents his classic paper "On Faraday's Line of Force," describing Faraday's lines of force using mathematics. His work, known as Maxwell's equations, describing magnetic and *electric fields,* gives a mathematical framework to electromagnetic theory.

(P)

1856

William Ferrel explains wind currents.

The movement of winds and currents are affected by the rotation of the Earth. The middle *latitudes* of both the Northern and Southern Hemispheres have prevailing westerly winds. In 1856, American geologist William Ferrel (1817–91) models the wind currents and describes the wind as flowing toward the poles and eastward at low altitudes and toward the equator and westward at high altitudes. His work is described in the article "An Essay on the Winds and Currents of the Ocean" published in *The Nashville Journal.*

(W)

Claude Bernard discovers glycogen.

Animals extract the *energy* they need from the food they eat. When an animal consumes more food than necessary, most of the excess energy is stored in the form of fat. Humans store some of this energy in the liver in the form of *carbohydrates*. In the first half of the 19th century, however, most biologists believed that animal cells were incapable of synthesizing carbohydrates. In 1856, French physiologist Claude Bernard (1813–78) discovers that animals make a carbohydrate he calls glycogen.

(B)

William Thomas Blanford finds evidence of an ice age in India.

During the 19th century, geologists found evidence that glaciers once extended into central Europe, suggesting that there was a time when the climate was extremely cold. In 1856, English geologist William Thomas

French physiologist Claude Bernard shows that animal cells can make and store carbohydrates. *(G. Terry Sharrer, National Museum of Science Technology and Culture, National Cancer Institute)*

Blanford (1832–1905) demonstrates that such periods of cold, known as ice ages, probably occurred in Asia as well. While working on a geological survey of India, Blanford finds evidence that glaciers had once extended across that country as well. Blanford's findings show that ice ages occurred across the Earth.

(ES, W)

1857

Rudolf Albert von Kölliker describes the mitochondria in muscle cells.

Eukaryotic cells have specialized compartments with specific functions, called *organelles. Mitochondria* are organelles that are involved in generating cellular energy. In 1857, German biologist Rudolf Albert von Kölliker (1817–1905) first identifies the mitochondria while studying muscle cells under the microscope. Soon biologists discover that the vast majority of energy in animal cells is produced in the mitochondria.

(B)

Daniel Kirkwood observes gaps in the asteroid belt.

During the 19th century, astronomers discovered the *asteroid* belt, an area of small, planet-like, satellites orbiting the Sun between Mars and Jupiter. In 1857, American astronomer Daniel Kirkwood (1814–95) observes gaps in the asteroid belt. He publishes his discovery of what are now called Kirkwood gaps in 1866. Today, astronomers realize that the Kirkwood gaps are a result of the influence of Jupiter on the asteroids.

(SA)

Scientists identify the remains of "Neanderthal man."

Scientists in the 19th century pondered the origin of life. In 1857, evidence for the *evolution* of man is uncovered when workers discover the remains of a manlike creature while digging a quarry in Germany. The skeleton, dubbed "Neanderthal man," appears to be the link between man and apes. Although the discovery was controversial at the time, today scientists believe Neanderthal man to be ancestor of humans that dates back more than 100,000 years.

(B)

James Maxwell describes Saturn's rings.

The invention of the telescope allowed Galileo Galilei to discover the rings that surround Saturn (*See* entry for 1610). During the 19th century, astronomers believed that the rings were solid. In 1849, Édouard Roche proposed that rings formed when an object orbiting the planet broke apart (*See* entry for 1849). In 1857, Scottish physicist James Maxwell (1831–79) publishes a paper that supports Roche's theory. He demonstrates mathematically that the only way Saturn's rings can be stable is if they are made of small particles.

(P, SA)

1858

Julius Wilhelm Richard Dedekind gives a rigorous definition of irrational numbers.

Mathematicians have developed a number of different ways to classify numbers. *Real numbers* are made up of *rational numbers,* or numbers that can be represented as a fraction of *integers,* and *irrational numbers,* which cannot. In 1858, German mathematician Julius Wilhelm Richard Dedekind (1831–1916) gives a more rigorous definition of irrational numbers, using what are known as Dedekind cuts. His work, *Stetigkeit und irrationale zahlen* (Continuity and irrational numbers), is published in 1858.

(M)

Archibald Scott Couper proposes notation for molecular structures.

During the 19th century, chemists began writing the composition of compounds using standard chemical formulas that denote the identity and quantity of all the *atoms.* Soon, chemists realized that two compounds with the same chemical formula can have vastly different properties. Such sets of compounds are called *isomers.* In 1858, Scottish chemist Archibald Scott Couper (1831–92) writes the formulas for chemicals in a way that denotes molecular structure. He uses the symbols for each atom, and then draws lines between them to denote chemical bonds. His notation is particularly useful for describing isomers.

(C)

Rudolph Virchow claims diseases originate at a cellular level.

Physicians in the 19th century used the modern tools of biological research to help them understand disease. Microscopes became particularly important, both in the search for microorganisms and for comparing healthy and diseased cells. In 1858, German physician Rudolph Virchow (1821–1902) publishes *Die cellularpathologie* (Cellular pathology) describing the appearance of disease cells and proposing that abnormal cells arise from healthy ones.

(B)

Julius Plücker studies electricity in a vacuum.

Improvements in the ability to generate vacuums in Geissler tubes (*See* entry for 1854) allowed physicists to perform experiments under vacuum conditions in the laboratory. In 1858, German physicist Julius Plücker (1801–68) adds electrodes to a Geissler tube and detects *fluorescence* when the current flows. When he added a *magnetic field,* the fluorescence shifted. Plücker's experiment leads to a number of studies that try to understand fluorescence, which comes to be known as a *cathode ray.*

(P)

Stanislao Cannizzaro systemizes atomic weight.

Advances in chemistry throughout the 18th and 19th centuries gave chemists insight into the chemical formula of many different compounds. Unfortunately, at this time there was no consensus on how to represent chemical structures or how to define *atomic weights.* In 1858, Italian chemist Stanislao Cannizzaro (1826–1910) uses an *atom* of hydrogen as the standard for atomic weight, and defines its atomic weight as one. He presents his method at the First International Chemical Conference in 1860. Soon,

Cannizzaro's method standardizes the calculations of atomic weights.

(C)

July 1

Charles Darwin and Alfred Wallace present the theory of natural selection.

As described in the sidebars "Theories of Geological Change" and "Theories of Evolution," 19th-century geologists debated how the Earth changes over time, while biologists of the era began to study how organisms change over time as well. On July 1, 1858, English naturalists Charles Darwin (1809–82) and Alfred Wallace (1823–1913) present papers outlining the theory of *natural selection* (*See* entry for 1859). Just as Darwin had

developed his theory during his voyage on the HMS *Beagle,* Wallace began formulating his similar theory while observing species on a voyage to Indonesian islands.

(B)

1859

James Maxwell describes the kinetic theory of gases.

Chemists and physicists in the 19th century worked out the relationship between the temperature, pressure, and volume of gases. In 1859, Scottish physicist James Maxwell (1831–79) provides a mathematical treatment of gas behavior in his kinetic theory of gases. He derives equations that allow scientists to

THEORIES OF EVOLUTION

Just as geologists in the 18th and 19th centuries debated how the Earth changes over time, biologists of the same era began to describe and debate how changes in species occur. Since the Renaissance, scholars such as Conrad Gesner studied fossils and noted how they resemble modern-day animals. By the 18th century, attempts to explain the origin of these fossils, and describe how species could change over time led to the development of theories of *evolution.*

One of the first biologists to offer a theory of how species change is French biologist Jean-Baptiste de Lamarck. Beginning in 1801, Lamarck studies fossils and notes how species appear to change over time. He proposes that organisms change in response to their environment, and that such changes can be passed down from one generation to the next. Over time, small adjustments to the environment will lead to significant changes, as the parts of the organism that are necessary for survival in a

particular environment grow more prominent, and those that are not needed in the organism's environment become less prominent, or disappear all together. The classic example of Lamarckian evolution is the long neck of a giraffe. According to Lamarck, the giraffe's neck becomes longer as it stretches to reach leaves high in the trees. While Lamarck was correct in his hypothesis that the organisms evolve in response to their environment, his idea that such changes can occur in a single generation is now known to be incorrect.

Lamarck's contemporary, French naturalist Georges Cuvier, did not believe that organisms could change over time. Instead, Cuvier argues that the fossils represent species that have become extinct. A proponent of the *catastrophist theory* of change, Cuvier believes that a series of sudden events lead to geological changes and the extinction of many species that are now known only through fossils. Unlike Lamarck and later evolutionists, Cuvier believes that new spe-

understand the distribution of gas particles in a vessel at a given temperature and pressure. His equations also show the average kinetic *energy* of a gas is related to its temperature.

(C, P)

Charles Darwin publishes *On the Origin of Species by Means of Natural Selection.*

As described in the sidebar "Theories of Evolution," English naturalist Charles Darwin (1809–82) described *natural selection* in a joint paper with Alfred Wallace in 1858 (*See* entry for JULY 1858). Darwin's theory is the result of decades of study on how species change over time. In 1859, Darwin publishes his classic work *On the Origin of Species by Means of Natural Selection,* where he outlines his theory of natural selection. Darwin notes that while

the number of individuals in a population of animal remains relatively constant, each species produces far more eggs and larvae than organisms that survive to adulthood. He states that some of the larvae will be better suited to survive in a particular environment than in others. Those that survive are thus selected by the environment and pass their heartier traits to subsequent generations. Under natural selection, if the environmental conditions suddenly change, there is a mechanism for the species to survive.

(B)

Louis Pasteur shows that microorganisms are in the air.

For centuries, scholars believed that under certain conditions, organisms can come

cies arise by divine creation. Today, scientists know that species regularly become extinct as a result of both subtle and catastrophic changes in the environment. However, the explanation for the origin of modern-day species does not come until the 19th century.

Today, the theory of evolution is most closely associated with English naturalist Charles Darwin. In 1831, Darwin begins a voyage around the world, where he observes different species. When he returns, he begins to formulate his ideas of how species change over time. While Darwin discusses his work with colleagues, he does not immediately publish his theory. During the 1850s, English naturalist Alfred Wallace develops a theory similar to Darwin's after traveling to the Indonesian Islands. In 1858, the two scientists present a joint presentation of the theory of *natural selection.* The next year, Darwin publishes his classic work *On the Origin of Species,* outlining his theory of natural selection in more detail. Ironically, Darwin rarely uses the term *evolution* in his classic work.

Like Lamarck before them, Darwin and Wallace both state that species change over

time in response to changes in the environment. However, Darwin's theory of natural selection is predicated upon the assumption that certain individuals within a species are born with characteristics that make them more likely to survive in a given environment. Such individuals are selected through a process known as survival of the fittest. Over several generations, natural selection can lead to a species acquiring vastly different characteristic than its ancestors. In the *Origin of the Species,* Darwin focuses on nonhuman animals and plants. After his theory becomes more widely accepted, he advances his ideas on human evolution in *The Descent of Man, and Selection in Relation to Sex* (1871). Here, Darwin hypothesizes that man evolved from a more primitive primate, leading to the often-quoted misconception that Darwin says man evolved from the apes. During the 20th century, Darwin's theory of natural selection is combined with the theory of inheritance developed by the 19th-century scholar Gregor Mendel to explain how traits evolve and are passed down to subsequent generations.

from nonliving matter, a theory known as spontaneous generation. In the 17th century, Francisco Redi disproved one of the main examples of spontaneous generations (*See* entry for 1648); however, no one could definitively show that microorganisms do not arise by spontaneous generations, so the theory persisted into the 19th century. In 1859, French chemist Louis Pasteur (1822–95) places a broth in a flask with a twisted neck, allowing air to reach the broth but prohibiting particles from entering, and boils it. He shows that no microorganisms grow in the boiled broth, thus disproving spontaneous generation. Next, he turns the flask on its side so that the collected particles can enter the broth, and soon an entire culture of microorganisms are growing, demonstrating that microorganisms are found in the air.

(B)

September 1

Richard Carrington observes a solar flare.

Astronomers studying sunspots observe that they appear and disappear in cycles that follow the variations in the Earth's *magnetic field*. Another solar event that leads to magnetic disturbances is a solar flare. While studying sunspots on September 1, 1859, English astronomer Richard Carrington (1826–75) witnesses an intense burst of white bright light coming from the Sun. The light disappears after a few minutes. Carrington notes a magnetic disturbance at the same time as he observes the solar flare.

(SA)

1860

Gustav Kirchhoff and Robert Bunsen demonstrate that each element has a unique spectral line.

As described in the sidebar "Discovering the Elements," chemists searched for the *ele-*

ments that make up matter throughout the 18th and 19th centuries. Soon, chemists noticed that certain chemicals display unique colors when heated by a flame. In 1860, German scientists Gustav Kirchhoff (1824–87) and Robert Wilhelm Bunsen (1811–99) show that each element emits a unique *spectral line* when subjected to a flame test. The identification of new spectral lines becomes an important tool in identifying new elements.

(C)

Robert Bunsen and Gustav Kirchhoff discover cesium.

Many *elements* were discovered during the 18th and 19th centuries. In 1860, German scientists Gustav Kirchhoff (1824–87) and Robert Wilhelm Bunsen (1811–99) discover the element cesium while analyzing mineral water. They identify the element after separating mineral water into its known components, including salts of the elements sodium, potassium, and calcium, then analyzing the leftover liquid. Using a flame test, which analyzes elements based upon the characteristic light they emit upon absorbing *energy,* Kirchhoff and Bunsen show that the liquid contains a previously unknown element. They call the new element cesium.

(C)

January 24

Jean-Joseph-Étienne Lenoir patents the internal combustion engine.

The invention of the steam engine allowed production of a wide variety of machines, from pumps to steamboats. However, the original steam engine required that steam enter from an outside source. In 1860, French-Belgian inventor Jean-Joseph-Étienne Lenoir (1822–1900) patents an engine in which the steam is generated inside the engine, known as the internal combustion engine. Lenoir's engine is smaller than the traditional steam engine, and thus able to power vehicles. Later improvements to Lenoir's design by Nikolaus Otto leads to the widespread use of the internal combustion engine.

(P)

July 18

Warren De la Rue photographs a solar eclipse.

Today's astronomers study pictures of celestial bodies observed when using telescope. Nineteenth-century English astronomer Warren De la Rue (1815–89) was the first to use photography as part of his study of the stars. De la Rue devised a telescope with an attached camera, known as a photoheliograph, that could take pictures of the Sun. On July 18, 1860, he photographs a solar *eclipse*. His photographs show that the red flames surrounding the Sun, known as solar prominences, are part of the Sun and not merely scattered light, as others had previously proposed.

(SA)

1861

Sir William Crookes discovers thallium.

As described in the sidebar "Discovering the Elements," many of the *elements* that make up matter were identified during the 18th and 19th centuries. Some were discovered when scientists analyzed impurities in other chemicals. In 1861, English chemist Sir William Crookes studies preparations of sulfuric acid. He notes that the atomic spectra of the sample contain a green line that had not been previously detected. Crookes deduces that the sample contains a new element and names it thallium. The next year, French physicist Claude-Auguste Lamy (1820–87) isolates a sample of thallium.

(C)

Ignaz Phillipp Semmelweis describes how hand washing can prevent childbed fever.

During the 19th century, more than 10 percent of women contracted potentially fatal infections after giving birth, a condition known as childbed fever. Hungarian physician Ignaz Phillipp Semmelweis (1818–65) realized that physicians who performed autopsies before examining women in labor could transmit such infections. He institutes a policy of hand washing before examining laboring women and reduces the cases of childbed fever in his hospital by 80 percent. Although he publishes his method in 1861, the medical community does not embrace it, and hand washing does not become common practice until later in the century.

(B)

Karl Weierstrass finds a function that is continuous but does not have a derivative.

The development of *calculus* in the 17th century led mathematicians to study *functions*. In its simplest definition, a function $f(x)$ is said to be continuous if a change in f results in a change in x. A change in a function is known as its *derivative*. In 1861, German mathematician Karl Weierstrass (1815–97) finds a continuous function that does not have a derivative.

(M)

Anders Jonas Ångström identifies hydrogen in the Sun.

The discovery of *spectral lines* gave scientists a tool to study *elements* found in space. In 1861, Swedish astronomer Anders Jonas Ångström (1814–74) studies the spectrum of the Sun. He notes the presence of the spectral line corresponding to hydrogen, and identifies it as an important element in the Sun. Ångström goes on to detect more than 1,000 spectral lines in the Sun and describes them in his 1868 work *Recherches sur le spectre solaire* (Research on the solar spectrum).

(SA)

Thomas Andrews describes critical temperatures.

During the 19th century, scientists developed methods to cool gases, such as carbon dioxide, to form a liquid. Since the temperature of a gas is related to its pressure, it is possible to liquefy a gas by increasing pressure as well. In 1861, Irish chemist Thomas Andrews (1813–85) proposes that there is a critical temperature at which it cannot be liquefied using pressure alone. In 1869, he shows that the critical temperature of carbon dioxide is 87.6°F (30.9°C).

(P)

Louis Pasteur describes fermentation.

Microorganisms are critical for the breakdown of sugars to form alcohol, known as *fermentation*. In 1861, French chemist Louis Pasteur (1822–95) describes the role of different strains of yeast in fermentation. Specifically, the yeast responsible for fermenting grapes into wine is different from those that cause wine to go bad. He shows that more alcohol is produced when the fermenting wine is kept out of the air, known as *anaerobic* conditions, than when oxygen is present—a phenomenon known as the Pasteur effect.

(B, C)

Christian Erich Hermann von Meyer describes the link between dinosaurs and birds.

Naturalists identified the first dinosaur fossils in the 19th century and used them to identify a group of ancient reptiles (*See* entry for AUGUST 2, 1841). In 1861, German paleontologist Christian Erich Hermann von Meyer (1801–69) announces the discovery of the complete skeleton and the impression of a feather from an ancient bird called *Archaeopteryx lithographica*. As the discovery comes soon after the publication of English naturalist Charles Darwin's *On the Origin of Species* (*See* entry for 1859), many conclude *Archaeopteryx* represents the "missing link" between birds and dinosaurs. Over the next hundred years, paleontologists debate whether the fossil is an ancient bird or a feathered dinosaur.

(B)

February 23

Robert Bunsen and Gustav Kirchhoff discover rubidium.

As described in the sidebar "Discovering the Elements," scientists analyzing the components of different ores and minerals identified many *elements* that make up matter. On February 23, 1861, German scientists Gustav Kirchhoff (1824–87) and Robert Wilhelm Bunsen (1811–99) discover the element rubidium while analyzing a mineral containing the metal lithium. They perform a series of chemical reactions to purify the components of the mineral. One of the substances they purify has an atomic spectrum that had never been seen before. They call the new element rubidium, for the ruby red color of the *spectral lines*.

(C)

April 17

Pierre-Paul Broca finds the region of the brain responsible for speech.

The brain controls both voluntary and involuntary movement in humans. During the 19th century, scientists began to believe that different regions of the brain are responsible for different activities. The first proof of this theory comes in 1861. French physician Pierre-Paul Broca (1824–80) identifies a patient with brain damage that had led to significantly impaired speech. After the patient's death on April 17, Broca studies his brain and localizes the damage to a specific region, now known as Broca's region.

(B)

1862

Louis Pasteur develops pasteurization.

Yeast are microorganisms that break down sugars to form alcohol, a process known as *fermentation*. French chemist Louis Pasteur (1822–95) discovered that wine spoils when a specific type of yeast grows and produces lactic acid. In 1862, he develops a method to protect wine from spoiling by killing the offending yeast with *heat*. The process, known as pasteurization, also kills *bacteria*. Soon, pasteurization is used to protect milk from spoiling as well.

(B)

Gustav Robert Kirchhoff introduces the concept of a black body.

A *black body* is defined as a body that absorbs light without reflecting it, giving it a black appearance. The perfect black body is only theoretical, but it plays an important role in the history of physics. In 1862, German physicist Gustav Robert Kirchhoff (1824–87) introduces the concept of a black body. While a black body does not reflect light, it will emit *radiation*. The study of black bodies and black-body radiation leads to the development of *quantum mechanics* in the 20th century.

(P)

Julius von Sachs shows that photosynthesis occurs in chloroplasts.

Eukaryotic cells are divided into distinct compartments called *organelles*. Each organelle performs a specific function in the cell. Plant cells have an organelle called the *chloroplast*, which is not found in animal cells. In 1862,

French scientist Louis Pasteur makes many pioneering discoveries in chemistry and biology. This portrait depicts Pasteur investigating the law of fermentation. *(Jean-Loup/Photo Researchers Inc)*

Polish botanist Julius von Sachs (1832–97) shows that *photosynthesis,* the process whereby sunlight is converted to chemical *energy,* takes place in the chloroplast.

(B)

Felix Hoppe-Seyler describes hemoglobin.

Blood shuttles oxygen from the lungs to the tissues, then picks up the cellular by-product, carbon dioxide, and carries it from the tissues back to the lungs to be excreted from the body. The red blood cells perform this function. In 1862, German physiologist Felix Hoppe-Seyler (1825–95) discovers the molecule responsible for carrying oxygen and calls it *hemoglobin.*

(B)

1863

Sir William Huggins observes the spectra of stars.

The discovery that *elements* can be identified by their characteristic *spectra* led to advances in chemistry, where new elements were identified, and astronomy. Astronomers used spectra to identify the elements that make up the universe. In 1863, English astronomer Sir William Huggins (1824–1910) publishes, "Report on the Spectra of Stars," detailing the spectra he observes. Huggins finds that many of the elements found on Earth, such as hydrogen and carbon, are also found in the universe.

(SA)

John Tyndall shows how carbon dioxide and water vapor control the Earth's temperature.

As scientists understood more about the air around us, they began to question how the atmosphere maintains the ambient temperatures found on Earth. In 1863, Irish scholar John Tyndall (1820–93) shows that the gases of the atmosphere, specifically carbon dioxide and water vapor, can absorb *heat.* He concludes that water vapor bears most of the responsibility for maintaining the Earth's temperature. Tyndall also proposes that fluctuations in the level of carbon dioxide in the atmosphere could lead to changes in the climate—the first articulation of the *greenhouse effect.*

(W)

Ferdinand Reich and Hieronymus Theodor Richter discover indium.

During the 19th century, chemists discovered many of the *elements* that make up matter by examining the characteristic *spectral lines* that they emit. In 1863, German chemists Ferdinand Reich (1799–1866) and Hieronymus Theodor Richter (1824–98) study zinc ores. In one sample, they notice a previously unseen spectral line that is bright violet. Reich and Richter purify the metal, which they call indium after the color of its spectral line.

(C)

John Wesley Hyatt invents celluloid.

In the 19th century, advances in chemistry began to be applied to industry. In 1863, inventor John Wesley Hyatt (1837–1920) searches for a material that can replace ivory. He notices that when three chemicals, cellulose nitrate, camphor, and alcohol, are mixed together they form a hard plastic. In 1870, he is awarded the patent for the first synthetic plastic, which he calls celluloid. Soon, celluloid is used in a variety of household items, from buttons to pens.

(C)

Alfred Russel Wallace describes the geographical distribution of species.

During the second half of the 18th century, biologists studied how species change. English naturalist Alfred Russel Wallace (1823–

1913) independently arrived at the theory of *natural selection* from observations made during his voyages to the Indonesian islands (*See* entry for JULY 1858). During the voyage, he noted the geographical distribution of species in that region of the world. In 1863, he describes what becomes known as the Wallace line, an imaginary line that runs between Asia and Australia, separating zoologically distinct species.

(B, ES)

1864

John Newlands arranges the elements into groups of eight.

Chemists organize *elements* into groups based upon their chemical properties. In 1864, English chemist John Newlands (1837–98) arranges the known elements into groups of eight, or octaves. He notes similar properties in every eight elements. Although Newlands system is not widely adopted, it represents one of the first efforts to classify elements based upon their chemical properties, a pursuit that culminates in the development of the periodic table of the elements in 1869.

(C)

Cato Maximilian Guldberg and Peter Waage describe the law of mass action.

Chemical reactions occur at *equilibrium,* meaning that there is a distribution among the *reactants* and the *products.* In 1864, Norwegian chemists Cato Maximilian Guldberg (1836–1902) and Peter Waage (1833–1900) study chemical equilibrium and discover that by increasing the amount, or total mass, of the reactants they could force the chemical reaction to occur, creating more products. Their work, known as the law of mass action, continues to be studied today.

(C)

August 29

Sir William Huggins shows that nebulae are made up of gas.

Today, *nebulae* are recognized as celestial structures that are formed from gases and dust found in the universe. However, astronomers in the 19th century assumed that they were masses of stars. On August 29, 1864, English astronomer Sir William Huggins (1824–1910) analyzes a nebula by taking its spectra. Huggins had pioneered the study of stars by looking at characteristic spectra (*See* entry for 1863) and observing that the *elements* found on Earth are found in stars. When he turns to a nebula, he is surprised to find it is composed of a single gas. Huggins's observation shows that nebulae are masses of gas and not groups of stars.

(SA)

1865

Friedrich August Kekule von Stradonitz describes the structure of benzene.

The chemical properties of molecules depend upon the arrangement of *atoms* in three dimensions. In the 1860s, chemists tried to determine the structure of benzene, a molecule that has six carbon atoms and six hydrogen atoms. In 1865, German chemist Friedrich August Kekule von Stradonitz (1829–96) proposes that the carbon atoms in benzene are arranged in a ring structure. He later claims his discovery is inspired by a dream. Today, *organic* chemists work with a wide range of compounds that contain a ring structure similar to benzene. These so-called aromatic compounds are important components of industrial products, such as dyes and drugs.

(C)

Johann Loschmidt determines the number of molecules in a fixed volume of gas.

Scientists studying gases know that the volume of a gas affects its temperature and pressure. In 1811, Italian scientist Amedeo Avogadro stated that two gases held under the same conditions have the same number of molecules. In 1865, Czech scholar Johann Loschmidt (1829–95) calculates the number of molecules in a fixed volume, known as a mole of gas. The quantity, approximately 6.03×10^{23} molecules, becomes known as Avogadro's number.

(C)

Joseph Lister introduces antiseptics to surgery.

The discovery of microorganisms and their role in disease explains why surgical patients often contract infections. In 1865, English surgeon Joseph Lister studies the germ theory of disease and realizes that infections could be reduced if surgical instruments are properly cleaned. Lister establishes a cleaning protocol for his instruments that consists of cleaning them with an *acid* then heating the instruments. Lister's method, known as an antiseptic technique, kills most microorganisms, and leads to a reduction in the number of postsurgical infections. Although he publishes his results in 1867, it takes several years for his antiseptic techniques to be widely applied.

(B)

Adolf von Baeyer begins his work on organic dyes.

Indigo is a bright blue dye derived from plants. In 1865, German chemist Adolf von Baeyer (1835–1917) studies the chemistry of indigo, an *organic* molecule. Von Baeyer's studies on indigo uncover the chemical composition of the dye and leads to the development of a method to synthesize the dye in an industrial setting. He is honored with the Nobel Prize in chemistry in 1905 "in recognition of his services in the advancement of organic chemistry

and the chemical industry, through his work on organic dyes and hydroaromatic compounds."

(C)

February 8

Gregor Mendel describes laws of heredity.

The science of *genetics* was born during the 19th century, when Australian scientist Gregor Mendel (1822–84) performed studies on the inheritance of traits in pea plants. During the 19th century, botanists debated the role of sexual reproduction in plants and studied *hybrids*. Mendel generated thousands of pea plant hybrids and carefully recorded the appearance of both the parents and the offspring. His work showed that traits segregate independently of one another. Although he presents his findings in a talk on February 8, 1865, entitled "Versuche über pflanzen-hybriden" (Experiments in plant hybridization), they are not widely accepted until the 20th century.

(B)

1866

Alfred Nobel invents dynamite.

Nitroglycerine is an explosive molecule that was used for military purposes in the 19th century. In the 1860s, the family of Swedish inventor Alfred Nobel (1833–96) ran a factory that produced nitroglycerine. In 1864, Nobel is inspired to devise a safe way to contain nitroglycerine after an accidental explosion in the family factory kills his brother. In 1866, he reaches this goal with the invention of dynamite. Upon his death in 1896, Nobel endows a foundation that awards the Nobel Prize each year (*See* sidebar "Awarding Science").

(C)

Alfred Nobel invents dynamite in the 19th century. This photograph depicts dynamite being used by a United States Marine demolition crew to destroy a Japanese cave in May 1945. *(Department of Defense/ National Archives)*

July 27

A transatlantic cable connects Ireland to Canada.

The invention of the telegraph allowed rapid communication across long stretches of land. On July 27, 1866, the first transatlantic cable is completed, allowing communication between Europe and North America. The more than 3,100 miles (5,000 km) of cable begins in Ireland and ends in Newfoundland.

(P)

1868

Johann Friedrich Miescher discovers nucleic acids.

Cells depend upon thousands of different chemical reactions to survive and thrive. During the 19th century, chemists began to discover the molecules involved in these reactions. In 1868, chemist Johann Friedrich Miescher (1844–95) studies an *organelle* of *eukaryotic cells* called the *nucleus*. He finds that there is an abundance of a substance he calls nucleins. Further analysis shows that nucleins has two components, *proteins* and a phosphorus-containing acid he calls nucleic acid. In the 20th century, scientists will show that nucleic acids, specifically *deoxyribonucleic acid* (DNA), carry the genetic information in the cell.

(B)

March

Cro-Magnon man skeleton is discovered in Europe.

The discovery of fossils that resemble manlike animals spurred research into human *evolution* during the 19th and 20th centuries. In March 1868, railroad workers find the skeletons of four adults and one infant that are estimated to be 30,000 years old. The skeletons are identified as early humans, and called Cro-Magnon man.

(B)

August 18

Pierre-Jules-César Janssen identifies helium.

As described in the sidebar "Discovering the Elements," scientists examined the characteristic *spectral lines* emitted by different *atoms* to identify new elements. Spectral lines can be observed from the Sun, allowing scientists to identify some of the *elements* that are present there. French astronomer Pierre Janssen (1824–1907) was particularly interested in identifying elements associated with the Sun. On August 18, 1868, he examines the spectral lines given off from the Sun during an *eclipse*. He identifies a new element, the *noble gas* helium.

(C, SA)

1869

The periodic table of the elements becomes the classification system for the elements.

As the *elements* that make up all matter were being identified, chemists sought a logical

Russian chemist Dmitry Mendeleyev develops a version of the periodic table of the elements in 1869. *(Museum of the History of Science, Oxford)*

system to classify them. In 1869, two scientists, Russian chemist Dmitry Mendeleyev (1834–1907) and German chemist Julius Lothar Meyer (1830–95), independently demonstrate that when the *atoms* are organized by their *atomic weight* they can be easily arranged into a table that also reflects their physical properties. Thus, the early version of the *periodic table* of the elements is born. A version of this table remains a cornerstone of chemistry.

(C)

1870

Eduard Hitzig and Gustav Fritsch map the motor area of the brain.

Specialized regions of the brain control specific physiological functions. In 1870, German physiologists Eduard Hitzig (1838–1907) and Gustav Fritsch (1838–1927) perform a series of experiments that allows them to map the region of the brain that controls the movement of arms and legs, known as the motor area, by stimulating different regions of the cerebral cortex with *electricity.* Hitzig and Fritsch show that the stimulation of the motor area leads to the movement of specific parts of the body.

(B)

1871

Charles Darwin describes the evolution of man.

As described in the sidebar "Theories of Evolution," English naturalist Charles Darwin (1809–82) presented his theory of *natural selection* in 1859. His book *On the Origin of Species by Means of Natural Selection* focuses on nonhuman animals (*See* entry for 1859). In 1871, he extends his arguments to man in *The Descent of Man, and Selection in Relation to Sex.* Darwin argues that man descended from a more primitive primate, an argument that is popularly characterized as being descended from apes. He also describes how mating patterns contribute to natural selection.

(B)

John William Strutt explains why the sky is blue.

In the 19th century, the study of *optics* brought a greater understanding of the nature of light. In 1871, English physicist John William Strutt (also known as Lord Rayleigh, 1842–1919) uses optics to explain why the sky appears blue. Strutt states that the blue color is a result of particle-scattering light. He uses mathematical equations to relate the degree of scattering to the wavelength of light perceived by the eye. Today, scientists recognize that the particles are in fact molecules of the gases that make up the atmosphere.

(P)

1872

Christian Felix Klein presents a unified view of geometry.

Geometry is based upon a set of assumptions or *axioms.* During the 19th century, mathematicians developed a number of *non-Euclidean geometries* based upon different axioms than those based on the classical geometry of Euclid (*See* entry for CA. 300 B.C.E.). In 1872, German mathematician Christian Felix Klein (1849–1925) presents the "Erlanger Program," describing how all known geometries can be unified. Today, the Erlanger Program is accepted as a standard view of the field.

(M)

Ferdinand Cohn classifies bacteria.

During the 18th and 19th centuries, scientists classified everything from clouds to organisms. Advances in microscopy allowed biologists to develop a system of classification for microorganisms based upon their structures. In 1872, German botanist Ferdinand Cohn (1828–98) classifies *bacteria,* arguing in his paper "Untersuchungen über bacterien" (Investigations over bacteria) that they are related to plants. Although today bacteria are recognized as being distinct from both plants and animals, Cohn's work leads to the development of bacteriology as a field of study.

(B)

August

Henry Draper photographs the spectrum of a star.

The study of astronomy benefited from some new technologies of the 19th century, particularly photography and *spectroscopy.* In August 1872, American astronomer Henry Draper (1837–82), son of William Draper (*See* entry for 1839), becomes the first person to photograph the spectrum of a star. He devises a spectrograph, or camera devised to photograph spectra, for this purpose.

(SA)

December 21

Sir Charles Wyville Thomson departs on HMS *Challenger,* finding life on the bottom of the sea.

Ocean life ranges from the plants, fish, and marine mammals visible from the shore to rarely seen animal and plant life that live deep in the sea. As 19th-century schol-ars began to study the oceans, Scottish naturalist Sir Charles Wyville Thomson (1830–82) participated in many deep-sea dredging voyages. On December 21, 1872, he de-parts on the HMS *Challenger,* where he is director of the scientific staff. During the three-and-a-half-year voyage, Thomson discovers that there is life deep in the sea—up to 3,000 fathoms. He publishes his findings in the 1877 work *The Voyage of the Challenger.*

(ES, MS)

Scottish naturalist Sir Charles Wyville Thomson discovers deep-sea life during his travels aboard the *Challenger.* This picture, from his 1878 work *The Voyage of the Challenger—The Atlantic* Volume I, depicts the dredging and sounding arrangements on the ship. *(Steve Nicklas/ NOS, NGS/NOAA)*

1873

Wilhelm Wundt describes biological basis of psychology.

While experiments have been a critical element of scientific pursuits since the Renaissance, the field of psychology remained theoretical until the 19th century. At this time, German psychologist Wilhelm Wundt (1832–1920) began conducting scientific experiments designed to explain psychological phenomena. In 1873, he publishes *Grundzüge der physiologischen psychologie* (Principles of physiological psychology), which becomes the standard text for the field.

(B)

Charles Hermite shows that *e* is transcendental.

Irrational numbers are numbers that cannot be written as fractions of *integers*. Some irrational numbers belong to a special class known as *transcendental numbers*. Examples of known transcendental numbers include *pi,* the *ratio* of the *circumference* of circle to its diameter, and *e,* the *base* of natural *logarithms.* In 1873, French mathematician Charles Hermite (1822–1901) proves that *e* is transcendental.

(M)

James Maxwell publishes his theory of electromagnetism.

The discovery of the relationship between *electricity* and *magnetism* in 1820 set off a wave of research on these two physical phenomena (*See* entry for 1820). Scottish physicist James Maxwell (1831–79) studied the problem and approached it using mathematics. In 1873, he publishes *Treatise on Electricity and Magnetism,* a culmination of a decade's worth of work in the field. Maxwell reduces his theory of electromagnetism to eight equations, known as Maxwell's equations, and proves the existence of electromagnetic waves.

(P)

Gerhard Hansen discovers the bacterium that causes leprosy.

As described in the sidebar "Finding the Microorganisms That Cause Disease," many 19th-century physicians and scientists showed that infectious diseases are caused by *bacteria, viruses,* and other pathogens too small to see. One example is leprosy, a debilitating infectious disease that causes disfiguring skin lesions and permanent nerve damage. Until the 19th century, physicians believed that leprosy was an inherited disease. In 1873, the Norwegian microbiologist Gerhard Hansen (1841–1912) identifies a bacterium, *Mycobacterium leprae,* in infected tissues. By the 1880s, Hansen and others successfully show that the bacterium causes leprosy.

(B)

Johannes van der Waals describes weak attractive forces in gases.

Physicists and chemists studied the fundamental properties of gases during the 19th century. In 1873, Dutch physicist Johannes van der Waals (1837–1923) modifies the gas law to include weak attractive *forces* between molecules. His work explains the existence of critical temperature, or temperatures above which a gas cannot be liquefied using pressure alone. Today, the weak *forces* he described are known as van der Waals forces. Van der Waals was honored with the Nobel Prize in chemistry in 1910 "for his work on the equation of state for gases and liquids."

(C, P)

December

Georg Cantor describes the mathematics of infinite sets.

Mathematicians classify numbers into various categories, such as *natural numbers* and *real numbers*. The set of all real numbers is *infinite*. In December 1873, Russian mathematician Georg Cantor (1845–1918) proves that the real numbers cannot be counted. His paper describing the proof lays the basis for the mathematics of infinite sets. Over the next two decades, Cantor continues his work on set theory.

(M)

1874

September

Jacobus Hendricus van't Hoff describes carbon atoms.

Organic chemistry is the study of carbon-containing molecules. One feature of many organic molecules is their *chirality,* which allows seemingly similar molecules to have slightly different physical and biological properties. In 1874, Dutch chemist Jacobus Hendricus van't Hoff (1852–1911) explains chirality by describing the asymmetry in the carbon *atom*. He states that carbon makes four separate chemical bonds, forming a tetrahedron. The four bonds carbon allows organic molecules with the same chemical formula and structure to have different three-dimensional arrangement of atoms.

(C)

1875

Oskar Wilhelm August Hertwig describes the process of fertilization.

The invention of the microscope allowed scientists to discover the male sperm cells and female egg cells that are involved in the process. Similar to other *eukaryotic cells,* the reproductive cells of animals are divided into different compartments or *organelles.* In 1875, German zoologist Oskar Wilhelm August Hertwig (1849–1922) uses a microscope to observe the fertilization of sea urchin eggs. He finds that during fertilization, the *nucleus* of the egg fuses with that of the sperm. Today, scientists know this fusion event is critical for combining the genetic information of the mother with that of the father.

(B)

August

Paul-Émile Lecoq de Boisbaudran discovers gallium.

As described in the sidebar "Discovering the Elements," during the 19th century chemists discovered many *elements* that make up matter. Russian chemist Dmitry Mendeleyev (1834–1907) arranged these elements into the *periodic table* of the elements (*See* entry for 1869). His table predicted the existence of elements not yet discovered. In August 1875, French chemist Paul-Émile Lecoq de Boisbaudran (1838–1912) discovers one of these predicted elements, gallium, as a contaminant of a sample of zinc. Lecoq de Boisbaudran first notices that the contaminant has an unusual *spectral line.* Soon after, he uses *electrolysis* to isolate a pure preparation of gallium.

(C)

1876

Josiah Willard Gibbs describes the thermodynamics of chemical reactions.

Chemists studying *thermodynamics* are interested in the effect of *heat* and other forms of energy on chemical reactions. In 1876, American chemist Josiah Willard Gibbs publishes the first part of his classic study on thermodynamics "On the Equilibrium of Heterogeneous Substances." Gibbs considers a wide range of factors that influence chemical reactions, including *equilibrium,* electrochemical potential, and free energy. His work gives chemists the tools to predict whether or not a chemical reaction is likely to take place spontaneously.

(C)

Robert Koch shows that anthrax is caused by bacterial infection.

As described in the sidebar "Finding the Microorganisms that Cause Disease," 19th-century biologists showed that bacterial infections lead to some of the diseases found in humans and animals. During the 1870s, German microbiologist Robert Koch (1843–1910) showed that the bacterium *Bacillus anthraces* causes anthrax. Koch grew cultures of the *bacteria* and used them to infect sheep. The sheep infected with the cultures contracted anthrax, while the sheep that were not infected with the bacteria remained disease-free. He announces his results in the 1876 paper "The Etiology of Anthrax, Based upon the Lifecycle of *Bacillus anthraces.*"

(P)

March 10

Alexander Graham Bell invents the telephone.

Advances in physics throughout the 19th century led to a revolution in communications, beginning with the telegraph. The telegraph allows communication over long distances by transmitting electromagnetic waves over wires. In the 1870s, American inventor Alexander Graham Bell (1847–1922) worked to transmit sound electrically. On March 10, 1876, he successfully demonstrates the telephone, using it to speak to an assistant in the next room.

(P)

1877

Charles Friedel and James Crafts develop a method to prepare hydrocarbons.

During the 19th century, chemists began looking for ways to synthesize complex molecules in the laboratory. Hydrocarbons are *organic* molecules used as fuel for motorized vehicles and as precursors for the synthesis of plastics. In 1877, French chemist Charles Friedel (1832–99) and American chemist James Crafts (1839–1917) develop a method to prepare hydrocarbons. The so-called Friedel-Craft reaction allows chemists to synthesize different hydrocarbons.

(C)

Wilhelm Pfeffer describes osmotic pressure.

In a vessel separated by a semipermeable membrane, water will move from an area with a high concentration of dissolved substances, known as solutes, to an area with a lower solute concentration via a process known as *osmosis* (*See* entry for 1748). In 1877, German chemist Wilhelm Pfeffer (1845–1920) performs a series of experiments measuring the pressure exerted by this moving water, known as osmotic pressure. He finds that osmotic pressure depends upon the concentration of chemicals dissolved in the water as well as the temperature. Osmosis plays an important role in many biological processes, such as the movement of molecules in and out of cells and the uptake of nutrients by plants.

(C)

Othniel Charles Marsh describes the *Apatosaurus*.

Paleontologists identified the first dinosaur fossils and began to classify them into differ-

ent species during the 19th century (*See* entry for AUGUST 2, 1841). In 1877, American paleontologist Othniel Charles Marsh (1831–99) discovers the *Apatosaurus,* a large dinosaur commonly (and incorrectly) known as the Brontosaurus. The first *Apatosaurus* fossils are discovered in Colorado. Based upon a nearly six-foot-long fossilized leg bone, Marsh states that the *Apatosaurus* is the largest known land animal.

(B)

May 3

John William Strutt describes sound waves.

Hearing occurs when the ear detects sound waves that travel through the air. Physicists interested in *acoustics* study the properties of sound waves and how they affect human hearing. On May 3, 1877, English physicist John William Strutt (also known as Lord Rayleigh, 1842–1919) considers the properties of sound waves in his paper "On the Amplitude of Sound Waves." Strutt's work on acoustics culminates with the two-volume *Theory of Sound* (1877), describing various sound vibrations, the *reflection* and *refraction* of sound waves, and the propagation of sound waves through various media.

(P)

September 12

Giovanni Schiaparelli begins observations of the surface of Mars.

Astronomers studying the surface of Mars in the 19th century believed landmasses and seas, similar to on Earth, covered it. On September 12, 1877, Italian astronomer Giovanni Schiaparelli (1835–1910) begins a series of observations of the surface of Mars that culminates in the mapping of various seas, rivers (or canali as he calls them), and landmasses. He continues studying the surface Mars until 1891, drawing detailed maps and naming the various features he observes.

Although it turns out that Mars is not covered with seas, Schiaparelli's maps and nomenclature continue to be used into the 20th century.

(SA)

1878

Chemists discover holmium.

As described in the sidebar "Discovering the Elements," 19th-century chemists discovered a number of *elements* known as the rare earth elements, or *lanthanides*. Often, these elements were isolated from preparations of other lanthanides that were previously thought to be pure. In 1878, chemists Marc Delafontaine and Jacques Louis Soret working together, and Swedish chemist Per Teodor Cleve (1840–1905) (*See* entry for 1874) working independently, find a new element, holmium, in a sample of the lanthanide erbium. Later, scientists purify dysprosium from holmium.

(C)

Jean-Charles-Galissard de Marignac isolates ytterbium.

As described in the sidebar "Discovering the Elements," 19th-century chemists discovered a group of chemicals called the rare earth elements, or *lanthanides*. In 1878, Swiss chemist Jean Charles Galissard de Marignac (1817–94) studies the lanthanide erbium. Erbium itself was discovered in a sample of yttrium (*See* entry for 1843), an abundant element often found with lanthanides. Through a series of chemical reactions, Galissard de Marignac isolates a new element from erbium, which he calls ytterbium.

(C)

Wilhelm Friedrich Kühne calls biological catalysts enzymes.

Enzymes catalyze the wide range of chemical reactions that are required in cells. During the 19th century, the first of these catalysts was isolated from yeast and animal sources. In 1878, German physiologist Wilhelm Friedrich Kühne (1837–1900) calls these molecules enzymes. Today, the study of enzymes is a major focus of biochemical research.

(B, C)

Hendrik Antoon Lorentz proposes the electromagnetic theory of light.

Electromagnetic radiation is caused by oscillation of electric charges. In 1878, Dutch physicist Hendrik Antoon Lorentz (1853–1928) proposes that the electromagnetic theory of light, which states that light is a result of similar electric oscillations. Lorentz shares the Nobel Prize in physics in 1902 with Pieter Zeeman "in recognition of the extraordinary service they rendered by their researches into the influence of magnetism upon radiation phenomena."

(P)

April 29

Louis Pasteur presents his germ theory of disease.

As described in the sidebar "Finding the Microorganisms That Cause Disease," the vast influence that microorganisms have on our world began to become clear during the 19th century. On April 29, 1878, French chemist Louis Pasteur (1822–95) presents his germ theory of disease in his paper "Germ Theory and its Applications to Medicine and Surgery." Pasteur, who had been developing his germ theory since the 1860s, describes the accumulating evidence that microorganisms are responsible for a number of diseases, including cholera and anthrax.

(B)

1879

Lars Fredrik Nilson discovers scandium.

As described in the sidebar "Discovering the Elements," 19th-century scientists identified

FINDING THE MICROORGANISMS THAT CAUSE DISEASE

While the idea that some diseases are contagious was developed during the time of ancient Greece, it was not until the 19th century that scientists discovered the causes of infectious diseases, such as anthrax and tuberculosis. During the Renaissance, Italian physician Girolamo Fracastoro put forth the theory that contagious diseases are caused by tiny infectious agents. Although Dutch microscopist Antoni van Leeuwenhoek discovered *bacteria* and other microorganisms in 1674, scientists could not definitively show that that specific diseases are caused by particular microorganisms until the 19th century.

By the middle of the 19th century, physicians and scientists strongly suspect that microorganisms cause a number of diseases, even if they cannot prove it. Hungarian physician Ignaz Phillipp Semmelweis is one of the first to attempt to eliminate contamination with microorganisms in a medical setting. He institutes a hand-washing policy for all physicians attending to childbirths. Semmelweis's hand-washing procedure drastically reduces the number of maternal deaths following childbirth, but unfortunately his practice does not remain in practice. In 1854, more evidence that microscopic agents cause disease accumulates when an epidemic of the infectious disease cholera breaks out in a neighborhood of London. English scholar John Snow identifies a public water pump as the source of the disease. While he hypothesizes that an agent in the water is responsible for the disease, he cannot identify the agent nor confirm that one actually exists.

The first articulation of the germ theory of disease comes from French scientist Louis Pasteur. Pasteur had previously demonstrated that microorganisms are present in the air around us and described the role of microorganisms in the process of *fermentation,* as well as in the spoiling of wine and milk. During the 1860s, he turns his attention to the role of microorganisms in disease, realizing that if microorganisms can cause milk and wine to spoil, they could also play a role in disease. In 1878, he presents his germ theory of disease, describing the role of microorganisms in diseases such as anthrax and cholera.

While Pasteur establishes the germ theory of disease, the rules for determining that a particular microorganism causes a specific disease are laid out by German microbiologist Robert Koch. In 1876, Koch shows that the disease anthrax is caused by bacterial infection, followed by the discovery of the bacteria that causes tuberculosis in 1882. Koch follows a defined protocol, now known as Koch's *postulates,* for proving that a microorganism causes a disease. First, the microorganism must be found in all patients with the disease. Second, the microorganism must be isolated and grown in the laboratory. Third, a scientist must be able to use the culture of the microorganism grown in the laboratory to infect another organism that has not been exposed to the disease. Finally, the same microorganism must be found in all newly infected animals, isolated, and shown to be identical to the original organism.

With Pasteur's germ theory of disease and Koch's postulates in hand, physicians and scientists in the late 19th century begin a wave of studies to find diseases that are caused by microorganisms. In addition, physicians begin to institute measures to prevent infections in a medical setting, from the hand washing originally proposed by Semmelweis, to sterilizing surgical instruments as advocated by physician Joseph Lister.

many of the *elements* that make up matter. Russian chemist Dmitry Mendeleyev (1834–1907) organized the elements into the *peri-* *odic table* of the elements, which allows chemists to predict their properties (*See* entry for 1869). In 1879, Swedish chemist Lars

Fredrik Nilson (1840–99) studies a complex mineral. He finds that one of the components has an atomic spectrum that had not been seen previously. He shows the new element is one that had been predicted by Dmitry Mendeleyev when he established the periodic table of the elements. Nilson calls the new element scandium.

(C)

Per Teodor Cleve discovers thulium.

As described in the sidebar "Discovering the Elements," 19th-century scientists discovered many of the *elements* that make up matter. The series of elements known as the rare earth elements, or *lanthanides,* proved difficult to identify, and a number of early preparations of lanthanides were subsequently shown to be impure. Swedish chemist Per Teodor Cleve (1840–1905) studied a sample of the lanthanide erbium (*See* entry for 1878), believing it contaminated with other elements. In 1879, he extracts a new lanthanide from the sample, thulium.

(C)

Paul-Émile Lecoq de Boisbaudran discovers samarium.

As described in the sidebar "Discovering the Elements," the rare-earth elements, now called *lanthanides,* proved to be challenging to purify. Minerals found in mines often contained a mixture of many different lanthanides. By the late 19th century, chemists found other elements in cerium minerals, such as didymium. In 1879, French chemist Paul-Émile Lecoq de Boisbaudran (1838–1912) isolates samarium, a new lanthanide, from the sample.

(C)

Charles Lapworth describes the Ordovician period.

Geologists study fossils found in different *strata* of the Earth and assign them to different periods in geological history. Without modern methods of dating ancient objects, the boundaries of these periods are difficult to determine. In fact, a controversy ensued over the boundary between the Cambrian and the Silurian periods. In 1879, English geologist Charles Lapworth (1842–1920) realizes that a third geologic era lies between the two periods. He calls the era the Ordovician period and shows that fossils from this era are distinct from both the Cambrian and Silurian periods. Today, paleontologists recognize the Ordovician period as the time between 490 million years ago and 443 million years ago.

(ES)

Josef Stefan quantitatively describes the effects of temperature on heat radiation.

Physicists distinguish temperature from *energy* radiated in the form of *heat.* Clearly, a body radiates more heat at a high temperature than at a lower temperature. In 1879, Austrian physicist Josef Stefan (1835–93) quantitatively describes the effects of temperature on *radiation,* showing that the radiation of a body is proportional to the temperature raised to the fourth power.

(P)

Albert Abraham Michelson measures the speed of light.

Since the Renaissance, scholars have devised methods to measure the speed of light. French physicist Jean-Bernard-Léon Foucault (1819–68) calculated the speed of light to within 5 percent in 1850. His method is improved in 1879 by American physicist Albert Abraham Michelson (1852–1931), who obtains the first accurate measurement. Later, Michelson repeats his experiment in a vacuum tube and determines the speed of light in a vacuum, an important value in many physical calculations.

(P)

December

Thomas Alva Edison demonstrates the lightbulb.

Advances in the understanding of *electricity* in the 19th century led to a number of useful inventions from communications aids such as the telephone and telegraph to the lightbulb. During December 1879, American inventor Thomas Alva Edison (1847–1931) demonstrates the first practical lightbulb. Edison's incandescent bulb generates light for over 13 hours. As the electric industry grows in the 1880s, electric lightbulbs soon replace gaslights.

(P)

1880

Louis Pasteur creates a vaccine using an attenuated strain of cholera.

Smallpox was the only disease that could be prevented by vaccination until 1880, when French chemist Louis Pasteur (1822–95) creates a vaccine to prevent cholera in chickens. Pasteur identifies the bacterium that causes cholera, and then develops a weakened, or attenuated, strain. When he administers the attenuated strain to uninfected chickens, they became resistant to the disease. Soon, attenuated strains are used to create vaccines against other diseases, including anthrax and rabies.

(B)

Charles Galissard de Marignac discovers gadolinium.

As described in the sidebar "Discovering the Elements," during the 19th century chemists discovered a group of *elements* known as the rare earth elements, or *lanthanides*. Some of these elements were first found as contaminants in preparations of other lanthanides that were previously thought to be pure. By heating the preparations and analyzing the characteristic spectral lines they give off, many new lanthanides were discovered. In 1880, Charles Galissard de Marignac uses this method to discover the element now called gadolinium.

(C)

Friedrich Wilhelm Ostwald describes the rate of chemical reactions.

A number of factors, such as pressure, temperature, and concentration, influence the course of chemical reactions. In 1881, German chemist Friedrich Wilhelm Ostwald (1853–1932) describes the rate of a reaction catalyzed by an *acid*. His studies culminate in his finding that the rate of acid-catalyzed reactions is proportional to the square of the strength of the acid. Ostwald is honored with the Nobel Prize in chemistry in 1909 "in recognition of his work on catalysis and for his investigations into the fundamental principles governing chemical equilibrium and rates of reaction."

(C)

John Venn develops a method to represent symbolic logic.

During the 19th century, mathematicians developed methods to symbolically represent logic. In 1881, English mathematician John Venn (1834–1923) publishes *Symbolic Logic*. His work is notable for the use of diagrams, now called Venn diagrams, to represent sets and where they intersect. Venn diagrams are so clear and easy to follow that they are still commonly seen in elementary school textbooks.

(M)

May 5

Louis Pasteur creates a vaccine that protects against anthrax.

Edward Jenner's discovery of a vaccine for smallpox inspired 19th-century physicians and scientists to search for other diseases that could be eradicated by vaccination. French chemist Louis Pasteur (1822–95) was instrumental in extending Jenner's work. He discovered a way to attenuate disease-causing microbes so that they could be used to inoculate animals. In 1880, he creates the first attenuated vaccine, which protects chickens from cholera. Next, he tackles anthrax, a disease that can be spread from farm animals to humans. On May 5, 1881, he begins inoculating cows and sheep with a vaccine against the disease anthrax.

(B)

Summer

Josef Breuer describes the unconscious mind.

One of the dominant theories in 20th-century psychology was the distinction between the conscious and unconscious mind. During summer 1880, Austrian physician Josef Breuer (1842–1925) treats a patient with severe psychological disturbances. Upon hypnotizing her, he finds she articulates memories that she did not discuss in her normal state. He cures her by allowing her to discuss these memories, the first such "talking therapy." Breuer's ideas and therapies surrounding the unconscious mind influences his coworker, Sigmund Freud.

(B)

September 30

Henry Draper studies the Orion nebula.

During the 19th century, astronomy benefited from the invention of photography, which allowed the images of celestial bodies to be recorded, and the development of *spectroscopy*, which helped scientists identify the elements that make up the universe. American astronomer Henry Draper (1837–82) turned these two powerful tools to the study of the Orion *nebula*. On September

30th, he obtains the first photograph of the nebula.

(SA)

1882

Walther Flemming describes cell division.

Advances in microscopy gave 19th-century biologists new insight into the molecular processes that underlie life. In 1882, German anatomist Walther Flemming (1843–1905) describes his observations of the process of cell division, known as mitosis, in his work *Zellsubstanz, kern und zeltheilung* (Cytoplasm, nucleus, and cell division). Flemming uses a special dye to visualize structures in the nucleus he calls *chromosomes* and describes their behavior during cell division.

(B)

Carl Louis Ferdinand Lindemann shows that π is transcendental.

Mathematicians define *transcendental numbers* as numbers that are not the root of any algebraic equation with *rational* coefficient. Therefore, *irrational* numbers can be transcendental, but this is difficult to prove. In 1882, German mathematician Carl Louis Ferdinand Lindemann (1852–1939) proves that π, the *ratio* of the circumference of a circle to its diameter, is transcendental.

(M)

Élie Metchnikoff describes how the body defends against microorganisms.

During the 19th century, physicians and scientists discovered that microorganisms cause many diseases, including tuberculosis and malaria. Soon, biologists realized that the body must have some means to protect against these invisible invaders. In 1882, Russian biologist Élie Metchnikoff (1845–1916) discovers that mammals have cells that protect the body by engulfing microorganisms. His discovery of these cells, called phagocytes, is controversial at the time. Today, his work is recognized as one of the earliest descriptions of cells involved in the immune system. Metchnikoff shared the 1908 Nobel Prize in physiology or medicine with Paul Ehrlich "in recognition of their work on immunity."

(B)

Clarence Dutton describes the history of the Grand Canyon.

Today, Arizona's Grand Canyon is a huge tourist attraction in the western United States. However, this was not the case when the region was first being settled. The Grand Canyon first captures the imagination of naturalists after American geologist Clarence Dutton (1841–1912) of the United States Geological Survey publishes *The Tertiary History of the Grand Cañon District*. Dutton's combines artists' rendering of the canyon alongside scientific explanations of the geography.

(ES)

March 24

Robert Koch identifies the bacterium that causes tuberculosis.

Tuberculosis is a potentially fatal infectious disease that spreads through the air. On March 24, 1882, German microbiologist Robert Koch (1843–1910) announces that he has identified the cause of tuberculosis—a bacterium known as *Mycobacteria tuberculosis*. Koch grows cultures of the *bacteria* and uses them to infect guinea pigs, which subsequently contract tuberculosis. Although over a century has passed since Koch's discovery, tuberculosis remains a public health problem today. Koch was honored with the Nobel Prize in physiology or medicine in 1905 "for his investigations and discoveries in relation to tuberculosis."

(B)

1883

Emil Theodor Kocher shows the importance of the thyroid gland.

The thyroid gland, the largest gland in the body, is located in the neck of humans. In the late 19th century, physicians began to treat a disease called goiter, where the thyroid becomes enlarged, by removing the entire gland. The surgery resulted in the death of nearly 40 percent of patients and caused the other patients to become lethargic. In 1883, Swiss physician Emil Theodor Kocher (1841–1917) realizes that the thyroid is playing a vital role in the body's metabolism. By removing only part of the thyroid gland, Kocher reduces the mortality rate to 13 percent. He is honored with the Nobel Prize in physiology or medicine in 1909 "for his work on the physiology, pathology and surgery of the thyroid gland."

(B)

Nikola Tesla invents an alternating current generator.

As physicists understood the properties of *electricity*, inventors began to create devices powered by *electric currents*. Early inventions used the direct current (DC) supplied by a battery. In 1883, American inventor Nikola Tesla (1856–1943) develops a way to generate an alternating current using electromagnetic induction. Tesla's generator, which uses a rotating *magnetic field* to generate an electrical current, serves as the basis for many electrical devices.

(P)

Charles Fritts invents the solar cell.

Advances in physics in the 19th century led to the invention of various means to power machines, from batteries to steam engines. In 1883, American inventor Charles Fritts devises a way to power machines using the *energy* of the Sun. His solar cell is quite inefficient, converting less than 1 percent of the energy it collects. However, his invention is the first step toward developing solar energy.

(P)

Eduard Suess describes the formation of geological features.

As described in the sidebar "Theories of Geological Change," during the 19th century

Grand Canyon of the Colorado River at the foot of the Toroweap, Arizona *(Department of the Interior, Geological Survey/National Archives)*

Earth scientists debated the origin of different geological features, such as mountain ranges. In 1883, Austrian geologist Eduard Suess (1831–1914) publishes the first volume of his *Das antlitz der Erde* (The faces of the Earth). He describes the formation of mountain ranges and the floor of the oceans in terms of movement in the Earth's crust. His work marks the beginning of the study of *plate tectonics*.

(ES, MS)

Ludwig Boltzmann mathematically describes black body radiation.

At the end of the 19th century, physicists began considering how *energy* is radiated as heat. In 1879, the Austrian physicist Josef Stefan quantitatively described the effects of temperature on *radiation*, showing that the radiation of a body is proportional to the temperature raised to the fourth power (*See* entry for 1879). His work is expanded by Austrian physicist Ludwig Boltzmann (1844–1906) in 1883, who uses *statistics* to show that it applies only to theoretical bodies that absorb light, without reflecting it, and then emit energy at every frequency, called *black bodies*. His work, known as the Stefan-Boltzmann law, lays the foundation for the development of *quantum mechanics* in the 20th century.

(P)

1884

Emil Fischer describes the chemical structure of sugars.

Advances in chemistry throughout the 19th century allowed scientists to study the structure and function of biologically important molecules. Sugars are a family of chemically similar molecules that are used by organisms for *energy*. In 1884, German chemist Emil Fischer (1852–1919) begins a series of studies in which he uncovers the structures and relationship between different sugars, including glucose, the major fuel used by cells, and

fructose, the sugar found in fruits. Fischer was honored with the Nobel Prize in chemistry in 1902 "in recognition of the extraordinary services he has rendered by his work on sugar and purine syntheses."

(B, C)

Robert Koch describes the rules for determining whether a microorganism causes disease.

As described in the sidebar "Finding the Microorganisms That Cause Disease," during the 19th century physicians and scientists discovered that microorganisms cause communicable diseases. One of the leaders in the field was German microbiologist Robert Koch (1843–1910), who discovered that *bacteria* cause tuberculosis. In 1884, Koch outlines the rules for rigorously establishing that a microorganism causes a disease. The rules, known as Koch's *postulates*, state that the microorganism must be found in all patients with the disease, and can be isolated and grown in the laboratory. In addition, the laboratory culture must be able to infect a new healthy animal. Koch's postulates are instrumental in helping physicians prove that a particular microorganism causes a specific disease.

(B)

Charles-Louis-Alphonse Laveran discovers that a parasite causes malaria.

As described in the sidebar "Finding the Microorganisms That Cause Disease," during the 19th century physicians and scientists began to realize that microorganisms cause many diseases, including tuberculosis and cholera. Beginning in 1879, French physician Charles-Louis-Alphonse Laveran (1845–1922) investigated the cause of malaria, a potential fatal infectious disease that is prevalent in tropical climates. He found that the disease is caused by microscopic parasites, called protozoa, that enter the victim's red blood cells and destroy them. In 1884, he publishes his finding in *Traité des fièvres palustres* (Treatise on paludal fever). Laveran is honored with the Nobel Prize in physiology or medicine in 1907 "in recognition of his work on the role played by protozoa in causing diseases."

(B)

German scientists conclude that the cell nucleus is critical for heredity.

The major cell structures known today, including the large *organelle* known as the *cell nucleus,* were identified during the 19th century. In 1884, a number of German scientists, including botanist Eduard Adolf Strasburger (1844–1912), zoologist Oskar Wilhelm August Hertwig (1849–1922), and zoologist August Friedrich Weismann (1834–1914), independently come to the conclusion that the nucleus is critical for passing down genetic traits from parent to offspring.

(B)

Svante August Arrhenius describes how salts dissolve in water.

Salts can be dissolved in water to form mixtures known as solutions. In 1884, Swedish chemist Svante August Arrhenius (1859–1927) presents his doctoral dissertation, arguing that when salts dissolve they break apart into positively and negatively charged particles, now known as *ions.* His theory is controversial, but eventually gains widespread acceptance. Arrhenius is honored with the Nobel Prize in chemistry in 1903 "in recognition of the extraordinary services he has rendered to the advancement of chemistry by his electrolytic theory of dissociation."

(C)

Swedish chemist Svante August Arrhenius is honored with the Nobel Prize for his theory describing how salts dissociate into ions. *(Museum of the History of Science, Oxford)*

1885

Carl Auer discovers neodymium and praseodymium.

As described in the sidebar "Discovering the Elements," 19th-century chemists discovered a number of *elements* known as the rare earth elements, or *lanthanides*. Many of these elements were isolated from preparations of other lanthanides that were previously thought to be pure. In 1885, Austrian chemist Carl Auer (1858–1929) studies the lanthanide didymium. He isolates two new elements from the sample. He calls the elements neodymium and praseodymium.

(C)

Jacobus Hendricus van't Hoff describes osmotic pressure.

Many chemicals can be dissolved in water to form mixtures called solutions. During the 19th century, scientists showed that if two solutions are separated by a barrier that will allow water to pass, but not other molecules, the water will move from the more dilute solution to the more concentrated solution, a process known as *osmosis*. Halting osmosis requires the application of pressure, known as osmotic pressure. In 1885, Dutch chemist Jacobus Hendricus van't Hoff (1852–1911) studies osmotic pressure and notices its similarities to gas pressure. His work leads to the realization that the gas laws can apply to dilute solutions. Van't Hoff is honored with the first Nobel Prize in chemistry in 1901 "in recognition of the extraordinary services he has rendered by the discovery of the laws of chemical dynamics and osmotic pressure in solutions."

(B, P)

Albrecht Kossel studies the molecules found in the cell nucleus.

Eukaryotic cells are divided into different compartments called *organelles*. Many organelles, including the *nucleus*, were identified during the 19th century. In 1885, German chemist Albrecht Kossel (1853–1927) begins a series of studies of the molecules found in the cell nucleus. He isolates large molecules called nucleoproteins, and the smaller molecules that serve as building blocks for nucleoproteins. He eventually identifies the *nucleotides* that make up the DNA and a specialized family of DNA-binding *proteins* called histones. Kossel is honored with the Nobel Prize in physiology or medicine "in recognition of the contributions to our knowledge of cell chemistry made through his work on proteins, including the nucleic substances."

(B, C)

February 1

The Blue Hills Observatory begins maintaining weather records.

A typical weather report includes the record high and low temperature for that day.

Weather records have been kept sporadically throughout history. However, continuous weather records were not kept until the 19th century. On February 1, 1885, the Blue Hills Observatory in Milton, Massachusetts, begins keeping daily weather records. The observatory has the longest continuous records of weather observations in the United States, and continues to maintain records today.

(W)

July 6

Louis Pasteur uses the rabies vaccine on humans.

Rabies is a deadly infectious disease that can be passed from animals to humans. During the 19th century, European physicians searched for a treatment of the disease, which is carried by stray dogs and other street animals. French chemist Louis Pasteur (1822–95) had developed vaccines against other diseases that infect animals, such as cholera and anthrax (*See* entries for 1880 and 1881, respectively). In the 1880s, he turned his attention to rabies and soon developed a rabies vaccine that could be given to infected dogs. On July 6, 1885, Pasteur administers his rabies vaccine to a young boy who had been bitten by a rabid dog. The boy survives and news of Pasteur's vaccine spreads throughout the world.

(B)

1886

Hermann Hellriegel discovers that bacteria help some plants take up nitrogen.

All organisms require the *element* nitrogen to build a variety of molecules, such as *amino acids,* which play critical roles in cell growth and function. Animals obtain nitrogen from the food they eat, while plants absorb it from the soil. In 1886, German chemist Hermann Hellriegel (1831–95) studies legumes, plants such as beans and peas, which can grow in nitrogen-deficient soil. He finds that if he sterilizes the nitrogen-deficient soil, the legumes no long grow well. From this experiment, he concludes that a microorganism must be helping the plant absorb nitrogen. Today, scientists know that a specific type of *bacteria* lives in the root of legumes, forming a nitrogen-fixing nodule.

(B)

Theodor Escherich discovers the bacterium *Escherichia coli.*

During the 19th century, physicians and scientists discovered many new microorganisms that cause diseases, such as tuberculosis and anthrax. In 1886, German physician Theodor Escherich (1857–1911) studies *bacteria* found in the intestinal tract. He discovers a new bacterium, called *Escherichia coli,* commonly known as *E. coli.* Escherich describes the bacterium and its relationship to digestion. In the 20th century, *E. coli* becomes a widely used model system for studying *molecular biology.*

(B)

Paul-Émile Lecoq de Boisbaudran discovers dysprosium.

As described in the sidebar "Discovering the Elements," during the 18th and 19th centuries scientists began to identify and isolate many of the *elements* that make up matter. The processes were not perfect, and in some cases substances were either incorrectly identified as elements, or what was believed to be a pure preparation of an element was found to be contaminated with another substance. In 1886, through a series of careful experiments, Paul-Émile Lecoq de Boisbaudran (1838–1912) identifies the element dysprosium as a contaminant of a preparation of another element called holmium.

(C)

Henri Moissan isolates fluorine.

As described in the sidebar "Discovering the Elements," chemists in the 18th and 19th centuries searched for new *elements* and developed methods to isolate them. Some elements evaded isolation for many years after their initial identification. For example, the element fluorine was known in the 18th century, but for decades, no chemist was able to isolate this highly toxic substance. In 1886, French chemist Henri Moissan (1852–1907) uses a technique known as *electrolysis* to isolate fluorine. Moissan is honored with the Nobel Prize in chemistry in 1906 "in recognition of the great services rendered by him in his investigation and isolation of the element fluorine, and for the adoption in the service of science of the electric furnace called after him."

(C)

January 29

Carl Benz patents the gas-powered automobile.

Advances in physics were translated into the invention of motors and electrical devices during the second half of the 19th century. Inventors used these motors to improve transportation, developing the steamboat and locomotive. Some tried to use steam engines to power a horseless vehicle, or automobile; however, steam engines proved to be too cumbersome to power small automobiles. On January 29, 1886, German inventor Carl Benz (1844–1929) patents an automobile powered by gasoline rather than by steam. The gas-powered automobile is much more practical than its steam-powered predecessors and begins to be widely used in the 20th century.

(P)

February

Clemens Alexander Winkler discovers germanium.

As described in the sidebar "Discovering the Elements," 19th-century scientists discovered many of the *elements* that make up matter. Russian chemist Dmitry Mendeleyev (1834–1907) arranged these elements into the *periodic table* of the elements and predicted the existence of elements that were not yet discovered (*See* entry for 1869). In February 1886, German chemist Clemens Winkler (1838–1904) finds a new element in a mineral sample that is taken from a silver mine. He shows that the sample is made of silver, sulfur, and a third unidentified element. Soon he discovers that the element, which he calls germanium, is one that had been predicted by Mendeleyev.

(C, ES)

March 20

William Stanley uses an electrical transformer to power lightbulbs.

As physicists expanded their understanding of *electricity,* inventors applied it to build devices from the lightbulb to the telegraph. Electrical devices require an outside source of electricity. American inventor William Stanley (1858–1916) devised an electrical transformer that generates an alternating current (AC). On March 20, 1886, he uses his transformer to generate enough power to light the stores and offices along Main Street in Great Barrington, Massachusetts.

(P)

1887

Heinrich Rudolf Hertz observes the photoelectric effect.

Physicists explored the relationship between *electricity* and *magnetism* throughout the 19th century. Scottish physicist James Maxwell (1831–79) put forth the *electromagnetic* theory of light, stating that light can be described using the concept of an *electromagnetic field.* In 1887, German physicist Heinrich Rudolf Hertz (1857–94) proves Maxwell's theory when he demonstrates the *photoelectric effect.* Hertz shows that light can extract an *electron* from a metal. The photoelectric effect cannot be explained using the wave theory of light, and its discovery leads to a new understanding of light in the 20th century.

(P)

Albert Abraham Michelson and Edward Williams Morley try to measure the motion of the Earth.

Some experiments are famous for what they fail to show rather than what they prove. In 1887, American physicist Albert Abraham Michelson (1852–1931) and American chemist Edward Williams Morley (1838–1923) attempt to measure the speed of the Earth as it travels through space. Despite several different experimental designs, their results always suggest that the Earth is not moving. Of course, they know the Earth is moving, so the failure of their work, which becomes known as the Michelson-Morley experiment, becomes an active field of investigation for many physicists. Over the next several decades, attempts to explain the Michelson-Morley experiment lead to many advances in physics, including Albert Einstein's Special Theory of Relativity.

(P, SA)

Heinrich Rudolf Hertz discovers radio waves.

During the 19th century, physicists discovered that *energy* travels though the air in the form of waves. Waves outside of the *visible spectrum* were discovered, known as ultraviolet light and infrared light, or *heat* rays. In 1887, German physicist Heinrich Rudolf Hertz (1857–94) discovers another form of wave that has less energy and a longer wavelength than the previously characterized form of *radiation*. The radiation Hertz discovers is now known as *radio waves*.

(P)

1888

Sofya Kovalevskaya describes the rotation of a solid around a point.

While *calculus* was developed centuries before, many questions in this field remained unanswered in the 19th century. One problem, the rotation of a solid around a fixed point, continued to be studied by the great mathematicians of the era. Russian mathematician Sofya Kovalevskaya (1850–91) completes the problem in 1888. She presents her solution in her 1888 work *On the Rotation of a Solid Body about a Fixed Point.*

(M)

Henry-Louis Le Châtelier describes chemical equilibrium.

In a chemical reactions, molecules known as *reactants* undergo a chemical change to form one or more molecules known as *products*. Many reactions, particularly those that occur in biological systems, do go to completion, but reach *equilibrium* with a set proportion of products to reactants. In 1888, French chemist Henri-Louis Le Châtelier (1850–1936) articulates "Le Châtelier's principle," describing how systems at equilibrium change as a result of external *forces,* such as adding more reactants, taking away products, or changing the temperature and/or pressure.

(C)

1889

Svante August Arrhenius describes the energy needed to start a chemical reaction.

Chemists investigate how chemical reactions begin and take place. Svante August Arrhenius (1859–1927) examined the effect of increasing temperature on the rate of chemical reactions. In the course of his studies, he realized that a certain amount of *energy,* in the form of *heat,* is required to start a chemical reaction. In 1889, he derives what is now known as the Arrhenius equation, describing the mathematical relationship between this energy, known as activation energy, and the rate of the reaction.

(C)

Giuseppe Peano expands symbolic logic.

Mathematicians in the 19th century developed new ways to represent basic mathematical operations and functions. In 1847, George Boole introduced a system of symbolic logic for mathematics, known as Boolean logic (*See* entry for 1847). Italian mathematician Giuseppe Peano (1858–1932) developed his own system of symbolic logic based upon five assumptions or *axioms* about number systems. In 1889, he publishes *Arithmetices principia, nova methodo exposita* (Principles of arithmetic, presented by a new method). Peano's system is widely adopted by his contemporaries.

(M)

October

Santiago Ramón y Cajal describes the structure of the nervous system.

Nerve cells were difficult for 19th-century scientists to study because they have long extensions called axons that connect one nerve to another. In the 1880s, biologists debated whether these axons were a part of a network of continuous filaments or if each was a part of a discrete nerve cell. In October 1889, Spanish biologist Santiago Ramón y Cajal (1852–1934) stains tissues from the brain of infant and shows that each axon is connected to a single nerve cell. His work sets the foundation for today's understanding of the nervous system. Ramón y Cajal shares the Nobel Prize in physiology or medicine in 1906 with Italian pathologist Camillo Golgi (1844–1926) "in recognition of their work on the structure of the nervous system."

(B)

1890

Emil von Behring develops serum therapy for tetanus and diphtheria.

As described in the sidebar "Finding the Microorganisms That Cause Disease," 19th-century physicians and scientists realized that microorganisms cause many diseases. Beginning in 1890, German biologist Emil von Behring (1854–1917) develops serums made from animals treated with the agents that cause tetanus and diphtheria. He uses these serums to treat a separate population of animals that are afflicted with these diseases. He believes the serums contain the antidote to the toxins produced by microorganisms. Over the next five years, Behring and German biologist Paul Ehrlich (*See* entry for 1891) improve serum therapy, and it becomes a popular treatment for these diseases. Behring is honored with the first Nobel Prize in physiology or medicine in 1901 "for his work on serum therapy, especially its application against diphtheria, by which he has opened a new road in the domain of medical science and thereby placed in the hands of the physician a victorious weapon against illness and deaths."

(B)

Otto Wallach develops a method to characterize terpenes.

Terpenes are *organic* compounds found in the oils of various plants, notably coniferous trees such as pines. By the end of the 19th century, chemists had identified hundreds of terpenes from different plants. How these molecules were chemically related, however, remained a mystery. In 1890, German chemist Otto Wallach (1847–1931) develops a method to characterize terpenes base upon their chemical structure. His work is honored with the Nobel Prize in chemistry in 1910 "in recognition of his services to organic chemistry and the chemical industry by his pioneer work in the field of alicyclic compounds."

(B, C)

1891

Paul Ehrlich describes antitoxins.

As scientists realized that microorganisms cause disease, it became clear that the body must have some mechanism to protect itself from these invaders. One of the pioneers of immunology was German biologist Paul Ehrlich (1854–1915). In 1891, he begins a series of studies on antitoxins—substances produced by the body to defend against *bacteria*. Ehrlich makes antiserums to the infectious disease diphtheria and uses them to treat children with the disease. Ehrlich shares the 1908 Nobel Prize in physiology or medicine with Ilya Ilyich Mechnikov "in recognition of their work on immunity."

(B)

Hermann Henking observes the X chromosome.

When scientists observe cell division under the microscope, structures known as *chromosomes* appear in the cell *nucleus*. During the 19th century, biologists noticed that chro-

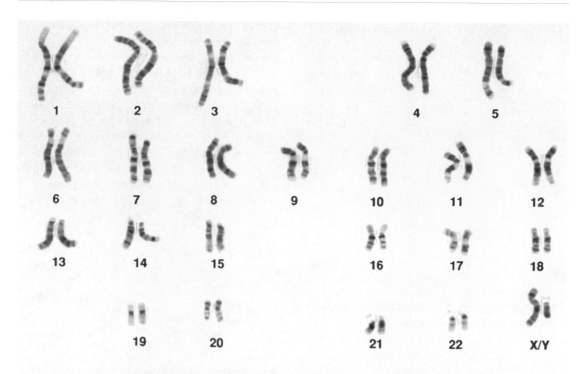

Normal Karyotype

Chromosomes, structures within the nuclei of eukaryotic cells that contain an organism's genetic material, are identified at the end of the 19th century. This photograph shows the full complement (or karyotype) of human chromosomes. *(National Cancer Institute)*

mosomes are found in seemingly identical pairs. In 1891, German zoologist Hermann Henking (1858–1942) observes the separation of chromosomes during the production of sperm and notes that one type of chromosome does not have a counterpart. Since it is unpaired, the X chromosome is distributed only to half of the sperm produced. Soon, scientists show that the X chromosome is one of two sex-determining chromosomes. Henking was unable to see second sex-determining chromosome, called the Y chromosome.

(B)

Gabriel Lippmann produces stable color photographs.

In some of the earliest experiments that led to the development of photography, scientists were able to reproduce not just images but also colors. However, these colors were not retained for long, and until 1891, no one could explain how color worked. In that year, French scientist Gabriel Lippmann (1845–1921) publishes *Color Photography,* explaining a method to obtain and fix color images. Lippmann is honored with the Nobel Prize in physics in 1908 "for his method of reproducing colours photographically based on the phenomenon of interference."

(P)

August

Eugène Dubois discovers Java man.

As scientists embraced English naturalist Charles Darwin's theory of *natural selection,* some looked for fossils that served as the "missing link" between man and other primates. In the 1880s, Dutch scholar Eugène Dubois (1858–1940) traveled to the Indonesian island of Java to look for fossils of early man. In August 1891, Dubois discovers a tooth, and later a skull of what appeared to be a manlike ape. Despite his claims to have found the missing link, Dubois's contemporaries rightly recognize them to be of an early man. Today, the fossils are classified as *Homo erectus* and are popularly known as Java man.

(B, ES)

1892

Jules-Henri Poincaré describes celestial mechanics.

The movement of heavenly bodies can be described using the laws of physics, known as celestial *mechanics.* In the 19th century, scholars pondered how orbits of various celestial bodies influence one another, known as the three-body problem. In 1892, French mathematician Jules-Henri Poincaré (1854–1912) publishes a partial solution of the three-body problem as part of his work *Les méthodes nouvelles de la mécanique céleste* (The new methods of celestial mechanics).

(M, SA)

Dmitri Iosifovich Ivanovski discovers a plant virus.

As described in the sidebar "Finding the Microorganisms That Cause Disease," 19th-century physicians and scientists discovered that microorganisms cause many communicable diseases. In 1892, Russian botanist Dmitri Iosifovich Ivanovski (1864–1920) describes his work on mosaic disease that affects tobacco plants. He shows that a microscopic agent that can pass through a laboratory filter causes the disease. Since such a filter retains *bacteria,* it appears that the agent responsible for mosaic disease is not a bacterium. Today, scholars realize that Ivanovski was one of the first to identify a disease caused by a *virus.*

(B)

John Milne develops the modern seismograph.

Scholars have developed devices to monitor and measure earthquakes since ancient times. In 1892, English seismologist John Milne (1850–1913) invents the modern *seismograph.* Milne's seismograph differs from its predecessors, having a greater sensitivity for recording ground motion, and a more compact design. Soon, Milne's seismographs are set up across at stations across the globe, allowing worldwide monitoring of seismic activity.

(ES)

Sir Charles Scott Sherrington describes reflexes.

The nervous system controls all conscious and unconscious movements. During the 1890s, English physiologist Charles Scott Sherrington (1857–1952) studies reflexive movement of the leg when the knee is hit, known as the knee-jerk reflex. He maps the nerves leading away from the knee that tell the brain that the knee has been hit, and the nerves coming from the spinal cord that transmit the orders to move to the knee. Sherrington shares the 1932 Nobel Prize in physiology or medicine with Edgar Adrian (1889–1977) "for their discoveries regarding the functions of neurons."

(B)

1893

Philipp Eduard Lenard generates cathode rays in the open air.

Physicists in the late 19th century used vacuum tubes to study *electricity*. *Cathode rays* are formed as the current passes through the tube. In 1893, German physicist Philipp Eduard Lenard (1862–1947) devises a vacuum tube with a thin metal "window" at one end. The metal window stops gas molecules from entering the tube, maintaining the vacuum while allows the rays to exit. Lenard's experiments are instrumental in understanding the structure of the *atom*. Lenard is honored with the Nobel Prize in physics in 1905 "for his work on cathode rays."

(P)

Alfred Werner describes metal ions.

During the 19th century, chemists began to discover how *atoms* and molecules interact with one another. Some atoms can take the form of charged particle known as *ions*. In 1893, Swiss chemist Alfred Werner (1866–1919) publishes his coordination theory, explaining how metal ions form compounds. Werner shows that metal ions have two states, one that interacts with other ions and a second that can interact with neutral molecules. He uses his theory to predict the existence of several compounds that are discovered years later. Werner is honored with the Nobel Prize in chemistry in 1913 "in recognition of his work on the linkage of atoms in molecules by which he has thrown new light on earlier investigations and opened up new fields of research especially in inorganic chemistry."

(C)

Theobald Smith shows that ticks can transmit disease.

As physicians and scientists recognized that microorganisms cause communicable diseases, the search for the agent that causes these diseases began. During the 1880s and 1890s, American microbiologist Theobald Smith (1859–1934) studied a number of diseases that affect livestock. In 1893, he publishes *Investigations into the Nature, Causation, and Prevention of Texas or Southern Cattle Fever*, describing his discovery of the parasite *Babesia bigemina* that causes Texas cattle fever. He is the first person to show that ticks can transmit an infectious disease, spreading Texas cattle fever among the cattle and then to humans.

(B)

Wilhelm Wien describes the distribution of black body radiation.

At the end of the 19th century, physicists tried to explain an idealized type of *radiation* known as *black body* radiation, using the laws of physics outlined by Sir Isaac Newton and James Maxwell. They found that black body radiation has a low intensity at very long or very short wavelengths, and it reaches its peak intensity toward the middle of the visible light spectrum. In 1893, German physicist Wilhelm Wien (1864–1928) shows that wavelength of peak intensity is dependent upon temperature, with the peak coming at shorter wavelengths at higher temperatures. Wien is honored with the Nobel Prize in physics in 1911 "for his discoveries regarding the laws governing the radiation of heat."

(P)

1894

Sir Edward Albert Sharpey-Schafer discovers the first hormone.

Hormones are molecules produced by specific cells in the body that help regulate a variety of physiological processes, from sexual maturation to regulation of blood pressure. In 1894, English physiologist Sir Edward Albert

Sharpey-Schafer (1850–1935) works with George Oliver (1841–1915) to isolate a molecule from adrenal glands. When they inject the substance back into animals, the animals experience a rise in blood pressure. The hormone becomes known as adrenaline, after the gland from which it was isolated.

(B)

1895

Charles Thomson Rees Wilson invents the cloud chamber.

As physicists began to consider the behavior and properties of small particles, they required more sophisticated instruments to perform experiments. In 1895, Scottish physicist Charles Thomson Rees Wilson (1869–1959) invents the cloud chamber, a vessel where water vapor can condense in dust-free air. As the name implies, Wilson first uses his device to study cloud formation. Within a few years, Wilson shows that the cloud chamber can be used to study the behavior of charged particles, or *ions*. Later, he and others use the original cloud chamber, as well as improved versions of the device, to study *subatomic particles*. Wilson is honored with the 1927 Nobel Prize in physics "for his method of making the paths of electrically charged particles visible by condensation of vapour."

(P, W)

Niels Ryberg Finsen treats bacterial diseases with light.

As described in the sidebar "Finding the Microorganisms That Cause Disease," 19th-century physicians and scientists showed that microorganisms cause a wide range of illnesses, from malaria to tuberculosis. Danish physician Niels Ryberg Finsen (1860–1904) attempted to treat these infectious diseases by killing the microorganism. In 1895, he shows that ultraviolet light can be used to treat a bacterial infection of the skin, called lupus vulgaris. Soon Finsen opens a clinic where patients can receive light therapy. With the invention of *antibiotics* in the 20th century, light therapy falls out of favor, but at the time it provided a viable treatment for some bacterial infections. Finsen is honored with the Nobel Prize in physiology or medicine in 1903 "in recognition of his contribution to the treatment of diseases, especially lupus vulgaris, with concentrated light radiation, whereby he has opened a new avenue for medical science."

(B)

January 31

John Strutt and Sir William Ramsay announce the discovery of argon.

The group of *elements* known as the inert or *noble gases* occurs naturally as single *atoms* rather than as a part of a compound. Argon is a noble gas that makes up nearly 1 percent of the Earth's atmosphere. On January 31, 1895, English physicist John William Strutt (also known as Lord Rayleigh, 1842–1919) and Sir William Ramsay (1852–1916) announce the discovery of argon gas. In 1904, Strutt is honored with the Nobel Prize in physics "for his investigations of the densities of the most important gases and for his discovery of argon in connection with these studies," and Ramsay receives the Nobel Prize in chemistry "in recognition of his services in the discovery of the inert gaseous elements in air, and his determination of their place in the periodic system."

(C, P)

March 26

Sir William Ramsay announces the discovery of helium on Earth.

Scientists discovered the *noble gas* helium by examining the *spectral lines* of gases surrounding the Sun (*See* entry for AUGUST 18, 1868). However, no one found helium on Earth until the 1890s, when English chemist Sir William Ramsay (1852–1916) analyzes the gases given off by a uranium ore. He finds that one of the gases has the same spectral lines as solar helium. Ramsay announces the discovery of helium on Earth on March 26, 1895. He is honored with the Nobel Prize in chemistry in 1904 "in recognition of his services in the discovery of the inert gaseous elements in air, and his determination of their place in the periodic system."

(C)

December 28

Wilhelm Conrad Röntgen announces the discovery of X-rays.

At the end of the 19th century, experimental physicists studied various forms of *radiation*. On December 28, 1895, physicist Wilhelm Conrad Röntgen (also known as Roentgen,

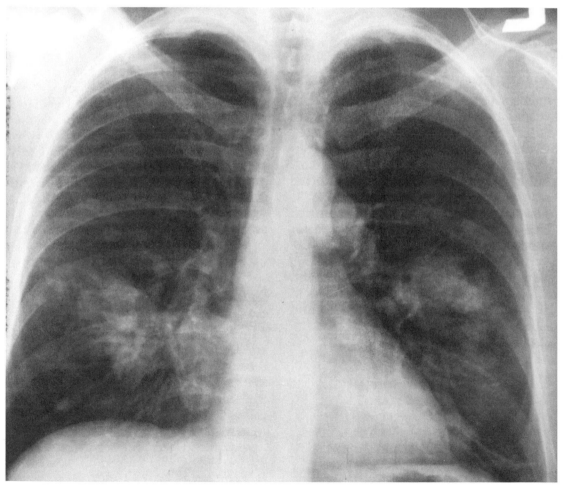

Wilhelm Conrad Röntgen's discovery of X-rays in the 19th century impacts both physics and medicine. This chest X-ray shows a growth on the left side of the lung. *(National Cancer Institute)*

1845–1923) discovers the high-*energy* electromagnetic rays known as X-rays. Röntgen notices the penetrating rays when performing an experiment using a discharge tube. He follows this discovery with a series of experiments showing that the rays can penetrate a variety of substances and remove electrons from the atoms and molecules in the air. He is honored with the Nobel Prize in physics in 1901 "in recognition of the extraordinary services he has rendered by the discovery of the remarkable rays subsequently named after him."

(P)

1896

Pieter Zeeman shows that spectral lines are split in the presence of a magnetic field.

Elements give characteristic *spectral lines* when heated. Spectral lines have characteristic colors corresponding to the wavelength of light emitted from the *atoms*. In 1896, Dutch physicist Pieter Zeeman (1865–1943) shows that spectral lines are split when a strong *magnetic field* is applied to the material. He shares the Nobel Prize in physics in 1902 with Hendrik Lorentz "in recognition of the extraordinary service they rendered by their researches into the influence of magnetism upon radiation phenomena."

(P)

Christiaan Eijkman discovers that beriberi is caused by a nutritional deficiency.

As described in the sidebar "Finding the Microorganisms That Cause Disease," during the 19th century physicians and scientists showed that microorganisms cause many diseases. During the 1890s, physician Christiaan Eijkman (1858–1930) studies a degenerative muscle disease known as beriberi that is prevalent in the Dutch East Indies. Eijkman initially tries to prove that the disease

is the result of bacterial infection. However, after several experiments, Eijkman and his colleagues realize that beriberi is prevalent in animals and humans who are fed processed rice. When affected individuals are given unprocessed rice, they recover from the disease, suggesting the disease is caused by a nutritional deficiency. Soon, scientists determine that the coat of rice, which is removed during processing, contains vitamin B_1, an essential nutrient. Eijkman is honored with the Nobel Prize in physiology or medicine in 1929 "for his discovery of the antineuritic vitamin."

(B)

May

Sir Ronald Ross uncovers the role of mosquitoes in transmitting malaria.

Malaria is a potentially fatal disease that is endemic in tropical climates. During the 19th century, physicians determined that it is caused by a parasite. In May 1896, English physician Sir Ronald Ross (1857–1932) begins a series of experiments that eventually proves that mosquitoes carry the malaria-causing parasite. His work leads to a mosquito-control measure that reduces the number of malaria cases worldwide. Ross is honored with the Nobel Prize in physiology or medicine in 1902 "for his work on malaria, by which he has shown how it enters the organism and thereby has laid the foundation for successful research on this disease and methods of combating it."

(B)

1897

Eduard Buchner performs fermentation without a living yeast cell.

Chemists and biologist show that the *fermentation* of sugar into alcohol occurs through the action of living microorganisms called

At the end of the 19th century, English physician Sir Ronald Ross uncovers the role of mosquitoes in transmitting disease. This World War II–era poster encourages citizens to mosquito-proof their homes. *(Office for Emergency Management/ National Archives)*

yeast. In 1897, German chemist Eduard Buchner isolates a component of yeast that can ferment sugars outside of a living cell. He calls the component zymase, and compares it to other *enzymes* that are isolated in the late 1900s. His work is instrumental in proving that the actions of living cells can be reduced to simple chemical reactions that can be reproduced in the laboratory. Buchner is honored with the Nobel Prize in chemistry in 1907 "for his biochemical researches and his discovery of cell-free fermentation."

(B, C)

Sir Joseph John Thomson discovers the electron.

In the second half of the 19th century, physicists began to realize that *electricity* might be generated from the movement of particles. In 1897, English physicist Sir Joseph John Thomson (1856–1940) performs a series of experiments designed to uncover the nature of particles that carrier electricity. He finds that the particles are much smaller than hydrogen atoms and have an overall negative charge. The particles that Thomson describes are later called *electrons*. Thomson is honored with the Nobel Prize in physics in 1906 "in recognition of the great merits of his theoretical and experimental investigations on the conduction of electricity by gases."

(C, P)

April 10

David Hilbert describes algebraic number theory.

Mathematicians have studied the properties of numbers, known as *number theory,* for centuries. On April 10, 1897, German mathematician David Hilbert (1862–1943) presents his report *Der zahlbericht* (Commentary on numbers), summarizing what is known about algebraic number theory and lays the foundation for class field theory.

(M)

June

Paul Sabatier uses nickel to add hydrogen to organic compounds.

Synthetic chemists look for ways to make specific molecules through a series of chemical reactions. Many *organic* compounds have hydrogen *atoms* covalently attached to carbon atoms. In June 1897, French chemist Paul Sabatier (1854–1941) shows that the metal nickel can be used to catalyze the addition of hydrogen to certain organic compounds. Over the next three years, he develops a generalized method for such hydrogenation reactions. Sabatier is honored with the Nobel Prize in chemistry in 1912 "for his method of hydrogenating organic compounds in the presence of finely disintegrated metals whereby the progress of organic chemistry has been greatly advanced in recent years."

(C)

1898

Martinus Willem Beijerinck shows that a virus causes tobacco mosaic disease.

As described in the sidebar "Finding the Microorganisms That Cause Disease," 19th-century scientists identified a number of diseases in humans, animals, and plants that are caused by microorganisms. In 1898, Dutch botanist Martinus Willem Beijerinck (1851–1931) studies tobacco mosaic disease. Like Dmitri Iosifovich Ivanovski before him (*See* entry for 1892), Beijerinck finds that the agent that causes the disease can pass through a laboratory filter. Since such filters retain bacteria and other known microorganisms, Beijerinck believes that the agent is a new type of organism, which he calls a *virus*.

(B)

Friedrich Löffler and Paul Frosch show that a virus causes foot-and-mouth disease in cattle.

By the end of the 19th century, scientists showed that a wide range of microorganisms can cause disease in humans, animals, and plants. In the 1890s, Martinus Willem Beijerinck and Dmitri Iosifovich Ivanovski independently determined that an infectious agent smaller than a *bacteria*, known as a *virus*, causes mosaic disease in tobacco plants (*See* entries for 1898 and 1892, respectively). In 1898, German microbiologist Friedrich

Löffler (1852–1915) shows that a virus causes foot-and-mouth disease, which is commonly found in cattle.

(B)

Jules Bordet explains the interactions between antiserum and its targets.

In the last decade of the 19th century, physicians began developing antiserums to treat microbial infections (*See* entries for 1890 and 1891). In 1898, Belgian bacteriologist Jules Bordet (1870–1961) studies how antiserums kill microorganisms. He isolates a serum capable of breaking apart red blood cells and shows that it is similar to the antiserums that fight bacterial infections. The molecules that Bordet describes are *proteins* called antibodies, which specifically bind foreign materials in the body. Bordet is honored with the Nobel Prize in physiology or medicine in 1919 "for his discoveries relating to immunity."

(B)

Antoine-Henri Becquerel discovers radioactivity.

At the end of the 19th century, physicists began studying various forms of *radiation*. French physicist Antoine-Henri Becquerel (1852–1908) was particularly interested in *fluorescence,* the phenomenon whereby certain materials can absorb light, then emit it at a different time. While looking for evidence that fluorescent molecules generate *X-rays,* Becquerel studies a uranium-containing molecule. He finds that the molecule emits radiation regardless of the experimental conditions, which is the first demonstration of *radioactivity.* Becquerel is honored with the Nobel Prize in physics in 1903 "in recognition of the extraordinary services he has rendered by his discovery of spontaneous radioactivity."

(C, P)

Emil Fischer describes the chemicals derived from purines.

During the 19th century, chemists began to understand the structure of complex, carbon-containing compounds, called *organic* molecules. In 1884, German chemist Emil Fischer (1852–1919) studies a family of chemically similar compounds, including caffeine, vegetable produces, and adenine, a common molecule found in cells. He realizes that these molecules are all derivatives of a compound he calls a purine. In 1898, Fischer chemically synthesizes a purine in the laboratory. His work leads to the industrial production of purine derivatives, including some pharmaceuticals. Fischer is honored with the Nobel Prize in chemistry in 1902 "in recognition of the extraordinary services he has rendered by his work on sugar and purine syntheses."

(B, C)

Pierre and Marie Curie show that radioactivity is an atomic property.

The discovery of *radioactivity* by Antoine-Henri Becquerel (*See* entry for 1898) began a series of experiments aimed at understanding this new phenomenon. French chemist Pierre Curie (1859–1906) and his wife, chemist Marie Curie (1867–1934), were among the first to confirm and extend Becquerel's work. In 1898, they show that radioactivity is a property of single *atoms* rather than entire molecules, then demonstrate that each radioactive atom in a sample emits a single ray. The Curies share the Nobel Prize in physics in 1903 "in recognition of the extraordinary services they have rendered by their joint researches on the radiation phenomena discovered by Professor Henri Becquerel."

(C, P)

April

Camillo Golgi uncovers a new cell organelle.

Under the microscope, biologists observe that *eukaryotic cells* are divided into several discrete compartments known as *organelles*. Italian pathologist Camillo Golgi (1844–1926) studied cells from the nervous system. He developed new methods to stain the cells, giving him a better view of its inner workings. In April 1898, he shows that nerves have a previously unidentified structure, which he calls the internal reticular apparatus. Today, the organelle is called the Golgi apparatus, or Golgi bodies, in his honor. Golgi shares the Nobel Prize in physiology or medicine with Spanish biologist Santiago Ramón y Cajal (1852–1934) in 1906 "in recognition of their work on the structure of the nervous system."

(B)

May 30

Sir William Ramsay and Morris Travers discover krypton.

As described in the sidebar "Discovering the Elements," scientists identified many of the *elements* that make up matter by looking at the characteristic *spectral lines* that they emit. This technique is particularly useful for identifying a group of elements known as the inert or *noble gases*. By 1898, two of these gases, helium and argon, had been identified. On May 30, 1898, English chemists Sir William Ramsay (1852–1916) and Morris Travers (1872–1961) analyze a sample of argon and find that it is contaminated with another type of gas. When they look at its spectral lines, they find that it is a new element, which they name krypton. Ramsay is honored with the Nobel Prize in chemistry in 1904 "in recognition of his services in the discovery of the inert gaseous elements in air, and his determination of their place in the periodic system."

(C)

June

Sir William Ramsay and Morris Travers discover the element neon.

Scientists identified many of the inert or *noble gases* by examining the characteristic

CELLULAR ORGANELLE DISCOVERED DURING THE NINETEENTH CENTURY

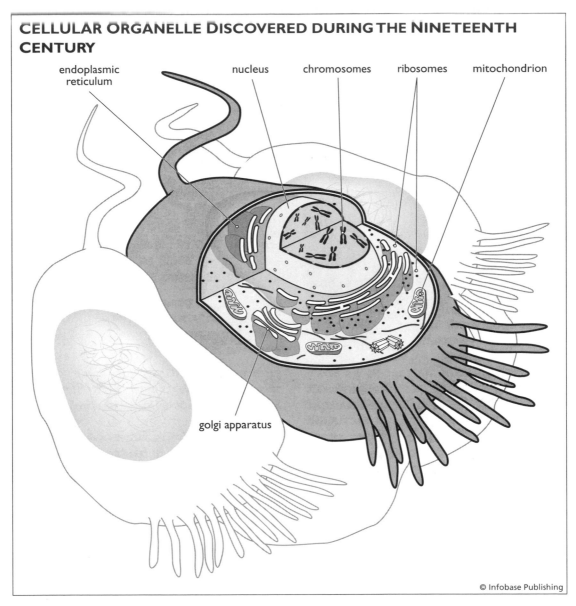

endoplasmic reticulum — nucleus — chromosomes — ribosomes — mitochondrion

golgi apparatus

© Infobase Publishing

Many of the specialized compartments or organelle and other important structures found in eukaryotic cells are discovered at the end of the 19th century. Among the discoveries are the plasma membrane, nucleus, chromosomes, Golgi apparatus, and mitochondria.

spectral lines that they emit. In 1898, English chemists Sir William Ramsay (1852–1916) and Morris Travers (1872–1961) study a sample of the *noble gas* argon. They form solid argon, and then let it evaporate and collect the gas it gives off. By analyzing the spectral lines of the new gas, they see that it is a previously unidentified element, and they call the new element neon. Ramsay is honored with the Nobel Prize in chemistry in 1904 "in recognition of his services in the discovery of the inert gaseous elements in air, and his determination of their place in the periodic system."

(C)

July

Pierre and Marie Curie announce the discovery of polonium.

The creation of the *periodic table* of the elements predicted the existence of many elements that were not known at the time (*See* entry for 1869). In July 1898, French chemist Pierre Curie (1859–1906) and his wife, chemist Marie Curie (1867–1934), publish an account of a new radioactive element that they isolated from a sample of uranium. They call the element, which had been predicted by the periodic table of the elements, polonium. Marie Curie is honored with the Nobel Prize in chemistry for this and other work (*See* entry for DECEMBER 1898) in 1911, five years after Pierre's death, "in recognition of her services to the advancement of chemistry by the discovery of the elements radium and polonium, by the isolation of radium and the study of the nature and compounds of this remarkable element."

(C, P)

July 12

Sir William Ramsay and Morris Travers discover xenon.

The group of *elements* known as the inert or *noble gases* occur naturally as single *atoms* rather than as a part of a compound. At the end of the 19th century, English chemists Sir William Ramsay (1852–1916) and Morris Travers (1872–1961) isolated three of these gases: neon, argon, and krypton. On July 12, 1898, the pair isolates a fourth noble gas

from a sample of krypton. They name this new gas xenon. Ramsay is honored with the Nobel Prize in chemistry in 1904 "in recognition of his services in the discovery of the inert gaseous elements in air, and his determination of their place in the periodic system."

(C)

December 26

Pierre and Marie Curie discover radium.

The creation of the *periodic table* of the elements predicted the existence of many *elements* that were not known at the time (*See* entry for 1869). In 1898, French chemist Pierre Curie (1859–1906) and his wife, chemist Marie Curie (1867–1934), study the material in pitchblende, an ore of the radioactive element uranium. They are able to extract

Polish chemist Marie Curie's work on radioactive elements is honored with Nobel Prizes in both physics and chemistry. *(Museum of the History of Science, Oxford)*

a small amount of a new element from the sample. They announce the discovery of the new element, which they call radium, on December 26 of that year. Marie Curie is honored with the Nobel Prize in chemistry for this and other work (*See* entry for JULY 1898) in 1911, five years after Pierre Curie's death, "in recognition of her services to the advancement of chemistry by the discovery of the elements radium and polonium, by the isolation of radium and the study of the nature and compounds of this remarkable element."

(C, P)

1899

André-Louis Debierne isolates actinium.

The discovery of *radioactivity* in the 19th century led many chemists to look for undiscovered radioactive *elements*. In 1899, French scientist André-Louis Debierne (1874–1949) isolates the element actinium from a uranium ore. Actinium is a highly radioactive element that occurs naturally in the Earth's crust, albeit in trace quantities. Today, researchers prepare actinium in the laboratory by bombarding an *isotope* of the element radium with *neutrons*.

(C)

David Hilbert describes the foundations of geometry.

Geometry has been studied since the days of ancient Greece. In 1899, German mathematician David Hilbert (1862–1943) writes *Grundlagen der geometrie* (The foundations of geometry), describing the assumptions or *axioms* that underlie *Euclidian geometry* and explaining their significance. Hilbert's work is widely read and serves as guide to geometry throughout the 20th century.

(M)

Karl Ferdinand Braun improves radio transmission.

The transmission of *radio waves* across the Atlantic Ocean required more than antennas to accept them; it required powerful transmitters. In 1899, German physicist Karl Ferdinand Braun (1850–1918) improves Italian physicist Gugielmo Marconi's (1874–1937) transmitting system, greatly increasing the distance that radio waves could be transmitted. Braun's improved transmitters combined with the large antennas developed by Gugielmo Marconi allows radio waves to be transmitted across the Atlantic Ocean. In 1909, Braun and Marconi share the Nobel Prize in physics "in recognition of their contributions to the development of wireless telegraphy."

∽ CONCLUSION ∾

Many of the scientific discoveries of the late 19th century had great consequences in the 20th century. In medicine, the discovery that microorganisms cause disease leads to effective methods to prevent diseases such as malaria through the control of mosquitoes, as well as the development of antibiotics to kill disease-causing microbes. The two other important advances in biology of the era, Charles Darwin's theory of *evolution* and Gregor Mendel's theory of heredity, also have medical impact in the 20th century. In the early decades of the 20th century, biologists will reconcile the works of Darwin and Mendel, then use their work as a starting point to understand how genetics influence normal development as well as diseases.

Work in physics at the end of the 19th century, particularly early studies of black box *radiation* and the discoveries of *X-rays, radioactivity,* and the *electron,* lay the basis for the revolution in physics and the development of quantum mechanics that occurs at the beginning of the 20th century. Twentieth-century physicists will soon uncover other *subatomic particles* and within 50 years learn to harness the forces that hold the *atom* together.

The last half of the 19th century also sees the first suggestion, by geologist Eduard Suess, that geological formations such as mountains are formed by the movement of landmasses—the first articulation of what will become *plate tectonics* in the 20th century. The next century will see a clear articulation of the *continental drift theory,* the discovery of ridges in the world's oceans, and a greater understanding of how the Earth's landmasses move.

7

New Theories and Old

1900–1945

∾ INTRODUCTION ∾

The beginning of the 20th century marks a new era for science and technology. The field of physics is on the verge of a change that no one could have predicted. Biology and chemistry are applied to the treatment of human diseases. Through the study of earthquakes, geologists begin to understand the different layers that make up the Earth. Scientific advances even shed some light into the most unpredictable of natural phenomena, weather.

Some argue that no scientific discipline witnesses as much change in the first half of the 20th century as the field of physics. The discovery of *radioactivity* and *X-rays* in the late 19th century had set off a wave of experiments that fundamentally altered the understanding of the *atom*. During the 19th century, physicists identified the *electron*. Ernst Rutherford and James Chadwick identified two more fundamental components of the atom, the *proton* and *neutron*. With this new understanding came a realization

of the *energy* harnessed within the atomic *nucleus*. In 1942, Italian-American physicist Enrico Fermi (1901–54) performs the first controlled nuclear reaction in the laboratory. His work is predicated upon research in *quantum mechanics* that dominates physics during this era. Through the work of physicists Max Planck (1858–1947), Niels Bohr (1885–1962), Werner Heisenberg (1901–76), Erwin Schrödinger (1887–1961), and others, the world is introduced to new concepts that describe the behavior of *subatomic particles*. One of the most famous physicists of the era, (1879–1955) Albert Einstein, makes his mark on quantum theory when he describes the particle nature of light. Also during this era, Einstein makes his most famous contribution to physics—his two theories of *relativity*.

Biology and chemistry join forces in the first half of the 20th century to help elucidate the chemical reactions that are vital to sustaining life. New insights are gained into how *energy* is harnessed from food and stored in the body. Through the work of biochemists Carl (1896–1984) and Gerty (1896–1957) Cori, Sir Hans Krebs (1900–81), Fritz Lipmann (1899–1986), and others, many of the basic mechanisms of energy metabolism are uncovers. Biology and chemistry are also used to tackle diseases. The origins of a number of infectious diseases, including yellow fever and typhus, are identified, leading the way for vaccine development. Scottish microbiologist Sir Alexander Fleming (1881–1955) discovers penicillin, the first antibiotic. The development of other antibiotics, such as sulfa drugs and streptomycin, mean once fatal bacterial infections can be treated. Chemists also discover the chemical structure of a number of biologically important molecules, including the oxygen-carrying molecule *hemoglobin,* a number of *hormones,* and vitamins.

The understanding of the Earth and its atmosphere is dramatically changed at the beginning of the century. The work of seismologists, including Richard Dixon Oldham (1858–1936), Andrija Mohorovičić (1857–1936), Beno Gutenberg (1889–1960), and Inge Lehman (1888–1993) identifies the different layers of the Earth, from the *crust* to the core. Meteorologists make similar findings, notably Léon-Phillippe Teisserenc De Bort (1885–1931) who divides the atmosphere into two layers, the *stratosphere* and *troposphere.* Later, French physicist Charles Fabry (1867–1945) discovers the *ozone layer,*

and scientists begin to understand its role in protecting the Earth from ultraviolet rays.

Beyond the Earth's atmosphere, astronomers identify new heavenly bodies and begin to gather data that the universe is expanding. Pluto, the ninth planet in the solar system, is discovered. Astronomers also find the nearest star to the Earth. Astronomers Edwin Hubble (1889–1953) and Vesto Slipher (1875–1969) both observe galaxies moving away from the Earth. Soon other astronomers begin collecting evidence that the universe is expanding. Such observations lead mathematician Alexander Friedmann (1888–1925) to propose that the universe began with a giant explosion, also known as the big bang.

Current scientific advances are widely applied by inventors and engineers at the beginning of the 20th century. As the century opens, American inventors Orville (1871–1948) and Wilbur (1867–1912) Wright draw the plans that lead to the first flight in 1903. Engineers and mathematicians begin developing the circuits needed to create simple computers. In 1943, English mathematician Alan Turing (1912–54) and colleagues design Colossus, the first electronic computer. The British use Colossus to help decode messages during World War II. World War II also brings about the development of the most powerful weapon ever seen, the nuclear bomb.

TIME LINE OF SCIENTIFIC ACHIEVEMENTS FROM 1900 TO 1945

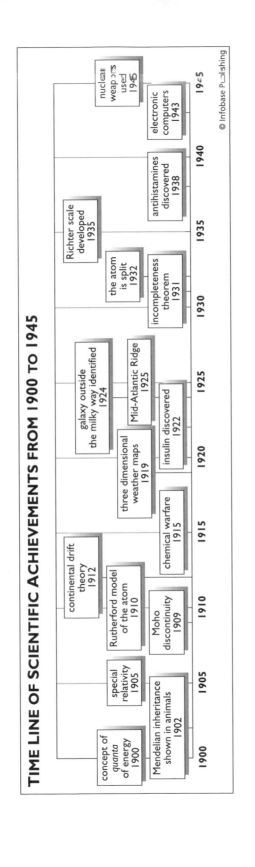

concept of *quanta* of energy 1900

Mendelian inheritance shown in animals 1902

special relativity 1905

Moho discontinuity 1909

Rutherford model of the atom 1910

continental drift theory 1912

chemical warfare 1915

three dimensional weather maps 1919

galaxy outside the milky way identified 1924

insulin discovered 1922

Mid-Atlantic Ridge 1925

incompleteness theorem 1931

the atom is split 1932

Richter scale developed 1935

antihistamines discovered 1938

nuclear weapons used 1945

electronic computers 1943

1900 1905 1910 1915 1920 1925 1930 1935 1940 1945

❧ CHRONOLOGY ❧

1900

Friedrich Ernst Dorn discovers radon.

The group of *elements* known as the inert or *noble gases* occur naturally as single *atoms* rather than as a part of a compound. In 1900, German physicist Friedrich Ernst Dorn (1848–1916) studies the radioactive element radium. He notes that a gas builds up when radium is kept in tightly sealed containers. He shows that the gas is a previously unknown element, with 86 *protons,* now known as radon. While radon is a noble gas that does not readily react with other chemicals, the element is also highly radioactive, and thus short-lived.

(C, P)

Karl Pearson applies statistics to the study of heredity.

At the end of the 19th century, biologists began applying mathematical treatments to their observations. Mathematics began to be used to test the validity of observations, particularly by scientists studying *evolution* and heredity. English mathematician Karl Pearson (1858–1936) pioneered the application of *statistics* to biology. In 1900, he develops the chi-squared test. The chi-squared test allows scientists to compare the theoretical results of an experiment to the actual data and draw conclusions as to whether the theory is valid. Pearson's test remains one of the most widely used statistical tests in biology.

(B, M)

A virus causes yellow fever.

Yellow fever is a potentially fatal infectious disease prominent in tropical climates. In 1900, the Yellow Fever Board headed by American army surgeon Walter Reed (1851–1902) discovers that the disease is caused by a *virus.* They also find that mosquitoes passed on the virus. These two facts are vital to the control of yellow fever, leading to efforts to control the mosquito population and reduce the number of yellow fever outbreaks. Today, a vaccine is available, which confers immunity to the virus. However, the World Health Organization still considers it to be an important threat to public health in tropical regions.

(B)

A new alloy of nickel steel improves weight measurements.

Every system of weights and measures requires a set of standards that defines each unit. Unfortunately, such standards can be difficult to develop because the same material may have different a volume at different temperatures. In 1900, Swiss physicist Charles Édouard Guillaume (1861–1938), a scientist at the International Bureau of Weights and Measured, finds an *alloy* of nickel steel that expands very little in a wide range of temperature. The alloy is useful not only as a weight standard, but also as a material in precision instruments. Guillaume is honored with the Nobel Prize in physics in 1920 "in recognition of the service he has rendered to precision measurements in Physics by his discovery of anomalies in nickel steel alloys."

(P)

Moses Gomberg isolates a new reactive molecule.

As the structure of the *atom* was uncovered, chemists looked to explain how atoms interact with one another to form compounds. One mechanism is elucidated in 1900, when American chemist Moses Gomberg (1866–1947) discovers the *organic* free radical. A free radical is a highly reactive chemical that contains an unpaired *electron.* At the time of the discovery, chemists think it is impossible to isolate such a molecule. Thus, many chemists dismiss Gomberg's work for nearly 30 years, until they became used in the synthesis of plastics. Today, organic free radicals remain important chemicals in the manufacture of plastics, latex, and other *polymers*.

(C)

Biologists rediscover Mendelian genetics. Gregor Mendel's work on genetics remained largely unnoticed for nearly 40 years. The renewed interest in his work is tradition- ally attributed to three scientists who inde-

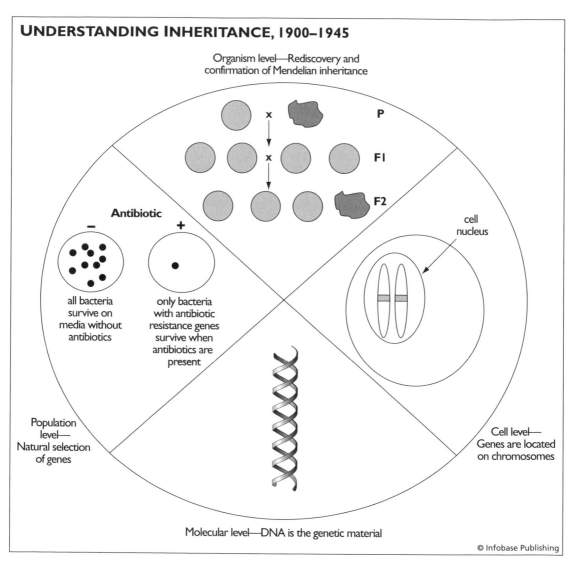

UNDERSTANDING INHERITANCE, 1900–1945

Organism level—Rediscovery and confirmation of Mendelian inheritance

P

F1

F2

Antibiotic

−   +

all bacteria survive on media without antibiotics

only bacteria with antibiotic resistance genes survive when antibiotics are present

cell nucleus

Population level— Natural selection of genes

Cell level— Genes are located on chromosomes

Molecular level—DNA is the genetic material

© Infobase Publishing

From 1900 to 1945, a number of events changed our understanding of inheritance. Clockwise from top: Gregor Mendel's work on inheritance became widely accepted. Genes were shown to reside on chromosomes in the cell nucleus. Avery and colleagues demonstrated that DNA is the genetic material in cells. Scientists began to reconcile Mendel's work on inheritance with Charles Darwin's theory of natural selection.

pendently repeated and extended his theories in 1900. German botanist Karl Correns (1864–1933) shows that sex is inherited in Mendelian fashion. Meanwhile, Dutch botanist Hugo de Vries (1848–1935) uses Mendelian genetics to support *evolution*. Austrian botanist Erich Tschermak von Seysenegg (1871–1962) is one of the first to apply Mendel's laws to crop breeding. Their work marks the beginning of the wide acceptance of Mendel and his theory of inheritance.

(B)

Paul Villard discovers gamma rays.

Many physicists and chemists at the turn of the 20th century eagerly pursued questions involving *radioactivity*. In 1900, French physicist Paul Villard (1860–1934) notices that some radioactive *elements* emit a different type of *energy* than the previously characterized *alpha* and *beta radiation*. The rays he identifies are later called *gamma rays*. Today, gamma rays are important components in a number of medical imaging tests, such as PET scans.

(P)

Karl Landsteiner identifies the four major blood groups.

The risk of blood loss is inherent in major surgeries, particularly those on the heart and lungs. Such procedures often require transfusions. However, the body's immune system will often, but not always, reject the blood of another person. In 1900, American biologist Karl Landsteiner (1868–1943) finds one of the keys to successful blood transfusion when he identifies the four human blood groups: A, B, AB, and O. These groups identify the presence and type of particular *proteins*, called *antigens*, in the blood. Blood typing allows successful transfusions between two people with the same blood type. Landsteiner is honored with the Nobel Prize in physiology

or medicine in 1930 "for his discovery of human blood groups."

May 11

The Grignard reagent improves the synthesis of many chemicals.

One of the goals of *organic* chemistry is to synthesize complex chemicals from simple starting materials. In 1900, chemists looked for methods to create specific molecules called organic halides. In research toward his Ph.D., French chemist Victor Grignard (1871–1935) develops a useful reagent, called the Grignard reagent to make these molecules. The Grignard reagent can be made at room temperature and used right away, making it useful in the synthesis of a wide variety of molecules. In 1912, Grignard is awarded the Nobel Prize in chemistry "for the discovery of the so-called Grignard reagent, which in recent years has greatly advanced the progress of organic chemistry."

(C)

August 8

David Hilbert poses mathematical problems to be solved in the next century.

Advances in science do not come just from discoveries, but from the clear articulation of the problems that need to be solved. At the turn of the 20th century, German mathematician David Hilbert was considered one of the world's finest mathematicians. In 1900, he is asked to address the Second International Congress of Mathematicians. He uses the occasion to speak about the future problems of mathematics. In a speech on August 8 of that year, and in subsequent papers, he outlines 23 problems that should be solved during the 20th century. One hundred years later, a number of them remain unsolved.

(M)

December 14

Max Planck states that energy radiates in discrete portions.

The discovery of *radiation* was the beginning of a radical change in physics. At the turn of the 20th century, physicists strived to understand the *energy* of the *atom;* however, classical physics could not explain the data that were being observed. On December 14, 1900, German physicist Max Planck proposes that radiated energy exists in discrete portions he called *quanta*—an idea that marks the birth of quantum physics. Planck is honored with the Nobel Prize in physics in 1918 "in recognition of the services he rendered to the advancement of Physics by his discovery of energy quanta."

(P)

1901

Eugène-Anatole Demarçay isolates europium.

The series of *elements* known as the rare earth elements, or *lanthanides,* proved to be difficult to identify. Many early preparations were subsequently shown to be impure. One of the first lanthanides to be discovered was cerium. A series of studies found cerium samples to contain a number of other elements, including didymium, praseodymium, neodymium, samarium, and gadolinium. In 1901, French scientist Eugène-Anatole Demarçay (1852–1904) finds another element in these preparations, which he names europium.

(C)

Sigmund Freud describes the unconscious mind.

Austrian physician Sigmund Freud (1856–1939) began his career as a medical doctor who specialized in diseases of the nervous system. This led him to an interest in the scientific investigation of psychological conditions. Over time he developed his widely known theories of psychoanalysis. In 1901, he publishes *Interpretation of Dreams.* Freud describes the functioning of the unconscious mind and how it influences conscious behavior. This and other works by Freud fuel the psychoanalytic movement.

(B)

Sir Frederick Hopkins discovers an essential amino acid.

As techniques in chemistry and biology became more sophisticated, scientists tried to identify the exact nutrients required to maintain a healthy body. One of the pioneers in this field was English biochemist Sir Frederick Hopkins (1861–1947), who studied *amino acids,* the building blocks of *proteins.* In 1901, he discovers the amino acid tryptophan. Hopkins shows that humans must get this amino acid from food, making tryptophan the first essential amino acid to be identified. Today, scientists know that a number of amino acids must be obtained from people's diets. Hopkins is honored with the Nobel Prize in physiology or medicine in 1929 for "for his discovery of the growth-stimulating vitamins."

(B, C)

Sir Owen Richardson shows that heat causes electrons to be emitted from metals.

Many scientists at the turn of the 20th century were interested in the ability of metals to conduct *electrons.* Studies had shown that metals could also emit electrons at high temperatures. How this occurred remained a subject of debate. Some thought that the emission was a result of a chemical reaction between the metal and the gases surrounding it, while others believed it was solely due to the high temperatures. In 1901, English physicist Sir Owen Richardson settles this debate by showing that electron emission occurred under high vacuum, and thus must be caused by heat. Richardson is honored with the Nobel Prize in physics in 1928 "for his work on the thermionic phenomenon and especially for the discovery of the law named after him."

(P)

AWARDING SCIENCE

For a week each fall, news reports describe the important discoveries in science that have been honored with the Nobel Prize. The Nobel Prize was set up in the will of the inventor of dynamite, Alfred Nobel. Nobel amassed a sizable estate through patents on his inventions and the laboratories he set up around the world. In his will, he specified that a portion of his estate be set aside to fund five international prizes to be given to individuals who excelled in physics, chemistry, physiology or medicine, literature, and work toward international peace. The Nobel Foundation was soon established to coordinate the awarding of the prize. In 1968, a sixth prize, the Bank of Sweden Prize in Economic Science in Memory of Alfred Nobel, was added.

Alfred Nobel's will specified the organization that would select the recipient and some criteria they should use in the selection process. The physics and chemistry prize recipients are awarded by the Swedish Academy of Science, while the Karolinska Institute in Stockholm awards the physiology or medicine prize. Nobel's will states that the prize is given to the person who made the most important discoveries in their respective field in the past year. However, scientific discoveries must be reviewed, published, and repeated by others before they are widely accepted. Therefore, the selection committees for the three science prizes normally award discoveries that happened years earlier, but their importance is apparent in the year of the award. Another complication is the overlap between the fields. Some discoveries could be equally considered chemistry or physics. Other candidates for the chemistry prize might just as easily fall under the category of physiology or medicine. For instance, the polymerase *chain reaction,* (PCR) developed by American biochemist Kary Mullis (b. 1944) in the 1980s, relied on a chemical reaction that amplified biological samples. PCR has a great impact in the fields of biology and forensics. Mullis received the Nobel Prize in chemistry, but one could easily argue that he could have received the award for physiology or medicine. Another striking example is Polish scientist Marie Curie. She was awarded two Nobel Prizes for different aspects of her work on *radioactivity.* The first award was for physics and the second was for chemistry.

The selection criteria for the Nobel Prize states that the recipient must be living and that the prize can be divided between no more than three people each year. These rules have led to some controversy over who should receive the prize for a specific discovery. Most scientific discoveries are not individual events, but are developments that occur over time and with the contributions of many researchers. When this work culminates in an important discovery, it can be hard to narrow the list to three scientists who contributed to it. The stipulation that the honoree be living at the time the prize is announced also means that some great discoveries are not honored with Nobel Prizes. For example, the work of American biologist Oswald Avery (1877–1955) identifying DNA as the genetic material was not honored with a Nobel Prize because Avery had died before his work was widely accepted and its great significance had become apparent.

(continues)

(continued)

Does having a Nobel Prize attached to a discovery signify that it is among the best of its time? While certainly a great number of prizes have been given to the most important work of the era, there are conspicuous omissions, as well as prizes awarded for work that is now considered of questionable value. In addition, many fields are often left out of Nobel consideration. Many have noted that there is not a Nobel Prize awarded for achievement in mathematics. The closest equivalent to a mathematics Nobel Prize is the Fields Medal awarded for superior achievement in mathematics by a scholar under the age of 40. In addition, a number of mathematicians have been awarded the memorial prize in Economics. Similarly, Nobel Prizes are not awarded in the vibrant fields of Earth science or ecology, leaving many great scientists out of Nobel consideration. Despite these notable omissions, the list of Nobel Prize winners makes it clear it includes the names of many of the greatest scientists of the past century.

Arthur Kennelly discovers the ionosphere.

The first transmission of *radio waves* across the Atlantic Ocean fascinated scientists as well as the general public. American Arthur Kennelly (1861–1939), an electrical engineer, was particularly interested in how the waves traveled beyond the curvature of the Earth. In 1901, he proposes that the waves do not follow the path of the Earth, but rather bounce off a layer of electrical charge in the atmosphere. He calls this layer the *ionosphere*. Today, Earth scientists study changes in the ionosphere to monitor changes in the Earth's atmosphere.

(P, SA, W)

Walter Sutton proposes that chromosomes hold genetic information.

As Mendelian genetics gained in acceptance, the search for the material responsible for transmitting genetic information began. From 1901 to 1903, American physician Walter Sutton (1877–1916) was a graduate student studying this problem. He proposes that *chromosomes* found in the cell's *nucleus* hold this genetic information. Once the cellular home of genetic information is established, scientists move on to finding the chemical basis of heredity. Today, biologists have clearly established that the DNA in the chromosomes holds the genetic information essential for life.

(B)

December 12

Guglielmo Marconi transmits radio waves across the Atlantic Ocean.

Physicists demonstrated the existence of *radio waves*, short-lived electromagnetic waves that can travel through air, in the 1880s. At the turn of the 20th century, Italian physicist Guglielmo Marconi set out to make these waves useful by devising a means to transmit these waves over a long distance. He did this by building larger antennas. On December 12, 1901, Marconi transmits radio waves across the Atlantic Ocean, opening up lines of rapid communication between the United States and Europe. Marconi shares the Nobel Prize in physics with Karl Ferdinand Braun "in recognition of their contributions to the development of wireless telegraphy."

(P)

1902

Ernst Rutherford and Frederick Soddy describe radioactive disintegration.

Radioactivity was widely studied by chemists and physicists at the turn of the 20th century.

In 1901, Guglielmo Marconi transmits radio waves across the Atlantic Ocean. This illustration depicts the experimental design Marconi used. (*SPL/Photo Researchers, Inc*)

In 1902, British physicist Ernest Rutherford (1871–1937) studies the radioactive element thorium. Working with English chemists Frederick Soddy (1877–1956), Rutherford notices that thorium loses its radioactive activity over time, and a new form of thorium appears in that same time. When they graph the disappearance of radioactivity and the appearance of thorium over time, they uncover a fundamental property of radioactivity, radioactive disintegration. Their work demonstrates that radioactive *elements* disintegrate into new elements when radiation is released. Rutherford is honored with the Nobel Prize in chemistry in 1908 "for his investigations into the disintegration of the elements, and the chemistry of radioactive substances."

(C, P)

William Bayliss and Ernest Starling discover the first hormone.

Within a multicellular organism, cells must be able to communicate with one another and with groups of tissues and organs. In 1902, English biologists William Bayliss (1900–64) and Ernest Starling (1866–1927) study how the body knows to produce digestive *enzymes* after eating. They discover that the pancreas produces digestive enzymes not in response to nerve impulses but rather in response to a molecule secreted from the stomach lining. The molecule, which they call secretin, is the first *hormone* to be characterized.

(B)

Léon Teisserenc de Bort discovers that the atmosphere has different layers.

The invention of the hot-air balloon allowed meteorologists to study high reaches of the atmosphere. French scientist Léon Teisserenc de Bort conducted a series of experiments in which he sent balloons up into the atmosphere and measured the temperature at various distances from the Earth's surface. He found that the temperature decreased at higher altitudes until the balloon reached 6.8 miles (11 km) above the Earth. At this altitude, temperature stabilizes. Other meteorologists observed the same phenomena but attributed it to instrument error. In 1902, Teisserenc de Bort confirms that this was not an error and proposes that the Earth's atmosphere consisted of two parts: the *troposphere*, where temperatures change, and the *stratosphere*, where they remain constant. His findings influence other scientists who soon found similar layers in the Earth.

(ES, W)

William Bateson shows that Mendelian inheritance applies to animals.

The Mendelian laws of heredity were established and reintroduced to explain the reproduction of plants. In 1902, English biologist William Bateson (1861–1926) shows that the laws of Mendelian inheritance extends to animals. He adds to the rediscovery of Mendel's work by translating it into English. Later, in 1905, Bateson calls the study of inherited traits genetics and suggests most of the terms still used today.

(B)

Henri-Léon Lebesgue develops a new method of integration.

One of the primary problems in *calculus* is finding the area inside a curve for a given *function*. This process is known as *integration*. However, not all function can be represented by as a curve on a graph. In 1902, French mathematician Henri-Léon Lebesgue (1875–1941) develops a method to integrate these functions. The Lebesgue integral greatly influences mathematics by expanding the number of functions that could be integrated.

(M)

The electrocardiogram measures and records electrical activity in the heart.

The heart is responsible for pumping blood throughout the body. Electrical impulses are critical for the heart's action. Dutch physiologist Willem Einthoven (1860–1927) realized that one could assess the functioning of the heart by measuring its electrical activity. In 1902, he invents the electrocardiogram, an instrument that measures and records this activity. Today, electrocardiography remains an important diagnostic tool in cardiac medicine. Einthoven is honored with the Nobel Prize in physiology or medicine in 1924 "for his discovery of the mechanism of the electrocardiogram."

(B)

June

Alexis Carrel describes methods to reconstruct damaged blood vessels.

A key step in reattaching severed limbs or transplanting organs is to attach the cut blood vessels to the patient's existing vessels in a way that does not impede circulation. In June 1902, French surgeon Alexis Carrel (1873–1944) describes a method to replace or reconstruct damaged blood vessels. Carrel uses his technique to transplant organs in experimental animals. He is honored with the Nobel Prize in physiology or medicine in 1912 "in recognition of his work on vascular suture and the transplantation of blood vessels and organs."

(B)

1903

Charles-Robert Richet describes anaphylaxis.

For centuries, humans have recognized that substances made by plants and animals can act as poisons that harm or potentially kill other organisms. How these poisons exert their actions, on the other hand, was not always clear. In 1903, French physiologist Charles-Robert Richet (1850–1935) begins to unravel the mechanisms that some poisons use. Richet finds that exposure to a toxin extracted from a Portuguese man-of-war increases a person's sensitivity to the effects of that toxin. He called this effect *anaphylaxis*. Today, scientists know that anaphylaxis occurs when the immune system recognizes a foreign substance, like a toxin, and mounts a particularly strong immune response against it. Richet is honored with the Nobel Prize in physiology or medicine in 1913 "in recognition of his work on anaphylaxis."

(B)

Richard Zsigmondy describes the nature of colloidal gold.

Matter can take three forms, gas, liquid, and solid. Matter can also be mixed into solutions or dispersed into a *colloid*. An example of a colloid is fog, where water is dispersed through the air. German chemist Richard Zsigmondy (1865–1929) studied the colloids of gold. In 1903, he invents the ultramicroscope to investigate these solutions and uses his instrument to describe the nature of colloidal gold. Zsigmondy is honored with the Nobel Prize in chemistry in 1925 "for his demonstration of the heterogeneous nature of colloid solutions and for the methods he used, which have since become fundamental in modern colloid chemistry."

(C)

Konstantin Tsiolkovsky describes methods for exploring space.

By the early 20th century, advances in science and engineering made space exploration seem possible. In Russia, the father of space travel was scientist Konstantin Tsiolkovsky (1857–1935). Tsiolkovsky envisioned much of the space travel that occurred in the latter half of the 20th century. In 1903, he publishes *Research into Interplanetary Space by Means of Rocket Power,* which advocates the use of multistage rockets and liquid propellants to explore space. He continues his writing on the theory of space exploration until his death in 1932. Today, he is considered the father of cosmonautics.

(SA)

Charles Glover Barkla uses X-rays to identify gases.

The discovery of *X-rays* leads physicists to investigate their affect on matter. In 1903, English physicist Charles Glover Barkla (1877–1944) wonders what happens when gases are exposed to X-rays. He shows that when X-rays are aimed at an elemental gas, the gas gives off radiation. In fact, each element gives off radiation of a specific wavelength. This characteristic of each element can be used to identify the element that makes up the gas. Barkla is honored with the Nobel Prize in physics in 1917 "for his discovery of the characteristic Röntgen radiation of the element."

(C, P)

Johan Herman Lie Vogt studies the formation of igneous rocks.

Igneous rocks are glassy rocks formed from when hot magma solidifies. In 1903, Norwegian geologist Johan Herman Lie Vogt (1858–1931) publishes a study on the formation of these rocks called *The Molten Silicate Solution.* Vogt notes that by-products of industrial combustion, called slags, have similar properties as igneous rocks. He uses these slags as starting point of a chemical study of igneous rocks. His work inspires geologists to take similar approaches to studying rock formation.

(ES)

December 17

Orville and Wilbur Wright take the first airplane flight.

Humans dreamed that they could fly like the birds. Hot-air balloons allowed humans to travel in the air; however, they were difficult to control. Inventors began dreaming of a machine that would allow a controlled flight through the air. On December 17, 1903, American inventors Orville (1871–1948) and Wilbur (1867–1912) Wright realize that dream when they take the first flight in an airplane they both designed and built. The Wright Brothers airplane flies for 59 seconds and travels approximately 852 feet (260 m). Within a few years, airplanes are being produced for commercial and military uses.

(P)

1904

Hendrik Antoon Lorentz puts forth a proposal about objects moving near the speed of light.

Some of the most important discoveries are the result of experiments that appear, at first glance, to have failed. Such is the case of the so-called Lorentz transformations. In 1904, Dutch physicist Hendrik Antoon Lorentz

American inventors Wilbur and Orville Wright complete the first successful airplane flight in 1903. Here the Wright brothers are shown wih *Flyer II* at Huffmann Prairie. *(NASA)*

proposes an explanation for a famous experiment that failed to measure the motion of the Earth relative to space. Looking at this experiment, he realizes that objects moving near the speed of light have slightly different physical properties. Thus, properties such as mass, length, and time are relative. These ideas later form the basis for Einstein's special theory of relativity.

(P)

Christian Bohr studies the release of oxygen from the blood.

Animal cells require oxygen to carry out their many activities. The major by-product of these reactions is carbon dioxide. These gases are carried to and from the lungs via the bloodstream. In 1904, Danish physiologist Christian Bohr (1855–1911) studies the uptake and release of these gases by the blood protein *hemoglobin*. He finds that hemoglobin binds carbon dioxide more tightly than oxygen. Therefore, if a cell is releasing carbon dioxide, the hemoglobin will let go of the oxygen it is carrying from the lungs. This process is known today as the Bohr Effect.

(B)

Franz Knoop uses tracers to follow chemical reactions in the body.

In the 20th century, many chemists turned their attention to the chemical reactions that take place in the body. Many of these studies were performed using molecules that were first isolated from cells and tissues, then studied in the laboratory. In 1904, German biochemist Franz Knoop (1875–1946) develops a method to follow chemical reactions as they occurred in the body, using a biological tracer. Knoop studies fat metabolism by labeling fat molecules with a tracer, then feeding the labeled fat to dogs. He then analyzes the urine of these dogs, looking at what molecules carry the tracer. From these studies he determines how the fat was broken down. Today, tracers are routinely used in biology laboratories.

(B, C)

Sir Arthur Harden discovers that coenzymes are important for biological reactions.

The field of biochemistry was born as chemists began turning their attention toward reactions that occur in living systems. First, the chemists tried to learn how the *fermentation* of sugars occurred. Outside of living cells, biological catalysts, known as *enzymes,* carried out these reactions. In 1904, English chemist Sir Arthur Harden (1865–1940) discovers that inside the cell enzymes alone cannot efficiently carry out such reactions. He finds that they required an additional cofactor, now known as a coenzyme. Today, biologists realize that many enzymes require coenzymes to carry out their biological function. Harden shares the Nobel Prize in chemistry in 1929 with German chemist Hans Karl August Simon von Euler-Chelpin "for their investigations on the fermentation of sugar and fermentative enzymes."

(B, C)

December 20

Mount Wilson Observatory is founded.

As the field of astrophysics began to grow in the early 20th century, scientists required larger telescopes to collect data about the stars. On December 20, 1904, scientists interested in studying the Sun open the Mount Wilson Observatory in the mountains of Southern California. Within four years, it houses the largest telescopes in the world. Throughout the 20th century, the Mount Wilson Observatory remains a leading site for astronomical research.

(SA)

1905

Ernst Rutherford uses radioactive decay to estimate the age of the Earth.

The discovery and explosion of research into *radioactivity* affected many fields of science. For instance, the occurrence of natural radioactivity in rocks meant work in the field led to new research in geology. In 1905, British chemist Ernst Rutherford uses *radioactive decay* to estimate the age of the Earth. Rutherford proposes that the radioactive elements in rocks release helium gas as they decay. The helium is then trapped in the rock. Thus, by measuring the amount of helium, Rutherford deduces the age of the rock. Using this method, he estimates the age of the Earth to be approximately 500 million years.

(C, ES, P)

Fritz Haber synthesizes ammonia in the laboratory.

Nitrogen is one of the main components of the air around us. At the turn of the 20th century, chemists looked for methods to capture nitrogen from the air and incorporate it into useful compounds, such as ammonia. Ammonia is made up of *atoms* of nitrogen and hydrogen. In 1905, German chemist Fritz Haber (1868–1934) becomes the first person to synthesize ammonia from these two gases. His work leads to the industrial production of ammonia, an important component of a number of products ranging from fertilizers to weapons. Haber is honored with the Nobel Prize in chemistry in 1918 "for the synthesis of ammonia from its elements."

(C)

Sir Rowland Biffen shows the ability to resist infection is inherited.

Farmers working in the field have always recognized that certain plants seem to resist insects and infections better than others do. In 1905, British botanist Sir Rowland Biffen (1874–1949) shows that the ability to resist infection is inherited. He performs experiments on two different varieties of wheat and demonstrates that the ability to resist infection with a particular fungus is passed down from one generation to the next. This discovery sets off a flurry of activity aimed at producing hardier strains of agriculturally important plants. Today, genetic engineering has produced a number of plants that are resistant to a variety of pests and infections.

(B)

Robert Bárány recognizes the role of vestibular apparatus in maintaining equilibrium.

The anatomy of the ear is easy to determine by dissection. The physiology, on the other hand, is more difficult to discern since it is difficult to observe the functioning of an organ. In 1905, Austrian physician Robert Bárány (1876–1936) expands knowledge of a portion of the ear known as the vestibular apparatus. He notices that patients with ear infections who were being treated by irrigating the ear canal often became dizzy. He studies this phenomenon and concludes that water entering the ear canal has an effect on body balance. Physiologists now know that the vestibular apparatus plays a key role in maintaining equilibrium. For his insights, Bárány is awarded the Nobel Prize in physiology or medicine in 1914 "for his work on the physiology and pathology of the vestibular apparatus."

(B)

Nettie Stevens and Edmund Beecher Wilson show chromosomes determine the sex of an individual.

As the science of genetics blossomed, scientists began to ask how the sex of an organism is determined. This question is answered in 1905, when American biologist Nettie Stevens (1861–1912) and Edmund Beecher Wilson (1856–1972) independently show that the chromosomal makeup of an organism determines its sex. Specifically, they each observe that the male of a species has a chromosome, now known as the Y chromosome, that the females lack. Today, biologists know that different organisms employ a number of different mechanisms to determine the sex of an offspring; however, all these mechanisms are under genetic control.

(B)

Alfred Binet develops a means to measure intelligence.

Early in the 20th century, experimental psychologists searched for a means to measure intelligence. In 1905, French psychologist Alfred Binet (1857–1911) establishes an intelligence scale to investigate such problems. He measures the ability of children to perform a series of tasks, then compares their results to other children of the same age. He uses these results to calculate a mental age for each child. A higher mental age than chronological age is considered a sign of intelligence. Binet's work shows a means by which intelligence can be quantified, and his tests serve as the precursor to modern IQ tests.

(B)

March

Albert Einstein demonstrates the particle nature of light.

The early 20th century witnessed a reexamination of many aspects of the physical world. The discovery of the *photoelectric effect,* that is, the ability of light to stimulate the release of an *electron* from an *atom,* led to further research into the nature of light. While studying the photoelectric effect in 1905, German-American physicist Albert Einstein shows that light behaves in a manner similar to a molecular gas. Thus, the particle nature of light is established. Einstein is honored with the Nobel Prize in physics in 1921 "for his services to Theoretical Physics, and especially for his discovery of the law of the photoelectric effect."

(P)

June

Albert Einstein introduces his special theory of relativity.

During the late 19th century and early 20th century, physicists began obtaining data that cannot be explained by classical physics. Previous studies had assumed that physical measurements were independent of the position and motion of the person taking the measurements. In 1905, German-American physicist Albert Einstein states that this assumption is false when he proposes his special theory of relativity to describe objects moving at a constant velocity. The theory explains that measurements of distance and time are not absolute, but are affected by the motion of the observer. One of the important consequences of the theory is the relationship between mass and energy, summarized in the famous equation $E=mc^2$.

(P)

December 23

Walther Hermann Nernst proposes the third law of thermodynamics.

Chemical reactions lead to either the absorption or release of *energy* in the form of *heat.* The study of this aspect of a chemical reac-

tion is called *thermodynamics.* On December 23, 1905, German chemist Walther Nernst presents what is now known as the third law of thermodynamics, stating that the overall disorder of a system, known as its *entropy,* approaches zero as the temperature approaches absolute zero. This law allows a calculation of the overall entropy of a system and helps chemists predict chemical reactions. Nernst is honored with the Nobel Prize in chemistry in 1920 "in recognition of his work in thermochemistry."

(C, P)

1906

Bernard Brunhes discovers that the Earth's magnetic field can reverse itself.

Compasses point north in the direction of the Earth's *magnetic field.* However, this was not always the case. In 1906, French physicist Bernard Brunhes (1867–1910) uncovers evidence suggesting that the Earth's magnetic field has reversed direction throughout history. Brunhes studies magnetic ores in some rocks that are magnetized in a direction opposite the Earth's magnetic field. His observations are not widely accepted at first, but later studies show that Earth's magnetic field not only reverses over time but also becomes weaker and stronger over time.

(ES, P)

Daniel Barringer shows that a meteor crashing into the Earth formed a crater.

It was once widely believed that all craters were formed by volcanic activity. In 1906, American engineer Daniel Barringer (1860–1929) provides evidence that a meteor crashing into Earth formed at least one crater. Barringer studies the composition of minerals in and around the crater, and finds evidence of a meteor but no sign of volcanic rocks. Furthermore, he finds areas where the rock layers are inverted; suggesting a large amount of earth had been overturned. Eventually, the scientific community recognizes that the crater, now known as the Barringer Crater, was formed by meteor impact.

(ES)

Maurice-René Fréchet considers the mathematics of abstract spaces.

In the 20th century, mathematicians began working on a number of abstract problems. These problems frequently involved functions and matrices. In 1906, French mathematician Maurice-René Fréchet (1878–1973) aids the mathematical treatment of such objects. He shows that if one can define a distance between two mathematical objects of any kind, then mathematics can be performed in a manner analogous to real and *complex numbers*. This work leads to a rapid expansion of research into the mathematics of abstract spaces.

(M)

Richard Dixon Oldham describes the core of the Earth.

At the beginning of the 20th century, the various layers of the Earth begin to be identified. In 1906, British seismologist Richard Dixon Oldham identifies the *core* of the Earth. He notices that the waves given off by earthquakes, known as *seismic waves,* travel more slowly when they are far from the epicenter of the earthquake. He proposes that the waves are slowed down as they pass through a core that is composed of a different material from the rest of the Earth. Today, geologists know that the Earth has a number of different layers, including the central core identified by Oldham.

(ES)

Richard Willstätter uncovers the chemical structure of pigments.

In the early 20th century, many chemists turned their attention to the complicated molecules and reactions found in biological systems. German chemist Richard Willstätter began investigating the pigments found living systems. In 1906, he studies the animal pigment heme, an essential component of the oxygen-carrying molecule *hemoglobin,* and the plant pigment chlorophyll, an essential molecule for *photosynthesis*. His research elucidates a number of structural similarities between the molecules. His work is honored with a Nobel Prize in chemistry in 1915 "for his researches on plant pigments, especially chlorophyll."

(B, C)

1907

Georges Urbain discovers lutetium.

Throughout the 19th century, a number of *elements* known as the rare earth elements, or *lanthanides,* were discovered. Many were isolated from preparations of other lanthanides that were previously thought to be pure. In 1907, French chemist Georges Urbain (1872–1938) discovers lutetium, the last of the lanthanides, while analyzing a sample of thulium. Later studies show that lutetium is the heaviest lanthanides.

(C)

Ivan Petrovich Pavlov demonstrates the conditioned response.

After many years of studying the physiology of digestion, Russian physiologist Ivan Petrovich Pavlov (1849–1936) sought to understand the behavior. In 1907, he performs a famous experiment in which he rings a bell at the same time he feeds a group of dogs. As they are fed, the dogs excrete saliva to help with the digestion of the food. After a period of time, Pavlov finds that the dogs excrete saliva in response to the bell, even if there is no food present. He calls this a conditioned response.

(B)

Pierre Weiss describes how iron becomes magnetized.

Iron can become a magnet when exposed to a *magnetic field.* In 1907, French physicist Pierre Weiss (1865–1940) proposes a theory that explains how this happens. Weiss's "mean-field theory of ferromagnets" explains how iron can remain magnetized even after the magnetic field has been removed. As more is understood about *quantum mechanics,* Weiss's theory continues to hold true. Today, scientists continue to update his model as they conduct more experiments geared at understanding this type of *magnetism.*

(ES)

Bertram Borden Boltwood estimates the age of the Earth based upon radioactive decay.

In the early 20th century, physicists began using the properties of radioactive *elements* to calculate the age of materials. This method of dating depends upon *radioactive decay* of elements within an object. In 1907, American scientist Bertram Borden Boltwood (1870–1927), who had previously investigated the nature of uranium and radium, develops a dating method based on lead content. Using this method, he estimates that the Earth is 2.2 billion years old. While not widely accepted at the time, by the 1930s the scientific community accepts his estimate.

(C, ES)

The automatic sun-valve revolutionizes lighthouses.

One of the benefits of scientific research is that it is applied to solve problems in every-day life. In 1907, Swedish inventor Nils Gustaf Dalén applies his knowledge of *heat radiation* to invent an automatic sun-valve. Dalén's device automatically switches off the light beacons in the daylight. His valve is used in lighthouses, reducing the amount of fuel they consumes as well as the amount of maintenance they require. Dalén is honored with a Nobel Prize in physics in 1912 "for his invention of automatic regulators for use in conjunction with gas accumulators for illuminating lighthouses and buoys."

(CP)

Ross Granville Harrison shows how to grow tissues outside the body.

As biological investigations turned toward the inner workings of the cell, scientists began to look for methods to grow cells and tissues outside a living organism. In 1907, American biologist Ross Granville Harrison (1870–1959) publishes the handing drop method of tissue culture. Using this method, he is able to grow tissue taken from tadpoles in a test tube. His method allows scientists to grow tissues, and later cells, outside of a living organism, giving them the opportunity to observe their functions in a controlled environment. Cell and tissue culture techniques remain a vital part of modern cell biology research.

(B)

1908

Ernst Rutherford and Johannes Hans Wilhelm Geiger uncover the nature of the alpha particle.

The discovery that some *atoms* are radioactive led physicists to investigate the nature of *radiation.* Some *elements* release alpha particles that cannot travel far; some release beta particles that can penetrate more deeply; and others release high-energy *gamma rays*. Beta particles were previously shown to be *electrons*. In 1908, British scientist Ernest Rutherford and German physicist Johannes Hans Wilhelm Geiger (1882–1945) characterize the particles that make up *alpha radiation*. They find that the alpha particles are equivalent to a helium *nucleus* stripped of its two electrons.

(C, P)

Geneticists describe how often a specific trait is found in a population.

Mendelian genetics allowed scientists to make predictions as to the frequency that certain traits, called *alleles,* will be observed based upon whether that trait is dominant or recessive. In 1908, the mathematician English Godfrey Hardy (1877–1947), working with English geneticist Reginald Punnett (1875–1967), describes a mathematical

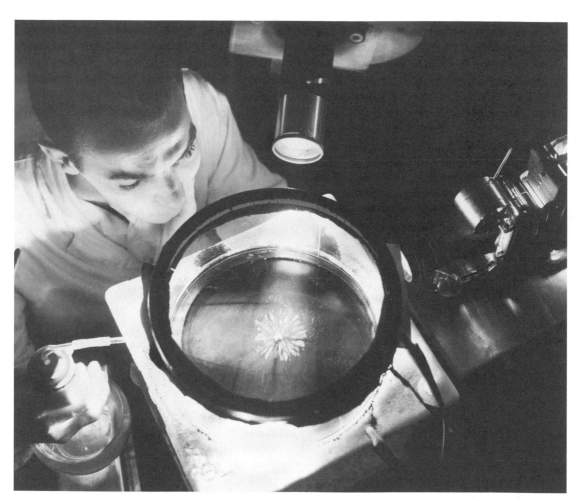

Scottish physicist Charles Thomson Rees Wilson invents the cloud chamber, which is used to study charged particles. In this photograph, physicists use the cloud chamber to study alpha particles. *(Bill Bowles/NASA)*

formula to calculate the frequency of a particular allele in the population. German physician Wilhelm Weinberg (1862–1937) publishes the same formula in 1908. The formula is now known as the Hardy-Weinberg law.

(B, M)

Jean-Baptiste Perrin shows that colloid particles obey the gas laws.

Scientists classify matter in one of three states, solid, liquid, and gas. However, in nature, matter is often found in mixtures, such as solutions or dispersions known as *colloids*. In 1908, French scientist Jean-Baptiste Perrin (1870–1942) studies the nature of colloids and discovers that the particles obeyed previously characterized gas laws. His experiments confirm the theoretical work on colloidal particles published by Albert Einstein. Perrin is honored with the Nobel Prize in physics in 1926 "for his work on the discontinuous structure of matter, and especially for his discovery of sedimentation equilibrium."

(P)

Allvar Gullstrand describes how the eye perceives images.

Early work on *optics* focused on how an object can be seen. How the eye actually perceives the world remained a subject of great interest. In 1908, Swedish physician Allvar Gullstrand (1862–1930) publishes the third of his great works describing how the eye perceives optical images. His work is honored with a Nobel Prize for physiology in medicine in 1911 "for his work on the dioptrics of the eye."

(B)

Frank Taylor proposes that the continents can move on the Earth's surface.

As more people easily traveled between the continents, scientists began to notice similarities between them. In 1908, American geologist Frank Taylor (1860–1939) proposes that the continents move on the earth's surface. He believes this explains the similarities between mountain ranges on opposite sides of the Atlantic Ocean. At the time, the scientific community largely ignores Taylor's ideas. A few years later, German geologist Alfred Lothar Wegener (1880–1930) presents a similar notion, with more evidence, in the form of his theory of *continental drift*. However, the notion that the continents are moving does not gain wide acceptance for several decades.

(ES)

July 10

Heike Kamerlingh-Onnes liquefies helium.

Scientists classify matter into three interconvertible states: solid, liquid, and gas. While a molecule such as water is readily found in all three states, many *atoms* and molecules change states only at extremely high or low temperatures. By the early 20th century, all atomic gases had been liquefied, except helium. In 1908, Dutch physicist Heike Kamerlingh-Onnes (1853–1926), who studies the properties of matter at extremely low temperatures, obtains liquid helium by bringing the gas down to a temperature of −452.4°F (−269°C or 4.2°K), just a few degrees above *absolute zero*. Kamerlingh-Onnes is honored with the Nobel Prize in physics in 1913 "for his investigations on the properties of matter at low temperatures which led, inter alia, to the production of liquid helium."

(P)

1909

Charles-Jean-Henri Nicolle describes the transmission of typhus.

Typhus is a highly infectious disease that usually occurs in large epidemics. In 1909,

French biologist Charles-Jean-Henri Nicolle (1866–1936) makes an important step toward controlling the disease when he uncovers its mechanism of transmission. Nicolle notices that when patients first enters the hospital with typhus, they are able to infect other people. However, once the patients have bathed and their clothes cleaned, they no longer pose a threat to others. Nicolle proposes that lice on the patients' bodies transmit the disease. Careful experiments with chimpanzees later confirm his hypothesis. Nicolle is awarded the Nobel Prize in physiology or medicine in 1928 "for his work on typhus."

(B)

Irving Langmuir describes surface chemistry.

The study of chemical reactions often occurs in a test tube. However, in the body many reactions occur at the interface between two states of matter, such as a surface where a solid meets a liquid. One of the pioneers into the chemistry that occurs at surfaces was American scientist Irving Langmuir (1881–1957). In 1909, he begins his groundbreaking research while working at General Electric Laboratories. He is honored with a Nobel Prize in chemistry in 1932 "for his discoveries and investigations in surface chemistry."

(C)

Andrija Mohorovičić describes the boundary between the Earth's crust and mantle.

The Earth is separated into several different layers. The first evidence for this is uncovered in 1909, when seismologist Russian Andrija Mohorovičić studies an earthquake in the Kupa Valley. Mohorovičić notes that *seismic waves* begin to travel more slowly at a depth of 31 miles (50 km). He proposes that this change in velocity is caused by discontinuity between two layers of the Earth. Thus, he discovers the boundary that separates the *crust* of the Earth from the *mantle*. This boundary is now known as the Mohorovičić discontinuity in his honor.

(ES)

Søren Sørenson develops a scale to describe acidity.

While ancient alchemists used *acids* and *bases* in their work, the modern understanding of them arose as chemists investigated the properties of solutions. Acids are solutions with higher concentrations of hydrogen *ions,* while bases contain a higher concentration of hydroxide ions. In 1909, Danish chemist Søren Sørensen (1868–1939) defines the modern measurement of the acidity of a solution when he introduces the *pH* scale. The pH scale is a logarithmic scale that tells a chemist the concentration of hydrogen ions in a given solution. The same scale is in use today.

(C)

Robert Millikan performs the oil drop experiment to determine the charge of an electron.

As the structure of the *atom* became apparent, scientists attempted to make precise measurements of its physical properties. In 1909, American physicist Robert Millikan (1868–1953) publishes the first precise measurement of the charge of an *electron*. In his famous "oil drop" experiment, Millikan observes the behavior of oil drops that have been passed through an *electric field*. He then determines the charge of each oil drop. In a series of such experiments, he measures the smallest difference possible between two drops, and thus determines the mass of a single electron. Millikan is honored with the

Nobel Prize in physics in 1923 "for his work on the elementary charge of electricity and on the photoelectric effect."

(P)

1910

Gerhard Jakob de Geer determines the date of ice ages by studying sediments.

Geologists study changes in the Earth by examining various *sediments* of soil and the fossils that are found within them. In 1910, Swedish geologist Gerhard Jakob de Geer (1858–1943) develops a method to determine the date of climate changes by studying a special type of sediment called a varve, which forms when *glaciers* move. He uses his method to determine the dates of ice ages.

(ES, W)

Mikhail Tsvet separates pigments using chromatography.

In 1910, Russian graduate student Mikhail Tsvet studied plant physiology. In the course of his research, he needed to separate plant pigments. He finds that he can exploit the chemical properties of these pigments to separate and isolate them. When he passes a mixture of pigments over a chemical matrix, some bind the matrix more tightly than others do. He could then determine the conditions whereby each pigment would dissociate from the matrix. He calls his method chromatography. Today, chromatography is used everyday in biochemistry laboratories to separate and isolate biologically important molecules.

(B, C)

Percy Bridgman creates high-pressure conditions in the laboratory.

Experimental physics often requires extremely high-pressure conditions. American physicist Percy Bridgman (1882–1961) pioneered work at high pressure. In 1910, he invents an apparatus that reaches pressures of 20,000 atmospheres. Previous investigators could reach only 3,000 atmospheres. As stronger materials become available, he achieves even higher pressures. For this advance, Bridgman is honored with the Nobel Prize in physics "for the invention of an apparatus to produce extremely high pressures, and for the discoveries he made therewith in the field of high pressure physics."

(P)

August Krogh describes how oxygen enters the blood.

Oxygen taken up by the lungs through breathing must enter the bloodstream in order to be delivered to the other cells and tissues of the body. At the turn of the 20th century, leading physiologists believed this important process to be active. In 1910, Danish physiologist August Krogh (1874–1949) shows that this was not true. Krogh carefully measures the concentration of oxygen in the lungs and compares it to that of the blood stream. He finds that the concentration is the same, demonstrating that simple *diffusion,* rather than a more complicated controlled process, is the mechanism by which oxygen enters the blood.

(B)

Ernst Rutherford proposes a model for the atom.

Investigations into the nature of *radioactivity* gave physicists in the 20th century a host of new data to incorporate into atomic theory. In 1910, British scientist Ernest Rutherford proposes a new model of the *atom* based on these data. In his model, the positively charged *nucleus* is very small, 10,000 times smaller than the atom itself. This means that the negatively charged *electrons* move in a large void of empty space. Today,

Rutherford's model of the atom is widely viewed as his greatest achievement.

(C, P)

Francis Peyton Rous shows a virus can cause cancer.

The search for the causes and cures for cancer has been going on for many years. In 1910, American scientist Francis Peyton Rous (1879–1970) discovers a *virus* that causes cancer in chickens, known as the Rous sarcoma virus. Scientists soon try to find viruses in tumors from mammals. When they do not find them, it is assumed that Rous's work would not apply to human cancers. However, over the next 40 years scientists begin to identify a number of viruses that cause specific cancers in mammals. Furthermore, studies on the mechanism by which the Rous sarcoma virus induces cancer lead to fundamental insights into cancer biology. Over a half century after his discovery, Rous is honored with the Nobel Prize in physiology or medicine in 1966 "for his discovery of tumour-inducing viruses."

(B)

Alfred North Whitehead and Bertrand Arthur William Russell publish a classic work in mathematical logic.

Mathematicians work to demonstrate that theorems and proofs can be reduced to logic. This convergence of philosophy and mathematics expands during the period 1910 to 1913, when English mathematicians Alfred North Whitehead (1861–1947) and Bertrand Arthur William Russell (1872–1970) publish *Principia Mathematica*. Their work inspires much of the research into mathematical logic that occurs later in the 20th century. Although some of their theories have been refuted, it remains a classic work in mathematics and logic.

(M)

1911

Heike Kamerlingh-Onnes discovers superconductivity.

The ability of metals to conduct *electrons* sparked many investigations in the early 20th century. In 1911, Dutch physicist Heike Kamerlingh-Onnes studies the conductivity of metals at very low temperatures. He finds that at temperatures below −452°F (−269°C or 4°K) the electrical resistance of the metal mercury drops to a tiny fraction of its normal value. He calls this phenomenon superconductivity. Investigations into the mechanism behind superconductivity and the search for more metal *alloys* that can become *superconductors* continue to this day.

(P)

Petroleum refinement improves with the thermal cracking method.

The invention of the automobile and its rapidly growing popularity vastly increased the need for petroleum-based fuels. In 1911, the process of obtaining these fuels is made more efficient by the development of the thermal cracking method to refine petroleum. Petroleum oils are made up of large molecules. By heating heavy oils in a high-pressure reactor, they can be split into smaller molecules, such as gasoline, that are suitable to fuel automobiles.

(C)

August 12

Victor Franz Hess discovers cosmic radiation.

The air above the Earth can be difficult for scientists to study. However, as technology increased the altitudes at which measurements could be accurately taken, studies of the atmosphere blossomed. In 1911, American physicist Victor Franz Hess (1883–1964) embarks on a series of experiments to understand the atmosphere. On August 12, 1911, he measures *radiation* by launching a balloon into the atmosphere. These experiments show that radiation in the upper atmosphere is 5,000 times higher than that at sea level. Rays from the Sun cannot account for such a large amount of radiation. Therefore, radiation must be coming from outer space. American physicist Robert Millikan later calls this radiation cosmic rays. Hess is honored with a Nobel Prize in physics in 1936 "for his discovery of cosmic radiation."

(P, W)

1912

Sir Frederick Hopkins discovers vitamins.

During the early 20th century, physicians and biologists realized that humans rely on food for more than just *energy*. Scientists began researching other nutritional factors found in food. In 1912, British chemist Sir Frederick Hopkins discovers that milk contains growth-promoting molecules known as vitamins. The vitamins he studies are required only in small amounts. Hopkins's work pioneers research into vitamins. Hopkins is honored with the Nobel Prize in physiology or medicine in 1929 for "for his discovery of the growth-stimulating vitamins."

(B, C)

Fritz Pregl develops techniques for analyzing chemicals in small quantities.

Chemists study the properties and reactions of matter. Often it is feasible to obtain only small quantities of chemicals. In 1912, Austrian chemist Fritz Pregl (1863–1930) makes these studies easier when he develops new technique for microanalysis. Pregl's techniques allow chemists to accurately measure small quantities of carbon, hydrogen, sulfur, and other common elements. These

techniques greatly aid chemists by allowing them to work with very small quantities of expensive and difficult to obtain chemicals. Pregl is honored with the Nobel Prize in chemistry in 1923 "for his invention of the method of micro-analysis of organic substances."

(C)

Alfred Lothar Wegener proposes that the continents were once a single landmass.

Although a few scientists had previously suggested that the continents of the Earth (*See* entry for 1908) could move, the idea does not begin to gain acceptance until German geologist Alfred Lothar Wegener proposes the *continental drift* theory in 1912. He eventually publishes several editions of his classic work, *The Origin of the Continents and Oceans*. In this work, he proposes that the continents were once a single landmass he called Pangaea. He cites physical evidence, such as the jigsaw puzzle nature of the landmasses, as well as fossil evidence. The scientific community, however, does not immediately embrace his theory. However, geologists soon begin uncovering evidence supporting his work. Today, Wegner is credited as the father of the continental drift theory.

(ES, MS)

Theodore William Richards accurately determines atomic weight.

Chemists study the properties of matter. One of the fundamental properties of any *atom* or molecule is its mass. However, the mass of a single atom is difficult to discern. A table of *atomic weights* was created in the mid-19th century. American chemist Theodore William Richards (1868–1928) continued this work, developing improved techniques for weighing atoms. In 1912, he publishes accurate atomic weights for 30 elements. These weights are used to determine the weight of other elements. Richards is honored with the

Nobel Prize in chemistry in 1914 "in recognition of his accurate determinations of the atomic weight of a large number of chemical elements."

(C)

Heinrich Otto Wieland describes oxidation-reduction reactions in living organisms.

In the 20th century, many chemists turned their attention to the chemical reactions that drive biological systems. They found that many of the reactions that occur in the test tube also occur in living systems. One common reaction is known as an oxidation-reduction, or redox, reaction. The reaction gets its name because the substance being oxidized often reacts with oxygen. In 1912, German chemist Heinrich Otto Wieland (1877–1957) proposes that in living systems the dominant process is not reaction with oxygen, but rather the loss of hydrogen from a biologically important molecule. Scientists now know that many of the redox reactions in living systems involve the removal of hydrogen and that living systems contain specialized molecules that mediate this process.

(B, C)

Heinrich Otto Wieland finds that bile acids are made of steroids.

Scientists have long been interested in how the body extracts *energy* and nutrients from food. In 1912, German chemist Heinrich Otto Wieland begins studying the chemicals that make up bile. He finds that the bile *acids* are derived from a class of molecules known as *steroids*. He shows that their chemical structure is similar to cholesterol. Wieland is honored with the Nobel Prize in chemistry in 1927 "for his investigations of the constitution of the bile acids and related substances."

(B, C)

Peter Debye measures the dipole moment of a molecule.

Chemists often classify molecules based on the separation of charges. A molecule with a large separation of charge between its *atoms* is known as a polar molecule. In 1912, American chemist Peter Debye (1884–1966) studies the effect of *electric fields* on polar molecules. He develops methods to measure the degree of charge separation in a molecule, known as the dipole moment. Today, the dipole moment of a molecule is expressed in units called debyes. Debye is honored with a Nobel Prize in chemistry in 1936 "for his contributions to our knowledge of molecular structure through his investigations on dipole moments and on the diffraction of X rays and electrons in gases."

(C, P)

X-rays reveal the atomic nature of a crystal.

In the decade following the discovery of *X-rays,* physicists sought to understand their nature. In 1912, German physicists Max von Laue (1879–1960) passes X-rays through crystals in order to show their wavelike nature. His experiment succeeds not only in showing that X-rays travel in waves but also in demonstrating that X-rays can be used to reveal the atomic nature of the crystal. This insight leads to an important technique in understanding the structure of molecules, *X-ray crystallography.* Von Laue is honored with the Nobel Prize in physics in 1914 "for his discovery of the diffraction of X rays by crystals."

(B, C, P)

Vesto Slipher observes nebula moving away from the Earth.

While observing the light emitted from certain *nebula,* American astronomer Vesto Slipher (1875–1969) noticed a phenomenon called redshifting. Redshifting occurs when an object is moving away from the Earth. In fact, nearly all the nebula he observed appeared to be moving away from the Earth at a high speed. His observations, made in 1912, are some of the first evidence that the universe is expanding.

(SA)

Niels Bohr proposes a model of the atom.

If the *atom* is made up of negatively charged electrons surrounding a positively charged *nucleus,* then how is it stable? Based on attraction, one would expect the electrons and nucleus to be attracted to each other, causing the orbiting *electron* to crash into the nucleus. In 1912, Danish physicist Niels Bohr (1885–1962) answers this question using the hydrogen atom as a model. He demonstrates mathematically that the electrons are confined to different *energy* levels or orbits. According to Bohr's model, energy from an outside source is required to move an electron from one orbit to another. Bohr is awarded the Nobel Prize in physics in 1922 "for his services in the investigation of the structure of atoms and of the radiation emanating from them."

(C, P)

March 3

Henrietta Swan Leavitt develops a method to measure the distance between stars.

A problem that astronomers faced through the ages was how to measure distances between objects in the heavens. On March 3, 1912, American astronomer Henrietta Swan Leavitt (1868–1921) publishes her finding that the brightness and period of brightness of certain *variable stars* is related. Specifically, Leavitt shows that brighter stars shine longer. She then devises a method to calculate the actual brightness of the star based upon its appearance in the sky. By studying these

quantities astronomers can estimate the distance of these stars.

(SA)

1913

Leonor Michaelis and Maud Menten describe enzyme-catalyzed reactions.

The discovery of biological catalysts known as *enzymes* led biologists to examine the chemistry and physics of biological reactions. In 1913, German chemists Leonor Michaelis (1875–1949) and Maud Menten (1879–1960) develop an equation that describes the interaction between an enzyme and the molecules it acts upon, called the substrate. The Michaelis-Menten constant, an important constant in enzyme kinetics, describes how well the enzyme will bind to its substrate. This allows scientists to compare enzymes that act upon the same substrate and predict which interaction is more likely to occur.

(B, C)

Fredrich Bergius revolutionizes oil preparation.

As technology expanded in the industrialized world, so did the need for large quantities of high-quality fuels. Chemists began looking for new ways to efficiently prepare oil. In 1913, German chemist Friedrich Bergius (1884–1949) develops a method that allows much larger amounts of oil to be extracted from coal. He accomplishes this by using high pressure, reducing the amount of oil consumed during the extraction process. By eliminating waste in the process, Bergius revolutionizes fuel preparation. He shares the Nobel Prize in chemistry in 1931 with Carl Bosch "in recognition of their contributions to the invention and development of chemical high pressure methods."

(C)

X-ray crystallography reveals the structure of molecules.

X-rays diffract when passed through a crystal. This diffraction pattern gives scientists insight into the atomic structure of the crystal. In 1913, English physicist Sir William Henry Bragg (1862–1942) and his son Sir William Lawrence Bragg (1890–1971) extend these studies by building a device called an X-ray spectrometer. Using this device, they elucidate the structure of the crystal. The procedure, known as *X-ray crystallography,* can be applied to minerals as well crystallized forms of biologically important molecules and remains an important tool in biology today. They share the Nobel Prize in physics in 1915 "for their services in the analysis of crystal structure by means of X-rays."

(B, C, P)

Johannes Andreas Grib Fibiger proposes a cause for stomach cancer.

Scientific investigations can result in false conclusions. Such was the case in 1913, when Danish pathologist Johannes Andreas Grib Fibiger (1867–1928) proposes that stomach cancer in mice is caused by an infection with a type of small worm called a nematode. Fibiger is awarded the Nobel Prize in physiology or medicine in 1926 "for his discovery of the Spiroptera carcinoma." However, scientists cannot replicate his results, and other causes are later found for this type of cancer.

(B)

Johannes Stark studies spectral lines.

Elements can be identified by a variety of techniques. Physicists often examine what are known as *spectral lines,* which that emit from an element under experimental conditions. Scientists showed during the late 19th century that these lines are affected by *magnetic fields.* In 1913, German physicist Johannes Stark (1874–1957) demonstrates that spectral lines are also affected by strong *electric fields.* This discovery opens up new avenues of research into the structure of the *atom.* Stark is honored with the Nobel Prize in physics in 1919 "for his discovery of the Doppler effect in canal rays and the splitting of spectral lines in electric fields."

(C, P)

Charles Fabry finds the ozone layer.

The atmosphere is divided into two layers, the *troposphere* and the *stratosphere.* In 1913, French physicist Charles Fabry (1867–1945) uncovers the function of the stratosphere when he discovers the *ozone layer.* Fabry specializes in making instruments capable of precision measurements. He uses one such instrument to show that ozone gas is plentiful in the upper atmosphere, known as the stratosphere. He also demonstrates that this layer of ozone filters out ultraviolet rays from the Sun.

(P, W)

The periodic table of the elements is organized by atomic number.

The *periodic table* of the elements as devised by Russian chemist Dmitry Ivanovich Mendeleyev organized the *elements* on the basis of their *atomic weight.* The discovery of *isotopes,* that is, versions of the same element with different atomic weights, made this system of classification obsolete. In 1913, English physicist Henry Moseley (1887–1915) modifies the periodic table of the elements such that it is organized by atomic number, that is the number of electrons in the *atom.* Since the behavior of atoms is strongly influenced by its atomic number, this system is a more realistic way to draw the table. Today, the periodic table of the elements remains in the form proposed by Moseley.

(C, P)

Frederick Soddy describes Isotopes.

Chemists study the properties of atoms and molecules that make up all matter. By the early 20th century, many *elements* were characterized, and chemists established an *atomic weight* for each. In 1913, English chemist Frederick Soddy (1877–1956) proposes that an element can be found in different forms with different atomic weights but otherwise chemically indistinguishable from one another. These forms are called *isotopes*. The study of isotopes has been important in many fields, including nuclear chemistry and biology. Soddy is honored with the Nobel Prize in chemistry in 1921 "for his contributions to our knowledge of the chemistry of radioactive substances, and his investigations into the origin and nature of isotopes."

(C, P)

1914

Carl Bosch develops a method to synthesize ammonia on a large scale.

During the 20th century, many industries began looking for methods to synthesize a number of chemicals on a large scale. Ammonia is a particularly important chemical in industrial settings as it can be used in the synthesis of compounds containing nitrogen. This process is greatly facilitated in 1914, when German chemist Carl Bosch (1874–1940) improves upon Fritz Haber's method for synthesizing ammonia (*See* entry for 1905). Bosch's improvements allow the large-scale synthesis of ammonia. The method is now known as the Haber-Bosch method. Bosch shares the Nobel Prize in chemistry in 1931 with Friedrich Berguis "in recognition of their contributions to the invention and development of chemical high-pressure methods."

(C)

Light is emitted when an electron strikes an atom.

In the late 19th century, physicists discovered that light could stimulate the release of electrons from a metal, a phenomenon known as the *photoelectric effect*. In 1914, American physicist James Franck (1882–1964) and German physicist Gustav Ludwig Hertz (1887–1975) show that the opposite is also true—when an *electron* of a specific *energy* strikes an *atom*, light is emitted. Mathematical treatment of their discovery leads to the verification of an important constant in physics known as Planck's constant. Franck and Hertz share the Nobel Prize in physics in 1925 "for their discovery of the laws governing the impact of an electron upon an atom."

(P)

Sir Henry Hallett Dale studies how nerves carry information to other parts of the body.

Nerves carry information from the brain to other parts of the body. In 1914, English biologist Sir Henry Hallett Dale (1875–1968) tries to understand how this happens. Previously, he found that chemicals released in the body are involved in controlling circulation. In 1914, he shows that some of the same chemicals, namely acetylcholine, can stimulate nerves. This fundamental insight into the nature of nerve impulses leads to the discovery of many *neurotransmitters*. In 1936, Dale shares the Nobel Prize in physiology or medicine with American pharmacologist Otto Loewi "for their discoveries relating to chemical transmission of nerve impulses."

(B, C)

Beno Gutenberg measures the distance to the Earth's core.

The discovery of the Earth's iron *core* led geologists to find the depth at which the

NEW UNDERSTANDING OF THE ATOM, 1900–1945

protons

neutrons

nucleus

electrons   orbit

Type of radioactive decay

alpha particle (helium nuclei stripped of its electrons)

beta particle (electron)

gamma ray (electromagnetic energy)

© Infobase Publishing

Simple model of the new understanding of the atom and subatomic particles developed during the early 20th century. The atomic nucleus contains protons and neutrons that make up most of the mass of the atom. A cloud of negatively charged electrons surrounds the nucleus. Radioactive atoms spontaneously give off one of three types of radiation. The first, alpha particles, is shown to be the equivalent of a helium nucleus without its electrons. Beta particles are an electron. Gamma rays are electromagnetic energy that is spontaneously emitted from the nucleus of a radioactive atom.

core begins. In 1914, American seismologist Beno Gutenberg (1889–1960) uncovers the boundary between the Earth's core and its *mantle.* He does this by analyzing the speed at which *seismic waves* travel large distances. He determines that the iron core lay 1,800 miles (2,900 km) beneath the Earth's surface. This value is later confirmed using more sophisticated instrumentation, and it is still used today.

(ES)

Ernest Rutherford identifies the proton.
The study of *radioactivity* gave physicists many insights into the structure of the *atom* and led English scientist Ernest Rutherford (1871–1937) to propose a widely accepted model of the atom whereby much of the mass is concentrated into a small space, known as

the *nucleus.* He then turned to understanding the nature of the nucleus. In 1914, he shows that the stable nucleus of an atom is made up of many particles that appear to be individual hydrogen nuclei. These particles, known as *protons,* are released when alpha waves hit the nuclei. Thus, Rutherford identifies the proton, one of the fundamental pieces of atomic nuclei.

(C, P)

1915

Fossils of ancient bacteria are found.
Studying fossils gives us an insight into ancient organisms that once populated the world, by allowing modern scientists to study plant and animals that have been extinct for millions of years. In 1915, American

geologist Charles Doolittle Walcott (1850–1927) identifies fossils of *bacteria*. Walcott studies fossils from the *Precambrian* era, 540 million years ago. Fossils are found in stromatolites, layers of calcium carbonate that can contain fossils of microscopic organisms. While his discovery is looked upon with skepticism at the time, today an extensive fossil record of bacteria has been established.

(B, ES)

Thomas Hunt Morgan studies genetics using fruit flies.

With the resurgence of Gregor Mendel's ideas on heredity, the field of genetics expanded rapidly at the beginning of the 20th century. At this time, American biologist Thomas Hunt Morgan (1866–1945) thought that a simple system was required to study genetics. He conducted his experiments using a model system, the fruit fly *Drosophila melanogaster*. In 1915, he publishes *The Mechanism of Mendelian Heredity*. In this seminal publication, he uses the fruit fly model to collect experimental evidence that *genes* are arranged on *chromosomes* in a linear fashion. This fundamental observation leads to the mapping and identification of specific genes. Morgan is honored with the Nobel Prize in physiology or medicine in 1933 "for his discoveries concerning the role played by the chromosome in heredity."

(B)

Scientists find viruses that kill bacteria.

Viruses infect both plants and animals. In 1915, English biologist Frederick Twort (1877–1950) discovers that there are viruses that also infect *bacteria*. He makes this discovery while trying to find out why some of his cultures of bacteria die. He isolates an agent from some of these dead cultures, then uses it to kill healthy cultures. Twort believes that the agent is a virus. Two years later, Canadian microbiologist Félix d'Hérelle (1873–1949) makes a similar discovery and calls the agent *bacteriophage*. Biologists employ bacteriophage in a number of crucial experiments that lead to much of what is known today about DNA.

(B)

The closest star to the Earth is found.

The Alpha Centauri star system shines brightly in the sky, and thus has been known to astronomers for centuries. Interestingly, the closest star to the Earth is part of this group, but it was not discovered until 1915. During this time, astronomers noticed a faint star while observing Alpha Centauri from a telescope in South Africa. Soon after, they show that although this star is faint, it is the closest of the three stars that make up Alpha Centauri. At approximately four light-years away, it is the closest star to Earth.

(SA)

April

Chemical weapons are used during World War I.

Advances in chemistry made it possible to amass weapons that contained and released deadly chemicals. The first instance of this modern chemical warfare occurred during World War I. In April 1915, the German army releases chlorine gas during an attack on French military units. Chemical attacks by both sides of the conflict continue throughout the war. Today, despite international treaties addressing the problem, chemical weapons remain a security concern.

(C)

1916

Einstein proposes his general theory of relativity.

German-American physicist Albert Einstein's special theory of *relativity* explained the nature of electric and magnetic *forces*. In 1916, he tackles another important force— *gravity*. At this time, Sir Isaac Newton's work on gravity still dominated the thinking of most physicists (*See* entry for 1687). In his general theory of relativity, Einstein proposes that like motion gravity could affect measurements of distance and time. Since the theory was introduced, a number of its predictions of have been confirmed.

(P)

Covalent bonds involve the sharing of electrons.

Understanding how the *elements* come together to form compounds is critical to the study of chemistry. As the structure of the *atom* began to be understood, chemists used it to explain chemical reactions. In 1916, American chemist Gilbert Newton Lewis (1875–1946) applies the new knowledge of atomic structure when he proposes that covalent bonds involve the sharing of *electrons*. He states that the outer shell of an atom is most stable when it is filled with eight electrons. He theorizes that atoms combine to share electrons such that the outer shell of each atom is filled with eight electrons. His view of covalent bonds influences chemistry throughout the 20th century.

(C)

Karl Manne Georg Siegbahn uses X-ray spectroscopy to understand the elements.

As the field of physics turned toward understanding the *atom*, the need for advanced instrumentation became crucial. In 1916, Swedish physicist Karl Manne Georg Siegbahn (1886–1978) improves a technique known as X-ray spectroscopy. His improvements to the technique allow him to precisely measure spectra for the elements. These measurements show that heavier *elements* have more shells filled with electrons than lighter elements. His work establishes the rules for transitions between electronic shells. Siegbahn is honored with the Nobel Prize in physics in 1924 "for his discoveries and research in the field of X-ray spectroscopy."

(P)

Jan Czochralski devises a new method to grow crystals in the laboratory.

Not all discoveries result from carefully planned experiments. Some happen when a researcher notices something unusual, then follows up on the observation. Such was the case of Polish scientist Jan Czochralski's (1885–1953) discovery of a method for growing crystals of metals. In 1916, Czochralski is studying metal alloys. When he stops to write some notes, he accidentally dips his pen into a container of molten tin. He notices a thin thread of metal hanging from the tip. He then reasons that if the metal could crystallize in the narrow tip of the pen, he could devise a narrow tube to grow crystals in the laboratory. His method is still used today.

(C)

Robert Millikan studies the photoelectric effect.

In the late 19th century, scientists demonstrated that light can induce metal to emit *electrons*, which is known as the *photoelectric effect*. Physicist Albert Einstein predicted that the *energy* released via the photoelectric effect is proportional to the wavelength of light. American experimental physicist Robert Millikan verifies his prediction in 1916. Millikan also uses his studies on the photoelectric effect to determine the value of an important physical constant known as Planck's constant.

(P)

Physicians induce fevers to treat paralysis.

Before *antibiotics* became widely used, syphilis was a major public health concern.

Advanced syphilis leads to insanity and a specific type of paralysis known as paresis. In 1917, Austrian physician Julius Wagner von Jauregg (1857–1940) develops a treatment for paresis. His treatment involves infecting patients with malaria-infected blood. Upon contracting malaria, the patient develops a high fever, thus it becomes known as the fever treatment. The treatment is widely used for several years, and Wagner von Jauregg is awarded the Nobel Prize in physiology or medicine in 1927 "for his discovery of the therapeutic value of malaria inoculation in the treatment of dementia paralytica." By the 1950s, antibiotics prove to be a better treatment for syphilis, and physicians no longer use the fever treatment.

(B)

1918

Lise Meitner isolates protactinium.

During the 20th century, chemists and physicists began to discover some of the *elements* that are predicted by the *periodic table* of the elements. In 1918, Austrian physicist Lise Meitner (1878–1968) discovers an element with 91 *protons*. While purifying a sample of uranium, she notes the presence of a radioactive element that decays into actinium. Today, the element is known as protactinium.

(C)

August Krogh shows that capillaries control blood flow to the muscles.

Small vessels called capillaries bring blood to the tissues and muscles. The circulation of blood through blood vessels increases during periods of intense work as muscles require more oxygen. Many physiologists believed that the blood flow through the capillaries was simply faster during these times. In 1918, Danish physiologist August Krogh shows that the amount of blood flow to the muscles is controlled by the opening and closing of the capillaries. His discovery is honored with the Nobel Prize in physiology or medicine in 1920 "for his discovery of the capillary motor regulating mechanism."

(B)

Jacob and Vilhelm Bjerknes find the cause of extratropical cyclones.

What causes changes in the weather? A small part of this question is answered in 1918, when American meteorologist Jacob Bjerknes (1897–1975) and his father, Norwegian physicist Vilhelm Bjerknes (1862–1951), identify the cause of extratropical cyclones. They see that rain clouds form along the boundaries separating masses of warm and cold air, known as *fronts*. They note that as the air moves it supplies the *energy* needed to form a cyclone. Thus, the cyclones form as the air from the polar regions of the Earth exchanges with air from the equator. Meteorologists today continue to identify and track extratropical cyclones, which are now viewed on satellite images.

(P, W)

Otto Meyerhof describes the role of oxygen in muscle metabolism.

How do the muscles of bodies get the *energy* to do their work? At the beginning of the 20th century, physiologists knew that they required fuel in the form of dietary *carbohydrates* and oxygen. During the period from 1918 to 1922, German biochemist Otto Meyerhof (1884–1951) describes how these components are metabolized in muscle tissue. Meyerhof finds that in the absence of oxygen muscles produce lactic acid. A small portion of lactic acid is subsequently broken down when oxygen is reintroduced to the muscles. Meyerof's thorough work on these aspects of muscle metabolism is honored with the Nobel Prize in physiology or medicine in 1922 "for his discovery of the fixed relationship between the consumption of oxygen and the metabolism of lactic acid in the muscle."

(B)

1919

Adolf Windaus identifies cholesterol as a precursor to many biologically important molecules.

In the 20th century, chemists began turning their attention to the reactions that occur in living systems. Many biologically important molecules are chemically quite complicated, and undergo reactions in the body that changes their chemical structure as well as their biological function. German chemist Adolf Windaus (1876–1959) believed that cholesterol was a biological molecule that served as a base from which other molecules were made. In 1919, he demonstrates that through a series of chemical reactions cholesterol could be transformed into a bile acid. Today, biologists know that many molecules, known as *steroids,* are synthesized in the body using cholesterol as a precursor. Windaus is honored with the Nobel Prize in chemistry in 1928 "for the services rendered through his research into the constitution of the sterols and their connection with the vitamins."

(B, C)

The mass spectrometer measures the mass of atoms.

Once John Dalton's *atomic theory* gained wide acceptance, scientists believed that all *atoms* of the same substance had the same mass. As instruments to analyze elements became more sophisticated, this belief was called into question. In 1912, English physicists Francis William Aston (1877–1945) and Sir

Joseph John Thomson (1856–1940) showed that heavier forms of an atom could exist. They called these forms *isotopes.* In 1919, Aston builds a device to detect and precisely measure the mass of stable isotopes—the mass spectrometer. Aston is honored with the Nobel Prize in chemistry in 1922 "for his discovery, by means of his mass spectrograph, of isotopes, in a large number of non-radioactive elements, and for his enunciation of the whole-number rule."

(C)

Three-dimensional mapping improves weather forecasting.

Norwegian scientist Vilhelm Bjerknes (1862–1951), considered the father of modern meteorology, applied physics predicting future conditions in the atmosphere. He established a weather forecasting service with his son American meteorologist Jacob Bjerknes (1897–1975) as its head. In 1919, the Bjerknes study the convergence of wind currents, using the established model of mapping them in two dimensions. They improve upon on the model by mapping in three dimensions. Thus, they can see surfaces of discontinuity separating different air masses. This modeling has become an important tool in weather forecasting.

(P, W)

Elwood Haynes invents stainless steel.

Mixtures of metals, known as *alloys,* have many important industrial uses. In 1919, American inventor Elwood Haynes (1857–1925) patents an alloy that would become widely used in a variety of applications, including nonrusting stainless steel. According to legend, he invents stainless steel so his wife could have dinnerware that did not tarnish. Today, stainless steel is used everywhere from surgical instruments to space equipment.

(C)

Ernst Rutherford shows that stable elements can undergo disintegration.

By 1919, physicists knew that radioactive *elements* are unstable, emitting particles during the process of *radioactive decay*. Stable elements, however, were believed to remain stable. In 1919, English scientist Ernest Rutherford shows that an element with a stable *nucleus* can be forced to disintegrate when bombarded with an alpha particle. Thus, he demonstrates that stable elements could be changed, or transmuted.

(C, P)

1920s

Leopold Ruzicka discovers the chemical structure of molecules from living organisms.

Some of the most interesting and complicated molecules are produced by living organisms. In the 20th century, chemists began investigating the structure of many large biologically active molecules. One of the pioneers in this field was Swiss chemist Leopold Ruzicka (1887–1976). During the 1920s, he elucidates the chemical structure of a number of biologically important molecules, including the chemical that gives musk its odor. Ruzicka also chemically synthesizes molecules normally isolated from living organisms, such as the *hormones* androsterone and testosterone and a class of plant compounds called terpenes. Ruzicka is honored with the Nobel Prize in chemistry in 1939 "for his work on polymethylenes and higher terpenes."

(B, C)

Pyotr Kapitsa discovers superfluidity.

Matter exists in one of three states: gas, liquid, or solid. All *atoms* and molecules, however, are not readily found in all three states. The element helium, for instance, exists as a liquid only at temperatures just above absolute zero. The *isotope* of helium, ^{4}He, for instance, liquefies at –452°F (–269°C or 4.2°K). During the 1920s, Russian physicist Pyotr Kapitsa (1894–1984) studies liquid helium. He finds that at even lower temperatures, specifically –456°F (–271°C or 2.2°K), liquid helium has an interesting property—it can flow through a vessel with virtually no *friction*. This phenomenon is now known as *superfluidity*. Kapitsa is honored with the Nobel Prize in physics in 1978 "for his basic inventions and discoveries in the area of low-temperature physics."

(P)

Polymers are shown to be made of long chains of repeating units.

Polymers are molecules made up of repeating units. In the 1920s, German chemist Hermann Staudinger (1881–1965) turns his attention to the structure of polymers. At this time, chemists are debating whether polymers are long chains of repeating units, or aggregates. Staudinger correctly favors the long-chain hypothesis. In his quest to prove this hypothesis, he synthesizes many synthetic polymers, including those that later became the basis for plastics. His work is honored with the Nobel Prize in chemistry in 1953 "for his discoveries in the field of macromolecular chemistry."

(C)

Walter Rudolf Hess describes the functional organization of the brain.

The nervous system controls the activity of the body's organs. Research in the field of neuroscience showed that the functions of a particular organ map to a specific region in the brain. During the 1920s, Swiss physiologist Walter Hess (1881–1973) expands this knowledge when he describes functional organization of the brain in fine detail. Hess is honored with the Nobel Prize in physiology or medicine in 1949 "for his discovery of the functional organization of the interbrain as a coordinator of the activities of the internal organs."

(B)

Cytochromes are involved in the breakdown of carbohydrates.

During the 20th century, many chemists turned their attention to the chemical reactions that occur in the body. Many focused on *energy* metabolism—how the body breaks down food and stores energy. During the 1920s, German biochemist Otto Heinrich Warburg (1883–1970) discovers a molecule critical for the breakdown of *carbohydrates*. The molecule, known as a cytochrome, has an iron-binding core similar to that of the oxygen-carrying molecule *hemoglobin* that is found in the blood. Cytochromes play important roles in the breakdown of carbohydrates by the body. Warburg is honored with the Nobel Prize in physiology or medicine in 1931 "for his discovery of the nature and mode of action of the respiratory enzyme."

(B)

William Francis Giauque measures the entropy of gases.

Many experimental investigations in chemistry and physics require extremely low temperatures. In the 1920s, American chemist William Francis Giauque (1895–1982) develops a method to cool a vessel to a fraction of a degree above *absolute zero*. This technique allows Giauque to experimentally measure the *entropy*, or degree of disorder, of a number of gases. These entropy measurements are important for a variety of thermochemical studies. Giauque is honored with a Nobel Prize in chemistry in 1949 "for his contributions in the field of chemical thermodynamics, particularly concerning the behaviour of substances at extremely low temperatures."

(P)

Karl Jansky discovers cosmic radio waves.

The invention of radio made wireless communication devices possible. In the late 1920s, scientists and engineers researched ways to create radiotelephone connections across the Atlantic Ocean. American engineer Karl Jansky (1905–1950) starts an investigation into possible sources of interference, that is *radio waves* that can be picked up from the atmosphere. In addition to known causes of background radio static, Jansky discovers faint static that apparently comes from the Sun. Further investigation shows the radio waves are in fact coming from the center of the Milky Way. Today, Jansky's discovery of cosmic radio waves serves as the basis for an entire field, radio astronomy.

(P, SA)

1920

Milutin Milankovitch explains ice ages.

The Earth has gone through periods known as ice ages, in which glaciers move farther away from the poles and much of the habitable land known today is frozen. In 1920, Serbian physicist Milutin Milankovitch (1879–1958) develops a theory to explain ice ages. The Earth's orbit around the Sun changes slightly over time. This means that the amount of *radiation* the Earth gets from the Sun varies. He uses mathematics to calculate that there are periods when the amount of radiation the Earth receives is low enough to cause an ice age. His theories are not embraced until decades later when scientists discover evidence that past ice ages occurred at the same times predicted by Milankovitch.

(ES, P, W)

Archibald Hill describes muscle contraction.

Muscles do their work through a series of contractions and relaxations. For many years, the basic physics and chemistry that underlie these processes were unclear. In 1920, English physiologist Archibald Hill (1886–1977) adds to the knowledge of muscle contraction with studies of *heat* production in muscle. Hill uses a specialized instrument to measure the development of heat in isolated frog muscles as they contract. His work leads to an increased understanding of the cycle muscles undergo as they contract then recover from performing work. Hill is honored with the Nobel Prize in physiology or medicine in 1922 "for his discovery relating to the production of heat in the muscle."

(B)

Scientists determine raw liver can cure anemia.

Blood carries oxygen to the body's organs and tissues. Severe blood loss can lead to a condition known as anemia. Anemia can also be the result of a number of diseases that affect blood production. In 1920, American pathologist George Whipple (1878–1976) searches for nutrients that can be used to treat anemia. He finds that he can treat dogs that have anemia as a result of blood loss with raw liver. This insight leads to a new treatment for anemia in humans. Whipple shares the Nobel Prize in physiology or medicine in 1934 with George Minot and William Murphy "for their discoveries concerning liver therapy in cases of anemia."

(B)

Mathematicians develop multiple-valued logic.

Exercises in logic depend on certain defined truths. In classical logic, statements are either true or false. In 1920 and 1921, respectively, Polish logician Jan Lukasiewicz (1878–1956) and American mathematician Emil Leon Post (1897–1954) independently extend classical logic to include a third possibility, namely, "We don't know." Thus, they lay the basis for multiple-valued logic. Multiple-valued logic

is more than an exercise in philosophy and mathematics. Its influence has been seen in hardware design and the development of artificial intelligence.

(M)

April 26

Harlow Shapley and Heber Curtis debate the size and extent of the universe.

American astronomer Harlow Shapley (1885–1972) began studying star clusters within our galaxy, the Milky Way, in 1914. His observations led him to calculate the size and structure of the Milky Way, stating that it is 300,000 light-years in diameter. He also proposed the center of the galaxy to be 60,000 light-years away from the Earth. He summarizes his work at a meeting of the National Academies of Science in Washington, D.C., on April 26, 1920. At the same meeting, renowned American astronomer Heber Doust Curtis (1872–1942) presents his own calculations of the size of the galaxy. Historians remember this meeting for the debate on the size and extent of the universe by these astronomers. Shapley argued for a large universe, composed of a single galaxy, while Curtis states that the universe is smaller but filled with multiple galaxies. Today, astronomers know that the universe is larger than either of these men had argued and contains many galaxies beyond the Milky Way.

(SA)

1921

Chemicals transmit nerve impulses.

Nerves transmit messages to the body's organs. English biologist Sir Henry Hallett Dale suggested that chemicals released by the nerves are responsible for their actions (*See* entry for 1914). In 1921, American pharmacologist Otto Loewi (1873–1961) confirms these studies, using isolated frog hearts bathed in a nutritive liquid known as Ringer solution. Loewi stimulates one of the hearts to beat. When he collects the solution from that heart and moved it to the second heart, it beats without stimulation. He surmises that a chemical now called a *neurotransmitter* must have been released that caused the heart to beat. Later experiments show that the nerves surrounding the heart release a chemical, proving that chemicals transmit nerve impulses. Loewi and Dale share the Nobel Prize in physiology or medicine in 1936 "for their discoveries relating to chemical transmission of nerve impulses."

(B)

Albert-Léon-Charles Calmette and Camille Guérin isolate an attenuated strain of tuberculosis.

Tuberculosis has been a public health scourge for hundreds of years. In the early 20th century, advances in microbiology and vaccine development gave scientists the hope they could control the disease. Microbiologist Robert Koch, who identified the strain of *bacteria* that causes tuberculosis, tried unsuccessfully to develop a vaccine. In 1921, French scientists Albert-Léon-Charles Calmette (1863–1933) and Camille Guérin (1872–1961) isolate a strain of tuberculosis that does cause disease. This attenuated strain is called BCG (Bacillus Calmette-Guérin). Within 10 years, BCG is widely used to vaccinate against tuberculosis. Unfortunately, BCG is not a completely effective vaccine against tuberculosis and millions of cases are still contracted each year.

(B)

1922

Lewis Fry Richardson incorporates mathematics into weather prediction.

Weather prediction has changed and improved over time. Modern weather forecast-ing depends upon mathematical models that predict the movement of the atmosphere. In 1922, British mathematician Lewis Fry Richardson (1881–1953) introduces mathematical models into weather forecasting in his paper "Weather Prediction by Numerical Processes." The calculations required to predict weather, however, are cumbersome, so mathematical modeling did not gain prominence until the use of computers became widespread.

(M, W)

Joseph Erlanger and Herbert Spencer Gasser study the action of a single nerve.

Messages from the brain travel throughout the body, using nerves. In 1922, American physiologists Joseph Erlanger (1874–1965) and Herbet Spencer Gasser (1888–1963) study how this occurs. They develop a technique that allows them to study the electrical impulses of a single nerve. Using this technique, they learn, in 1922, that the speed of a nerve impulse depends on the thickness of the nerve. In addition, their techniques are adapted for use in instruments that diagnose diseases of the brain and nervous system. They share the Nobel Prize in physiology or medicine in 1944 "for their discoveries relating to the highly differentiated functions of single nerve fibres."

(B)

Sir Chandrasekhara Venkata Raman explains why the ocean is blue.

If water itself is clear and colorless, then where does the blue color of the ocean come from? After a sea voyage in 1922, Indian physicist Sir Chandrasekhara Venkata Raman (1888–1970) wanted to find out. He conducts experiments in which he passes light through water and ice. He finds that the *diffusion* of sunlight causes the blue color of the ocean.

(P)

Arthur Holly Compton confirms the particle nature of light.

The nature of light is a classic question in physics. In the 20th century, physicists questioned the idea that light traveled in waves. Albert Einstein proposed that light traveled in units called *photons* that have both *energy* and *momentum*. In 1922, American physicist Arthur Holly Compton (1892–1962) confirms this theory. He measures the scattering of *X-rays* and finds that his data cannot be explained using classical physics. However, when he treats the problem using Einstein's proposal that light is a particle, his data makes senses. Thus, the particle nature of X-rays, and subsequently light, is confirmed. Compton is honored with the Nobel Prize in physics in 1927 "for his discovery of the effect named after him."

(P)

February

Insulin is shown to control blood sugar.

In February 1922, Canadian biologists Sir Frederick Grant Banting (1891–1941) and Charles Herbert Best (1899–1978) make a breakthrough in the control of diabetes when they isolated the *hormone* insulin. Banting and Best remove the pancreas from a dog and make an extract from it. They then give the extract to another dog that has high blood sugar. Immediately, the dog's blood sugar falls. They soon isolate the hormone in the pancreas responsible for this effect. Scottish physiologist John James Macleod (1876–1935), the head of their laboratory, calls the hormone insulin. The importance of their discovery is recognized immediately, and Banting and Macleod share the Nobel Prize in physiology or medicine in 1923 "for the discovery of insulin."

(B)

1923

György Hevesy discovers hafnium.

During the 19th century, Dimitri Mendeleyev arranged the *elements* into the *periodic table* of the elements. His table predicted the existence of elements that were not yet discovered. In 1923, Hungarian chemist György Hevesy (1885–1966) uses *X-rays* to examine a mineral. His study indicates that an unidentified element is present in the sample. Later analysis shows that the element, now called hafnium, has 72 *protons* and had been predicted to exist by Mendeleyev years earlier.

(C)

Chemists explain acids and bases.

Acids and *bases* have been known to scientists since the days of the alchemy. However, how they worked remained a mystery. As the structure of the atom became widely understood, chemists used it to explain the properties of many substances. In 1923, Danish chemist Johannes Niccolaus Brønsted (1879–1947) and English chemist Thomas Lowry (1874–1936) independently propose a concept of acids and bases that explains their function on an atomic level. They define an acid as any substance capable of donating a proton to another molecule. Similarly, a base is defined as a molecule that can accept a proton. This definition expands the list of known acids and bases.

(C)

Scientists discover how the body fights pneumonia.

The body's immune system is responsible for recognizing foreign substances, such as *bacteria,* and eliminating them from the body. How the immune system actually works was a long-standing question in biology. In 1923, American biologists Michael Heidelberger (1888–1991) and Oswald Avery (1877–1955) show that the immune system recognizes molecules on the outside of bacteria called polysaccharides. This critical observation in immunology leads to development of a vaccine against some forms of pneumonia, blood infection, and meningitis.

(B)

Hermann Oberth shows a rocket can overcome the Earth's gravity.

Travel beyond the Earth once existed only in the realm of science fiction. In 1923, German physicist Hermann Oberth (1894–1989) takes steps toward bringing it closer to reality in his work *By Rocket to Space*. His book shows mathematically that a rocket could be built that would generate enough thrust to escape the Earth's *gravity*. His book is based on his dissertation that was rejected the previous year for being too speculative. Oberth continues writing on the possibilities of space travel and building rockets based on his theories. Today, he is considered one of the fathers of space travel.

(SA)

Summer

Louis-Victor-Pierre-Raymond de Broglie expresses the wave-particle duality of matter.

During the 20th century, physicists reexamined old theories about the nature of *energy* and matter. In 1923, French physicist Louis-Victor-Pierre-Raymond de Broglie (1892–1987) proposes that matter, like energy, has some properties consistent with a wave and others consistent with a particle. He develops a mathematical expression for *wave-particle duality* of matter. His theories are experimentally supported by the experiments of others. De Broglie is honored with the Nobel Prize in physics in 1929 "for his discovery of the wave nature of electrons."

(P)

1924

Alexander Friedmann states that the universe is expanding.

Theories of how the universe was created are as old as humankind. In the early 20th century, advances in physics and astronomy gave scientists new tools to investigate this question. In 1924, Russian scientist Alexander Friedmann (1888–1925) proposes that the universe is expanding. He bases his theory on Albert Einstein's theory of *relativity*. Friedmann theorizes that the universe began with a large explosion, the "big bang." His work, and that of other scientists of the time who reach similar conclusions, still forms the basis of the *big bang theory*.

(P, SA)

Bose-Einstein statistics are used to count particles.

As quantum theory became more popular, physicists reexamined many classic problems in physics. In 1924, Indian scientist Satyendra Nath Bose (1894–1974) derives equations to describe *black body* radiation, using only *quantum mechanics*. His views become widely known when German-American physicist Albert Einstein publishes a generalization of his methods. Today, his methods are popularly known as Bose-Einstein *statistics*. Their work allows physicists to count some types of *subatomic particles*.

(P)

The polarograph allows chemists to determine the concentration of a chemical in solution.

Chemists are often faced with trying to understand the nature of chemicals in a solution. One common problem is trying to determine the concentration of a particular chemical within the solution. An easy way of measuring this is developed by Czech chemist Jaroslav Heyrovsky (1890–1967) in 1924. He designs the polarograph, an instrument that measures current and voltage passing through a solution. The concentration of the chemical in solution can be determined by measuring the change in voltage through the solution as an electric current is passed through it. This device becomes the basis for a number of analytical tools used in research, industry, and medical settings. Heyrovsky is honored with the Nobel Prize in chemistry in 1959 "for his discovery and development of the polarographic methods of analysis."

(C)

Hans Spemann describes the early development of an embryo.

Reproduction presents scientists with many fascinating questions. In the early 20th century, biologists began investigating how an embryo develops. In 1924, German biologist Hans Spemann (1869–1941) brings some insight into this process when he describes what is known as the organizer effect. Spemann took cells from the front of an amphibian embryo and transplanted them to the belly of another. When the animal was born, it had two heads. His experiments show that cells in certain regions serve as "organizers" directing the development of the surrounding cells. Spemann is awarded the Nobel Prize in physiology or medicine in 1935 "for his discovery of the organizer effect in embryonic development."

(B)

The ionosphere is shown to reflect radio waves.

As the use of radio began to spread, scientists and engineers investigated ways to improve reception, and they searched for the cause of interference. In 1924, English physicist Sir Edward Victor Appleton (1892–1965) proposes that the variations in signal happen because the waves are being reflected by something in the atmosphere. Others had proposed such a reflecting layer in the past. Appleton, however, proves that the layer, now known as the *ionosphere,* exists and measures its distance from the Earth's surface. He uses techniques that are later employed in the development of radar. For his work, Appleton is awarded the Nobel Prize in physics in 1947 "for his investigations of the physics of the upper atmosphere especially for the discovery of the so-called Appleton layer."

(ES, P)

Sir Arthur Stanley Eddington determines the mass of stars.

How does an astronomer determine the mass of a star when it is impossible to perform a physical measurement? In 1924, Sir Arthur Stanley Eddington (1882–1944) applies mathematics to this question and develops a method to determine the mass based on measuring its illuminated light. Using the mass-luminosity relation, he determines the mass of many types of stars.

(SA)

The Svedberg develops the ultracentrifuge.

Chemists often need to separate complex mixtures. One method commonly used is centrifugation. In a centrifuge, mixtures are spun at high speeds at which they separate on the basis of their physical properties. In 1924, Swedish chemist The Svedberg (1884–1971) develops a centrifuge in which the motion of particles can be optically monitored. He calls it an ultracentrifuge. In the years that follow, Svedberg uses his ultracentrifuge to study biologically important molecules such as *proteins* and polysaccharides. He is honored with the Nobel Prize in chemistry in 1926 "for his work on disperse systems." Ultracentrifugation remains an important analytical technique in laboratories today.

(C)

Gordon Dobson measures ozone levels in the atmosphere.

During the early 20th century, meteorologists determined that the temperature of one layer of the atmosphere, known as the *troposphere,* varies according to height from the Earth. English scientist Gordon Dobson (1889–1976) proposed that this variation is due to the absorption of ultraviolet rays from the Sun by ozone in the atmosphere. In 1924, he designs and builds an instrument that can measure ozone levels in the atmosphere. Over the next five years, he examines how the amount of ozone in the atmosphere changes depending on the season and the position on the Earth. Dobson's instruments are still used to measure ozone levels today.

(ES, P, W)

February

Edwin Hubble states that there are galaxies beyond the Milky Way.

During the early 20th century, astronomers debated whether or not there were galaxies outside of the Milky Way. In February 1924, American astronomer Edwin Hubble (1889–1953) measures the distance to the Andromeda *nebula* and finds that it is more than 100,000 times farther away from the Earth than the nearest stars. He proposes that it lies in a galaxy beyond the Milky Way. Throughout his life, Hubble continued to identify other galaxies and to measure their distance from the Earth.

(SA)

July 6

Hans Berger records electrical activity in the brain.

Electrical activity in the brain had been known since the late 19th century. German psychiatrist Hans Berger (1873–1941) tried to develop an instrument that would record these impulses. In 1924, he attaches electrodes that are normally used to stimulate brain activity to a device used in electrocardiogram recordings. After several tries, he finds the conditions in which he can record electrical impulses in the brain. These early experiments lead to the electroencephalograph or EEG, which remains one of the most widely used techniques in neurology.

(B)

1925

Sir Robert Robinson uncovers the structure of morphine.

Plants have served as a source of both food and medicines. Many medicines are derived from molecules found only in plants. One class of plant molecules, the alkaloids, is particularly interesting to *organic* chemists. In 1925, English chemist Sir Robert Robinson (1886–1975) determines the chemical structure of a pharmacologically important alkaloid, pain-killing morphine. Robinson is honored with the Nobel Prize in chemistry in 1947 "for his investigations on plant products of biological importance, especially the alkaloids."

(B, C)

Wolfgang Pauli describes the electronic shell of the atom.

As described in the sidebar "The Beginnings of Quantum Mechanics," by 1925 physicists knew that *atoms* are made up of a dense nucleus surrounded by electrons. Further studies showed that some electrons are held tightly in the atom, making up the core, while others are part of the outside or *valence* electrons. American physicist Wolfgang Pauli (1900–58) studied the *quantum* state of these electrons. In 1925, he develops what is known as the Pauli Exclusion Principle. Simply stated, it shows that an atom can have only one electron of a given quantum state.

His work expands the understanding of the electron shell of an atom. In 1945, Wolfgang Pauli is awarded the Nobel Prize in physics "for the discovery of the Exclusion Principle, also called the Pauli Principle."

(P)

Walther Bothe studies nuclear decay.
The first half of the 20th century saw a great expansion in the knowledge about the *atom*

THE BEGINNINGS OF QUANTUM MECHANICS

As the 19th century drew to a close, many believed that all the big questions in physics had been answered. Many felt that some of the underlying theories to explain matter, light, *gravity, electricity,* and other natural phenomena had been uncovered. However, this was not the case. Soon experiments that helped to elucidate the structure of the atom would generate data that could not be explained by classical mechanics and would soon lead physicists to a new way of looking at the world. The result of these studies is the development of *quantum mechanics,* which explains the physical behavior of very small particles.

Quantum theory was born in 1900, when the German physicist Max Planck attempted to explain *black body radiation* without making any assumptions and without breaking the laws of *thermodynamics.* A black body is one that absorbs all radiation that comes to it. Physicists had studied black bodies and the *energy* emitted from them, black body radiation, for 40 years. By 1900, Planck's early attempts to explain black body radiation had been proven incorrect by subsequent experiments. He then proposed that the energy emitted from a black body traveled in discrete units he called quanta. This assumption made Planck's calculation match the experimental data. While most physicists

accepted Planck's work as correct, it was not immediately apparent what impact the concept of quanta would have on modern physics.

Over the next 20 years, evidence mounted that energy traveled in quanta. Soon it appeared that some types of electromagnetic radiation behaved both like a wave and like a particle. This so-called *wave-particle duality* became apparent in 1905, when German-American physicist Albert Einstein presented his work explaining the nature of light. Classical *mechanics* held that light traveled in waves. Einstein concluded that light travels in discrete units, now known as *photons.* His theory was not widely accepted, despite experimental evidence supporting his conclusions. Regardless, Einstein continued his work on the nature of light, developing the important concept of wave-particle duality, that is light sometimes has the properties of a particle, and other times the properties of a wave. As time passed, the evidence supporting the wave-particle duality continued to mount. In 1924, French physicist Louis-Victor-Pierre-Raymond de Broglie suggested that matter exists as both a particle and a wave. Experiments by American physicist Clinton Davisson (1881–1958) confirmed de Broglie's hypothesis.

(continues)

(continued)

Physicists soon began applying quantum theory to the new knowledge being gained about the structure of the atom. In 1913, Danish physicist Niels Bohr developed a theory of atomic structure that relied upon quantum theory. In his model of the atom, the *electron* orbiting the *nucleus* was confined to one of a series of orbits. A discrete quantity of energy is either emitted or absorbed when an electron moves from one orbit or another. These assumptions were necessary to account for the experimentally determined spectra of atoms. However, Bohr argued that classical physics could not explain the energy released or emitted during the transitions. A quantum explanation of this phenomenon was required. Soon after Bohr's work, other physicists used quantum mechanics to describe the atom, including Wolfgang Pauli, who showed in 1925 that only one electron can occupy a given quantum state, and Robert Sanderson Mulliken, who extends the work of Bohr and others to entire molecules when developing his molecular orbital theory in 1927.

During the 1920s, quantum mechanics became firmly established. In 1926, Erwin Schrödinger applied de Broglie's theory that matter can act as a wave to Bohr's model of the atom. He viewed the electron in Bohr's model as a wave and worked out a physical and mathematical description of its behavior. A key component to the mathematics of Schrödinger's so-called wave mechanics is known as the Schrödinger equation. Schrödinger's wave mechanics gives a similar mathematical description of the atom as another description, matrix mechanics, proposed by German physicist Werner Heisenberg in 1925. Later in 1926, Max Born added a critical conceptual element to Schrödinger's wave mechanics. He believed that the motion of particles followed the laws of *probability,* and thus probability had to be accounted for in the mathematical description of the motion of an electron. Taken together, Schrödinger's wave mechanics, Heisenberg's matrix mechanics, and Born's probabilistic interruption gave rise to modern quantum mechanics.

Throughout the 20th century, physicists continued to gather evidence supporting quantum theory. Unlike classical mechanics, quantum mechanics explains physical behavior on a small scale. The ideas and experiments of many physicists combined to produce one of the greatest scientific achievements of the century.

and in particular the atomic *nucleus.* Theoretical physicists, who relied upon previously gathered data and mathematical models, as well as experimental physicists embraced these studies. Experimental physics depended upon the continual development of techniques that aided in the exploration of the atom. In 1925, German physicist Walther Bothe (1891–1957) adds to that arsenal of techniques when he develops the coincidence method for studying nuclear decay. He later uses the coincidence method to address problems in particle physics, as well as to study cosmic rays. His work is honored with the Nobel Prize in physics in 1954 "for the coincidence method and his discoveries made therewith."

(P)

Sonar is used to uncover the Mid-Atlantic Ridge.

From 1925 to 1927, a German Atlantic expedition aboard the *Meteor* collected data on the Atlantic Ocean. The scientists employ sonar, a technique that uses sound waves, to measure the depth of the ocean. In the course of these measurements, they detect an area in the middle of the Atlantic Ocean where the seafloor is not nearly so deep as it is closer to the continents. The area is now known as the Mid-Atlantic Ridge, a mountain range that lies beneath the Atlantic Ocean.

(ES, MS)

May

Walter Noddack and Ida Tacke discover rhenium.

During the 18th and 19th centuries, scientists identified many of the *elements* known today. They are organized into the *periodic table* of the elements, which allowed chemists to predict their properties. Early versions of the periodic table of the elements also predicted the existence of elements yet to be discovered. In May 1925, German chemists Walter Noddack (1893–1960) and Ida Tacke (1896–1979) discover one such element while studying manganese ores. The element, now called rhenium, has 75 *protons*. Rhenium is the last nonradioactive element to be found.

(C)

July

Werner Heisenberg develops matrix mechanics.

By the 1920s, quantum physicists turned their attention toward the workings of the *atom*. German physicist Werner Heisenberg makes great strides in establishing this field in July 1925, when he introduces *matrix mechanics*.

Early three-dimensional model of the Mid-Atlantic Ridge made from observations made on board the German research vessel *Meteor* between 1925 and 1927. This photograph is taken from Alexander Bessmertny's *Das atlantis ratsel* (1932). *(Steve Nicklas/NOS, NGS/NOAA)*

Heisenberg starts with the assumption that analysis of the atom should be done only with experimentally measurable properties. Along with coworkers, he then works out a mathematical matrix to solve such problems. This work is widely considered the starting point for *quantum mechanics*. Heisenberg is honored with the Nobel Prize in physics in 1932 "for the creation of quantum mechanics, the application of which has, inter alia, led to the discovery of the allotropic forms of hydrogen."

(P)

1926

The Milky Way is shown to rotate around its center.

In the 20th century, astronomers using modern techniques to chart and follow stars noticed that they appeared to be moving in one of two directions. In 1926, Swedish astronomer Bertil Lindblad (1895–1965) explains this observation when he proposes that the Milky Way rotates around its center. Dutch astronomer Jan Oort (1900–92) later proves Lindblad's theory.

(SA)

Fermi-Dirac statistics allow physicists to count subatomic particles.

Counting *subatomic particles* presents a difficult problem for physicists. In 1926, physicists realized that the method being used, Bose-Einstein *statistics,* did not apply to *protons, neutrons,* or *electrons*. American physicist Enrico Fermi (1901–54) and British physicist Paul Dirac (1902–84) develop a statistical method to count these particles. The method is known as Fermi-Dirac statistics, and particles that can be counted in this manner are collectively termed *fermions*. This method is still employed by physicists.

(P)

Geneticists use X-rays to induce mutations.

Geneticists understand *gene* functions by comparing a "normal" or wild-type gene to one that has an error, called a mutation. However, the rate of spontaneous mutation is very low in nature. Therefore, a scientist has to examine thousands of organisms in the wild to find a single mutant. In 1926, American biologist Hermann Muller (1890–1967) develops a method to speed up the process. He exposes fruit flies, a common model system in genetics, to *X-rays*. Since X-rays cause genetic mutations, he now has a larger population of mutants to study. Today, geneticists have a number of methods available to induce mutations. Muller's work is honored with the Nobel Prize in physiology or medicine in 1946 "for the discovery of the production of mutations by means of X-ray irradiation."

(B)

Raw liver is shown to treat pernicious anemia.

The body relies on red blood cells to carry oxygen to its organs and tissues. Anemia is a disease marked by a reduced number of red blood cells. In 1926, American physician George Minot (1885–1950) and American physician William Murphy (1892–1987) study a specific type of anemia called pernicious anemia. They read about George Whipple's 1920 work, in which he treated anemia in dogs by feeding them raw liver. Minot and Murphy set out to see if raw liver could be used to treat humans with pernicious anemia. The treatment is successful because, as scientists later determine, pernicious anemia is caused by a lack of vitamin B_{12}, a nutrient found in liver. They share the Nobel Prize in physiology or medicine with American biologist George Whipple "for their discoveries concerning liver therapy in cases of anemia."

(B)

Sir George Paget Thomson proves that electrons have the properties of a wave.

As described in the sidebar "The Beginnings of Quantum Mechanics," quantum theory expanded rapidly in the early decades of the 20th century, and experimental physicists began the quest for data to back up the theories. In 1926, English physicist Sir George Paget Thomson (1892–1975) begins work to prove French physicist Louis-Victor-Pierre-Raymond de Broglie's wave theory of *electrons* (*see* entry for SUMMER 1923). He observes the scattering of electrons as they pass through metals and finds that their diffraction patterns agree with that predicted by the wave theory. Thus, an important part of quantum theory is experimentally proven. Thomson shares the Nobel Prize in physics in 1937 with American physicist Clinton Davisson for "for their experimental discovery of the diffraction of electrons by crystals."

(P)

Max Born explains wave-particle duality.

As described in the sidebar "The Beginnings of Quantum Mechanics," development of *quantum mechanics* in the early 20th century led physicists to reexamine the nature of *energy* and matter. Physicists showed that both energy and matter display what is known as *wave-particle duality,* that is they both have some properties of waves and others of particles. In 1926, German physicist Max Born (1882–1970) extends this understanding with his work on interrupting the wave function. He shows that the wave is in essence the *probability* of finding the particle at a particular point. Born is honored with the Nobel Prize in physics in 1954 "for his fundamental research in quantum mechanics, especially for his statistical interpretation of the wave function."

(P)

Biologists obtain pure preparations of enzymes.

Biological systems depend on a large number of chemical reactions to sustain life. Specialized *proteins* known as *enzymes* catalyze these reactions. During the 20th century, chemists began investigating these reactions and the enzymes that allow them to occur. To replicate biological reactions in a test tube, chemists needed to obtain enzymes in a pure form. However, this proved to be extremely difficult, as living cells are composed of mixtures of a large number of proteins, and enzymes are extremely sensitive to changes in temperature, as well as physical manipulation. The task of obtaining a pure preparation of an enzyme is finally completed in 1926, when American biochemist James Sumner (1887–1955) purifies the enzyme urase, and demonstrates its purity by obtaining crystals of it. After several years and the work of other scientists, Sumner's work becomes generally accepted. However, it was clearly recognized as pioneering work in 1946, when he is honored with the Nobel Prize in chemistry "for his discovery that enzymes can be crystallized."

(B, C)

January 26

Images are transmitted through the air by television.

During the 1920s, physicists and engineers developed technology that allows pictures to be transmitted from a camera to a receiver. One inventor, American engineer Philo Farnsworth (1906–71), successfully transmitted the image of a white line. The realization of television as an efficient means to broadcast images over long distances comes on January 26, 1926, when Scottish inventor John Logie Baird (1888–1946) electrically transmits moving pictures. Baird later transmits television images across the Atlantic Ocean. Today,

Baird is considered one of the inventors of television.

(P)

May

Erwin Schrödinger develops wave mechanics.

As described in the sidebar "The Beginnings of Quantum Mechanics," during the early 20th century physicists reexamined many older theories in terms of the newly developed field of *quantum mechanics.* The work of French physicist Louis-Victor-Pierre-Raymond de Broglie and others had shown that matter itself had the characteristics of both a particle and a wave. In 1926, Austrian physicist Erwin Schrödinger (1887–1961) develops a mathematical treatment of this problem in his classic paper *Quantization as an eigenvalue problem.* His work marks the creation of wave mechanics, allowing a mathematical explanation of the motion of *electrons.* Schrödinger shares the 1933 Nobel Prize in physics with Paul Dirac "for the discovery of new productive forms of atomic theory."

(P)

1927

Ernst Munch explains nutrient transport in plants.

Plants, like animals, must take up nutrients from the environment and distribute them throughout their tissues. In 1927, botanist Ernst Munch (1876–1946) puts forth the mass flow hypothesis to explain nutrient transport in plant tissue. The mass flow hypothesis states that nutrients move into the plant phloem by an active mechanism. Water then moves into the phloem by *osmosis,* and the additional pressure causes movement of water and nutrients throughout the tissues. While there are cases where it does not apply, this hypothesis remains widely accepted today.

(B)

Molecular orbital theory explains chemical bonds.

The discovery of *subatomic particles* and the development of *quantum mechanics* gave chemists new ways to think about the nature of chemical bonds. In 1927, American physicist Robert Sanderson Mulliken (1896–1986) develops molecular orbital theory. Molecular orbital theory states that the electronic structure of a molecule extends over several atoms, and possibly across the entire molecule. This theory is particularly useful for understanding chemical bonds in large molecules. Mulliken is honored with the Nobel Prize in chemistry in 1966 "for his fundamental work concerning chemical bonds and the electronic structure of molecules by the molecular orbital method."

(C, P)

Charles Elton applies economic principles to ecology.

Naturalists examine the relationships between plants and animals. Eventually, their observations and studies evolved into the science of ecology. In 1927, English biologist Charles Elton (1900–91) publishes *Animal Ecology,* a book that defines many of the principles used in ecology today. Elton draws from the principles of economics, defining the relationships between species in terms of food chains, food cycles, and *niches.* He spends the rest of his career expanding on these important concepts that serve as the basis of animal ecology today.

(B)

Werner Heisenberg puts forth his uncertainty principle.

As described in the sidebar "The Beginning of Quantum Mechanics," advances in *quantum mechanics* occurred rapidly throughout the 1920s. During the development of *matrix mechanics* in 1925, German physicist Werner Heisenberg stated that quantum mechanics should consider only experimentally observable data. In 1927, he suggests how difficult this task is when he articulates his famous uncertainty principle. Heisenberg explains that at a given time one cannot measure both the energy and the position of a subatomic particle because once the energy is measured the particle will have moved. Since the physical properties of these particles cannot be precisely measured, physicists cannot accurately predict their motion.

(P)

A virus is shown to cause yellow fever.

Yellow fever is a potentially fatal disease that has been seen in tropical regions for hundreds of years. Symptoms of the disease include a high fever and the yellowing of the skin. In 1927, American physician Max Theiler (1899–1972) discovers that a *virus* causes yellow fever. Over the next 10 years he develops a model to study yellow fever in mice that leads to the development of a vaccine. In 1938, field tests of the vaccine against yellow fever begin. The vaccine is still in use today. Theiler is honored with the Nobel Prize in physiology or medicine in 1951 "for his discoveries concerning yellow fever and how to combat it."

(B)

Clinton Davisson shows electrons act like waves.

As described in the sidebar "The Beginnings of Quantum Mechanics," the development of *quantum mechanics* led to renewed investigations into the nature of both *energy* and matter. In 1923, French physicist Louis-Victor-Pierre-Raymond de Broglie proposed that matter displays properties of both particles and waves. In 1927, American physicist Clinton Davisson confirms de Broglie's theory. Davisson demonstrates that when electrons hit a *crystal* they are reflected in a manner similar to waves. Thus, the particle was exhibiting wavelike behavior. Davisson shares the Nobel Prize in physics with English physicist Sir George Paget Thomson in 1937 "for their experimental discovery of the diffraction of electrons by crystals."

(P)

May 21

Charles Lindbergh completes the first solo flight across the Atlantic Ocean.

Two decades after the Wright Brothers took their first flight, a $25,000 prize is offered to the first person to fly nonstop across the Atlantic Ocean. On May 20, 1927, American aviator Charles Lindbergh (1902–74) takes off from New York in his plane, *The Spirit of St. Louis*. Thirty-three and a half hours later, on May 21, 1927, Lindbergh arrives in Paris, France. His success heralds the start of transcontinental air travel.

(P)

1928

Sir Gilbert Walker describes the southern oscillation.

Meteorologists have always noticed that weather varies not only by season but year to year. In 1928, English mathematician Gilbert Walker (1868–1958) sets out to study annual variations in weather to see if he could discern a pattern. After looking at 40 years of weather records from across the globe, Walker proposes that when atmospheric pressure is high in one area it is reduced in another. He calls this phenomenon the southern oscillation.

(M, W)

Sir Chandrasekhara Venkata Raman describes the scattering of light.

Light travels in waves of a particular frequency. The colors that the eye perceives depend upon the frequency of light the eyes observe. In 1928, Indian physicist Chandrasekhara Venkata Raman (1888–1970) shows that when light of a single color hits a molecule, it is scattered at a different or shifted frequency. He further demonstrates that this effect, now known as Raman scattering, is caused by changes in the energy level of the molecule. His observations allow the development of an important technique in chemical analysis, Raman *spectroscopy*. He is honored with the Nobel Prize in physics in 1930 "for his work on the scattering of light and for the discovery of the effect named after him."

(P)

Sir Alexander Fleming discovers penicillin.

Bacterial infections are a major public health problem. Since their discovery, physicians have relied on techniques to minimize infections rather than treat them. In 1928, Scottish biologist Sir Alexander Fleming (1881–1955) makes a discovery that will allow physicians to treat a number of deadly bacterial infections. Fleming studies a bacterial strain called *Staphylococcus*. One day he finds mold growing on the plates that he used to grow the *bacteria*. He notices that no bacteria grew near the mold. He concludes that the mold contains a substance that inhibits the growth of the bacteria. He calls it penicillin. Fleming shares the Nobel Prize in physiology or medicine in 1945 with Sir Howard Florey and Ernst Chain "for the discovery of penicillin and its curative effect in various infectious diseases."

(B)

Fredrick Griffith describes bacterial transformation.

In the early 20th century, many microbiologists studied how *bacteria* cause disease. In 1928, British biologist Frederick Griffith (1881–1941) compares a virulent, or disease-causing, strain of the bacteria *Pneumococcus* to an attenuated strain that does not cause disease. He finds that if he mixes dead bacteria from the virulent strain with live bacteria from the attenuated strain, the attenuated strain is "transformed" into the virulent strain. This phenomenon is called transformation of bacteria. Historically, this observation is critical as it lays some of the groundwork leading up to the discovery that DNA is the genetic material.

(B)

Albert von Szent-Györgyi isolates vitamin C.

Inside the cell, biological molecules often undergo what are known as oxidation-reduction reactions. During the early 1920s, biochemists tried to define all the components of such reactions, known as oxidizing agents and reducing agents. In 1928, Hungarian biochemist Albert Von Szent-Györgyi (1893–1986) isolates a biologically active reducing agent, now known as vitamin C. Von Szent-Györgyi then shows that this is the same chemical that was shown to prevent scurvy several years earlier. For his pioneering work on vitamin C, von Szent-Györgyi is awarded the Nobel Prize in physiology or medicine in 1937 "for his discoveries in connection with the biological combustion processes, with special reference to vitamin C and the catalysis of fumaric acid."

(B, C)

Chemists synthesize ring-shaped molecules.

Synthetic chemists are always looking for new and more efficient ways to synthesize complex molecules in the laboratory. In 1928, German chemists Otto Diels (1876–1954) and Kurt Alder (1902–1958) develop an important and widely useful method to synthesize *organic* compounds with a particular ring-shaped structure. The Diels-Alder reaction, as scientists now know, is widely used and facilitates the development of plastics. Diels and Alder share the Nobel Prize in chemistry in 1950 "for their discovery and development of the diene synthesis."

(C)

Edgar Adrian measure the activity of a single nerve.

Nerves carry messages between the brain and the other organs of the body. How they accomplish this is an important field of research. In 1928, English physiologist Edgar Adrian (1889–1977) increases the understanding of nerve action by devising an apparatus that monitors the activity of a single nerve. Adrian finds that when stimulated, electrical activity in the nerve increases. However, with constant stimulation the electrical activity of the nerve declines. Adrian's work sets the stage for further understanding of nerve action. Adrian shares the Nobel Prize in physiology or medicine in 1932 with Sir Charles Sherrington "for their discoveries regarding the functions of neurons."

(B)

Georg von Békésy explains the workings of the inner ear.

How does the ear perceive sounds? In 1928, American biologist Georg von Békésy (1899–1972) tries to answer this question. He observes the cochlea or inner ear and explains the physical mechanisms that allow us to hear. Békésy dissects the cochlea and observes the vibrations of membranes within the ear in response to various sounds. His work elucidates hearing and sets the stage for

further studies on the biophysics of this process. Von Békésy is honored with the Nobel Prize in physiology or medicine in 1961 "for his discoveries of the physical mechanism of stimulation within the cochlea."

(B)

Hans Fischer synthesizes heme.

Synthetic chemists search for ways to synthesize complex molecules in the laboratory. Some of the most challenging molecules to synthesize come from living systems. In 1928, German chemist Hans Fischer (1881–1945) synthesizes heme, an important component of the oxygen-carrying blood protein *hemoglobin*. He then studies and synthesizes other biologically important compounds. Fischer is honored with the Nobel Prize in chemistry in 1930 "for his researches into the constitution of haemin and chlorophyll and especially for his synthesis of haemin."

(B, C)

Werner Forssmann demonstrates heart catheterization.

Diseases of the heart are often fatal because of its central role in keeping a human being alive. For centuries, physicians could not observe the heart of a patient directly because the process was too dangerous. In 1928, German physician Werner Forssmann (1904–79) makes the first steps toward allowing more direct observation of heart function when he demonstrates that heart catheterization was possible in humans. He inserts a catheter into his own vein and guides it to his heart. At first, his experiments are widely criticized and considered dangerous. After several years and more research, the technique is developed further and becomes accepted. Forssmann shares the Nobel Prize in physiology or medicine in 1956 with André Cournad and Dickenson Richards "for their discoveries concerning heart catheterization and pathological changes in the circulatory system."

(B)

Sir John Cockcroft and Ernest Walton develop the particle accelerator.

Theoretical physicists rely on mathematics and previously collected data to develop their theories. These theories must be proven with experiments. In a field such as nuclear physics, where scientists study particles smaller than *atoms* that are held together by extremely strong *forces,* such experiments can be hard to perform. In 1928, British physicist Sir John Cockcroft (1897–1967) and Irish physicist Ernest Walton (1903–95) make these experiments much easier when they develop the particle *accelerator.* Use of this early accelerator serves as the basis for the larger and more powerful accelerators used to study particle physics today. Cockcroft and Walton share the Nobel Prize in physics in 1951 "for their pioneer work on the transmutation of atomic nuclei by artificially accelerated atomic particles."

(P)

Sugar molecules are shown to form rings.

In the 20th century, many chemists turned their attention to the reactions that occur in living systems. An important family of molecules that provides *energy* for living organisms is sugars. To develop theories on how sugars are processed in the body, chemists need to understand their chemical structure. By 1928, English chemist Sir Walter Norman Haworth (1883–1950) establishes that sugar molecules form a ring. He confirms the chemical structure of a large number of biologically important sugars. Haworth is honored with the Nobel Prize in chemistry in 1937 "for his investigations on carbohydrates and vitamin C."

(B, C)

Hormones are shown to control sugar metabolism.

Diabetes, a disease characterized by excess sugar in the blood and urine, has been known for centuries. Research into the causes of diabetes has led to many insights on how the body breaks down and uses dietary sugars. In 1928, Argentine physiologist Bernardo Houssay (1887–1971) discovers that *hormones* play a role in the breakdown of sugars. Houssay finds that a hormone secreted by the pituitary gland controls the uptake of sugar from the blood into tissues and organs. Houssay is honored with the Nobel Prize in physiology or medicine in 1947 "for his discovery of the part played by the hormone of the anterior pituitary lobe in the metabolism of sugar."

(B)

The Earth's magnetic field can reverse directions.

Geologists have known that the Earth has a *magnetic field,* resulting on magnetic North and South Poles, since the invention of the compass. In 1929, Japanese geologist Matuyama Motonori (1884–1958) demonstrates that this magnetic field has reversed directions at a number of points in the Earth's history. In other words, from time to time the magnetic North Pole becomes the magnetic South Pole and, in turn, the magnetic South Pole becomes the magnetic North Pole. Motonori came to this conclusion by examining the polarity of rocks that have formed from volcanic eruptions. Today, the examination of magnetic reversals is an important tool in geology.

(ES)

Lars Valerian Ahlfors analyzes Riemann surfaces.

Mathematicians visualize equations by creating graphs along the appropriate axis. During the 19th century, German mathematician Bernhard Riemann (1826–1866) developed a new way to consider some equations, showing that when graphed they define a surface, known as a Riemann surface. In 1928, Finnish mathematician Lars Valerian Ahlfors (1907–1996) develops new methods to analyze Riemann surfaces. His work is honored with a Fields Medal in 1936.

(M)

NAD is shown to be an important cofactor in biological reactions.

The everyday actions of biological systems, such as the extraction of *energy* from food, occur through complex chemical reactions. The catalysts for these reactions are specialized proteins called *enzymes*. Enzymes, however, are not the only molecules required in many of these reactions. For instance, the *fermentation* of sugar by yeast requires a second component, known as coenzyme. In 1928, Swedish chemist Hans von Euler-Chelpin (1873–1964) identifies the coenzyme, a molecule now called nicotinamide adenine dinucleotide (NAD). Biologists now know that NAD is an important cofactor in many biological reactions. Von Euler-Chelpin shares the Nobel Prize in chemistry in 1929 with Arthur Harden "for their investigations on the fermentation of sugar and fermentative enzymes."

(B, C)

March

Paul Dirac predicts the existence of antimatter.

The identification of the *electron* in the late 19th century led to a surge in research into *subatomic particles*. Soon after, the *proton* and *neutron* were also identified. The parts of the atom are further dissected in 1928, when English physicist Paul Dirac (1902–1984) applies Albert Einstein's special theory of

relativity to the electron and predicts the existence of an "anti-electron" or positron as scientists now know it. Experiments conducted a few years later confirm the positron's existence. Dirac is the first to predict the existence of what is known as *antimatter*. He shares the Nobel Prize in physics with Erwin Schrödinger in 1933 for his achievement.

(P)

1929

Edwin Hubble claims the universe is expanding.

Astronomers are constantly looking farther into outer space—first beyond the Moon, then the solar system, and finally outside of the Milky Way. In 1929, American astronomer Edwin Hubble (1889–1953) analyzes light reflected from distant galaxies. He sees that these distant galaxies are moving away from the Milky Way. This critical observation is the first piece of evidence for what is now known as Hubble's law, which states that the universe is expanding, and provides evidence supporting the *big bang theory*. NASA later recognizes Hubble's pioneering contributions to astronomy by naming its space-based optical telescope in his honor.

(SA)

1930s

Adolf Butenandt isolates sex hormones.

Males and females differ not only in physical attributes but also in their biochemical makeup. One means by which the body controls development and the functioning of organs and tissues is by secreting specialized chemicals called *hormones*. In the late 1920s and early 1930s, German chemist Adolf Butenandt (1903–95) makes great advances in understanding the biochemical differences between men and women when he isolates three major sex hormones, the female hormones estrone and progesterone and male hormone androsterone. His work lays the basis for the future development of birth control pills and anabolic steroids. Butenandt is honored with the Nobel Prize in chemistry in 1939 "for his work on sex hormones."

(B, C)

Radio meteorographs aid weather forecasting.

Accurate weather forecasting relies on data from the upper atmosphere. Since the 18th century, scientists have used kites and balloons to get readings of atmospheric conditions. In the 1930s, the United States Weather Service expands the capacity of weather balloons when they add radio transmitters, creating the first radio meteorographs. The radio meteorographs are capable of measuring temperature, humidity, and pressure, then sending the readings back to a station on the Earth. Today, the U.S. Weather Service maintains a network of stations across the country.

(W)

Richard Kuhn discovers the chemical structure of vitamins.

Foods provide *energy* and nutrients that organisms need to survive. As chemists began turning their attention to biological systems, many investigated the chemical nature of vitamins. During the 1930s, Austrian chemist Richard Kuhn (1900–1967) uncovers the chemical structure of a number of vitamins, including the three forms of carotene (alpha, beta, and gamma), and vitamin B_2. Kuhn is honored with the Nobel Prize in chemistry in 1938 "for his work on carotenoids and vitamins."

(B, C)

Otto Stern measures the magnetic moment of protons.

Like *atoms* and molecules, *subatomic particles* have magnetic properties. During the 1930s, physicist German physicist Otto Stern (1888–1969) develops techniques to measure the magnetic moment of *protons*. Stern uses a molecular beam that sends atoms through a *magnetic field*. He is honored with the Nobel Prize in physics in 1943 "for his contribution to the development of the molecular ray method and his discovery of the magnetic moment of the proton."

(P)

During the 1930s, radio meteorographs are used by the United States Weather Service. The photograph depicts an early radio meteorograph launch. *(NOAA)*

Arne Tiselius uses electrophoresis to separate mixtures of proteins.

Biological systems depend on complex molecules called *proteins* to carry out many important functions. To study proteins in the laboratory, biochemists must separate them from the large mixture that exists in each cell. In the 1930s, Swedish biochemist Arne Tiselius (1902–71) introduces electrophoresis, an important technique that allowed scientists to separate proteins based on their physical characteristics. Using electrophoresis, scientists can separate proteins and nucleic acids based on their size and charge. Electrophoresis is used daily in biology and biochemistry laboratories. Tiselius is honored with the Nobel Prize in chemistry in 1948 "for his research on electro-phoresis and adsorption analysis, especially for his discoveries concerning the complex nature of the serum proteins."

(B, C)

Odd Hassel shows that compounds can exist in more than one conformation.

Chemists are interested in the properties and reactions of matter. The *atoms* that make up the molecules dictate a reaction between two molecules. During the 1930s, Norwegian chemist Odd Hassel (1897–1981) shows that in large molecules another property is important, the molecule's *conformation*. He studies the *organic* compound cyclohexane and finds that it can exist in more than one form or conformation. Today, scientists know that biological systems recognize differences in a molecule's conformation and specifically use one conformation over another. Hassel shares the Nobel Prize in chemistry in 1969 with Sir Derek Barton "for their contributions to the development of the concept of conformation and its application in chemistry."

(C)

1930

Sir Ronald Fisher reconciles the works of Mendel and Darwin.

The rediscovery of Gregor Mendel's work on inheritance led biologists to think about genetics and an effort to reconcile Mendel's work with Charles Darwin's theory of *natural selection* (*See* entry for 1859). In 1930, English mathematician Sir Ronald Aylmer Fisher (1890–1962) synthesizes the ideas of these men when he publishes *The Genetical Theory of Natural Selection*. This book expands upon his earlier work, arguing that variation and changes in *genes* leads to traits that can then be selected. Fisher's work shows that the two theories are complementary, not mutually exclusive. In fact, the convergence of these two theories provides the basis for *molecular biology* today.

(B, M)

Paul Karrer discovers the chemical structure of carotene.

In the early 20th century, biochemists began identifying and studying vitamins. In 1930, Swiss chemist Paul Karrer (1889–1971) increases the understanding of vitamins when he uncovers the chemical structures of carotene, a precursor to vitamin A. Understanding the chemical structure of vitamins is the first step both in discerning their function in the body as well as in synthesizing them to create vitamin supplements. Karrer's work is honored with a Nobel Prize in chemistry in 1937 "for his investigations on carotenoids, flavins and vitamins A and B_2."

(B, C)

Enzymes are shown to be proteins.

In the early 20th century, many chemists studied the chemistry of living systems. One of the first problems they addressed was how food is broken down and utilized by the body. In 1930, American biochemist John Northrop (1891–1987) studies molecules that speed up the digestion, known as *enzymes*. Northrop crystallizes three of these enzymes, pepsin, trypsin, and chymotrypsin, and shows they are *proteins*. His observations are critical in ending the debate about the chemical makeup of enzymes. In 1946, Northrop shares the Nobel Prize in chemistry with Wendall Stanley "for their preparation of enzymes and virus proteins in a pure form."

(B, C)

Ernest Lawrence develops the cyclotron.

A major focus of nuclear physics in the early 20th century was the development of instruments that could be used for more accurate experiments. The study of *subatomic particles* required the generation of extremely large amounts of *electricity*. In the 1920s, the particle *accelerator* was developed to perform such experiments. In 1930, American physicist Ernest Lawrence (1901–58) takes another approach when he develops the cyclotron. The cyclotron produces millions

Photograph taken in 1939 of the 60-inch cyclotron at the University of California Lawrence Radiation Laboratory, Berkeley *(Department of Energy/National Archives)*

of volts of electricity. Lawrence is honored with the Nobel Prize in physics in 1939 "for the invention and development of the cyclotron and for results obtained with it, especially with regard to artificial radioactive elements."

(P)

Isidor Rabi studies the magnetic properties of atoms and molecules.

Magnetism can be seen on a large scale, such as the magnetic poles of the Earth, or in a space as small as an *atom*. In 1930, American physicist Isidor Rabi (1898–1988) develops a method to measure the magnetic properties of atoms and molecules. His method, known as radio frequency resonance, leads to the creation of instruments that lend insight into the structure of molecules based upon their magnetic properties. Such instruments continue to be a vital tool in modern chemical analysis. Rabi is honored with the Nobel Prize in physics in 1944 "for his resonance method for recording the magnetic properties of atomic nuclei."

(P)

Corneille-Jean-François Heymans studies the control of respiration.

In the early 20th century, medical scientists deduced a relationship between blood pressure and *respiration*. How this process happened, however, remained a mystery. In 1930, Belgian physiologist Corneille-Jean-François Heymans (1892–1968) discovers how this process is regulated. In the course of experiments on dogs, Heymans finds molecules that sense the release of chemicals, known as chemoreceptors, in regions in the carotid sinus region, an area along the side of the neck. These receptors, along with others, are involved in the control of respiration. Heymans is honored with the Nobel Prize in physiology or medicine in 1938 "for the discovery of the role played by the sinus and aortic mechanisms in the regulation of respiration."

(B)

Patrick Blackett explains the nature of cosmic rays.

The 20th century saw many critical discoveries in physics that helped elucidate the structure of the *atom*. The discovery of *antimatter* was one of these critical findings. The antielectron, or *positron*, was discovered in 1928. In 1930, English physicist Patrick Blackett (1897–1974) shows that cosmic rays contain *electron* positron pairs. He is honored with the Nobel Prize in physics in 1948 "for his development of the Wilson cloud chamber method, and his discoveries therewith in the fields of nuclear physics and cosmic radiation."

(P)

Sir Cyril Norman Hinshelwood explains how water is formed.

Water has captured the attention of scientists throughout history. In 1930, English chemist Sir Cyril Norman Hinshelwood (1897–1967) commences experiments that lead to the first true understanding of how water is formed on a molecular level. Specifically, he studies how water molecules are formed from atoms of oxygen and hydrogen. He shares the Nobel Prize in chemistry in 1956 with Nikolay Nikolaevich Semenov "for their researches into the mechanism of chemical reactions."

(C)

February 18

Astronomers discover Pluto.

Most of the planets in the solar system are identified either by eye or telescope. However, in the 19th century astronomers predicted the existence of the planet Neptune. After Neptune's discovery, there appeared to be yet another planet orbiting the Sun. American astronomer Percival Lowell (1855–1916) devoted much energy to photographing the sky, looking for the ninth planet; however, he died without finding it. After searching photographs taken of its predicted location, Clyde Tombaugh (1907–97) discovers the planet Pluto in 1930.

(SA)

1931

Georges-Henri Lemaître proposes the big bang theory.

Throughout history, the origin of the universe has been a question most often tackled by religion. In 1931, Belgian physicist Georges-Henri Lemaître (1894–1966) begins formulating a scientific explanation for the birth of universe. He proposes that the world began as radioactive degradation of a primeval atom. His proposal lays the groundwork for what is known today as the *big bang theory*.

(P, SA)

Kurt Gödel introduces his incompleteness theorems.

For nearly a century, mathematicians have tried to establish a list of propositions, known as *axioms*, that would serve as a basis of all mathematics. In 1931, American mathematician Kurt Gödel (1906–78) proves that this quest is impossible when he introduces his incompleteness theorems. Simply put, these theorems demonstrate that an axiom can be true but not provable. Thus, any axiomatic system is incomplete. Gödel's theorems represent an important step in mathematical logic.

(M)

Lars Onsager describes irreversible reactions.

Chemical reactions either consume or release *energy* in the form of heat. In the early 20th century, chemists studied this process, describing the *thermodynamics* of different reactions. The reactions commonly studied occurred at *equilibrium*, a state where there is a balance between the *reactants* and the *products* of the reactions. In 1931, American chemist Lars Onsager (1903–76) describes the thermodynamics of reactions that are not in equilibrium. Such irreversible reactions are found in many biological systems. His work is honored with a Nobel Prize in chemistry in 1968 "for the discovery of the reciprocal relations bearing his name, which are fundamental for the thermodynamics of irreversible processes."

(C)

Harold Urey discovers heavy water.

The discovery that *elements* exist in different forms, known as *isotopes*, led to a search for isotopes of experimentally important elements. In 1931, American chemist Harold Urey (1893–1981) and colleagues isolate deuterium, an isotope of the simplest element, hydrogen, in the form of "heavy water." Heavy water contains two *atoms* of deuterium and one of oxygen. Since deuterium can be distinguished from hydrogen, it is often used as a biological tracer. In addition, deuterium is an important component of early nuclear *fusion* reactions. The significance of this discovery is immediately recognized, and Urey is honored with the Nobel Prize in chemistry in 1934 "for his discovery of heavy hydrogen."

(C)

Jesse Douglas solves the plateau problem.

Some mathematical problems go unanswered for more than 100 years. Such was the case of the plateau problem posed by French mathematician Joseph-Louis Lagrange in 1760. The plateau problem attempted to show the existence of a surface of minimal area with a given boundary curve. A general solution to this problem eluded mathematicians until 1931, when American mathematician Jesse Douglas (1897–1965) gives a complete solution to the problem. His work is honored with a Fields Medal in 1936.

(M)

Sir James Chadwick discovers the neutron.
During the early 20th century, physicists began to uncover the structure of the *atom*. They identified two *subatomic particles,* the small negatively charged *electron* and the much larger positively charged *proton*. However, the mass of the protons and electrons did not add up to the total mass of the atom. Thus, scientists concluded there must be another particle. In 1931, English physicist Sir James Chadwick (1891–1974) identifies a third subatomic particle, the *neutron*. He shows that the subatomic particle has the same mass as a proton but does not have an overall charge. Chadwick is honored with the Nobel Prize in physics in 1935 "for the discovery of the neutron."

(P)

April

Ernst Ruska invents the electron microscope.
Advances in *quantum mechanics* have implications for many different branches of science. One of the clearest examples of this is the invention of the electron microscope in 1931. German physicist Ernst Ruska (1906–88) uses short wavelengths of *electrons* to greatly increase the magnification of his microscope. Today, electron microscopes are powerful enough to visualize large biologically important molecules. Ruska is honored with the Nobel Prize in physics in 1986 "for his fundamental work in electron optics, and for the design of the first electron microscope."

(B, P)

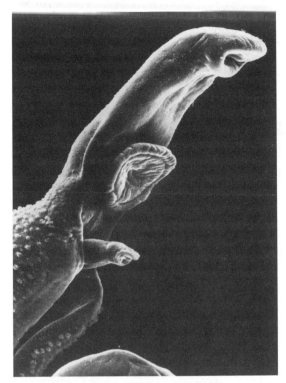

Electron microscopy allows biologists to visualize fine details of cells and organisms. This scanning electron micrograph depicts the schistosome parasite magnified 256 times. *(Bruce Wetzel and Harry Schaefer/National Cancer Institute)*

1932

Sir Hans Krebs describes the urea cycle.
All animals must have a way to excrete excess nitrogen, an important component of *proteins* consumed in their diets. Humans and a number of other vertebrates excrete it in a chemical known as urea. The mechanism by which the liver converts excess nitrogen into urea, called the urea cycle, is elucidated by a young biochemist named Sir Hans Krebs (1900–81) in 1932. The urea cycle is one of the first important metabolic pathways to be discovered.

(B, C)

Artturi Ilmari Virtanen develops a method to preserve cattle fodder.

The products of scientific research are applied to all facets of life, from technology to agriculture. One example is the research aimed at improving the preservation of vegetables that are used as cattle fodder. Cows get all of their protein from clover and other plant matter that they eat. When cows are raised in an agricultural setting, they must be fed the highest-quality food, no matter what the season. In 1932, Finish chemist Artturi Ilmari Virtanen (1895–1973) develops a method to preserve cattle fodder that assures the maximum retention of protein and other nutrients. The method, known as the AIV, improves the living conditions of cows as well as the quality of the milk they produce throughout the year. Virtanen is honored with the Nobel Prize in chemistry in 1945 "for his research and inventions in agricultural and nutrition chemistry, especially for his fodder preservation method."

(B, C)

John Van Vleck develops crystal field theory.

As physicists began to understand more about the structure of the *atom,* new theories on how molecules are formed and held together emerged. American physicist John Van Vleck (1899–1980) applied these theories as he tried to understand the effects of *magnetism* on molecules in a *crystal* form. He developed what is known as crystal field theory to describe the behavior of electrons under these conditions. In 1932, he publishes *The Theory of Electric and Magnetic Susceptibilities.* His theories are particularly useful in understanding molecules that contain metal *ions,* such as biologically important molecules. Van Vleck shares the Nobel Prize in physics in 1977 with Phillip Warren Anderson and Sir Nevill Francis Mott "for their fundamental theoretical investigations

of the electronic structure of magnetic and disordered systems."

(P)

John Burdon Sanderson Haldane synthesizes the work of Mendel and Darwin.

Biologists in the early 20th century studied Gregor Mendel's theory of inheritance. Soon biologists tried to reconcile his work with Charles Darwin's theory of *natural selection.* In 1932, Scottish biologist John Burdon Sanderson Haldane (1892–1964) publishes his attempt to synthesize the two theories, *The Causes of Evolution.* Along with other works published at the time (in particular the work of Roland Fisher) Haldane shows that natural selection and Mendelian inheritance can both explain the passing of traits from parent to off-spring, and the selection of evolutionarily favorable traits.

(B)

Carl David Anderson detects antimatter in cosmic showers.

The *atom,* once thought to be the smallest form of matter, is made up of even smaller particles. By the 1930s, physicists identified *subatomic particles* and predicted the existence of an anti-electron, or *positron.* In 1932, American physicist Carl David Anderson (1905–91) detects positrons while studying cosmic showers. Anderson's discovery is honored with the Nobel Prize in physics in 1936 "for his discovery of the positron."

(P, SA)

The phase-contrast microscope allows transparent objects to be visualized.

The invention of the microscope allowed scientists to study a wide variety of living things that could not be seen before. However, to view an object under light microscopy it must have color, either naturally or by staining the sample in the laboratory. In 1932, Dutch physicist Frits Zernike (1888–1966) develops a method that allows transparent objects to be visualized. His invention, the phase-contrast microscope, is widely used in biology. Zernike is honored with the Nobel Prize in physics in 1953 "for his demonstration of the phase contrast method, especially for his invention of the phase contrast microscope."

(B, P)

Subramanyan Chandrasekhar explains the origin of stars.

Scientists have been observing the stars since ancient times. In the 20th century, a number of different types of stars were identified. How these stars came about remained a question. In 1932, Indian physicist Subramanyan Chandrasekhar (1910–95) proposes a theory of how certain small stars known as white dwarfs and *neutron* stars came about. His work on the origins of stars is honored with the Nobel Prize in physics in 1983 "for his theoretical studies of the physical processes of importance to the structure and evolution of the stars."

(P, SA)

The Cori cycle describes how glucose cycles between the liver and muscle.

Where do muscles get the *energy* to do their work? During the 1930s, American biologists Carl (1896–1984) and Gerty (1896–1957) Cori answer this question. They uncover a biochemical process now known as the Cori cycle. The Cori cycle describes the relationship between the liver, which releases glucose to the bloodstream, and muscle, which uses glucose as fuel. The muscle converts glucose to a storage molecule called glycogen. When muscles perform work, glycogen is converted to a molecule called lactate. Lactate is then released to the bloodstream, where it is taken up by the liver and used to produce more glucose. The Coris are honored with the Nobel

Prize in physiology or medicine in 1947 "for their discovery of the course of the catalytic conversion of glycogen."

(B, C)

April

Sir John Cockcroft and Ernest Walton split the atom.

As the 20th century progressed, physicists became increasingly interested in studying the particles that make up an atom. English physicist Sir John Cockcroft and Irish physicist Ernest Walton developed a device known as the particle *accelerator* to aid in these studies (*See* entry for 1928). In 1932, they use the accelerator to split a lithium atom into two helium atoms. This is the first time an atom is split without the use of radioactivity. Later, they split 15 other atoms using their particle accelerator, establishing it as an important tool for the study of nuclear physics.

(P)

1933

Eugene Wigner describes forces within atomic nuclei.

At the beginning of the 20th century, physicists became increasingly interested in studying *subatomic particles* within the atomic *nucleus*. American physicist Eugene Wigner (1902–95) was particularly interested in the *forces* that hold these subatomic particles together. In 1933, he shows that the force between particles in the nucleus is weak unless they are very close together. His work lays the basis for understanding elementary particles. Wigner is honored with the Nobel Prize in physics in 1963 "for his contributions to the theory of the atomic nucleus and the elementary particles, particularly through the discovery and application of fundamental symmetry principles."

(P)

Fritz Zwicky proposes that galaxies are made up of dark matter.

Astronomers rely upon the light reflected from stars to analyze the universe. In 1933, Swiss astronomer Fritz Zwicky (1898–1974) theorizes that there was more to some galaxies than the visible stars. Zwicky measures the rate at which galaxies move. He notes that the rate does not agree with what astronomers predict based on the calculated mass of the galaxy. He proposes that these galaxies are made up of *dark matter* that neither emits nor absorbs light. Zwicky believes that dark matter makes up approximately 90 percent of these galaxies. Today, cosmologists are still searching for the identity of dark matter.

(P, SA)

Axel Theorell and Otto Heinrich Warburg describe the oxidation of sugars.

During the first half of the 20th century, biologists and biochemists tried to discover how organisms get *energy* from complex molecules. From 1933 to 1935, Swedish biochemist Axel Theorell (1903–82) and German biochemist Otto Heinrich Warburg (1883–1970) investigate specialized biological molecules called *enzymes* that are involved in the oxidation of sugars. They isolate the enzyme and find that it contains two parts, a protein component and a chemical cofactor, vitamin B_2. They later describe the exact chemical reaction carried out by this enzyme. For his work on oxidation of sugars, Theorell receives the Nobel Prize in physiology or medicine in 1955 "for his discoveries concerning the nature and mode of action of oxidation enzymes."

(B, C)

Georgyi Frantsevitch Gause states that only one species can hold a specific niche.

Ecologists describe the ecological *niche* held by a species as the conditions within a habitat that it requires and uses to survive. In a given habitat, many species exist and compete for resources. In 1932, Russian biologist Georgyi Frantsevitch Gause (1910–86) proposes that only one species can hold a specific ecological niche in a given habitat. If two different species can potentially fill that niche, they will compete and one will eventually thrive while the other is excluded. Gause's principle, also known as the "competitive exclusion principle," is still accepted by ecologists today.

(B)

1934

Paul Flory begins his study of the physical chemistry of macromolecules.

Macromolecules, the general term for large complex molecules, are important in wide array of chemistry from biochemistry to the synthesis of *polymers* such as plastics. In 1934, American chemist Paul Flory (1910–85) begins a decades-long investigation into the physical chemistry of macromolecules. His work uncovers some of the chemical properties of plastics and gives chemists a better understanding of the chemical reactions that produce polymers. Flory is honored with the Nobel Prize in chemistry in 1974 "for his fundamental achievements, both theoretical and experimental, in the physical chemistry of the macromolecules."

(C)

Lord Todd begins his work on the chemistry of coenzymes.

Enzymes are biological molecules that catalyze chemical reactions in cells. Some enzymes, including those involved in the synthesis and degradation of molecules in cells, require other molecules or coenzymes. Humans obtain many of these coenzymes from food, where these molecules are better known as vitamins. In 1934, British chemist Lord Todd (1907–97) begins his work on the chemistry of coenzymes by studying the chemical structures of B vitamins. Todd is honored with the Nobel Prize in chemistry in 1957 "for his work on nucleotides and nucleotide co-enzymes."

(B, C)

Radioactive elements are created in the laboratory.

After decades of studies, scientists uncovered a number of radioactive elements and radioactive *isotopes* of elements. In 1934, French scientists Frédéric (1900–58) and Irène Joliot-Curie (1897–1956), daughter of chemists Pierre and Marie Curie, create artificial radioactive elements. These elements emit a particle known as a *positron*. They share the Nobel Prize in chemistry in 1935 for their discovery "in recognition of their synthesis of new radioactive elements."

(C, P)

Enrico Fermi uses neutrons to create radioactive elements.

In 1934, Italian physicist Enrico Fermi (1901–54) sets out to expand the number of artificially radioactive *elements*. Rather than use

SOME OF THE CHEMICAL STRUCTURES OF VITAMINS ELUCIDATED BY CHEMISTS FROM 1900 TO 1945

Vitamin C

Vitamin K₁

Beta carotene

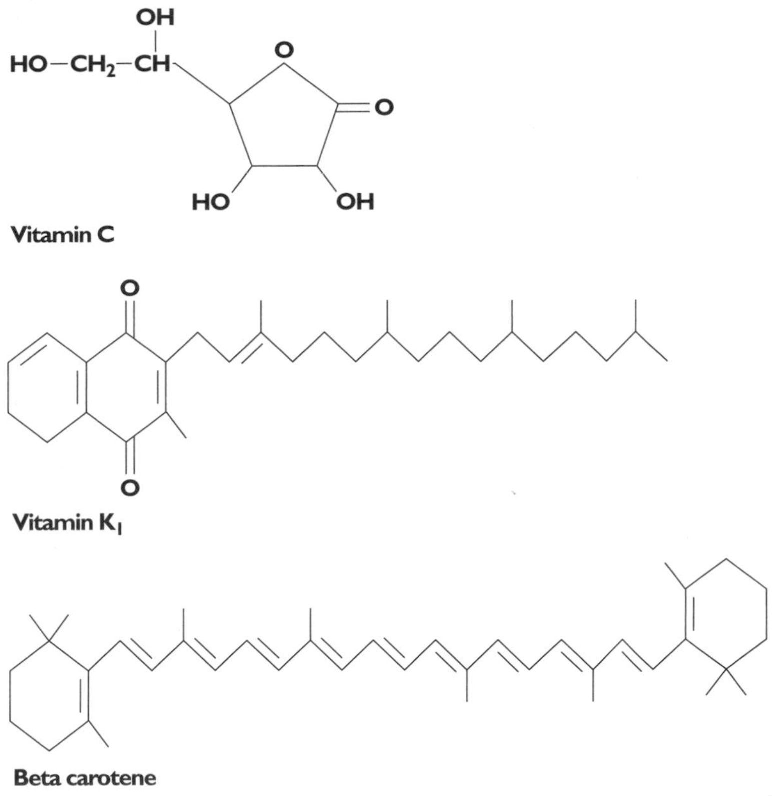

© Infobase Publishing

The chemical structure of three important vitamins, vitamin C, vitamin K₁, and beta-carotene, studied by chemists from 1900 to 1945

alpha particles to bombard nuclei, as the Joliots had, Fermi uses *neutrons*. Fermi proceeds to bombard a number of elements with neutrons and discovers artificial *radioactivity* in more than 30 of them. He shows that neutrons are much more efficient in carrying out this process. Fermi is honored with the Nobel Prize in physics in 1938 "for his demonstrations of the existence of new radioactive elements produced by neutron irradiation, and for his related discovery of nuclear reactions brought about by slow neutrons."

(P)

The Cherenkov effect serves as the basis for new detectors.

The study of particle physics depends upon technological advances that allow scientists to detect particles and measure their physical properties. In 1934, Russian physicist Pavel Alekseyevich Cherenkov (1904–90) notices an interesting property of charged particles moving at high velocities. Subsequent work on the "Cherenkov effect" by Russian physicists Ilya Mikhaylovich Frank (1908–90) and Igor Yevgenyevich Tamm (1895–1971) provides the basis for developing detectors that are used to study nuclear physics. Cherenkov, Frank, and Tamm share the Nobel Prize in physics in 1958 "for the discovery and the interpretation of the Cherenkov effect."

(P)

Sir Marcus Oliphant discovers tritium.

During the first half of the 20th century, scientists discovered that *elements* could exist in more than one form. The different forms of the elements are called *isotopes*. The heavier isotopes of an element have the same number of *protons* but more *neutrons* than the stable isotope. One such isotope is a heavier form of hydrogen, called deuterium. In 1934, Australian physicist Sir Marcus Oliphant (1901–2000) bombards deuterium with neutrons and produces

an even heavier form of hydrogen called tritium. Today, tritium is used in biological laboratories as a radioactive tracer, allowing researchers to follow the incorporation of hydrogen into biologically important molecules.

(P)

Ladislaus Marton views biological samples using the electron microscope.

Understanding the workings of living cells requires biologists to use microscopes that allow them to see the cell's structure under a number of different conditions. Advances in physics led to the construction of more powerful microscopes, allowing scientists to view small objects at high resolution. One such advance was the invention of the electron microscope (*See* entry for 1930). In 1934, Belgian scientist Ladislaus Marton (1901–79) uses the electron microscope to visualize biological samples. These experiments are the first in a long line of studies in biology that use the electron microscope. Such studies continue to this day.

(B, P)

Scientists use radioactivity to follow biological reactions.

The discovery of *isotopes*, different forms of *elements* that had the same chemical properties, had consequences beyond chemistry. In 1934, Hungarian chemist Georg Karl von Hevesy (1885–1966) uses radioactive isotopes as tracers in a series of biological experiments. Hevesy injects a solution containing radioactive phosphorus into animals, then follows its path from the bloodstream into the body. Today, radioactive tracers are essential tools in biological research. Hevesy is honored with the Nobel Prize in chemistry in 1943 "for his work on the use of isotopes as tracers in the study of chemical processes."

(B, C, P)

1935

Sir Arthur Tansley defines an ecosystem.

Ecologists study the interaction between organisms within a given environment. The systematic study of ecology began in the 20th century. One of the pioneers was British biologist Sir Arthur Tansley (1871–1955), who was the first to use the term *ecosystem*. In 1935, Tansley advocates a reductionist approach to ecology, examining each species as an individual within an ecosystem, rather than considering groups of related species as part of a community. His quantitative approach to studying ecology is still used today.

(B)

Nikolay Nikolayevich Semenov describes chain reactions.

Chemists in the 20th century tried to understand the mechanism behind chemical reactions. One particularly interesting type of reaction is called the *chain reaction*. In a chain reaction, the reaction between molecules serves as a trigger for other molecules to react. One of the pioneers in this field was Russian chemist Nikolay Nikolayevich Semenov (1896–1986), who showed that the combustion of phosphorus vapor and oxygen is a chain reaction. In 1935, he publishes an important work describing the field, *Chemical Kinetics and Chain Reactions*. Semenov shares the Nobel Prize in chemistry in 1956 with Sir Cyril Norman Hinshelwood "for their researches into the mechanism of chemical reactions."

(C)

Sulfa drugs are shown to treat bacterial infections.

With the discovery of penicillin, the search for other *antibiotics* began. In 1935, German chemist Gerhard Domagk (1895–1964) uncovers another important class of antibiotics, the sulfonamides or sulfa drugs. Domagk tests the bacterial killing ability of a type of chemical known as azo dyes. He finds a dye that kills *bacteria* from the Streptococcus family. These bacteria cause a variety of diseases, including scarlet fever and rheumatic fever. The importance of sulfa drugs is recognized immediately, and Domagk is honored with the Nobel Prize in physiology or medicine in 1939 "for the discovery of the antibacterial effects of prontosil."

(B)

Hideki Yukawa proposes that an exchange particle holds together the atomic nucleus.

The 20th century saw research into the structure of the *atom* with the discovery of *subatomic particles*. The atomic *nucleus* is made up of positively charged *protons* and uncharged *electrons*. However, at first scientists were unsure how these particles are held together. In 1935, Japanese physicist Hideki Yukawa (1907–81) proposes that an exchange particle carries the force necessary to hold together the nucleus. He states that such a particle must be larger than an electron, but smaller than a proton. Initially, these particles are thought to be *mesons*, but subsequent studies disprove that theory. Yukawa is honored with the Nobel Prize in physics in 1949 "for his prediction of the existence of mesons on the basis of theoretical work on nuclear forces."

(P)

Linus Pauling describes chemical bonds.

The discovery of *subatomic particles* and the development of *quantum mechanics* in the early 20th century led to increased research into chemical bonds. In 1935, American chemist Linus Pauling (1901–94) applies quantum mechanics to chemistry and develops his *valence* bond method for studying chemical bonds. In 1939, he publishes the widely read book on the subject, *The Nature of the Chemical Bond.* Pauling is awarded the Nobel Prize in chemistry in 1939 "for his research into the nature of the chemical bond and its application to the elucidation of the structure of complex substances."

(C, P)

Wendell Stanley describes the nature of viruses.

After the discovery of *viruses,* microbiologists tried to understand the nature of these agents of disease. American biologist Wendell Stanley (1904–71) studied a plant pathogen called tobacco mosaic virus. In 1935, Stanley finds that the virus behaves chemically like the biological molecules called *proteins.* Subsequent studies by other laboratories show the virus also contains nucleic acids. Stanley shares the Nobel Prize in chemistry in 1944 with John Northrop "for their preparation of enzymes and virus proteins in a pure form."

(B)

The Richter scale measures the strength of earthquakes.

News report of earthquakes always state the earthquake's magnitude on the Richter scale. The Richter scale, developed in 1935 by American seismologist Charles Richter (1900–85), assigns a value of zero to the smallest detectable earthquake detectable at that time. The scale is logarithmic, so each point above one represents an earthquake 10 times stronger. The scale is still used today to compare the size of different earthquakes.

(ES)

Konrad Lorenz describes how newborn birds recognize their mother.

The ability of a newborn animal to recognize its parents is critical for its survival. In 1935, Austrian zoologist Konrad Lorenz (1903–89) describes the mechanism by which newborn birds recognize their mother, a process known as imprinting. Lorenz shows that newly hatched ducklings follow the first moving animal they see, and regard it as its parent. Lorenz continues his work in ethology, a field he pioneered. He shares the Nobel Prize in physiology or medicine in 1973 with Nikolaas Tinbergen and Karl von Frisch "for their discoveries concerning organization and elicitation of individual and social behaviour patterns."

(B)

Tadeus Reichstein and Edward Kendall isolate cortisone.

The secretion of specialized molecules called *hormones* regulates many physiological processes. During 1935 and 1936, Swiss scientist Tadeus Reichstein (1897–1996) and American scientist Edward Kendall (1886–1992) independently isolate the hormone cortisone from the adrenal gland. Cortisone is later used as a drug to decrease inflammation in serious conditions such as rheumatoid arthritis. Reichstein and Kendall share the Nobel Prize in physiology or medicine in 1950 with Phillip Showalther Hench "for their discoveries relating to the hormones of the adrenal cortex, their structure and biological effects."

(B)

1936

Inge Lehmann describes the Earth's core.

Earth scientists began noticing that the Earth and its atmosphere can be separated into layers with different properties. Seismologists uncovered the Earth's *crust, mantle,* and *core* by studying *seismic waves.* The core was believed to be liquid. In 1936, Danish geologist Inge Lehmann shows that seismic waves of deep

LAYERS OF THE EARTH AND ITS ATMOSPHERE DISCOVERED, 1900–1945

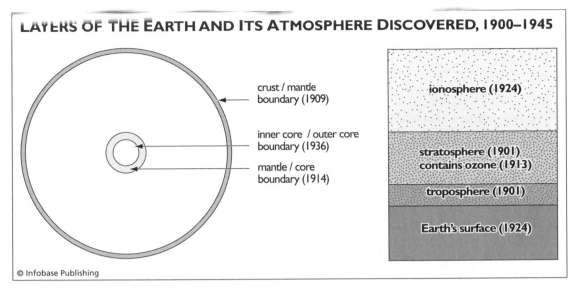

crust / mantle
boundary (1909)

inner core / outer core
boundary (1936)

mantle / core
boundary (1914)

ionosphere (1924)

stratosphere (1901)
contains ozone (1913)

troposphere (1901)

Earth's surface (1924)

© Infobase Publishing

During the early 20th century, scientists realized that the Earth and its atmosphere can be divided into several distinct layers. The boundaries between the Earth's crust, mantle, and core were all discovered. The atmosphere was divided into two major layers, the stratosphere and troposphere. The stratosphere was shown to contain a layer of ozone. The ionosphere, a third layer that could reflect radio waves, was found above the stratosphere.

earthquakes are reflected, suggesting that there is a solid inner core within the Earth's liquid core. Scientists conducting underground nuclear tests verify her work and calculate the size of the inner core during the 1960s.

(ES)

Walter Elsasser describes the formation of the Earth's magnetic field.

Where does the Earth's *magnetic field* come from? During the early 20th century, geologists proposed that the Earth's magnetic field is generated from what are known as self-sustaining *dynamos*. Dynamos occur when an *electric current* passes through a magnetic field. In 1936, German physicist Walter Elsasser (1904–91) suggests that a dynamo is created in the Earth's *core* by electric currents passing through the liquid iron core.

(ES, P)

António Egas Moniz develops the lobotomy.

Psychoses are severe mental diseases that are often difficult to treat. This was particularly true before the invention of tranquilizers and other drugs that alter a patient's mental state. In 1936, Portuguese neurologist António Egas Moniz (1874–1955) pioneers a surgical treatment for severe mental disorders, the prefrontal lobotomy. Surgeons cut nerves connecting two regions of the brain in the hope of stopping abnormal brain function. Despite severe side effects, the treatment is used widely for the next 20 years. Today, mental illness is generally treated with drugs, and lobotomies are no longer performed. However, at the time lobotomies are considered a revolutionary technique, and Egas Moniz is honored with the Nobel Prize in physiology or medicine in 1949 "for his discovery of the therapeutic value of leucotomy in certain psychoses."

(B)

1937

Emilio Segrè and Carlo Perrier discover technetium.

During the 18th and 19th centuries, scientists identified many of the *elements* known today. They are organized into the *periodic table* of the elements, which allows chemists to predict their properties (*See* entry for 1869). Earlier versions of the periodic table of the elements also predicted the existence of elements yet to be discovered. In 1937, physicists Emilio Segrè (1905–89) and Carlo Perrier (1886–1948) discover a new element after bombarding molybdenum *atoms* with an *isotope* of hydrogen. The element, now known as technetium, has 43 *protons* and was predicted to exist by the periodic table of the elements.

(C, P)

Grote Reber invents the radio telescope.

During the 20th century, *radio waves* were discovered in outer space. In 1937, American engineer Grote Reber (1911–2002) builds the first device designed to record radio waves, the radio telescope. He uses it to generate a radio map of the stars, demonstrating that the greatest amount of radio waves emanate from the Milky Way. His work serves as the basis for the field of radio astronomy.

(SA)

The citric acid cycle describes the metabolism of carbohydrates.

How does the body extract *energy* from food? In 1937, English biochemist Sir Hans Krebs (1900–81) answers a significant part of this question when he uncovers the citric acid cycle or Krebs cycle. The citric acid cycle is one of the means by which the body extracts energy from *carbohydrates*. Krebs is honored with the Nobel Prize in physiology or medicine in 1953 "for his discovery of the citric acid cycle."

(B, C)

Carl David Anderson finds muons in cosmic rays.

During the 20th century, physicists began to understand the particles that make up the *atom*. Physicists soon discovered that the basic components of the atom—the *proton, neutron,* and *electron*—are made up of even smaller elementary particles. In 1937, American physicist Carl David Anderson (1905–91) discovers one such particle, the muon, in cosmic rays. The muon is about the size of an electron but heavier. Research on these interesting particles continues today.

(P)

Wallace Carothers invents nylon.

Polymers are large molecules that contain repeating units. The study of the chemistry of polymers has led to the development of many useful synthetic materials. American chemist Wallace Carothers (1896–1937) was one of the innovators of such technologies in the 1930s. In 1937, he develops nylon, a synthetic material that is used to make a variety of industrial and household items, including textiles, plastics, and rugs.

(C)

November

George Stibitz creates the binary circuit.

Mathematicians and inventors have designed many different models of calculating machines. In November 1937, American inventor George Stibitz (1904–95) uses telephone relays to create the first binary circuit. Stibitz's machine performs division to eight decimal places in under a minute. He later demonstrates remote computing by sending the machine a problem to be solved across telephone lines. Stibitz is widely considered the father of digital computing.

(M, P)

1938

Daniele Bovet discovers antihistamines.

The immune system is designed to rid the body of foreign organisms and substances. Sometimes the reaction to a foreign agent can be more dangerous than the substance itself, resulting in a severe immune response called *anaphylaxis*. In 1938, Italian pharmacologist Daniele Bovet (1907–92) makes progress in treating this condition when he discovers a drug that could stop anaphylaxis in dogs. This drug, and ones that work by a similar mechanism, are known as antihistamines. Antihistamines remain important agents in the treatment of both mild allergies and severe anaphylaxis. Bovet is honored with the Nobel Prize in physiology or medicine in 1957 "for his discoveries relating to synthetic compounds that inhibit the action of certain body substances, and especially their action on the vascular system and the skeletal muscles."

(B)

Otto Hahn demonstrates nuclear fission.

The first half of the 20th century saw a great expansion in the understanding of the *atom*. Scientists discovered that the atom is made up of *electrons* surrounding a *nucleus* composed of *protons* and *neutrons*. The nuclei of some atoms are spherical in shape and stable, while others are deformed. In 1938, German scientist Otto Hahn (1879–1968) shows that bombarding an atom with a deformed nucleus, namely uranium, with neutrons leads to a nuclear *fission* reaction. The result of the reaction is the element barium. Hahn

is honored with the Nobel Prize in chemistry in 1944 "for his discovery of the fission of heavy nuclei."

(P)

DTT is shown to kill mosquitoes.

As physicians and scientists determined that insects spread a number of tropical diseases, the quest to control insect populations became a public health problem as well as an agricultural one. In 1938, Swiss chemist Paul Müller (1899–1965) develops a powerful insecticide known as DDT. DDT gains widespread use during World War II as it wipes out mosquito populations that carry diseases such as malaria. Müller is honored with the Nobel Prize in physiology or medicine "for his discovery of the high efficiency of DDT as a contact poison against several arthropods." By the 1970s, however, the use of DDT is greatly reduced as governments become concerned with its environmental effects. Today, its use is banned in the United States and many other countries.

(C)

1939

Marguerite Perey isolates francium.

The *elements* that make up all matter are organized into the *periodic table* of the elements, which allows chemists to predict their properties (*See* entry for 1869). Early versions of the periodic table of the elements also predicted the existence of elements yet to be discovered. One such element, now known as francium, has 87 *protons*. In 1939, French scientist Marguerite Perey (1909–75) discovers francium as a contaminant in a sample of actinium. Today, scientists know that francium has an extremely short half-life, which explains why the element was not discovered sooner.

(C, P)

Blood clotting requires vitamin K.

A number of diseases are caused by the lack of a particular nutrient or vitamin. In the 1920s and 1930s, Danish chemist Carl Peter Henrik Dam (1895–1976) searched for a nutritional factor that would prevent diseases marked by excess bleeding. He noticed that chicks fed a fat-free diet bled excessively. He realized that a fat-soluble vitamin must be required for blood clotting. In 1939, he isolates the factor and calls it vitamin K. Vitamin K is soon used to treat bleeding disorders in humans. Dam is honored with the Nobel Prize in physiology or medicine in 1939 "for his discovery of vitamin K."

(B)

Edward Adelbert Doisy discovers the chemical makeup of vitamin K.

The discovery of vitamin K and its role in blood clotting led biochemists to investigate its chemical nature. In 1939, American biochemist Edward Adelbert Doisy (1893–1986) isolates vitamin K from two sources, alfalfa and fish. He purifies the vitamins and describes their chemical makeup, noticing slight differences between the vitamin K from the two sources. He later synthesizes vitamin K from simpler chemicals in the laboratory, allowing large quantities of it to be made for medical treatments. Doisy is honored with the Nobel Prize in physiology or medicine in 1943 "for his discovery of the chemical nature of vitamin K."

(B)

Specialized cells in the eye are shown to allow color perception.

Twentieth-century scientists knew that the eyes take in light and relay images to the brain. However, the mechanism by which the eye perceives colors remained a mystery. In 1939, Swedish chemist Ragnar Granit (1900–91) discovers specialized cells in the retina that allow color perception. He identifies three different types of these specialized cells, called cone cells. Each of the three types of cone cells has a specific spectrum of light they can perceive. Together, they allow for color vision. Granit shares the Nobel Prize in physiology or medicine in 1967 with Haldan Keffer Hartline and George Wald "for their discoveries concerning the primary physiological and chemical visual processes in the eye."

(B)

January 1

Hans Bethe describes nuclear fusion in the stars.

The Sun and other stars are fueled by massive amounts of *energy*. Where this energy comes from was a mystery for centuries. As scientist studied nuclear reactions, it became clear that the energy of the stars is powered by nuclear *fusion*. On January 1, 1939, American physicist Hans Bethe (1906–2005) publishes "Energy Production in Stars" in the journal *Physical Review,* describing the cycle by which *protons* are fused into helium nuclei via a process now known as the carbon-nitrogen-oxygen cycle. This process releases enough energy to fuel the stars. Bethe is honored with the Nobel Prize in physics in 1967 "for his contributions to the theory of nuclear reactions, especially his discoveries concerning the energy production in stars."

(P, SA)

1940s

Ilya Prigogine puts forth the theory of dissipative structures.

Chemists seek to understand the properties and reactions of matter. Many physical chemists are interested in the *energy* associated with chemical reactions, often measured in the form of *heat absorbed or released*. This field of study, known as *thermodynamics*, has produced three fundamental laws that govern chemical reactions. These laws, however, describe chemical reactions that occur at *equilibrium*, where there is a balance between the starting materials and products of a reaction. Many biological reactions do not occur at equilibrium. In the 1940s, Belgian chemist Ilya Prigogine (1917–2003) begins to study the thermodynamic of this type of reaction. He develops what is known as the theory of dissipative structures to describe these reactions. Prigogine is honored with the Nobel Prize in chemistry in 1977 "for his contributions to non-equilibrium thermodynamics, particularly the theory of dissipative structures."

1940

Physicists produce astatine in the laboratory.

During the 20th century, chemists and physicists began to find and create *elements* that are predicted by the *periodic table* of the elements. In 1940, physicists Dale Corson (b. 1914), Kenneth Mackenzie (b. 1912), and Emilio Segré create an element with 85 *protons* in the laboratory. They call the element astatine. Today, scientists recognize that astatine is a highly radioactive element that occurs in only minute quantities in the Earth's crust.

(C, P)

Blood cells are shown to contain Rh factor.

Blood contains specific identifying markers, called *antigens*, that make up what is known as the blood type. The most common of these is the ABO group, discovered in 1900 by American biologist Karl Landsteiner (1868–1943) (*See* entry for 1900). In 1940,

Landsteiner and Alexander Wiener (1907–76) discover another important blood antigen, the Rh factor. This antigen is responsible for fatal reactions that occur in infants when their blood type is different from the mothers. Blood is now commonly identified both by the ABO group and the presence or absence of Rh factor.

(B)

Neptunium is created in the laboratory.

The ancient alchemists tried to transform one element into another. As *alchemy* gave way to chemistry, scientists searched for previously uncharacterized elements. The discovery of new *elements* continued in the 20th century as chemists tried to create larger elements in the laboratory. In 1940, American scientist Edwin McMillian (1907–91) succeeds at this task when he creates the first transuranium element by bombarding uranium nuclei with *neutrons*. He names the element neptunium. McMillian shares the Nobel Prize in chemistry in 1951 with Glenn Seaborg "for their discoveries in the chemistry of the transuranium elements."

(C, P)

Chemists generate plutonium in the laboratory.

In 1940, the search for new *elements* was renewed when Edwin McMillian produced a new element, neptunium, in the laboratory. Neptunium, however, is relatively unstable. Glenn Seaborg (1912–99), a coworker of McMillian, finds that when neptunium disintegrates, yet another new element is created. They name this element plutonium. Plutonium proves to be very stable and becomes an important fuel for nuclear reactions. Seaborg shares the 1951 Nobel Prize in chemistry with McMillian "for their discoveries in the chemistry of the transuranium elements."

(C, P)

Carbon-14 is made in the laboratory.

In the early 20th century, scientists discovered that forms of *elements* with different *atomic weights,* known as *isotopes* are both found in nature and can be generated in the laboratory. In 1940, American chemist Martin Kamen (1913–2002) discovers one of the most useful radioactive isotopes, carbon-14. He generates carbon-14 in the laboratory for use as a radioactive tracer. Later, carbon-14 is found in nature and becomes a useful tool in determining the age of ancient artifacts.

(B, C, P)

The *J-B Tables* help locate earthquakes.

Geologists studying earthquakes often need to pinpoint their exact location. When an earthquake occurs, *seismic waves* quickly travel from its center. Specialized instruments called *seismographs* measure the waves created by the earthquake. Seismologists then commence a series of calculations to determine where the earthquake started. To do these calculations, they must know the travel time of seismic waves from various points to the location of their seismograph. In 1940, English geologist Sir Harold Jeffreys (1891–1989) and New Zealander geologist Keith Bullen (1906–76) publish the *J-B Tables* of travel times. The calculation of such information is a painstaking process, but it has stood the test of time. Data from the *J-B Tables* are still used in locating earthquakes today.

(ES)

May

Penicillin is used to treat bacterial infections.

Bacterial infections can be fatal if not treated. Sir Alexander Fleming discovered that a substance made by mold, which he called penicillin, kills some types of *bacteria* growing in laboratory (*See* entry for 1928). In May 1940, British pathologist Howard Florey (1898–1968) and British biochemist Sir Ernest Boris Chain (1906–79) demonstrate that penicillin kills bacteria in infected mice. This demonstration that penicillin works in a living animal rapidly leads to the testing and use of penicillin in humans and ushers in the age of *antibiotics.* Florey and Chain are awarded the Nobel Prize in physiology or medicine in 1945 with Fleming "for the discovery of penicillin and its curative effect in various infectious diseases."

(B)

1941

Archer Martin and Richard Synge use partition chromatography to separate complex mixtures.

Chemists try to understand biological systems by looking at the chemical makeup and reactions that occur inside tissues and cells. To do this, they need methods to separate specific molecules from the complex mixtures that make up cells. In 1941, British chemists Archer Martin (1910–2002) and Richard Synge (1914–94) develop a technique to help separate the components of a sample of biological material. Their technique, called partition chromatography, separates substances on the basis of their solubility in different liquids. Partition chromatography is later used to identify many of the components of a cell. Martin and Synge share the Nobel Prize in chemistry in 1952 "for their invention of partition chromatography."

(B, C)

George Wells Beadle and Edward Lawrie Tatum propose that a gene encodes a single protein.

In the 20th century, biologists accepted that traits are inherited by the passing down of genes from one generation to the next. Traits that can be seen, such as hair color, or measured in the laboratory, such as blood cholesterol levels, are the end result of chemical reactions in the body. Specialized *proteins* called *enzymes* carry out these reactions. In 1941, American geneticist George Beadle (1903–89) and American biochemist Edward Tatum (1900–75) discover that mutating a gene can lead to the alteration of the specific enzyme in the body that is responsible for that trait. To explain this data, they propose what is known as the "one gene one protein" hypothesis. Although biologists later show that some genes could encode more than one protein, Beadle and Tatum's work is critical for much of the early research in *molecular biology*. They share the Nobel Prize in physiology or medicine in 1958 "for their discovery that genes act by regulating definite chemical events."

(B)

André Frédéric Cournand and Dickinson Richards perform heart catheterization.

Diseases of the heart and circulatory system are often hard to assess and treat. In 1941, American physicians André Frédéric Cournand (1898–1988) and Dickinson Richards (1895–1973) perform a procedure known as heart catheterization to more directly examine a diseased heart. The procedure involves inserting a small tube, or catheter, into the heart via a vein in the patient's arm. Heart catheterization allows physicians to better diagnose a variety of heart diseases and defects. Cournand and Richards share the Nobel Prize in physiology and medicine in 1956 with Werner Forssmann "for their discoveries concerning heart catheterization and pathological changes in the circulatory system."

(B)

Hormones affect the growth of prostate cancer cells.

Cancer is a disease in which abnormal cells grow and spread through the body in an uncontrolled fashion. In 1941, American physician Charles Brenton Huggins (1901–77) shows that prostate cancer cells grow more rapidly in the presence of male *hormones,* and would stop growing in the presence of female hormones. His work not only results in a treatment for prostate cancer but also gives biologists insight into the mechanism of cancer cell growth. He is honored with the Nobel Prize in physiology or medicine in 1966 "for his discoveries concerning hormonal treatment of prostatic cancer."

(B)

Lev Davidovich Landau explains superfluidity.

During the 20th century, scientists developed methods to study matter at extremely low temperatures. The elemental gas helium was often used in such studies because it does not become a liquid until the temperature is reduced to just above absolute zero. Liquid helium has a unique property; it can flow through a tube with virtually no *friction*. This property is called *superfluidity*. In 1941, Russian physicist Lev Davidovich Landau (1908–68) develops a theory of condensed matter to explain superfluidity. He is honored with the Nobel Prize in physics in 1962 "for his pioneering theories for condensed matter, especially liquid helium."

(P)

1942

Konrad Bloch explains the synthesis of cholesterol.

Biological molecules are often large and complex. In the 20th century, chemists and biochemists began studying how organisms synthesize these complex molecules. In 1942, American scientist Konrad Bloch (1912–2000) researches how organisms synthesize cholesterol. He finds that the body uses a small molecule, acetic acid, as building blocks for a series of complex molecules, including cholesterol. His work greatly increases understanding of how the body makes cholesterol. He shares the Nobel Prize in physiology or medicine in 1964 with Feodor Lynen "for their discoveries concerning the mechanism and regulation of the cholesterol and fatty acid metabolism."

(B)

George Snell discovers genes that control tissue rejection.

The immune system must differentiate between foreign bodies and its own cells and tissues. This makes it difficult to transplant tissues from one individual to another. In 1942, American biologist George Snell (1903–96) shows that whether or not a tissue will be rejected is determined by the organism's *genes*. He studies tissue transplantation in mice and identifies genes that control tissue rejection, called histocompatibility genes. Tissues can be transplanted between mice that have the same histocompatibility genes, but the tissue is rejected if the mice have different genes. Snell shares the Nobel Prize in physiology or medicine in 1980 with Baruj Benacerraf and Jean Dausset "for their discoveries concerning genetically determined structures on the cell surface that regulate immunological reactions."

(B)

Raymond Lindeman describes energy flow through ecosystems.

Many species of plants, animals, and *bacteria* come together and live in a given *ecosystem*. To sustain it, some of these organisms must produce *energy* while others must get their energy from consuming organisms that are lower on the food chain. In 1942, ecologist Raymond Lindeman studies how energy flows through an ecosystem. He divides the ecosystem into trophic levels, based upon what an organism consumes to get its energy.

(B)

December 2

Enrico Fermi performs a controlled nuclear chain reaction.

In the early decades of the 20th century, physicists learned much about the *atom* and the *energy* of the atomic *nucleus*. They found that by bombarding a radioactive element, uranium, with *neutrons,* the atom splits and releases more neutrons. Soon physicists realize that a *chain reaction* could be set up whereby the bombardment of a uranium atom releases neutrons that then split more atoms. The reaction would then continue in a self-sustaining manner. On December 2, 1942, American physicist Enrico Fermi (1901–54) performs the first controlled nuclear chain reaction at the University of Chicago. This marks a critical milestone in the development of atomic energy.

(P)

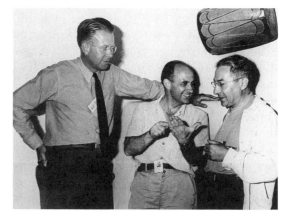

Pioneers of atomic physics Ernst O. Lawrence (left), Enrico Fermi (center), and Isidor Rabi (right) *(Department of Energy/National Archives)*

Dorothy Crowfoot Hodgkin determines the structure of biologically important molecules.

The development of *X-ray crystallography* allowed chemists to determine the exact three-dimensional structure of many chemicals. Nevertheless, determining the structure of a complex biologically important molecule remained an arduous task. In 1942, British chemist Dorothy Crowfoot Hodgkin (1910–94) determines the structure of the *antibiotic* penicillin. Throughout the decade, Hodgkin solves the structure of other complex biologically important molecules, including vitamin B$_{12}$. She is honored with the Nobel Prize in chemistry in 1964 "for her determinations by X-ray techniques of the structures of important biochemical substances."

(B, C)

1943

Frederick Sanger begins sequencing the hormone insulin.

Proteins are large molecules that carry out a wide array of functions in biological systems, including mediating communication between cells and organs or tissues. These molecules are *polymers,* consisting of *amino acids* linked together in a specific order. The order or sequence of amino acids in a protein dictates both the three-dimensional structure and biological function of the molecule. The *hormone* insulin is a protein that is essential for regulating blood glucose levels. In 1943, American chemist Frederick Sanger (b. 1918) begins the arduous task of determining the amino acid sequence of this critical hormone. His work establishes protein-sequencing techniques that become widely used in biological research. Sanger is honored with the Nobel Prize in chemistry in 1958 "for his work on the structure of proteins, especially that of insulin."

(B, C)

Max Delbrück and Salvador Luria establish bacteriophage genetics.

As the 20th century progressed, biologists became increasingly interested in genetics as a means to uncover the fundamental processes of living organisms. However, performing detailed studies on humans or other complex organisms could be difficult. In 1943, American scientists Max Delbrück (1906–81) and Salvador Luria (1912–91) decide to use simple *viruses* known as *bacteriophages* as a model system. By establishing bacteriophage genetics, they set the stage for important advances in the understanding of genetics and *molecular biology*. Delbrück and Luria share the Nobel Prize in physiology or medicine in 1969 with Alfred Hershey "for their discoveries concerning the replication mechanism and the genetic structure of viruses."

(B)

Colossus is the first electronic computer.

As described in the sidebar "Computers and Science," 20th-century inventors and engineers worked for decades toward building machines that could perform calculations and other logical tasks. In 1943, these plans are realized when English mathematician Alan Mathison Turing (1912–54) and colleagues create Colossus, an electronic computer. Colossus is built in Great Britain as a machine that could break German codes during World War II. Colossus serves as the model for more elaborate electronic computers of the future.

(M)

Selman Waksman discovers streptomycin.

In the 20th century, microbiologists discovered that some *bacteria* make agents that kill other species of bacteria. These agents became known as *antibiotics*. American biochemist Selman Waksman (1888–1973) set out to find some of these agents and use them to treat diseases caused by bacteria.

In 1943, his quest leads him to discover the antibiotic streptomycin. Streptomycin is one the first effective treatments for the potentially fatal disease tuberculosis. Waksman is honored with the Nobel Prize in physiology or medicine in 1952 "for his discovery of streptomycin, the first antibiotic effective against tuberculosis."

(B)

November 4

The first nuclear reactor opens.

The discovery of nuclear *fission* in 1939 led to the rapid realization that scientists can harness the *energy* of the *atom* and use it to build a powerful weapon (*See* entry for 1939). Physicists in the United States feared that such research was being conducted in Nazi Germany and pushed for an American facility to conduct similar research. Such research requires large amounts of plutonium. On November 4, 1943, the first nuclear reactor was opened in Oak Ridge, Tennessee. The reactor produces the plutonium used by Los Alamos scientists, who develop the first nuclear weapons. Today, Oak Ridge National Laboratory remains a research institution specializing in energy and environmental research.

(P)

Selman Waksman discovers the antibiotic streptomycin, one of the first effective treatments for tuberculosis. In this photograph, Waksman (center) and colleagues test the ability of an antibiotic to kill bacteria in the laboratory. *(National Cancer Institute)*

1944

Economists study game theory.

Mathematics is often used to support theories in both physical and social sciences. In 1944, American mathematician John von Neumann (1903–57) and American economist Oskar Morgenstern (1902–77) apply a specialized type of mathematics called game theory to economics. In 1926, von Neumann developed game theory, a way of looking at people's interactions that depend on some level of strategy. However, its application becomes widely recognized in 1944, when von Neumann and Morgenstern write *Theory of Games and Economic Behavior.* Since the publication of this landmark work, game theory has been applied to other fields such as political science and behavioral science.

(M)

Howard Hathaway Aiken creates an automatic calculator.

As described in the sidebar "Computers and Science," during the early 20th century mathematicians and engineers strived to create machines that could perform complex calculations, the forerunners to today's computers. In 1944, American mathematician Howard Hathaway Aiken (1900–73) and colleagues construct an automatic calculator that can perform four different mathematical operations and remember past results. The machine, called the Mark-I, weighs more than 35 tons. Mark-I is considered one of the important predecessors to today's electronic computers.

(M)

Barbara McClintock discovers mobile genetic elements.

During the 20th century, biologists studying a wide variety of organisms turned to genetics. American geneticist Barbara McClintock (1902–92) studied the genetics of the plant maize. In 1944, she discovers that some *genes* can move from one *chromosome* to another. Many years pass before her discovery of mobile genetic elements is widely accepted. Now biologists recognize that genes in organisms from *bacteria* to humans can move within or between chromosomes, and that the process is important in contributing to genetic variation. McClintock is honored with the Nobel Prize in physiology or medicine in 1983 "for her discovery of mobile genetic elements."

(B)

Robert Burns Woodward synthesizes natural products.

Chemists try to synthesize complex molecules from simple chemicals in the laboratory. Some of the most difficult chemicals to synthesize are natural products. The synthesis of such compounds is often important in discovering and producing drugs to treat a variety of diseases. In 1944, American chemist Robert Burns Woodward (1917–79) synthesizes the antimalarial drug quinine entirely from simple chemicals. He later synthesizes a variety of natural products, including cholesterol, cortisol, and vitamin B_{12}. For his groundbreaking work in the synthesis of natural products, Woodward is honored with the Nobel Prize in chemistry in 1965 "for his outstanding achievements in the art of organic synthesis."

(B, C)

February

Oswald Avery and colleagues show that DNA is the genetic material.

Microbiologists uncovered a phenomenon whereby a *bacterium* that does not cause disease in mice can be "transformed" into a virulent, or disease-causing strain. Biologists believed that bacterial transformation was a result of an exchange of *genes* between bacteria. In 1944, American biologists Oswald Avery (1877–1955), Colin Macleod (1909–72), and Maclyn McCarty (1911–2005) isolate the transforming material and show that it is DNA. The results suggest that DNA is the genetic material. This conclusion is viewed with skepticism, as scientists did not think DNA had sufficient complexity to be the genetic material. However, later experiments using different organisms confirm Avery's results, and the focus of *molecular biology* turns to DNA.

(B)

1945

Scientists discover promethium.

During the 20th century, chemists and physicists began to discover *elements* that are predicted by the *periodic table* of the elements. For years, scientists predicted that there is an element with 61 *protons*. A few scientists claimed to have isolated the element, but they were unable to prove it. In 1945, scientist Charles Coryell (1912–71) and colleagues isolate an *isotope* of the element and show that it is indeed the missing element with 61 protons. They name the element promethium, after the figure from Greek mythology Prometheus. Today, scientists realize that the difficulty in isolating promethium stems from the element's highly radioactive nature.

(C, P)

Felix Bloch and Edward Mills Purcell measure the magnetism of the atomic nucleus.

The study of *subatomic particles* requires instruments that can measure their activity and properties. In 1945, American physicists Felix Bloch (1905–83) and Edward Mills Purcell (1912–97) independently develop a method to measure the *magnetism* of the atomic *nucleus*. The two scientists share the Nobel Prize in physics in 1952 "for their development of new methods for nuclear magnetic precision measurements and discoveries in connection therewith."

(P)

Fritz Lipmann discovers coenzyme A.

Energy metabolism, the study of how food is broken down and used by the body, poses a number of interesting biological question. The 20th century saw a great increase in knowledge in this field. In 1945, American biologist Fritz Lipmann (1899–1996) discovers a molecule that serves as a critical cofactor in the breakdown of *carbohydrates*, coenzyme A. Lipmann is honored with the Nobel Prize in physiology or medicine in 1953 "for his discovery of co-enzyme A and its importance for intermediary metabolism."

(B)

Alfred Hershey discovers a process that corrects genetic errors.

As the 20th century progressed, more biologists turned to genetics as a means to understand life processes. Geneticists often induced mutations in *genes* to help uncover their function. In 1945, American biologist Alfred Hershey (1908–97) discovers that organisms can correct mutation through a process known as recombination. Hershey shares the Nobel Prize in physiology or medicine in 1969 with Max Delbrück and Salvador Luria "for their discoveries concerning the replication mechanism and the genetic structure of viruses."

(B)

Albert Claude studies cells, using the electron microscope.

For many years, biologists' desire to understand how cells function was aided by advances in technology. The invention of the electron microscope let biologists look at cells under higher magnifications than ever (*See* entry for 1930). One of the pioneers of using electron microscopy to study cells was Belgian biologist Albert Claude (1898–1983). In 1945, he publishes the first pictures of cells, using electron microscopy. Electron microscopy remains an important tool in cell biology research today. Claude shares the Noble Prize in physiology or medicine in 1974 with Christian de Duve and George Palade "for their discoveries concerning the structural and functional organization of the cell."

(B)

John von Neumann describes a stored program computer.

As described in the sidebar "Computers and Science," one of the hallmarks of today's computers is the ability to store data. As computer technology grew, memory distinguished more sophisticated computers from early calculating machines. In 1945, American mathematician John von Neumann (1903–57) describes the theory that allows the creation of a stored program computer. Von Neumann's ideas are influential in the design of more modern electronic computers.

(M)

August 6

Nuclear weapons are used in Japan.

The first half of the 20th century saw great advances in the understanding of the *atom.* Physicists realized that this knowledge could be applied toward making more powerful weapons. During World War II, the United States initiated the Manhattan Project, enlisting the country's top physicists to create and build nuclear *fission* bombs. A test conducted in July 1945 confirmed that they had succeeded. The bomb they built had the energy

of more than 20,000 tons of the explosive TNT. On August 6, 1945, the Japanese city of Hiroshima is attacked using a nuclear fission bomb, killing an estimated 140,000 people. On August 9, 1945, a second nuclear weapon is used to attack the city of Nagasaki, killing approximately 70,000 people.

(P)

November 11

Glenn Seaborg and colleagues prepare americium in the laboratory.

Physicists can prepare *elements* that do not occur naturally on the Earth. On November 11, 1945, American physicist Glenn Seaborg announces that he and his colleagues have prepared an element with 95 *protons* by bombarding plutonium with *neutrons.* They call the element americium. Today, americium is used in smoke detectors.

(C, P)

Glenn Seaborg and colleagues make curium in the laboratory.

During the 20th century, physicists began creating *elements* in the laboratory. In 1944, a group of scientists led by American physicist Glenn Seaborg bombards plutonium *atoms* with alpha particles. They create a new element with 96 *protons.* They call the element curium, in honor of Pierre and Marie Curie. Seaborg announces the creation of curium on November 11, 1945.

(C, P)

❧ CONCLUSION ❧

The early decades of the 20th century saw an enormous amount of scientific discoveries. In many cases, the work in one field benefited many. Physicists developed new and important theories, and explored the physics of the atomic *nucleus.* Chemists benefited from the insights into *atoms* and molecules that physicists provide. Many chemists also turned their attention to the chemical reactions that occur in living systems. Many important biological molecules were isolated and synthesized by chemists. Astronomers also benefited from advances in physics, as *radio waves* were detected from outer space and evidence supporting the *big bang theory* began to be collected. In geology, scientists debated a new theory, *continental drift,* while other earth scientists uncovered the different layers of the Earth and its atmosphere.

Medical science benefited from research in chemistry and biology. New techniques, such as *X-ray crystallography,* allowed scientists to analyze the complex molecules that exist in biological systems. Chemists isolated a number of biologically active molecules such as *hormones* and vitamins. *Antibiotics* were discovered, giving physicians powerful new tools to combat otherwise fatal infections. Research in biology set the stage for new research in molecular medicine. Genetics became a more popular field of study, and the discovery that DNA is the genetic material led to genetic engineering.

Science also benefited from new technologies developed during the early 20th century. This era saw the first airplane flight leading to transatlantic flight. Building on the technology developed during this era, scientists and engineers extended manned flight to outer space in later decades. Mathematicians and engineers developed calculating machines and computers that would be the forerunners of the more powerful computers used today.

8

SCIENCE IN THE POST-ATOMIC WORLD

1946–1979

❧ INTRODUCTION ❧

A number of world events influenced the pace of science after World War II. The ensuing cold war between the United States and the Soviet Union acted as a catalyst, speeding up research in a number of scientific fields including physics, computer science, and space travel. For instance, invention and detonation of the atomic bomb, and the spread of that technology to the Soviet Union and other countries, resulted in the United States expanding its research into weapons systems. Such research relies on continual advances in the field of physics. Just as physics benefited from the weapons research brought about by the cold war, many astronomy advances stemmed from the space race between the two countries that began when the Soviet Union launched the *Sputnik* space satellite. Soon both countries were launching space probes that sent back new information about the planets of the solar system.

Scientific research in all fields and the discovery of new technologies during the last half of the 20th century was aided by the rapid advances in computer science that occurred after World War II. In the period described in this section, computers shrink from the size of a room to something that will fit on a desk. A number of critical innovations including the computer chip and the microprocessor make computers increasingly useful to scientific researchers as well as the public. During the 1970s, the power of computing is used to model chemical reactions and solve long-standing mathematical problems. Of course, this is just a prelude to the information age. The first hints of what is to come occur during this era when the United States Defense Department sets up the APRANET, a computer networking system that is the forerunner to the Internet.

One scientific discipline that benefits significantly from the rapid advance of technology is physics. During this era, many physicists study the *subatomic particles* that make up matter. They build particle accelerators and powerful detectors that lead to the discovery of more subatomic particles than anyone had previously imagined. Soon, order is brought to the field as a classification system is established, and physicists discover what they believe to be the most basic form of matter of all—the *quark*. Much of the research in physics is aimed at understanding these particles and the *forces* that govern their behavior and interactions.

While some physicists study the smallest particles that make up matter, others look to the stars. The close relationship between physics and astronomy continues after World War II. Astronomers studying cosmic radio waves discover *pulsars*. Others find background *radiation* that supports the idea that the universe is expanding. Astronomers also get their first close look at the solar system. As part of their space program, the United States and the Soviet Union send unmanned space probes to study the planets of the solar system. In addition to pictures, scientists collect data on the atmosphere, *magnetic field,* and effect of solar wind on the planets in the solar system. These missions result in the discovery of an active volcano on one of Jupiter's moons, and an analysis of the rings that surround Jupiter, Uranus, Neptune, and, most prominently, Saturn. While most of these missions are flybys, the United States lands unmanned probes that study the surface of Mars, and the Soviet Union sends a probe to the surface of Venus. The crowning achievement of this era is the lunar landing, which allows astronauts to explore and study the Moon directly.

Here on Earth, geologists and oceanographers develop a new theory to explain the movement of the continents. By studying underwater mountain ridges and the composition of the seafloor, it soon becomes apparent that the seafloor is spreading. As magna rises from the Earth, it solidifies, creating new land on the ocean floor and spreading the old toward the landmasses. Soon, Earth scientists looking at this and other data develop the concept of *plate tectonics*. Plate tectonics takes into account the data supporting *seafloor spreading* and uses it to explain a number of geological phenomena from earthquakes to the *continental drift*. It states that Earth's surface is made up of seven rigid plates. The movement of these plates powers the separation of the continents and results in earthquakes, volcanoes, and the formation of mountain ranges. While many Earth scientists ponder the land and the ocean, still others remain fascinated with the atmosphere. This era sees increased understanding in the movement of air currents, giving us explanations of meteorological phenomena such as El Niño, as well as a greater understanding of why the weather is so hard to predict.

Meteorologists are not the only scientists interested in the atmosphere. Chemists begin to study the chemical reactions that occur when industrial gases enter the atmosphere. During this time, chemists explain how some forms of air pollution breakdown the *ozone layer*. Other advances in chemistry lead to a better understanding of chemical reaction and the creation of new catalysts that help industrial chemists synthesize a variety of molecules needed to make everything from plastics to pharmaceuticals. In fact, the pharmaceutical industry thrives during this era. Chemists begin synthesizing more drugs based upon natural products, and biologists and chemists work together to understand the underlying defects in a number of diseases, and design drugs to correct them.

While discoveries in drug development are exciting, the biggest advance in biology comes when the three-dimensional structure of DNA is determined. Within years of this discovery, biologists gain a greater understanding of how genetic information is read by cells and used to direct the synthesis of *proteins*. Other biologists study how DNA is replicated and passed on to subsequent generations. In the course of these studies, biochemists learn to modify DNA in the laboratory. Soon they can create *recombinant DNA* molecules and use them to produce proteins. Such findings mark the dawn of a new era in biology, in which DNA technology is routinely used to make discoveries about fundamental biological processes. Soon DNA technology will be applied outside of biology, ranging from forensic science to anthropology.

The post–World War II era sees rapid advancement in many areas of science, including landmark achievements in the understanding of everything from the smallest subatomic particle to the ever-expanding universe. Perhaps even more important, the development of technologies from computers to genetic information assures that scientific discoveries will continue to come at this rapid pace in the future.

TIME LINE OF SCIENTIFIC ACHIEVEMENTS FROM 1946 TO 1979

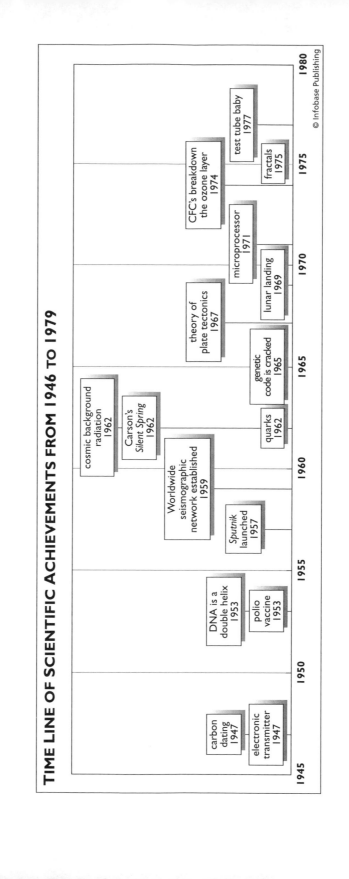

© Infobase Publishing

❦ CHRONOLOGY ❧

1946

Melvin Calvin describes carbon dioxide fixation in plants.

Living organisms require *energy* to grow and sustain them. Plants convert energy from light through a process known as *photosynthesis*. In the first half of the 20th century, scientists recognized that plants assimilate carbon dioxide from the air around them, and release oxygen into the environment. How this occurs remained a mystery until

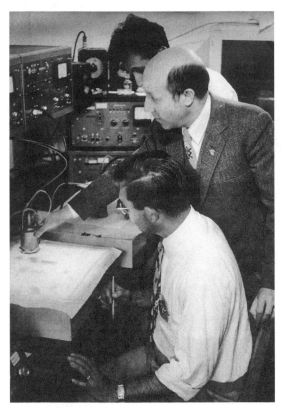

In the 1940s, American Melvin Calvin shows how plants use carbon dioxide from the atmosphere to synthesize carbohydrates. Calvin (center) is shown here working in the laboratory. *(NCI)*

1946, when American chemist Melvin Calvin (1911–97) begins his studies tracing the metabolism of carbon dioxide in plants. His work demonstrates that several *enzymes* are involved in the process. Calvin is awarded the Nobel Prize in chemistry in 1961 for his research on the "carbon dioxide assimilation in plants."

(B, C)

Clifford Shull determines the structure of complex chemicals.

In the 20th century, chemists began to go beyond investigation into the properties of matter to examining the actual structure of molecules. The discovery of *X-rays* and the development of *X-ray crystallography* allowed such studies to be pursued. In 1946, American physicist Clifford Shull (1915–2001) begins work that leads to the development of another powerful technique to uncover molecular structures, *neutron* diffraction. Shull finds that he could use neutrons rather than X-rays to determine the *crystal* structure of magnetic materials. He is honored with the Nobel Prize in physics in 1994 "for the development of the neutron diffraction technique."

(P)

February 14

John Mauchly and John Eckert introduce the first electronic digital computer.

As described in the sidebar "Computers and Science," during the early 20th century engineers and mathematicians began to design and build computers. The United States military became increasingly involved in computer research as World War II progressed. During that time, American engineer John Mauchly (1907–80) developed a design for an electronic digital computer. He builds it with American engineer John Eckert (1919–95), and together they introduce the electronic integrator and computer (ENIAC) on

February 14, 1946. ENIAC is more than 1,000 times faster than previous computers. In the next decade, Mauchly and Eckert design and build the first commercially available computer, UNIVAC. Today, they are considered pioneers in the field of computer science.

(M, P)

October 14

Joshua Lederberg discovers sexual reproduction in bacteria.

Genetic variation is critical for living organisms to adapt to their environment. One of the best ways to assure genetic variation in higher organisms is the mixing of *genes* that occurs in sexual reproduction. For a long time, scientists believed that this important mechanism was not available to *bacteria*. Then, on October 14, 1946, American biologist Joshua Lederberg (b. 1925) shows that some bacteria can exchange genetic information in a process known as bacterial conjugation. His work has implications beyond microbiology and leads to the discovery of genetic recombination, the process by which genes are exchanged between distinct pieces of DNA. Genetic recombination occurs in all organisms. Lederberg is honored with the Nobel Prize in physiology or medicine in 1958 "for his discoveries concerning genetic recombination and the organization of the genetic material of bacteria."

(B)

1947

Carbon-14 dating allows scientists to measure the age of ancient artifacts.

How do archaeologists know the age of ancient artifacts? Scientists have developed a number of methods to answer this question. In 1947, American chemist Willard Libby (1908–80) exploits the discovery of radioactive *isotopes* when he develops carbon-14 dating. The technique relies upon the observation that carbon, which has a long half-life, is incorporated into plant tissues by a process known as carbon fixation. A known portion of the carbon dioxide that plants acquire from the atmosphere contains radioactive carbon. Once a plant dies, it can no longer take up carbon from the environment. Libby shows that one can estimate the age of a material made from plant products by analyzing the amount of radioactive carbon in the material. The more radioactive carbon in the material, the more recently the plant died. Libby is honored with the Nobel Prize in chemistry in 1960 "for his method to use carbon-14 for age determination in archaeology, geology, geophysics, and other branches of science."

(B, C, ES)

Ronald George Wreyford Norrish and George Porter develop flash photolysis to study fast chemical reactions.

Chemical reactions occur at different rates. Some extremely rapid reactions occur within fractions of a second and can be very difficult to measure in the laboratory. In 1947, British physicists Ronald George Wreyford Norrish (1897–1978) and George Porter (1920–2002) begin work that leads to the development of a technique known as flash photolysis to study these rapid reactions. Flash photolysis allows researchers to study reactions that were previously uncharacterized, such as chemical reactions that occur in the atmosphere. Norrish and Porter share the Nobel Prize in chemistry in 1967 with Manfred Eigen "for their studies of extremely fast chemical reactions, effected by disturbing the equilibrium by means of very short pulses of energy."

(C)

Paleontologists discover fossils of *Coelophysis*.

Our understanding of ancient animals comes from the study of fossils. In 1947, Amerioan paleontologists George Whitaker and Edwin Colbert (b. 1905) discover a quarry of dinosaur fossils in New Mexico. The quarry contains more than 100 skeletons of the dinosaur known as *Coelophysis*. The fossils date to the Triassic period. *Coelophysis* fossils show that the dinosaur had a birdlike posture with long hind limbs and shorter forelimbs. The existence of the large quarry of fossils suggests that the dinosaurs traveled in herds. Today, *Coelophysis* is one of the most well studied dinosaurs.

(B, ES)

Radio waves are detected from the Crab Nebula.

In 1054, astronomers from many cultures recorded the appearance of a bright star, visible during daylight (*See* entry for 1054). The star they observed was a *supernova* that formed when what is now called the Crab Nebula was created. In 1947, British astronomer John Bolton (1922–93) uses a powerful radio telescope to identify the source of cosmic *radio waves*. He then correlates the source of the waves with specific objects in the sky. He finds that one of the largest sources of radio waves comes from the Crab Nebula.

(SA)

Willis Lamb refines the structure of the hydrogen atom.

Hydrogen *atoms* have a single *electron* that orbits the atomic *nucleus*. Many 20th-century physicists used the hydrogen atom as a simple model to model the behavior of *subatomic particles*. In 1947, American scientist Willis Lamb (b. 1913) uses experimental techniques to check and refine the theoretical structure of the hydrogen atom. He is honored with the Nobel Prize in physics in 1955 "for his discoveries concerning the fine structure of the hydrogen spectrum."

(P)

May 24

Cecil Powell discovers the pion.

The atomic *nucleus* is made up of *protons* and *neutrons*. Protons have a positive charge and would normally repel one another. The physicist Hideki Yukawa predicted that there must be an exchange particle that holds atomic nuclei together. On May 24, 1947, British physicist Cecil Powell (1903–69) discovers the exchange particle, known as the pi-*meson* or pion. As Yukawa had predicted, it has a mass similar to that of an *electron*. Today, scientists recognize that pions interact with both protons and neutrons. Powell is honored with the Nobel Prize in physics in 1950 "for his development of the photographic method of studying nuclear processes and his discoveries regarding mesons made with this method."

(P)

October

Polykarp Kusch measures the magnetic moment of the electron.

The development of *quantum mechanics* in the early 20th century led to many predictions about the properties and behavior of *subatomic particles*. As instrumentation became more sophisticated, physicists could make precise measurements of these properties. In October 1947, American physicist Polykarp Kusch (1911–93) measures a property known as the magnetic moment of the *electron*. The value he obtains differs from the one predicted by theoretical physicists. Kusch's work, along with the work of other experimental physicist of his era, leads to new research on the application of quantum mechanics to *electromagnetism*. Kusch is honored with the Nobel Prize in physics "for his precision determination of the magnetic moment of the electron."

(P)

December 23

The transistor improves electronic devices.

The first computers and other electronic devices were large machines that easily filled an entire room. One reason for their size was their use of vacuum tubes to control the electrical current. Vacuum tubes pose other problems. They need to warm up before use and lose *energy* while running, creating many problems for engineers trying to design efficient electronic devices. On December 23, 1947, American physicists John Bardeen (1908–91) and Walter Houser Brattain (1902–87) solve these problems when they invent the point-contact *transistor*. Their design revolves around the discovery that *electrons* act differently at the surface of a particular type of material known as a *semiconductor*. American engineer William Shockley (1910–89) later improves upon their invention. The three scientists are awarded the Nobel Prize in physics in 1956 "for their researches on semiconductors and their discovery of the transistor effect."

(P)

1948

Dennis Gabor develops holography.

Physicists use a number of techniques to understand the behavior of individual *atoms*. During the 1940s, British scientist Dennis Gabor (1900–79) tried to develop a microscope powerful enough to see an atom. While pursuing this goal, he develops holography, a method to take three-dimensional photographs or holograms, in 1948. Today, holography is used everywhere from scientific laboratories to credit cards. Gabor is honored with the Nobel Prize in physics in 1971 "for his invention and development of the holographic method."

(P)

Physicists develop a new theory to explain the interactions among electrons.

As described in the sidebar "Quantum Mechanics," physicists in the 20th century developed *quantum mechanics* to describe the behavior of small *subatomic particles*. A number of physicists focused their studies on the interactions among negatively charged *electrons*, a field known as quantum electrodynamics. In 1948, Japanese physicist Sin-Itiro Tomonaga (1906–79), and American physicists Julian Schwinger (1918–94) and Richard Feynman (1918–88) show that these interactions are more complicated than most researchers had originally thought. They new develop a model of *electron* interactions. Later experiments show their model to be highly accurate. They share the Nobel Prize in physics in 1965 for this pioneering work "for their fundamental work in quantum electrodynamics, with deep-ploughing consequences for the physics of elementary particles."

(P)

Louis Néel explains some of the properties of certain magnetic ores.

Magnets have been known since the Chinese first used the compass. Physicists have discovered that there are different classes of magnetic ores. Each becomes magnetic by a different physical mechanism. In 1948, French physicist Louis Néel (1904–2000) describes the *magnetism* of a specific type of magnet, known as ferrimagnets. Today, ferrimagnets are used widely in computers. Néel is honored with the Nobel Prize in physics "for fundamental work and discoveries concerning antiferromagnetism and ferrimagnetism which have led to important applications in solid state physics."

(P)

Some cosmologists argue that the universe remains a constant size.

After American astronomer Edwin Hubble observed stars moving away from the Milky Way, cosmologists began to believe that the universe is expanding. Soon astronomers began collecting data to support the *big bang theory*. In 1948, a group of scientists led by British astronomers Sir Fred Hoyle (1915–2001) and Sir Hermann Bondi (1919–2005), and American astronomer Thomas Gold (1920–2004) argues that the universe is not expanding. Their proposal, known as steady-state cosmology, states that the size of the universe is constant. They claim that any observed expansion of the universe is accompanied by destruction somewhere else. Steady-state cosmology remains a viable alternative to the big bang theory until the 1960s, when the discovery of *cosmic background radiation* convinces most scientists that the universe is indeed expanding.

(SA)

July

Claude Shannon develops information theory.

By the middle of the 20th century, engineers had developed many devices, from telegraphs to television, that increased the capacity for communication. Rapid advances in computing made it clear that the trend would continue throughout the century. In July 1948, American mathematician Claude Shannon (1916–2001) was working in communication at Bell Laboratory. He develops a method to measure the efficiency of communications systems, now known as information theory. His work shows how much information can be transmitted over a cable and lays the basis for data compression. Information theory continues to guide telecommunication research today.

(M)

September 21

Cortisone treats rheumatoid arthritis.

Rheumatoid arthritis is a painful and debilitating disease. In 1948, American physician Philip Hench (1895–1965) searched for treatments that would help patients suffering from the disease. Years earlier, American biologist Edward Kendall (1886–1972) and Swiss scientist Tadeus Reichstein (1897–1996) had isolated a new *hormone* from the adrenal cortex (*See* entry for 1935). On September 21, 1948, Hench uses this hormone, called cortisone, to successfully treat patients with rheumatoid arthritis. The three scientists share the Nobel Prize in physiology or medicine in 1950 "for their discoveries relating to the hormones of the adrenal cortex, their structure and biological effects."

(B)

October

Lyman Aldrich and Alfred Nier develop argon/potassium dating to determine the age of ancient artifacts.

Archaeologists and paleontologists search for methods to determine the age of the artifacts and fossils that they study. One well-known method, carbon-14 dating, measures the decay of a radioactive element (*See* entry for 1947). Unfortunately, carbon dating is useful only for dating objects less than 50,000 years old. In October 1948, American geologists Lyman Aldrich and Alfred Nier (1911–94) discover that radioactive argon is released during the radioactive decay of potassium becomes trapped in some ancient rocks. Radioactive argon has an extremely long half-life, more than 4 billion years, making it a useful marker to date ancient rocks. Argon/potassium dating has been used to determine the age of many fossils, including those of early man.

(C, ES, P)

1949

Herbert Hauptman and Jerome Karle develop a method to determine the three-dimensional structure of a molecule.

Many molecules have complex structures that are critical for their function. A powerful technique known as *X-ray crystallography* allows scientists to deduce the three-dimensional structure of a molecule. In its early days, X-ray crystallography was a painstakingly slow process. In 1949, American scientists Herbert Hauptman (b. 1917) and Jerome Karle (b. 1918) develop a new method to determine a molecule's three-dimensional structure. They apply mathematics to measurements of the analysis of *X-ray crystal* structures. Their work allows scientists to pinpoint the positions of atoms in a molecule much more quickly than previous techniques. Hauptman and Karle share the Nobel Prize in chemistry in 1985 "for their outstanding achievements in the development of direct methods for the determination of crystal structures."

(B, C)

Luis Leloir describes the chemistry of carbohydrate synthesis in the body.

Animals get the majority of their *energy* from breaking down the *carbohydrates* they consume. However, during times when there is plenty of food, the body stores some carbohydrates so that it will have an easily accessible supply. In 1949, Argentine chemist Luis Leloir (1906–87) describes how the body synthesizes these carbohydrates, and identifies key molecules in the pathway. Leloir is honored with the Nobel Prize in chemistry in 1970 "for his discovery of sugar nucleotides and their role in the biosynthesis of carbohydrates."

(B)

Albert Szent-Györgyi shows where muscles get the energy to contract.

Physiologists try to understand how the various organs and tissues of the body function. Muscle tissue, which is capable of performing work, is particularly interesting. In 1949, Hungarian scientist Albert Szent-Györgyi (1893–1986) shows that isolated muscle cells will contract when the energy-storing molecule ATP is added. In the course of his studies, Szent-Györgyi identifies a number of molecules that are critical for muscle contraction. His work lays the foundation for the understanding of muscle contraction today.

(B)

Atle Selberg provides a simple proof of the prime number theorem.

A *natural number* that is divisible only by itself and the number 1 is called a *prime number*. Mathematicians have studied prime numbers for centuries, searching for prime numbers and asking how many there are. During the 18th century, the prime number theorem was proposed to calculate the number of primes in a given set of numbers (say 1 through 10,000). A complicated proof to the prime number theorem was given in 1896. In 1949, Norwegian mathematician Atle Selberg (b. 1917) provides a simple proof of the prime number theorem. For this and other works, Selberg is honored with the Fields medal in 1950.

(M)

The shell model is shown to explain stable atomic nuclei.

The first half of the 20th century saw a deeper understanding of the *atom*. First, three major *subatomic particles* were discovered, the *electron*, *proton*, and *neutron*. Then, physicists began investigating the structure of the atomic *nucleus*. Physicists realized that stable nuclei have what was termed a *magic num-*

ber of protons and neutrons; however, they were not sure why this was the case. In 1949, American physicist Maria Goeppert Mayer (1906–72) and German physicist Johannes Hans Daniel Jensen (1907–73) independently develop the shell model of the atomic nucleus, explaining how the magic number of protons and neutrons leads to a stable nuclei. They share the Nobel Prize in physics in 1963 "for their discoveries concerning nuclear shell structure."

(P)

Karl von Frisch describes how bees communicate.

Animals do not have the capacity for language, so they must have another means of communication. Biologists interested in animal behavior study how they communicate with one another. One of the pioneers in this field was German biologist Karl von Frisch (1886–1982). He devoted decades of his career studying how bees tell one another where they can find honey. He found that bees use their perception of light as a means to tell direction, demonstrating that bees have complex, genetically programmed means of communication. Von Frisch shares the Nobel Prize in physiology or medicine in 1973 with Konrad Lorenz and Nikolaas Tinbergen "for their discoveries concerning organization and elicitation of individual and social behaviour patterns."

(B)

June

Scientists isolate the poliovirus.

Polio, also known as infantile paralysis, is an infectious disease caused by a *virus* that can result in paralysis or even death. In the 1940s, scientists had difficulty obtaining pure samples of poliovirus to study in the laboratory, making the search for a cure difficult. In 1949, American physicians John

Enders (1897–1985), Thomas Huckle Weller (b. 1915), and Frederick Chapman Robbins (1916–2003) develop a method to grow viruses in the laboratory. They use their technique to isolate the poliovirus, a critical step in developing a vaccine against this fatal disease. Enders, Weller, and Robbins share the Nobel Prize in physiology or medicine in 1954 "for their discovery of the ability of poliomyelitis viruses to grow in cultures of various types of tissue."

(B)

December

Glenn Seaborg creates berkelium and californium in the laboratory.

In 1940, scientists began to create new *elements* in the laboratory. These new elements had a larger number of *protons*. One of the leaders in the field was American physicist Glenn Seaborg, who created plutonium. In December 1949, Seaborg and colleagues make elements with 97 protons. Soon after, in early 1950, they create an element with 98 protons. They call the elements berkelium and californium, respectively, to honor their discovery at the University of California at Berkeley.

(C, P)

1950s

Sir Frank MacFarlane Burnet describes how the body tells the difference between its own cells and tissues and foreign materials.

The immune system is critical for protecting the body from dangerous microorganisms. To function properly, it must be able to discriminate between the cells and tissues that belong in the body and those that are foreign and potentially harmful. During the 1950s, Australian physician Sir Frank MacFarlane Burnet (1899–1985) shows that the immune system is not fully formed when an animal is born, but rather develops during the early part of life. During this time, the body learns what material belongs there. His clonal selection theory of the immune system describes how the immune system develops. Burnet shares the Nobel Prize in physiology or medicine in 1960 with Peter Medawar "for discovery of acquired immunological tolerance."

(B)

1950

Hannes Alfvén describes a new type of magnetic wave.

Physicists study matter in a variety of different forms. During the middle of the 20th century, Swedish physicist Hannes Alfvén (1908–95) pioneered work in plasma physics. Plasmas are gases in which the *atoms* exist as charged particles known as *ions*. Alfvén was particularly interested in the affect of *magnetic fields* on plasmas. In 1950, he discovers a new type of magnetic wave that is created when plasmas pass through a magnetic field. His work has important implications for astrophysics. Alfvén is honored with the Nobel Prize in physics "for fundamental work and discoveries in magneto-hydrodynamics with fruitful applications in different parts of plasma physics."

Derek Barton demonstrates the importance of a molecule's three-dimensional structure.

During the 20th century, chemists studied the molecules that make living systems work. They identified a number of biologically important molecules and began to understand the chemical reactions that are required for life. In 1950, British chemist Sir Derek Barton (1918–98) studies the chemistry of a class of molecules called *steroids*. In the

course of his work, he shows that the three-dimensional structure of a steroid is critical for its biological function. His observation is later expanded to other biologically important molecules. Barton shares the Nobel Prize in chemistry in 1969 with Odd Hassel "for their contributions to the development of the concept of conformation and its application in chemistry."

(B, C)

André Lwoff describes how a virus infects a cell.

A *virus* must infect a cell to replicate itself. Some of these infections result in the death of the cell, while others allow the cell to survive. Viruses that infect *bacteria*, known as *bacteriophage*, are often used to study viral infections in the laboratory. In 1950, French biologist André Lwoff (1902–94) uses bacteriophage to show how a virus can remain dormant in the cell it infects until outside event induces it to replicate and kill the cell. In a process known as lysogeny, the virus incorporates itself into the genetic material of the cell it infects, where it can be passed down to subsequent generations as the cell divides. When Lwoff treats the infected cells with ultraviolet light, the virus begins to replicate itself and kills the infected cell. Lwoff shares the Nobel Prize in physiology or medicine in 1965 with French biologists Franáois Jacob and Jacques Monod "for their discoveries concerning genetic control of enzyme and virus synthesis."

(B)

Gertrude Elion and George Hitchings develop drugs by comparing normal cells to diseased cells.

One of the goals of some scientific research is the discovery of new drugs to treat diseases. During the early 20th century, most scientists working in drug development took an approach similar to looking for a needle in a haystack. They treated diseased cells with a variety of different molecules and looked for those that might be effective drugs. Beginning in the late 1940s, American biochemists Gertrude Elion (1918–99) and George Hitchings (1905–98) developed a new method for drug discovery. They compared diseased cells to normal cells and looked for important biochemical differences. In 1950, they exploit these differences to develop drugs to treat leukemia. Their approach yields many effective drugs to treat diseases, ranging from cancers to viral infection. Elion and Hitchings share the Nobel Prize in physiology or medicine in 1988 with British scientist Sir James Black "for their discoveries of important principles for drug treatment."

(B, C)

Alfred Kastler uses polarized light to excite electrons.

Many physicists in the 20th century were interested in the behavior of the *subatomic particles* that make up the *atom.* They found that *electrons,* which orbit the atomic *nucleus,* can exist in a number of different states. When *energy* is added to an atom, the electron can be excited into a higher energy state. In 1950, French physicist Alfred Kastler (1902–84) shows that *polarized light* can be used to excite electrons. His work is critical to the subsequent development of *lasers.* Kastler is honored with the Nobel Prize in physics in 1966 "for the discovery and development of optical methods for studying Hertzian resonances in atoms."

(P)

George Wald describes the chemical reactions in the eye that allow vision.

To understand vision, scientists study both the physics of light and the biology of the eye. Vision occurs when the eye takes in light and then transmits the visual image to the brain. How this process occurs has been an active field of research. In 1950, American biologist George Wald (1906–97) begins a set of experiments that elucidates the series of chemical reactions that occur when light hits the eye. He shares the Nobel Prize in physiology or medicine in 1967 with Ragnar Granit and Haldan Keffer Hartline "for their discoveries concerning the primary physiological and chemical visual processes in the eye."

(B)

Edwin Chargaff develops his rules for DNA composition.

During the early 20th century, biologists and chemists began to analyze the molecules that make up biological systems. As described in the sidebar "The Science of DNA," scientists discovered that the genetic material is made up of a relatively simple molecule, *deoxyribonucleic acid,* or DNA. DNA is made up of combinations of four different *nucleotides.* In 1950, Austrian chemist Edwin Chargaff (1905–2002) analyzes DNA from a number of organisms. He discovers that DNA from all organisms has a similar composition. His develops what become known as Chargaff's rules for DNA composition, describing the proportion of nucleotides in DNA. His rules play a critical role in the elucidation of the structure of DNA.

(B, C)

Rita Levi-Montalcini discovers nerve growth factor.

Biologists who study the development of organisms are interested in how cells know when to begin growing. Understanding how and why cells grow also affects cancer research, as tumors result from cells that grow out of control. In 1950, Italian biologist Rita Levi-Montalcini (b. 1909) makes great strides in understanding cell growth when she discovers nerve growth factor while studying nerve growth in chick embryos. She adds tumors to the embryos in the laboratory and finds that nerves grow. She then determines that the tumor is releasing a molecule, known as nerve growth factor, that stimulates nerve growth. Levi-Montalcini shares the Nobel Prize in physiology or medicine in 1986 with Stanley Cohen "for their discoveries of growth factors."

(B)

Vitaly Ginzburg and Lev Landau divide superconductors into two classes.

At extremely low temperatures, some metals and *alloys* can conduct *electricity* without electrical resistance. Mercury was the first of these *superconductors* shown to have this property (*See* entry for 1911). In 1950, Russian physicists Vitaly Ginzburg (b. 1916) and Lev Landau (1908–68) mathematically demonstrate that there are two distinct classes of superconductors. Thirty-five years after Landau's death, Ginzburg shares the Nobel Prize in physics in 2003 with Alexi Abrikosov and Anthony Leggett "for pioneering contributions to the theory of superconductors and superfluids."

(P)

January 13

Jan Oort suggests that a cloud of comets surrounds the solar system.

Astronomers have been observing masses of dust and ice that travel through space, called *comets,* for centuries. Where do these celestial bodies come from? On January 13, 1950, Dutch astronomer Jan Oort (1900–92) publishes a paper proposing that the solar system must be surrounded by a cloud of comets left over from the creation of the Sun. He believes that periodic changes in the gravitational pull of nearby stars causes some

of the comets to break away and enter the solar system.

(SA)

April

Leo James Rainwater proposes that the atomic nucleus is not spherical.

Advances in the study of *subatomic particles* developed rapidly in the 20th century. Physicists began to understand the atomic *nucleus.* Many calculations were predicated on the belief that the atomic nucleus assumes the shape of a sphere. In April 1950, American physicist Leo James Rainwater (1917–86) proposes that not all nuclei are spherical. Instead, he states that *electrons* influence the shape of the atomic nucleus. Later work by Danish physicists Aage Bohr and Ben Mottelson confirms his hypothesis (*See* entry for 1952). The three scientists share the Nobel Prize in physics in 1975 "for the discovery of the connection between collective motion and particle motion in atomic nuclei and the development of the theory of the structure of the atomic nucleus based on this connection."

(P)

1951

Manfred Eigen develops a method to follow extremely rapid chemical reactions.

Chemists study the properties of matter and the reactions that they undergo. Chemical reactions occur at various speeds, with some occurring in an extremely short period—as little as one millionth of a second. Obviously, such reactions are extremely difficult to study in the laboratory. In 1951, German chemist Manfred Eigen (b. 1927) begins a series of experiments that culminate in the development of methods to follow such rapid chemical reactions. His so-called relaxation techniques are particularly useful for studying the rapid chemical reactions that charged particles known as *ions* undergo. Eigen shares the Nobel Prize in chemistry in 1967 with Ronald George Wreyford Norrish and George Porter "for their studies of extremely fast chemical reactions, effected by disturbing the equilibrium by means of very short pulses of energy."

(C)

Bertram Brockhouse develops the neutron spectrometer.

Scientists use a variety of technique to probe the structures of *atoms* and molecules. Techniques that use *magnetism* to examine molecular structures are known collectively as spectrometry. In 1951, Canadian physicist Bertram Brockhouse (1918–2003) and colleagues use the *magnetic fields* generated by *neutrons* to develop the neutron spectrometer. His technique is widely used by physicists studying solid-state matter. Brockhouse is honored with the Nobel Prize in physics in 1994 "for the development of neutron spectroscopy."

(P)

Nikolaas Tinbergen studies the role of instinct in animal behavior.

During the 20th century, biologist systematically studied animal behavior. One of the pioneers in this field, known as ethology, was British biologist Nikolaas Tinbergen (1907–88). Throughout his career, he studied the social behavior of animals, ranging from birds to primates, arriving at his theories from careful experimentation and observations of animals in their natural habitats. In 1951, Tinbergen publishes his classic work *The Study of Instinct*. He extends many of his observations to human behavior; however, many of these ideas have been challenged. He shares the Nobel Prize in physiology or medicine in 1973 with Karl

von Frisch and Konrad Lorenz "for their discoveries concerning organization and elicitation of individual and social behaviour patterns."

(B)

Dirk Brouwer uses a computer to calculate planetary orbits.

Early astronomers contributed to the development of mathematics, as they needed increasingly more sophisticated means to calculate the movement of heavenly bodies. In the 20th century, astronomers used computers in their studies. Dutch astronomer Dirk Brouwer (1902–66) was one of the first scientists to apply computers to astronomy. In 1951, he publishes *The Coordinates of the Five Outer Planets, 1653–2060*, the first work to use computers to calculate planetary orbits.

(M, SA)

Robert Burns Woodward synthesizes cholesterol.

Natural products are among the most challenging molecules for chemists to synthesize in the laboratory. One such molecule is the *steroid* cholesterol. The structure of cholesterol includes four rings, making it a challenging molecule to synthesize from simpler chemicals. In 1951, American chemist Robert Burns Woodward completes the total synthesis of cholesterol. Woodward later completes the synthesis of many others important natural products, including the antimalarial drug quinine and the *hormone* cortisone. He is honored with the Nobel Prize in chemistry "for his outstanding achievements in the art of organic synthesis."

(B, C)

Feodor Lynen discovers an important molecule in fat metabolism.

Many 20th-century biochemists were interested in how the body extracts *energy* from food. They uncovered a variety of metabolic pathways and the *enzymes* that allow these important reactions to occur. In 1951, German biologist Feodor Lynen (1911–79) studies the breakdown of fat, following the work of Fritz Lipmann, who found an important molecule, coenzyme A, required for fatty acid metabolism. Lynen discovers a molecule that acts as an intermediary when coenzyme A is transferred from one molecule to another, which he calls acetyl coenzyme A. Lynen shares the Nobel Prize in physiology or medicine in 1964 with Konrad Bloch "for their discoveries concerning the mechanism and regulation of the cholesterol and fatty acid metabolism."

(B, C)

March 25

Edward Purcell detects radiation from interstellar hydrogen.

Astronomers look for ways to detect and analyze the *atoms* and molecules that exist in space. In 1944, Hendrik van de Hulst proposed that hydrogen atoms in space would emit *radio waves* as a result of changes in the surrounding magnetic field. Even though such an event is extremely rare, there are so many hydrogen atoms in the universe that the radio waves should be detectable. On March 25, 1951, American physicist Edward Purcell (1912–97) detects radio waves, showing that they can be used to detect atoms in interstellar space.

(P, SA)

1952

Fukui Kenichi explains the reactivity of molecules.

Chemists are interested in how *atoms* and molecules react to form new molecules. As the structure of the atom was elucidated during the 20th century, many scientists tried to explain chemical reactions in terms of atomic structure. In 1952, Japanese chemist Fukui Kenichi (1918–98) develops frontier orbital theory to explain the reactivity of molecules. Fukui's theory explains how many chemical reactions take place. Fukui shares the Nobel Prize in chemistry in 1981 with Roald Hoffmann "for their theories, developed independently, concerning the course of chemical reactions."

(C)

Ernst Fischer and Geoffrey Wilkinson describe sandwich molecules.

Chemists study the properties and reactions of matter. Many chemists are particularly interested in the structure of molecules because of the important influence that structure has on the types of reactions that a molecule will undergo. In 1952, German chemist Ernst Fischer (b. 1918) and British chemist Geoffrey Wilkinson (1921–96) independently describe the makeup of a new type of molecular structure, the so-called sandwich molecule. Sandwich molecules consist of two carbon rings flanking a metal *ion* like slices of bread on a sandwich. They share the Nobel Prize in chemistry in 1973 "for their pioneering work, performed independently, on the chemistry of the organometallic, so called sandwich compounds."

(C)

Renato Dulbecco develops a model of virally induced cancer.

Biologists studying diseases such as cancer develop models that allow them to study the disease in the laboratory. In 1952, American biologist Renato Dulbecco (b. 1914) shows interest in *viruses* that cause cancer in some animals. He wants to study these viruses and how they affect cells in the laboratory. To do this, he develops methods to infect cells outside the body, and studies the effects of viral infection on these cells. Later, he uses these techniques to show that the DNA of some tumor viruses can be found in cancer cells. For his pioneering work, Dulbecco shares the Nobel Prize in physiology or medicine in 1975 with David Baltimore and Howard Temin "for their discoveries concerning the interaction between tumour viruses and the genetic material of the cell."

(P)

Alfred Hershey and Martha Chase confirm that DNA is the genetic material.

How is information passed from one generation to the next? As described in the sidebar "The Science of DNA," scientists studying biochemistry in the early 20th century looked for the molecules that carry genetic information. At first, many believed that only *proteins* were sufficiently complex. In the 1940s, Oswald Avery and colleagues performed experiments that suggested DNA is the genetic material. After these seminal experiments, many others worked to confirm their results. In 1952, American biologists Alfred Hershey (1908–97) and Martha Chase (1930–2003) use *bacteriophage* to confirm that DNA is the genetic material. These experiments end the debate as to the nature of the genetic material.

(B, C)

Scientists create the maser.

Physicists in the early 20th century realized that *atoms* could both absorb and emit *energy*. Some began looking for ways to stimulate such energy emissions. In 1952, American physicist Charles Townes (b. 1915) develops a way to stimulate the emission of *microwaves*. He calls his device a *maser* for "microwave amplification by stimulated emission of radiation." At the same time, Russian physicists Aleksandr Prokhorov (1916–2002) and Nikolai Basov (1922–2001) independently develop a maser. Townes later works with Arthur L. Schawlow to use light instead of microwaves, to create an optical maser, or *laser*, as scien-

tists now recognize. Townes, Prokhorov, and Basov share the Nobel Prize in physics "for fundamental work in the field of quantum electronics, which has led to the construction of oscillators and amplifiers based on the maser-laser principle."

(P)

Donald Glaser develops the bubble chamber to detect subatomic structures.

During the early 20th century, physicists began to discover the components of the *atom*, known as *subatomic particles*. One of the challenges of this research was finding ways to detect these extremely small particles. In 1952, American physicist Donald Glaser (b. 1926) develops the bubble chamber to detect subatomic particles. The bubble chamber is filled with a liquid kept at its boiling point. When a particle is passed through the liquid, a bubble forms. The bubble chamber allows physicists to monitor the formation of subatomic particles and the path they take as they travel through the liquid. Glaser is honored with the Nobel Prize in physics in 1960 "for the invention of the bubble chamber."

(P)

Aage Bohr and Ben Mottelson demonstrate that atomic nuclei are not perfect spheres.

The 20th century saw many advances in the understanding of the *atom*. For many years, physicists studying the atomic *nucleus* believed that it was a perfect sphere. In 1950, James Rainwater proposed that the shape of the nuclei is not spherical, but rather influenced by the *electrons* that surround it (*See* entry for APRIL 1950). Danish physicist Aage Bohr (b. 1922) also believed that nuclei are not perfect spheres. In 1952, he and Danish physicist Ben Mottelson (b. 1926) conduct a series of experiments that clearly demonstrate that the shape of the atomic nucleus is affected by electrons.

Bohr and Mottelson share the Nobel Prize in physics in 1975 with Leo James Rainwater "for the discovery of the connection between collective motion and particle motion in atomic nuclei and the development of the theory of the structure of the atomic nucleus based on this connection."

(P)

March

Alan Hodgkin and Alexander Huxley describe the excitation of nerve cells.

One of the most interesting problems in physiology is how nerve cells transmit information throughout the body. Scientists have demonstrated that electrical impulses are carried through nerves. Where do these impulses come from? In the early 20th century, some believed that the movement of charged particle called *ions* across the nerve's *membrane* generates the electrical impulses. In March 1952, British biologists Alan Hodgkin (1914–98) and Alexander Huxley (b. 1917) report experiments that demonstrate that this is true. Today, biologists study the molecules devoted to making sure this exchange of ions occurs at the right time. Hodgkin and Huxley share the Nobel Prize in physiology or medicine in 1963 with Sir John Carew Eccles "for their discoveries concerning the ionic mechanisms involved in excitation and inhibition in the peripheral and central portions of the nerve cell membrane."

(B)

May 2

Rosalind Franklin obtains X-ray pictures of DNA.

During the 20th century, chemists began applying their expertise to biologically important molecules. One important property of these molecules is their structure. *X-ray crystallography* is a powerful technique that many chemists use to elucidate the

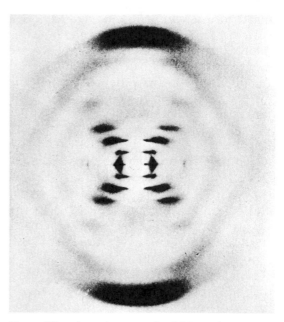

X-ray diffraction photograph of DNA taken by Rosalind Franklin in May 1952. Franklin's photographs are used by James Watson and Francis Crick to uncover the double helix nature of DNA. *(Omikron/Photo Researchers, Inc)*

three-dimensional structure of molecules. On May 2, 1952, English biophysicist Rosalind Franklin (1920–58) studies the molecule that carries genetic information in the cell, *deoxyribonucleic acid,* or DNA, using X-ray crystallography. She obtains X-ray photographs of DNA in many different forms. As described in the sidebar "The Science of DNA," James Watson and Francis Crick refer to her photographs as they develop their double helix model of DNA (*See* entry for APRIL 2, 1953).

(B, C)

November 1

The United States tests the first hydrogen bomb.

When the Soviet Union tested an atomic bomb in 1949, the United States realized

It had to research more powerful nuclear weapons. American physicist Edward Teller (1908–2003) leads a group that develops a thermonuclear device, or hydrogen bomb. The hydrogen bomb relies upon nuclear *fission*. In general, thermonuclear devices are thousands of times more powerful than atomic bombs. The United States tests the first hydrogen bomb on November 1, 1952. Less than one year later, the Soviet Union tests its own thermonuclear device.

(P)

December

Scientists isolate einsteinium.

During the 20th century, advances in physics led to many new *elements* being discovered. In 1952, a group of scientists analyzes the debris from a thermonuclear explosion. In the debris, they find a previously unknown element with 99 *protons*. They call the element einsteinium after physicist Albert Einstein. Scientists recognize that thermonuclear explosions lead to the creation of many different elements.

(C, P)

1953

Vincent du Vigneaud synthesizes oxytocin in the laboratory.

Hormones are molecules that mediate communication between cells, tissues, and organs. Some hormones are short chains of *amino acids* called peptides. One such peptide hormone is oxytocin, which is responsible for inducing uterine contraction during labor and milk letdown during lactation. In 1953, American chemist Vincent du Vigneaud (1901–78) synthesizes oxytocin in the laboratory. He is honored with the Nobel Prize in chemistry in 1955 "for his work on biochemically important sulphur com-

pounds, especially for the first synthesis of a polypeptide hormone."

(B, C)

Henry Taube begins investigating electron transfer between metal complexes.

Advances in physics at the beginning of the 20th century provided new avenues of research that helped chemists understand chemical reactions. One mechanism of a chemical reaction is the transfer of an *electron* between metal ions. Electron transfer reactions are particularly important in biological systems. In 1953, American chemist Henry Taube (1915–2005) begins his pioneering investigations into the mechanism of electron transfer between metal complexes. He is honored with the Nobel Prize in chemistry in 1983 "for his work on the mechanisms of electron transfer reactions, especially in metal complexes."

(B, C)

March 2

Jonas Salk develops a vaccine against polio.

Polio, a disease that can lead to paralysis and death, is caused by a *virus* and thus cannot be treated with antibiotics. Scientists in the mid-20th century searched for a vaccine that would keep people from catching polio. On March 28, 1953, American physician Jonas Salk (1914–95) reports that he has found a way to make polioviruses less contagious. He grows three such viruses, known attenuated strains, in the laboratory and uses them to create a polio vaccine. His vaccine is tested and approved for use in 1955. Soon the cases of polio are dramatically reduced, and today polio has been eradicated in the United States.

(B)

April 2

Watson and Crick show that DNA is a double helix.

Many chemists and biologists work toward understanding the structure of biologically important molecules. As described in the sidebar "The Science of DNA," *deoxyribonucleic acid,* or DNA, is the molecule that carries the genetic information in the cell. On April 2, 1953, a group of scientists describe the three-dimensional structure of DNA. American scientist James Watson (b. 1928)

and British scientist Francis Crick (1916–2004) use data collected and analyzed by British scientists Rosalind Franklin (1920–58) and Maurice Wilkins (1916–2004) to build a model of a DNA molecule. Their model reveals that DNA looks like a double helix. Watson, Crick, and Wilkins share the Nobel Prize in physiology or medicine in 1962, four years after Franklin's death, "for their discoveries concerning the molecular structure of nucleic acids and its significance for information transfer in living material."

(B, C)

SCIENCE OF DNA

Nearly every day the news reports scientific advances that stem from our understanding of DNA. New drugs, methods of diagnosis, forensic technology that helps solve crimes, and analysis of ancient material that gives us a view of *evolution* have all been possible because scientists have learned to analyze and manipulate DNA. Yet at the beginning of the 20th century, scientists did not even know the function of DNA. A series of landmark studies in biology, beginning with the identification of DNA as the genetic material, brought about a biology revolution in few decades.

At first, biologists believed that DNA was not sufficiently complex to be the genetic material. DNA is a long molecule made from combinations of four different molecules called nucleotides. The four nucleotides are structurally similar except for a region of the molecule known as the base. The nucleotides that make up DNA have one of four bases: adenine, cytosine, guanine, or thymidine. For many years, biologists believed that *proteins,* more complex molecules made up of a combination of 20 different small molecules called *amino acids,* carried genetic information. However, by the

middle of the 20th century, a series of experiments by Oswald Avery and Alfred Hershey demonstrated beyond a doubt that DNA is the genetic material.

The next great advance was the elucidation of the double helix structure of DNA. Chemists and biologists tried to model the molecule following what are known as "Chargaff's rules." The chemist Edwin Chargaff analyzed the chemical composition of DNA and found that two of the bases, adenine and thymidine, always occur in the same concentration, and the other two, cytosine and guanine, also occur in the same proportion. Chargaff's work gave chemists an insight into the composition of DNA, but more information was needed to uncover its structure. The next leap forward happened in 1953, when Rosalind Franklin obtained *X-ray* photographs of a DNA molecule. Her colleague, Maurice Wilkins shared her photographs with James Watson and Francis Crick. After noting that the photograph indicates the molecule takes a helical form, they used this data, along with Chargaff's rules, to build a model of DNA. Their model showed that DNA forms a double helix, composed of two strands of DNA held together

May 15

Stanley Miller and Harold Urey show how biologically active molecules can form from gases.

During the 20th century, scientists conducted experiments aimed at understanding how life began. One of the important questions they tried to address was how molecules for life form. On May 15, 1953, American scientists Stanley Miller (b. 1930) and Harold Urey (1893–1981) show that one type of molecules critical for living systems, *amino acids,* can be formed from the gases believed to make up the primeval atmosphere. When they add an electric spark to a vessel filled with a mixture of gases including water vapor and natural gas, they find that *amino acids* are formed. Their experiment suggests that lightning hitting the primordial atmosphere could have been the first step in developing life on Earth, providing insight into the possible origin of life.

(B, C)

by hydrogen bonds between the bases. The double helix conformed to Chargaff's rules, with adenine always pairing with thymidine, and guanine always pairing with cytosine. Watson and Crick also noted that this model suggested the means by which DNA is replicated. Since the bases always pair in the same manner, one strand can serve as a template to replicate the new strand.

Over the next few years, scientists use their knowledge of the double helix to learn how cells use the genetic information. They discover that through base pairing, DNA directs the formation of a *ribonucleic acid* (RNA) intermediate. Specific RNAs known as messenger RNA (mRNA) are synthesized using DNA as a template. The mRNA is then transported to large molecules called ribosomes that synthesize proteins by reading the genetic code on the mRNA. The message is translated when sequences of three nucleotides are matched with the proper amino acid. This sequence of events—DNA to RNA to protein—is known as the central dogma.

Scientist studying DNA and how it transmits genetic information in the cell also discover a number of proteins that modify DNA. Many of these studies are carried out using simple systems such as *bacteria* and *viruses*.

Biologists studying how bacteria defend against infection by a virus notice that, in many cases, the viral DNA is specifically degraded while the bacterial DNA remains intact. This observation leads to the discovery of restriction *enzymes*—proteins that cut DNA at specific sequences. Soon, many other important and useful enzymes are discovered, including ligases that join two pieces of DNA together and DNA polymerases that can be used to synthesize DNA and sequence it in the laboratory. Biologists use these enzymes as tools to fuse DNA from one organism to that of another. The so-called recombinant DNA molecules they create have been used in a wide variety of experiments and industrial applications.

As scientists learn more about DNA, they apply that knowledge to a range of biological problems. The ability to cut, paste, and analyze DNA is useful also in fields beyond biology. Forensic scientists analyze DNA left at crime scenes and compare it to victims and suspects. Physicians can now look for *genes* that predispose patients to breast cancer and other inherited diseases. Finally, medical scientists apply these techniques to uncover more secrets hidden away in cells. The continued use of DNA technology will bring more advances in future.

September 4

Eugene Aserinsky and Nathaniel Kleitman describe REM sleep.

Physiologists have described the different stages that occur during sleep. On September 4, 1953, sleep researchers Eugene Aserinsky (1912–98) and Nathaniel Kleitman (1895–1999) describe an important stage of sleep characterized by rapid eye movements (REM). During the so-called REM phase of sleep, people move more and exhibit greater heart rate, blood flow, and other physiological activities. By studying sleeping patients Aserinsky and Kleitman show that REM sleep is more physiologically similar to wakefulness than non-REM sleep. Scientists continue to study the function and importance of this stage of sleep.

(B)

October 3

Peter Medawar demonstrates immunological tolerance.

The immune system protects animals from *viruses, bacteria,* and other foreign matter. During the 20th century, biologists began to understand how the immune system works. Sir Frank Macfarlane Burnet showed that immunity develops after an animal is born (*See* entry for 1950s). On October 3, 1953, British biologist Peter Medawar (1915–87) publishes experiments suggesting that the immune system could be coaxed into believing a foreign tissue is not dangerous if the animal is exposed to it early in development. Through a series of experiments, he later shows that such immunological tolerance indeed takes place. Medawar and Burnet share the Nobel Prize in physiology or medicine in 1960 "for discovery of acquired immunological tolerance."

(B)

November

Karl Ziegler shows that metals can be used to help create polymers.

Many 20th-century chemists studied reactions that lead to chains of molecules with repeating subunits known as *polymers*. In 1953, German chemist Karl Ziegler (1898–1973) studied ways to catalyze or speed up the reactions that create polymers. He discovered that some metals will speed up polymerization reactions. In November 1953, his catalyst is used for the first time. Later, Italian chemist Giulio Natta (1903–79) applies Ziegler's technique to the production of plastics. Ziegler and Natta share the Nobel Prize in chemistry in 1963 "for their discoveries in the field of the chemistry and technology of high polymers."

(C)

1954

Wolfgang Paul invents the atomic trap.

Scientists are constantly trying to develop new techniques and instruments that will allow them to study the physical world. Studying the interactions of charged particles known as *ions* requires specialized instruments. In 1954, German physicist Wolfgang Paul (1913–93) invents the atomic trap, a device that captures ions. Paul's trap allows scientists to study the behavior of ions. His technique is widely used by physicists. Paul shares the Nobel Prize in physics in 1989 with Hans Dehmelt (b. 1922) "for the development of the ion trap technique."

(P)

Georg Wittig develops a method to synthesize carbon-carbon double bonds in the laboratory.

During the 20th century, many chemists worked to synthesize biologically important molecules in the laboratory. A number of these molecules have a type of bond called carbon-carbon double bonds. In 1954, German chemist Georg Wittig (1897–1987) develops a method to catalyze or help reactions that create carbon-carbon double bonds. Using the so-called Wittig reaction, scientists are able to synthesize a wide range of molecules. Industrial chemists use the Wittig reaction to manufacture vitamins. Wittig shares the Nobel Prize in chemistry in 1979 with Herbert Brown "for their development of the use of boron- and phosphorus-containing compounds, respectively, into important reagents in organic synthesis."

(C)

Kunihiko Kodaira and Jean-Pierre Serre receive the Fields medal.

As described in the sidebar "Awarding Science," the Fields medal is given out every four years to outstanding young mathematicians. In 1954, Japanese mathematician Kunihiko Kodaira (1915–97) and French mathematician Jean-Pierre Serre (b. 1926) receive the honor. Kodaira is honored for his work on harmonic analysis. Serre works on the homotopy groups on spheres.

(M)

Robert Hofstadter describes the structure of protons and neutrons.

Many 20th-century physicists were interested in the *subatomic particles* that make up the *atom*. They recognized that the atomic *nucleus* is made up of *protons* and *neutrons*. Beginning in 1954, American physicist Robert Hofstadter (1915–90) devises techniques that allow him to determine the structure of the proton and neutron. His studies, which continue through 1957, reveal the size, shape, and distribution of electrical charge in these particles. Hofstadter is honored with the Nobel Prize in physics in 1961 for "for his pioneering studies of electron scattering in atomic nuclei and for his thereby achieved

discoveries concerning the structure of the nucleons."

(P)

Christian de Duve discovers the lysosome.

Eukaryotic cells are divided into a number of different sections, called *organelles,* which perform a variety of tasks. A membrane separates each organelle from the rest of the cell. In 1954, Belgian biologist Christian de Duve (b. 1917) studies cells by breaking them apart and separating them into their various components. During these studies, he discovers a new organelle, the lysosome. Later studies show that the lysosome is the site in the cell where nutrients are broken down after being brought in from outside the cell. De Duve shares the Nobel Prize in physiology or medicine in 1974 with Albert Claude and George Palade "for their discoveries concerning the structural and functional organization of the cell."

(B)

Stanley Tyler and Elso Barghoorn describe fossils of ancient bacteria.

Fossils give scientists a way of studying the organisms that populated the world before humans. Fossils of plants and animals have been known for centuries. During the 20th century, it became clear that some rocks hold fossils of *bacteria* as well. In 1954, American geologist Stanley Tyler (1906–63) discovers the oldest known fossilized bacteria, dating to the *Precambrian* era. Tyler and American anthropologist Elso Barghoorn (1915–84) report the discovery of the 2 billion-year-old bacteria, but it is not widely accepted until after Tyler's death in 1963.

(B, ES)

William Lipscomb begins his study of borane chemistry.

Boranes, also known as boron hydrides, are compounds that contain the *elements* boron and hydrogen. These molecules are difficult to study because they are highly reactive, unstable, and toxic. In 1954, American chemist William Lipscomb (b. 1919) begins his studies of borane chemistry. His work elucidates the structure of boranes and allows chemists to predict chemical reactions involving boron hydrides. Lipscomb is honored with the Nobel Prize in chemistry in 1976 "for his studies on the structure of boranes illuminating problems of chemical bonding."

(C)

Vladimir Prelog begins his investigations into the chirality of natural products.

Many biological molecules, including the *amino acids* that are the building blocks for proteins, exhibit a specific three-dimensional structure known as chirality. Two molecules are *chiral* if they are non-superimposable mirror images of one another (*See* entry for 1815). In 1954, Swiss chemist Vladimir Prelog (1906–98) begins a series of investigations into the chirality of various natural products, including antibiotics. Prelog is honored with the Nobel Prize in chemistry in 1975 "for his research into the stereochemistry of organic molecules and reactions."

(B, C)

December

Joseph Murray performs a successful kidney transplant.

When vital organs stop working, some patients can be treated by transplanting a new organ. Organ transplantation is hindered by the immune system, which recognizes the foreign tissue and rejects the transplantation. American physician Joseph Murray (b. 1919) realized that transplantation might be possible if the donor is genetically identical to the recipient. In December

1954, he performs a successful kidney transplant between identical twins. Murray's work leads to many important studies that allow organ transplantation to succeed today. He shares the Nobel Prize in physiology or medicine in 1990 with E. Donnall Thomas "for their discoveries concerning organ and cell transplantation in the treatment of human disease."

(B)

Stanford Moore and William Stein determine the chemical makeup of proteins.

Proteins carry out a number of critical functions in cells. They are complex molecules made up of a number of smaller molecules called *amino acids*. In December 1954, American chemists Stanford Moore (1913–82) and William Stein (1911–80) help scientists study proteins when they build an instrument that analyzes the amino acid content of proteins. They use their amino acid analyzer to determine the sequence of a protein. Amino acid sequencing remains a valuable tool in biochemistry today. Moore and Stein share the Nobel Prize in chemistry in 1972 "for their contribution to the understanding of the connection between chemical structure and catalytic activity of the active centre of the ribonuclease molecule."

(B, C)

1955

Severo Ochoa discovers the enzyme that helps cells synthesize RNA.

A class of biologically important molecules called *nucleic acids* is important in the storage and transmission of genetic information. *Ribonucleic acids,* or RNA, are critical molecules that help the cell use the genetic information coded in DNA. In 1955, American biochemist Severo Ochoa

(1905–93) isolates an *enzyme* from cells and uses it to synthesize RNA in the laboratory. The enzyme becomes an important tool in *molecular biology* laboratories. Ochoa shares the Nobel Prize in physiology or medicine in 1959 with American biochemist Arthur Kornberg "for their discovery of the mechanisms in the biological synthesis of *ribonucleic acid* and *deoxyribonucleic acid.*"

(B, C)

Scientists discover fermium.

During the 20th century, physicists discovered many *elements* that either do not occur naturally, or are present only at low levels. In 1955, two groups announce the discovery of an element with 100 *protons*. Scientists analyzing the debris from a thermonuclear explosion first discover the element, named fermium after Italian-American physicist Enrico Fermi. Later, physicists in Sweden create the same element in the laboratory by bombarding an *isotope* of uranium with oxygen nuclei.

(C, P)

Henry Kettlewell proposes that industrial pollution is driving evolution.

Most biologists since the time of Darwin believed that *natural selection* drives evolutionary changes. In 1955, English biologist Henry Kettlewell (1907–79) proposes that industrial pollution serves as a selective force, driving the *evolution* of moths. He notes that a particular species of moth is darker in areas near polluting factories than in the countryside. He proposes that the darker moths survive because they are camouflaged when they land on trees covered in industrial pollution. In the countryside, the lighter moths thrive because the clean trees camouflage them. His theory is known as industrial melanism.

(B)

Edmond Fischer and Edwin Krebs uncover an important mechanism for controlling the activity of cellular proteins.

Chemists and biologists studying the chemical reactions that occur in cells have identified a number of biologically important molecules. *Proteins* are a particularly important class of molecules that carry out many tasks within the cell. In 1955, American biologist Edwin Krebs (b. 1918) and Swiss-American scientist Edmond Fischer (b. 1920) uncover an important mechanism that cells use to regulate the activity of cellular proteins. They find that the activity of some proteins is either turned on or turned off by a specific chemical modification called phosphorylation. Today, scientists recognize that many cellular processes from the breakdown of nutrients to communication between cells rely upon phosphorylation. Fischer and Krebs share the Nobel Prize in physiology or medicine in 1992 "for their discoveries concerning reversible protein phosphorylation as a biological regulatory mechanism."

(C)

Niels Jerne proposes a theory of immune system development.

The immune system uses an array of cells and molecules to protect organisms from invading organisms. Among these molecules are *antibodies, proteins* that specifically recognize molecules that do not belong in the body. How does this occur? In 1955, Danish immunologist Niels Jerne (1911–94) writes *Natural Selection Theory of Antibody Generation,* proposing that all antibodies are present before birth. Then, as the body is exposed to different foreign molecules, the antibodies that recognize those molecules the best are selected to be produced in greater numbers. Jerne's theory changes the view of antibody generation. He shares the Nobel Prize in physiology or medicine in 1984 with Georges Köhler and César Milstein "for theories concerning the specificity in development and control of the immune system and the discovery of the principle for production of monoclonal antibodies."

(B)

February 18

Glenn Seaborg and colleagues produce mendelevium.

During the 20th century, physicists created many *elements* that are not found on the Earth. The properties of these so-called *transfermium elements* are not well understood because they usually exist for only a short period of time. On February 18, 1955,

American physicist Glenn T. Seaborg produces a number of transfermium elements, including plutonium. This photograph shows Seaborg working in his Berkeley laboratory in 1956. *(LBNL/Photo Researchers, Inc)*

a group of scientists led by American physicist Glenn Seaborg creates an element with 101 *protons* by bombarding an *isotope* of einsteinium with *alpha particles*. The element is named mendelevium, after Russian chemist Dmitry Mendeleyev, who created an early version of the *periodic table* of the elements (*See* entry for 1869).

(C, P)

October 11

Erwin Muller observes a single atom using a field ion microscope.

Microscopes allow scientists to view objects that are far too small to be seen by eye. Early microscopes let biologists see the components of pond water and body fluids. Improvements were continually made, and by the 20th century, scientists used microscopes to visualize individual molecules such as large proteins and DNA. On October 11, 1955, American physicist Erwin Muller (1911–77) becomes the first person to see an *atom* when he uses a field *ion* microscope to visualize the atoms on the tip of a metal.

(C, P)

October 24

Owen Chamberlain and Emilio Segrè discover the antiproton.

Many 20th-century physicists devoted their careers to the study of *subatomic particles*. The invention of the particle *accelerator* allowed scientists to study the components of the *atom*. On October 24, 1955, American physicists Owen Chamberlain (b. 1920) and Emilio Segrè (1905–89) describe experiments in which they use a particle accelerator to identify a new type of particle, the antiproton. The antiproton has the same mass as a *proton*, but it has a net negative charge. They share the Nobel Prize in physics in 1959 "for their discovery of the antiproton."

(P)

1956

Norman Phillips develops a new method of weather prediction.

Weather prediction is an important application of science. Meteorologists use a combination of data collection and models to forecast the weather. In 1956, American meteorologist Norman Phillips develops a way to use numerical models to predict weather. His work leads to the development of computer programs that are used in weather forecasting today.

(M, W)

Earl Sutherland uncovers a mechanism of hormone actions.

Cells and tissue communicate with one another by releasing molecules called *hormones*. Biologists work to understand how cells interrupt the signals sent by hormones. In 1956, American biochemist Earl Sutherland Jr. (1915–74) discovers that after cells bind a particular hormone they produce a molecule called cyclic AMP (cAMP). He calls cAMP a second messenger, as it is the second molecule involved in transmitting information to the cell. Today, a number of different second messengers are known to be involved in transmitting signals to the cell. Sutherland is honored with the Nobel Prize in physiology or medicine in 1971 "for his discoveries concerning the mechanisms of the action of hormones."

(B)

Rudolph Marcus explains how electron transfer reactions occur.

Research into the structure of the *atom* helped 20th-century chemists gain a better understanding of many chemical reactions. One important type of reaction, known as oxidation-reduction reactions, involves the transfer of an *electron* from one molecule to another. Beginning in 1956, American chemist Rudolph Marcus (b. 1923) conducts a series of studies that unveil how these reactions take place. His work is particularly useful in understanding the rate at which these reactions occur. Marcus is honored with the Nobel Prize in chemistry in 1992 "for his contributions to the theory of electron transfer reactions in chemical systems."

(C)

Maurice Ewing and Bruce Heezen describe the mid-oceanic ridge.

In the early part of the 20th century, the German research vessel called the *Meteor* discovered a tall ridge in the middle of the Atlantic Ocean. The ridge is actually an underwater mountain range that circles the globe. In 1956, American geologists Bruce Heezen (1924–77) and Maurice Ewing (1906–74) provide a more thorough description of mid-oceanic ridge, which passes through all the world's oceans. Today, scientists recognize that the mid-oceanic ridge was formed during *seafloor spreading*.

(ES, MS)

January 21

Mahlon Hoagland and Paul Zamecnik discover molecules that allow genetic information to be translated into proteins.

Once biologists clearly demonstrated that *deoxyribonucleic acid,* or DNA, is the genetic material in cells, scientists began trying to find out how cells read the genetic information it holds. They learned that the DNA directs the synthesis of *proteins* in a process known as translation. On January 21, 1956, American biologists Mahlon Hoagland (b. 1921) and Paul Zamecnik (b. 1913) publish a paper describing their discovery of tRNA, an important molecule in the process of translation. Later experiments show that tRNA has a *nucleic acid* component that recognizes the genetic code and an attached *amino acid* that is incorporated into the protein being synthesized.

(B)

May

Tsung-Dao Lee and Chen-Ning Yang discover important properties of subatomic particles.

Many 20th-century physicists were interested in the study of the *subatomic particles* that make up *atoms*. Throughout the century, they devised experiments and instruments that allowed them to study these particles and understand how they work. Physicists believed that the physical interactions between particles were symmetrical. In 1956, Chinese physicists Tsung-Dao Lee (b. 1926) and Chen-Ning Yang (b. 1922) show that this is not always the case. Their work changes the way physicists understand the behavior of many subatomic particles. They share the Nobel Prize in physics in 1957 "for their penetrating investigation of the so-called parity laws which has led to important discoveries regarding the elementary particles."

(P)

Ulf von Euler shows that neurotransmitters are stored in particles within cells.

Neurons transmit messages by releasing small molecules called *neurotransmitters* into the *synapse,* the space between the neuron and another cell. In order for messages to be sent rapidly, the neuron must have a ready supply of neurotransmitters at all times. In 1956, Swedish biologist Ulf von Euler (1905–83) shows that neurotransmitters are stored in small particles within cells. These particles are located near the outer *membrane* of the neuron, allowing neurotransmitters to be quickly released into the synapse. Von Euler

shares the Nobel Prize in physiology or medicine in 1970 with Sir Bernard Katz and Julius Axelrod "for their discoveries concerning the humoral transmittors in the nerve terminals and the mechanism for their storage, release and inactivation."

(B)

John Polanyi begins his work on a method to study chemical reactions.

The new understanding of *atoms* and atomic structure in the 20th century served as the basis for many techniques used to analyze atoms, molecules, and chemical reactions. In 1956, Canadian scientist John Polanyi (b. 1929) begins his work on infrared chemiluminesence, a technique use to study chemical reactions. Polanyi's work serves as the basis for instruments used in chemistry laboratories today. Polanyi shares the Nobel Prize in chemistry with Dudley Herschbach and Yuan Lee "for their contributions concerning the dynamics of chemical elementary processes."

(C)

July

George Palade discovers how cells make proteins.

During the 20th century, many biologists and chemists tried to understand the chemical reactions that underlie the basic functions of the cell. All cells must synthesize many different *proteins* that will carry out various functions in the cell, from catalyzing chemical reactions to helping cells communicate. American biologist George Palade (b. 1912) studied the different compartments of the cell known as *organelles*. In July 1956, he publishes his work on the organelle known as the endoplasmic reticulum, showing that ribosomes, complex molecules that are associated with the organelle, make proteins. Palade shares the Nobel Prize in physiology or medicine in 1974 with Albert Claude and Christian de Duve "for their discoveries concerning the structural and functional organization of the cell."

(B)

July 21

Arthur Kornberg discovers the enzyme that makes DNA.

The discovery that DNA is the genetic material led many scientists to try to understand how DNA is made in the cell. DNA is made from many individual molecules called nucleotides. American biochemist Arthur Kornberg (b. 1918) was interested in how these nucleotides are brought together to form DNA. On July 21, 1956, he publishes a paper describing his discovery of an *enzyme* that catalyzes the synthesis of DNA. He soon isolates this enzyme and names it DNA polymerase. Kornberg shares the Nobel Prize in physiology or medicine in 1959 with Severo Ochoa "for their discovery of the mechanisms in the biological synthesis of ribonucleic acid and deoxyribonucleic acid."

(B)

October 13

Vernon Ingram discovers how to get the "fingerprint" of a protein.

Proteins are a class of biologically important molecules that carry out a number of critical functions in the cell. The information for making proteins is carried in the DNA of cells. Many genetic diseases result from mutations in the DNA that in turn lead to production of proteins that do not function correctly. In 1956, American biochemist Vernon Ingram (b. 1924) developed a method to look at the "fingerprint" of proteins. On October 13 of that year, he uses protein fingerprinting to show that the oxygen-carrying protein *hemoglobin* from patients with a genetic disease called sickle cell anemia has a different fingerprint than hemoglobin from healthy people. His work leads to a greater understanding of the effects of genetic mutations on the proteins produced by the mutant genes.

(B, C)

October 15

Nicolaas Bloembergen develops new methods to determine the structure of molecules.

Chemists and physicists are often interested in the structures of the *atoms* and molecules that make up matter. During the 20th century, a number of techniques, known collectively as *spectroscopy*, were used to elucidate these structures. The invention of *lasers* improved spectroscopic techniques. Lasers can be used in spectroscopy because of pioneering work done by American physicist Nicolaas Bloembergen (b. 1920) on a forerunner of the laser, known as the *maser*. On October 15, 1956, he publishes a method to amplify the maser. His method is applied to lasers and used in laser spectroscopy. Bloembergen shares the Nobel Prize in physics in 1981 with Arthur Leonard Schawlow "for their contribution to the development of laser spectroscopy."

(P)

John Backus develops the FORTRAN programming language.

A computer uses a specific set of rules, known as a programming language, to understand the instructions that programmers give it. Early computer programs were written in machine language, making computer programming a difficult and expensive endeavor. On October 15, 1956, American mathematician John Backus (b. 1924) introduces the widely used programming language known as formula translation, or FORTRAN. Programmers working with scientific applications quickly adopt FORTRAN. A version of the language is still used today.

(M)

1957

Sir John Carew Eccles describes nerve impulses.

Many physiologists are interested in how nerves transmit information throughout the body. Studies by Hodgkin and Huxley demonstrated that nerve impulses cause an exchange of charged particle called *ions* across the *membrane* of nerve cells. During the 1950s, British biologist Sir John Carew Eccles (1903–97) demonstrated that when two nerve cells meet at a junction known as a *synapse,* the nerve transmitting information releases a factor that in turn causes the nerve receiving the information to allow ions to flow into the cell. In 1957, he describes his work in the classic book *The Physiology of Nerve Cells.* Eccles shares the Nobel Prize in physiology or medicine in 1963 with Alan Hodgkin and Andrew Huxley "for their discoveries concerning the ionic mechanisms involved in excitation and inhibition in the peripheral and central portions of the nerve cell membrane."

(B)

Kai Siegbahn develops high-resolution electron spectroscopy.

Spectroscopy is a technique that allows scientists to analyze the structure of molecules by studying how they absorb electromagnetic *radiation.* In 1957, Swedish physicist Kai Siegbahn (b. 1918) and colleagues develop a method to use the *electrons* emitted upon treatment with ultraviolet light to determine the substance's electronic structure. Their work becomes the basis of high-resolution electron spectroscopy, a technique used in many chemistry laborato-

ries. Siegbahn is honored with the Nobel Prize in physics in 1957 for "for his contribution to the development of high-resolution electron spectroscopy."

(C, P)

John Warcup Cornforth synthesizes cholesterol in the laboratory.

Chemists who specialize in synthetic chemistry try to develop ways to synthesize complex chemical from simple precursors in the laboratory. Some of the most challenging syntheses involve biologically active molecules. The *atoms* in many of these molecules not only have to be in the correct position, but they also must have the proper orientation in space, known as stereochemistry. From 1957 to 1958, Australian biochemist John Cornforth (b. 1917) reports the use of biological catalysts called *enzymes* to synthesize cholesterol in the laboratory. His work is honored with the Nobel Prize in chemistry in 1975 "for his work on the stereochemistry of enzyme-catalyzed reactions."

(B, C)

The BCS theory is shown to explain superconductivity.

When *electricity* passes through a conducting metal, it generates *friction. Superconductors* are materials that can conduct electricity without friction, usually at extremely low temperatures (*See* entry for 1911). After superconductors were first discovered, physicists tried to determine how they work. In 1957, American physicists John Bardeen (1908–91), Leon Cooper (b. 1930), and John Robert Schrieffer (b. 1931) propose the BCS theory to explain superconductivity. The three scientists share the Nobel Prize in physics in 1972 "for their jointly developed theory of superconductivity, usually called the BCS-theory."

(P)

Sune Bergström isolates prostaglandins.

The complex physiological and chemical reactions that occur in biological systems must be regulated so that cells and organs do their jobs at the correct time. In 1957, Swedish scientist Sune Bergström (1916–2004) discovers two members of a new class of regulatory molecules called prostaglandins. Prostaglandins are made from fatty acids in the body. Today, scientists recognize that the prostaglandins are important in a number of biological processes, including uterine contractions, pain, and blood vessel constriction. Bergström shares the Nobel Prize in physiology or medicine in 1980 with Bengt I. Samuelsson and John R. Vane "for their discoveries concerning prostaglandins and related biologically active substances."

(B)

Alexei Abrikosov explains why some materials are superconductors.

Superconductors are materials that conduct electricity without resistance (*See* entry for 1911). In 1957, American physicists John Bardeen (1908–91), Leon Cooper (b. 1930), and J. Robert Schrieffer (b. 1931) propose the BCS theory to explain the superconductivity of some pure metals, known as type-1 superconductors (*See* entry for 1957). In that same year, Russian physicist Alexi Abrikosov (b. 1928) proposes a theory to explain how superconducting *alloys,* known as type-2 superconductors, work. His work is demonstrated experimentally 10 years later. Abrikosov shares the Nobel Prize in physics in 2003 with Vitaly Ginzburg and Anthony Leggett "for pioneering contributions to the theory of superconductors and superfluids."

(P)

Jens Skou shows how cells maintain the proper salt concentrations.

A semipermeable *membrane* surrounds cells, helping to maintain a consistent intercellu-

lar environment. *Proteins* embedded in the membrane allow specific *ions* or molecules to enter or exit the cell. Two of these ions, sodium and potassium, are found in stable concentrations inside the cell. In 1957, Danish biologist Jens Skou (b. 1918) discovers the protein within the cell membrane that transports sodium and potassium ions across the cell membrane. He is honored with the Nobel Prize in chemistry in 1997 "for the first discovery of an ion-transporting enzyme, $Na+, K+ -ATPase.$"

(B, C)

Francis Crick describes the flow of genetic information.

As described in the sidebar "The Science of DNA," by the middle of the 20th century biologists had established that DNA is the genetic material and it encodes a variety of *proteins* that carry out important functions in the cell. A number of biologists began to study RNA, which helps transmit genetic information throughout the cell. In 1958, British biologist Francis Crick describes the flow of genetic information. He states that genetic information is encoded in the DNA, which is then transcribed into a messenger RNA (mRNA). These molecular messengers then carry the genetic information from DNA, and that message is translated into a protein. He calls this flow of information the central dogma, and it becomes a guiding principle in *molecular biology.*

(B)

April

Christian Anfinsen describes how proteins get their structure.

Proteins carry out many important functions in biological systems—from catalyzing reactions to acting as *hormones.* Proteins are encoded in DNA, the genetic information in the cell, and are synthesized from precursor

CENTRAL DOGMA

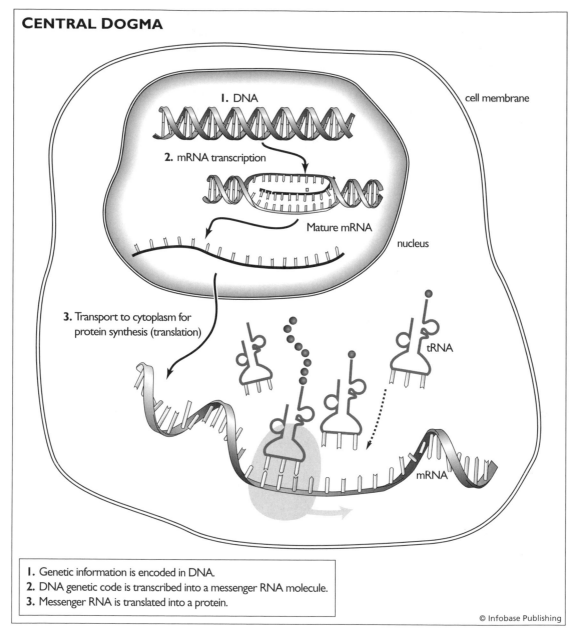

1. DNA

cell membrane

2. mRNA transcription

Mature mRNA

nucleus

3. Transport to cytoplasm for protein synthesis (translation)

tRNA

mRNA

1. Genetic information is encoded in DNA.
2. DNA genetic code is transcribed into a messenger RNA molecule.
3. Messenger RNA is translated into a protein.

© Infobase Publishing

The elucidation of the double helix structure of DNA (1) helps scientists uncover the mechanism by which genetic information stored in DNA is expressed in cells, commonly known as the central dogma. Cellular DNA unwinds, exposing a single strand or template that is used to transcribe the coded genetic message (2). The molecule that carries this transcribed messages is called messenger RNA (mRNA). The genetic code is written in three base sets of codons. Genetic messages are decoded or translated by ribosomes, large molecular machines that bring together mRNA and tRNA and direct protein synthesis.

molecules called *amino acids*. Each protein has a unique three-dimensional structure that is critical for its function in the cell. How does the protein fold into the proper structure? In April 1957, American biochemist Christian Anfinsen (1916–95) demonstrates that the structure of a protein is inherent in its amino acid sequence. He treats a protein with strong chemicals that cause it to be denatured into a linear sequence of amino acids. When the chemical is removed, the protein refolds into its active structure. Anfinsen is honored with the Nobel Prize in physiology or medicine in 1957 "for his work on ribonuclease, especially concerning the connection between the amino acid sequence and the biologically active conformation."

(B, C)

July

Clyde Cowan and Frederick Reines discover neutrinos.

Many physicists in the 20th century were interested in the *subatomic particles* that make up *atoms*. Early atomic physicists postulated the existence of a tiny particle called a *neutrino*. Neutrinos are as small as *electrons* but have no net charge. In 1957, American physicists Clyde Cowan (1919–74) and Frederick Reines (1918–98) devise a method to detect neutrinos. They succeed in capturing neutrinos that are emitted from a nuclear reactor. Reines is honored with the Nobel Prize in physics in 1995, 21 years after Cowan's death, "for the detection of the neutrino."

(P)

September

Alick Isaacs and Jean Lindemann discover a way that cells protect against viral infections.

The immune system has a variety of ways to protect the body against infections. In Sep-

tember 1957, Scottish biologist Alick Isaacs (1921–67) and Swiss biologist Jean Lindemann report the discovery of interferon, an important molecule used to guard against *viruses*. Their experiments show that when a cell is infected with a virus it releases interferon. Interferon, in turn, helps the surrounding cells resist infection. Today, three different types of interferons are known. Commercially produced interferon is used to treat of a variety of diseases.

(B)

October

William Fowler describes how elements are formed by nuclear reactions in stars.

All molecules are made from a combination of *elements*. Where do these elements come from? In October 1957, American physicist William Fowler (1911–95) develops a theory that describes how the *elements* are formed. Based on both mathematical calculations and experiments, he proposes that the nuclear reactions that occur in stars leads to the formation of heavier elements. Fowler is honored with the Nobel Prize in physics in 1983 "for his theoretical and experimental studies of the nuclear reactions of importance in the formation of the chemical elements in the universe."

(P, SA)

October 4

The Soviet Union launches *Sputnik I*.

Space exploration became a reality in the 1950s. As described in the sidebar "Exploring Space," the space age begins on October 4, 1957, when the Soviet Union launches the satellite *Sputnik I*. The satellite weighs only 183 pounds (83 kg) and takes 93 minutes to orbit the Earth. *Sputnik I* remains in orbit until 1958. The launch of *Sputnik* is the beginning of the space race between the Soviet Union and the United States.

The United States embarks upon the *Explorer* program and launches its own satellite in 1958. Throughout the next decades, the two countries continue to explore space.

(SA)

November

Daniel Carleton Gajdusek describes the transmission of kuru.

Physicians look for the causes of disease, hoping that they can prevent future cases. During the 1950s, American biologist Daniel Carleton Gajdusek (b. 1923) traveled to New Guinea and observed a rare disease called kuru, found only in the Fore people. Patients afflicted with kuru slowly lose weight, begin to tremble, and eventually die. Gajdusek believed the disease is transmitted by the Fore custom of eating the brains of kuru victims. In November 1957, he proposes that a *virus* found in the brains of infected individuals causes kuru. Today, scientists recognize that kuru is actually caused by an infectious agent known as a *prion* (*See* entry for 1982). Scientists recognize as well that prions cause other neurological conditions such as mad cow disease. Gajdusek shares the Nobel Prize in physiology or medicine in 1976 with Baruch Blumberg "for their discoveries concerning new mechanisms for the origin and dissemination of infectious diseases."

(B)

Herbert Kroemer increases the performance of semiconductors.

Advances in computing and electronics created a need for *semiconductors* that could rapidly transmit information. In November 1957, German physicist Herbert Kroemer (b. 1928) shows that components known as heterostructures can greatly increase the performance of semiconductors. His observations lead to the development of high-speed electronics. He shares the Nobel Prize

in physics in 2000 with Russian physicist Zhores Alferov "for developing semiconductor heterostructures used in high-speed- and opto-electronics."

(P)

1958

Leo Esaki invents the tunnel diode.

Physicists in the early part of the 20th century discovered that matter has the properties of both a particle and wave. Such *wave-particle duality* suggests that some matter should be able to pass through another, a phenomenon known as tunneling. In 1958, Japanese physicist Leo Esaki (b. 1925) demonstrates that tunneling can occur with solids. He applies this work to electronics and invents the tunnel diode. Esaki shares the Nobel Prize in physics in 1973 with Ivar Giaever "for their experimental discoveries regarding tunneling phenomena in semiconductors and superconductors, respectively."

(P)

Phillip Anderson describes how electrons move through disordered systems.

Electrons are *subatomic particles* that orbit the *nucleus* of an *atom*. Studying the behavior of atoms and electrons in an ordered system, such as a *crystal*, is relatively easy because atoms are held in predictable locations. However, physicists in the middle of the 20th century had trouble predicting the behavior of atoms in disordered systems that do not have a crystalline structure. In 1958, American physicist Phillip Anderson (b. 1923) publishes a paper describing the behavior of electrons in disordered system. His work lays the basis for technological advance in electronics later in the century. Anderson shares the Nobel Prize in physics in 1977 with Sir Nevill Mott and John van Vleck "for their fundamental theoretical investigations of the electronic structure of magnetic and disordered systems."

(P)

Glenn Seaborg and colleagues create nobelium in the laboratory.

During the 20th century, physicists began to create many *elements* that are not found on Earth in the laboratory. A group led by American physicist Glenn Seaborg at the University of California in Berkeley created many of these elements, so-called *transfermium elements*, using a linear *accelerator*. In 1958, they bombard two different *isotopes* of the element curium with carbon *atoms* to create atoms with 102 *protons*, now known as nobelium.

(C, P)

Rudolf Mössbauer shows that crystals emit a sharp beam of gamma rays.

Gamma rays are high-energy rays emitted during some forms of *radioactive decay*. When *atoms* emit gamma rays, they can excite surrounding atoms. In 1958, German physicist Rudolf Mössbauer (b. 1929) shows that at low temperatures atoms can emit gamma rays without exciting the surrounding atoms. Known as "the Mössbauer effect," his discovery allows scientists to produce gamma rays of a specific wavelength and leads to a new method for determining the electronic structures of atoms and molecules. His work is honored with the Nobel Prize in physics in 1961 "for his researches concerning the resonance absorption of gamma radiation and his discovery in this connection of the effect which bears his name."

(P)

Klaus Roth and René Thom receive the Fields medal.

As described in the sidebar "Awarding Science," the Fields medal is awarded every four years to outstanding young mathematicians.

In 1958, the medal is awarded to German mathematician Klaus Roth (b. 1925) and French mathematician René Thom (1923–2002). Roth receives the honor for his solution of a problem known as the Thue-Siegel problem. Thom is honored for his work on cobordism theory, and important theory in the field of *topology*.

(M)

François Jacob and Jacques Monod describe how genes control protein synthesis.

During the 20th century, biologists learned that genetic material is made of DNA and that *proteins* carry out a number of important functions in the cell. The genetic information in DNA directs the synthesis of proteins. In 1958, French biologists François Jacob (b. 1920) and Jacques Monod (1910–76) begin a series of experiments that explain the genetic control of protein synthesis. By studying *gene* regulation in *bacteria,* they show that genes encoding proteins that work together in the cell are arranged next to one another. Thus, genes can be regulated such that the proteins are only made when they are needed. Jacob and Monod share the Nobel Prize in physiology or medicine in 1965 with French biologist André Lwoff "for their discoveries concerning genetic control of enzyme and virus synthesis."

(B)

February

Arvid Carlsson reveals the role of dopamine in Parkinson's disease.

Today, neurological diseases are some of the most challenging for physicians to treat. Parkinson's disease is a neurological disorder that renders patients unable to control their own movements. Some of the first clues to the causes of Parkinson's disease come in

February 1958, when Swedish physician Arvid Carlsson (b. 1923) studies a *neurotransmitter* called dopamine. He finds that when mice are treated with dopamine, they are unable to move. Subsequent research shows that Parkinson's disease patients are missing dopamine in critical regions of the brain. His work leads to the use of the drug L-Dopa to replace the missing dopamine and alleviate some of the symptoms of this disease. Carlsson shares the Nobel Prize in physiology or medicine in 2000 with Paul Greengard and Eric Kandell "for their discoveries concerning signal transduction in the nervous system."

(B)

March 8

Sir John Cowdery Kendrew unveils the three-dimensional structure of a protein.

Proteins perform many vital functions in living organisms. Like other biologically important molecules, the three-dimensional structure of proteins is important for their proper function. *X-ray crystallography* is a powerful technique for determining the three-dimensional structure of molecules. On March 8, 1958, Sir John Cowdery Kendrew (1917–97) reports the three-dimensional structure of the oxygen-carrying molecule myoglobin. He is able to describe both the overall shape of the molecule and the exact arrangement of its *amino acids*. He shares the Nobel Prize in chemistry in 1962 with Max Perutz "for their studies of the structures of globular proteins."

(B)

May

Explorer I provides evidence for the Earth's magnetosphere.

The Earth's *magnetic field* has been known since the invention of the compass in ancient China. In the early 20th century, American astronomer Thomas Gold hypothesized that the Earth's atmosphere is enclosed by a magnetic layer he called the magnetosphere. Gold's hypothesis is confirmed in May 1958, when experiments conducted by the United States's first satellite, *Explorer I,* shows that belts of particles and *ions* surround the Earth. The existence of these belts, called Van Allen belts, demonstrate that the magnetosphere exists. Today, scientists recognize that the magnetosphere protects the Earth by capturing particles from the solar wind.

(ES, SA)

Matthew Meselson and Franklin Stahl describe DNA replication.

The 20th century saw a rapid expansion in the knowledge of how traits are passed from parents to offspring. As described in the sidebar "The Science of DNA," the discovery that DNA carries genetic information and the uncovering of its double helix structure led to increased research in the field. One of the first questions biologists asked was how DNA is replicated and passed from one generation to the next. In May 1958, American biologists Matthew Meselson (b. 1930) and Franklin Stahl (b. 1929) begin to answer that question when they describe the semiconservative replication of DNA. They show that before a cell divides, the DNA double helix unwinds and each strand serves as a template for replication.

(B)

July

Jean Dausset discovers immunological markers in humans.

The immune system protects animals from a variety of foreign organisms and tissues. Unfortunately, the immune response presents a problem when physicians want to treat a patient with an organ transplant.

Often, the immune system recognizes that the transplanted tissue is foreign, and attacks it. How does the immune system discriminate between its own tissue and the transplanted tissue? In July 1958, French biologist Jean Dausset (b. 1916) begins to answer this question when he identifies a specific marker on human tissues, known as the HLA *antigen*. His discovery eventually helps researchers find ways to get around the immune system and successfully complete organ transplants. Dausset shares Nobel Prize in physiology or medicine in 1980 with Baruj Benacerraf and George D. Snell "for their discoveries concerning genetically determined structures on the cell surface that regulate immunological reactions."

(B)

July 29

The United States government forms NASA.

As described in the sidebar "Exploring Space," the 1950s saw the beginnings of the United States and the Soviet Union racing for supremacy in outer space. When the Soviet Union successfully launched the *Sputnik* satellites (*See* entry for OCTOBER 4, 1957), the U.S. government reevaluated its space program. As a result, the National Advisory Committee for Aeronautics (NACA) and other similar government bodies are reorganized into the National Aeronautics and Space Agency (NASA) on July 29, 1958. NASA scientists immediately begin working toward human space travel.

(ES, SA)

September 12

Jack Kilby invents the microchip.

Early computers were so large they required entire rooms to house them. Today, computers are smaller and more powerful. How is this possible? On September 12, 1958, American engineer Jack Kilby (1923–2005) takes the first step toward shrinking the size of computers when he demonstrates his new invention—the microchip. The microchip contains an entire circuit that is smaller than a paper clip. Kilby's pioneering work in computer science is honored with the Nobel Prize in physics in 2000 "for his part in the invention of the integrated circuit."

(P)

1959

E. Donnall Thomas treats leukemia by transplanting bone marrow.

Leukemia is a cancer characterized by the uncontrolled growth of white blood cells, which are produced in the bone marrow. In 1959, American physician E. Donnall Thomas (b. 1921) successfully treats leukemia by performing a bone marrow transplant. To prevent rejection of the new bone marrow, he obtains the bone marrow from the identical twin of the patient. Later, he successfully uses a drug that suppresses the immune system in patients who need a bone marrow transplant. Thomas shares the Nobel Prize in physiology or medicine in 1990 with Joseph Murray "for their discoveries concerning organ and cell transplantation in the treatment of human disease."

(B)

Sir Martin Ryle maps radio sources in the universe.

In the early 20th century, astronomers began noticing *radio waves* coming from space. Radio telescopes were soon developed, allowing astronomers to map radio sources. English astronomer Sir Martin Ryle (1918–84) developed a number of radio telescopes and techniques to map sources of cosmic radio waves. In 1959, he publishes a catalog of radio sources called *The Third Cambridge*

Catalogue. His work contributes to the discovery of *pulsars* in the 1960s. Ryle shares the Nobel Prize in physics in 1974 with Antony Hewish "for their pioneering research in radio astrophysics: Ryle for his observations and inventions, in particular of the aperture

The United States opens the National Aeronautics and Space Agency (NASA) in July 1958. One of the centers under NASA is the Goddard Space Flight Center, named after the father of American rocketry Robert Hutchings Goddard. Goddard is shown here with the vacuum apparatus he developed in 1916. *(NASA)*

synthesis technique, and Hewish for his decisive role in the discovery of pulsars."

(P, SA)

Gerhard Herzberg determines the structure of free radicals.

The increased knowledge of atomic structure gained during the early 20th century helped many chemists understand how chemical reactions proceed. In a number of chemical reactions, short-lived intermediates, called free radicals, are formed. Since free radicals cannot be isolated, they are difficult to study. In 1959, Canadian chemist Gerhard Herzberg (1904–99) develops a technique that allows him to determine the structure of free radicals. He is honored with the Nobel Prize in chemistry in 1971 "for his contributions to the knowledge of electronic structure and geometry of molecules, particularly free radicals."

(C)

Worldwide Standardized Seismographic Network is established.

Earthquakes occur along fault lines across the globe. After the invention of the *seismograph* to measure activity along fault lines, many countries with active faults opened seismographic stations to monitor movements in the Earth. In 1959, the Worldwide Standardized Seismographic Network is established to monitor seismic activity across the globe. The network assures that all its stations have six well-calibrated seismographs capable of measuring seismic activity over short and long time periods.

(ES)

Max Perutz unveils the structure of hemoglobin.

A *protein* called *hemoglobin* carries oxygen through the blood stream. The ability of hemoglobin to bind oxygen in the lungs and release it to the cells and tissues of the body is related to its three-dimensional structure.

In 1959, British scientist Max Perutz (1914–2002) uses *X-ray crystallography* to determine the overall structure of hemoglobin, and shows that it is made up of four identical subunits. He shares the Nobel Prize in chemistry in 1962 with Sir John Cowdery Kendrew "for their studies of the structures of globular proteins."

(B, C)

Bruce Merrifield develops a method to synthesize proteins in the laboratory.

Proteins are large molecules that carry out a wide array of chemical reactions in cells. Researchers who wish to study proteins usually have to purify the molecules from cells because they are too large to synthesize in the laboratory. In 1959, American scientist Bruce Merrifield (b. 1921) conceives of a relatively simple method to synthesize peptides and small proteins in the laboratory. He is honored with the Nobel Prize in chemistry in 1984 "for his development of methodology for chemical synthesis on a solid matrix."

(B, C)

January 4

Soviet spacecraft reach the Moon.

The 1950s saw the beginning of the race between the United States and the Soviet Union to explore space. In 1959, the Soviet Union launches the unmanned spacecraft *LUNA 1*, which passes above the Moon on January 4, 1959. Data from the *LUNA 1* mission show that the Moon does not have a *magnetic field*. On September 14, 1959 a second Soviet spacecraft, *LUNA 2*, crashes into the Moon.

(SA)

November 21

Rosalyn Yalow develops a method to analyze the chemicals in blood.

Physicians often run blood tests on patients to help them diagnose a variety of diseases and conditions. During the 1950s, American scientist Rosalyn Yalow (b. 1921) developed an important technique that medical laboratories use to analyze blood, the radioimmunoassay. On November 21, 1959, she publishes a paper showing how radioimmunoassay can be used to determine the amount of the *hormone* insulin in the blood of patients with diabetes. Radioimmunoassays are soon adapted to analyze a variety of hormones, drugs, and toxins. Yalow is honored with the Nobel Prize in physiology or medicine in 1977 "for the development of radioimmunoassays of peptide hormones."

(B)

1960s

Elias J. Corey develops new methods of synthesizing organic molecules.

Many *organic* compounds are large molecules with complex structures. They are useful in a variety of industrial applications from pharmaceuticals to paints and dyes. Since making these molecules in the laboratory can be difficult, synthetic chemists are constantly developing new methods to combine simple chemicals to create complex organic molecules. During the 1960s, American chemist Elias J. Corey (b. 1928) develops a new approach to organic synthesis called retro synthetic analysis. Before synthesizing a molecule, he considers its final structure. He then scans the molecules, looking for the best bonds to break, and the easiest components to synthesize separately, then brings together the final product. His approach yields new synthesis for hundreds of *organic* molecules, including many natural products. He is honored with the Nobel Prize in chemistry in 1990 "for his development of the theory and methodology of organic synthesis."

(C)

John Tuzo Wilson describes plate tectonics.

Throughout the 1960s, Earth scientists began to understand how mountain ridges below the ocean form. Evidence points to *seafloor spreading,* a process where volcanic lava comes to the surface at ridges in the ocean, causing the seafloor to spread. In the late 1960s, Canadian geologist John Tuzo Wilson (1908–93) proposes that the seafloor spreads at faults in the ocean. He states that the landmasses move on plates that cover the Earth, providing a mechanism for the movement of the continents proposed by the *continental drift* theory. Today, the field is known as *plate tectonics.*

(ES, MS)

Sir Nevill Francis Mott describes semiconductors.

Advances in physics have been used by engineers to advance technology. Electronics depends upon the study of how different materials conduct *electricity.* During the 1960s, Sir Nevill Francis Mott (1905–96) describes the rules that determine how some materials can conduct electricity under certain conditions and act as insulators under other conditions. Such materials, known as *semiconductors,* are important components in a number of different electronic devices. Mott shares the Nobel Prize in physics in 1977 with Philip Warren Anderson and John Hasbrouck van Vleck "for their fundamental theoretical investigations of the electronic structure of magnetic and disordered systems."

(P)

Scientists show that weak nuclear forces behave like electromagnetic forces.

Physicists study the various *forces* that lead to interactions between the particles that make up all matter. In the 1960s, three scientists studying the weak nuclear forces between *subatomic particles* demonstrate that

SEAFLOOR SPREADING

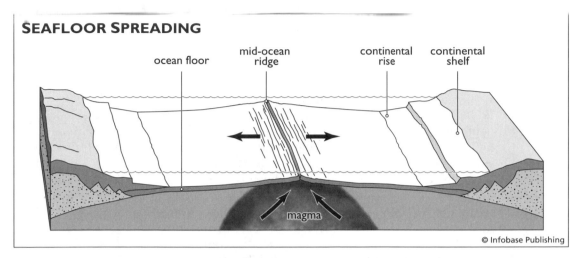

New regions of the ocean floor are generated by seafloor spreading, a process that occurs at sites where two tectonic plates meet. In the region between the plates, hot magma travels to the surface and becomes rapidly cooled by the ocean waters.

these forces are the same as the *electromagnetic* forces. Pakistani physicist Abdus Salam (1926–96) and American physicist Steven Weinberg (b. 1933) use different approaches to show that this is true for particles such as *electrons*. American physicist Sheldon Glashow (b. 1932) extends their findings to a number of other particles, including *protons* and *neutrons*. The three share the Nobel Prize in physics in 1979 "for their contributions to the theory of the unified weak and electromagnetic interaction between elementary particles, including, inter alia, the prediction of the weak neutral current."

(P)

Roald Hoffmann and Robert Woodward explain the formation of molecules with ring structures.

Many chemists are interested in synthesizing complex molecules using simpler chemicals in the laboratory. Some of the most challenging of these *organic* syntheses are biologically important molecules. Often, these molecules have *atoms* connected to one another in a way that forms a ring structure. During the early 1960s, American chemist Roald Hoffmann (b. 1937) and Robert Woodward try to synthesize vitamin B_{12}, but they have difficulty finding chemical reactions that lead to the formation of some of the rings. By studying these reactions, they establish the Woodward-Hoffman rules for reactivity. Hoffman is honored with the Nobel Prize in chemistry in 1981, "for their theories, developed independently, concerning the course of chemical reactions."

(C)

1960

Peter Mitchell explains how cells store energy.

Many 20th-century chemists and biologists studied how cells extract *energy* from food. They found that this energy is stored in the form of a molecule called *ATP*, and that ATP is synthesized in an *organelle* called the *mito-*

chondria. At an international meeting held in 1960, British scientist Peter Mitchell (1920–92) outlines his theory on how energy is captured and stored as ATP. He proposes that the formation of ATP is linked to the transport of *protons* across the *membrane* that surrounds mitochondria. Biologists later work out the details of this process (*See* entry for OCTOBER 1973). Mitchell is honored with the Nobel Prize in chemistry in 1978 "for his contribution to the understanding of biological energy transfer through the formulation of the chemiosmotic theory."

(B, C)

Leon Lederman, Melvin Schwartz, and Jack Steinberger begin building a neutrino beam.

Neutrinos are *subatomic particles* that are produced during *fusion* reactions. Beginning in the late 1950s, physicists argued whether there is more than one type of neutrino. In 1960, American physicists Leon Lederman (b. 1922), Melvin Schwartz (b. 1932), and Jack Steinberger (b. 1921) begin building a neutrino beam, an instrument that allows them to study the interactions of neutrinos without interference from other subatomic particles. Soon after, the three scientists use the neutrino beam to discover the muon neutrino. In 1988, they share the Nobel Prize in physics "for the neutrino beam method and the demonstration of the doublet structure of the *leptons* through the discovery of the muon neutrino."

(P)

Abraham Robinson studies infinitesimals.

Any number can be divided by two an infinite number of times without disappearing. Eventually these numbers get extremely small. Mathematicians define infinitesimals as numbers that are so small they approach zero without reaching it. In 1960, German mathematician Abraham Robinson (1918–

74) develops nonstandard analysis, which allows mathematicians to study infinitesimals.

(M)

The Leakeys discover *Homo habilis.*

Paleontologists studying the *evolution* of human beings have found evidence of a number of different species of humans that existed millions of years ago. In 1960, British anthropologists Louis (1903–92) and Mary Leakey (1913–96) identify a new species, *Homo habilis,* from remains found in Tanzania. Scientists believe that *Homo habilis* lived nearly 2 million years ago. Fossils of *Homo habilis* have been found with many artifacts that appear to be tools.

(B)

April 1

The first weather satellite is launched.

Accurate weather forecasting relies upon measurements of atmospheric conditions such as pressure and temperature, as well as data on the movement of clouds and air masses. The successful launch of satellites that orbit the Earth suggests that weather forecasting could be improved. On April 1, 1960, the first weather satellite, called *TIROS* (television infrared observational satellite), is launched. *TIROS* provides valuable pictures of the atmosphere, greatly improving understanding of atmospheric conditions.

(SA, W)

April 22

Ivar Giaever demonstrates tunneling of electrons through superconductors.

Certain materials known as *superconductors* can conduct *electricity* with almost no resistance (*See* entry for 1911). On April 22, 1960, American physicist Ivar Giaever (b. 1929) uses superconductors to create a

The United States launches the weather satellite, television infrared observation satellite (TIROS), in 1960. *(NASA)*

tunnel junction. He shows that *electrons* will "tunnel" or travel through the superconductor. His work leads to a better understanding of superconductors and how they can be used in electronic applications. Leo Esaki and Ivar Giaever share the Nobel Prize in physics in 1973 "for their experimental discoveries regarding tunneling phenomena in semiconductors and superconductors, respectively."

(P)

August 6

Theodore Maiman builds the first functional laser.

Engineers in the 20th century applied many of the advances in physics to create useful products. Physicists had discovered that *atoms* can emit *energy*. Later, they used *microwaves* to stimulate such energy emission, creating a device known as a *maser*. Some theorized that light could be used to stimulate similar emissions. On August 6, 1960, American physicist Theodore Maiman (b. 1927) reports the creation of the first functional *laser*. He uses a ruby to create a beam of light with a single wavelength. Today, lasers are used in applications ranging from barcode readers to surgery.

(P)

December

Luis Alvarez detects new subatomic particles.

In order to study *subatomic particles,* physicists must devise and build complex instruments capable of generating and detecting short-lived particles. In December 1960, American physicist Luis Alvarez (1911–88) describes improvements to one such instrument, known as the bubble chamber. A bubble chamber detects subatomic particles by following the path of the bubbles they create when passed through liquid kept at its

boiling point. Alvarez creates a large bubble chamber and uses it to detect particles that exist for less than a trillionth of a second. Nearly 150 different particles are detected using his bubble chamber. Alvarez is honored with the Nobel Prize in physics in 1968 "for his decisive contributions to elementary particle physics, in particular the discovery of a large number of resonance states, made possible through his development of the technique of using hydrogen bubble chamber and data analysis."

(P)

1961

Scientists prove that tuberculosis is transmitted through the air.

Tuberculosis is a devastating infectious disease that leads to death for many patients. In the 1950s, biologists recognized that a *bacterium* causes the disease and that patients can spread the disease to others. In 1961, a group of scientists led by Richard Riley completes a study that shows the disease is transmitted through the air. They expose guinea pigs to air piped in directly from the tuberculosis ward of the hospital. The animals contract the disease with no other exposure, proving that the disease can be disseminated by air.

(B)

Roger Sperry discovers that different sides of the brain have different functions.

The brain is divided into two sides, called hemispheres. American scientist Roger Sperry (1913–94) was interested in how these two hemispheres function. He performed experiments in monkeys that suggested that each side of the brain has its own function. Then, in 1961, he discovers a group of human patients who had the connection between the left and right hemisphere severed. Through a series of studies on these patients, he details the specialization of each side of the brain. Sperry is honored with the Nobel Prize in physiology or medicine in 1981 "for his discoveries concerning the functional specialization of the cerebral hemispheres."

(B)

Albert Ghiorso produces lawrencium in the laboratory.

In the laboratory, physicists can produce *elements* that are not found on Earth. In 1961, American scientist Albert Ghiorso (b. 1915) and his colleagues generate several *isotopes* of an element with 103 *protons* by bombarding *atoms* of californium with boron *ions*. The newly discovered element is named lawrencium after Ernst Lawrence, who developed the cyclotron (*See* entry for 1930).

(C, P)

January 7

Julius Axelrod describes the reuptake of neurotransmitters.

During the 20th century, neurobiologists began to understand how nerves carry information through the body. Nerve impulses lead to the release of chemicals called *neurotransmitters* at the *synapses,* where two nerves meet. Many believed that neurotransmitters were destroyed after sending their messages. On January 7, 1961, American biologist Julius Axelrod (1912–2004) publishes experiments that show this is not true. He shows that rather than being destroyed, the neurotransmitter is taken back up by the nerve cell. His finding leads to a new class of drugs that act on the nervous system, reuptake inhibitors, which are used to treat depression. Axelrod shares the Nobel Prize in physiology or medicine in 1970 with Sir Bernard Katz and Ulf von Euler "for their discoveries concerning the humoral transmittors in the nerve terminals

and the mechanism for their storage, release and inactivation."

(B)

April 12

Yury Gagarin is the first man to orbit the Earth.

As described in the sidebar "Exploring Space," throughout the late 1950s and 1960s the United States and the Soviet Union rushed to explore space. On April 12, 1961, Soviet cosmonaut Yury Gagarin (1934–68) becomes the first man to travel in space. His spacecraft, *Vostok I,* orbits the Earth in a trip that takes one hour and 48 minutes. After completing its orbit, *Vostok I* returns to Earth, and Gagarin parachutes out to avoid being injured on impact.

(SA)

1962

Harry Hammond Hess proposes that the seafloor spreads.

As the 20th century proceeded, scientists embraced many aspects of the *continental drift* theory, which states that the continents were once joined and then moved apart. Scientists considering this theory wondered how the continents move. In 1962, Harry Hammond Hess (1906–69) provides insight into the mechanism of *continental drift* when he puts forth his theory of *seafloor spreading* in the paper "History of Ocean Basins." Hess proposes that the seafloor spreads by molten rock from the inner Earth coming up to the ocean floor at the ocean ridges. Upon reaching the ocean, the rock solidifies, creating new seafloor. The force of this *seafloor spreading* will push the continents, allowing them to move. Geologists today continue gathering data supporting Hess's theory.

(ES, MS)

Lars Hörmander and John Milnor receive the Fields medal.

As described in the sidebar "Awarding Science," the Fields medal is awarded every four years to young mathematicians. In 1962, Swedish mathematician Lars Hörmander (b. 1931) and American mathematician John Milnor (b. 1931) receive the honor. Hörmander's award-winning work involves partial differential equations. Milnor's work leads to the creation of the field of differential *topology*.

(M)

Murray Gell-Mann classifies subatomic particles.

During the mid-20th century, advances in particle physics led to the discovery of many different *subatomic particles*. In 1962, American physicist Murray Gell-Mann (b. 1929) devises a scheme to classify these particles by separating them into eight different groups based on their properties. He calls his system "The Eightfold Way." Gell-Mann proposes that the subatomic particles that scientists had uncovered are made from even smaller particles that he calls *quarks*. He is honored with the Nobel Prize in physics in 1969 "for his contributions and discoveries concerning the classification of elementary particles and their interactions."

(P)

George Olah isolates a stable reaction intermediate.

Many chemical reactions involve the creation of an unstable intermediate that is destroyed before the reaction is complete. One such intermediate, the carbocation, is a positively charged fragment of a carbon-containing molecule. In 1962, American chemist George Olah (b. 1927) shows that carbocations can be prepared in the laboratory. His work allows carbocations to be studied and leads to their use in industrial applications such as petroleum cracking. Olah is honored with the Nobel Prize in

chemistry in 1994 "for his contribution to carbocation chemistry."

(C)

Rachel Carson describes pollution from pesticides.

Rapid advances in chemistry throughout the 20th century were applied to a number of industries. Agriculture benefited from the production of pesticides that save crops from insects. In 1962, American ecologist Rachel Carson (1907–64) publishes her controversial book *Silent Spring* describing the environmental impact of agricultural chemicals. The book quickly becomes a best seller and helps spur the environmentalist movement throughout the 1960s and 1970s.

(B)

Herbert Brown publishes a description of borohydrides.

Some chemists devote their careers to synthesizing new compounds in the laboratory, starting with simple chemicals—a field known as *organic* synthesis. They study the chemical bonds they want to make and look for reactions that will create them. In 1962, American chemist Herbert Brown (1912–2004) helps this field when he describes in his book *Hydroboration* new molecules that he created containing the element boron. The molecules he creates, called borohydrides, are used to remove impurities from the products of organic synthesis. Brown shares the Nobel Prize in chemistry in 1979 with Georg Wittig "for their development of the use of boron- and phosphorus-containing compounds, respectively, into important reagents in organic synthesis."

(C)

Brian Josephson describes electron behavior at the junction of two superconductors.

The discovery that matter has the properties of both a wave and a particle led to the discovery of a phenomenon called *electron* tunneling. Physicists demonstrated that electrons can pass through a solid. This work was particularly applicable to materials that conduct *electricity* with little or no *friction,* known as *superconductors* (*See* entry for 1911). In 1962, British physicist Brian Josephson (b. 1940) shows that the behavior of electrons will change at the junction of two superconductors. This so-called Josephson effect is later experimentally proven. Josephson is honored with the Nobel Prize in physics in 1973 for his work "for his theoretical predictions of the properties of a supercurrent through a tunnel barrier, in particular those phenomena which are generally known as the Josephson effects."

(P)

Neil Bartlett produces a compound using an inert gas.

The *elements* have been arranged into the *periodic table* of the elements based upon their properties. Chemists later discovered that that the number of *electrons* in the outer shell of an element determines the types of reactions it will undergo. One family of elements, the inert or *noble gases,* do not have free electrons in their outer shell, and thus there were no known compounds containing these elements. In 1962, British chemist Neil Bartlett (b. 1932) prepares a compound using the inert gas xenon. His works leads to the synthesis of a number of xenon containing compounds.

(C)

Stanley Cohen discovers a new growth factor.

Cells grow in response to chemical signals, or growth factors, secreted by other cells. In 1952, Rita Levi-Montalcini discovered nerve growth factor (NGF) the first such chemical to be identified (*See* entry for 1952). While studying NGF, American scientist Stanley Cohen (b. 1922) discovers a second factor that stimulates growth of epidermal cells in the skin. Later studies show that the epidermal growth factor (EGF) stimulates a wide array of cells including cells in the liver and ovaries. Cohen and Levi-Montalcini share the Nobel Prize in physiology or medicine in 1986 for their discoveries of growth factors.

(B)

January

David Hubel and Torsten Wiesel explain how the brain processes vision.

A number of different factors work together to allow vision. The eye perceives light, setting off series of chemical reactions that culminate in information being sent to the brain, where it is processed. In January 1962, American biologists David Hubel (b. 1926) and Torsten Wiesel (b. 1924) report studies that show how nerve impulses are carried from the eye to the visual processing centers in the brain. They map several key regions in the brain that are required for vision. Hubel and Wiesel share the Nobel Prize for physiology or medicine in 1981 "for their discoveries concerning information processing in the visual system."

(B)

December

Riccardo Giacconi detects X-rays from outside the solar system.

Astronomers in the 20th century studied the various forms of *radiation* found in space. American astrophysicist Riccardo Giacconi (b. 1931) was particularly interested in *X-rays*. He constructed a variety of telescopes to map and measure cosmic X-rays. In December 1962, he detects X-rays that come from outside the solar system. He later proves that background X-ray radiation exists in the universe. Giacconi is awarded the Nobel Prize in physics in 2002 "for pioneering contributions to astrophysics, which have led to the discovery of cosmic X-ray sources."

(P, SA)

December 14

Mariner 2 flies by Venus.

As described in the sidebar "Exploring Space," throughout the 1960s NASA led the United States in space exploration. One goal was to send spacecrafts to study other planets. On December 14, 1962, the unmanned spacecraft *Mariner 2* becomes the first to encounter another planet, when it flies within 22,000 miles (35,000 km) of the planet Venus. Using data collected by *Mariner 2,* NASA scientists learn that Venus rotates in the opposite direction of the Earth. *Mariner 2* also reveals that Venus has an extremely hot carbon dioxide–based atmosphere, and that most of the planet is covered in clouds.

(SA)

1963

Roy Glauber describes the behavior of light particles.

Physicists at the beginning of the 20th century explained that light could be thought of as both a particle and a wave (see sidebar "The Beginnings of Quantum Mechanics"). Further work during this century showed that light could take on different forms. Light that comes from a lightbulb is a mixture of frequencies, while light emitted from a *laser* is a single frequency. In 1963, American physicist Roy Glauber (b. 1925) explains the difference between these two types of light. His work lays the basis for *quantum optics.* Glauber is honored with the Nobel Prize in physics in 2005 "for his contribution to the quantum theory of optical coherence."

(P)

Allan Cormack and Godfrey Hounsfield develop the CAT scan.

The discovery of *X-rays* has had a great impact on medical diagnosis. During the 1960s, American physicist Allan Cormack (1924–98) wanted to improve the ability of X-rays to distinguish soft tissues. He develops a method known as computer axial tomography (CAT) in 1963. His technique uses computers to analyze and compile X-ray photographs taken at a variety of different angles, giving physicians a three-dimensional view of the body. Unfortunately, the computing power at the time of his invention was not sufficient to make the method widely applicable. In 1968, British physicist Godfrey Hounsfield (1919–2004) independently develops the CAT scan. Soon his invention is widely used in medical practices. Cormack and Hounsfield share the Nobel Prize in physiology or medicine in 1979 "for the development of computer assisted tomography."

(B, P)

Arno Penzias and Robert Wilson discover cosmic microwave background.

Cosmologists in the 20th century debated two different theories of the universe. Adherents of the *big bang theory* believed that the universe is expanding. Others believed in so-called steady-state cosmology, arguing that the universe remains the same size. In 1963, German physicist Arno Penzias (b. 1933) and American physicist Robert Woodrow Wilson (b. 1936) refute the steady-state theory of the universe when they discover cosmic microwave background. Such *radiation* was predicted by the *big bang theory* and could not be explained by the steady-state theory. Penzias and Wilson are honored with the Nobel Prize in physics in 1978 "for their discovery of cosmic microwave background radiation."

(P, SA)

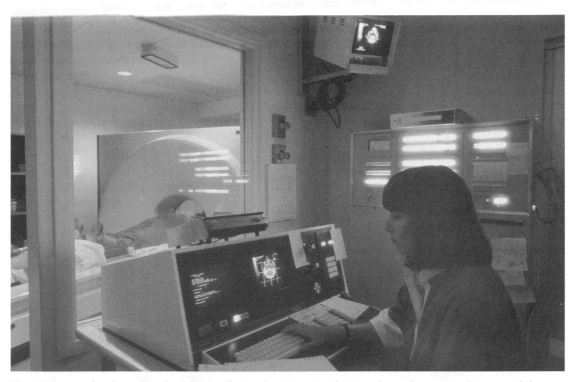

The CAT scan, developed in the 1960s, allows physicians to obtain a three-dimensional image of the human body. *(NCI)*

Baruch Blumberg discovers hepatitis B virus in the blood of patients.

A number of different *viruses* infect the liver and cause varying degrees of inflammation. These viruses are commonly known as hepatitis viruses. In 1963, American physician Baruch Blumberg (b. 1925) discovers markers or *antigens* from the hepatitis B virus in the blood of infected patients. His discovery allows scientists to screen donated blood for the presence of the hepatitis B virus. Blumberg shares the Nobel Prize in physiology or medicine in 1976 with Daniel Carleton Gajdusek "for their discoveries concerning new mechanisms for the origin and dissemination of infectious diseases."

(B)

Roy Kerr solves Einstein's Field Equations.

Einstein's General Theory of *relativity* attempts to describe the affects of gravitational *forces* on space and time. A number of mathematical equations, known as Einstein's Field Equations, can be derived from the theory. These equations proved to be immensely difficult to solve. In 1963, New Zealander mathematician Roy Kerr (b. 1934) discovers a solution to Einstein's Field Equations. His work leads to a description of *black holes*.

(M, P)

Baruj Benacerraf studies the genetics of the immune system.

The immune system protects the body from a variety of microorganisms. One of the hallmarks of the immune system is its ability to specifically recognize foreign molecules, called *antigens*. In 1963, American immunologist Baruj Benacerraf (b. 1920) studies the genetics of the immune system. He finds that some guinea pigs have immune systems that are better at fighting off infections than others. He then maps the *gene* responsible for this trait. Benacerraf shares the Nobel Prize in physiology or medicine in 1980 with Jean Dausset and George D. Snell "for their discoveries concerning genetically determined structures on the cell surface that regulate immunological reactions."

(B)

Zhores Alferov develops the heterostructure laser.

Modern electronic devices rely upon specialized *semiconductors* composed of thin layers of differing sized gaps called heterostructures. In 1963, Russian physicist Zhores Alferov (b. 1930) patents a *laser* made of heterostructures. Soon the technology is improved, and heterostructure lasers become key components in electronic devices such as barcode readers and compact disc players. Alferov shares the Nobel Prize in physics in 2000 with Herbert Kroemer for "for developing semiconductor heterostructures used in high-speed- and opto-electronics."

(P)

Richard Doell and Allan Cox describe reversals in the Earth's magnetic field.

The Earth's *magnetic field* undergoes periodic reversals, meaning that sometimes what is today considered the magnetic North is actually South. During the 1920s, Earth scientists noted that rocks dating to different time periods have different magnetic polarities. In 1963, American geologists Richard Doell (b. 1923) and Allan Cox (1926–87) commence a program to map the changes in the magnetic polarity. They examine volcanic rock,

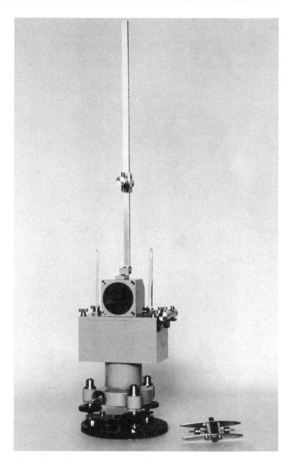

The Z-variometer was one of the instruments used by scientists studying changes in the Earth's magnetism during the 1950s and 1960s. *(NOAA, Historic C&GS Collection)*

correlating its magnetic polarity with its age. By 1966, they create a time line of magnetic reversals that dates back over 3 million years.

(ES)

February 5

Maarten Schmidt discovers quasars.

During the 20th century, some astronomers used radio telescopes to map sources of *radio waves* in space. Dutch astronomer Maarten

Schmidt (b. 1929) examined these radio sources with a light telescope. On February 5, 1963, he finds that not all radio sources can be directly correlated with visible objects. These points are called "quasi stellar radio sources" or *quasars*. Schmidt shows that quasars are objects moving rapidly away from the Earth, providing more evidence that the universe is expanding.

(SA)

March

Edward Lorenz mathematically expresses the limits to predicting weather.

Meteorologists study atmospheric conditions, satellite images, and the movements of *air currents*, yet they still cannot always accurately predict the weather. In March 1963, American meteorologist Edward Lorenz (b. 1917) shows mathematically that the weather cannot be predicted accurately. He uses a computer program to show that extremely small variations in initial conditions have a huge effect on the predicted weather. When explaining his work, he offers the now famous example that a butterfly flapping its wing in one part of the world changes the weather across the globe. His prediction is often referred to as the "Butterfly Effect."

(W)

June 16

Valentina Tereshkova becomes the first woman to travel in space.

As described in the sidebar "Exploring Space," the United States and the Soviet Union were locked in a space race during the 1960s. At that time, the Soviet Union trained four women as cosmonauts. On June 16, 1963, Russian cosmonaut Valentina Tereshkova (b. 1937) becomes the first woman to travel in space. In *Vostok* 6, she orbits the Earth 48 times during a 70-hour flight. She is the only female cosmonaut from that group to orbit the Earth. It will be 20 years before another woman, American astronaut Sally Ride (b. 1951), travels in space.

(SA)

1964

Val Logsdon Fitch and James Watson Cronin study symmetry.

Physicists have noted that most *forces* have symmetry, meaning the interactions occur in the same way if the process is reversed. Particle physicists study symmetry to see if it holds true for *subatomic particles*. Two forms of symmetry were shown to not hold true for weak forces between subatomic particles (*See* entry for 1957). In 1964, American physicists James Watson Cronin (b. 1931) and Val Logsdon Fitch (b. 1923) study symmetry by observing the decay of a particle called the K-*meson*. They show that symmetry does not hold when matter is converted to *antimatter*. Fitch and Cronin are honored with the Nobel Prize in physics in 1980 "for the discovery of violations of fundamental symmetry principles in the decay of neutral K-mesons."

(P)

Georgy Flerov and colleagues create the element rutherfordium.

During the 20th century, physicists began to create in the laboratory many *elements* that are not found on Earth. The discovery of these so-called *transfermium elements* was often controversial, perhaps because they usually exist for only a short period of time. In 1964, Russian physicist Georgy Flerov (1913–1990) and colleagues bombard an *isotope* of plutonium with neon *ions* to create *atoms* with 104 *protons*. Their claim is not widely accepted. Five years later, a group of physicists in California create the same element using a different method. Eventually, chemists acknowledge that both groups created the element, and it is named rutherfordium after the chemist Ernst Rutherford.

(C, P)

Walter Kohn provides a mathematical explanation of atomic structure.

Advances in *quantum mechanics* in the 20th century allowed scientists to develop structural models of *atoms* and how they interact to form molecules. In 1964, American chemist Walter Kohn (b. 1923) simplifies the calculations that describe atoms involved in chemical bonds. He shows that the total *energy* of the system can be calculated if the *electron* density is known. Kohn is honored with the Nobel Prize in chemistry in 1998 "for his development of the density-functional theory."

(C)

May 16

Sir James Black develops beta-blockers.

Diseases of the heart and circulatory system affect many people in developed countries. On May 16, 1964, British physician Sir James Black (b. 1924) provides a powerful treatment for many of these conditions when he develops a class of drugs called beta-blockers. Black recognizes that physiological affects are regulated by *neurotransmitters* binding receptors on the surface of tissues. He reasons that he can control overstimulation of certain tissues, such as the heart, by developing a drug that will block the receptor. Today, many drugs work by blocking a variety of receptors, including drugs that regulate blood pressure and control heartburn. Black shares the Nobel Prize in physiology or medicine in 1988 with Gertrude Elion and George Hitchings "for their discoveries of important principles for drug treatment."

(B)

Summer

Richard Ernst improves nuclear magnetic resonance.

During the 20th century, physicists and chemist developed a number of different techniques to determine the structure of molecules. One technique, nuclear magnetic resonance (NMR), works by measuring the interaction of individual *atoms* in a molecule as it is passed through a *magnetic field*. In its early form, NMR could be used only to study a few atoms. In summer 1964, Swiss chemist Richard Ernst (b. 1933) begins a series of experiments that improve NMR. His work allows researcher to use NMR to determine the structure of more complex molecules, such as *proteins*. Today, high-resolution NMR is used by chemists regularly. Ernst is honored with the Nobel Prize in chemistry in 1991 "for his contributions to the development of the methodology of high-resolution nuclear magnetic resonance (NMR) spectroscopy."

(C)

July 15

Sune Bergström and Bengt Samuelsson describe the synthesis of prostaglandins.

Biologists have discovered a number of different molecules that regulate physiological process. In the 1950s, Swedish scientist Sune Bergström discovered a class of regulatory molecules derived from fatty acids called prostaglandins (*See* entry for 1957). Prostaglandins are important for regulating a variety of physiological processes from blood pressure to the onset of labor in pregnant women. On July 15, 1964, Bergström and Swedish scientist Bengt Samuelsson (b. 1934) publish a paper showing how the body makes prostaglandins. They share the Nobel Prize in physiology or medicine in 1982 for their work "for their discoveries concerning prostaglandins and related biologically active substances."

(B)

1965

Gordon Moore predicts the course of technological development.

Throughout the late 20th century, advances in the field of computer science continued at a rapid pace. In 1965, American engineer Gordon Moore (b. 1929) accurately predicts the pace of advances. He looks at the history of silicon chip development and states that the power of a silicon chip will double every 18 months. His prediction, known as Moore's Law, drives the computer industry through the end of the century.

(M, P)

Sir Aaron Klug uses electron microscopy to determine the three-dimensional structure of a virus.

Many biologists and chemists are interested in the three-dimensional structure of molecules and its effect upon their biological function. A number of techniques and methods have been developed that allow these structures to be elucidated. In 1965, British chemist Sir Aaron Klug (b. 1926) develops crystallographic *electron* microscopy and uses the technique to determine the three-dimensional structure of a *virus*. The method has since been used to determine the structure of a number of *proteins*. Klug is honored with the Nobel Prize in chemistry in 1982 "for his development of crystallographic electron microscopy and his structural elucidation of biologically important nucleic acid-protein complexes."

(B, C)

Har Gobind Khorana and Marshall Nirenberg crack the genetic code.

Genetic information is passed from parent to offspring through *deoxyribonucleic acid* (DNA). DNA encodes the *proteins* that carry out vital functions in biological systems. How is the genetic information translated into proteins? In 1965, American biochemists Har Gobind

Khorana (b. 1922) and Marshall Nirenberg (b. 1927) separately carry out a series of experiments that elucidate the genetic code. They show how the building blocks of DNA, called nucleosides, are arranged to form a code. Nucleotides are arranged to form a triplet code that correlates to one of the 20 different *amino acids*. Amino acids are then joined together in the order dictated by DNA to form *proteins*. Khorana and Nirenberg share the Nobel Prize in physiology or medicine in 1968 with Robert Holley "for their interpretation of the genetic code and its function in protein synthesis."

(B)

Thomas Brock discovers bacteria living in hot springs.

Bacteria have evolved to live in a variety of different conditions. In 1965, Thomas Brock begins searching hot springs for bacteria that can survive at high temperatures. Among the strains of thermophillic, or heat-loving, bacteria that he identifies is one called *Thermus aquaticus*. These bacteria thrive in water that is nearly 212°F (100°C), the temperature at which water boils. Scientists later study the heat-stable *proteins* made by this bacteria. Later, one of its proteins, called a heat-stable DNA polymerase, becomes a critical part of the valuable laboratory technique known as the polymerase chain reaction (PCR).

(B)

February

Werner Arber shows that bacterial DNA is modified at specific sites.

Viruses called *bacteriophage* can infect *bacteria*. During the 1960s, researchers studying bacteriophage infections noticed that some bacteria resist infection by specific bacteriophage. In February 1965, Swiss biologist Werner Arber (b. 1929) publishes his work on the system *bacteria* use to protect against bacteriophage infection. Through the next decade, Arber's work shows that bacteriophage DNA is specifically destroyed by the bacteria. He describes a system with two components, one that modifies the bacterial DNA at specific sites, and the other that destroys unmodified DNA. His work leads to the isolation of *enzymes* that specifically cleave DNA, called restriction enzymes. Arber shares the Nobel Prize in physiology or medicine in 1978 with Daniel Nathans and Hamilton Smith "for the discovery of restriction enzymes and their application to problems of molecular genetics."

(B)

March 8

Linus Pauling and Emile Zuckerkandl use genes to time evolution.

During the 20th century, there were rapid advances in the understanding of *genes* and how they affect various traits in organisms. Biologists showed that *evolution* occurs as *genes* change or mutate. On March 8, 1965, Austrian biologist Emile Zuckerkandl and American chemist Linus Pauling publish a paper proposing that genes can be used to determine when different organisms evolutionarily diverge. They compare similar molecules from different species and estimate how long ago they diverged from one another. Their theory, known as the molecular clock, remains an important part of evolutionary biology.

(B)

March 18

Alexei Leonov becomes the first man to "walk" in space.

As described in the sidebar "Exploring Space," the Soviet Union and the United States vied to be the first to explore space throughout the 1960s. After both countries successfully sent people to orbit the Earth,

the next step was to have someone leave the spacecraft. On March 18, 1965, Soviet cosmonaut Alexei Leonov (b. 1934) becomes the first man to walk in space. He leaves the spacecraft *Voskhod 2* for 12 minutes. Almost three months later, Edward White becomes the first American to complete a spacewalk.

(SA)

March 19

Robert Holley describes the structure of tRNA.

Genetic information passes from parent to offspring through a molecule called *deoxyribonucleic acid* (DNA). DNA encodes the many *proteins* that play vital roles in cells. The link between DNA and proteins are small molecules called tRNA. tRNAs read the genetic code and bring the correct *amino acids* together to form *proteins*. On March 19, 1965, American biologist Robert Holley (1922–93) publishes a paper describing describes the structure of a tRNA molecule. Holley shares the Nobel Prize in physiology or medicine in 1968 with Har Gobind Khorana and Marshall Nirenberg "for their interpretation of the genetic code and its function in protein synthesis."

(B)

June

Lotfi Zadeh invents fuzzy logic.

The rapid development of computers in the 20th century led scientists and engineers to look for ways to make them respond more like humans. Computers use a system of logic that looks at a piece of information and decides if it is true or false. In June 1965, logician Lotfi Zadeh (b. 1921) devises a system known as fuzzy logic, in which computers act more like humans, considering a range of possibilities.

(M)

July 14

Mariner 4 takes pictures of Mars.

As described in the sidebar "Exploring Space," in the 1960s the United States and the Soviet Union began exploring space. They both sent manned spacecraft to orbit the Earth and explore the Moon, and unmanned crafts to study the planets. In 1964, the United States sends the unmanned spacecraft *Mariner 4* mission to take pictures of Mars. On July 14 and 15, 1965, *Mariner 4* takes the first pictures of the surface of Mars.

(SA)

1966

Sir Bernard Katz describes the mechanism of neurotransmitter release.

Scientists studying the brain have long been interested in how nerves transmit information to the various tissues of the body. They found molecules known as *neurotransmitters* that are released when nerves are stimulated. In 1966, Sir Bernard Katz (1911–2003) describes the mechanism of neurotransmitter release in his book *Nerve, Muscle, and Synapse*. He shows that upon stimulation, nerves that control muscles release a discrete quantity of neurotransmitters, and proposes that all types of nerves work by a similar mechanism. Katz shares the Nobel Prize in physiology or medicine in 1970 with Ulf von Euler and Julius Axelrod "for their discoveries concerning the humoral transmittors in the nerve terminals and the mechanism for their storage, release and inactivation."

(B)

Michael Atiyah, Paul Cohen, Alex Grothendieck, and Stephen Smale receive the Fields medal.

As described in the sidebar "Awarding Science," the Fields medal is presented to outstanding young mathematicians. In 1966, the honorees are British mathematician Michael Atiyah (b. 1929), American mathematician Paul Cohen (b. 1934), German mathematician Alexander Grothendieck (b. 1928), and American Stephen Smale (b. 1930). Atiyah worked on the interaction between the fields of *geometry* and analysis. Cohen worked in set theory. Grothendieck studied algebraic geometry. Smale worked on differential geometry and tackled many famous problems, including the Poincaré conjecture.

(B)

October 15

The United States establishes the endangered species list.

During the 1960s, many people began to realize the impact that human activity has on the environment. One of the most

The United States establishes the Endangered Species List in 1966. Among the protected animals are the stilt birds, shown here in the Kanahe Pond, Hawaii. *(Environmental Protection Agency/National Archives)*

obvious problems was the disappearance of animal species. To stop species from becoming extinct, the United States Congress passes the Endangered Species Preservation Act on October 15, 1966. As a part of the law, the U.S. Department of Interior issues the first Endangered Species List, naming animals that are protected under the law. Later legislation protects endangered plants and habitats as well.

(B)

1967

Dan McKenzie and W. Jason Morgan model plate movement.

During the 1960s, Earth scientists began gathering data that suggested landmasses move across the Earth on plates (*See* entry for 1960s). In 1967, British geologist Dan McKenzie and American geologist William Jason Morgan provide a mathematical explanation of how this plate movement can occur on a spherical planet. Their model gives mathematical credibility to the theory of *plate tectonics*.

(ES)

Jerome Friedman, Henry Kendall, and Richard Taylor prove that matter is made of quarks.

During the 20th century, physicists began to understand the *subatomic particles* that make up the *atom*. In the 1960s, Murray Gell-Mann proposed that all the known subatomic particles are made from building blocks he calls *quarks* (*See* entry for 1962). In 1967, American physicists Jerome Friedman (b. 1930) and Henry Kendall (1926–99), and Canadian physicist Richard Taylor (b. 1929) begin a series of experiments using a two-mile-long linear *accelerator* to determine the inner structure of *protons* and *neutrons*. Over the next six years, they gather evidence to demonstrate the existence of quarks. The three

scientists share the Nobel Prize in physics in 1990 "for their pioneering investigations concerning deep inelastic scattering of electrons on protons and bound neutrons, which have been of essential importance for the development of the quark model in particle physics."

(P)

Georgy Flerov produces dubnium.

During the 20th century, scientists began producing new *elements* by colliding *atoms* and *subatomic particles* in the laboratory. The properties of these so-called *transfermium elements* are not well understood because they usually exist for only a short period of time. In 1967, Russian physicist Georgy Flerov and colleagues report that they have produced a new element with 105 *protons* by bombarding the element americium with *ions* of neon. In 1970, a second group produces this element as well. For many years, the discovery and name of this new element is controversial. Finally, in 1997 the element is officially named dubnium to honor Dubra, the city of its discovery.

(C, P)

Charles Pederson synthesizes crown ethers.

In biological systems, *proteins* play a number of vital roles from catalyzing chemical reactions to facilitating communication between cells. Protein function depends upon the ability to specifically recognize and bind a variety of different molecules. Many chemists try to synthesize molecules that can bind a variety of molecules in a similar matter. In 1967, American chemist Charles Pederson (1904–89) synthesizes a class of molecules called crown ethers, which have the ability to bind a number of different metals. His discovery leads to the creation of molecules that react in a manner similar to proteins. Pederson shares the Nobel Prize in chemistry in 1987 with Donald Cram and Jean-Marie

Lehn "for their development and use of molecules with structure-specific interactions of high selectivity."

(C)

The cesium clock becomes the time standard.

The quest for accurate timekeeping devices has captured the imagination of scientist since antiquity. In 1967, the new standard becomes the cesium or atomic clock. Based upon the work of American physicist Norman Ramsey (b. 1915), atomic clocks rely on the passage of an *isotope* of cesium through a *magnetic field*. Ramsey is honored with the Nobel Prize in physics in 1989 for "for the invention of the separated oscillatory fields method and its use in the hydrogen maser and other atomic clocks."

(P)

January 1

The World Health Organization effort to eradicate smallpox begins.

Smallpox is a deadly infectious disease that can be prevented by vaccination. In 1967, the disease affected nearly 15 million people worldwide and killed an estimated 2 million people. On January 1 of that year, the World Health Organization begins a program to eradicate the disease by mass vaccination.

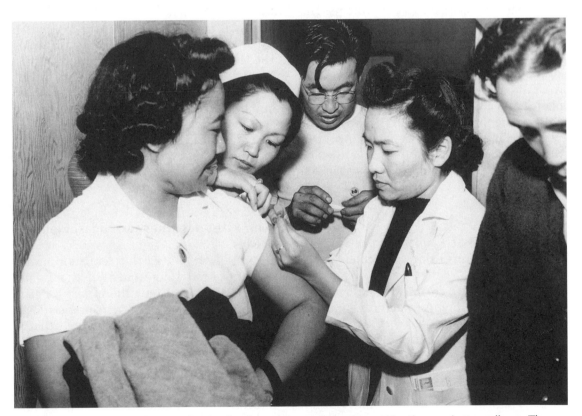

In 1967, the World Health Organization begins a program of mass vaccination against smallpox. The disease is eradicated by 1980. This photograph depicts an adult receiving a smallpox vaccination in 1942. *(Department of the Interior/ National Archives)*

By 1980, the disease is eradicated around the world.

(B)

February 17

Marshall Nirenberg and colleagues demonstrate that the genetic code is universal.

Genetic information is encoded in DNA, which is the template for the synthesis of the *proteins* that carry out vital functions in biological systems. As described in the sidebar "The Science of DNA," the genetic information is "transcribed" from DNA and carried out of the cell *nucleus* by a molecule known as mRNA. The mRNA is made up of a number of subunits called *nucleotides,* which form a code that is translated to form proteins. This process depends upon the correct reading of the genetic code. On February 17, 1967, American biologist Marshall Nirenberg and colleagues publish a paper showing that the same genetic code is shared by *bacteria,* plants, and animals—that is, the same mRNA will encode the same protein in all biological systems. Subsequent works have shown that there are some exceptions to this rule and that the genetic code is nearly universal.

(B)

March

Dudley Herschbach and Yuan Lee study chemical reactions using molecular beams.

Chemists studying chemical reactions need specialized instruments to help them understand how they take place. In March 1967, American chemists Dudley Herschbach (b. 1932) and Yuan Lee (b. 1936) begin a series of experiments using a technique known as molecular beams to study chemical reactions. The technique is particularly useful for studying short-lived reactions, such as the reaction between sodium and oxygen.

Herschbach and Lee share the Nobel Prize in chemistry in 1986 with John Polanyi "for their contributions concerning the dynamics of chemical elementary processes."

(C)

November 28

Anthony Hewish and Jocelyn Bell discover pulsars.

During the 20th century, astronomers began to map cosmic *radio waves*. On November 28, 1967, Irish astronomer Jocelyn Bell (b. 1943), a graduate student working with British astronomer Anthony Hewish (b. 1924), finds pulses of radio waves that occur at regular intervals. Bell and Hewish later show that these regular pulses of radio waves, which they call *pulsars,* come from distant stars. Today, astronomers have shown that pulsars originate from *neutron* stars. Hewish shares the Nobel Prize in physics in 1974 with Sir Martin Ryle "for their pioneering research in radio astrophysics: Ryle for his observations and inventions, in particular of the aperture synthesis technique, and Hewish for his decisive role in the discovery of pulsars."

(P, SA)

1968

Lynn Sykes describes earthquakes in the oceans.

During the 1960s, Earth scientists collected evidence that suggested that the Earth's landmasses move along the surface on giant plates. The theory of *plate tectonics* was developed from studying mountain ranges that lie beneath the ocean, the seafloor, and earthquakes (*See* entry for 1960s). In 1968, geophysicist Lynn Sykes studies the earthquakes that occur in the oceans. He tests a theory put forth by Canadian geologist John Tuzo Wilson that earthquakes in the ocean occur at the large ridges where plates meet. Sykes determines that this is true; earthquakes in the oceans occur in earthquake zones encompassing the mid-oceanic ridge and surrounding areas. His work provides more evidence for *plate tectonics.*

(ES, MS)

Lynn Margulis proposes that the mitochondria and chloroplasts arose from endosymbiosis.

Eukaryotic cells have many specialized compartments, called *organelles,* where specific cellular functions are performed. *Mitochondria* and *chloroplasts* are organelles that produce *energy* in cells. Unlike other organelles, both mitochondria and chloroplasts have their own DNA. In 1968, American biologist Lynn Margulis (b. 1938) proposes that these organelles were originally *bacteria.* Known as the endosymbiotic hypothesis, her theory states that during *evolution* certain bacteria began living inside of eukaryotic cells. In exchange, they provided energy to the cell. While her theory is criticized at first, it is now generally accepted.

(B)

William Knowles makes chiral molecules.

The function of many biologically important molecules depends upon the correct three-dimensional arrangement of *atoms.* In particular, the orientation of atoms around a carbon atom, known as its *chirality,* can determine if a molecule is biologically active or not. This poses a problem for chemists who wish to synthesize biologically active molecules because they must make sure that all of the atoms are in the correct spatial arrangement. In 1968, American chemist William Knowles (b. 1917) produces a catalyst that helps generate molecules of a specific chirality. His work leads to the production of the drug L-DOPA, which is used to treat Parkinson's disease. Knowles shares the Nobel Prize in chemistry in 2001 Ryoji Noyori "for their

work on chirally catalysed hydrogenation reactions."

(C)

June 22

Raymond Davis Jr. captures solar neutrinos.

Physicists studying *subatomic particles* have identified small-uncharged particles called *neutrinos.* Neutrinos are generated during nuclear reactions. By the 1960s, physicists captured neutrinos from nuclear power plants. During this time, American physicist Raymond Davis Jr. (b. 1914) believed that he could capture neutrinos generated from the nuclear reactions in the Sun. He built a large tank and devised a method to detect the particles by measuring the product of their interaction with certain *atoms.* On June 22, 1968, he obtains the first evidence that he has captured solar neutrinos. He reports his data in September of that year, although the number he finds is nearly three times lower than others had predicted. Davis shares the Nobel Prize in physics in 2002 with Masatoshi Koshiba "for pioneering contributions to astrophysics, in particular for the detection of cosmic neutrinos."

(P)

July 1

Georges Charpak invents the wire chamber.

Physicists in the 20th century studied the different *subatomic particles* that make up *atoms.* Studying such tiny particles required sophisticated instruments that are capable of detecting and recording their presence. On July 1, 1968, French physicist Georges Charpak (b. 1924) publishes a paper describing his new invention, the wire chamber. His wire chamber is capable of detecting up to 1 million particles per second, far more than the two particles per second that previous detectors could follow. Charpak is honored with the Nobel Prize in physics in 1992 "for his invention and development of particle detectors, in particular the multiwire proportional chamber."

(P)

December 24

Apollo 8 orbits the Moon.

As described in the sidebar "Exploring Space," during the 1960s the United States and the Soviet Union raced to explore outer space. In 1963, the United States initiated the Apollo program with the goal of sending a manned spacecraft to explore the Moon. On December 24, 1968, an important step toward this goal is taken when *Apollo 8* successfully orbits the Moon. The crew returns on December 27, just over six days after the spacecraft launched.

(SA)

1969

The U.S. Department of Defense creates ARPANET.

As computers became more powerful, they were used in a variety of scientific and government functions. During the 1960s, United States Department of Defense wanted to be able to join different computers in a network. In 1969, U.S. Advanced Research Project Agency (ARPA) develops a way for computers to communicate with one another. The ARPANET, as it becomes known, connects a handful of government and academic research labs together. Today, scientists recognize it as the predecessor of the Internet.

(M)

Paul Greengard begins his study of protein kinases in the brain.

Cells in the nervous system communicate with one another by sending chemicals across the space between two cells known as the *synapse*. These chemicals, called *neurotransmitters,* set off a cascade of events within the cell. In 1969, American biologist Paul Greengard (b. 1925) begins his study of the role of protein kinases in the brain. Subsequent studies show that protein kinases are the key molecules inside of neurons that convey the messages sent by neurotransmitters. Greengard shares the Nobel Prize in physiology or medicine in 2000 with Arvid Carlsson and Eric Kandel "for their discoveries concerning signal transduction in the nervous system."

(B)

Jean-Marie Lehn synthesizes complex crown ethers.

In 1967, Charles Pedersen discovered that some cyclic molecules, called crown ethers, can specifically bind *ions* (See entry for 1967). Two years later, French chemist Jean-Marie Lehn (b. 1939) synthesizes new crown ethers that are more complex and bind ions with greater specificity than the crown ethers discovered by Pedersen. Lehn's work is the basis for synthesizing molecules that mimic the action of *enzymes*, providing a model used by chemists to study the chemistry of some biological molecules. Lehn shares the Nobel Prize in chemistry in 1987 with Donald Cram and Charles Pederson "for their development and use of molecules with structure-specific interactions of high selectivity."

(C)

January

Roger Guillemin and Andrew Schally describe peptide hormones in the brain.

Different cells in the body produce and release *hormones* that are used to communicate with other tissues and organs. Beginning in the 1950s, American biologists Roger Guillemin (b. 1924) and Andrew Schally (b. 1926) devoted themselves to the study of hormones released in a particular region of the brain called the hypothalamus. While they were able to isolate the hormones from animal brains and showed how they function, the chemical nature of the hormones remains a mystery. In January 1969, they demonstrate that one of the hormones is a small peptide made of three *amino acids*. Scientists now recognize that the brain makes a variety of different peptide hormones, including growth hormone. Guillemin and Schally share the Nobel Prize in physiology or medicine in 1977 "for their discoveries concerning the peptide hormone production of the brain."

(B)

March

Jacob Bjerknes describes global climate patterns.

A variety of atmospheric conditions combine to make the weather. During the 1960s, meteorologists began to realize that certain changes in air pressure and ocean temperature lead to severe changes in the weather. The most famous of these weather patterns is known as El Niño. In 1969, American meteorologist Jacob Bjerknes describes how a cycle of changes in air pressure in South America, known as the Southern Oscillation, leads to changes in the weather in North America. His work shows that there is a pattern of global climate oscillations.

(W)

May

Gerald Edelman and Rodney Porter make a model of an antibody.

The immune system uses a variety of cells and molecules to protect the body from infection by microorganisms. One such molecule, the *antibody*, specifically recognizes foreign substances that the body has seen before. The three-dimensional structure of antibodies is critical for their proper function in the body. Beginning in 1959, American scientist Gerald Edelman (b. 1929) and British scientist Rodney Porter (1917–85) independently began stud-

ies on the structure of antibodies by cleaving the molecule into smaller parts that are easier to study. They continued making progress on the model throughout the 1960s, and in May 1969, Edelman completes the structure of an antibody. They share the Nobel Prize in physiology or medicine in 1972 "for their discoveries concerning the chemical structure of antibodies."

(B, C)

July 20

First manned lunar landing occurs.

As described in the sidebar "Exploring Space," the 1960s saw the United States and the Soviet Union race to explore space. In 1963, the United States initiated the Apollo program to explore the Moon. On July 16, 1969, *Apollo 11* launches, and on July 20, 1969, the United States successfully lands a manned

Apollo 11, the first manned spaceflight to land on the Moon, launches at 9:32 EDT on July 16, 1969. *(NASA)*

EXPLORING SPACE

Astronomers have been studying the stars for centuries. During the 20th century, the convergence of science and engineering allowed people to explore space. In less than two decades, space exploration went from calculations on paper to the landing of a manned mission on the Moon. The rapid pace of space exploration was the result of advances in technology and a strong political drive to explore space as the United States and the Soviet Union raced to dominate space.

The space age begins on October 4, 1957, when the Soviet Union launches the *Sputnik* space satellite. The launch shocks the American public, and the United States speeds the development of its own satellite program. Less than four months later, on January 31, 1958, the United States launches the *Explorer I* satellite. Each country continues to launch satellites and uses them to collect a variety of scientific data on the Earth and its atmosphere. The Explorer satellite program leads to the discovery of the Earth's magnetosphere. The Soviet Union uses the Sputnik program to study the effects of

space travel on living organisms by sending a dog into space. As a result of the Sputnik and Explorer programs, satellites become common tools used in weather prediction and communications within a few years.

The ability to successfully launch unmanned spacecrafts opens the possibility of direct observation of the solar system. During the 1960s and 1970s, a number of unmanned space probes are sent out to collect data from the other planets in the solar system. Both the United States and the Soviet Union send missions to Earth's closest neighbors, Mars and Venus. In 1975, the United States successfully lands an unmanned spacecraft, *Viking I*, on the surface of Mars. Other missions such as the *Voyager 1* and *2*, and the *Pioneer 10* are sent to the outer planets, and collect data on Jupiter, Saturn, Uranus, and Neptune.

While the photographs and data from unmanned space probes is exciting, few things capture the public's imagination like manned space missions. On April 12, 1961, the Soviet cosmonaut Yuri Gagarin becomes the first man

---

spacecraft on the Moon. Just over six hours later, American astronaut Neil Armstrong (b. 1930) becomes the first man to walk on the Moon. He and American astronaut Buzz Aldrin (b. 1930) spend the next 21 hours exploring the Moon and collecting rocks to bring back to Earth.

(SA)

September 15

Sir John Pople designs a computer program that analyzes chemical reactions. During the 20th century, advances in physics influenced our understanding of chemistry.

British chemist Sir John Pople (1924–2004) designed the Gaussian computer program, based on the laws of *quantum mechanics,* to analyze molecules and the chemical reactions they undergo. On September 15, 1969, he publishes a paper describing his work. In 1970, the first version of the program, Gaussian 70, becomes available. Over the next decades, Pople improves his program, and it is widely used in the field of theoretical chemistry. Pople is honored with the Nobel Prize in chemistry in 1998 "for his development of computational methods in quantum chemistry."

(C)

to travel in space. Nearly a year later, the United States sends American astronaut John Glenn (b. 1921) in the Mercury space capsule *Friendship 7* to orbit the Earth on February 20, 1962. In 1963, the Soviets send a female cosmonaut, Valentina Tereshkova, into space. Having successfully sent men (and a woman) into space, the programs turn to making crafts that can maneuver in space. In 1965, the Soviet *Voskhod I* is launched with a two-man crew. At one point during the mission, *Voskhod I* stops and allows one of the cosmonauts, Aleksey Leonov to "walk" in space. Soon the United States counters with the *Gemini 4* mission, in which a similar space walk is performed.

Soon, the United States space program turns its attention to sending a manned mission to the Moon. NASA scientists and engineers design the Apollo spacecrafts for this purpose. The spacecrafts consist of three modules, one of which, the lunar module is designed to detach from the craft and carry astronauts to the Moon. In February 1967, the first Apollo mission, *Apollo 1,* ends in tragedy when the craft catches fire on the launch pad, killing all three astronauts aboard. Despite the tragedy, the Apollo program soon resumes, carrying out a number of missions that test the spacecrafts' ability to orbit the Earth and reach the Moon. Finally, on July 16, 1969, the *Apollo 11* mission is launched, and four days later the lunar module carries American astronauts Neil Armstrong and Buzz Aldrin to the surface of the Moon. The United States sends four more Apollo missions to the Moon before discontinuing the program.

During the 1970s, the United States and the Soviet Union work toward establishing manned space stations. The Soviet Union launches a number of Salyut space stations in the early 1970s with limited success. By the late 1970s, however, cosmonauts inhabit the *Salyut 6* and *Salyut 7* space stations for up to 200 days at a time. The United States counters with the *Sky Lab* space station, which launches in 1973 and is manned and operational from May through November of that year.

In a period of 20 years, space exploration advances from the successful launching of a single satellite to the operation of a manned space station. The space programs leads to discoveries about the Earth and its atmosphere, the other planets in the solar system, as well as the effects of weightlessness on humans.

November 22

Jon Beckwith isolates a gene in the laboratory.

Genetic information, encoded by DNA, is found in discrete units called *genes*. On November 22, 1969, American biologist Jon Beckwith publishes a report showing that he has isolated a gene while studying the genetic control of sugar metabolism in *bacteria*. First, he moves the gene to a *virus* that infects bacteria, known as a *bacteriophage;* then he isolates the DNA encoding the gene itself and views it under the *electron* microscope. Beckwith's work ushers in an age in which DNA can be moved between organisms, making genetic engineering possible.

(B)

1970s

Sir Peter Mansfield develops a method to obtain MRI images.

Magnetic Resonance Imaging (MRI) is a widely used medical technique that allows physicians to obtain two-dimensional images of the human body. During the 1970s, British physicist Sir Peter Mansfield (b. 1933) develops a method to rapidly convert the raw data generated during an MRI to a visible image of tissues and body parts. Mansfield shares the Nobel Prize in physiology or medicine in 2003 with Paul Lautenbur "for their discoveries concerning magnetic resonance imaging."

(B, P)

Eric Kandel shows that learning is associated with changes in synapses.

Nerves transmit messages to one another and other tissues in the body by sending chemicals across small spaces called *synapses*. During the 1970s, American biologist Eric Kandel (b. 1929) studies the events that occur in neurons during learning, using the sea slug as a model. He finds that learning is associated with changes in synapse. If such changes are blocked, long-term memory and learning cannot occur. Kandel shares the Nobel Prize in physiology or medicine in 2000 with Arvid Carlsson and Paul Greenberg "for their discoveries concerning signal transduction in the nervous system."

(B)

1970

Alan Baker, Heisuke Hironaka, Serge Novikov, and John Thompson receive the Fields medal.

As described in the sidebar "Awarding Science," the Fields medal is awarded every four years to a group of outstanding young mathematicians. In 1970, British mathematician Alan Baker (b. 1939), Japanese mathematician Heisuke Hironaka (b. 1931), Russian mathematician Serge Novikov (b. 1938), and American mathematician John Thompson (b. 1932) are honored. Baker is honored for identifying new *transcendental numbers,* and his work on Diophantine equations. Hironaka's work focuses on algebraic geometry. Novikov states a fundamental problem in differential *topology,* known

as Novikov's conjecture. Thompson studies finite groups.

(M)

Stephen Hawking shows that black holes can emit radiation.

Black holes are celestial bodies where the force of *gravity* is so strong that even light cannot escape. For years, scientists assumed that they did not emit *radiation*. In 1970, British theoretical physicist Stephen Hawking (b. 1943) shows that black holes actually can emit a certain type of radiation. Using *quantum mechanics* and *relativity,* he derives an equation that describes this *radiation*.

(P, SA)

June

Leland Hartwell identifies genes that control cell growth.

For an organism to function properly, cells must grow in a controlled manner. Cancer is an example of a disease that occurs when cells grow out of control. In June 1970, American biologist Leland Hartwell (b. 1939) publishes the first of a series of studies designed to uncover how cells control their growth. He identified *genes* encoding *proteins* that are responsible for keeping cell growth in check. Hartwell shares the Nobel Prize in physiology or medicine in 2001 with Timothy Hunt and Sir Paul Nurse "for their discoveries of key regulators of the cell cycle."

(B)

June 27

Howard Temin and David Baltimore discover reverse transcriptase.

The flow of genetic information from the genetic material, DNA, to the *proteins* that do the work of the cell, uses another molecule called RNA. As described in the sidebar "The Science of DNA," the pathway of DNA to RNA to protein is known as the central dogma. On June 27, 1970, American biologists Howard Temin (1934–94) and David Baltimore (b. 1938) independently publish papers showing that the central dogma is not always true. They study a family of *viruses* called retroviruses. Retroviruses carry their genetic information on RNA rather than DNA. Once they infect a cell, they use the RNA as a template to synthesis DNA, which is a reversal of the central dogma. Temin and Baltimore share the Nobel Prize in physiology or medicine in 1975 with American biologist Renato Dulbecco "for their discoveries concerning the interaction between tumour viruses and the genetic material of the cell."

(B)

July

The United States government creates the Environmental Protection Agency.

During the 1960s, people began to become aware of dangerous pollution in the air, water, and food supply, and they searched for a way to bring it under control. In July 1970, the United States government creates the Environmental Protection Agency (EPA) to oversee environmental issues. The EPA works on environmental regulations, performs scientific research on environmental issues, funds projects to understand and clean up the environment, and educates the public on environmental issues.

(B)

July 28

Hamilton Smith isolates a restriction enzyme.

Bacteria have evolved a mechanism to recognize their own DNA by making modifications at specific sequences. *Proteins,* known as restriction *enzymes,* cut any DNA that is not modified. On July 28, 1970, American scientist Hamilton Smith (b. 1931) publishes a report stating that he has isolated a restric-

tion enzyme and shown that it can be used to cut DNA at a specific sequence. Since his discovery, many other restriction enzymes have been isolated. Today, they are used every day to manipulate DNA in the laboratory. Smith shares the Nobel Prize in physiology or medicine in 1978 with Werner Arber and Daniel Nathans "for the discovery of restriction enzymes and their application to problems of molecular genetics."

(B)

1971

Kenneth Wilson describes the mathematics of some phase transitions.

Matter can exist as a solid, a liquid, or a gas, and transitions occur between these three phases. Normally, these phase transitions occur over time, such as steam arising from a pot of boiling water. However, under certain conditions the phase transition can occur throughout the entire volume of matter at the same time. In 1971, American physicist Kenneth Wilson (b. 1936) provides a mathematical basis used to study these types of phase transitions. He is honored with the Nobel Prize in physics in 1982 "for his theory for critical phenomena in connection with phase transitions."

(P)

Günther Blobel describes how proteins find their proper home in the cell.

Proteins play a variety of important roles in biological organisms from catalyzing chemical reactions to providing cellular structure. Once a protein is synthesized, it must be directed to the proper location in the cell. How does a protein know where it ultimately belongs? In 1971, American biologist Günther Blobel (b. 1936) answers this question when he develops the signal hypothesis. He notes that all proteins contain a signal within their *amino acid* sequence that directs them to the proper location in the cell. Blobel is honored with the Nobel Prize in physiology or medicine in 1999 "for the discovery that proteins have intrinsic signals that govern their transport and localization in the cell."

(B)

Yves Chauvin presents a mechanism for metal-containing catalysts.

Chemists use catalysts, substances that accelerate the rate of chemical reactions, to synthesize new molecules in the laboratory. Catalysts with metals bound to a molecule that includes a carbon-carbon double bond are useful in metathesis reactions—chemical reactions where atoms bound to one part of an *organic* molecules are moved to another part of the same molecule. In 1971, French chemist Yves Chauvin (b. 1930) presents a mechanism explaining how metal-containing compounds catalyze metathesis reactions. He shares the Nobel Prize in chemistry in 2005 with Robert H. Grubbs and Richard R. Schrock "for the development of the metathesis method in organic synthesis."

(B)

March 25

Martin Rodbell discovers G-proteins.

Within an organism, individual cells must communicate with one another. Biologists call such communication, and the molecular pathways that they travel through, signal transduction. On March 25, 1971, American biologist Martin Rodbell (1925–98) publishes his discovery of a new type of *protein* involved in signal transduction. At the time, he recognizes that a signal is transmitted when a *hormone* binds to a receptor in the cell *membrane*, which leads to the formation of a molecule called a second messenger

(*See* entry for 1956). He realizes that a third protein must also be involved, one that carries the message from the receptor to the second messenger. He calls this a G-protein. Scientists now recognize that G-proteins are critical in a number of signal transduction pathways. Rodbell shares the Nobel Prize in physiology or medicine in 1994 with Alfred Gilman "for their discovery of G-proteins and the role of these proteins in signal transduction in cells."

(B)

April

The Soviet Union launches the first space station.

As described in the sidebar "Exploring Space," the United States and the Soviet Union raced to explore space in the 1960s and 1970s. In April 1971, the Soviet Union launches the first space station, *Salyut I.* A crew traveling in a Soyuz capsule docks with the station in June 1971 and inhabits it for three weeks. The Soviet Union continues developing space station technology throughout the century. Their work culminates in the launching of the International Space Station.

(SA)

October

Paul Crutzen describes ozone destruction.

The Earth's atmosphere is covered with a layer that contains the gas ozone. The *ozone layer* protects the planet from *ultraviolet radiation* from the Sun. In October 1971, Dutch chemist Paul Crutzen (b. 1933) publishes a paper describing the chemical mechanism of ozone destruction. He shows how gases called nitrogen oxides can catalyze or speed up the destruction of ozone. Later that year, American chemist Harold Johnston uses Crutzen's work to argue that supersonic airplanor that release nitrogen oxides could have a detrimental effect on the environment. Crutzen shares the Nobel Prize in chemistry in 1998 with Mario J. Molina and F. Sherwood Rowland "for their work in atmospheric chemistry, particularly concerning the formation and decomposition of ozone."

(C, ES)

October 1

Martinus Veltman and Gerardus 't Hooft provide a mathematical foundation for particle physics.

During the 20th century, many physicists studied the properties and interactions of *subatomic particles*. They discovered a host of subatomic particles and proposed the electroweak theory to describe the *forces* that hold them together. On October 1, 1971, Dutch physicists Gerardus 't Hooft (b. 1946) and Martinus Veltman (b. 1931) publish a mathematical foundation of the electroweak theory. They devise a computer model that allows physicists to calculate the physical properties of subatomic particles. Veltman and 't Hooft share the Nobel Prize in physics in 1999 "for elucidating the quantum structure of electroweak interactions in physics."

(P)

November

Ted Hoff invents the microprocessor.

During the 1950s and 1960s, computers became smaller and more powerful. The invention of the computer chip spread rapidly, helping to reduce the size of computers. A young American engineer named Ted Hoff (b. 1937) decided to make a chip that is programmable. The result of his work, the microprocessor, is introduced in November 1971. Hoff's microprocessor is as powerful as the ENIAC computer, which was big enough to fill a room (*See* entry for 1946). Today, microprocessors are fundamental components of computers.

(P)

November 24

Douglas Osheroff, Robert Richardson, and David Lee demonstrate superfluidity in ³He.

In the early 20th century, physicists observed that when an *isotope* of helium, ⁴He, is cooled to nearly *absolute zero,* it loses *friction* and becomes a superfluid. In 1971, American physicists Douglas Osheroff (b. 1945), David Lee (b. 1931), and Robert Richardson (b. 1937) investigate the properties of a lighter isotope of helium, ³He. On November 24, 1971, Osheroff makes an unexpected finding while trying to obtain helium ice by cooling the isotope to a fraction of a degree above absolute zero. The three scientist later show that ³He becomes a superfluid at this temperature. Superfluid ³He is later used to study a variety of physical phenomenon. Lee, Osheroff, and Richardson share the Nobel Prize in physics in 1996 "for their discovery of superfluidity in helium-3."

(P)

December

Dan Nathans creates a genetic map of a virus.

DNA carries genetic information in cells. During the 1960s, biologists discovered that *bacteria* make *enzymes* that will cut DNA at specific sites, called restriction enzymes. In December 1971, American biologist Dan Nathans (1928–99) publishes a paper showing how he used one of these enzymes to make a genetic map of a *virus* known as SV40. He isolates DNA from the virus, then treats it with the restriction enzyme. He shows that it cleaves the viral DNA into 11 discrete pieces. The cleavage pattern forms a map of the viral DNA, known as restriction map, which soon become powerful tools for studying DNA. Nathans shares the Nobel Prize in physiology or medicine in 1978 with Werner Arber and Hamilton Smith "for the discovery of restriction enzymes and their application to problems of molecular genetics."

(B)

December 23

Richard Nixon signs the National Cancer Act.

In 1971, cancer is recognized as the second-leading cause of death in the United States. During his State of the Union address, President Richard Nixon (1913–94) discusses cancer, and pledges more money aimed at eliminating the disease. He signs the National Cancer Act on December 23, 1971. The legislation gives an additional $100 million to the National Cancer Institute. While researchers have not yet eliminated cancer, many patients live much longer with the disease today than they would have in 1971.

(B)

1972

Anthony Leggett explains how atoms interact with one another in a superfluid.

During the 1920s, physicists discovered that when *isotopes* of helium are cooled to extremely low temperatures they lose all viscosity, a property called *superfluidity*. In 1972, British physicist Anthony Leggett (b. 1938) proposes a theory that explains how *atoms* of ^{3}He interact in a superfluid. His theory also helps physicists understand how matter transitions from one phase to another. Leggett shares the Nobel Prize in physics in 2003 with Vitaly Ginzburg and Alexei Abrikosov "for pioneering contributions to the theory of superconductors and superfluids."

(P)

René Thom introduces catastrophe theory.

Some mathematicians try to apply their work to real-life problems, such as computing or engineering. In 1972, French mathematician René Thom attempts to use mathematics to explain abrupt changes in either physical or social behavior. He introduces his catastrophe theory in his work *Structural Stability and Morphogenesis*. While once touted as a powerful theory, it has been criticized for, among other things, being more qualitative than quantitative.

(M)

October

Paul Berg constructs a recombinant DNA molecule.

As described in the sidebar "The Science of DNA," many 20th-century biologists and chemists studied DNA and how cells use the genetic information that it encodes. These studies led to the discovery of *enzymes* that modify DNA. In October 1972, American biologist Paul Berg (b. 1926) publishes a paper describing the use of these enzymes to construct a *recombinant* DNA molecule. He fuses DNA from a *virus* that infects apes to DNA from *bacteria*, forming a recombinant DNA molecule. He then introduces this new molecule into bacteria cells and shows that they now produce the *protein* encoded by the viral DNA. Today, recombinant DNA technology is a vital tool in biology laboratories. Berg is honored with the Nobel Prize in chemistry in 1980 "for his fundamental studies of the biochemistry of nucleic acids, with particular regard to recombinant-DNA."

(B, C)

1973

Paul Doherty and Rolf Zinkernagel describe how T cells work.

The immune system protects animals from a variety of foreign microorganisms. A number of different cells, collectively known as white blood cells, each play unique roles during an immune response. One of the most powerful components of the human immune system is the T cell. T cells kill other cells that are infected by microorganisms, limiting the infection from spreading throughout the body. In 1973, Australian biologist Peter Doherty (b. 1940) and Swiss biologist Rolf Zinkernagel (b. 1944) begin work that describes how T cells recognize infected cells. They share the Nobel Prize in physiology or medicine in 1996 "for their discoveries concerning the specificity of the cell mediated immune defense."

(B)

Paul Lauterbur develops a new imaging technique.

Advances in physics and chemistry often lend themselves to important new technologies. During the 1970s, American scientist Paul Lauterbur (b. 1929) worked on a technique called nuclear magnetic resonance (NMR), which is used by chemists to determine the structure of molecules. After observing biologists using NMR to study tissue samples, Lauterbur set out to apply NMR in a way that allows scientists to obtain two-dimensional images of tissues. He succeeds in 1973, and his work lays the basis for magnetic resonance imaging (MRI), a powerful noninvasive method to look inside the body. Lauterbur shares the Nobel Prize in physiology or medicine in 2003 with Sir Peter Mansfield "for their discoveries concerning magnetic resonance imaging."

(C, P)

June

David Gross, David Politzer, and Frank Wilczek describe the forces between quarks.

All matter is made of fundamental particles called *quarks*. Within the *atomic nucleus,* quarks are held together by strong *forces,* also known as the color force. In June 1973, David Gross (b. 1941), David Politzer (b. 1949), and Frank Wilczek (b. 1951) show that the color force between quarks is weaker when the quarks draw closer together and stronger when the quarks are farther apart. Their work establishes the basis of a new field, quantum chromodynamics (QCD). The three scientists share the Nobel Prize in physics in 2004 for "for the discovery of asymptotic freedom in the theory of the strong interaction."

(P)

October

Paul Boyer describes how cells synthesize ATP.

Cells must extract *energy* from food in the environment in order to power the many chemical reactions that are needed to sustain life. During the 20th century, biochemists discovered that ATP is generated in *organelles* called *mitochondria*. Peter Mitchell proposed that ATP synthesis is coupled to the transport of *protons* across the mitochondrial *membrane* (*See* entry for 1960). In October 1973, American biochemist Paul Boyer (b. 1918) proposes a mechanism to explain how the ATP synthesis reaction is actually carried out. His work is controversial at first, and he spends many years collecting data to support it. British biochemist John Walker (b. 1941) later confirms his theory. Boyer and Walker share the Nobel Prize in chemistry in 1997 "for their elucidation of the enzymatic mechanism underlying the synthesis of adenosine triphosphate (ATP)."

(B, C)

Michael Brown and Joseph Goldstein describe how cholesterol is regulated.

Cholesterol serves many important functions in living organisms. However, too much cholesterol in the bloodstream has been associated with heart disease. During the 1970s, American biologists Michael Brown (b. 1941) and Joseph Goldstein (b. 1940) studied families with a genetic predisposition to high cholesterol. In October 1973, their studies lead to the discovery of the molecule responsible for bringing cholesterol into the cell—called the LDL receptor. They go on to describe how cells take up cholesterol from the bloodstream, uncovering an important pathway in cell biology. Brown and Goldstein share the Nobel Prize in physiology or medicine in 1985 "for their discoveries concerning the regulation of cholesterol metabolism."

(B)

November 19

Hans Dehmelt isolates a single electron.

Physicists studying *subatomic particles* rely upon the development of powerful instruments that allow them to conduct their research. During the 1950s, German physicist Wolfgang Paul developed a trap that allows physicists to isolate charged molecules or *ions* (See entry for 1954). On November 19, 1973, American physicist Hans Dehmelt (b. 1922) publishes a paper describing the use of this trap to isolate a single *electron*. He then directly assesses a number of its physical properties. Dehmelt and Paul share the Nobel Prize in physics in 1989 "for the development of the ion trap technique."

(P)

December 3

Pioneer 10 reaches Jupiter.

As described in the sidebar "Exploring Space," a number of different crafts were sent to explore the solar system during the 1960s and 1970s. In 1972, NASA launched *Pioneer 10* on a course to the planet Jupiter. On December 3, 1973, the spacecraft comes within 125,000 miles (201,000 km) of the planet. In addition to taking pictures of Jupiter and its moons, *Pioneer 10* conducts a number of experiments that study the *magnetic field,* solar winds, atmosphere, and physical properties of the planet.

(SA)

1974

Burton Richter and Samuel Ting find the charm quark.

During the 20th century, many physicists investigated the properties and interactions of *subatomic particles*. During the 1960s, Murray Gell-Mann predicted that all particles are made up of even smaller building blocks he calls *quarks* (See entry for 1962). In 1974, American physicist Burton Richter (b. 1931) and Samuel Ting (b. 1936) independently discover the charm quark in the form of a particle made from the quark and its antiquark. The charm quark proves to be the first of many such particles to be discovered. Richter and Ting share the 1976 Nobel Prize in physics "for their pioneering work in the discovery of a heavy elementary particle of a new kind."

(P)

Mario Molina and F. Sherwood Rowland describe the destruction of the ozone layer.

The Earth's atmosphere is covered with a *ozone layer* that protects the planet from the ultraviolet rays of the Sun. During the 1970s, scientists began studying the effects of pollution on various components of the atmosphere. In 1974, American chemists Mario Molina (b. 1943) and F. Sherwood Rowlands (b. 1927) show that a family of chemicals called chlorofluorocarbons (CFCs) can break

DESTRUCTION OF THE OZONE LAYER BY AIR POLLUTANTS

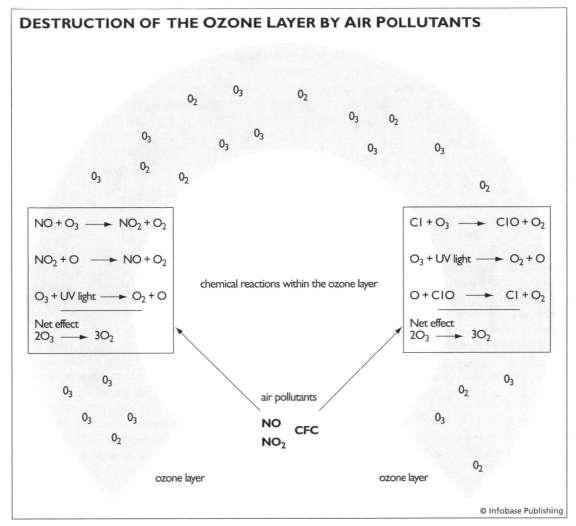

A series of chemical reactions between air pollutants, notably nitrous oxide (NO), chlorine aerosols (Cl), and atmospheric ozone (O_3), causes ozone to be degraded into oxygen molecules, leading to the destruction of the ozone layer.

down ozone. Their work leads to a movement to ban CFCs. Molina and Rowland share the Nobel Prize in chemistry in 1995 with Paul Crutzen "for their work in atmospheric chemistry, particularly concerning the formation and decomposition of ozone."

(C, ES)

Pierre-Gilles de Gennes describes the physics of liquid crystals.

Many physicists study the different phases of matter and how transitions occur between phases. During the 1920s, physicists discovered liquid crystals, a form of matter that has properties of both a liquid and a solid.

During the 1970s, French chemist Pierre-Gilles de Gennes (b. 1932) studied liquid crystals. In 1974, he publishes *The Physics of Liquid Crystals,* which becomes the standard text for scientists interested in the topic. Gennes is honored with the Nobel Prize in physics in 1991 "for discovering that methods developed for studying order phenomena in simple systems can be generalized to more complex forms of matter, in particular to liquid crystals and polymers."

(P)

Enrico Bombieri and David Mumford are awarded the Fields medal.

As described in the sidebar "Awarding Science," the Fields medal is awarded to outstanding young mathematicians every four years. In 1974, Italian mathematician Enrico Bombieri (b. 1940) and British mathematician David Mumford (b. 1937) receive the honor. Bombieri had studied a wide range of important mathematical problems, including *prime numbers, functions* of complex variables, and partial differential equations. Mumford is honored for his work on algebraic geometry.

(M)

Edward O. Wilson describes the biology of social behavior.

The intersection of biology and physiology is an active field of research. Some scientists try to correlate animal behavior to humans. In 1974, American biologist Edward O. Wilson publishes *Sociobiology: The New Synthesis.* In this work, he uses studies of animal behavior to explain human social behavior. He suggests that some behavior is genetically influenced. Although his book is quite controversial at the time of its publication, today neuroscientists have found that some behaviors, particularly those associated with mental illness, have a genetic basis.

(B)

Donald Cram describes an approach to synthesizing complex crown ethers.

Crown ethers are molecules that can bind specific *ions* forming molecular complexes (*See* entry for 1969). In 1974, American chemist Donald Cram (1919–2001) and colleagues publish their approach to synthesizing these interesting molecules in the laboratory. Cram calls the study of crown ethers and the complexes formed with ions host-guest chemistry. He shares the Nobel Prize in chemistry in 1987 with Jean-Marie Lehn and Charles Pedersen "for their development and use of molecules with structure-specific interactions of high selectivity."

(C)

Donald Johnson and colleagues discover "Lucy," an early hominid.

Our understanding of human origins depends upon the discovery of fossilized human ancestors. In 1974, American anthropologist Donald Johnson (b. 1943) and colleagues discover 40 percent of the skeleton of an early hominid in Ethiopia. The fossil, which they dub "Lucy," is one of the most complete skeletons ever found. Lucy lived approximately 2.8 million years ago.

(B)

March 29

Mariner 10 sends back images of Mercury.

As described in the sidebar "Exploring Space," the United States launched a series of successful missions to photograph and study the planets of the solar system. In 1973, *Mariner 10* was launched with the goal of visiting both Venus and Mercury. After a successful flight past Venus, the craft reached the planet Mercury on March 29, 1974, passing within a half a mile of the planet's surface. *Mariner 10* encounters the planet two more times. The spacecraft sends back pictures of Mercury and scientific data showing that the planet has no atmosphere and a small *magnetic field*.

(SA)

May

Sydney Brenner shows the roundworm can be used as a model for development.

Biologists who are interested in how an organism develops look for simple systems to aid their studies. Many use the fruit fly, an organism that is easy to manipulate genetically. In May 1974, British biologist Sydney Brenner (b. 1927) demonstrates that an even simpler system can be used, the roundworm known as *Caenorhabditis elegans*. He shows that the roundworm is easy to grow in the laboratory, and that treating the worm with carcinogens can induce mutations. Today, the roundworm is a powerful experimental model that has led to many discoveries in how organisms develop. Brenner shares the Nobel Prize in physiology or medicine in 2002 with H. Robert Horvitz and John E. Sulston "for their discoveries concerning 'genetic regulation of organ development and programmed cell death.'"

(B)

Charles Sibley shows that similar-looking birds have different ancestors.

For centuries, biologists have classified animals into families based upon their appearance. Another approach is to examine the molecules each animal uses. Such molecular analysis provides scientists with a view of how closely related two species are to each other. In May 1974, American biologist Charles Sibley (1917–98) publishes his first account of his work on *molecular biology* relating to the study of bird species. By examining the DNA of different birds he discovers that birds that appear to be closely related are actually the descendants of different ancestors. At first his work was controversial, but over the years, it has gained wider acceptance.

(B)

June

Georgy Flerov and Yuri Oganessian create seaborgium.

During the 20th century, physicists began to create many *elements* that are not found on Earth. The properties of these so-called *transfermium elements* are not well understood because they usually exist for only a short period of time. In June 1974, Russian physicists Georgy Flerov and Yuri Oganessian (b. 1933) create an element with 106 *protons* by fusing different *isotopes* of lead with an isotope of chromium. Soon after, the same element is created in California using a different method. Today, the element is called seaborgium after the physicist Glenn Seaborg, who led a group that synthesized many transfermium elements.

(C, P)

July 2

Russell Hulse and Joseph Taylor discover a double pulsar.

During the 20th century, astronomers began mapping cosmic *radio waves*. This led to discovery of *pulsars*, distant stars that emit regular radio waves. In 1974, American physicists Russell Hulse (b. 1950) and Joseph Taylor (b. 1941) observe a double pulsar, or two such stars locked in orbit with each other. Their discovery leads to the detection of *gravity* waves and provides the first evidence of gravitational *radiation*. They share the Nobel Prize in physics in 1993 "for the discovery of a new type of pulsar, a discovery that has opened up new possibilities for the study of gravitation."

(P)

1975

Benoit Mandelbrot describes fractal geometry.

Euclidean geometry does not accurately describe all types of figures. In 1975, Polish mathematician Benoit Mandelbrot (b. 1924) introduces the geometry of fractals in his book *Les objets fractals, forn, hasard et dimension* (Fractals, form, chance, and dimension). Fractals are figures that are not represented by classical geometry because they occur in a noninteger dimension. Many natural phenomena, such as *erosion,* can be described by fractals.

(M)

August

Mitchell Feigenbaum discovers a fundamental constant for chaos theory.

Advances in computing throughout the 20th century led to a number of important discoveries. In 1975, American mathematician Mitchell Feigenbaum (b. 1944) has a computer perform calculations, using an equation that describes chaos dynamics. This equation must go through several calculations, and the slow computing speed at the time allows him to see many of the intermediates. He notes that the same number, which can be approximated to 4.6692, comes up in all the calculations. The number becomes known as the Feigenbaum number, an important constant for chaos theory.

(M)

August 7

Georges Köhler and César Milstein produce monoclonal antibodies.

The immune system uses a wide range of cells and molecules to protect the body from foreign organisms and molecules. Certain immune cells secrete *proteins* called *antibodies* that specifically recognize proteins made by microorganisms. Biologists realize that these antibodies are useful tools for studying proteins in the laboratory. In 1975, Argentine biologist César Milstein (1927–2002) and German biologist Georges Köhler (1946–95) develop a method to produce antibodies that

recognize a single protein, called monoclonal antibodies, in the laboratory. Monoclonal antibodies have become useful tools in biomedical research, disease diagnosis, and treatment. Köhler and Milstein share the Nobel Prize in physiology or medicine in 1984 with Niels Jerne "for theories concerning the specificity in development and control of the immune system and the discovery of the principle for production of monoclonal antibodies."

(B)

December

Martin Perl discovers tau particles.

Physicists in the 20th century began to study the components of the *atom.* They created a variety of instruments to break atoms down to smaller *subatomic particles.* By the 1960s, scientist recognized that there are fundamental particles that make up matter. Beginning in 1974, American physicist Martin Perl (b. 1927) uses a powerful linear *accelerator* to produce one of these particles by colliding an *electron* with an antielectron. In December 1975, he publishes a paper suggesting the presence of a new particle. He later calls the particle tau. Subsequent work by his group and others over the next two years confirms the existence of these previously undetected particles. Perl is honored with the Nobel Prize in physics in 1977 "for the discovery of the tau lepton."

(P)

1976

Thomas Cech and Sidney Altman discover catalytic RNA.

Biological systems rely upon countless chemical reactions that occur in a regulated manner. *Enzymes* are molecules made by cells that catalyze these reactions. For many years, scientists believed that all *enzymes* are *proteins.*

In 1976, American biologists Thomas Cech (b. 1947) and Sidney Altman (b. 1939) independently discover that another biologically important molecule, *ribonucleic acid,* or RNA, can catalyze chemical reactions as well. Cech and Altman are honored with the Nobel Prize in chemistry in 1989 "for their discovery of catalytic properties of RNA."

(B, C)

March 11

Michael Bishop and Harold Varmus discover oncogenes.

Cancer is a disease characterized by uncontrolled cell growth. Physicians and scientists studying cancer often look at animal models of the disease. *Viruses* cause a number of animal cancers. These tumor viruses have genes that allow the infected cell to grow uncontrollably. On March 11, 1976, American biologists J. Michael Bishop (b. 1936) and Harold Varmus (b. 1939) publish a paper showing that animal cells have versions of the same genes present in their *genomes.* They call these cancer-causing genes oncogenes. Bishop and Varmus are honored with the Nobel Prize in physiology or medicine in 1989 "for their discovery of the cellular origin of retroviral oncogenes."

(B)

April 29

Erwin Neher and Bert Sakmann measure the activity of an individual molecule in a nerve cell.

Biologists have long been interested in the mechanism by which nerve impulses are transmitted. During the 20th century, scientists discovered that nerve impulses result in the opening of molecules in the nerve *membrane* called *ion* channels. These channels let sodium and/or potassium ions flow in and out of the nerve cell. On April 29, 1976, German biologists Erwin Neher (b. 1944) and Bert Sakmann (b. 1942) publish an account of the technique they developed to measure the activity of an individual ion channel. Their patch-clamp technique is widely used to study neurotransmission. Neher and Sakmann share the Nobel Prize in physiology or medicine in 1991 "for their discoveries concerning the function of single ion channels in cells."

(B)

June 17

Sir John Vane discovers prostacyclin.

Cells make a variety of molecules, including *hormones* and *neurotransmitters,* that regulate physiological processes. The prostaglandins are short-lived molecules that play a role in the regulation of blood pressure, pain, and the onset of labor in pregnant women. On June 17, 1976, British biologists Sir John Vane (1927–2004) publishes the discovery of prostacyclin, a prostaglandin that relaxes blood vessels. His discovery leads to new treatments for cardiovascular diseases. Later this year, Vane describes how the drug aspirin exerts its biological effects by interacting with prostaglandins. Vane shares the Nobel Prize in physiology or medicine in 1982 with Sune Bergström and Bengt Samuelsson for their discoveries concerning prostaglandins and related biologically active substances.

(B)

July 20

Viking 1 lands on Mars.

As described in the sidebar "Exploring Space," in the early 1970s several spacecrafts were sent to study the planets of the solar system. These vessels performed their studies as they flew by the planets. On July 20, 1976, *Viking 1* becomes the first spacecraft to land on Mars and begins to explore the planet. *Viking 2* follows on September 3, 1976. The

Viking missions take pictures of the planet's surface, look for signs of life, and conduct a series of scientific experiments. They both maintain communications with the Earth until the early 1980s.

(SA)

July 23

Sir Paul Nurse identifies a key factor in regulating cell growth and division.

Cells must grow in a controlled manner for an organism to function properly. They replicate and divide in a regulated process known as the cell cycle. *Eukaryotic cells* have developed systems that look for any abnormalities during the cell cycle and will halt cell growth and division if the conditions are not right. On July 23, 1976, Sir Paul Nurse (b. 1949) publishes a paper that identifies a key *gene* in the regulation of the cell cycle. His works leads to the discovery of many of the molecules required for cell cycle regulation. Nurse shares the Nobel Prize in medicine in 2001 with Timothy Hunt and Leland Hartwell "for their discoveries of key regulators of the cell cycle."

(B)

October

Susumu Tonegawa describes antibody genes.

The immune system comprises a number of cells and molecules that protect the body from a wide range of microorganisms and foreign substances. Some immune cells secrete *antibodies,* which are *proteins* that specifically recognize foreign molecules. After the discovery of the diversity of antibodies, scientists were unsure how *genes* could encode the large number of antibodies needed to mount an effective immune response. In October 1976, Japanese biologist Susumu Tonegawa (b. 1949) publishes his discovery that antibodies are produced

from genes that are rearranged in immune cells. These genetic rearrangements allow for the production of the wide range of diverse antibodies necessary to mount an effective immune response. Tonegawa is honored with the Nobel Prize in physiology or medicine in 1987 "for his discovery of the genetic principle for generation of antibody diversity."

(B)

1977

Walter Gilbert and Fredrick Sanger develop methods to determine the sequence of DNA.

DNA encodes genetic information that directs the function of all cells. The molecule is a *polymer,* made up of different combinations of four *nucleotides*. These nucleotides make up the genetic code that directs protein synthesis. As scientists learned to isolate and manipulate individual *genes,* they looked for ways to determine their nucleotide sequences. In 1977, American biochemist Walter Gilbert (b. 1932) and British chemist Fredrick Sanger (b. 1918) independently develop methods to determine the sequence of DNA. The two scientists are honored with the Nobel Prize in chemistry in 1980 "for their contributions concerning the determination of base sequences in nucleic acids."

(B, C)

Richard Roberts and Phillip Sharp show that some genes split.

The *genes* that encode *proteins* required in biological systems are found in an organism's DNA. Scientist once believed that the genes reside as discrete units on DNA. In 1977, American biologist Phillip Sharp (b. 1944) and British biologist Richard Roberts (b. 1943) independently show that some genes are interrupted by large stretches of DNA that do not code for the protein. These noncoding sequences become known as introns. Today, scientists have established that the genes of most higher organisms contain introns, and that they play an important role in the regulation of genes and the *evolution* of organisms. Roberts and Sharp share the Nobel Prize in physiology or medicine in 1993 "for their discoveries of split genes."

(B)

Ferid Murad shows the drugs that open blood vessels act by releasing nitric oxide.

Cardiovascular diseases are among the leading causes of death in industrialized nations. Physicians often give the drug nitroglycerine to help open up constricted blood vessels. In 1977, American biologist Ferid Murad (b. 1936) publishes a paper showing that nitroglycerin works by releasing the gas nitric oxide. Subsequent studies by a number of different researchers demonstrate that nitric oxide is also released by cells and used to control a variety of physiological processes, including blood vessel dilation. Murad shares the Nobel Prize in physiology or medicine in 1998 with Robert Furchgott and Louis Ignarro "for their discoveries concerning nitric oxide as a signaling molecule in the cardiovascular system."

(B)

John Corliss and Robert Ballard discover organisms in deep-sea vents.

Living organisms can adapt to wide variety of conditions. In 1977, a group including John Corliss and Robert Ballard (b. 1942) explore deep-sea vents off the Galápagos Islands. The vents are found along ridges in the ocean. Seafloor vents are extremely hot because of their proximity to the hot magna that creates the ridges and dark because they are too deep for light to penetrate. Corliss and Ballard find a number of organisms living in the vents, despite these harsh conditions. Scientists continue to study how these organisms survive in the absence of light.

(B, MS)

March

Sir John Sulston maps the lineage of roundworm cells.

Biologists interested in how organisms develop use a variety of different model systems in their experiments. In the 1970s, many turned to the roundworm (*See* entry for 1974). In March 1977, Sir John Sulston (b. 1942) aids all scientists working on the roundworm when he publishes the lineage of every cell in the developing organism. He notes that during development the death of many cells is regulated or programmed. He goes on to isolate one of the *genes* responsible for this programmed cell death. Sulston shares the Nobel Prize in physiology or medicine in 2002 with Sydney Brenner and Robert Horvitz "for their discoveries concerning 'genetic regulation of organ development and programmed cell death.'"

(B)

March 10

Astronomers discover that Uranus has rings.

For centuries, astronomers have known that rings surround the planet Saturn. On March 10, 1977, scientists observe the planet Uranus as it passes between a star and the Earth—an event known as a stellar occultation. They discover that Uranus also has rings. The *Voyager 2* spacecraft subsequently photographs the rings. Today, scientists recognize that planetary rings are composed of small pieces of solid matter, and also surround Jupiter and Neptune.

(SA)

August 5

Carl Woese identifies archea.

Biologists have divided living organisms in many different ways. In the 1970s, all organism were thought to fall into one of five classes: *bacteria,* animal, plant, protozoa, or fungus. On August 5, 1977, American biologist Carl Woese (b. 1928) publishes a paper suggesting that bacteria can be dividing into two classes—bacteria and archeabacteria, or archea. Archea appear to be bacteria, genetic analysis showing they are an evolutionarily distinct group of organisms. Many archea live in extreme conditions, such as hot water vents or *acid* waters in caves. Later, Woese proposes that all organisms be divided into one of three domains, eukaryota, eubacteria, or archea.

(B)

October 24

Alan Heeger, Alan MacDiramid, and Hideki Shirakawa make a plastic that conducts electricity.

Physicists and engineers study the properties of different metals that make them good conductors of *electricity.* Traditionally, plastics are classified as insulators, or materials that do not conduct electricity. On October 24, 1977, American chemist Alan Heeger (b. 1936), New Zealander chemist Alan MacDiramid (b. 1927), and Japanese chemist Hideki Shirakawa (b. 1936) change this view when they announce the synthesis of a plastic that can conduct electricity. These so-called semiconductive *polymers* are used in a variety of devices, including flat-screen televisions. The three chemists share the Nobel Prize in chemistry in 2000 "for the discovery and development of conductive polymers."

(C)

1978

Pierre Deligne, Charles Fefferman, Gregori Margulis, and Daniel Quillen receive the Fields medal.

As described in the sidebar "Awarding Science," the Fields medal is awarded every four years to a group of outstanding young mathematicians. The award is often thought of as the equivalent of the Nobel Prize in mathematics. In 1978, four mathematicians receive the medal. Belgian mathematician Pierre Deligne (b. 1944) is honored for his work on algebraic geometry and algebraic *number theory.* American mathematician Charles Fefferman (b. 1949) makes advances in multidimensional complex analysis. Russian mathematician Gregori Margulis (b. 1946) works on Lie groups. American mathematician Daniel Quillen (b. 1940) solves problems in algebraic theory.

(M)

Michael Smith develops a method to specifically change DNA sequences.

As described in the sidebar "The Science of DNA," biologists learned to manipulate DNA *genes* during the 20th century. In 1978, Canadian scientist Michael Smith (1932–2000) develops a method to specifically change the sequence of a given piece of DNA. His technique, called site-directed mutagenesis, allows molecular biologists to examine the effects of different gene sequences on molecular and/or cellular functions in an experimental organism. Smith is honored with the Nobel Prize in chemistry in 1993 "for his fundamental contributions to the establishment of oligonucleotide-based, site-directed mutagenesis and its development for protein studies."

(B, C)

Mary Leakey and colleagues discover preserved hominid footprints.

Anthropologists analyze fossils to investigate the origins of human beings. In 1978, paleontologist Mary Leaky (1913–96) finds preserved hominid footprints in volcanic beds in Laetoli, Tanzania. Analysis of the 3.5-million-year-old footprints suggests that the hominids walked upright, making them the oldest-known bipedal human ancestors.

(B)

July 25

First human baby conceived by in vitro fertilization is born.

Advances in the isolation and storage of human egg cells made in vitro fertilization, the conceiving of a human embryo in a test tube, a possibility by the 1970s. Similar procedures were already commonplace in animal breeding. In 1977, British physicians Patrick Steptoe (1913–88) and Robert Edwards (b. 1925) carried out the first successful in vitro fertilization. On July 25, 1978, Louise Brown, the first baby conceived by in vitro fertilization, is born. Although the procedure is a success and gives hope to many infertile couple, the ethical questions surrounding the procedure are debated for years to come.

(B)

December 7

Edward Lewis describes the genetic basis of fruit fly development.

Biologists interested in how complex organisms develop use a variety of model systems. One of the most popular is the fruit fly, which has been used in genetic experiments for decades. On December 7, 1978, American biologist Edward Lewis (1918–2004) publishes an analysis of years of research into how *genes* control the development of the fly. Specifically, he studies mutations that lead to one segment of the fly's body behaving as if it were another. He shows that key developmental genes are clustered on *chromosomes*. His work has given scientists insight into the causes of some congenital mutations in humans, such as DiGeorge syndrome. Lewis shares the Nobel Prize in physiology or medicine in 1995 with Christiane Nüsslein-Volhard and Eric F. Wieschaus "for their discoveries concerning the genetic control of early embryonic development."

(B)

1979

***Voyager 1* and *Voyager 2* fly by Jupiter and its moons.**

As described in the sidebar "Exploring Space," throughout the 1970s the United States launched a number of spacecrafts destined to explore the planets of the solar system. In 1979, two crafts called *Voyager 1* and *Voyager 2* fly by the planet Jupiter. The Voyager missions take thousands of pictures of Jupiter and its moons. They also collect scientific data about the planet's *magnetic field* and atmosphere. The missions discover an active volcano on one of its moons, Io, the first active volcano discovered outside of the Earth. The Voyager missions continue and fly by Saturn, Uranus, and Neptune before leaving the solar system.

(SA)

January

Gerd Binnig and Heinrich Rohrer invent the scanning tunneling microscope.

Many scientists are interested in the chemical reactions and molecular interactions that occur on surfaces. In January 1979, German physicist Gerd Binnig (b. 1947) and Swiss physicist Heinrich Rohrer (b. 1933) develop the scanning tunneling microscope to study surfaces. Rather than magnifying an image, the scanning tunneling microscope traces a surface using a conducting probe that comes within a few *atoms* of a sample. The movement of *electrons* between the probe and the sample is measured, and then used to produce an image. Binnig and Rohrer use their technique to map the surface of a *semiconductor*. They are honored with the Nobel Prize in physics in 1986 "for their design of the scanning tunneling microscope."

(B, C, P)

September 1

Pioneer 11 observes Saturn.

As described in the sidebar "Exploring Space," the United States launched a number of spacecraft that will explored the planets of the solar system during the 1970s. On September 1, 1979, *Pioneer 11* becomes the first spacecraft to observe Saturn, passing within approximately 13,000 miles (21,000 km) of its surface. The spacecraft conducts a number of experiments to analyze the atmosphere and surface of Saturn and its moons, and then travels out of the solar system. The spacecraft continues reporting back to Earth until 1995.

(SA)

∽ CONCLUSION ∾

The era spanning the end of World War II to 1979 was a time of great scientific and technical advances. The cold war and the launch of the Soviet *Sputnik* satellite sparked science in the United States. This renewed focus on science and engineering led to the establishment of NASA and the technological advances that allowed a man to land on the Moon and spacecrafts to be sent to explore the solar system. Such advances laid the foundation for

the construction and operation of the Hubble Space Telescope at the end of the 20th century, which awed scientists and the public alike with beautiful pictures of distant stars and galaxies; and the successful landing of a series of Mars Rovers that explored the surface of Mars. Cold war–era technology also spurred the U.S. Defense Department to create a network of government and academic computers, foreshadowing the Internet, which became as common as radio or television by the mid-1990s.

During this period, scientists and the public alike become increasingly aware of the effects of human activity on the environment. The publication of Rachel Carson's *Silent Spring,* as well as other arguments that man has had a detrimental effect on the planet, call many in the general public to action. By the 1970s, scientists begin to understand exactly how different types of pollution harm the atmosphere. In the last decades of the 20th century, scientific data is used to argue for banning some air pollutants and reducing others. Activists and politicians join in the debate as the century draws to a close.

The seeds for more public debate are sowed in the post–World War II era as revolutionary advances in *molecular biology* soon give man the power to manipulate genetic material of organisms from *viruses* to humans. Within 50 years of the elucidation of the structure of DNA, scientists sequence the human *genome* and identify people based upon their genetic "fingerprint." During this era, bioethicists and the public also debate in vitro fertilization with the birth of the first "test tube baby" in 1978. Such debates revived and amplified at the turn of the century, when biologists learn how to clone mammals and isolate stem cells from human embryos.

9

THE EXPANSION OF SCIENCE IN THE INFORMATION AGE

1980–2006

∽ INTRODUCTION ∽

Science at the end of the 20th century and beginning of the 21st century is profoundly influenced by new technologies that allow researchers to explore everything from tiny *subatomic particles* to a "Great Wall" of galaxies. High-powered computers influence the course of discovery in fields from astronomy to biology. New technologies help scientists make advances that sound like science fiction: NASA sends a series of robots called Rovers to study the surface of Mars, the cloning of mammals becomes a reality, and the stage is set for *nanotechnology*.

The field of chemistry sees advances in the synthesis of complex molecules and the development of compounds that will form the basis of nanotechnology. Research in synthetic chemistry leads to the synthesis of new drugs that are now widely used to treat diseases such as high blood pressure

and arthritis. Another exciting development in chemistry is the discovery of a previously unknown form of elemental carbon, dubbed the Buckminster fullerene (or simply fullerene), in which 60 individual carbon *atoms* form a structure that resembles a soccer ball. In the 1990s, scientists notice during the production of fullerenes in the laboratory tiny tubes formed by rings of fullerenes. These tubes, now known as carbon nanotubes, can conduct *electricity*. Carbon nanotubes are one of the chemicals that scientists consider using to make tiny molecular circuits, launching the field of nanotechnology.

Cells are also studied at the molecular level during this era. Advances in the manipulation of *genes* allow biologists to probe the function of genes and learn more about complex processes such as the development of embryos. As DNA sequencing becomes increasingly easier and less expensive, companies and government agencies launch programs to sequence the complement of DNA in a single organism, known as its *genome.* The most heralded achievement of these efforts is the sequencing of the human genome, completed in 2003. By comparing sequences from genomes of species from yeast to man, biologists find that organisms have striking similarities at the genetic level. The sequencing of the human genome and discovery of *gene* mutations that lead to diseases from cystic fibrosis to breast cancer raises a number ethical questions surrounding the availability of genetic information and how that information is used. Two other advances in biology, the cloning of mammalian cells and the isolation of stem cells from human embryos, spark ethical and political debates that will likely continue well into the 21st century.

Just as biologists probe the inner workings of cells, physicists continue to dissect the inner world of atoms. Particle physicists detect subatomic particles, such as the top *quark,* whose existence had been theorized but never demonstrated, as well as three types of particles called *bosons* that carry the weak *forces* that dictate the interaction between subatomic particles. Others find particles beyond the boundaries of Earth, such as *neutrinos.*

Astronomers and physicists work together to uncover more evidence to support the *big bang theory,* a theory that explains the origin of the universe. These and many other investigations of the cosmos are aided by the construction of unmanned spacecraft that explore the solar system and beyond, as well telescopes that scan the universe from a vantage point much closer to Earth. In 1993, the Hubble Space Telescope, which orbits the Earth 380 miles (610 km) above the surface, becomes operational. The Hubble telescope has a wide array of instruments to study distant stars and galaxies. Closer to Earth, scientists and engineers at NASA develop, launch, and successfully land a series of robots, known collectively as the Mars Rovers, equipped with instruments that sample and analyze the planet's surface. In 2004, data sent back to Earth from the Mars Rover reveal further evidence that there was once water on surface of Mars.

While geologists learn more about the composition of the Earth's neighbors and ponder the possibility of life on other planets, others study the affects of man on the atmosphere of Earth. During this period, scientists discover a hole in the *ozone layer,* an important component of the Earth's atmosphere that absorbs much of the *ultraviolet radiation* from the Sun. As news of the hole spreads, nations work together to write and ratify an international treaty that bans the release of many chemicals that can chemically react with ozone released into the air. A second international group of scientists shows that man's activities have also directly influenced the climate of Earth. Over the 25 years detailed in this section, scientists, government officials, and environmental activists become increasingly concerned with global climate change. Their efforts culminate in the Kyoto Protocol, an international treaty limiting the release of gases that promote the *greenhouse effect* and thus lead to climate change.

TIME LINE OF SCIENTIFIC ACHIEVEMENTS FROM 1980 TO 2006

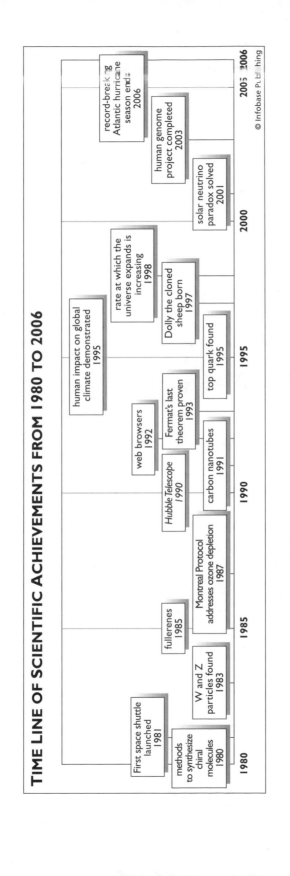

methods to synthesize chiral molecules 1980

First space shuttle launched 1981

W and Z particles found 1983

fullerenes 1985

Montreal Protocol addresses ozone depletion 1987

Hubble Telescope 1990

carbon nanotubes 1991

web browsers 1992

Fermat's last theorem proven 1993

human impact on global climate demonstrated 1995

top quark found 1995

rate at which the universe expands is increasing 1998

Dolly the cloned sheep born 1997

solar neutrino paradox solved 2001

human genome project completed 2003

record-breaking Atlantic hurricane season ends 2006

1980   1985   1990   1995   2000   2005   2006

CHRONOLOGY

1980

Ryoji Noyori develops a catalyst used to synthesize chiral molecules.

Many biologically important molecules, such as the building blocks for *proteins* called *amino acids,* exist in two forms that are mirror images of each other. These *chiral* molecules are difficult to synthesize in the laboratory using smaller chemicals because most chemical reactions yield both forms of the molecule. In 1980, Japanese chemist Ryoji Noyori (b. 1938) develops a catalyst that helps specifically synthesize one form of a chiral molecule. His catalyst is used in the synthesis of pharmaceuticals, including the painkiller naproxen. Noyori shares the Nobel Prize in chemistry with William Knowles (*See* entry for 1968) in 2001 for "for their work on chirally catalyzed hydrogenation reactions."

(B, C)

Barry Sharpless develops a method to synthesize heart drugs in the laboratory.

One problem in manufacturing pharmaceuticals is that biologically important molecules are often found in two forms that are mirror images of each other. The body generally recognizes only one form of these *chiral* molecules. In 1980, American chemist Barry Sharpless (b. 1941) makes a breakthrough in the synthesis of some types of chiral molecules. His work leads to the manufacture of an important class of drugs, called beta-blockers, used to treat heart disease. Sharpless is honored with the Nobel Prize in chemistry in 2001 for "for his work on chirally catalyzed oxidation reactions." work on chirally catalyzed oxidation reactions."

(B, C)

Walter and Luis Alvarez speculate that a meteor crash led to the demise of the dinosaurs.

Since the discovery of dinosaurs in the 19th century (*See* entry for AUGUST 2, 1841), scientists have wondered how they became extinct. In 1980, American geologists Walter (b. 1940) and Luis Alvarez (1911–88) discover a layer of the rare metal iridium in *sediment* of clay at the boundary between the Cretaceous and Tertiary periods. They believe that a dust cloud formed when a meteor that crashed into the Earth produced the layer and speculate that this dust cloud blocked out the Sun. According to Alvarez, this sequence of events could have caused the death of plant life and ultimately the extinction of the dinosaurs.

(ES)

Aaron Ciechanover, Avram Hershko, and Irwin Rose describe how cellular proteins are degraded.

Proteins carry out the majority of cellular tasks, from catalyzing chemical reactions to transporting substances across biological *membranes*. The synthesis of proteins is highly regulated to assure that cells only make the proteins needed for the tasks at hand. In the 1970s, scientists began to realize that another way to regulate the amount and types of proteins in a cell was to have a mechanism by which proteins are targeted for degradation. In 1980, Israeli scientists Aaron Ciechanover (b. 1947) and Avram Hershko (b. 1937) along with American scientist Irwin Rose (b. 1926) publish a series of papers describing the mechanism by which proteins are targeted for degradation in the cell. The three share the Nobel Prize in chemistry in 2004 for "for the discovery of ubiquitin-mediated protein degradation."

(B, C)

Spring

Klaus von Klitzing discovers the quantized Hall effect.

Physicists began studying the relationship between *electricity* and *magnetism* in 1820. By the end of the 19th century, American physicist Edwin Hall (1855–1938) applied a *magnetic field* to a strip of gold carrying an *electric current* and showed that a *voltage* is generated in the same direction as the magnetic field. Other physicists studied this phenomenon, known as the Hall effect, throughout the 20th century. German physicist Klaus von Klitzing (b. 1943) studied the Hall effect in a new system: the thin surface between a metal and a *semiconductor.* In spring 1980, von Klitzing uses this system to show that the conductivity that results from Hall effect is not even, but rather occurs in discrete groups called *quanta*. He is honored with the Nobel Prize in physics in 1985 for "for the discovery of the quantized Hall effect."

(P)

June 16

United States Supreme Court states that microorganisms can be patented.

Rapid developments in *molecular biology* during the 1970s led to a host of unresolved legal questions. Chief among them was the issue of whether living organisms that have been genetically engineered can be patented. In 1972, inventors filed a patent for a strain of genetically engineered *bacteria* that breaks crude oil down into simpler chemicals. When the United States Patent Office rejected the patent, stating that living organisms cannot be patented, an eight-year legal battle ensued. On June 16, 1980, the United States Supreme Court rules on this case, establishing that genetically engineered organisms can be patented.

(B)

Fall

Christiane Nüsslein-Volhard and Eric Wieschaus describe how genes control development.

Biologists use model systems to study how organisms develop. For example, the fruit fly, *Drosophila melanogaster,* can be used as a model organism to study how *genes* control biological processes such as the development of a complex multicellular organism. In fall 1980, developmental biologists Christiane Nüsslein-Volhard (b. 1942) and Eric Wieschaus (b. 1947) publish a paper describing a variety of genetic mutations that led to changes in fruit fly embryos. Their work leads to the discovery of many genes critical for the development of organisms. Nüsslein-Volhard and Wieschaus share the 1995 Nobel Prize in physiology or medicine with Edward Lewis "for their discoveries concerning the genetic control of early embryonic development."

(B)

November 7

Alfred Gilman isolates a protein critical for cell communication.

In multicellular organisms, cells secrete molecules that allow them to communicate with one another, and thus coordinate physiological activities such as movement. During the 1970s, Martin Rodbell discovered that a common biological molecule called GTP is critical for disseminating information within a cell, a process known as signal transduction (*See* entry for MARCH 25, 1971). In November 1980, American biologist Alfred Gilman (b. 1941) publishes a paper describing the isolation a cellular *protein* that works with GTP to send messages through the cell. Subsequently, a family of these signaling *proteins*, collectively known as G-proteins, is discovered. Gilman shares the 1994 Nobel Prize in physiology or medicine with Rodbell "for their discovery of G-proteins and the role of these proteins in signal transduction in cells."

(B)

November 27

Robert Furchgott describes how blood vessels dilate.

Blood vessels dilate and constrict in response to a variety of biological signals, from changes in temperature to physiological changes. In November 1980, American biologist Robert Furchgott (b. 1916) publishes studies on how the body controls the dilation of blood vessels. When he tries to study blood vessel dilation in the laboratory, he finds he needs intact living cells to perform his experiments. He deduces that the cells are secreting a factor that tells the blood vessel to dilate. Subsequent studies find that the factor is the gas nitric oxide (*See* entry for APRIL 1986). Furchgott shares the Nobel Prize in physiology or medicine with Louis J. Ignarro and Ferid Murad in 1998 "for their discoveries concerning nitric oxide as a signaling molecule in the cardiovascular system."

(B)

1981

Peter Armbruster and colleagues generate bohrium in the laboratory.

Physicists in the laboratory can generate *elements* that are not found on the Earth. In 1981, German physicist Peter Armbruster and his colleagues fuse an *isotope* of lead with an isotope of chromium to produce an *atom* with 107 *protons*. The atoms rapidly decay and therefore cannot be isolated. The element is named bohrium after Danish physicist Niels Bohr.

(C, P)

April 12

NASA launches the space shuttle *Columbia.*

As described in the sidebar "Exploring Space," the space race between the United States and the Soviet Union began with the launch of the *Sputnik* satellite (*See* entry for OCTOBER 4, 1957) and continued as each country developed space stations and new vehicles. On April 12, 1981, the United States space agency NASA launches the first space shuttle, a reusable spacecraft that can orbit the Earth. The space shuttle *Columbia* launches from Florida, orbits the Earth for two days, and then lands like an airplane at Edwards Air Force Base in California. The space shuttle *Columbia* completes 27 successful flights over 21 years, before being tragically destroyed upon reentering the Earth's atmosphere in 2003 (*See* entry for FEBRUARY 2003).

(SA)

1982

Timothy Hunt discovers a group of proteins that are produced and destroyed as cells replicate.

Eukaryotic cells divide through a process called *mitosis.* A number of events must occur before the cell divides, and biologists have shown that these events occur in a series of regulated stages known collectively as the cell cycle. In 1982, Timothy Hunt (b. 1943) and colleagues study the biochemical changes in sea urchin cells as they pass through the cell cycle. He discovers a *protein* that is produced at specific stages during the cell cycle and destroyed at other stages. Later research by Hunt and others shows that this protein, now known as a cyclin, helps control the progression of cells through the cell cycle and ultimately cell division. Cyclins are later found in all *eukaryotic cells,* including

The space shuttle program allows the United States to regularly conduct experiments in space. Here the Alpha Magnetic Spectrometer, used to search for cosmic antimatter, is being prepared for a flight on the space shuttle *Discovery* in 1998. *(NASA)*

humans, where they have been implicated in the development of cancer. Hunt shares the Nobel Prize in physiology or medicine in 2001 with Leland Hartwell and Paul Nurse for "for their discoveries of key regulators of the cell cycle."

(B)

Hartmut Michel crystallizes a membrane protein.

The function of proteins is intimately related to their three-dimensional structures. Chemists and biologists use a method called *X-ray crystallogragphy* to uncover the structure of biologically important molecules from drugs to the *proteins* that perform the majority of tasks in cells. Many important proteins are embedded in cellular *membranes*, and are only in their active form when surrounded by fatty molecules. For many years, chemists were unable to determine the structure of such proteins because they did not readily form crystals. In 1982, German scientist Hartmut Michel (b. 1948) succeeds in crystallizing a membrane protein required for *photosynthesis*. He shares the Nobel Prize in chemistry in 1988 with Johann Deisenhofer and Robert Huber "for the determination of the three-dimensional structure of a photosynthetic reaction centre."

(B, C)

Alain Connes, William Thurston, and Shing-Tung Yao receive the Fields medal.

As described in the sidebar "Awarding Science," the Fields medal is awarded every four years to young mathematicians who have made significant advances in their field. In 1982, the Fields medal is given to French mathematician Alain Connes (b. 1947), American mathematician William Thurston (b. 1946), and Chinese mathematician Shing-Tung Yao (b. 1949). Connes's work centers on the theory of operator *algebra*. Thurston studies *topology* in two and three dimensions. Yao makes contributions in the field of differential equations.

(M)

Stanley Prusiner shows that proteins called prions cause some infectious diseases.

Louis Pasteur and other 19th-century biologists described how a variety of different microorganisms cause communicable disease (*See* sidebar "Finding the Microorganisms That Cause Disease"). By the early 20th century, scientists described a number of neurological diseases, including Creutzfeldt-Jakob disease and mad cow disease, that are transmitted by eating the brain of an infected organism. However, the exact agent that causes these diseases remained elusive for decades. In 1982, American biologist Stanley Prusiner (b. 1942) shows that the agent responsible for transmitting Creutzfeldt-Jakob disease is not a microorganism but rather a single *protein*. He calls this new class of infectious agents *prions*. Prusiner is honored with the Nobel Prize in physiology and medicine in 1997 "for his discovery of "Prions—a new biological principle of infection."

(B)

Daniel Tsui and Horst Störmer discover a new quantum fluid.

Early investigations into the relationship between *electricity* and *magnetism* showed that when an *electric field* is applied to a thin strip of metal conducting electricity, a voltage can be generated in the same direction as the electric field. This phenomenon is known as the Hall effect. German physicist Klaus von Klitzing later showed that when electrons are conducted between a metal and a *semiconductor,* the Hall effect is quantized (*See* entry for 1980). In 1982, American physicist Daniel Tsui (b. 1939) and German physicist Horst Störmer (b. 1949) repeat von Klitzing's experiments at low temperatures using stronger *magnetic fields* and find that the electron's behave in a different manner. Their work leads to the discovery of a new quantum fluid. Tsui and Störmer share the Nobel Prize in physics in 1998 with Robert Laughlin "for their discovery of a new form of quantum fluid with fractionally charged excitations."

(P)

Peter Armbruster and colleagues generate unnilennium in the laboratory.

During the 20th century, advances in physics allowed scientists to create a number of *elements* that are not found on Earth. In 1982, a group led by German scientists Peter Armbruster (b. 1931) and Gottfried Münzenberg (b. 1940) create an element with 109 *protons* by bombarding an *isotope* of the element bismuth with iron *ions*. The *atom* has a half-life of less than a second, then decays into lighter atoms. The scientist use highly sensitive detectors to prove that they did indeed generate unnilennium.

(C, P)

1983

Swiss scientists discover W and Z particles.

The discovery of *radioactivity* during the 19th century led to physicists' discovering *subatomic particles.* For example, when a *neutron* radioactively decays, an *electron* and a *neutrino* are released. In the 1970s, physicists proposed that two types of particles, termed W and Z, are formed after the decay but before the electron and *neutrino* are generated. In 1983, scientists at CERN in Switzerland find and measure the W and Z particles, using an instrument designed specifically for this experiment. Years earlier, Swiss scientist Carlo Rubbia (b. 1934) had proposed the experiment that led to the discovery of the particles and Dutch physicist Simon van der Meer (b. 1925) designed the instrument used in his experiment. The actual discovery is the culmination of a large project involving many scientists and technicians. Rubbia and van der Meer are honored with the Nobel Prize in physics in 1984 for "their decisive contributions to the large

project, which led to the discovery of the field particles W and Z, communicators of weak interaction."

(P)

Luc Montagnier and Robert Gallo discover the virus that causes AIDS.

Acquired immunodeficiency syndrome (AIDS) first appeared in the 1980s, and physicians and scientists immediately looked for the infectious agent that causes the disease. In 1983, French scientist Luc Montagnier (b. 1933) and American microbiologist Robert Gallo (b. 1937) independently announce the isolation of a new *virus* from patients with AIDS. Controversies immediately surround the discovery of the virus. While some question whether or not the virus, now known as the human immunodeficiency virus (HIV) actually causes AIDS, Montagnier and

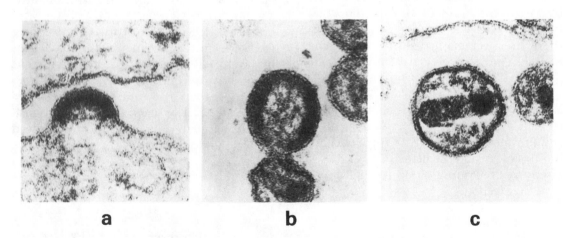

Human Immunodeficiency Virus (HIV-I)

a   b   c

The human immunodeficiency virus (HIV) is shown to cause AIDS during the 1980s. These electron micrographs show newly synthesized HIV virions budding from an infected cell. *(Matthew Gonda/ National Cancer Institute)*

Gallo disagree over who should be credited with the discovery. Today, the scientific and medical communities agree that HIV causes AIDS.

(B)

Robert Laughlin develops a theory explaining a quantum fluid.

Physicists began studying the relationship between *electricity* and *magnetism* in the 19th century. In 1982, American physicist Daniel Tsui and German physicist Horst Störmer discovered a quantum fluid by exposing *electrons* flowing along the interface of a metal and a *semiconductor* to a strong *magnetic field* at low temperature (*See* entry for 1982). In 1983, American physicist Robert Laughlin (b. 1950) develops a theory to explain their discovery. Laughlin shares the Nobel Prize in physics in 1998 with Tsui and Störmer "for their discovery of a new form of quantum fluid with fractionally charged excitations."

(P)

1984

Physicists generate hassium in the laboratory.

Advances in physics in the 20th century allowed scientists to generate *elements* that are not found on Earth, known as *transfermium elements*. The discovery of many of the transfermium elements were controversial. In 1984, two groups of physicists, one in Germany and the other in Russia, report that they have generated an element with 108 *protons*. Both groups prepare the element in the same way, by bombarding an *isotope* of lead with *ions* from an isotope of iron. The German group names the element hassium after the state where it is discovered.

(C, P)

June 16

Barry Marshall and J. Robin Warren find bacteria in ulcer patients.

During the 19th century, medical scientists demonstrated that microorganisms cause a wide variety of communicable diseases, from malaria to tuberculosis. For many years, physicians believed that stomach ulcers were caused by stress or eating acidic foods. In 1984, Australian physicians Barry Marshall (b. 1951) and J. Robin Warren (b. 1937) showed that the *bacterium Heliobacter pylori* also causes stomach ulcers. On June 16, 1984, Marshall and Warren published a paper describing the bacterium. Later, Marshall proves that it causes disease by drinking a culture of *H. pylori*, giving himself a stomach ulcer, then treating his disease with *antibiotics*. Today, antibiotics are routinely used to treat stomach ulcers. Marshall and Warren share the Nobel Prize in physiology or medicine in 2005 "for their discovery of the bacterium *Helicobacter pylori* and its role in gastritis and peptic ulcer disease."

(B)

October 1984

NASA launches satellites to study the Earth's radiation budget.

As described in the sidebar "Climate Change," scientists at the end of the 20th century worked to understand the factors that lead to climate changes over time. Global climate is influenced, in part, by the Earth's *radiation* budget, defined as the difference in *energy* absorbed from the Sun and the energy leaving the Earth. In 1984, NASA puts three satellites into orbit that monitor the energy radiating from the Earth as well as the solar energy absorbed by the Earth. For more than 10 years, the satellites supply data used by climatologists to understand how clouds, gases, and aerosols affect weather patterns.

(W)

December 5

Hartmut Michel, Johann Deisenhofer, and Robert Huber determine the three-dimensional structure of the photosynthetic reaction center.

Photosynthesis is the process whereby plants and some single-cell organisms convert *energy* from sunlight into a form that can be used by cells. Scientists studying the mechanism by which photosynthesis occurs have identified many *proteins* involved in this process. One of these proteins, the photosynthetic reaction center, is surrounded by *membranes* and is thus difficult to purify and crystallize. In 1983, German scientist Hartmut Michel successfully crystallized the photosynthetic reaction center from algae (*See* entry for

CLIMATE CHANGE

As the 20th century drew to a close, scientists, government officials, and environmental activists from around the world became increasingly concerned with the effects of human activity on the global climate. Research in the 1980s and 1990s focused on the increased release of a number of gases that contribute to global temperature by inducing the *greenhouse effect.* These gases, known collectively as *greenhouse gases,* stop *heat* from leaving the Earth's surface while simultaneously allowing the Sun to warm the planet. The greenhouse effect, first noted by Irish scientist John Tyndall (*See* entry for 1863), is an essential process that helps make the Earth's environment suitable for human life. However, research in the last decades of the 20th century showed that human activity has led to an increase in the overall concentration of a number of greenhouse gases, particularly carbon dioxide, methane, and chlorofluorocarbons. At the same time, climatologists developed models that show that climate change could have potentially devastating effects in countries near the equator, as well as on agriculture in many industrialized nations. These studies began an international effort to curb the impact of humans on global climate by calling for reductions in the amount of greenhouse gases released into the atmosphere.

Global climate change is not a recent phenomenon, but a natural process that has occurred throughout the Earth's history. Scientists studying climate change have shown that global temperatures have fluctuated at the beginnings and ends of different ice ages. These periods of climate change occurred well before recorded history. Studies on glaciers and polar ice sheets have given scientists a picture of past climate changes. Each year, a new layer is formed in the polar ice sheet. This formation captures samples of the atmosphere at the time the layer forms. By studying these layers, climate scientists learn about the climate condition in the year the layer was formed, specifically the average temperatures, the snowfall levels, and even the carbon dioxide levels in the surrounding atmosphere. Using these and other data, climate scientists have reconstructed how the average temperature has changed over thousands of years.

Recent climate change can be easily assessed using weather records that have been kept in the past few centuries. These data have shown that average global temperature has increased between $0.5°F–1.1°F$ $(0.3°C–0.6°C)$ over the past century. Scientists use the data of climate conditions in the distant past as well as the present to generate and test models of potential climate change in the future. If the model can accurately reproduce past changes, then the same model might also be able to project future global temperatures. However, just as no one can definitively predict the weather for a

1983). He worked with two other German scientists, Johann Deisenhofer (b. 1943) and Robert Huber (b. 1937), to determine its structure, which they publish in December 1984. The three scientists share the Nobel Prize in chemistry in 1988 "for the determination of the three-dimensional structure of a photosynthetic reaction centre."

(B, C)

1985

Steven Chu uses lasers to slow the movement of atoms.

Physicists develop a number of sophisticated instruments to help them study the properties and behavior of *atoms* and *subatomic particles*. Atoms are constantly moving at high speeds, making them difficult to study.

week ahead, no scientist can say with certainty what types of climate change will occur in the future.

In 1995, the Intergovernmental Panel on Climate Change (IPCC), an international working group dedicated to study global climate change, issued a report detailing the increases in global temperatures and atmospheric concentrations of a number of greenhouse gases, including carbon dioxide. Their report concluded that human activity has directly affected global temperature. The IPCC report sparked an international movement to reduce the amount of greenhouse gases released into the atmosphere. In 1997, representatives from 160 nations drafted the Kyoto Protocol, an international treaty to reduce the emission of greenhouse gases. In the 1980s, a similar treaty, the Montreal Protocol, effectively reduced the release of chlorofluorocarbons, gases that both promote the greenhouse effect and contribute to the depletion of ozone in the atmosphere. The Kyoto Protocol, however, faced strong opposition from industrialized nations, particularly the United States and Australia. Eventually, enough industrialized countries signed the treaty and the Kyoto Protocol took effect in February 2005.

Modern scientists studying climate change often have to go to the ends of the Earth. The Clean Air Facility on the South Pole, shown here in 1978, is used for atmospheric sampling. *(Commander John Bortniak/NOAA Corps)*

In 1985, American physicist Steven Chu (b. 1948) uses *lasers* to slow the motion of atoms so that they could be studied in the laboratory. Chu shares the Nobel Prize in physics in 1997 with Claude Cohen-Tannoudji, and William Phillips "for development of methods to cool and trap atoms with laser light."

(P)

American microbiologists find a drug that can treat AIDS.

AIDS was first characterized in the 1980s, and physicians and scientists immediately began searching for its cause and for an effective treatment. In 1983, scientists discovered human immunodeficiency virus (HIV), the *virus* that causes AIDS (*See* entry for 1983). In 1985, a group of American scientists including Robert Gallo, one of the scientists involved in HIV's discovery, shows that a drug called AZT inhibits HIV infection in the laboratory. Physicians soon begin giving AZT to patients, and in 1987 it becomes the first anti-HIV drug approved for use in the Untied States. Unfortunately, the drug is not an effective treatment because the virus rapidly develops resistance.

(B)

March

Scientists discover a "hole" in the ozone layer.

The upper region of the Earth's atmosphere is characterized by a high concentration of the chemical ozone. The *ozone layer,* absorbs *ultraviolet radiation* from the Sun. During the 20th century, environmental scientists noted that some types of air pollutants, such as chlorofluorocarbons (CFCs), undergo chemical reactions with ozone and lead to the depletion of this important molecule (*See* entry for 1974). In March 1985, environmental scientists report that nearly half of the ozone in the layer above Antarctica has

been depleted. The discovery of this depletion, widely known as the hole in the ozone layer, leads to regulation of the use of CFCs and other ozone-depleting compounds.

(ES, W)

March 20

Kurt Wüthrich applies a new method to the study of protein structures.

Proteins perform the majority of tasks in cells, from obtaining *energy* to helping the cell divide. The function of proteins is intimately related to their three-dimensional structure. Chemists and biologists often use a technique called *X-ray crystallography* to determine the structures of *proteins*. However, this technique cannot be applied to all proteins. On March 20, 1985, Swiss scientist Kurt Wüthrich (b. 1938) publishes a paper describing the use of nuclear magnetic resonance (NMR) to solve the structure of proteins. Previously, NMR had been used to determine the structure of smaller molecules. Today, nearly 20 percent of all known protein structures are determined by using NMR. Wüthrich is honored with the Nobel Prize in chemistry in 2002 "for his development of nuclear magnetic resonance spectroscopy for determining the three-dimensional structure of biological macromolecules in solution."

(B, C)

July 4

Sir Alec Jeffreys and colleagues publish a method to analyze human DNA "fingerprints."

Genetic information is passed along on *genes* that are found on large molecules of DNA. The sequence of *nucleotides* in a given *gene* or in regions of DNA that are not part of genes can vary greatly among different individuals. Such differences are called DNA polymorphisms. On July 4, 1985, Sir Alec Jeffreys (b. 1950) publishes a paper describing a method to distinguish individuals based upon their DNA polymorphisms. His technique, commonly known as DNA fingerprinting, becomes an important tool in forensics and medical science.

(B)

November 14

Robert F. Curl, Harold W. Kroto, and Richard E. Smalley discover fullerenes.

Elemental carbon can take a number of different forms, such as graphite and diamonds. In 1985, American chemists Robert Curl (b. 1933) and Richard Smalley (1943–2005) and British chemist Sir Harold Kroto (b. 1939) discover that carbon *atoms* can cluster into closed shells containing 60 carbon atoms, with a structure that closely resembles that of a soccer ball. They call the new structures buckminsterfullerene, or simply fullerenes, after the architect who designed a dome with a similar shape. They describe the discovery in a paper published on November 14, 1985. Subsequent studies show that fullerenes have a number of interesting properties, opening up a new field of investigation. The three scientists share the Nobel Prize in chemistry in 1996 "for their discovery of fullerenes."

(C)

December 20

Kary Mullis develops a method to amplify DNA.

As the genetic defects that cause many diseases were identified, biologists needed a method to quickly analyze DNA from a patient and determine if the patient carries the defective gene. In 1985, American scientist Kary Mullis (b. 1944) develops the polymerase chain reaction (PCR) for this purpose. He describes the technique as part of a paper published on December 20, 1985. PCR allows scientists to make millions of copies of a specific piece of DNA. Given a small sample of

DNA, biologists can now easily expand it and look for genetic defects. Almost immediately, PCR becomes an important tool for scientists performing medical research, disease diagnosis, and forensic analysis. Mullis is honored with the Nobel Prize in chemistry in 1993 for "for his invention of the polymerase chain reaction (PCR) method."

(B, C)

1986

Robert Furchgott and Louis Ignarro show that nitric oxide can transmit signals in organisms.

Organisms use a variety of molecules, such as *hormones* and *neurotransmitters,* to transmit signals between different organs within the body. During the 1980s, American biologist Robert Furchgott studied the signals that tell blood vessels to dilate. In 1986, he and American scientist Louis Ignarro (b. 1941) independently show that the molecule responsible for blood vessels dilation is the gas nitric oxide. Their work explains how nitroglycerine helps patients with cardiovascular disease and leads to the development of new drugs. Furchgott and Ignarro share the Nobel Prize in physiology of medicine in 1998 with Ferid Murad "for their discoveries concerning nitric oxide as a signaling molecule in the cardiovascular system."

(B)

Simon Donaldson, Gerd Faltings, and Michael Freedman receive the Fields medal.

As described in the sidebar "Awarding Science," the Fields medal is awarded every four years to young mathematicians who have made significant advances in their field. In 1986, British mathematician Simon Donaldson (b. 1957), German mathematician Gerd Faltings (b. 1954), and American mathematician Michael Freedman (b. 1951) receive the Fields medal. Donaldson and Freedman study the *topology* of four-fold manifolds. Faltings is honored for his proof of the Mordell Conjecture.

(M)

January 24

Voyager II flies by Uranus.

As described in the sidebar "Exploring Space," during the 1970s the United States sent out a number of unmanned spacecrafts to study the solar system. On January 24, 1986, the spacecraft *Voyager II* reaches the planet Uranus. *Voyager II* sends back photographs of the planet's rings, as well as data showing that 10 moons orbit Uranus, and demonstrating that the planet has a strong *magnetic field.*

(SA)

January 28

Space shuttle *Challenger* explodes after liftoff.

The United States developed space shuttles as reusable spacecrafts that can shuttle between the Earth and orbiting bodies such as satellites and space stations (*See* entry for APRIL 1981). After nearly five years of flying successful missions, the space shuttle *Challenger* explodes shortly after launch, killing all seven passengers aboard. The terrible accident leads to a reevaluation of the shuttle program, and flights are suspended until September 1988.

(SA)

February 20

The Soviet Union launches the *Mir* space station.

The United States and the Soviet Union continued their "space race" into the 1980s (*See* the sidebar "Exploring Space" for more

details). On February 20, 1986, the Soviet Union launches the *Mir* space station. *Mir* is manned by a series of cosmonauts from March 1986 to June 2000. After the end of the cold war, *Mir* becomes a site of cooperation between Russia and the United States when, in 1995, the nations agree to a joint venture in which a space shuttle flies missions and supplies astronauts to *Mir.*

(SA)

March 28

H. Robert Horvitz isolates genes that control cell death.

Biologists studying the development of multicellular organisms used the worm *Caenorhabditis elegans* (*C. elegans*) as a model system (*See* entry for MAY 1974). During the development, some cells died in a regulated manner by a process called apoptosis or programmed cell death. On March 28, 1986, American biologist H. Robert Horvitz (b. 1947) publishes a paper identifying two *genes* that control programmed cell death in *C. elegans.* Horvitz shares the Nobel Prize in physiology or medicine in 2002 with Sydney Brenner and John E. Sulston "for their discoveries concerning genetic regulation of organ development and programmed cell death."

(B)

April

J. Georg Bednorz and K. Alexander Müller discover new superconductors.

Physicists at the beginning of the 20th century showed that at extremely low temperatures some materials become *superconductors,* conducting *electricity* with little or no resistance (*See* entry for 1911). For the next several decades, researchers looked for materials that would become superconductors at higher temperature. In 1986, the highest temperature of known superconductors is −482°F (−250°C). In April of that year, German physicist J. Georg Bednorz (b. 1950) and K. Alexander Müller (b. 1927) show that lanthanum-copper oxide is a superconductor at −460°F (−238°C). Their work leads to an explosion in the use of oxides as superconductors. Bednorz and Muller are honored with the Nobel Prize in physics in 1987 "for their important breakthrough in the discovery of superconductivity in ceramic materials."

(P)

1987

Ahmed Zewail shows how atoms move during a chemical reaction.

When two molecules react with each other, the arrangement of the *atoms* involved in the reaction changes. All reactions go through a transition state in which the molecules have a different structure than either the initial reactants or the final products. Chemists have to deduce the structures of transition states because they are short-lived and cannot be isolated. In 1987, Egyptian chemist Ahmed Zewail (b. 1946) develops a technique called femtosecond *spectroscopy,* which allows scientists to study transition states and see how atoms move during chemical reactions. Zewail is honored with the Nobel Prize in chemistry in 1999 "for his studies of the transition states of chemical reactions using femtosecond spectroscopy."

(C)

February 23

Masatoshi Koshiba detects and captures neutrinos from a supernova explosion.

Neutrinos are *subatomic particles* that are formed during *fusion* reactions. These particles are difficult to detect because they do not interact with matter. American physicist Raymond Davis first captured neutrinos from the Sun in the 1960s (*See* entry for JUNE 22, 1968). Japanese physicist Masatoshi Koshiba

(b. 1926) and colleagues who detect and capture neutrinos from a distant *supernova* explosion on February 23, 1987, confirm his work decades later. Their work establishes the study of neutrinos as an important branch of astrophysics. Davis and Koshiba share the Nobel Prize in physics in 2002 "for pioneering contributions to astrophysics, in particular for the detection of cosmic neutrinos."

(P)

September

The Montreal Protocol on Substances that Deplete the Ozone Layer is finalized.

The Earth's upper atmosphere contains a layer with a high concentration of ozone molecules. Ozone absorbs solar *radiation,* protecting the Earth from dangerous ultraviolet light. By the middle of the 1980s, scientists realized that a number of air pollutants, particularly chlorofluorocarbons (CFCs), undergo chemical reactions that lead to the depletion of the *ozone layer* (*See* entry for 1974). In September 1987, an international treaty called The Montreal Protocol on Substances that Deplete the Ozone Layer is finalized. The Montreal Protocol, as it comes to be known, is signed by more than 100 country and leads to marked reduction in the use of CFCs.

(C, W)

1988

William Phillips cools atoms below the known limit.

Studying the behavior and properties of *atoms* is difficult because they are constantly in motion. The motion of particles is proportional to temperature, with particles moving faster at high temperatures and slower at low temperatures. In the 1980s, American physicist William Phillips (b. 1948) developed a method to slow the movement of atoms, using a *magnetic field*. In 1988, he reduces the temperature of atoms slowed by a magnetic field and shows that he could cool the atoms to mere fractions of a degree above *absolute zero*, six times lower than the theoretical limit. He collaborates with French physicist Claude Cohen-Tannoudji (b. 1933) to explain why these temperatures could be achieved in the laboratory. Phillips and Cohen-Tannoudji share the Nobel Prize in physics in 1997 with Steven Chu "for development of methods to cool and trap atoms with laser light."

(P)

John Fenn and Koichi Tanaka adapt mass spectrometry to study proteins.

Proteins are large biological molecules that perform much of the work that is essential for cells to survive and thrive. Chemists routinely use a technique called mass spectrometry to determine the size of molecules. However, for many years this technique could not be used to study proteins because the molecules were too big to be analyzed. In 1988, American chemist John Fenn (b. 1917) and Japanese chemist Koichi Tanaka (b. 1959) independently adapt mass spectrometry so that the technique could be applied to proteins. Their techniques are not used to study individual proteins and complexes of proteins that are critical for life. Fenn and Tanaka share the Nobel Prize in chemistry in 2002 for "for their development of soft desorption ionization methods for mass spectrometric analyses of biological macromolecules."

(B, C)

Peter Agre discovers a channel that allows water flow into cells.

A semipermeable *membrane* surrounds cells, controlling the flow of molecules into and out of the cell. Embedded within these membranes are a variety of *proteins* that allow some molecules or *ions* to cross the membrane while prohibiting the movement of others. One of the most important molecules in the cell is water, which is the primary component of the cell cytoplasm. Without a mechanism to control the flow of water into and out of the cell, cells would not maintain a constant volume. In 1988, American scientist Peter Agre (b. 1949) discovers a channel protein in the cell membrane that is responsible for transporting water. He is honored with the Nobel Prize in chemistry in 2003 "for the discovery of water channels."

(B, C)

1989

John Huchra and Margaret Geller discover the "Great Wall of Galaxies."

Galaxies move as the universe expands, a property that astronomers study by measuring the shift in wavelength of *radiation* emitted as they move, known as the redshift. In the 1970s, astronomers began to map the galaxies of the universe, using redshift data. In 1989, astronomers John Huchra and Margaret Geller (b. 1947) announce that in the course of redshift mapping, they have discovered the largest-known structure in the universe. Huchra and Geller describe a cluster of galaxies 600 million light-years long, 250 million light-years high, and 30 million light-years deep. The structure is known as the "Great Wall of Galaxies."

(SA)

August 24

Voyager II flies by Neptune.

As described in the sidebar "Exploring Space," during the 1970s and 1980s the United States used a series of unmanned spacecrafts to study the solar system. On August 24, 1989, the spacecraft *Voyager II* reaches the planet Neptune. Data from *Voyager II* shows that Neptune is surrounded by three rings and is orbited by six previously undiscovered moons. The spacecraft also studies the *magnetic field* that surrounds Neptune.

(SA)

1990

Richard Schrock develops new metal-containing catalysts.

Organic chemists use metathesis reactions to synthesize new molecules (*See* entry for 1971). These reactions require metal-containing catalysts to accelerate the reaction so that it is useful in an industrial setting. In 1990, American chemist Richard Schrock (b. 1945) develops a molybdenum containing catalyst that could be used in the synthesis of carbon chains with double bonds. His work allows for the routine synthesis of such molecules in the laboratory. Schrock shares the Nobel Prize in chemistry in 2005 with Yves Chauvin and Robert Grubbs "for the development of the metathesis method in organic synthesis."

(C)

The United States launches the Human Genome Project.

Throughout the 1970s and 1980s, biologists made great strides in understanding and manipulating DNA. By 1990, scientists routinely analyzed the DNA sequences of *genes* and began turning their attention to all of the genetic information in an organism, known as a *genome*. In that year, the United States government begins to fund a project to sequence the entire human genome. Over the next 13 years, scientists working on the Human Genome Project improve the sequencing of DNA and eventually sequence the majority of DNA in human cells.

(B)

Vladimir Drinfeld, Vaughan Jones, Shigefumi Mori, and Edward Witten receive the Fields medal.

As described in the sidebar "Awarding Science," the Fields medal is awarded every four years to young mathematicians who have made significant advances in their field. In 1990, Ukrainian mathematician Vladimir Drinfeld (b. 1954), New Zealander Vaughan Jones (b. 1952), Japanese mathematician Shigefumi Mori (b. 1951), and American mathematician Edward Witten are awarded the Fields medal. Drinfeld's work centers on quantum groups and *number theory*. Jones studies geometric *topology*. Mori works in the field of algebraic geometry. Witten studies mathematics as it relates to theoretical physics.

(M)

April 25

NASA places the *Hubble Space Telescope* into orbit.

As scientists asked more complex questions about the universe, they required more powerful and sophisticated telescopes to research their problems. On April 25, 1990, NASA places a powerful telescope into orbit around the Earth. The telescope,

The *Hubble Space Telescope* begins orbiting the Earth in the 1990s. *(NASA)*

named Hubble after American astronomer Edwin Hubble, detects visible, ultraviolet, and infrared light, and can visualize images with about 10-fold higher resolution than telescopes located on the Earth. The telescope becomes operational in 1993 and is scheduled to remain in use for 20 years.

(SA)

1991

Iijima Sumio discovers carbon nanotubes.

During the 1980s, chemists showed that *atoms* of elemental carbon can group together forming a domelike structure called a fullerene. In 1991, Japanese scientist Iijima Sumio (b. 1939) finds extremely small cylinders of carbon, known as nanotubes, left behind as a by-product of fullerene formation. Carbon nanotubes can act as *semiconductors* and are used in high-powered microscopes and consumer electronic devices such as flat-screen display panels.

(C, P)

April 5

Linda Buck and Richard Axel describe the genetic basis of smell.

The ability of animals to take in information via the five senses is based on the function of the nervous system. Sensory organs contain receptors that stimulate *neurons* that send signals to the brain. Each receptor binds to a specific chemical in the air, which is then perceived as smell. On April 5, 1991, American biologists Linda Buck (b. 1947) and Richard Axel (b. 1946) jointly publish a paper showing that nearly 3 percent of human genes encode receptors involved in the sense of smell. The two scientists share the Nobel Prize in physiology or medicine in 2004 "for their discoveries of odorant receptors and the organization of the olfactory system."

(B)

1992

Robert Grubbs develops a new catalyst used in the synthesis of carbon chains with double bonds.

Synthetic chemists use a variety of catalysts to accelerate the rate of chemical reactions and make new molecules. Metal-containing catalysts are used in metathesis reactions—synthetic reactions that are used to make molecules that contain carbon chains with double bonds. American chemist Richard Schrock developed a molybdenum-containing catalyst for this purpose (*See* entry for 1990). In 1992, American chemist Robert Grubbs (b. 1942) published his work on a ruthenium-containing catalyst for metathesis reactions that was less reactive, and thus more widely useful. Grubbs shares the Nobel Prize in chemistry in 2005 with Schrock and Yves Chauvin "for the development of the metathesis method in organic synthesis."

(C)

George Smoot detects "ripples" from the big bang.

By the 1940s, astronomers proposed that the universe formed from an explosion widely known as the big bang. Evidence for the *big bang theory* includes the discovery of *cosmic background radiation* that was released as a by-product of the explosion. In 1992, American cosmologists George Smoot (b. 1945) analyzes data from the Cosmic Background Explorer (COBE) satellite and detects variation in the cosmic background radiation, popularly known as "ripples" from the big bang. Scientists continue mapping these variations, hoping they will provide more clues as to the origin of the universe.

(SA)

January

Tim Berners-Lee introduces the first Web browser.

Primarily, government and academic scientists first used the Internet, which was

MODEL OF THE COSMIC BACKGROUND EXPLORER (COBE)

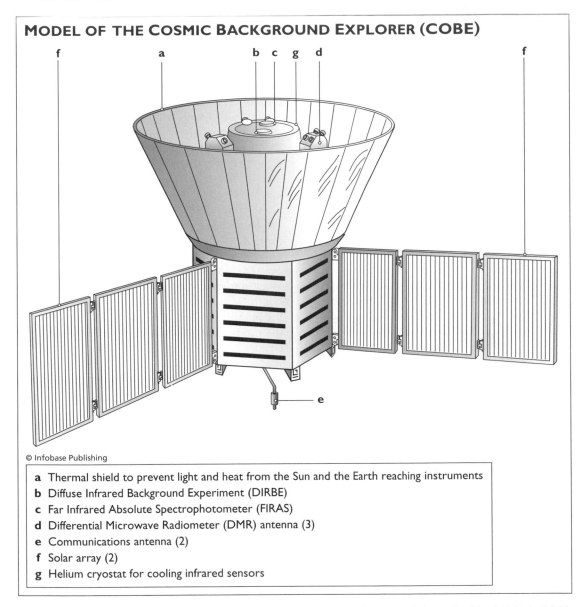

© Infobase Publishing

a Thermal shield to prevent light and heat from the Sun and the Earth reaching instruments
b Diffuse Infrared Background Experiment (DIRBE)
c Far Infrared Absolute Spectrophotometer (FIRAS)
d Differential Microwave Radiometer (DMR) antenna (3)
e Communications antenna (2)
f Solar array (2)
g Helium cryostat for cooling infrared sensors

Model of the cosmic background explorer (COBE), an unmanned spacecraft launched by NASA in 1989 that measures cosmic background radiation

established in the 1970s. In January 1992, scientists and engineers at CERN in Switzerland, led by British scientist Sir Tim Berners-Lee (b. 1955), introduce the first Web browser, establishing the World Wide Web. Berners-Lee bases his browser on links written in the hypertext markup language (HTML). With the introduction of the Web browser, the Internet immediately becomes accessible to people without sophisticated computer knowledge.

(M)

COMPUTERS AND SCIENCE

At the start of the 20th century, computers were still merely ideas in the heads of forward-thinking mathematicians and inventors. By the close of the century, computers were essential tools used throughout the industrialized world. Computers and traditional scientific research have a symbiotic relationship—the continued improvement to computers depends upon scientific research just as many current scientific investigations could not occur without powerful computers. This strong relationship between computers and science will likely continue into the next century as nanotechnology, a field of research dedicated to building and studying extremely small devices, becomes increasingly common and as sciences such as biology and astronomy continue generating massive amounts of data that require complex computer algorithms to analyze and interpret.

The development of the modern computer began in the 19th century. English mathematician Charles Babbage drew a design for an analytical engine that could be used to calculate large numbers. While Babbage never built his machine, today many consider the analytical engine to be a forerunner to the modern computer. Also during the 19th century, mathematician George Boole developed a method to represent logic using *algebra.* His Boolean logic is the basis of many modern computer programs.

Scientists and engineers built the first modern computers in the early 1940s. Early computers included the 35-ton Mark I, a calculator that could perform mathematical operations and remember the results, and Colossus, a code-breaking machine used in World War II. During this decade, the frenzied pace that characterizes the development of new computing technology begins. Within three years, engineers develop the first electronic computer, electronic integrator and computer (ENIAC), which is 1,000 times faster than early computers. Over the next decade, the invention of the *transistor* and the development of new programming languages such as FORTRAN, make computers increasingly useful to scientists, such as astronomers who use computers to predict orbits. By the end of the 1950s, the invention of the microchip allows computers to shrink from the room-filling machines of the 1940s to the desktops and laptops used at the end of the century.

Today, one of the most common uses of computers is the daily exchange of information that occurs across the Internet. The roots of the Internet are traced to a project by the U.S. Advanced Research Project Agency (ARPA) that developed a way for computers to communicate with one another. The computer network, called the ARPANET, connects government and academic computers, allowing scientists and researchers to easily communicate with one another. For the next 25 years, the Internet remains primarily a research tool. The widespread used of the Internet begins in the 1990s

1993

Andrew Wiles proves Fermat's Last Theorem.

Some scientific problems endure for centuries. One example is the proof of "Fermat's Last Theorem," the statement that given the equations $x^n + y^n = z^n$ the value of n cannot be a *natural number* greater than 2. In 1637, French mathematician Pierre Fermat wrote his theorem in the margin of a book, adding that he had found a proof but does not have the space to write it in the margin (*See* entry for 1637). For the next three centuries, mathematicians attempted to prove Fermat's

with the development of the Web browser, a tool that makes the Internet accessible to people without highly specialized computer training.

With the invention of the microchip in the 1950s, computers went from being the size of a room to a relatively small box that can sit on a desk. Today, scientists are working to build even smaller machines using nanochips. At the end of the 20th century, scientists and engineers work to find materials suitable for building circuits thousands of times smaller than tradi-tional computer chips. Researchers in the field of *nanotechnology* are working toward build-ing components that are smaller than 100 nm, roughly 0.000004 inch! The first nanochips, built in 2000, contain some features that are 0.000002 inch (50 nm) or smaller. These chips are found in computers built at the beginning of the 21st century. In the future, researchers hope to find new materials and use them to make nanodevices for use in fields from com-puting to medicine.

Electronic Numeric Integrator and Calculator, or ENIAC, is one of the first digital calculators and a forerunner to the modern computer. *(SPL/Photo Researchers, Inc)*

Last Theorem. In 1900, mathematician David Hilbert included the search for a proof on his list of mathematical problems to be addressed in the 20th century (*See* entry for 1900). The search ends in 1993, when British mathematician Andrew Wiles finally proves Fermat's Last Theorem.

(M)

1994

Jean Bourgain, Pierre-Louis Lions, Jean-Christophe Yoccoz, and Efim Zelmanov receive the Fields medal.

As described in the sidebar "Awarding Sci-ence," the Fields medal is awarded every four years to young mathematicians who have made significant advances in their field. In 1994, Belgian mathematician Jean Bourgain (b. 1954), French mathematicians Pierre-Louis Lions (b. 1956) and Jean-Christophe Yoccoz (b. 1957), and Russian mathematician Efim Zelmanov (b. 1955) receive the Fields medal. Bourgain is honored for his work in the *geometry* Banach spaces. Lions's work is in the field of nonlinear partial differential equations. Yoccoz studies dynamic systems. Zelmanov is honored for his solution to the restricted Burnside problem.

(M)

July 16

The comet Shoemaker-Levy 9 crashes into Jupiter.

Astronomers have observed *comets,* celestial bodies made of ice and dirt, for centuries. Like *asteroids,* a comet can crash into a planet when their orbits overlap. In 1993, the astronomers Gene (b. 1928) and Carolyn (b. 1929) Shoemaker and David Levy (b. 1948) studied a family of comets known as the Shoemaker-Levy comets. They noted that one of them, Shoemaker-Levy 9, was on a path to collide with the planet Jupiter. The crash takes place on July 16, 1994.

(SA)

August 25

John Walker determines the structure of the ATP synthesizing complex.

Cells require *energy* to perform tasks from replicating their DNA to communicating with other cells. In biological systems, cells break down storage molecules from food, such as *carbohydrates,* and store the energy in the form of a molecule called ATP. One of the major questions addressed by 20th-century biologists was how do cells store the energy they obtain from food into ATP. In 1978, American chemist Paul Boyer proposed that a *membrane* protein called the ATP synthase synthesizes

molecules of ATP in the cell by a novel mechanism (*See* entry for 1978). On August 25, 1994, British chemist John Walker (b. 1941) publishes the three-dimensional structure of the ATP synthase. His structure provides the evidence needed to confirm Boyer's model. Walker and Boyer share the Novel Prize in chemistry in 1997 "for their elucidation of the enzymatic mechanism underlying the synthesis of adenosine triphosphate (ATP)."

(B, C)

1995

IPCC states that humans have influenced the global climate.

As described in the sidebar "Climate Change," at the end of the 20th century scientists across the world became increasingly concerned about global climate changes. In 1988, an international group of panel called the Intergovernmental Panel on Climate Change (IPCC) convened to study climate change. In 1995, the IPCC releases a report called *Climate Change 1995,* describing the increase in the atmospheric concentration of *greenhouse gases* and detailing the 0.5°F–1.1°F (0.3–0.6°C) increase in global air temperature over the past century. The report cites evidence that human activities such as the use of aerosols and the release of carbon dioxide into the atmosphere has contributed to the observed increase in global air temperature. The IPCC report serves as the basis of international treaties to fight climate change.

(ES, W)

March 2

Scientists at the Fermi National Laboratory discover the top quark.

Advances in particle physics during the 20th century led to the theory that *subatomic particles* are composed of even smaller particles called *quarks* (*See* entry for 1964). Different types or "flavors" of quarks were proposed to exist. One of these flavors, the top quark, was proposed in the 1970s. On March 2, 1995, scientists at the Fermi National Accelerator Laboratory use the collision between a *proton* and an antiproton to produce the top quark.

(P)

June 5

Eric Cornell and Carl Wieman achieve the Bose-Einstein condensate.

The first decades of the 20th century saw a revolution in physics as advances in *quantum mechanics* changed the way scientists view matter and *energy*. In 1924, Indian physicist S.N. Bose performed theoretical calculations showing that when a given number of particles come in close enough contact with one another they will form a new form of matter. His work was translated and extended by Albert Einstein, thus the matter is known as the Bose-Einstein condensate (*See* entry for 1924). On June 5, 1995, American physicists Eric Cornell (b. 1961) and Carl Wieman (b. 1951) achieve the first Bose-Einstein condensation in the laboratory. Soon after, German physicist Wolfgang Ketterle (b. 1957) also makes a Bose-Einstein condensate. The three scientists share the Nobel Prize in physics in 2001 for "for the achievement of Bose-Einstein condensation in dilute gases of alkali atoms, and for early fundamental studies of the properties of the condensates."

(P)

October

Michael Mayor and Didier Queloz discover a planet outside of the solar system.

Astronomers discovered the planet Pluto, the farthest from the Sun in the solar system, in 1930. Soon, the attention of planet hunters turned outside the solar system. For many years, the claims of planets outside the solar system proved false. Then, in October 1995, Swiss astronomers Michael Mayor (b. 1942) and Didier Queloz (b. 1966) discover a small planet orbiting the star 51 Pegasi. Their discovery begins a new era of planetary discovery, with more than 50 extrasolar planets found by the year 2000.

(SA)

1997

February 27

Ian Wilmut clones a sheep.

For most of the 20th century, the generation of cloned animals was a part of science fiction. In 1997, the cloning of a mammal becomes a reality with the February 27 announcement that Ian Wilmut (b. 1944) and colleagues had produced Dolly, the first sheep cloned from cells of an adult animal. Wilmut uses the *nucleus* of a cell taken from the mammary gland of one sheep and injects it into an unfertilized egg, a process known as nuclear transfer. The embryo is implanted in the womb of another sheep, which gives birth to Dolly. This work sparks a debate of the ethics of cloning as many realize that the cloning of humans could also be possible in the not so distant future.

(B)

July 4

Pathfinder lands on the surface of Mars.

As described in the sidebar "Exploring Space," the United States sent a host of unmanned spacecraft to investigate the planets of the solar system. On July 4, 1997, a robot called *Pathfinder* lands on the surface of the planet Mars. NASA scientists are able to control the movements of *Pathfinder* from Earth. The Mars Rover, as it is also known, sends back stunning pictures of the surface of Mars and collects samples of soil and rock.

(ES, SA)

Beginning in the 1990s, NASA scientists use a series of robots or rovers to study the surface of Mars. *(NASA)*

July 11

Biologists announce the sequencing of DNA from a Neanderthal fossil.

Beginning in the 19th century, biologists found and studied fossils of early humans. Advances in *molecular biology* at the end of the 20th century allowed scientists to extract from these fossils. On July 11, 1997, two groups of scientists announce that they have successfully extracted and sequenced small pieces of mitochondrial DNA from Neanderthal fossils. By comparing the DNA from the fossils to mitochondrial DNA from living humans, the groups provide evidence that Neanderthals are not direct ancestors of humans but a separate species that is now extinct.

(B)

December

The Kyoto Protocol on Climate Change lays out a plan to reduce greenhouse gases.

As described in the sidebar "Climate Change," at the end of the 20th century scientists and policy makers became increasingly concerned with the increase of global air temperatures. In December 1997, representatives from 160 nations meet in Kyoto, Japan, to draft an agreement to fight global warming by reducing emissions of gases implicated in climate change, known as *greenhouse gases*. The Kyoto Protocol on Climate Change sets reduction targets for each industrialized country. The Kyoto Protocol meets stiff political resistance in the United States because of concern for the economic implications of such a drastic reduction in greenhouse gases.

(ES, W)

1998

Astronomers suggest that the universe is expanding at an increasing rate.

Astronomers in the 20th century collected evidence that the universe is expanding; however the rate of expansion remained a mystery. In 1998, scientists at Lawrence Berkeley National Laboratory in California and the Mount Stromlo and Siding Spring Observatories in Australia independently conclude that the rate of expansion is increasing. Each group reaches their conclusions by studying different *supernovae*. Their data contradict the popular model that the rate at which the universe is expanding is slowing over time.

(SA)

Richard Borcherds, William Gowers, Maxim Kontsevich, and Curtis McMullen receive the Fields medal.

As described in the sidebar "Awarding Science," the Fields medal is awarded every four years to young mathematicians who have made significant advances in their field. In 1998, British mathematician Richard Borcherds (b. 1959) and William Gowers (b. 1963), French mathematician Maxim Kontsevich (b. 1964), and American mathematician Curtis McMullen (b. 1958) are honored with the Fields medal. Borcherds is cited for his work on automorphic forms and mathematical physics. Gowers is honored for his work in functional analysis. Kontsevich works in the fields of algebraic *geometry*. McMullen's work centers on the geometry of three-dimensional manifolds.

(M)

Roderick Makinnon reveals the three-dimensional structure of an ion channel.

Cell *membranes* contain embedded proteins that control the flow of *ions* and molecules into and out of the cell. These proteins are critical for maintaining the volume and proper chemical environment of the cell. For example, cells have a variety of ion channels that allow only one or few types of ions to cross the cell membrane in a regulated fashion. How do these channels discriminate between ions with similar size and charge? In 1998, American biologist Roderick Makinnon (b. 1956) answers this question when he solves the three-dimensional structure of an ion channel that allows potassium ions to cross cell membranes. Makinnon is honored with the Nobel Prize in chemistry in 2003 "for structural and mechanistic studies of ion channels."

(B, C)

February 19

Andrew Fire and Craig Mello use small RNA molecules to block the expressions of genes.

As biologists understand more about the genetic basis of disease, it becomes apparent that the expression of certain *genes* causes some genetic diseases. Medical researchers look for ways to specifically block the expression of genes involved in disease without blocking the expression of the genes are that needed for cells and organisms to survive and thrive. On February 19, 1998, biologists Andrew Fire (b. 1959) and Craig Mello show that the presence of double-stranded RNA in cells can block *gene* expression by interfering with protein synthesis. Today, researchers are trying to use RNA interference to treat diseases, including genetic disorders and cancers.

(B)

March 26

Scientists observe the connection between gamma ray bursts and supernova explosions.

Astronomers have observed bright bodies in the sky called *supernovae* for centuries. By the end of the 20th century, scientists realized that supernovae are actually exploding stars. Using powerful telescopes, they studied the cosmic events that surround supernovae. While observing the explosion of a supernova on March 26, 1998, three groups of scientists independently note that the explosion occurs at the same time as three bursts of *gamma rays*. Previous studies had linked bursts of these high-energy rays with supernovae; however this explosion provides the first clear connection.

(SA)

November 6

James Thomson announces the isolation of embryonic stem cells.

During development, cells are not as specialized as they are in an adult organism. Certain populations of cells called stem cells have not yet committed to becoming one type of cell or another. For example, stem cells from embryos are the most immature, and thus have the potential to differentiate into a wide array of different cell types. At the end of the 20th century, biologists began to think that such cells could be used in the laboratory to generate new cells and tissues to treat a variety of degenerative diseases. On November 6, 1998, American biologist James Thomson (b. 1958) announces that he has isolated human embryonic stem cells. During his procedure, human blastocysts are destroyed, which leads to controversy as to whether or not public money should be used to fund this research in the United States.

(B)

December

Scientists announce the complete sequence of the genome of a multicellular organism.

Advances in *molecular biology* at the end of the 20th century made it possible for biologists to sequence the entire DNA in an organism. The study of entire *genomes* of a multicellular organism began in 1998, when scientists published the DNA sequence of the *Caenorhabditis elegans* genome. *C. elegans* is a microscopic worm that biologists study as a model system for the development of multicellular organisms (*See* entry for MAY 1974). As the genomes of more organisms are sequenced, scientists are able to better understand the vast genetic similarities among organisms, as well as the genetic differences that lead to the visible differences between species.

(B)

1999

Physicists produce cold fermion gases.

During the 20th century, physicists began to discover a variety of *subatomic particles* and studied their properties. One group of subatomic particles, called *fermions,* includes

electrons and nuclei with odd masses. Unlike *bosons* (*See* entry for 1924), when gases of fermions are cooled to extremely low temperatures, they do not form a condensate. Instead, the particles are believed to form pairs. Physicists became interested in the properties of these pairs, and in 1999 make the first step toward studying them when several groups independently announce the production of a cold *fermion* gas.

(P)

August

Geologists find fossil evidence of 2.7-billion-year-old eukaryotes.

Eukaryotic cells are divided into several cellular compartments or *organelles*. Biologists believe that eukaryotes evolved from more simple organisms such as archea around 2 billion years ago. In August 1999, geologists discover fossil evidence suggesting that eukaryotes lived on Earth 2.7 billion years ago.

(B, ES)

2000

Theodor Hänsch and John Hall develop laser-based precision spectroscopy.

Experimental science depends on the ability of researchers to make precise and accurate measurements. One important measurement made by physicists is the frequency of light. In the second half of the 20th century, physicists began using lasers to make these measurements. By 2000, German physicist Theodor Hänsch (b. 1941) and American physicist John Hall (b. 1934) independently made advances that led to the development of laser-based precision spectroscopy. This technique allows scientists to accurately measure frequencies up to 15 decimal places. Hänsch and Hall share the Nobel Prize in physics in 2005 "for their contributions to the development of laser-based precision spectroscopy, including the optical frequency comb technique."

(P)

June 26

Scientists announce the completion of the "rough draft" of the human genome.

Advances in *molecular biology* at the end of the 20th century made it possible for biologists to obtain the entire DNA sequence of an organism. By comparing the complete genetic information, known as *genomes,* of different species, scientists began to understand the similarities among living organisms. In June 2000, American biologists Francis Collins (b. 1950) of the Human Genome Project and J. Craig Venter (b. 1946) of the private company Celera, jointly announce the completion of a "rough draft" of the human genome. Their work shows that humans have 35,000 genes and vast regions of repetitive DNA.

(B)

August

Data from the spacecraft *Galileo* suggests that there is water on Europa.

Galileo first sighted Europa, one of the moons orbiting the planet Jupiter, in the 17th century (*See* entry for 1610). Nearly 400 years later, a spacecraft bearing Galileo's name studied the surface of Jupiter and Europa, sending data back to Earth that suggest that Europa is covered with a salty ocean. Equipment aboard *Galileo* measured the *magnetic fields* surrounding both Jupiter and Europa and found that the orientation of the magnetic field on Europa is related to the magnetic field of Jupiter. In August 2000, scientists deduce that this could happen only if the surface of Europa is covered with a liquid capable of conducting *electricity,* such as a salty ocean.

(SA)

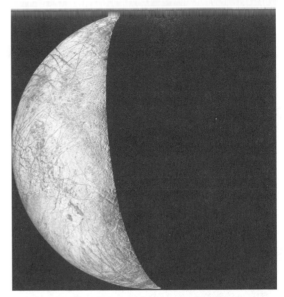

Image of Jupiter's moon Europa, taken by *Voyager 2 (NASA)*

2001

The Food and Drug Administration approves a rationally designed anticancer drug.

Cancer occurs when the normal regulation of cell growth fails, allowing cells to rapidly divide and form tumors. For many years, anticancer chemotherapy consisted primarily of poisons that kill both cancer cells and normal cells. Such drugs led to the severe side effects associated with chemotherapy such as hair loss and immune system suppression. At the end of the 20th century, medical researchers tried to apply their knowledge of how cells work to rationally design drugs that would kill cancer cells while allowing normal cells to live. In 2001, the United States Food and Drug Administration approves the use of Gleevec, a rationally designed drug that specifically kills certain leukemia cells. The approval of Gleevec heralds a new age in cancer treatment.

(B)

January

IPCC announces that climate change is caused by an increase in greenhouse gases.

As described in the sidebar "Climate Change," scientists noted an increase in the global air temperatures at the end of the 20th century. An international working group called the Intergovernmental Panel on Climate Change (IPCC) studied this problem. In January 2001, the IPCC announces that the observed global warming of the previous 50 years was likely caused by an increased concentration of *greenhouse gases,* such as carbon dioxide. Their study puts pressure on nations to ratify the Kyoto Protocol (*See* entry for DECEMBER 1997), but many countries, including the United States, fail to sign the treaty.

(ES, W)

April

James Heath announces the invention of a functioning nanocircuit.

As described in the sidebar "Computers and Science," during the second half of the 20th century manufacturers made smaller computers as electronics technology improved. Some engineers began to believe that electronic circuits could be made from single molecules. Such ideas spawned the field of *nanotechnology.* In April 2001, James Heath announces that he and his colleagues have made a functioning nanocircuit using molecules called rotaxanes. The molecules act a *transistor* for a 16-bit memory circuit. Heath's work is soon followed by announcements of working nanocircuits developed by other groups.

(C, P)

2002

Laurent Lafforgue and Vladimir Voevodsky receive the Fields medal.

As described in the sidebar "Awarding Science," the Fields medal is awarded every four years to young mathematicians who have made significant advances in their field. In 2002, French mathematician Laurent Lafforgue (b. 1966) and Russian mathematician Vladimir Voevodsky (b. 1966) are awarded the Fields medal. Lafforgue is honored for his work on the Langlands Problem. Voevodsky is honored for his work in algebraic *geometry.*

(M)

April

Sudbury Neutrino Observatory solves the solar neutrino paradox.

During the 20th century, physicists studied the properties of the various *subatomic particles* found in the universe. One of these particles, the *neutrino,* proved to be difficult to study. Neutrinos come in three flavors: electron, mu, and tau. Physicists know that the Sun produces electron neutrinos, but only one-third of these particles appear to reach the Earth—an observation known as the solar neutrino paradox. In April 2002, scientists at the Sudbury Neutrino Observatory (SNO) show the electron neutrinos from the Sun can change flavors on their journey to the Earth. When researchers added the electron, mu, and tau neutrinos together, they found the expected number of solar neutrinos, thus solving the solar neutrino paradox.

(P, SA)

July 11

Michel Brunet announces the discovery of the oldest-known hominid.

Paleoanthropologists study the fossils of ancient primates to understand the origin of humans. The oldest-known hominid fossils were found in East Africa and appeared to be nearly 3 million years old. On July 11, 2002, Michel Brunet (b. 1940) and colleagues announce the discovery of human ancestor that is between 6 and 7 million years old. The fossil, which they call Toumaï, is found in western Africa. Their discovery is controversial, as other researchers argue that Toumaï is an early ape, rather than an early species of man.

(B)

September 23

Scientists report polarization in cosmic microwave background.

The discovery of the cosmic microwave background in 1965 gave cosmologists an important piece of evidence that the universe is expanding. Astronomers continued to study cosmic microwave background, looking for clues to how the events after the big bang occurred. On September 23, 2002, scientists report a study using Degree Angular Scale Interferometer (DASI) that detected polarization in the cosmic microwave background. This finding confirms the prediction of scientists studying the origins of the universe.

(P, SA)

2003

February

Images from the Wilkinson Microwave Anisotropy Probe show the universe is made up of dark energy.

Cosmologists investigating the beginnings of the universe have shown that universe is expanding. In 1998, astronomers showed that the rate of expansion is actually increasing. A force known as dark energy was thought to mediate this expansion by overcoming the force of *gravity* that would naturally bring bodies together. In 2003, the Wilkinson Microwave Anisotropy Probe (WMAP) sends images back to Earth that show that 73 percent of the universe is made of dark energy. Data from the WMAP also helps cosmologists estimate the age of

the universe to be 13.7 billion years old, calculate the rate at which the universe is expanding, and determine that the universe is flat.

(SA)

February 1

The space shuttle *Columbia* explodes upon reentering the Earth's atmosphere.

As described in the sidebar "Exploring Space," the United States developed the space shuttle as a reusable spacecraft for manned flight. On April 12, 1981, NASA successfully launched *Columbia,* the first space shuttle (*See* entry for APRIL 12, 1981). After a fatal accident in 1986, the space shuttles returned to regular mission. On February 1, 2003, a second fatal accident occurs when the space shuttle *Columbia* explodes upon reentering the Earth's atmosphere. All seven crewmembers are killed in the accident, and the United States once again reevaluates the space shuttle program.

(SA)

April 14

Scientists complete the sequencing of the human genome.

At the end of the 20th century, biologists determined the DNA sequence of *genomes* from a wide variety of organisms. In June 2000, two large groups announced that they had obtained a "rough draft" of the DNA sequence from humans (*See* entry for JUNE 2000). The completion of this project is announced on April 14, 2003. The "final draft" of the human genome accounts for 99 percent of the DNA in humans and is 99.99 percent accurate. The sequences are freely available to other scientists who continue to use data from the Human Genome Project to study human diseases.

(B)

Biologists in the 21st century working in the field of genomics use computers to analyze the information from thousands of genes in a single experiment. *(NCI)*

2004

January 25

NASA scientists announce that data from the Mars Rover suggest there was once water on Mars.

Beginning in 1998, the United States sent a series of robots to photograph and analyze the surface of Mars. On January 25, 2004, NASA scientists announce that geological samples taken by the Mars Rover *Opportunity* suggest that there was once water on Mars. By studying *sediments* in the Martian bedrock, *Opportunity* shows that the pattern of sedimentation is similar to that which occurs with gradual drying.

(ES, SA)

February

Scientists in Russia produce element 115 and element 113.

Physicists can produce *elements* that do not naturally occur in the laboratory. In February 2004, a group of Russian scientist published a paper reporting that they produced four nuclei of an element with 115 *protons* by fusing calcium nuclei with americanium nuclei. These nuclei quickly decay to an element with 113 protons.

(C, P)

October 4

***SpaceShipOne* completes flight as the first privately funded manned spacecraft.**

The success of manned space programs, from the lunar landing to the space shuttle, stimulates entrepreneurs to dream of space tourism. To stimulate the development of private spaceflight, a private foundation offered a $10 million prize for the first private spacecraft to fly into space twice within a span of two weeks. On October 4, 2004, *SpaceShipOne,* designed by American engineer Burt Rutan, completed its second flight, 367,500 feet (112 km) into the air.

(SA)

December 26

An earthquake in the Indian Ocean triggers a tsunami.

On December 26, 2004, the fourth-largest earthquake since 1900, measuring 9.0 on the Richter scale, occurs in the Indian Ocean. The earthquake triggers a devastating tsunami that affects 12 East Asian countries, notably Sri Lanka, Indonesia, and Thailand, and reaches as far as the east coast of Africa and kills an estimated 300,000 people. The tragedy prompts the nations that border the Indian Ocean to set up a tsunami early warning system similar to the one that exists in the Pacific Ocean.

(ES, MS)

2005

January 14

Huygens becomes the first spacecraft to land on the moon of another planet.

Dutch astronomer Christiaan Huygens discovered Titan, the largest of Saturn's 18 moons, in 1655 (*See* entry for 1655). The European Space Agency (ESA) named the probe it sent to Titan after the astronomer. On January 14, 2005, *Huygens* lands on Titan, sending back pictures and scientific data to scientists on Earth. Data collected by the probe includes temperature, pressure, and wind speeds, as well as data on the composition of the soil on the surface of Titan.

(SA)

February 16

Kyoto Protocol on Climate Change enters into force.

In December 1997, representatives from 160 nations drafted an agreement to fight global warming by reducing emissions of *greenhouse gases* that impact climate change (*See* entry for DECEMBER 1997). The Kyoto Protocol to the United Nations Framework on Climate Change set reduction targets for each industrialized country. The Kyoto Protocol meets stiff political resistance in the United States because of concern for the economic implications of such a drastic reduction in greenhouse gases and is not ratified by Congress. On February 16, 2005, the agreement goes into force after 156 countries ratify the treaty.

(ES, W)

July 3

Deep Impact studies the collision of a spacecraft with a comet.

Comets, balls of dust, ice, and gas that orbit the Sun, were first observed by ancient astronomers and continue to be studied by 21st-century scientists. On July 3, 2005, NASA scientists participating in the *Deep Impact* mission fly a spacecraft into the comet Tempel 1. The experiment captured images of the comet's nucleus and showed that the gravitational forces that hold the comet together are much weaker than had been previously believed.

(SA)

July 26

Space shuttle *Discovery* returns to space.

NASA placed the space shuttle program on hold for two and half years after the explosion of the space shuttle *Columbia* in 2003 (*See* entry for FEBRUARY 1, 2003). On July 26, 2005, the program resumed with the launching of the space shuttle *Discovery*. The successful mission included docking at the *International Space Station*, and the first in-orbit repair of damaged heat shields. *Discovery* successfully returned to Earth on August 9, 2005.

(SA)

September 1

Scientists publish the sequence of the chimpanzee genome.

The chimpanzee is the closest relative to humans, with evolutionary biologists calculating that the two species evolved from a common ancestor 6 million years ago. Their work shows that the genomes of humans and chimpanzees differ by only 4 percent. This work both confirms the close relationship between the two species and serves as a springboard for research into the genetic changes that allowed humans to evolve into a species with dramatically different appearance and behavior than other primates.

(B)

December 20

Judge rules that intelligent design cannot be taught in science class.

Despite being a widely accepted theory in biology for over 100 years, *evolution* is still challenged by religious critics. In the 21st century, proponents of intelligent design, a theory that says that life is so complex it could not have evolved but had to be designed, asked that their theory be taught in public schools alongside evolution. In 2004, the Dover Area School District administrators in Pennsylvania instructed the district's teachers to preface the teaching of evolution with a disclaimer saying that evolution is not a fact. Their directive generated an uproar throughout the United States, pitting scientists against intelligent-design proponents. On September 26, 2005,

a group of parents sued the school district to stop the disclaimer from being read. After a lengthy trial, the judge rules on December 20 that intelligent design is not a scientific theory but a repackaged form of creationism and as such cannot be taught in science class.

(B)

2006

January 6

Record-breaking Atlantic hurricane season ends.

Meteorologists have tracked hurricanes in the Atlantic Ocean since 1851. The 2005 Atlantic hurricane season was one of the longest and most active seasons in 150 years, setting records with 27 named tropical storms and 14 hurricanes. The season also included the costliest hurricane on record, Hurricane Katrina, which made landfall on the Gulf Coast of the United States on August 29, 2005. The hurricane caused a breach in the levies protecting the city of New Orleans, leading to widespread flooding and the death of more than 1,000 people.

(W)

January 10

A committee at Seoul National University finds that researchers fabricated data in a report of isolating embryonic stem cells from cloned human blastocysts.

The major advances in biology at the end of the 20th century included the first cloning of a mammal (*See* entry for FEBRUARY 27, 1997) and the isolation of human embryonic stem cells (*See* entry for NOVEMBER 6, 1998). These advances led to the hope that one day embryonic stem cells could be generated to match any individual. This controversial field of research appeared to have advanced in 2004, when Korean scientist Woo Suk Hwang and colleagues reported two important firsts: cloning of a human blastocyst and using it to generate an embryonic stem cell line. In 2005, questions about their research arose, prompting an investigation of two critical papers. On January 10, 2005, a committee at Seoul National University, where the research was conducted, finds that the researchers fabricated some of the data, discrediting their reported discoveries.

(B)

❧ CONCLUSION ❧

At the end of the 20th century, the pace of scientific discovery quickened as advances in computers and *molecular biology* allowed researchers to develop and test hypotheses faster than in any other era. These experiments generated an immense amount of data. At the beginning of the century, research was reported in a handful of scientific journals; by the end of the century, libraries and Web sites were filled with hundreds of journals chronicling the research achievements of the world scientific community. With so much information available, key findings might, for a time period, get overlooked. In any era, sometimes the importance of a scientific discovery is not immediately apparent. Recall that Gregor Mendel's seminal work in genetics did not enter mainstream biology for nearly 50 years. Thus, one could imagine, or even expect, that a seminal discovery recently made at the end of the 20th century has not yet been recognized.

In the introduction to his book *What Remains to be Discovered,* John Maddox, longtime editor of the scientific journal *Nature,* imagines what discoveries an author writing a similar volume in 1900 might have anticipated. Citing examples such as *quantum mechanics* and molecular biology that could not have been predicted at the end of the 19th century, Maddox shows that while the scientific advances of the future stem from the research of today, no one can accurately predict the discoveries that will change the world in the next hundred years. The experiments of the 21st century will yield data supporting many of today's theories, and also uncover strange phenomena, exceptions to known "rules," and contradictions that might lead to the next revolution in science that will change the way people think about nature and the world around them. What field will see such a revolution? A common sports cliché reminds fans, "That is why they play the game." In the laboratory, this cliché is modified to "That is why they do the experiments."

APPENDIX 1

Units and Measurements

FUNDAMENTAL UNITS

The system of measurements most commonly used in science is called both the SI (for Système International d'Unités) and the International System of Units (it is also sometimes called the MKS system). The SI system is based upon the metric units meter (abbreviated m), kilogram (kg), second (sec), kelvin (K), mole (mol), candela (cd), and ampere (A), used to measure length, time, mass, temperature, amount of a substance, light intensity, and electric current, respectively. This system was agreed upon in 1974 at an international general conference. There is another metric system, CGS, which stands for centimeter, gram, second; that system simply uses the hundredth of a meter (the centimeter) and the hundredth of the kilogram (the gram). The CGS system, formally introduced by the British Association for the Advancement of Science in 1874, is particularly useful to scientists making measurements of small quantities in laboratories, but it is less useful for space science. In this set, the SI system is used with the exception that temperatures will be presented in Celsius (C), instead of Kelvin. (The conversions between Celsius, Kelvin, and Fahrenheit temperatures are given below.) Often the standard unit of measure in the SI system, the meter, is too small when talking about the great distances in the solar system; kilometers (thousands of meters) or AU (astronomical units, defined below) will often be used instead of meters.

How is a unit defined? At one time a "meter" was defined as the length of a special metal ruler kept under strict conditions of temperature and humidity. That perfect meter could not be measured, however, without changing its temperature by opening the box, which would change its length, through thermal expansion or contraction. Today a meter is no longer defined according to a physical object; the only fundamental measurement that still is defined by a physical object is the kilogram. All of these units have had long and complex histories of attempts to define them. Some of the modern definitions, along with the use and abbreviation of each, are listed in the table here.

Mass and weight are often confused. Weight is proportional to the force of gravity: Your weight on Earth is about six times

445

FUNDAMENTAL UNITS

MEASUREMENT	UNIT	SYMBOL	DEFINITION
length	meter	m	The meter is the distance traveled by light in a vacuum during 1/299,792,458 of a second.
time	second	sec	The second is defined as the period of time in which the oscillations of cesium atoms, under specified conditions, complete exactly 9,192,631,770 cycles. The length of a second was thought to be a constant before Einstein developed theories in physics that show that the closer to the speed of light an object is traveling, the slower time is for that object. For the velocities on Earth, time is quite accurately still considered a constant.
mass	kilogram	kg	The International Bureau of Weights and Measures keeps the world's standard kilogram in Paris, and that object is the definition of the kilogram.
temperature	kelvin	K	A degree in Kelvin (and Celsius) is 1/273.16 of the thermodynamic temperature of the triple point of water (the temperature at which, under one atmosphere pressure, water coexists as water vapor, liquid, and solid ice). In 1967, the General Conference on Weights and Measures defined this temperature as 273.16 kelvin.
amount of a substance	mole	mol	The mole is the amount of a substance that contains as many units as there are atoms in 0.012 kilogram of carbon 12 (that is, Avogadro's number, or 6.02205×10^{23}). The units may be atoms, molecules, ions, or other particles.
electric current	ampere	A	The ampere is that constant current which, if maintained in two straight parallel conductors of infinite length, of negligible circular cross section, and placed one meter apart in a vacuum, would produce between these conductors a force equal to 2×10^{-7} newtons per meter of length.
light intensity	candela	cd	The candela is the luminous intensity of a source that emits monochromatic radiation with a wavelength of 555.17 nm and that has a radiant intensity of 1/683 watt per steradian. Normal human eyes are more sensitive to the yellow-green light of this wavelength than to any other.

your weight on the Moon because Earth's gravity is about six times that of the Moon's. Mass, on the other hand, is a quantity of matter, measured independently of gravity. In fact, weight has different units from mass: Weight is actually measured as a force (newtons, in SI, or pounds, in the English system).

The table "Fundamental Units" lists the fundamental units of the SI system. These are units that need to be defined in order to make other measurements. For example, the meter and the second are fundamental units (they are not based on any other units). To measure velocity, use a derived unit, meters per second (m/sec), a combination of fundamental units. Later in this section there is a list of common derived units.

The systems of temperature are capitalized (Fahrenheit, Celsius, and Kelvin), but the units are not (degree and kelvin). Unit abbreviations are capitalized only when they are named after a person, such as K for Lord Kelvin, or A for André-Marie Ampère. The units themselves are always lowercase, even when named for a person: one newton, or one N. Throughout these tables a small dot indicates multiplication, as in N • m, which means a newton (N) times a meter (m). A space between the symbols can also be used to indicate multiplication, as in N • m. When a small letter is placed in front of a symbol, it is a prefix meaning some multiplication factor. For example, J stands for the unit of energy called a joule, and a mJ indicates a millijoule, or $10{-3}$ joules. The table of prefixes is given at the end of this section.

COMPARISONS AMONG KELVIN, CELSIUS, AND FAHRENHEIT

One kelvin represents the same temperature difference as 1°C, and the temperature in kel-vins is always equal to 273.15 plus the temperature in degrees Celsius. The Celsius scale was designed around the behavior of water. The freezing point of water (at one atmosphere of pressure) was originally defined to be 0°C, while the boiling point is 100°C. The kelvin equals exactly 1.8°F.

To convert temperatures in the Fahrenheit scale to the Celsius scale, use the following equation, where F is degrees Fahrenheit, and C is degrees Celsius:

$$C = (F - 32)/1.8$$

And to convert Celsius to Fahrenheit, use this equation:

$$F = 1.8C + 32$$

To convert temperatures in the Celsius scale to the Kelvin scale, add 273.16. By convention, the degree symbol (°) is used for Celsius and Fahrenheit temperatures but not for temperatures given in Kelvin, for example, 0°C equals 273K.

What exactly is temperature? Qualitatively, it is a measurement of how hot something feels, and this definition is so easy to relate to that people seldom take it further. What is really happening in a substance as it gets hot or cold, and how does that change make temperature? When a fixed amount of energy is put into a substance, it heats up by an amount depending on what it is. The temperature of an object, then, has something to do with how the material responds to energy, and that response is called entropy. The entropy of a material (entropy is usually denoted S) is a measure of atomic wiggling and disorder of the atoms in the material. Formally, temperature is defined as

$$\frac{1}{T} = \left(\frac{dS}{dU} \right)_N,$$

DERIVED UNITS

MEASUREMENT	UNIT SYMBOL (DERIVATION)	COMMENTS
acceleration	unnamed (m/sec^2)	
angle	radian rad (m/m)	One radian is the angle centered in a circle that includes an arc of length equal to the radius. Since the circumference equals two pi times the radius, one radian equals $1/(2\ pi)$ of the circle, or approximately $57.296°$.
	steradian sr (m^2/m^2)	The steradian is a unit of solid angle. There are four pi steradians in a sphere. Thus one steradian equals about 0.079577 sphere, or about 3282.806 square degrees.
angular velocity	unnamed (rad/sec)	
area	unnamed (m^2)	
density	unnamed (kg/m^3)	Density is mass per volume. Lead is dense, styrofoam is not. Water has a density of one gram per cubic centimeter or 1,000 kilograms per cubic meter.
electric charge or electric flux	coulomb C $(A \cdot sec)$	One coulomb is the amount of charge accumulated in one second by a current of one ampere. One coulomb is also the amount of charge on 6.241506×10^{18} electrons.
electric field strength	unnamed $[(kg/m)/(sec^3 \cdot A) = V/m]$	Electric field strength is a measure of the intensity of an electric field at a particular location. A field strength of one V/m represents a potential difference of one volt between points separated by one meter.
electric potential, or electromotive force (often called voltage)	volt V $[(kg/m^2)/(sec^3 \cdot A) = J/C = W/A]$	Voltage is an expression of the potential difference in charge between two points in an electrical field. Electric potential is defined as the amount of potential energy present per unit of charge. One volt is a potential of one joule per coulomb of charge. The greater the voltage, the greater the flow of electrical current.
energy, work, or heat	joule J $[N \cdot m\ (= kg \cdot m^2/sec^2)]$	
	electron volt eV	The electron volt, being so much smaller than the joule (one $eV = 1.6 \times 10^{-17}$), is useful for describing small systems.

MEASUREMENT	UNIT SYMBOL (DERIVATION)	COMMENTS
force	newton N $(kg·m/sec^2)$	This unit is the equivalent to the pound in the English system, since the pound is a measure of force and not mass.
frequency	hertz Hz (cycles/sec)	Frequency is related to wavelength as follows: kilohertz x wavelength in meters = 300,000.
inductance	henry H (Wb/A)	Inductance is the amount of magnetic flux a material produces for a given current of electricity. Metal wire with an electric current passing through it creates a magnetic field; different types of metal make magnetic fields with different strengths and therefore have different inductances.
magnetic field strength	unnamed (A/m)	Magnetic field strength is the force that a magnetic field exerts on a theoretical unit magnetic pole.
magnetic flux	weber Wb $[(kg·m^2)/(sec^2·A) = V·sec]$	The magnetic flux across a perpendicular surface is the product of the magnetic flux density, in teslas, and the surface area, in square meters.
magnetic flux density	tesla T $[kg/(sec^2·A) = Wb/m^2]$	A magnetic field of one tesla is strong: The strongest artificial fields made in laboratories are about 20 teslas, and the Earth's magnetic flux density, at its surface, is about 50 microteslas (μT). Planetary magnetic fields are sometimes measured in gammas, which are nanoteslas (10^{-9} teslas).
momentum, or impulse	unnamed [N·sec (= kg·m/sec)]	Momentum is a measure of moving mass: how much mass and how fast it is moving.
power	watt W $[J/s (= (kg·m^2)/sec^3)]$	Power is the rate at which energy is spent. Power can be mechanical (as in horsepower) or electrical (a watt is produced by a current of one ampere flowing through an electric potential of one volt).
pressure, or stress	pascal Pa (N/m^2)	The high pressures inside planets are often measured in gigapascals (10^9 pascals), abbreviated GPa. ~10,000 atm = one GPa.
	atmosphere atm	The atmosphere is a handy unit because one atmosphere is approximately the pressure felt from the air at sea level on Earth; one standard atm = 101,325 Pa; one metric atm = 98,066 Pa; one atm ~ one bar.
radiation per unit mass receiving it	gray (J/kg)	The amount of radiation energy absorbed per kilogram of mass. One gray = 100 rads, an older unit.

(continues)

(continued)

MEASUREMENT	UNIT SYMBOL (DERIVATION)	COMMENTS
radiation (effect of)	sievert Sv	This unit is meant to make comparable the biological effects of different doses and types of radiation. It is the energy of radiation received per kilogram, in grays, multiplied by a factor that takes into consideration the damage done by the particular type of radiation.
radioactivity (amount)	becquerel Bq	One atomic decay per second
	curie Ci	The curie is the older unit of measure but is still frequently seen. One Ci = 3.7×10^{10} Bq.
resistance	ohm Ω (V/A)	Resistance is a material's unwillingness to pass electric current. Materials with high resistance become hot rather than allowing the current to pass and can make excellent heaters.
thermal expansivity	unnamed (/°)	This unit is per degree, measuring the change in volume of a substance with the rise in temperature.
vacuum	torr	Vacuum is atmospheric pressure below one atm (one torr = 1/760 atm). Given a pool of mercury with a glass tube standing in it, one torr of pressure on the pool will press the mercury one millimeter up into the tube, where one standard atmosphere will push up 760 millimeters of mercury.
velocity	unnamed (m/sec)	
viscosity	unnamed [Pa·s (= kg/(m·sec))]	Viscosity is a measure of resistance to flow. If a force of one newton is needed to move one square meter of the liquid or gas relative to a second layer one meter away at a speed of one meter per second, then its viscosity is one Pa·s, often simply written Pa·s or Pas. The cgs unit for viscosity is the poise, equal to 0.1 Pa·s.
volume	cubic meter (m^3)	

meaning one over temperature (the reciprocal of temperature) is defined as the change in entropy (dS, in differential notation) per change in energy (dU), for a given number of atoms (N). What this means in less technical terms is that temperature is a measure of how much heat it takes to increase the entropy (atomic wiggling and disorder) of a substance. Some materials get hotter with less energy, and others require more to reach the same temperature.

The theoretical lower limit of temperature is −459.67°F (−273.15°C, or 0K), known also as absolute zero. This is the temperature at which all atomic movement stops. The Prussian physicist Walther Nernst showed that it is impossible to actually reach absolute zero, though with laboratory methods using nuclear magnetization it is possible to reach 10^{-6}K (0.000001K).

USEFUL MEASURES OF DISTANCE

A *kilometer* is a thousand meters (see the table "International System Prefixes"), and a *light-year* is the distance light travels in a vacuum during one year (exactly 299,792,458 m/sec, but commonly rounded to 300,000,000 m/sec). A light-year, therefore, is the distance that light can travel in one year, or:

299,792,458 m/sec x 60 sec/min x
60 min/hr x 24 hr/day x 365 days/yr =
9.4543 x 10^{15} m/yr.

For shorter distances, some astronomers use light minutes and even light seconds. A light minute is 17,998,775 km, and a light second is 299,812.59 km. The nearest star to Earth, Proxima Centauri, is 4.2 light-years away from the Sun. The next, Rigil Centaurs, is 4.3 light-years away.

An *angstrom* (10^{-10}m) is a unit of length most commonly used in nuclear or particle physics. Its symbol is Å. The diameter of an atom is about one angstrom (though each element and isotope is slightly different).

An astronomical unit (AU) is a unit of distance used by astronomers to measure distances in the solar system. One astronomical unit equals the average distance from the center of the Earth to the center of the Sun. The currently accepted value, made standard in 1996, is 149,597,870,691 meters, plus or minus 30 meters.

One kilometer equals 0.62 miles, and one mile equals 1.61 kilometers.

The preceding table gives the most commonly used of the units derived from the fundamental units mentioned previously (there are many more derived units not listed here because they have been developed for specific situations and are little-used elsewhere; for example, in the metric world, the curvature of a railroad track is measured with a unit called "degree of curvature," defined as the angle between two points in a curving track that are separated by a chord of 20 meters).

Though the units are given in alphabetical order for ease of reference, many can fit into one of several broad categories: dimensional units (angle, area, volume), material properties (density, viscosity, thermal expansivity), properties of motion (velocity, acceleration, angular velocity), electrical properties (frequency, electric charge, electric potential, resistance, inductance, electric field strength), magnetic properties (magnetic field strength, magnetic flux, magnetic flux density), and properties of radioactivity (amount of radioactivity and effect of radioactivity).

DEFINITIONS FOR ELECTRICITY AND MAGNETISM

When two objects in each other's vicinity have different electrical charges, an *electric field* exists between them. An electric field also forms around any single object that is electrically charged with respect to its environment. An object is negatively charged (–) if it has an excess of electrons relative to its surroundings. An object is positively charged (+) if it is deficient in electrons with respect to its surroundings.

An electric field has an effect on other charged objects in the vicinity. The field strength at a particular distance from an object is directly proportional to the electric charge of that object, in coulombs. The field strength is inversely proportional to the distance from a charged object.

Flux is the rate (per unit of time) in which something flowing crosses a surface perpendicular to the direction of flow.

An alternative expression for the intensity of an electric field is *electric flux density*. This refers to the number of lines of electric flux passing at right angles through a given surface area, usually one meter squared (1 m^2). Electric flux density, like electric field strength, is directly proportional to the charge on the object. But flux density diminishes with distance according to the inverse-square law because it is specified in terms of a surface area (per meter squared) rather than a linear displacement (per meter).

A *magnetic field* is generated when electric charge carriers such as electrons move through space or within an electrical conductor. The geometric shapes of the magnetic flux lines produced by moving charge carriers (electric current) are similar to the shapes of the flux lines in an electrostatic field. But there are differences in the ways electrostatic and magnetic fields interact with the environment.

Electrostatic flux is impeded or blocked by metallic objects. *Magnetic flux* passes through most metals with little or no effect, with certain exceptions, notably iron and nickel. These two metals, and alloys and mixtures containing them, are known as ferromagnetic materials because they concentrate magnetic lines of flux.

Magnetic flux density and *magnetic force* are related to *magnetic field strength*. In gen-

INTERNATIONAL SYSTEM PREFIXES

SI PREFIX	SYMBOL	MULTIPLYING FACTOR
exa-	E	10^{18} = 1,000,000,000,000,000,000
peta-	P	10^{15} = 1,000,000,000,000,000
tera-	T	10^{12} = 1,000,000,000,000
giga-	G	10^9 = 1,000,000,000
mega-	M	10^6 = 1,000,000
kilo-	K	10^3 = 1,000
hecto-	h	10^2 = 1000
deca-	da	10 = 10
deci-	d	10^{-1} = 0.1
centi-	c	10^{-2} = 0.01
milli-	m	10^{-3} = 0.001
micro-	µ or u	10^{-6} = 0.000,001
nano-	n	10^{-9} = 0.000,000,001
pico-	p	10^{-12} = 0.000,000,000,001
femto-	f	10^{-15} = 0.000,000,000,000,001
atto-	a	10^{-18} = 0.000,000,000,000,000,001

A note on nonmetric prefixes: In the United States, the word "billion" means the number 1,000,000,000, or 10^9. In most countries of Europe and Latin America, this number is called "one milliard" or "one thousand million," and "billion" means the number 1,000,000,000,000, or 10^{12}, which is what Americans call a "trillion." In this set, a billion is 10^9.

NAMES FOR LARGE NUMBERS

NUMBER	AMERICAN	EUROPEAN	SI PREFIX
10^9	billion	milliard	giga-
10^{12}	trillion	billion	tera-
10^{15}	quadrillion	billiard	peta-
10^{18}	quintillion	trillion	exa-
10^{21}	sextillion	trilliard	zetta-
10^{24}	septillion	quadrillion	yotta-
10^{27}	octillion	quadrilliard	
10^{30}	nonillion	quintillion	
10^{33}	decillion	quintilliard	
10^{36}	undecillion	sextillion	
10^{39}	duodecillion	sextilliard	
10^{42}	tredecillion	septillion	
10^{45}	quattuordecillion	septilliard	

This naming system is designed to expand indefinitely by factors of powers of three. Then, there is also the googol, the number 10^{100} (one followed by 100 zeroes). The googol was invented for fun by the eight-year-old nephew of the American mathematician Edward Kasner. The googolplex is $10^{googol,}$ or one followed by a googol of zeroes. Both it and the googol are numbers larger than the total number of atoms in the universe, thought to be about $10^{80.}$

eral, the magnetic field strength diminishes with increasing distance from the axis of a magnetic dipole in which the flux field is stable. The function defining the rate at which this field-strength decrease occurs depends on the geometry of the magnetic lines of flux (the shape of the flux field).

PREFIXES

Adding a prefix to the name of that unit forms a multiple of a unit in the International System (see the table "International System Prefixes"). The prefixes change the magnitude of the unit by orders of 10 from 10^{18} to 10^{-18}.

Very small concentrations of chemicals are also measured in parts per million (ppm) or parts per billion (ppb), which mean just what they sound like: If there are four parts per million of lead in a rock (4 ppm), then out of every million atoms in that rock, on average four of them will be lead.

APPENDIX 2

Periodic Table of the Elements

PERIODIC TABLE OF ELEMENTS

| 1 — atomic number |
| H — symbol |
| 1.008 — atomic weight |

Numbers in parentheses are the atomic mass numbers of radioactive isotopes.

1 H 1.008																	2 He 4.003
3 Li 6.941	4 Be 9.012											5 B 10.81	6 C 12.01	7 N 14.01	8 O 16.00	9 F 19.00	10 Ne 20.18
11 Na 22.99	12 Mg 24.31											13 Al 26.98	14 Si 28.09	15 P 30.97	16 S 32.07	17 Cl 35.45	18 Ar 39.95
19 K 39.10	20 Ca 40.08	21 Sc 44.96	22 Ti 47.88	23 V 50.94	24 Cr 52.00	25 Mn 54.94	26 Fe 55.85	27 Co 58.93	28 Ni 58.69	29 Cu 63.55	30 Zn 65.39	31 Ga 69.72	32 Ge 72.59	33 As 74.92	34 Se 78.96	35 Br 79.90	36 Kr 83.80
37 Rb 85.47	38 Sr 87.62	39 Y 88.91	40 Zr 91.22	41 Nb 92.91	42 Mo 95.94	43 Tc (98)	44 Ru 101.1	45 Rh 102.9	46 Pd 106.4	47 Ag 107.9	48 Cd 112.4	49 In 114.8	50 Sn 118.7	51 Sb 121.8	52 Te 127.6	53 I 126.9	54 Xe 131.3
55 Cs 132.9	56 Ba 137.3	57-71* ☐ ☐	72 Hf 178.5	73 Ta 180.9	74 W 183.9	75 Re 186.2	76 Os 190.2	77 Ir 192.2	78 Pt 195.1	79 Au 197.0	80 Hg 200.6	81 Tl 204.4	82 Pb 207.2	83 Bi 209.0	84 Po (210)	85 At (210)	86 Rn (222)
87 Fr (223)	88 Ra (226)	89-103‡	104 Rf (261)	105 Db (262)	106 Sg (263)	107 Bh (262)	108 Hs (265)	109 Mt (266)	110 Ds (271)	111 Uuu (272)	112 Uub (285)	113 Uut (284)	114 Uuq (289)	115 Uup (288)			

*lanthanide series

57 La 138.9	58 Ce 140.1	59 Pr 140.9	60 Nd 144.2	61 Pm (145)	62 Sm 150.4	63 Eu 152.0	64 Gd 157.3	65 Tb 158.9	66 Dy 162.5	67 Ho 164.9	68 Er 167.3	69 Tm 168.9	70 Yb 173.0	71 Lu 175.0

‡actinide series

89 Ac (227)	90 Th 232.0	91 Pa 231.0	92 U 238.0	93 Np (237)	94 Pu (244)	95 Am (243)	96 Cm (247)	97 Bk (247)	98 Cf (251)	99 Es (252)	100 Fm (257)	101 Md (258)	102 No (259)	103 Lr (260)

© Infobase Publishing

Each electromagnetic wave has a measurable wavelength and frequency.

THE CHEMICAL ELEMENTS

element	symbol	a.n.	element	symbol	a.n.	element	symbol	a.n.	element	symbol	a.n.
actinium	Ac	89	erbium	Er	68	molybdenum	Mo	42	selenium	Se	34
aluminum	Al	13	europium	Eu	63	neodymium	Nd	60	silicon	Si	14
americium	Am	95	fermium	Fm	100	neon	Ne	10	silver	Ag	47
antimony	Sb	51	fluorine	F	9	neptunium	Np	93	sodium	Na	11
argon	Ar	18	francium	Fr	87	nickel	Ni	28	strontium	Sr	38
arsenic	As	33	gadolinium	Gd	64	niobium	Nb	41	sulfur	S	16
astatine	At	85	gallium	Ga	31	nitrogen	N	7	tantalum	Ta	73
barium	Ba	56	germanium	Ge	32	nobelium	No	102	technetium	Tc	43
berkelium	Bk	97	gold	Au	79	osmium	Os	76	tellurium	Te	52
beryllium	Be	4	hafnium	Hf	72	oxygen	O	8	terbium	Tb	65
bismuth	Bi	83	hassium	Hs	108	palladium	Pd	46	thallium	Tl	81
bohrium	Bh	107	helium	He	2	phosphorus	P	15	thorium	Th	90
boron	B	5	holmium	Ho	67	platinum	Pt	78	thulium	Tm	69
bromine	Br	35	hydrogen	H	1	plutonium	Pu	94	tin	Sn	50
cadmium	Cd	48	indium	In	49	polonium	Po	84	titanium	Ti	22
calcium	Ca	20	iodine	I	53	potassium	K	19	tungsten	W	74
californium	Cf	98	iridium	Ir	77	praseodymium	Pr	59	ununbium	Uub	112
carbon	C	6	iron	Fe	26	promethium	Pm	61	ununpentium	Uup	115
cerium	Ce	58	krypton	Kr	36	protactinium	Pa	91	ununquadium	Uuq	114
cesium	Cs	55	lanthanum	La	57	radium	Ra	88	ununtrium	Uut	113
chlorine	Cl	17	lawrencium	Lr	103	radon	Rn	86	unununium	Uuu	111
chromium	Cr	24	lead	Pb	82	rhenium	Re	75	uranium	U	92
cobalt	Co	27	lithium	Li	3	rhodium	Rh	45	vanadium	V	23
copper	Cu	29	lutetium	Lu	71	rubidium	Rb	37	xenon	Xe	54
curium	Cm	96	magnesium	Mg	12	ruthenium	Ru	44	ytterbium	Yb	70
darmstadtium	Ds	110	manganese	Mn	25	rutherfordium	Rf	104	yttrium	Y	39
dubnium	Db	105	meitnerium	Mt	109	samarium	Sm	62	zinc	Zn	30
dysprosium	Dy	66	mendelevium	Md	101	scandium	Sc	21	zirconium	Zr	40
einsteinium	Es	99	mercury	Hg	80	seaborgium	Sg	106			

a.n. = atomic number

GLOSSARY

absolute zero the lowest possible temperature defined as 0°K or –273.15°C

accelerator instrument used to study subatomic particles by increasing their energy

acid a substance that releases hydrogen ions when dissolved in water, thus reducing the pH of a solution

acoustics the study of sound

aerobic a biological process involving oxygen

air current moving stream of air

alchemy a forerunner of chemistry concerned with transforming metals into gold or finding a substance that can confer eternal life

algebra the study of the relationship between numbers and equations; algebra uses variables denoted by letters to represent unknown quantities

alloy a mixture of two or more metals; alloys have different properties than the metals from which they are composed

alpha radiation disintegration in which a positively charged particle composed of two protons and two neutrons is released from the nucleus of a radioactive element

amicable numbers pairs of numbers where the sum of the proper divisors of each number is the value of the other

amino acids small molecules that are the building blocks for proteins

anaerobic a biological process that takes place in the absence of oxygen

anaphylaxis severe biological reaction to a substance

anatomy the study of the structure of plants or animals

antibiotic a naturally occurring molecule that harms or kills bacteria, often used to treat bacterial infections

antibody a biologically important molecule that recognizes foreign molecules or antigens in the bloodstream

antigen a foreign substance that is recognized by the immune system; an antigen can be a molecule or a cell

antimatter a form of matter in which the electric and mathematical properties of the particles are reversed

arithmetic mathematical discipline that studies the relationship between numbers

armillary sphere an ancient tool used to determine the position of stars

asteroid bodies smaller than planets that orbit the Sun

astrolabe ancient device used to measure the position of the Sun and other celestial bodies

astrology ancient discipline concerned with the position of planets and stars

astronomy   the study of all aspects of celestial bodies

atom   the smallest subunit of matter that cannot be broken apart without permanently changing its chemical composition

atomic theory   theory that all matter is composed of small subunits called atoms

atomic weight   the weight of a single atom of an element

ATP (adenosine triphosphate)   the primary molecule used to carry energy in biological systems

axiom   a basic unproven assumption from which other ideas are derived

bacteria (singular bacterium)   single-celled microorganisms that do not have a membrane-enclosed nucleus

bacteriophage   a virus that infects bacteria

base (chemistry)   a substance that releases a hydroxyl ion, thus raising the pH of a solution, when dissolved in water

base (mathematics)   the number on which a given place value notation system is based

beta particle   an electron released from a radioactive element

big bang theory   theory explaining the origin of the universe through an explosion of matter millions of years ago

binary stars   a pair of stars that revolve around the same center of gravity

binary system   a place value notation system based on the number two

black body   a theoretical physical body that absorbs all radiation

black hole   a celestial object formed when a star dies, characterized by a strong gravitational pull

boson   an elementary particle that transmits forces between subatomic particles

botany   the study of plants

Brownian motion   random, nonspecific movement of small particles in a liquid or gas

calculus   mathematical discipline that deals with changing quantities

capacitor   a device that stores electric charge

carbohydrate   biological molecules composed of carbon, hydrogen, and oxygen; carbohydrates are often used to store energy in organisms

catastrophist theory   theory stating that geological changes occur through sudden events

cathode ray   rays of electrons in a vacuum tube

chain reaction   a chemical or nuclear reaction that, once started, is self-sustaining

chiral   molecules with the same chemical composition and three-dimensional structure that are mirror images of one another

chloroplast   membrane-bound compartment in some cells where light energy is harnessed through photosynthesis

chromosome   structures composed of DNA and proteins within the cell nucleus that appear during cell division

circumference   the distance around the boundary of a circle

colloid   a substance consisting of particles suspended in a gas, liquid, or solid

comet   celestial body consisting of ice and dust that orbits the Sun

complex numbers   numbers of the form $a + bi$ where a is a real number and i is an imaginary number defined as $i^2 = -1$.

conic section   a curve formed at the intersection of a plane with a cone.

conformation   the three-dimensional structure of a molecule; a molecule's conformation is intimately related to its function

continental drift   movement of the Earth's landmasses

core   the center of Earth, composed of iron and nickel

cosecant   the ratio of the hypotenuse of a right triangle to the side opposite the acute angle

cosmic background radiation   microwave radiation believed to be left behind after the big bang

cotangent   in a right triangle, the ratio of the side adjacent to the acute angle to the side opposite

cosine   in a right triangle, the ratio of the side opposite the acute angle to the hypotenuse

crust   outer layer of the Earth

crystal   a solid unit in which an atom or molecule is arranged in a characteristic pattern

cubic equation   an equation in which the highest unknown quantity is a cube (a^3)

dark matter   matter that comprises approximately 90 percent of the universe; dark matter neither reflects or emits radiation and thus is difficult to detect

decimal system   number system based on units of 10

derivative   the measure of the rate of change of a function with respect to its variable

deoxyribonucleic acid (DNA)   molecule found in cells and viruses that carries genetic information

diffusion   the spreading of atoms and molecules from an area of high concentration to one of lower concentration

distillation   method to separate a mixture of liquids or solids by converting one of the substances to a gas, then condensing the gas to obtain a pure sample

Doppler effect   a perceived change in the frequency of waves with respect to an observer when the source of waves and/or the observer is moving

dynamo   a device that generates an electric current through motion

eclipse   the blocking of light that occurs when one heavenly body passes between two others; commonly refers to events when the Moon passes between the Sun and Earth (solar eclipse)

ecliptic   the annual path of the Sun and other planets with respect to the Earth

ecosystem   a group of interrelated organisms and the environment in a defined area

electric current   flow of electric charge through a material; the rate of charge flow is expressed in ampere or amp

electric field   a space containing a force generated by an electric charge

electric potential   the amount of work required to move a positive charge through an electric field, measured in volts

electricity   form of energy consisting of charged particles

electrolysis   a process that breaks compounds into their components by passing an electric current through a liquid

electromagnetic spectrum   range of electromagnetic waves from low-frequency radio waves to high-frequency X-rays

electromagnetism   the relationship between electricity and magnetism

electron   an elementary particle with a negative charge; electrons orbit the nucleus of an atom

element   a chemical that cannot be separated into a simpler substance

energy   the capacity to do work, commonly measured in joules or calories

entropy   a measure of the randomness of a system

enzymes   proteins that catalyze chemical reactions in biological systems

equilibrium   for a chemical reaction, the point at which the forward reaction and reverse reaction occur at the same rate and thus no measurable change occurs in the system

equinox one of two points in the solar year when the center of Sun passes over the Earth's equator

erosion the gradual wearing away of soil or rock by water, glaciers, or wind

Euclidian geometry the branch of geometry based upon Euclid's *Elements*

eukaryote cell that contains a membrane-bound nucleus

evolution gradual changes in the characteristics of a species over successive generations

fermentation biological process in which sugars are converted to carbon dioxide and alcohol

fermion elementary particles that conform to Fermi-Dirac statistics; protons, neutrons, and electrons are all fermions

fission splitting the nucleus of an atom; usually refers to the breaking apart the nuclei of heavy atoms such as uranium and concomitant release of massive amounts of energy

fluorescence describes a substance that gives off energy of one wavelength after absorbing energy of a different wavelength

force something that causes an object to move, expressed in Newtons or dynes

friction the resistance of a moving body to the substance that it contacts

front the surface that divides two different air masses

function a mathematical value that is dependant upon the value of another quantity

fusion an energy-releasing process in which two atomic nuclei are combined

gamma ray electromagnetic ray released from atomic nuclei during radioactive decay

gene a segment of DNA that codes for a particular heritable trait in an organism

genome the complete set of genetic information for an organism

geocentric a view of the universe that puts the Earth as the center around which other celestial bodies revolve

geometry branch of mathematics dealing with the relationships among figures (e.g. points, lines, and shapes) in space

gnomon a vertical pole or stick that casts a shadow when placed in the Sun, used as a timekeeping device in ancient cultures

gravity force of attraction that causes objects to move toward one another

greenhouse effect the warming of the Earth caused by the ability of Earth's atmosphere to absorb more radiation than it emits

greenhouse gases gases found in the Earth's atmosphere that produce the greenhouse effect

heat energy from the motion of molecules

heliocentric a view of the universe that states that the Sun is the center around which other bodies, including the Earth, revolve

hemoglobin a protein in red blood cells that carries oxygen; hemoglobin has been used as a model in many biochemical studies

histology the study of tissues within a multicellular organism

hormone a substance released by one cell that regulates the biological activity of specific organs, tissues, or cells

hydrostatics the study of fluids at rest and under pressure

hypotenuse the side opposite the right angle of a right triangle

imaginary number a number that includes the square root of a negative number, expressed as bi where b is a real number and $i^2 = -1$

integer a number whose absolute value is a whole number; includes positive and negative numbers as well as zero

inertia   the tendency for a body in motion to stay in motion and a body at rest to stay at rest

infinity   a quantity greater than any value that can be assigned

infrared radiation   electromagnetic radiation that is longer than the end of the visible spectrum

inorganic   substances that do not contain organic groups, including many salts, minerals, and water

integration   the mathematical process of finding the values of an integral, often applied to solve quantities such as area or volume

ion   a charged atom or compound

ionosphere   a layer of the Earth's atmosphere characterized by atoms and molecules ionized by the Sun's ultraviolet radiation

irrational number   a real number that cannot be expressed as a ratio between two integers

isomers   two compounds that have the same chemical makeup but differ in the three-dimensional arrangement of their atoms

isotope   forms of the same atom with different atomic weight stemming from the number of neutrons within the nucleus

lanthanide   rare earth elements

laser   a device that emits an intense beam of light at a single wavelength

latitude   a distance north or south of the Earth's equator

lepton   a subatomic particle that undergoes weak interactions; examples of leptons include electrons and muons

limit   a mathematical value that a function approaches without ever reaching

lodestone   a magnetic stone used in ancient China as an early compass

logarithms   the power to which a base in a given number system must be raised

to give a specified quantity; used to simplify calculations

longitude   distance east or west on the Earth's surface

magic square   numbers arranged in a square such that the sum in any direction (vertical, horizontal, and diagonal) is the same

magnetic field   the space around a magnet where the electromagnetic force is present

magnetism   a force that causes some metals, such as iron, to attract or repel one another

mantle   the layer between the Earth's crust and core

maser   a device that generates electromagnetic waves

matrix   a set of numbers or variables arranged in an array in order to show relationships between the quantities

mechanics   the study of forces on bodies at rest and/or in motion

membrane   a layer separating distinct regions of a cell or organism

meson   unstable subatomic particles composed of a quark and an antiquark

metallurgy   the study of metals

microwave   high-frequency electromagnetic wave; microwaves are lower energy than visible waves but higher energy than radio waves

mitochondria (sing. mitochondrion)   organelles in eukaryotic cells where many reactions involved in energy metabolism take place and most of the energy-carrying molecule ATP is synthesized

mitosis   the process whereby eukaryotic cell divide, rendering two cells that are genetically identical to the first

molecular biology   the study of the molecules and molecular interactions that are essential for life

molecular weight   the weight of a single molecule; equal to the sum of the atomic weights of the atoms that make up the molecule

momentum   an expression of the motion of an object; defined as the product of the object's mass and velocity

nanotechnology   the development of devices with components that work on the nanometer scale

natural numbers   positive integers; natural numbers do not include zero

natural selection   the process whereby organisms adapt to their environment over many generations

nebula (pl. nebulae)   a diffuse mass of dust and gas found in space

Neptunism   the belief that the movement of water produces geological changes

neurotransmitter   molecules released by nerve cells that send messages to organs or other nerve cells

neutrino   subatomic particle with no charge

neutron   subatomic particle found in the atomic nucleus

niche   the specific role of an organism within an ecosystem

noble gas   one of six inert elemental gases

non-Euclidean geometry   a form of geometry that does not adhere to Euclid's postulate that there is only one line parallel to a given a line

nucleus (atom)   the center of an atom

nucleus (cell)   a membrane-bound compartment in eukaryotic cells that holds the cell's genetic material

number theory   the study of the relationship between integers

obliquity   the tilt of a planet's axis of rotation

optics   the study of light

organelle   a specialized compartment in eukaryotic cells, separated from the rest of the cell by a membrane

organic   a chemical containing carbon

osmosis   the movement of water across a membrane until the solutions on either side of the membrane are of equal concentration

ozone layer   a layer in the Earth's atmosphere that is rich in the chemical ozone, which absorbs much of the Sun's ultraviolet radiation

parallax   the apparent change in the position of an object when viewed from two different locations

Pascal's triangle   a triangular array of numbers arrayed in rows such that each number is equal to the sum of the two numbers diagonally above it

perfect number   a number that is equal to the sum of its factors

periodic table   the table in which the chemical elements are arranged according to atomic number

pH   a measure of the overall acidity of a solution

pharmacology   the study of drugs and their interactions

phlogiston   a substance believed by early chemists to be found in all combustible materials

photoelectric effect   the release of an electron from a material upon exposing that material to light

photon   a discrete quantity of light or other electromagnetic radiation

photosynthesis   the process whereby plants, algae, and some bacteria convert light energy to chemical energy

pi (π)   the ratio of the circumference of a circle to the diameter; approximately 3.1416

place value notation   a system of expressing numbers where the value of a digit depends upon its place in the number

plasma (physics)   an ionized gas

plate tectonics   the theory that the Earth's continents and oceans lie on plates that move independent of one another

Plutonist the theory that geological change is brought about by heat

polarized light light that travels within a single plane

polygon a closed geometrical figure with three or more sides

polymer a large molecule made up of several smaller subunits

positional notation a way of expressing numbers where the value of a digit depends upon its position within the number

positron a subatomic particle with the same mass as an electron that carries a positive charge

postulate an assumption from which other ideas are deduced

Precambrian the earliest era of geological time

prime number a whole number that is not evenly divisible by any whole number other than one and itself

prion an infectious protein found in a number of neurodegenerative diseases

probability the mathematical likelihood that an event will occur

product (chemistry) the substance produced via a chemical reaction

projective geometry the geometry of figures that do not change when projected

prokaryote a cell that lacks a membrane-bound nucleus

protein biologically important molecule composed of amino acids; proteins perform most critical tasks in cells

proton subatomic particle with a positive charge; protons and neutrons make up the atomic nucleus

pulsar neutron star that emits radio waves in short bursts or pulses at regular intervals

Pythagorean theorem name given to the mathematical relationship between the sides of a right triangle; expressed as $a^2 + b^2 = c^2$, where c is the length of the hypotenuse, and a and b are the lengths of the sides

quadratic equation mathematical equation that takes the form $ax^2 + bx + c = 0$.

quantum (pl. quanta) a discrete quantity of energy

quantum mechanics the study of mechanics on a small scale

quarks subatomic particles that are believed to be the fundamental particles from which larger particles are built

quasar a bright celestial object that emits light and radio waves

radiation energy emitted in the form of waves or particles

radioactive decay the spontaneous decay of unstable atomic nuclei, resulting in the emission of a particle or energy

radioactivity the emission of particles or energy from an unstable atomic nucleus

radio wave electromagnetic waves that are longer than light

ratio relationship between two numbers expressed as a fraction

reactant the chemical or chemicals at the start of a chemical reaction

real numbers the set of numbers that includes all rational and irrational numbers

recombinant DNA DNA that has been altered in the laboratory by joining DNA from one or more organisms or from different parts of a single organism's genome

reflection the act of changing the direction of light or other particles or waves, sending them back to the spot from which they came

refraction the bending of waves or a stream of particles that occurs when they pass from one medium to another

relativity theory that explains how physical observations change based upon the motion of the observer

respiration the process by which an organism takes in oxygen and excretes carbon dioxide

ribonucleic acid (RNA) biologically important molecules that are critical for the dissemination of genetic information

right angle an angle that measures 90°

right triangle a triangle with a 90° angle

seafloor spreading the process by which the seafloor is formed by the pulling apart of oceanic plates and the rise and cooling of magna

secant in a right triangle, the ratio of the length of the hypotenuse to the length of side adjacent to the acute angle

sediment a layer of matter, usually stones and soil, deposited by water, wind, or glacier movement

sedimentation the process by which layers of soil, stones, and other matter are deposited

seismic waves waves that travel along the surface or the interior of the Earth, normally caused by an earthquake or an explosion

seismograph a device that measures seismic activity

semiconductor a material that conducts electricity with less efficiency than a metal but more than an insulator

sextant an instrument used in navigation to measure latitude and in astronomy to measure the altitude of celestial bodies

sine in a right triangle, the ratio of the length of the side opposite the acute angle to the length of the hypotenuse

smelt to extract metals from a mixture by heating

spectral line line in a spectrum generated when an atom transitions from one energy level to another; used to identify chemical elements

spectroscopy a method of chemical analysis that relies upon the study of spectra

spherical triangle a triangle formed by the intersection of the arcs of three circles on a sphere

statistics the study of the collection, analysis, and interpretation of numerical data

steroid one of a family of structurally related molecules that are the building blocks of many hormones and other biologically important molecules

stratum (pl. strata) a bed of rock containing primarily one type of material

stratosphere layer of the atmosphere 11–31 miles above the Earth's surface

subatomic particle one of the particles that make up an atom

superconductor a material that conducts electricity with no resistance

superfluid a fluid that lacks viscosity when cooled to temperatures near absolute zero

supernova an extremely bright nova caused by the destruction of a star

synapse the region between a nerve cell and the cell with which it communicates

tangent in a right triangle, the ratio of the length of the side opposite the acute angle to the length of the side adjacent

thermodynamics the study of the relationship between heat and other forms of energy

topology the study of the properties of figures or solids that are preserved when the object is deformed

transcendental number an irrational number that is not the root of a polynomial equation with integer coefficients; π is a common example of a transcendental numbers

transfermium element one of the elements with atomic numbers higher than 100 that are not naturally found on the Earth

transistor a device made from a semiconductor that modulates the flow of current

translation   the process whereby genetic information is used to build proteins in cells

trigonometry   the study of the relationship between the sides and angles of triangles

troposphere   the lowest region of the Earth's atmosphere

ultraviolet radiation   electromagnetic radiation that has shorter wavelengths than visible light but longer wavelengths than X-rays

Uniformitarianism   theory of geological change that states that changes in the Earth occur gradually over long periods of time

valence   the number of electrons available to donate or share with another atom in a chemical reaction

variable star   a star that varies periodically in brightness

ventricle   one of the two lower chambers of the heart

virus   infectious agent that must enter a living cell in order to replicate

visible spectrum   the region of the electromagnetic spectrum that can be seen by human eyes

Vulcanist theory   theory of geological change that claims rocks formed from a universal fluid

wave-particle duality   the principle that both light and matter exhibit the properties of both a wave and a particle

X-ray   electromagnetic radiation with an extremely short wavelength

X-ray crystallography   a method to analyze the three-dimensional structure of molecules using X-rays

FURTHER READING

REFERENCE WORKS

Asimov, Isaac. *Asimov's Biographical Encyclopedia of Science and Technology.* Garden City, N.Y.: Doubleday, 1964.

Asimov, Isaac. *Asimov's Chronology of Science and Discovery.* New York: Harper & Row, 1989.

Barnhart, Robert K. *The American Heritage Dictionary of Science.* Boston: Houghton Mifflin, 1986.

Bynum, W. F., E. J. Browne, and Roy Porter, eds. *Dictionary of the History of Science.* Princeton, N.J.: Princeton University Press, 1981.

Concise Dictionary of Scientific Biography, 2nd Edition. New York: Charles Scribner's Sons, 2000.

Encyclopaedia Britannica. Encyclopaedia Britannica Premium Service, 2002–2005.

Glut, Donald. *Dinosaurs: The Encyclopedia.* Jefferson, N.C.: McFarland, 1997.

Gorini, Catherine A. *The Facts On File Geometry Handbook.* New York: Facts On File, 2003.

Hellemans, Alexander, and Bryan Bunch. *The Timetables of Science: A Chronology of the Most Important People and Events in the History of Science.* New York: Simon & Schuster, 1988.

Lambert, David, and The Diagram Group. *Encyclopedia of Prehistory.* New York: Facts On File, 2002.

Meyers, Robert A. *Molecular Biology and Biotechnology: A Comprehensive Desk Reference.* New York: VHC Publishers, 1995.

Milner, Richard. *The Encyclopedia of Evolution.* New York: Facts On File, 1990.

Rosner, Lisa. *Chronology of Science: From Stonehenge to the Human Genome Project.* Santa Barbara, Calif.: ABC-CLIO Hutchinson, 2002.

Saari, Peggy, and Stephen Allison, eds. *Scientists: The Lives and Works of 150 Scientists (Volumes 1–4).* Detroit, Mich.: UXL Gale Research, 1996.

Sebastian, Anton. *A Dictionary of the History of Science.* New York: Parthenon Publishing Group, 2001.

BOOKS

Alic, Margaret. *Hypatia's Heritage: A History of Women in Science from Antiquity through the Nineteenth Century.* Boston: Beacon Press, 1986.

Alley, Richard B. *The Two-mile Time Machine: Ice Cores, Abrupt, Climate Change, and Our Future.* Princeton, N.J.: Princeton University Press, 2000.

Amato, Ivan, ed. *Science: Pathways of Discovery.* New York: John Wiley and Sons, 2002.

Atkins, P. W. *Physical Chemistry, Fourth Edition.* New York: W. H. Freeman, 1990.

Begon, Michael, John L. Harper, and Colin R. Townsend. *Ecology: Individuals, Populations, and Communities Second Edition.* Boston: Blackwell Scientific Publications, 1990.

Bell, E. T. *Men of Mathematics: The Lives and Achievements of the Great Mathematicians from Zeno to Poincaré*. New York: Simon & Schuster, 1965.

Brock, William H. *The Norton History of Chemistry*. New York: W. W. Norton, 1992.

Burroughs, William J., Bob Crowder, Ted Robertson, Eleanor Vallier-Talbot, and Richard Whitaker. *The Nature Company Guides Weather*. Sydney: Time Life Books, 1996.

Calle, Carlos I. *Superstrings and Other Things*. Bristol: Institute of Physics Publishing, 2001.

Carlson, Neil R. *Foundations of Physiological Psychology, Second Edition*. Boston: Allyn and Bacon, 1992.

Close, Frank, Michael Marten, and Christine Sutton. *The Particle Odyssey: A Journey to the Heart of Matter*. Oxford: Oxford University Press, 2002.

Cohen, I. Bernard. *Album of Science: From Leonardo to Lavoisier, 1450–1800*. New York: Charles Scribner's Sons, 1980.

Commission on Geosciences, Environment, and Resources. *Reconciling Observations of Global Temperature Change*. Washington, D.C.: National Academy Press, 2000.

Crick, Francis. *What Mad Pursuit*. New York: Basic Books, 1988.

Crombie, A. C. *The History of Science from Augustine to Galileo, Volumes 1 and 2*. New York: Dover Publications, 1995.

Debus, A. G. *Man and Nature in the Renaissance*. Cambridge: Cambridge University Press, 1978.

Ebbing, Darrel R. *General Chemistry, Second Edition*. Boston: Houghton Mifflin, 1987.

Emsley, John. *Nature's Building Blocks: An A-Z Guide to the Elements*. Oxford: Oxford University Press, 2001.

Eves, Howard. *Great Moments in Mathematics (After 1650)*. Washington, D.C.: Mathematical Association of America, 1983.

Faul, Henry, and Carol Faul. *It Began with a Stone: A History of Geology from the Stone Age to the Age of Plate Tectonics*. New York: John Wiley & Sons, 1983.

Frangsmyer, Tore, and Gosta Ekspong, eds. *Nobel Lectures in Physics, 1981–1990*. Singapore: World Scientific, 1993.

Grant, Edward. *The Foundations of Modern Science in the Middle Ages: Their Religious, Institutional, and Intellectual Contexts*. Cambridge: Cambridge University Press, 1996.

Grenthe, Ingmar. *Nobel Lectures, Chemistry, 1996–2000*. River Edge, N.J.: World Scientific, 2003.

Hall, Thomas S. *History of General Physiology 600 B.C. to A.D. 1900, Volume 1: From Pre-Socratic Times to the Enlightenment*. Chicago: University of Chicago Press, 1969.

Hall, Thomas S. *History of General Physiology 600 B.C. to A.D. 1900, Volume 2: From the Enlightenment to the End of the Nineteenth Century*. Chicago: University of Chicago Press, 1969.

Hancock, Paul L., and Brian J. Skinner. *The Oxford Companion to the Earth*. Oxford: Oxford University Press, 2000.

Harré, Rom. *Great Scientific Experiments: Twenty Experiments That Changed Our View of the World*. Oxford: Phaidon, 1981.

Hawking, Stephen W. *A Brief History of Time: From the Big Bang to Black Holes*. Toronto: Bantam Books, 1988.

Janeway, Charles A., and Paul Travers. *Immunobiology: The Immune System in Health and Disease*. London: Current Biology Ltd., 1994.

Joseph, George Gheverghese. *The Crest of the Peacock: Non-European Roots of Mathematics*. Princeton, N.J.: Princeton University Press, 2000.

Kragh, H. *Quantum Generations: A History of Physics in the Twentieth Century*. Princeton, N.J.: Princeton University Press, 1999.

Lanham, Url. *Origins of Modern Biology*. New York: Columbia University Press, 1968.

Levinovitz, Agneta Wallin, and Nils Ringertz, eds. *The Nobel Prize: The First 100 Years*. Singapore: World Scientific Publishing, 2001.

Levy, David H., and Wendee Wallach-Levy. *Cosmic Discoveries*. Amherst, Mass.: Prometheus Books, 2001.

Lindberg, David C. *The Beginnings of Western Science: The European Scientific Tradition in*

Philosophical, Religious, and Institutional Context, 600 B.C. to A.D. 1450. Chicago: University of Chicago Press, 1992.

Lloyd, G. E. R. *Early Greek Science: Thales to Aristotle*. New York: W. W. Norton, 1970.

Macrone, Michael. *Eureka! What Archimedes Really Meant: 80 Other Key Ideas Explained*. New York: Cader Books, 1994.

Maddox, John. *What Remains to be Discovered: Mapping the Secrets of the Universe, the Origins of Life, and the Future of the Human Race*. New York: Martin Kessler Books, 1998.

Malmstrom, B. G. *Nobel Lectures, Chemistry, 1991–1995*. Singapore: World Scientific, 1997.

Mathez, Edmond A., and James D. Webster. *The Earth Machine: The Science of a Dynamic Planet*. New York: Columbia University Press, 2004.

McGrayne, Sharon Bertsch. *Nobel Prize Women in Science: Their Lives, Struggles, and Momentous Discoveries*. New York: Birch Lane Press, 1993.

Merriam-Webster's Biographical Dictionary. Springfield, Mass.: Merriam-Webster, 1995.

Motz, Lloyd, and Jefferson Hane Weaver. *The Story of Physics*. New York: Plenum Press, 1989.

Nahin, Paul J. *When Least Is Best: How Mathematicians Discovered Many Clever Ways to Make Things as Small (or as Large) as Possible*. Princeton, N.J.: Princeton University Press, 2004.

National Research Council. *Learning to Predict Climate Variations Associated with El Niño and the Southern Oscillation: Accomplishments and Legacies of the TOGA Program*. Washington, D.C.: National Academy Press, 1996.

Needham, Joseph. *Science in Traditional China*. Cambridge, Mass.: Harvard University Press, 1981.

Neugebauer, Otto. *The Exact Sciences in Antiquity, 2nd Edition*. New York: Dover Publications, 1969.

Purves, William K., David Sadava, Gordon H. Orians, and H. Craig Heller. *Life: The Science of Biology, Seventh Edition*. Sutherland, Mass: Sinauer Associates, 2004.

Radetsky, Peter. *Invisible Invaders: The Story of the Emerging Age of Viruses*. Boston: Little, Brown, 1991.

Ringertz, Nils. *Nobel Lectures in Physiology or Medicine, 1991–1995*. Singapore: World Scientific, 1997.

Roberts, Royston M. *Serendipity: Accidental Discoveries in Science*. New York: John Wiley and Sons, 1989.

Strathern, Paul. *Mendeleyev's Dream: The Quest for the Elements*. New York: St. Martin's Press, 2000.

Struik, D. J. *The Concise History of Mathematics, 4th Revised Edition*. New York: Dover Publications, 1987.

Tarbuck, Edward J., and Frederick K. Lutgens. *Earth Science, Ninth Edition*. Upper Saddle River, N.J.: Prentice Hall, 2000.

Temple, R. *The Genius of China: 3,000 Years of Science, Discovery, and Invention*. London: Prion Books, 1998.

Teresi, Dick. *Lost Discoveries: The Ancient Roots of Modern Science—from the Babylonians to the Maya*. New York: Simon & Schuster, 2002.

Toulmin, S., and J. Goodfield. *The Fabric of the Heavens: The Development of Astronomy and Dynamics*. Chicago: University of Chicago Press, 1961.

Wolpert, Lewis, and Alison Richards. *Passionate Minds: The Inner World of Scientists,* Oxford: Oxford University Press, 1997.

MAGAZINE AND JOURNAL ARTICLES

Alley, Richard B. "Abrupt Climate Change." *Scientific American* 291 (2004): 62.

Brush, Alan H. "Charles Gald Sibley 1917–1998: A Biographical Memoir." *Biographical Memoirs* 83. Washington, D.C.: National Academies Press, 2003.

Buchanan, J. W. "Biochemistry during the Life and Times of Hans Krebs and Fritz Lipmann." *Journal of Biological Chemistry* 277 (2002): 33,531–33,536.

Chung, K. T., and C. J. Biggers. "Albert Leon Charles Calmette (1863–1933) and the Antituberculous BCG Vaccination." *Perspectives in Biology and Medicine* 44 (2001): 379–389.

Diamond, J. M. "Peeling the Chinese Onion." *Nature* 391 (1998): 433.

Dixon, H. B. F. "Frederick Gowland Hopkins and the Unification of Biochemistry." *Trends in Biochemical Science* 22 (1997): 184–187.

Doty, R. W. "Two Brains, One Person." *Brain Research Bulletin* 50 (1999): 423.

Giebultowicz, T. "Breathing Life into an Old Model." *Nature* 408 (2000): 408.

Gillham, N. W. "Evolution by Jumps: Francis Galton and William Bateson and the Mechanism of Evolutionary Change." *Genetics* 159 (2001): 1,383–1,392.

Grattan-Guinness, I. "A Sideways Look at Hilbert's Twenty-three Problems of 1900." *Notices of the AMS* 47 (2000): 752–757.

Gray, J. "Ivan Petrovich Pavlov and the Conditioned Reflex." *Brain Research Bulletin* 59 (1999): 433.

Greene, M. T. "High Achiever: The Discovery of the Stratosphere Laid the Foundations of Geophysics." *Nature* 407 (2000): 947.

Gross, L. "How Charles Nicolle of the Pasteur Institute Discovered That Epidemic Typhus Is Transmitted by Lice: Reminiscences from My Years at the Pasteur Institute in Paris." *Proceedings of the National Academy of Sciences, USA* 93 (1996): 10,539–10,540.

Haas, L. F. "Charles Robert Richet (1850–1935)." *Journal of Neurology Neurosurgery and Psychiatry* 70 (2001): 255.

Heilbron, J. L., and W. F. Bynum. "Millennial Highlights . . . from Gerbert d'Aurilac to Watson and Crick." *Nature* 403 (2000): 13–16.

Hutcheson, G. Dan. "The First Nanochips." *Scientific American* 290 (2004): 76.

Karl, Thomas R., and Kevin E. Trenberth "Modern Global Climate Change." *Science* 302 (2003): 1,719–1,723.

Kornberg, A. "Century of the Birth of Modern Biochemistry." *Trends in Biochemical Sciences* 22 (1997): 282–283.

Kristensson, K. "The Discovery of Poliovirus," *Brain Research Bulletin* 50 (1999): 461.

Li, Q. "Chinese Astronomy." In *Encyclopedia of Astronomy and Astrophysics.* Bristol, U.K.: Nature Publishing Group, 2001.

Manchester, K. L. "Arthur Harden: An Unwitting Pioneer of Metabolic Control Analysis." *Trends in Biochemical Sciences* 25 (2000): 89–92.

Millet, D. "Hans Berger: From Psychic Energy to the EEG." *Perspectives in Biology and Medicine* 44 (2001): 522–542.

Ottoson, D. "The Unraveling of the Code of Nerve Growth: A Modern Saga of the Dedication to Science." *Brain Research Bulletin* 50 (1999): 473–474.

Parnes, O. "Trouble from Within: Allergy, Autoimmunity, and Pathology in the First Half of the Twentieth Century." *Studies in the History and Philosophy of Biological and Biomedical Sciences* 34 (2003): 425–454.

Paul, D. "A Double-edged Sword." *Nature* 405 (2000): 515.

Peyrieras, N., and M. Morange. "The Study of Lysogeny at the Pasteur Institute (1950–1960): An Epistemologically Open System." *Studies in the History and Philosophy of Biological and Biomedical Sciences* 33 (2002): 419–430.

Raju, T. N. K. "The Nobel Chronicles 1914: Robert Barany (1876–1936)." *The Lancet* 352 (1998): 1,156.

Raju, T. N. K. "The Nobel Chronicles 1926: Johannes Andreas Grib Fibiger (1867–1928)." *The Lancet* 352 (1998): 1,635.

Riley, R. L. "What Nobody Needs to Know about Airborne Infection." *American Journal of Respiratory and Critical Care Medicine* 163 (2001): 7–8.

Saliba, G. "Islamic Astronomy." In *Encyclopedia of Astronomy and Astrophysics.* Bristol, U.K.: Nature Publishing Group, 2001.

Serge, G. "The Big Bang and the Genetic Code." *Nature* 404 (2000): 437.

Sheehan, William. "Giovanni Schiaparelli: Vision of a Color Blind Astronomer." *Journal of the British Astronomical Association* 107 (1997): 11–15.

Short, R. V. "Where Do Babies Come From?" *Nature* 403 (2000): 705.

Wald, George. "How the Theory of Solutions Arose." *Journal of Chemical Education* 23 (1986): 8.

Wolpert, L. "The Well-spring." *Nature* 405 (2000): 887.

SELECTED WORKS DISCUSSED IN ENTRIES

Section One

Apollonius. *Conics Books V to VII. Arabic Translation of the Lost Greek Original in the Version of the Banu Musa. Volume 1.* Edited by Gerald J. Toomer. New York: Springer-Verlag, 1990.

———. *Conics Books V to VII. Arabic Translation of the Lost Greek Original in the Version of the Banu Musa. Volume II.* Edited by Gerald J. Toomer. New York: Springer-Verlag, 1990.

Archimedes. *The Works of Archimedes.* Translated by Sir Thomas Little Heath. Cambridge: Cambridge University Press, 1897.

Aristotle. *History of Animals Books 1-3.* Translated by A. L. Peck. Cambridge, Mass.: Harvard University Press.

———. *History of Animals Books 4-6.* Translated by A. L. Peck. Cambridge, Mass.: Harvard University Press.

———. *History of Animals Books 7-10.* Translated by D. M. Balme. Cambridge, Mass.: Harvard University Press, 1991.

The Classic of Mountains and Seas. Translated by Anne Birrell. New York: Penguin Putnam, 1999.

Diocles. *On Burning Mirrors.* Edited by G. J. Toomer. New York: Springer-Verlag, 1976.

Han, Ying. *Han shi wai zhuan.* Translated by James Robert Hightower. Cambridge, Mass.: Harvard University Press, 1952.

Hippocrates. *Nature of Man. Regimen in Health. Humours. Aphorisms. Regimen 1-3. Dreams.*

Heracleitus. *On the Universe.* Translated by W. H. S. Jones. Cambridge, Mass.: Harvard University Press, 1931.

Hui, Lui. *The Nine Chapters on the Mathematical Art Companion and Commentary.* Translated and edited by Shen Kangshen, John Crossley, and Anthony Lun. New York: Oxford University Press, 1999.

Laozi. *The Classic of the Way and Virtue: A New Translation of the Tao-te ching of Laozi.* Interpreted by Wang Bi. Translated by Richard John Lynn. New York: Columbia University Press, 1999.

Lucretius. *On the Nature of Things.* Translated by W. H. D. Rouse. Revised by Martin F. Smith. Cambridge, Mass.: Harvard University Press, 1924.

Mo di. *Mo Tzu: Basic Writings.* New York: Columbia University Press, 1963.

Philo of Byzantium. *Pneumatica.* Translated by Frank D. Prager. Wiesbaden: Reichert. 1974.

Strabo. *Geography, I, Books 1–2.* Translated by Horace L. Jones. Cambridge, Mass.: Harvard University Press, 1917.

———. *Geography, II, Books 3–5.* Translated by Horace L. Jones. Cambridge, Mass.: Harvard University Press, 1923.

———. *Geography, III, Books 6–7.* Translated by Horace L. Jones. Cambridge, Mass.: Harvard University Press, 1924.

———. *Geography, IV, Books 8–9.* Translated by Horace L. Jones. Cambridge, Mass.: Harvard University Press, 1927.

———. *Geography, V, Books 10–12.* Translated by Horace L. Jones. Cambridge, Mass.: Harvard University Press, 1928.

———. *Geography, VI, Books 13–14.* Translated by Horace L. Jones. Cambridge, Mass.: Harvard University Press, 1929.

———. *Geography, VII, Books 15–16.* Translated by Horace L. Jones. Cambridge, Mass.: Harvard University Press, 1930.

———. *Geography, VIII, Books 17 and General Index.* Translated by Horace L. Jones. Cambridge, Mass.: Harvard University Press, 1932.

Su wen. Translated by Maoshing Ni. Boston: Shambhala, 1995.

Vitruvius. *On Architecture, I, Books 1–5.* Translated by Frank Granger. Cambridge, Mass.: Harvard University Press, 1931.

———. *On Architecture, II, Books 6–10.* Translated by Frank Gardner. Cambridge, Mass.: Harvard University Press, 1934.

Section Two

Abu Kamil Shuja ibn Aslam. *The Algebra of Abu Kamil Shuja ibn Aslam.* Madison: University of Wisconsin Press, 1966.

Abu Mashar. *Kitab ith-bat 'ilm al-nujum.* Edited by Keiji Yamamoto. Translated by Keiji Yamamoto and Charles Burnett. Boston: Brill, 2000.

Hero of Alexandria. *The Pneumatics of Hero of Alexandria.* Translated by Joseph Gouge Greenwood. Edited by Bennet Woodcroft. New York: American Elsevier, 1971.

Jabir ibn Hayyan. *The Works of Geber, the Most Famous Arabian Prince and Philosopher.* Translated by Richard Russel. London: Printed by Thomas James, 1678.

Al-Khwarizmi, Muhammad ibn Musa. *The Algebra of Mohammed ben Musa.* Edited and translated by Frederic Rosen. London: Oriental Translation Fund, 1831.

Muqaddasi, Muhammad ibn Ahmad. *Ahsan Altaqsim Fi Ma Rifat Al Aqalim* (The best division for knowledge of the regions: a translation of Ahsan al-taqasim fi marifat al-aqualim). Reading, U.K.: Garnet Publishing, 1994.

Nicomachus of Gerasa. *Introduction to Arithmetic.* Translated by Martin Luther D'Ooge. New York: Macmillan, 1926.

Pliny the Elder. *Natural History I, Books 1–2.* Translated by H. Rackham. Cambridge, Mass.: Harvard University Press, 1938.

———. *Natural History II, Books 3–7.* Translated by H. Rackham. Cambridge, Mass.: Harvard University Press, 1942.

———. *Natural History III, Books 8–11.* Translated by H. Rackham. Cambridge, Mass.: Harvard University Press, 1940.

———. *Natural History IV, Books 12–16.* Translated by H. Rackham. Cambridge, Mass.: Harvard University Press, 1945.

———. *Natural History V, Books 17–19.* Translated by H. Rackham. Cambridge, Mass.: Harvard University Press, 1950.

———. *Natural History VI, Books 20–23.* Translated by W. H. S. Jones. Cambridge, Mass.: Harvard University Press, 1951.

———. *Natural History VII, Books 24–27.* Translated by W. H. S. Jones and A. C. Andrews. Cambridge, Mass.: Harvard University Press, 1956.

———. *Natural History VIII, Books 28–32.* Index of Fishes. Translated by W. H. S. Jones. Cambridge, Mass.: Harvard University Press, 1963.

———. *Natural History IX, Books 33–35.* Translated by H. Rackham. Cambridge, Mass.: Harvard University Press, 1952.

———. *Natural History X, Books 36–37.* Translated by D. E. Eichholz. Cambridge, Mass.: Harvard University Press, 1962.

Ptolemy. *The Almagest.* Translated by G. J. Toomer. London: Duckworth. 1984.

———. *Geographia.* Mineola, N.Y.: Dover, 1991.

Seneca, Lucius Annaeus. *Naturales quaestiones.* Translated by Harry M. Hine. New York: Arno Press, 1981.

Sesiano, Jacques. *Books IV to VII of Diophantus' Arithmetica in Arabic Translation Attributed to Qusta ibn Luqa.* New York: Springer-Verlag, 1982.

Sigler, Laurence. *Fibonacci's Liber Abaci: A Translation into Modern English of Leonardo Pisano's Book of Calculation.* New York: Springer, 2002.

Wang, Chong. *Lunheng.* New York: Paragon Book Gallery, 1962.

Section Three

Agricola, Georg. *De re metallica.* Translated by Herbert Clark and Lou Henry Hoover. New York: Dover Publications, 1950.

Bacon, Francis. *Novum Organum.* Translated and edited by John Gibson and Peter Urbach. Chicago: Open Court Publishing, 1994.

Biringucci, Vannoccio. *The Pirotechnia of Vannoccio Biringuccio.* Translated by Cyril Stanley Smith and Martha Teach Gnudi. New York: American Institute of Mining and Metallurgical Engineers, 1942.

Cardano, Girolamo. *The Book on Games of Chance (Liber de ludo aleae).* Translated by

Sydney Henry Gould. New York: Holt, Rinehart, and Winston, 1961.

Copernicus, Nicolaus. *On the Revolutions.* Translated by Edward Rosen. Edited by Jerry Dobzycki. Baltimore: Johns Hopkins University Press, 1978.

Fabricius. *De venarum ostiolis.* Translated by K. J. Franklin. Springfield, Ill.: C. C. Thomas, 1933.

Fracastoro, Girolamo. *Hieronymi Fracastorii De contagione et contagiosis morbis et eorum curatione, libri III.* Translated by Wilmer Cave Wright. New York: G. P. Putnam's Sons, 1930.

Galilei, Galileo. *On Motion and On Mechanics.* Translated by I. E. Drabkin and Stillman Drake. Madison: University of Wisconsin Press, 1960.

———. *Dialogue Concerning the Two Chief World Systems, Ptolemaic and Copernican.* Translated by Stillman Drake. Foreword by Albert Einstein. Introduction by J. L. Heilbron. New York: Modern Library, 2001.

———. *Sidereus nuncios.* Translated by Albert van Helden. Chicago: University of Chicago Press, 1989.

Gilbert, William. *De magnete.* Translated by P. Fleury Mottelay. New York: Dover Publications, 1958.

Harvey, William. *De motu cordis.* Translated and annotated by Chauncey D. Leake. Springfield, Ill.: C. C. Thomas, 1941.

Huygens, Christiaan. *Treatise on Light.* Translated by Silvanus P. Thompson. London: Macmillan, 1939.

Kepler, Johannes. *Astronomia nova. English.* Translated by William H. Donahue. Cambridge: Cambridge University Press, 1992.

Napier, John. *Rabdologœ.* Cambridge, Mass.: MIT Press, 1990.

Regiomontanus, Joannes. *De triangulis omnimodis* (On triangles). Translated by Barnabas Hughes. Madison: University of Wisconsin Press, 1967.

Stevin, Simon. *Principle Works.* Edited by Ernst Crone. Translated by C. Dikshoorn. Amsterdam: C. V. Swets & Zeitlinger, 1966.

Vesalius, Andreas. *On the Fabric of the Human Body. Book II, The Ligaments and Muscles.* Translated by William Frank Richardson and John Burd Carman. San Francisco: Norman Publishing, 1999.

Viète, Franáois. *The Analytic Art: Nine Studies in Algebra, Geometry, and Trigonometry from the Opus restitutae mathematicae analyseos, seu, Algebra nova.* Translated by T. Richard Witmer. Kent, Ohio: Kent State University Press, 1983.

Section Four

Boyle, Robert. *The Skeptical Chymist.* New York: Dutton, 1964.

Buffon, Georges Louis Leclerce, comte de. *Historie naturelle des quadrupeds ovipares et des serpents.* New York: Arno Press, 1978.

Descartes, René. *Discourse on Method, Optics, Geometry, and Meteorology.* Translated by Paul J. Olscamp. Indianapolis, Ind.: Hackett Publishing, 2001.

Euler, Leonhard. *Foundations of Differential Calculus. Chapters 1–9.* Translated by John D. Blanton. New York: Springer, 2000.

———. *Introduction to Analysis of the Infinite.* Translated by John D. Blanton. New York: Springer-Verlag, 1988.

Hales, Stephen. *Statical Essays, Containing Haemastaticks.* Introduction by Andre Cournand. New York: Hafner Publishing, 1964.

———. *Vegetable Staticks.* Foreword by M. A. Hoskin. New York: American Elsevier, 1969.

Hooke, Robert. *Micrographia.* New York: Dover Publications, 1961.

Huygens, Christiaan, and Richard J. Blackwell. *Horologium oscillatorium.* Ames: Iowa State University Press, 1986.

Lenhoff, Sylvia G., and Howard Lenhoff. *Hydra and the Birth of Experimental Biology, 1744: Abraham Trembley's Mémoires Concerning the Polyps.* Pacific Grove, Calif.: Boxwood Press, 1986.

Linné, Carl von. *Linnaeus' Philosophia Botanica.* Translated by Stephen Freer. Oxford: Oxford University Press, 2003.

MacLaurin, Colin. *An Account of Sir Isaac Newton's Philosophical Discoveries*. New York: Johnson Reprint Corporation, 1968.

Newton, Isaac. *Philosophiae Naturalis Principia Mathematica*. Edited by Alexandre Koyré and I. Bernard Cohen. Cambridge, Mass.: Harvard University Press, 1972.

Pascal, Blaise. *The Physical Treatise of Pascal; The Equilibrium of Liquids and the Weight of the Mass of the Air*. Translated by I. H. B. and A. G. H. Spiers. New York: Octagon Books. 1973.

Redi, Francesco. *Experiments on the Generation of Insects*. Translated by Mab Bigelow. Chicago: Open Court Publishing, 1909.

Steno, Nicolaus, John Garrett Winter, William H. Hobbs, and George W. White. *The Prodromus of Nicolaus Steno's Dissertation Concerning a Solid Body Enclosed by Process of Nature within a Solid*. New York: Hafner Publishing, 1968.

Wallis, John. *The Arithmetic of Infinitesimals*. Translated by Jacqueline A. Stedall. New York: Springer, 2004.

Section Five

Agassiz, Louis. *Etudes Sur les Glaciers*. New York: Hafner, Pub., 1967.

Bergman, Torbern. *A Dissertation on Elective Attractions*. New York: Johnson Reprint, 1968.

Berthollet, Claude-Louis. *An Essay on Chemical Statics; With Copious Explanatory Notes, and an Appendix on Vegetable and Animal Substances*. Translated by B. Lambert. London: J. Mawman, 1804.

Boole, George. *The Mathematical Analysis of Logic*. Oxford: B. Blackwell, 1948.

Carnot, Sadi. *Reflexions on the Motive Power of Fire*. Translated and edited by Robert Fow. Manchester: Manchester University Press, 1986.

Conybeare, William Daniel. *Outlines of the Geology of England and Wales*. London: W. Phillips, 1822.

Darwin, Charles. *The Structure and Distribution of Coral Reefs*. Tucson: University of Arizona Press, 1984.

Faraday, Michael, Hermann von Helmholz, William Thomson Kelvin, Simon Newcomb, and Archibald Geikie. *Scientific Papers: Physics, Chemistry, Astronomy, and Geology*. New York: P. F. Collier, 1910.

Fourier, Jean Baptiste Joseph. *The Analytical Theory of Heat*. Translated by Alexander Freeman. New York: Dover Publishers, 1955.

Hutton, James. *Theory of the Earth: With Proofs and Illustrations*. New York: Hafner Publishing, 1959.

Lavoisier, Antoine Laurent. *Elements of Chemistry, in a New Systematic Order, Containing all the Modern Discovery*. Translated by Robert Kerr. New York: Dover Publications, 1965.

Lyell, Charles. *Principles of Geology*. New York: Johnson Reprint, 1969.

May, Lawrence A. *Withering on the Foxglove and other Classics in Pharmacology*. Oceanside, N.Y.: Dabor Science Publications, 1977.

Murchison, Roderick. *The Silurian System*. London: J. Murray, 1839.

Pinel, Philippe. *Traité médico-philosophique sur l'aliénation mentale*. Translated by D. D. Davis. Washington, D.C.: University Publications of America, 1977.

Schwann, Theodor. *Microscopical Researches into the Accordance in the Structure and Growth of Animals and Plants*. Translated by Henry Smith. New York: Kraus Reprint, 1969.

Sylvester, James Joseph. *The Collected Mathematical Papers of James Joseph Sylvester*. Edited by Henry Frederick Baker. New York: Chelsea Publishing, 1973.

Section Six

Darwin, Charles. *The Descent of Man, and Selection in Relation to Sex*. New York: Penguin Books, 2004.

———. *On the Origin of the Species by Means of Natural Selection*. Edited by Joseph Carroll. Orchard Park, N.Y.: Broadview Press, 2003.

Dedekind, Richard. *Essays on the Theory of Numbers: I. Continuity and Irrational Numbers. II. The Nature and Meaning of Numbers.* New York: Dover Publications, 1963.

Gibbs, J. Williard. *The Collected Works of J. Willard Gibbs.* Edited by W. R. Longley and R. G. Van Name. New York: Longmans, Green, 1928.

Hilbert, David. *Foundations of Geometry.* Translated by Leo Unger. Revised by Paul Bernays. La Salle, Ill.: Open Court, 1992.

Huggins, William. *The Scientific Papers of Sir William Huggins.* Edited by Sir William Huggins and Lady Huggins. London: W. Wesley and Son, 1909.

Kelvin, William Thomson. *Mathematical and Physical Papers by Sir William Thomson. Collected from Different Scientific Periodicals from May, 1841 to the Present Time.* Cambridge: Cambridge University Press, 1882–1991.

Koch, Robert. *The Aetiology of Tuberculosis.* Prepared by Dr. and Mrs. Max Pinner. New York: National Tuberculosis Association, 1932.

———. *Essays of Robert Koch.* Translated by K. Codell Carter. New York: Greenwood Press, 1987.

Maury, Matthew Fontaine. *The Physical Geography of the Sea.* New York: Harper & Brothers, 1855.

Maxwell, James. *A Treatise on Electricity and Magnetism.* New York: Oxford University Press, 1998.

Mendel, Gregor. *Experiments in Plant Hybridisation: Mendel's Original Paper in English Translation with Commentary and Assessment by Sir. Ronald Fisher, Together with a Reprint of W. Bateson's Biographical Notice of Mendel.* Edited by J. H. Bennett. Edinburgh: Oliver and Boyd, 1965.

Poincaré, Henri. *New Methods of Celestial Mechanics.* Edited and introduced by Daniel L. Goroff. Woodbury, N.Y.: American Institute of Physics, 1993.

Rayleigh, John William Strutt. *Scientific Papers.* New York: Dover Publications, 1964.

———. *The Theory of Sound.* Historical introduction by Robert Bruce Lindsay. New York: Dover Publications, 1945.

Smith, Theobald, and F. L. Kilborne. *Investigations into the Nature, Causation, and Prevention of Texas or Southern Cattle Fever.* Washington D.C.: United States Department of Agriculture, Bureau of Animal Industry, 1893.

Snow, John, B. W. Richardson, and Wade Hampton Frost. *Snow on Cholera: Being a Reprint of Two Papers by John Snow.* New York: Commonwealth Fund, 1936.

Suess, Eduard. *The Face of the Earth.* Translated by Hertha B. C. Sollas. Oxford: Clarendon Press, 1904.

Thomson, C. Wyville. *The Voyage of the Challenger.* New York: Harper & Brothers, 1878.

Venn, John. *Symbolic Logic, 2nd edition, revised and rewritten.* New York: Chelsea Publishing, 1971.

Virchow, Rudolf Ludwig Karl. *Cellular Pathology as based upon Physiology and Pathological History.* Translated by Frank Chance. Birmingham, Ala: Classics of Medicine Library, 1978.

Wundt, Wilhelm Max. *Principles of Physiological Psychology.* Translated by Edward Bradford Titchener. New York: Kraus Reprint, 1969.

Section Seven

Bohr, Niels Henrik David. *Collected Works.* Edited by L. Rosenfeld. Amsterdam: North-Holland Publishing, 1972.

Chandrasekhar, Subrahmanyan. *A Quest for Perspective: Selected Works of S. Chandrasekhar.* Edited by Kameshwar C. Wali. River Edge, N.J.: World Scientific Publishing, 2001.

Einstein, Albert. *Relativity: The Special and the General Theory.* Translated by Robert W. Lawson. New York: Routledge, 2001.

Elton, Charles S., Mathew A. Leibold, and J. Timothy Wootton. *Animal Ecology*. Chicago: University of Chicago Press, 2001.

Fisher, Ronald Aylmer. *The Genetical Theory of Natural Selection: A Complete Variorum Edition*. Edited by J. H. Bennet. Oxford: Oxford University Press, 1999.

Freud, Sigmund. *The Interpretation of Dreams*. Translated by Joyce Crick. Introduction and notes by Ritchie Robertson. Oxford: Oxford University Press, 1999.

Haldane, John Burdon Sanderson, and Egbert G. Leigh. *The Causes of Evolution*. Princeton, N. J.: Princeton University Press, 1990.

Hubble, Edwin Powell. *Red-shifts in the Spectra of Nebulae; being the Halley Lecture Delivered on 8 May 1934*. Oxford: Clarendon Press, 1934.

Morgan, Thomas Hunt, Hermann Joseph Muller, Calvin Blackman Bridges, and Alfred Henry Sturtevant. *The Mechanism of Mendelian Heredity, Revised Edition*. New York: Henry Holt, 1923.

Oberth, Hermann. *Man into Space; New Projects for Rocket and Space Travel*. Translated by G. P. H. De Freville. New York: Harper, 1957.

Pauling, Linus. *The Nature of the Chemical Bond and the Structure of Molecules and Crystals: An Introduction to Modern Structural Chemistry, 2nd Edition*. Ithaca, N.Y.: Cornell University Press, 1940.

Semenov, N. N. *Chemical Kinetics and Chain Reactions*. Oxford: Clarendon Press, 1935.

Tsiolkovsky, Konstantin. *Selected Works of Konstantin E. Tsiolkovsky*. University Press of the Pacific, 2004.

Van Vleck, J. H. *The Theory of Electric and Magnetic Susceptibilities*. Oxford: Clarendon Press, 1932.

Von Neumann, John, Oskar Morgenstern, Harold W. Kuhn, and Ariel Rubinstein. *Theory of Games and Economic Behavior, 60th anniversary edition*. Princeton, N.J.: Princeton University Press, 2004.

Wegener, Alfred. *The Origin of Continents and Oceans*. Translated by John Biram. Introduction by B. C. King. London: Methuen, 1968.

Whitehead, Alfred North, and Bertrand Russell. *Principia Mathematica, 2nd Edition*. Cambridge: Cambridge University Press, 1950.

Section Eight

Brown, Herbert Charles. *Hydroboration*. New York: W. A. Benjamin, 1962.

Calvin, Melvin. *The Path of Carbon in Photosynthesis*. Notre Dame, Ind.: University of Notre Dame, 1949.

Carson, Rachel. *Silent Spring, 40th anniversary edition*. Introduction by Linda Lear and afterword by Edward O. Wilson. Boston: Houghton Mifflin, 2002.

Eccles, John C. *The Physiology of Nerve Cells*. Baltimore: Johns Hopkins University Press, 1957.

Feynman, Richard Phillips. *Selected Papers of Richard Feynman: with Commentary*. Edited by Laurie M. Brown. River Edge, N.J.: World Scientific, 2000.

Gennes, Pierre G. de. *The Physics of Liquid Crystals*. New York: Oxford University Press, 1975.

Gell-Mann, Murray. *The Eightfold Way*. Edited by Murray Gell-Mann and Yuval Ne'eman. New York: W. A. Benjamin, 1964.

Katz, Bernard. *Nerve, Muscle, and Synapse*. New York: McGraw-Hill, 1966.

Lederberg, Joshua, comp. *Papers in Microbial Genetics; Bacteria and Bacterial Viruses*. Madison: University of Wisconsin Press, 1951.

Libby, Willard F. *Collected Papers*. Edited by Rainer Berger and Leona Marshall Libby. Santa Monica, Calif.: Geoscience Analytical, 1981.

Thom, René. *Structural Stability and Morphogenesis: An Outline of a General Theory of Models*. Translated by D. H. Fowler. Foreword by C. H. Waddington. Reading, Mass.: W. A. Benjamin, 1975.

Mandelbrot, Benoit B. *Fractals: Form, Chance, and Dimension*. San Francisco: W. H. Freeman, 1977.

Mayer, Maria Goeppert, and Johannes Jensen. *Elementary Theory of Nuclear Shell Structure.* New York: John Wiley, 1955.

Oort, Jan Hendrik. *The Letters and Papers of Jan Hendrik Oort: As Archived in the University Library.* Compiled by J. K. Katgert-Merkelijn. Boston: Kluwer Academic Publishers, 1997.

Schwinger, Julian Seymour. *A Quantum Legacy: Seminal Papers of Julian Schwinger.* Edited by Kimball A. Milton. River Edge, N.J.: World Scientific, 2000.

Selberg, Atle. *Collected Papers.* New York: Springer-Verlag, 1989.

Sibley, Charles Gald, and Jon E. Ahlquist. *Phylogeny and Classification of Birds: A Study of Molecular Evolution.* New Haven, Conn.: Yale University Press, 1990.

Szent-Györgyi, Albert. *Chemistry of Muscular Contraction, 2nd Edition.* New York: Academic Press, 1951.

Tinbergen, Niko. *The Study of Instinct.* New York: Oxford University Press, 1989.

Tomonaga, Shin'ichiro. *Scientific Papers of Tomonaga.* Edited by T. Miyazima. Tokyo: Misuzu Shobo Publishing, 1971.

Wilson, Edward Osborne. *Sociobiology: The New Synthesis, 25th anniversary edition.* Cambridge, Mass.: Belknap Press of Harvard University Press, 2000.

Zubay, Geoffrey, and Julius Marmur. *Papers In Biochemical Genetics, 2nd Edition.* New York: Holt, Rinehart, and Winston, 1973.

Section Nine

Berners-Lee, Tim, and Mark Fischetti. *Weaving the Web: The Original Design and Ultimate Destiny of the World Wide Web by its Inventor.* San Francisco: HarperSanFrancisco, 1999.

The Celera Genomics Sequencing Team. "The Sequence of the Human Genome." *Science* 291 (2001): 1,304–1,351.

Climate Change 1995: IPCC Second Assessment: A Report of the Intergovernmental Panel on Climate Change. Washington, D.C.: Intergovernmental Panel on Climate Change, 1999.

Collins, Francis S., Michael Morgan, and Aristides Patrinos. "The Human Genome Project: Lessons from Large-Scale Biology." *Science* 300 (2003): 290.

The International Human Genome Mapping Consortium. "A Physical Map of the Human Genome." *Nature* 409 (2001): 934–941.

McCarthy, James J. ed. *Climate Change 2001: Impacts, Adaptation, and Vulnerability: Contribution of Working Group II to the Third Assessment Report of the Intergovernmental Panel on Climate Change.* New York: Cambridge University Press, 2001.

SELECTED INTERNET RESOURCES

GENERAL

American Association for the Advancement of Science's Science Net Links: URL: http://www.sciencenetlinks.com Updated February 28, 2005. Resources for K-12 students and instructors, including weekly science updates, Internet-based classroom activities, science literacy, and a peer-reviewed list of Web resources.

American Chemical Society's Chemistry. org: URL: http://www.chemistry.org Updated February 28, 2005. Official Web site of the American Chemical Society, includes "Molecule of the Week" with information on various compounds and "chemistry. com/kids," featuring interactive features aimed toward students and educators.

American Mathematical Society's Math on the Web: http://www.ams.org/mathweb Updated October 15, 2004. The Web site contains a collection of links a variety of mathematical resources, including journals, books, articles, handbooks, dictionaries, and departments.

Center for the Study of Technology in Society: URL: http://www.tecsoc.org Updated February 28, 2005. Web site of the organization dedicated to studying the interaction between tech-

nological change and society. The site includes "This Date in Technology History" feature, as well as links to current articles chronicling the effects of technological advances on society.

Digital Library for Earth Science Education: URL: http://www.dlese.org Updated January 5, 2005. A user-produced collection of resources on all aspects of Earth Science geared toward educators from kindergarten through university.

Drexel University's Math Forum: URL: http://mathforum.org/students Updated February 28, 2005. Web site features information about mathematics that students encounter in their school-related studies. Includes interesting and challenging problems and solutions for students in grades K-12 as well as a fair amount of college-level information.

Ecological Society of America's Education Site: URL: http://esa.org/education Updated December 7, 2004. Resources for students and educators at all levels (K-12 and university) describing ecology, careers in ecology, curriculum information, and issues in ecology.

Encyclopaedia Britannica Online: URL: http://www.britannica.com Updated February 28, 2005. The official Web site of the classic reference features information free to the public, including classic articles from *Encyclopaedia Britannica*, interactive time lines, and links to news articles. Subscribers can readily access full-text articles from the encyclopedia and other reference books.

Geological Society of America Education Resources: URL: http://www.geosociety. org/educate Updated February 18, 2005. Resources for K-12 students and educators, including links to Earth Science lesson plans and award programs.

National Academies of Science: URL: http:// www.nationalacademies.org Updated February 28, 2005. The official Web site of the body assembled to advise the United States government on scientific issues. The Web site includes current science news and links to the National Academies Science Museum, free resources from the National Academies Press, articles from Beyond Discovery, and the journal Proceedings of the National Academies of Science USA.

National Aeronautics and Space Administration: URL: http://www.nasa.gov Updated February 28, 2005. The official Web site of NASA includes a wide range of resources for students, educators, journalists, and the general public. Highlights include information on current NASA missions and projects, historical information on space exploration, and NASA's Kids Science News Network.

National Geographic Society's NationalGeographic.com: URL: http://www.nationalgeographic.com Updated February 28, 2005. Information, photographs, and interactive features focusing on geography, plants and animals, and natural phenomena. Includes links geared toward K-12 students and educators.

National Oceanic and Atmospheric Administration (NOAA): URL: http://www.noaa. gov Updated February 28, 2005. The Web site for NOAA focuses on ocean and atmospheric

sciences, including historical information, time lines, an image library, and educational resources for both students and educators.

National Science Teachers Association: URL: http://www.nsta.org Updated October 18, 2005. Resources for science educators, including "Today in Science History," grade-level appropriate information on a wide variety of scientific disciplines, and links to science-related Web sites.

The National Zoo's Conservation Central: URL: http://nationalzoo.si.edu/Education/ ConservationCentral Updated 2004. An educational program from the National Zoo includes interactive features aimed at helping students understand biodiversity, habitats, and other conservation issues.

Physics Web.com: URL: http://www.physics web.org Updated 2005. General information on physics, including current physics news, historical articles, and physical constants.

PSIgate Physical Science Information Gateway: URL: http://www.psigate.ac.uk/newsite Updated February 24, 2005. A catalog of Web resources on physics, chemistry, material science, astronomy, and Earth Science. The site is updated monthly.

Smithsonian Education: http://www. smithsonianeducation.org The education site for the Smithsonian Institution includes extensive resources for educators, students, and families interested in studying science and technology. Resources include K-8 grade-level appropriate lesson plans, list of child-friendly museum exhibits, and games that teach important scientific concepts.

University of Arizona Biology Project: http:// www.biology.arizona.edu Updated July 2004. Information intended to complement an introductory biology course, suitable for advanced high school students and undergraduates.

Web Elements: The periodic table on the Web: URL: http://www.webelements.com An interactive periodic table of the elements that includes historical information as well as physical, biological, geological, nuclear, electronic, and structural data on each element.

Wolfram Research's Eric Weisstein's World of Science: URL: http://www.scienceworld. wolfram.com Updated February 28, 2005. The online encyclopedia features entries covering mathematics, astronomy, chemistry, and physics.

SCIENTIFIC AWARDS AND HONORS

Albert and Mary Lasker Foundation: URL: http://www.laskerfoundation.org Updated 2005. The Lasker Medical Research Awards have been awarded for outstanding medical research since 1946. The Lasker Foundation Web site includes a list of recipients of the Lasker Medical Research Awards and descriptions of their work.

The Bruce Medalists: URL: http://www.phys-astro.sonoma.edu/brucemedalists Updated June 8, 2004. The Astronomical Society of the Pacific has presented the Catherine Wolfe Bruce gold medal for lifetime achievement in astronomy since 1898. This site includes a list of medalists, biographical information, and links to references.

International Mathematics Union: URL: http://www.mathunion.org Updated September 10, 2004. The site includes a list of Fields medal honorees and a summary of their work.

Nobel Prize.org: URL: http://nobelprize.org Updated October 18, 2005. Extensive resources on the Nobel Prize and Nobel laureates, the site includes biographical information on the Nobel laureates, the Nobel Lectures, articles by and about Nobel Prize recipients, and interactive resources aimed at teaching students the concepts behind works honored with the Nobel Prize.

MUSEUMS

The Exploratorium: The Museum of Science, Art, and Human Perception: URL: http://www.exploratorium.edu Updated February 28, 2005. The Web site of the San Francisco science museum includes online exhibits covering all fields of science and an archive of Web casts.

The Franklin Institute: URL: http://www.sln.fi.edu Updated February 28, 2005. The Web site of the Philadelphia Science Museum features online exhibits and galleries, as well as resources and classroom activities for educators.

IEEE Virtual Museum: URL: http://www.ieee-virtual-museum.org Updated 2004. An online museum with exhibits on electronics and electricity.

Marian Koshland Science Museum of the National Academies of Science: URL: http://www.koshland-science-museum.org Updated 2005. The Web site for the Washington, D.C.–based science museum. Resources include online exhibits, "Science behind the headlines," and materials for educators.

Museum of Science, Boston: URL: http://www.mos.org Updated October 2005. The Web site for the Museum of Science in Boston includes virtual exhibits, video of current science and technology presentation, articles, and education tools.

Museum of Science and Industry: URL: http://www.msichicago.org Updated 2005. The Web site for the Museum of Science and Industry in Chicago includes online exhibits and educational resources geared toward students, educators, and parents.

National Museum of Science and Technology, Italy: URL: http://www.museoscienza.org Virtual museum section of the site includes an extensive collection of images detailing the scientific work of Leonardo da Vinci.

Science Museum: URL: http://www.science museum.org.uk Updated 2005. The Web site for London's Science Museum includes online exhibitions and "exhibitlets" that incorporate pieces from the museum's collections.

Smithsonian Institution's National Museum of Natural History: URL: http://www. mnh.si.edu Updated January 2005. The Web site includes online exhibits, in-depth single subject features in "Natural History Highlights," and Smithsonian TV, a collection of audio and video presentations.

Smithsonian National Zoological Park: URL: http://nationalzoo.si.edu Updated 2005. The Web site for the National Zoo in Washington, D.C., features information on a wide variety of animal species, teaching tools, and interactive resources geared toward children, including games and coloring pages.

University of California, Berkeley Museum of Paleontology: URL: http://www.ucmp. berkeley.edu Updated February 8, 2005. The site features online exhibits of geologic time and evolution as well as resources for K-12 educators.

Web Exhibits: URL: http://www.webexhibits. org Updated February 28, 2005. An online museum from the Institute for Dynamic Educational Advancement that includes scientific exhibits on calendars and vision.

SITES WITH HISTORICAL CONTENT

American Institute for Physics' *Center for History of Physics:* URL: http://www.aip.org/ history Updated June 23, 2005. The site presented by the American Institute for Physics includes online exhibits, a visual archive, and a catalog of resources available at the Niels Bohr Library in College Park, Maryland.

Chemical Heritage Foundation: URL: http:// www.chemheritage.org Updated 2005. Online exhibits include time lines of discovery and biographies of notable chemists. The site also includes Webquests designed to teach topics in the history of chemistry at a high school level and other educational resources.

Classic Chemistry: URL: http://web.lemoyne. edu/~giunta Updated September 4, 2003. Web site includes links to full-text classic papers in chemistry, a set of 50 quantitative exercises, and a glossary of chemical terms.

Mac Tutor History of Mathematics Archive: URL: http://www-history.mcs.st-andrews. ac.uk/history Updated February 2005. A valuable reference featuring encyclopedia-style articles on mathematicians and topics in the history of mathematics, including mathematics in other cultures and the history of number systems. Other features include a glossary of mathematics terms and a time line of events in the history of mathematics.

Mendel Web: URL: http://www.mendelweb. org Updated February 22, 1997. The site presents educational resources geared toward students and educators in the field of classical genetics. Highlights include links to the full text of Gregor Mendel's classic paper and links to articles on the history of genetics.

National Library of Medicine *Profiles in Science:* URL: http://profiles.nlm.nih.gov Updated February 2005. An online resource featuring biographies of biomedical scientists and links to selected lectures, papers, laboratory notebook entries, and photographs.

Neuroscience For Kids: URL: http://faculty. washington.edu/chudler/neurok.html Updated March 1, 2005. Web site geared toward students and educators interested in neuroscience. Highlights include features on the nervous system, teaching materials, neuroscience in the news, and

"The Neuroscientist Network," where students can send questions to a neuroscientist.

Stanford Encyclopedia of Philosophy: URL: http://www.plato.stanford.edu Updated March 1, 2005. Encyclopedia-style articles on philosophers and topics in philosophy. A valuable resource for information on the scientific works of the natural philosophers.

SITES FOCUSING ON CURRENT RESEARCH

American Association of the Advancement of Sciences' *EurekAlert!:* URL: http://www.eurekalert.org Updated March 1, 2005. The Web site features current science news in the form of official press releases as well as a "Science reporting for kids" portal and links to grade-level-appropriate science resources for students.

California and Carnegie Planet Search: URL: http://www.exoplanets.org Updated February 5, 2005. Web site dedicated to research on planets outside of our solar system includes current news, data on planets, and links to articles on the search for planets.

Leaky Foundation: URL: http://www.leakey-foundation.org Updated February 16, 2005. Web site for the foundation dedicated to research on human origins. Resources include an archive of audio lectures with scientists, a visual glossary, interactive time line, and suggested reading lists.

National Nanotechnology Initiative: URL: http://www.nano.gov Web site for the initiative for nanotechnology research in the United States features an Education Center with activities geared toward K-12 students, undergraduates, and teachers.

National Health Museum's *Access Excellence:* URL: http://www.accessexcellence.org Updated February 21, 2005. An online resource for information on biotechnology and biomedicine. Features include articles on current issues in biotechnology, historical articles on biotechnology and interviews with Nobel laureates, information on careers in biotechnology, and educational resources, including virtual experiments and science fair projects.

Particle Data Group—Resources for particle physics: URL: http://www.pdg.lbl.gov A resource for the study of particle physics features "Particle Adventure," an interactive tour of particle physics geared toward students.

Pew Charitable Trust: URL: http://www.pewtrust.org Updated February 25, 2005. Web site for the organization dedicated to finding research-based information and solutions for public policy issues. Current information and reports available for many scientific issues related to public policy, including food and biotechnology, climate change, genetics, and protecting ocean and wilderness life.

Protein Data Base's Molecule of the Month: URL: http://www.rcsb.org/pdb/molecules/molecule_list.html Updated October 2005. A resource for current information on various biologically important molecules includes three-dimensional structure, function, and relevance to human health.

Science Daily: URL: http://www.sciencedaily.com Updated March 1, 2005. The Web site features daily updates of breaking news in all fields of science and encyclopedia entries on a wide variety of pure and applied scientific topics.

The Why Files: Science Behind the News: URL: http://www.whyfiles.org Updated February 24, 2005. Web site features educational articles explaining the science behind current headlines. Highlights include articles geared toward educators written for specific grade levels (5–8 or 9–12) with science teaching standards in mind.

SOCIETIES AND ASSOCIATIONS

American Association for the Advancement of Science (AAAS)

(URL: http://www.aaas.org)
1200 New York Avenue, NW
Washington, DC 20005
Telephone: 202-326-6400

The world's largest scientific society, the American Association for the Advancement of Science serves all branches of science. Their major activities include publishing the journal *Science*, developing programs to advance science education and policy, and fostering communication between scientists and the public.

American Astronomical Society (AAS)

(URL: http://www.aas.org)
2000 Florida Avenue, NW
Suite 400
Washington, DC 20009
Telephone: 202-328-3010

The American Astronomical Society represents scientists and students in all disciplines of astronomy. Activities of the society include publishing journals, providing opportunities of career development, and promoting public policy issues of concern to astronomers.

American Chemical Society (ACS)

(URL: http://www.chemistry.org)
1155 Sixteenth Street, NW
Washington DC, 20036
Telephone: 800-227-5558

Founded in 1876, the American Chemical Society is a professional society serving all branches of chemistry. The activities of ACS provide members opportunities to interact with other chemists and chemistry students. The society publishes the prestigious *Journal of the American Chemical Society*.

American Mathematical Society (AMS)

(URL: http://www.ams.org)
American Mathematical Society
201 Charles Street
Providence, RI 02904
Telephone: 401-455-4000

Founded in 1888, the American Mathematical Society represents more than 20,000 mathematicians around the world. AMS works to promote mathematics through publications, career development for mathematicians, and public policy.

American Meteorological Society (AMS)

(URL: http://www.ametsoc.org)
5 Beacon Street
Boston, MA 02108
Telephone: 617-227-2425

The American Meteorological Society represents more than 10,000 members who are scientists, students, or laymen interested in atmospheric and oceanic studies. Among the society's activities are publishing scholarly journals, organizing national meetings, and providing career development opportunities for members.

American Physical Society (APS)

(URL: http://www.aps.org)
One Physics Ellipse
College Park, MD 20740
Telephone: 301-209-3200

Representing more than 40,000 physicists, the American Physical Society promotes communication among physicists by publishing prestigious journals such as *The Physical Review*. Other activities of the society include fostering communication among physicists and policy makers, the media, and the public, as well as monitoring the human rights of scientists.

Ecological Society of America (ESA)

(URL: http://www.esa.org)
1707 H Street, NW
Suite 400
Washington, DC 20006
Telephone: 202-833-8775

The Ecological Society of America represents more than 9,000 scientists and students working in the field of ecology. The society promotes the ecological sciences by fostering communication among ecologists, promoting public understanding of ecology, and highlighting the need for ecological science in public policy decision making.

Federation of American Societies for Experimental Biology (FASEB)

(URL: http://www.faseb.org)
9650 Rockville Pike
Bethesda, MD 20814
Telephone: 301-634-7000

The Federation of American Societies for Experimental Biology is a coalition of more than a dozen individual member societies that serve biomedical and life scientists. Activities of FASEB and its associated member societies include publishing scientific journals and promoting biological research through public policy.

Geological Society of America (GSA)

(URL: http://www.geosociety.org)
P.O. Box 9140
Boulder, CO 80301
Telephone: 303-447-2020

The Geological Society of America represents Earth scientists worldwide. The society works to promote Earth science education and foster communication among members working in the field.

INDEX

Page numbers set in *italics* indicate photographs or illustrations.